WORLD BEYOND REASON:

THE ORWELLIAN FACTOR

Has "1984" Arrived?

by

James C. Lewis

DORRANCE
PUBLISHING CO
EST. 1920
PITTSBURGH, PENNSYLVANIA 15238

Dorrance Publishing Co
585 Alpha Drive
Pittsburgh, PA 15238
Visit our website at *www.dorrancebookstore.com*

ISBN: 978-1-6480-4365-9
eISBN: 978-1-6480-4387-1

Contents

WANTED

Enemy of the state

GEORGE SOROS

WANTED FOR:

SEDITION
TRAITOR
COMPLICITY IN GENOCIDE
TERRORIST
FASCIST
CONSPIRATOR FOR THE OVERTHROW OF AMERICA
BILLIONAIRE AND FUNDER OF THE ABOVE

Foreword

The idea of coalescing the nations of the world into a single country, where peace and civility, where equality and multiculturalism, and where hunger and poverty can be achieved or overcome, is an intriguing thought. If a group of good-hearted, pure-spirited people, were in control, making the right decisions, unhinging all the barriers, and continuously striving for the betterment of all mankind, perhaps the idea of a one-government world could be realized without reservations. But we simply cannot look to the hearts of mankind for those answers and potentialities because, when we do, we always get disappointed. Some say that individuals are innately or inherently good and will usually respond in kind to the good-hearted outreach by others. Not that long ago, a man and his lady decided to take a bicycle ride together across Afghanistan with the belief that a smile and respect would be returned; their effort was to show the world that with a little love in your heart you can overcome just about any mood to the contrary. Yet, for them, on the side of the road, a car of Muslims stopped, beat them severely, raped the girl, brutally stabbed them to death, and cut off her head. So much for the offer of peace and love.

We exist on a planet of many races and cultures, a myriad of converging and conflicting belief systems, and different ideological and religious factions, and we expect in our modern times we can somehow overcome these deeply rooted divisive differences and all sit together and appreciate the sunset and roast marshmellows on an open fire singing "Kumbayah my Lord." We'd have more luck convincing a hungry lion not to eat us.

This is a troubled world, no doubt, and most of us try to ignore problems larger than we are and just go on about our daily lives. Live and let live is our motto. But this is not the way large powers in the nation or world are. So, we can't just ignore them and expect that they too will ignore us, because they won't. And they don't.

I would like to begin this trek to illumination or enlightenment by stating that I began my own journey to find the truth and reasons for the truth after accidently watching an online video. I don't recall the specific video after five years but it was the beginning of online research and investigation that included videos, news columns, mainstream and alternative media, comments, opinion pages, interviews, conversations, and articles. I am one of a growing chorus of voices who have realized our country is in dire trouble of being overthrown by forces from within our borders as well as from outside our borders. We have many enemies, and I want to talk about how the threat we face is of global proportions, and how it is orchestrated at the very highest levels, beyond our own government.

I originally came from a democrat background. I am now 70 years old. My parents were democrats, and politics did not interest me much. Besides, I felt I was just a nobody-person without any power or standing, so who was I to be interested in what was beyond my reach, as politics seemed to be. My parents were good solid Christian folk, hard-working, simple people. They weren't that educated. Mother worked in the WWII war effort making artillery shells. I never knew my biological father, and the Texas man she later married was a good father. So I will refer to him here as my father. In the war, Mirriam Lewis was with the 3rd Armored Division that hit the beach after Normandy was taken and with his Division swept through France, Belgium and on into German. I never knew those things while he was alive. When he passed on, with full military honors, mother gave me his military ring. Well-worn, the barely discernable words said "Spearhead Division", fondly and respectfully named because that tank division routed Nazi soldiers wherever they were, spearheading the charge. I researched online and learned all about the heroics of that division, and I was proud to be his son, even if adopted. I only regret he never talked about the war, because I could have grown to adulthood knowing my father was a war hero and only learning that after his death. Thinking of what I know now, it brought tears to my eyes to know my father had things about himself that he kept hidden from the rest of the family, perhaps he likely didn't want to tell of the horrors he witnessed, participated in, and endured in the war.

Neither Mom nor Dad were able to pass on knowledge of how to succeed in the world; all they ever said that one had to work hard in this life. But what I saw during my early life was that the poor and middle-class families had little to adequate from their hard work, while those who had the nicest cars, fine houses, and were considered high-class, well, they had lots of money and didn't seem to work hard at all. Of course, what did I know about them, or how they became wealthy? Nothing. I didn't realize that many wealthy people had worked hard to get what they had, and that to be in that class required a good education, setting goals, planning out one's future.

I suppose my life has been rather mundane. I missed the Vietnam 'war'. We came to live in separate states, Daddy Lewis died in 2000, and after my mother Sandy died in 2004, family visits became longer in between. My older brother was the proverbial 'dreamer', encouraged to be by our mother, but his life became a lineage of broken dreams and failures, one project after another. Darn, if he didn't remain a good man despite it all. When the current dream crashed, he went on to pursue another. I hope God will give him just one dream in this lifetime.

Me, well, I just lived in the netherworld of hope for a long time, suffering consequences of bad decisions, always feeling lost without direction until finally, dusting myself off, I learned from my mistakes and my life dramatically began changing for the better. While those earlier years were important in shaping who I evolved into, sometimes I wish they had not been so difficult. I eventually pushed through the sense of prevalent loss and self-depredation, and entered into a more productive reality. It was about "know-how" information I should have been taught at an earlier age.

I had worked at hard labor in the Louisiana oil fields as a roustabout, even worked as a sandblaster for a former New Orleans Saints quarterback who turned out to be a thief stealing from oil companies while the crew sandblasted. I worked offshore packing sand around the base of oil rigs, and also sandblasted and painted some of them. I worked hard, but didn't get rich. Life was a struggle for a few years.

I was tested to see what was my IQ level to see whether I qualified for possible membership in Mensa International. I scored at 142 and passed. For those of you who do not know about Mensa, Mensa International is an organization whose members test in the intelligence range as the top 5% of the world population in intelligence levels. On the test I took, one must qualify at least 140 score. I don't recall what the top is, but a 200 IQ is Einstein genius level. So I qualified at the low end of the "genius-level" Mensa scale.

But, my level of <u>knowledge</u> about life and worldly matters was about one on a scale of 1-1000. Success principles I never even knew existed until I was in my 20's saved me. I learned about courses in goal-setting and positive mental attitudes and the other attributes of successful people. I later enrolled in a success motivation program, and for the first time in my life information flooded in to fill my mental vacuum with knowledge of how to change one's life for the better and thereby become a successful and productive citizen in our merit-based economic system. I went through it several times, each time gaining higher understanding of what I would have liked to know in my youthful years. I wondered how different my life could have been had those things been taught early on and why they were not taught in the schools as tools we would need in our futures. Those who attended the course more than once were encouraged to give lectures on one topic or another; I went through enough times that I could, and did, teach the entire course. In later years I did, in fact, teach success motivation courses to others disadvantaged by lack of knowledge. I am a believer that teaching to others is a good way to cement such principles within oneself.

Another thing I got involved in was Transcendental Meditation (TM) and learned how to still the uncontrolled "chatter" of the mind until there were no thoughts, like calm pond water, as they say. Yet, that calmness gave me a surprising sense of awareness at a much higher level than before. My own life began to have meaning and opportunity. I learned that mental chatter caused stress, and basically "clouded" the mind in a way that hampered focus when one needed to concentrate.

That ability to concentrate and develop self-control helped me tremendously when I got involved in learning the martial arts, and after reaching a second degree level I had my sights set on getting a part in the martial arts movies. Unfortunately, a back injury shut all that down, and spiraled me into major disappointment, almost clinical depression. But that was short-lived as I embraced the disciplines I needed in order to move on.

As to politics, throughout the trials and significant, life-changing tribulations of my adult life, as most of us face in our lifetimes - which are not particularly relevant or important here - I was a Democrat in name only, as was my mother and father and brother. I didn't vote, didn't realize the importance of my vote, didn't think my vote even mattered, never put much thought into the different political parties, and I had my own problems and circumstances to deal with. In essence, I was not paying attention to that world of politics. I suspect millions of good Americans have been or are in that same situation. Americans today have all kinds of excuses, like, "politicians are all the same, crooked!", or "It doesn't matter who you elect, nothing good will ever get done!", or "I don't vote because it won't make any difference." Stuff like that. I thought the same way.

My back injury made me think in different ways for working, and I studied the law, eventually becoming a paralegal. I've always had a penchant for writing, so being a paralegal worked out just fine. I finally opened my own paralegal business. I was quite successful doing contract work, and worked for several law firms throughout California. I made excellent money, for a paralegal. I was still a Democrat, and still not paying any attention to the political scene, the government, or world affairs. I still naively thought all was well, my country was great, and it was OK to grumble about the greed of some politicians. I worked hard, made decent money, bought a new townhouse, enjoyed the occasional trade-in on a newer car, and took trips in-country and, a couple of time, to mainland China.

In 2014, I began to see things on the internet that got my attention. Lots of news sources, including alternative news sources, all raised red flags about a movement growing in the country that showed indicia of being a Socialist movement. Years of training in research and investigation helped me discern what was real and what was fiction, but I learned that most of the fiction and propaganda was coming from the Left, particularly the so-called "Progressives." I saw that the Democrat Party was not the same party I knew of in my younger days, not the same Party my parents were of. I remember believing that Democrat citizens were well-meaning and believed in God and Liberty and Justice for all. What I saw in 2014 among the Democrat leadership, and since, it is not that earlier Party anymore. But I also learned that what I thought the Democrat Party was back then did not serve the best interests of black Americans or any people of color. I recalled when I was a boy the schools in the South were segregated, the bathroom facilities said White Only and Colored Only, and restaurants often did not serve "colored" people at all. Where I had lived as a boy, blacks lived on the other side of the railroad tracks. Later in life, my brother married a black woman and I have a "binary" nephew. I hesitate saying he is "black" like traditionalists say, because I don't think that's fair to his "white" side; seems "binary" is more accurate.

But I did see institutionalized racism in the South I grew up in. I did not fall victim to that attitude, and during my life I have had great friends who were people of color. I am sorry to say that when I was about 9 years old, I met a "colored boy" (as they said in those days), and one day he came by the house and we had a great time playing in the yard, doing the same things boys often do, including wrestling and laughing in the grass. My mother stopped us, told the boy to go home, and forbid me from playing with him in the future. I did not understand why, but it left me with questions and no answers. I didn't realize this was racism. Years later, when my niece had a black boyfriend and got pregnant and bore a child, my mother removed her from her will as she neared her death. That's when I realized clearly my own mother had been a racist. But that's just the way it was in southern Louisiana.

But I digress. We all have our stories about something, and we all become the result of our environment and our response to it. None of us are the same as another because of the infinite differences in our individual lives. I just tried to hang on to the virtues and values I came to embrace in my life and be a decent person. So, while it may be unusual for a writer to talk about these personal things, I do so because I want you, the reader, to understand I am not some Harvard or Yale world scholar coughing up another book. I am YOU, just an American, John Q. Citizen, and I want you to know that I write for the truth and out of love for my country and countrymen.

After seeing the alt-Left's socialist agenda, I began to pay attention to Party politics. I spent a great deal of time doing research, investigating what was going on with my Party and in our nation. But, a lot of things I learned were confusing and/or raised new questions. Even using deductive reasoning left questions for which my method of investigation provided no logical connections or conclusions. How to connect the dots was the problem. A lot of local situations and events did not make a lot of sense, and I was confused about how these things were happening and why. Lots of things were just irrational.

Then I began to learn a great deal about affairs and events around the world, and I'm thinking, "What is going on?!" What was this "conspiracy theory" stuff they were talking about? I learned about international organizations, about the wars, about the history of Islam, about many things.

I began to see that most of what I was investigating lead to other events and organizations. I heard about the secret societies like the Illuminati many people say no longer exists, and that's just a "conspiracy theory." I learned that was not true. Throwing out the "conspiracy theory" accusation appeared to be the typical way the alt-Left, and even some folks on the right, tried to discredit that which they did not believe, or did not want to believe.

As I began to "connect the dots" I realized there is a much larger picture going on at the international level with tentacles deftly controlled by a small group of people who are so rich they actually own 80% of the world's currency as well as much of the land around the world. I realized they think in terms of "ownership" and the rest of the world are just temporary tenants who pay them money for the shelter they rent or own. They are the globalists, members of that secret society known as the Illuminati and including its Bilderberg group, which meets annually to discuss how their agenda is progressing and what the plans are for the upcoming year. These are the people who want a one-government world, run by them, which they call the New World Order, an Orwellian double-speak term. I learned the NWO agenda has been going on for a very long time, and is hardly a recent agenda.

This is a big book, far larger than I had intended. But there is so much information that ties to other relevant information, so my goal was to make those connections and draw the larger picture from the pieces I continued to find. I hope you bear with me, and I hope you realize I write with the most noble of intentions and concerns.

I came to the conclusion that the Democrat Party has been infiltrated and controlled by these globalist elites, who are the "puppetmasters" for a world-control agenda. They set up a pro-Socialist movement, well-funded, getting socialists into politics, but have no intent to end their success, if it is successful, at socialism. That is but a step, using the alt-Left stupidity to achieve that step. I came to see that some of our politicians were also a part of a greater, anti-capitalist movement.

I began to see that what was promised was actually quite the opposite from the mouthpiece politicians and Party officers, and then there were our Presidents, who we elect and entrust our own future as Americans in their hands. I wondered how we suffered ignorance while both Bush Presidents spoke of the New World Order coming, gushing the name as if it would be nothing short of Utopian. JFK was murdered because he intended to expose both the NWO and the military industrial complex (MIC).

And how did America elect Obama to the Presidency, when his birth certificate was proven to have been computer-created and false, and when his history showed a dedication to Marxism and a hatred for the history of colonialism he believed modern America represents? But more about that later.

So, my fellow patriots, as well as those anti-Americans who dare to read this book, this book is about my research and conclusions, which are based on irrefutable findings and conclusions of experts, as well as my own deductive reasoning and conclusions. For now, I'll just say, these globalist elites intend to destroy democracy around the world, they are using socialist methods to reach the socialist realm, and they will usher in totalitarianism where there are only two classes, the rich and powerful in control, and everybody else as mere working class, most likely nothing more than a slave class. They will decide who does what, who works where, who gets to eat and who starves, and who will get to live at all. Some people will accuse me of being a far-right conservative, or a conspiracy theorist. I intend this book as a non-partisan book, addressed to patriots mainly, and to the misguided pro-marxists calling for another revolution and socialism. I have learned they have been indoctrinated with false narratives, and that those manipulating them are true fascists seeking totalitarianism and a one-government world.

Ultimately, these power-elites intend to reduce the world population down to about one (1) billion people total; we are now over six (6) going on seven (7) billion. How do you think they will accomplish that depopulation project if they win their take-over goals?

I'll talk about Bill Gates "vaccines" as a method of genocide, 'testing' already underway (India and Africa). I'll talk about "chemtrails" that officially "do not exist" but which uses nano-aluminum and other particulates to poison and dumb-down Americans and other people around the world. And then there is the new 5G network, with transmitters everywhere, touted as newer and faster and amazing high-speed internet; but there is more to that, and right now I don't have all those answers, so I'll leave that to the experts who are investigating that. But I would suggest Americans should be very concerned about that. And then there is downright genocide too.

I ultimately concluded my Party has been hijacked by people who hate our Republic and want to change it to a socialist form of government. But, the puppeteers are not telling those who they, the puppeteers, are using to accomplish this this "Final Solution" that socialism is only a stepping stone to gain control. Instead, the alt-Left of the Democrats do not believe globalism or socialism is such a bad thing; they think of such a future with infantile starry eyes based solely on stated ideals about socialism or globalism. No facts enter the realm of their reasoning. The propaganda and efforts to brainwash have become alarmingly bad, with pro-socialist college professors teaching our children socialism is good, the "government takes care of them", and it will be the proverbial Utopia. Worse, a random poll of young people found that some 80% of them actually think that socialism is the best form of government. They seem to have no clue about the horrible reality that socialism always becomes, and they have no idea that will be temporary, with the very worst to come.

What is so scary about that is they are the future generation of politicians and teachers. I asked Democrats, like myself, and they just laughed and said, "What are you talking about?", and I realized they weren't paying attention beyond their own small world either. When I tried to engage a discussion about this "hijacking" with Democrats, often all I got was rejection that that was all false "conspiracy theory" alleged by those "damn republicans", and that I was either naïve or stupid to believe that "conspiracy stuff." Yet, I knew that was not true. I saw nothing to substantiate that dismissive mindset, nor understood why their minds were so closed to the information I had. Where they were mentally, it seemed to me, was a prime example of "secular humanism", which comes down to whatever the masses believe is the right thing. Hmmm, Nazism is a good example of that, and history shows us how that turned out. There's an old saying, "A person convinced against their will is of that opinion still." Brainwashing is a powerful method to do that, and with such brainwashing going on for many years now, I have learned that those "convinced against their will" by subtle forms of the overall media are likely to avidly, even violently, defend their beliefs even if their basis or result is wrong, a lie, or a fairy tale.

What we absolutely should know is every major media outlet around the world is owned by the transnational bankers and the Bilderberg group, who meets annually to review how their agenda is going and what needs to be done the next year, so as to ensure the propaganda machine stays revved up. Thus, all the propaganda that soaks into our minds is orchestrated from this owned media. This includes Facebook, Google, and other social networks that are set up to control our minds and keep us focused on the electronic devices that distract us from the reality of what is really going on.

So, I left the Democrat Party and registered as a Republican. I recognized in the interim that Republicans are generally constitutionalists, believed in morality, generally Christians in faith, and believed in a merit-based workplace and economy. I joined the local Party, became a local column writer, and am someone who often writes in Comment sections of various media. I have written and continue to write to enlighten Americans and the world about what the globalists are doing, and how they are doing it. Among other things, I have pointed out that, just as former President Truman cautioned, we need to fear the military industrial complex, because it is strongly influenced by the "shadow government" and because, accordingly, it must be "fed" by conflicts and war to remain productive and profitable. Donald Trump has called for an end to these endless military "small" wars since WW-II, costing many American lives and a great deal of money, yet since Vietnam these small skirmishes continue around the globe, always with an explanation of why we must be so involved.

Many responding commenters, particularly on the Left, proclaim with name-calling and eye-bulging tirades that I am wrong, yet give no facts or evidence, or even credible sources, that might support what they say or show that I am wrong.

The Left seems to see no challenge to the future of liberty and basic rights if socialism is to occur, and those who are not socialist will nonetheless reject outright my information, which is backed by credible sources, and accuse me of just lying about everything. I reply, "Well, prove me wrong." None of them make any effort to do so because they cannot prove me wrong.

In our merit-based capitalist republic, people have freedom to choose, liberty to move around, and unalienable rights. The Republic was initially established as a republic, not a democracy, and it called for small government who did the bidding of the population, a government of public servants doing public service things. We now have a huge government administered by people who no longer listen to the citizenry and think, instead, that they are our rulers. Democrats are especially guilty of that, but it is not limited to them. There are plenty RINOs in Congress (Republicans In Name Only) who serve the "shadow government" pulling the strings. We need to shut that problem down. Both Rothschild and Rockefeller once said, in different words, that it is of no matter who gets elected to Presidency, they already "own" them. (Fortunately, this was not the case with Donald Trump.) Going back to George Herbert W. Bush, he spoke publicly of taking America to a "new world order" as the best form of government. Both he and George W. Bush were members of the Illuminati's lower order called the Skull and Bones; George W., at a televised event, gave the S&B signal, crossed arms, hands shoulder to shoulder, and a bow of the head, which is available for anyone to see.

We are in a war, active right now, in our own political system. Democrats and Republicans cannot seem to agree on anything, hate each other, make generalized false conclusions about everyone in the other Party, and basically ignore or never consider that there are forces far above manipulating us against each other as a distraction. It is a war using propaganda and Orwellian methods to bring "change" that ushers in socialism if successful.

When we yield to ever-larger government, especially one infiltrated by shadow forces, we end up sacrificing parts of our unalienable rights to life, liberty, and the pursuit of happiness. Government tends to grow, with career bureaucrats constantly working on new ways to tax anything and everything, justifiable or not. Smaller money in our pockets means less freedom to choose, less liberty to move around, less freedom of expression, etc., because nearly everything we do, in some way, costs money, and with spending money comes the sales tax, ever rising. Things that tend to be more popular to do, are usually taxed higher. Things that are necessary to do require expensive licenses and permits, and if the project requires different approvals you can bet there is a department and agents and services who get your money.

And when we allow a government to cater to special interests, almost exclusively influenced by the multinational banks and corporations, the general population endures not "free trade agreements" on the international scale, like the TransAtlantic Trade and Investment Partnership (TTIP)[FN1.] but what has become known and described by Naom Chomsky, philosopher, as follows:

[FN1.] The Transatlantic Trade and Investment Partnership (TTIP) is a proposed trade agreement between the European Union and the United States, with the aim of promoting trade and multilateral economic growth. According to Karel de Gucht, European Commissioner for Trade between 2010 and 2014, the TTIP is the largest bilateral trade initiative ever negotiated, not only because it involves the two largest economies in the world but also because of its potential global reach in setting an example for future partners and agreements. The European Commission says that the TTIP would boost the EU's economy by €120 billion, the US economy by €90 billion and the rest of the world by €100 billion. The agreement has been criticized and opposed by some unions, NGOs and environmentalists, particularly in Europe. The *Independent* (a British online newspaper established in 1986) describes common criticisms of TTIP as "reducing the regulatory barriers for big business, things like food safety law, environmental legislation, banking regulations and the sovereign powers of individual nations", or more critically as an "assault on European and US societies by transnational corporations." The *Guardian* (another British newspaper) noted the criticism of TTIP's "undemocratic nature of the closed-door talks", "influence of powerful lobbyists", TTIP's potential ability to "undermine the democratic authority of local government", and described it as "the most controversial trade deal the EU has ever negotiated." German economist Max Otte argued that by putting European workers into direct competition with Americans (and in effect because of the North American Free Trade Agreement with Mexicans and Canadians), TTIP would negatively impact the European social models. An EU direct democracy mechanism, the European Citizens' Initiative, which enables EU citizens to call directly on the European Commission to propose a legal act, acquired over 3.2 million signatures against TTIP and CETA within a year. (Source, www.en.wikipedia.org/wiki/Transatlantic_Trade_and_Investment_Partnership.)

"The so-called free trade agreements are not free trade agreements. In fact, to a large extent they're not even trade agreements. These are <u>investor rights agreements</u>. There's a reason why they're kept secret from the public and as soon as you look at them you see why. Notice I say "secret from the public" not secret. They're not kept secret, they're not secret to the <u>corporate lawyers and lobbyists who are writing the detailed regulations</u>. Of course, the interests of their constituents don't happen to be the public of the world or their own countries. So, these are highly protectionist for the benefit of private power, so-called intellectual property rights, to effectively raise tariffs. They're called "patents" but which have an enormous impact on economies. (Great … wonderful for pharmaceutical and media court conglomerates and others.)

Investors/corporations are given the right to sue governments, something you and I can't do but a corporation can, to sue governments for harming their future, potentially future profits. You can figure out what that means and such cases already in the "courts" – they're not in the courts, they go to private trade adjudication groups made up largely of corporate representatives. They're already going on with NAFTA and we can expect more of them. There are provisions that undermine efforts at regulation including, incidentally, regulation of environmental dangers and rather striking the phrase "Climate Change" does not appear in these 280 pages (of the Greenpeace report about the TTIP), which are illustrative of the whole structure. So they have almost no … I should say that these agreements, so-called Pacific and Atlantic, have virtually no effect on tariffs. Tariffs are already quite low among the major trading partners. When you read the propaganda about it, it says "oh yeah sure, Vietnam is going to have to lower its tariffs." Yeah, almost no effect on trade. The major trading partners already have agreements that have reduced the tariffs very substantially.

There are few exceptions, not many. So these are basically …
we should disabuse our-self of the illusion that these are free
trade agreements, anything but. And, to a large extent not
even trade agreements. We have the experience of others like
NAFTA, many years of experience. So take, say NAFTA, it
has all of the aspects that I just described, but even more.
Consider even what is called trade. Interactions across the
US-Mexico border, they've increased substantially since
NAFTA. So economists will tell you trade is greatly increased
but have a look at them. So for example, suppose that General
Motors produces parts in Indiana, sends them to Mexico for
assembly and sells the car in Los Angeles. That's called trade
in both directions, but it's not. It is "interaction" internal to a
command economy. It's as if during the days of the Soviet
Union, parts were made, say in Leningrad, sent to Warsaw
for assembly and sold in Moscow. We wouldn't call that trade.
That's interactions internal to a command economy."

(Source: Noam Chomsky: Who Rules the World Now?, interview by Cathy
Newman of Channel 4 News, published May 14, 2016, currently on YouTube
at www.youtube.com/watch?v=P2lsEVlqts0, or, at YouTube search engine at
Noam Chomsky: Who rules the world now?)

So, even private citizens should have learned by now that large multinational
corporations do not necessarily serve the best interests of the population of
the country in which the corporation is primarily registered and domiciled.
We know, for sure, that a huge web of regulations imposed on businesses great
and small, have resulted in the smaller businesses becoming unable to make
sustaining profits as the regulations increase, thus putting them out of business. We know, also, that over-regulating large corporations result in the consumer class paying higher costs for their products. No one wins, except
perhaps the government bureaucracy. Yet, while some regulations are created
to protect the consumer from the great potential for abuse and dangers from
unregulated corporations, it is difficult to find the "fine line" so that both
benefit. That is made difficult by the thirst of bureaucracy to make money to
enrich the government at the expense of both taxpayer/consumer and the

business community. Just how do you think the government bureaucracy is able to continually expand, with sweetheart pensions for all the bureaucrats? (See also: Office of the United States Trade Representative, Executive Office of the President, Archive (www.ustr.gov/ttip).)

The TTIP has been described by Englishman John Hilary, Executive Director of campaign group "War on Want" who said the TTIP is "[a]n assault on European and US societies by transnational corporations."

The British paper, the Independent Minds, published a criticism of the TTIP in an article on October 6, 2015, by a Lee Williams | @leeroy112 |, who gave six reasons why the TTIP was not good and even dangerous to democratic nations. He wrote it could be that the TTIP would open up Europe's public health, education and water services to US companies, essentially resulting in the privatization of the National Health Service (NHS). Also, it is feared that the TTIP could loosen data privacy laws which is seen as an attack on individual privacy. (Just look at the "background check" companies who have basically eliminated privacy; even if the person being checked is not a criminal, these companies post everything that can be known about every person in their data base, which is now nearly every American!)

The biggest threat is, according to Williams, its inherent attack on democracy itself; the reason is this: One of the main aims of TTIP is the introduction of Investor-State Dispute Settlements (ISDS), which allow companies to sue governments if those governments' policies cause a loss of profits. In effect, it means unelected transnational corporations can dictate the policies of democratically elected governments. As of 2015, there were around 500 ISDS cases of business-versus-nations going on around the world, and they are all taking place before 'arbitration tribunals' made up of corporate lawyers appointed on an "ad hoc" basis which, according to War On Want's John Hilary, are "little more than kangaroo courts" with "a vested interest in ruling in favour of business." In sum, as concerned Williams in England, we may be forced to accept an attack on democracy, but knowing what the TTIP is actually all about can help the citizenry of America to at least fight against the conspiracy of silence within the TTIP, which operates without the public knowing what it is doing.

But again, I digress.

In trying to understand what was involved in this pro-socialist and globalist mess, I focused on the immediate events around me, on that everyday level. I became aware that something resembling insanity had overtaken European countries, where governments unilaterally determine what reality is going to be, what to say or not to say, and supporting the teaching of children that boys might be girls and girls might be boys. This is Orwellianism. Sadly, this last part has also arrived in the United States and is gaining ground. The transgender movement, and encouragement, is almost as insane as the Muslim's horrible treatment of homosexuals and females of all ages. The transgender movement will just wreak havoc within a tolerant society who will not all become politically subordinate to the idea that gender choice is normal or natural; a normal society may be restrained to giving tolerance of the abnormal activity, but they will not be silenced if they do speak out or believe otherwise about the issue. Yet, like in European countries, we are now seeing laws passed to make it illegal to speak against this kind of abnormal behavior, despite our right to object on religious conscience morality. There is no dialogue on differences of opinion, they just expect to shove it down our throats and tell us to shut up and accept it.

And then, the Muslim migrant swarm hit European countries. Hundreds of women and girls were raped and brutalized, and this is ongoing today. Some women were out the next day carrying signs with childlike drawings to 'educate' the Muslims that their type of bad treatment of girls and women were not the right thing to do in their host country. As if that made any difference whatsoever to a male-dominated culture that created a sort of caste system separating men and women, where men had total control and did pretty much what they want, including the raping of male or female prisoners. And, of course, they throw homosexuals off tall buildings. Criminal statistics in every country invaded by Muslim migrants showed an average of 3000% rise in violent crime and, especially, rapes of women and young boys. But, remember, such Muslims are not "homosexual." A bit of … kind of like, cognitive dissonance… going on there. Hypocrisy definitely. And, to this ideology looms the horror of allowing adult and old men to marry females as early as 5 years of age, in some provinces, younger than that. You know, what Americans call pedophilia, child abuse, and child-rape. We used to hang such folks not that many years ago. Yet, they are invading here by hook-and-crook and, not surprisingly, by "invitation." They were mostly young, military-aged young men, but also a lot of middle-aged and older men too. Hmmm. Crime going to go up here 3000% by them? We're not stopping it.

So, I began to realize this everyday level of life changes around the globe and here, on home ground, have causative connections higher than that just what occurs locally, or nationally, and so I followed that level higher. I learned that the beginnings of Europe's insanity started with this migrant swarm, but the swarm was orchestrated with premeditation by higher powers, and I'm not talking about God. The United Nations started it as a "population replacement" for "white" Western countries of Europe and America the UN decided how low birth and fertility rates and needed rejuvenation. I learned this was propaganda because the UN actually wanted to eliminate "white people" by integrating their bloodlines with people of color. I found that the UN was in favor of the New World Order of a one-government world.

What I found? A lot, but nothing that is not already available for everyone to see on their own volitional research. What I write about is what I learned in this ongoing research and investigation, and I have drawn some pretty clear perspectives and beliefs about what I have found. I am not a professional writer, I'm just a patriot who loves his country and wants to see it restored and made even better. The forces who intend to destroy the USA are strong, active, powerful, and wealthy. They are using every brainwashing technique in the book, and not the least of which is chemical warfare at the molecular level through some vaccines, aerosols, and geoengineering. They own all of the mainstream media.

I've tuned in to world affairs and events and found the world becoming unstable and dangerous all over the globe. Genocide not seen since the Stalin years in Russia (USSR) is occurring in African countries, focused mainly against Christians by the Arab and African Muslims. Then I began to hear about the Islamic agenda of world domination, and then about the "New World Order" group of the shadowy Illuminati and its 13 occultist families, families that were part of the top world bankers like the Rothschilds, Payseurs, and Warburgs. To my surprise I learned the Rockefeller family was part of that the organization, that the Bush family had supported Adolf Hitler, still supports the New World Order agenda (George H. and George W., both said so publicly), and that all of those forces were connected and working together. Two of our own Presidents (Bush) want to change America and replace it as just another part of a one-government world. They both were supported by the bankers of the Federal Reserve (FED).

I learned that our esteemed Yale college, where the "best" minds were groomed for the higher echelons of America, had a "club" or "fraternity" called "Skull and Bones" with the code number 332 and the code sign, crossed arms across the chest with head down, the very same code number and code sign in the Illuminati's pyramidal hierarchy group, Skull and Bones, not far from the top of the pyramid either.

And then along came Obama, promising "fundamental change", i.e., socialism first, ultimately Islamization, or so he thinks. He'd say things about these changes, first like a joke and the audience would laugh, and then he would say, "You think I'm joking", and then laugh, as would the audience. He was not joking. He just toyed with supporters who had really no clue he was a traitor and enemy of America. His mentor, George Soros, is a member of the Illuminati who wants his greatest achievement to be the destruction of the United States, and who helps crash countries around the world to force them to become socialist countries, all in preparation for the New World Order agenda.

George Soros, who is a front-man for the Illuminati, is a man who goes around the globe, helps destabilize a country's economy – especially if it is democratic or becoming democratic – and, when it is in real trouble, buys up its currency which crashes that country. Out of that country's ashes of its collapse, violence, and starvation, another socialist country is born. He is most famous for breaking the Bank of England and making a profit of $1-billion dollars in a single day doing that.

Soros was born a Jew; his father hid him with a German friend during Hitler's anti-Jew genocidal sweep, and then he profited greatly, posing as a German, from the confiscation and selling off of Jewish property of those sent to the gas chambers. In a public interview on 60 Minutes in 1998, when asked how he felt about that profiteering from Jewish property, he unashamedly said that was the most exciting time of his life. He said what he did was an "amoral" event, and that if he didn't take advantage of that situation, someone else would have. He financially supports and influences Organizing for Action headed by Obama, and is determined to destroy America. What does that make Obama?

America is a prime target for Soros and he has said publicly that his ultimate achievement will be the destruction of America.

Socialism is but a step towards totalitarianism, and in between, should it occur here, we'll see civil unrest, divisiveness, civil war, anarchy, martial law, disarmament of the citizenry, and dictatorship.

The Left, particularly women and children, looked up to Barack Obama like he was a God, even praying to him at night prayers or singing songs about him. Yet, Obama is part of that globalist plot, a willing part, funded by multibillionaire George Soros (Illuminati). Obama is a Marxist, an anti-colonialist, and he sees America's colonialist foundation as existing even now. He hates America, and his idea of "fundamental change" was its destruction. He was pro-Islam, and brought in members of the terrorist organization, the Muslim Brotherhood, and placed them in key spots in our government. He gave many millions of dollars in cash to Iran helping to fund terrorism against whoever, including America.

Faced with what I was discovering, I realized that a better method of investigating for answers was to start at the top, not the bottom, because what is going on from the bottom up is all orchestrated from the top down, including the pro-socialist movement in America, and the Islamic invasion in Europe and around the world. I realized that the difficulty with investigating from the bottom up was that it was confusing to connect the dots because there was so much distraction and misinformation. I found that certain assumptions I had earlier made about some things were changed by finding what the real fact was or truth, which was even larger and more complicated than I had thought. When I learned of this international banking cartel who owned the FED, and other banks on the world stage affiliated with the FED bankers, it all began to make sense.

Imagine, as in a story in the Twilight Zone, of a world owned a few extremely powerful families, or corporation even. The members own the entire world, obtaining ownership by hook-and-crook, by intimidation and murder, and by convincing the world that a one-government world would be like the proverbial Utopia.

Imagine, too, that the population of the world is war-torn, becoming more destitute and reliant on government hand-outs to survive. Their schools have been teaching children that Utopia awaits them, that a one-government world is good, it will take care of everyone, and everyone will be happy.

Imagine that the planet, controlled by these international societies, has reached the point where birth controls must be set in place because the planet is already over-populated to an almost unsustainable degree. Imagine that in some countries of ancient ancestries they have generally reduced having babies of their ethnicity and culture, to the point where the birth rate is so low that entire ethnicity and culture will die out completely. Imagine that the elites of this one-government world take a 'pragmatic' approach to the birthrate problem, since lower populations in some countries were adversely affecting the profits of the bank-owned government run by them. Would they not decide that the ethnicities across the globe have significant differences in IQ, as at least two careful studies have shown them to be? If depopulation be the goal, as it is, would not these elitists, in their godlike towers and sense of self, not take the pragmatic genocide action by killing off those of the lowest IQ first, unless they choose to keep them as labor slaves? And would they not kill off the other masses who were not producers or good workers next? Killing off 5 or 6 billion people might be easier than you might imagine in the Twilight Zone, because technology for genocide exists in military, medical, chemical, and infrastructural (turning off the electricity everywhere for about a year). I mean, the technology already exists, and if you think a small group who think themselves as Gods, or Disciples of Satan, are going to hesitate in any step of their one-government world project, you are mistaken! Lives are meaningless, except their own and those who will remain when the "culling" is over.

But, I'm getting ahead of myself.

This book represents a truncated factual summary of volumes of material I researched and investigated. I am not a person claiming some special expertise in research and investigation because what I found is available to anyone willing to take the time, with an open mind, and do the same research. This book is presented because there is confusion here in the USA about what is going on, and why. I could write volumes, but I tried to keep it short and simple as possible; yet, it is longer than I intended.

My goal is to awaken those good American people who just want answers, regardless of Party affiliation and membership. My objective is to alert everyone of the sinister evil heading our way. I want to let Americans know that their troubles, the troubles around the world, are all a part of a dangerous debacle, even satanic plot against the people of this planet, by the ones called "globalist elites" (which sounds innocuous) who are taking control, in an almost Orwellian fashion, of governments across the globe. Their plans include the depopulation of the planet from almost seven billion people to no more than one billion. How do you think they will accomplish that? Can history give us a clue? Yes, it can. Their largest obstacle to their goal is, yes, that's right, the United States, and they are busy working on that problem. We are seeing Orwellianism grow in the USA and around the Western world countries. You must realize how dangerous this is.

What do we need to counter this agenda? Right now, more than ever, we need a Trojan Horse and Sentries, formed inside the camps of the enemies of America. There is without doubt millions of middle-class, Christian, patriotic people who are Democrats and now on the fence about their Party. They are not liking what is going on within their Party either. They need to choose, if only for their own survival and the future of their own children and grandchildren.

We on the Right need to form an alliance with all patriots regardless of Party because none of us want socialism or the destruction of our nation. We need each other. This is a "common ground" matter. We both are victims of hate-mongering and brainwashing propaganda coming from the puppet-masters who seek to destroy this nation and control the world. We must put aside Party politics and come together to fight off this socialist movement because it is nothing more than a stepping stone to the totalitarian New World Order, i.e., a one-government world.

That's going to take dialogue, sit-down meetings, willingness to vote for the patriots, who are candidates, hoping to avert this madness against us. If they are Republican, so be it. The result is all that is important. We need Democrat patriots to remain inside the Democrat Party doing their part in their own meetings to stop the indoctrination by the far-Left leaders including the DNC. They need to stand against and argue with the Left's pro-socialist radicals, and take away their power by the simple act of rejecting their radical agenda, and kicking them out for fostering an ideology traditional Democrats do not support either.

If patriot Democrats do this, they become the Trojan Horse of our patriot alliance, and create paranoia in the far-Left. Second, we need "sentries" who are folks that are aware enough to help illuminate fake news broadcast our way from the media or other sources. We need to simply stop watching mainstream media, completely. Turn them off. Ignore them.

We need a collective to form in every State to pool knowledge and uniformly distribute it. If we are together on the same page, nothing can stop us from ridding our nation from those determined to destroy it. They claim freedom of speech to spread their treasonous intent, then we must claim OUR freedom of expression to reject their intent and agenda; it doesn't matter if the Left sees this proposed plan, once it is in place they won't know who is who anyway, with the result that paranoia reigns among them, and they won't be able to stop us at that point, regardless of the money behind them. Already we are seeing many Democrats backing away from the Left's radical agenda; we need more to do so. Our goal must be to shut down the Progressives who are essentially, knowingly or unknowingly, cooperating with the globalists' goal of chaos, anarchy, and takeover of the world to create their one government world.

It is hard for common folk, I think, to grasp the enormity of this agenda, strung across the globe like an insidious spider web of horrors, so I ask only that you consider what I bring to you here, avoid letting the mainstream media – owned by the elitists – brainwash you and dull your consciousness with their lies about all is well, or that the problem is Donald Trump and the Republicans, all lies. The globalists are dividing us, pushing the false narrative that white men and Republicans are to blame for everything gone wrong, pitting us against each other, all the while taking another step towards our mutual oblivion if they win. Part of this agenda is to eliminate all racial differences, so as to recreate humankind as a single bloodline. If you don't want this, then you need to step up. Complacency is, in our situation, akin to acquiescence, and works against us all. If we lose America, neither we nor our progeny will ever know freedom again. History will be re-written, and an Orwellian world will be created out of the ashes. Genocide by the billions will occur.

Finally, the on-going impeachment demands of the Left against President Trump is easy to understand. As I say further herein, from the Left's perspective, presidential candidate Donald Trump was a joke runner; they laughed about it, Hillary was happy because Trump's candidacy was a guarantee to her of winning. Or so she, and all her supporters, thought. No one on that side believed Trump had a prayer in hell of winning. On our side, few did either, but he resonated with our side well. I believed from the moment he threw his hat in the ring he would win.

The Left went after him immediately, before and after the election. They were desperate to unseat him. Why? Because he interrupted their pro-socialist plan led by the "shadow government" and assigned to Barack Obama and endorsed by Hillary Clinton, Bernie Sanders, and many others. They were so close to carrying out their plan that they were already rejoicing. Trump broke up that party atmosphere and sent them into a panic. Everything that the Left has done against Trump since then has been to get him out of office so they can get their socialist and, ultimately, their New World Order agenda back on track. There is not a single valid reason for the impeachment of Trump, so the Left's game card is to criticize and vilify Trump and all of his supporters. This is the hallmark of the Marxist "Critical Theory" method, i.e., criticize, lie, criticize, lie, over and over until the lie sticks if only by repetition. Everything the Left accuses the Right of is exactly what the Left is actually doing, another Marxist tool.

Support Donald Trump, vote out the RINOs who do not support him, and let's shut down this Marxist agenda. We cannot afford to lose the 2020 elections. Impeach, Cortez, Tlaib, and people like that. They are the true enemies of the State. Put them in prison.

Finally, don't over-generalize Democrats. There are plenty of disgruntled Democrats who are patriots and who love America. Help them to do the right thing at election time, and not support an out-of-control pro-socialist cartel who have taken over the Democrat Party.

All we patriots have to do is understand how Orwellianism works, and then everyone can see it working strongly in the Left's anti-America playbook.

I hope that you will read the entire book with an open mind, even if you are a democrat, or other, or just plain skeptical. I've tried to connect the dots accurately.

I'd like to close this (overlong) introduction with an incentive to go forward: The following is a recent event (today is 10/7/2019) about President Trump rolling back and discontinuing the post-World War II Marshall Plan. This is a fact, even if he has opposition to it, but he aims to get America out of this welfare-service to other countries who have abused America's generosity for many years. He alone has the guts to do the right thing by Americans.

TRUMP ENDING THE MARSHALL PLAN

The IMF is warning that global economies will contract by $455 billion next year due to the ongoing trade conflict between the U.S., China, the EU and to a lesser extent, Japan.

President Trump will cost the Global Economy $455 billion (that's almost half a trillion, folks!). because that money will be transferring back to the America First economy. That's what happens as MAGAnomics reverses the IMF trade (wealth distribution) model.

China and the EU have devalued their currency in an effort to block the impacts from President Trump and the America

First trade policy. Because those currencies are pegged against the dollar, the resulting effect is a rising dollar value. In essence, the globalist IMF is now blaming President Trump for having a strong economy that forces international competition to devalue their currency.

In the bigger picture is WHY President Trump is the most transformative economic President in the last 75 years. The post-WWII Marshall Plan was set up to allow Europe and Asia to place tariffs on exported American industrial products. Those tariffs were used by the EU and Japan to rebuild their infrastructure after a devastating war. However, there was never a built-in mechanism to end the tariffs. until President Trump came along and said: It's over!.

After about 20 years (+/-), say 1970 to be fair, the EU and Japan received enough money to rebuild. But instead of ending the one-way payment system, Asia and the EU sought to keep going and build their economies larger than the US. Additionally, the U.S. was carrying the cost of protecting the EU (via NATO) and Japan with our military. The EU and Japan didn't need to spend a dime on defense because the U.S. essentially took over that role. But that military role, just like the tariffs, never ended. Again, until Trump.

The U.S. economy was the host for around 50 years of parasitic wealth exfiltration, or as most would say distribution. The term exfiltration better highlights that American citizens paid higher prices for stuff, and paid higher taxes within the overall economic scheme, than was needed. President Trump is the first and only president who said: Enough!, and prior politicians who didn't stop the process were stupid etc. etc. Obviously, he is 100% correct.

For the past 30 years the U.S. was a sucker to keep letting the process remain in place while we lost our manufacturing base to overseas incentives. The investment process from Wall Street (removal of Glass-Steagall) only made the process much more severe and faster. Wall Street was now investing in companies whose best bet (higher profit return) was to pour money overseas. This process created the Rust Belt, and damned near destroyed the aggregate manufacturing industry.

Unfortunately, putting America First is now also against the interests of the multinationals on Wall Street; so President Trump has to fight adverse economic opponents on multiple fronts and their purchased mercenary army we know as DC politicians. No-one, EVER, could take on all these interests. Think about it. The EU, Asia, World Bank, International Monetary Fund, China, Russia, U.S. Chamber of Commerce, Iran, U.S. Congress, Democrats, U.S. Senate, Wall Street, the Big Club, Lobbyists, Hollywood, Corporate Media (foreign and domestic), and the ankle-biters in Never Trump. all of these financial interests are aligned against Main Street USA and against President Trump. Name one individual who could take them on simultaneously and still be winning, in a big way.

They say Trump is one man. They say they have him outnumbered. Yet somehow, as unreal as it seems, he's the one who appears to have them surrounded.

PATRIOTS, DON'T YOU JUST LOVE THIS PRESIDENT?

Now in looking for the source of the above, I did find another article in the September 5, 2018, edition of the Washington Times, written by Carlos Munoz, where he writes about Trump rejecting the long-standing Marshall Plan and other international gravy-train free-loader recipient countries.

In the July 13, 2017 edition of the HuffPost News, by Charles Kolb, Senior Public Policy Executive, there is a similar article about Trump going after these historic, post-war plans that were designed to help re-build war-torn countries but were never intended to be a free-loader-forever service, and he expressed his intention to put a stop to all that.

Also in 2017, a Bill Steil wrote an article in the Project Syndicate entitled "The Marshal Plan and America First" also discussing President Trump's intent to discontinue this "exfiltration" of American money to all of these countries who pay nothing to almost nothing to help themselves. So there is a lot of information out there about this. Steil, however, looks at it differently, characterizing it to say, it "is not that it places American interests first. It is the misguided way in which those interests are being defined."

In the April 17, 2018 edition of CDN (Communities Digital News), article by Terry Ponick, the Marshall Plan, which he writes as the Marshall Plan Ghost, he describes how the old MP is the real culprit behind 2018's trade war, and why if Trump dismantles the old MP and forces other countries to deal with America fairly and ethically, America will itself return to prosperity.

Americans have gotten caught in the web of politics that created and maintained the Marshall Plan some 70 years ago. All the recipient countries have prospered from our help, then continued to take advantage when they could easily stand on their own. Americans have gotten poorer because of unfair tariffs and trade agreements, most of which remain in place because of transnational corporations domiciled here in the USA. We have high unemployment because of this lop-sided relic still in place. We have seen our jobs taken as corporate America moved to other countries where manufacturing and consumer products could be made more cheaply. We have a huge number of welfare recipients burdening the working class because of this relic still in place. President Donald Trump is trying to dismantle it and help Americans return to prosperity. No other President has even attempted to do so. He is not letting us down, so how about we give him all of our support in 2020.

I don't mind borrowing tidbits of wisdom. Here is one: We need to take control of our destiny, not throw ourselves in the quagmire and accept it as our fate.

So, let's get started. I have given you an overview in this Introduction, so let's get down to the details, all of which, or nearly all of which, are interconnected in some way with the ultimate puppeteers who plan to destroy America, the Western world, and to bring us not to socialism – which is a mere stepping stone – but to a totalitarian regime run by elitists who will not be creating a Utopia, except for themselves, but a horror show for the citizens of the world, at least those who are left after they depopulate the planet to only one billion people.

This book needs to begin with George Orwell's "1984" so that we can begin to understand how "political correctness" is the new term for "double-speak" and other terms of Orwellianism that produce truth as lies and lies as truth, and force it upon the populations.

Can we fight back? Yes, but there is not much time left to organize, fund, and network enough patriots in all political parties to shut this socialist movement down peacefully, but with finality. We must try, and we must succeed. Neither we nor they will like the reality of socialism, or its final change, totalitarianism.

DO NOT LET THEM DESTROY THE SECOND AMENDMENT. This right to self-defense may become what saves us in the end.

I would like to close this Introduction with an admission. I have gotten angry at God from time to time, and I have yelled at Him, "Where the hell are you?" as I read about the atrocities going on today, especially against Christians by the Islamists. I saw the children Muslims slaughtered in the hundreds in North Africa because they were Christians. I have seen the evil rising here in the USA and around the world. Yes, I got angry with God for doing NOTHING to stop it. He said to me, "My son, I have give my children the jewel of the universe on which to live. I have given you the rules of life to live by. It is my children who must shepherd what I have given you. I have shown you how to clean your house by example, as I have cleaned mine. I am disappointed my children do not understand what they are tasked to do."

It is up to us to act. We must be the shepherds and caretakers.

Disclaimer

So, let's take a top down view. I may be a bit off on some things, but I have no reason at all to lie to you or intentionally publish inaccurate facts. Gathering facts is a process, and the problem is very huge, so I may inadvertently and unintentionally misstep somewhere. But know this; overall, I believe I am accurate about the intended outcomes of our enemies. I began writing this book several years ago, building it from several years of sound research. I didn't start with the idea of writing a book. I just wanted to know what was really going on. Now I pass what I have learned on to you, my fellow Americans. I believe every patriot and every enemy of America should read this because insight and wisdom may come late, but should never be rejected.

Please be patient as I have divided my book into parts, so you can take a break along the journey with me. I have told you in a summary fashion that we are all in serious trouble.

At 70 years old, I do not expect my life will last longer than 10 more years, if that. I am resigned to my own end, when it comes. I have no reason to lie, and I have tried to do my very best to uncover the truth about the things I write about here. I have watched many news shows, YouTube videos (archiving many of which for posterity), and relevant reading materials, all to compile what now appears in this book. I am a simple man who loves this country despite its squabbles and problems.

I have observed that most people tend to accept what their friends, their peers, their favorite media, and their Party leaders tell them. They seldom do the kind of research that I have done to get a more total view of all factors involved in what I tell you about here.

I've listed my sources as I went along, noting them in the appendix. Your future depends on what you know, and what you do about what you know. I'm here to give you in this book what has taken me several years to compile. I hope that you find yourself enlightened by the end. Knowledge is two-fold, and consists not only in an affirmation of what is true, but in the negation of that which is false.

Some of you may be familiar with Stansberry Research, one of the largest and most recognized financial research companies in the world, with hundreds of thousands of paid readers in nearly every country, an organization that regularly puts out notices, alerts, and publications about the economy and the stock market. A recent alert appeared in early September, 2019, entitled "The Female Obama: The Secret Force that will put a Socialist in the White House in 2020." (See, https://orders.cloudsna.com/?cid=MKT417512&eid=MKT421661&assetId=AST111548&page=1, or www.stansberryresearch.com) . It was narrated by Bill Shaw, a Senior Analyst at Stansberry Research, and with giving reference to him, I am quoting a brief part of what American patriots need to know:

> "There is a mysterious force that ignites the biggest social movements in history. Like the Labor movement of the 1930s, the Civil Rights movement of the 1960s, even Occupy Wall Street in 2011, only this time it's much bigger. The result: the most dramatic Presidential election of our generation. Once you understand this force and who's behind it, you'll understand why people like Alexandria Ocasio-Cortez and Bernie Sanders have millions of followers, why membership in the Democratic Socialists of America jumped nearly 500% in the past 2 years, and why 43% of Americans now say Socialism would be good for the country.
>
> More importantly, you'll understand why the next President is virtually guaranteed to be a Socialist Democrat who runs

on the most radical platform our nation has ever seen. How do I know? Simple. When the rich, a very small percentage of the population get in trouble with debt, it's an economic problem. But when the poor and middle class, a huge percentage of the population, get in trouble with debt, it's a political problem. I believe the next President will get elected by making Socialist promises to the poor and middle class.

Please understand I don't want to see this woman elected. But it will be her or someone even worse than her. This secret force cannot be stopped. It already has too much power. But there's still just enough time to prepare for the economic disasters that will follow her inauguration.

Most Americans don't believe that something like this could ever happen in America. But nobody predicted Trump would win in 2016 either. Frankly, I feel sorry for anyone who can't see what's coming, because if you sit on the sidelines and do nothing to prepare for the 2020 Election, you will fall victim to the next President's socialist agenda in ways you probably wouldn't even believe are legal.

As you'll see, the steps our next President takes during her first 100 days in office will create a nightmare for anyone with a 401(k), IRA, or any other savings. A massive movement brewing in America

My book is not predicated solely on Stansberry Research, inasmuch as my research traversed hundreds of sources over the last five years, but I find Bill Shaw's warnings to be consistent with and validating my own warnings in this book. I can't say Shaw was talking about AOC becoming president, perhaps he was talking about Elizabeth Warren, who is definitely an uninformed crackpot. About her, I'll quote something relevant from Charles Caleb Colton (1780-1832), to wit: "*Examinations are formidable even to the best prepared, for the greatest fool may ask more than the wisest man can answer.*"

This book is far larger than I ever anticipated, almost a mini-encyclopedia of world affairs and history. I hope you bear with me, and find the information enlightening. Colton also said, which applies to me here, that: *"Justice to my readers compels me to admit that I write because I have nothing to do; justice to myself induces me to add that I will cease to write the moment I have nothing to say."*

Chapter I:

What is "Orwellianism"?

PART 1: WHO WAS GEORGE ORWELL?

Premise: Orwellianism is alive and growing in America and in other Western countries.

Many of us are familiar with the books "Animal Farm" and "1984" by Eric Arthur Blair, better known by his pen name George Orwell. I will hereafter refer to him as Orwell. He was an English novelist and essayist, journalist and critic, whose work is characterized by lucid prose, awareness of social injustice, opposition to totalitarianism, and outspoken support of democratic socialism. He was born June 25, 1903 and died January 21, 1950, at the age of 46. He wrote a number of books, and although I may here refer to Animal Farm, I am particularly focused on "1984" which later, after his death, was made into the somewhat truncated-movie "1984" in the mid-50s. Orwell leaned toward socialism and had significant issues with the capitalist systems. However, it might be said that capitalism was relatively unknown around the world, and the United States's capitalist system, in the early 20's and through the 50's, was still evolving.

If you are not familiar with George Orwell's works, you can see online both "Animal Farm" and "1984", with the books also available online.[FN2.]

[FN2.] George Orwell's "1984" has repeatedly been banned and challenged in the past for its social and

Orwell, wrote his book "1984" to convey a totalitarian regime that obtained and retained power by the use of "double-speak" language. Orwell personally had spent years engaged in actual protests and battles with anti-democratic forces, right and left, and grew to understand both the overt and the subtle forms of totalitarianism. Initially, Orwell's books were banned in some countries, and publishers in the US during the early stages of WWII were reluctant to publish because initially the US viewed Russia as an ally against Germany. After the war, his books became highly popular.

Many scholars and ordinary people have read and discussed the book "1984." One of those people, Noah Tavlin, has become well-known for his "My Analysis of 1984" and the fictional government called "Oceania." I will reference this introduction to prepare my thoughts about our world of today, which I see becoming a "World Beyond Reason" largely reflecting the Orwellian Factor. Noah Tavlin's publications can be found in the link, https://ed.ted.com, search term "Orwellian" or https://ed.ted.com/search?utf8= &qs=Orwellian (References, #1). There are other publications and videos also finding that Orwellianism is alive and a threat not only to America but on the world stage as well.

There are two particular aspects indicative of the dystopian society characterized in Orwell's "1984." They are the rise of Collectivism and Hedonism, both of which are growing ever stronger in the United States and, indeed, around the globe in Westernized countries.

Collectivism is a doctrine, or set of ideologies, in which the goals of a certain collective, such as a state, a nation, or a society, are given precedence over the goals of the individual. Socialism, communism and fascism are all collectivist ideologies. Orwell believed that a precondition of the rise of totalitarianism was the emergence of a collectivist social structure as this permits the centralized rise of power needed to exert total societal control. Orwell's view of the connection between totalitarianism and collectivism has proved puzzling. Orwell was a staunch leftist, a critic of capitalism, and a socialist. How could

---

political themes, as well as for sexual content. Additionally, in 1981, the book was challenged in Jackson County, Florida, for being pro-communism. In 1950 it was banned in Russia under Stalin and the USSR with ownership subject to arrest for possible anti-communist thought.

someone who favored socialism, a collectivist ideology, at the same time write a dystopian novel which portrays a collectivist society in such a horrific manner? To understand his position, it must first be realized that Orwell did not consider capitalism to be a viable system. He wrote:

> "It is not certain that Socialism is in all ways superior to capitalism but it is certain that, unlike capitalism, it can solve the problems of production and consumption." (George Orwell, Complete Works – Vol. XII.)

Capitalism was such an inadequate system in Orwell's mind, that like many leftists of his day he believed that it was on its deathbed, and would soon be replaced by some form of collectivism. He saw this as inevitable. The issue for Orwell was what type of collectivism would take its place. He wrote:

> "The real question ... is whether capitalism, now obviously doomed, is to give way to oligarchy [totalitarianism] or to true democracy [democratic socialism]." (George Orwell, Complete Works – Volume XVIII.)

Assuming the impending death of capitalism, Orwell hoped that democratic socialism would be adopted in the West. Democratic socialists, like Orwell, advocated for essentially "planned economy", the nationalization of all major industry, and the radical decrease in wealth inequality. They were also supporters of civil liberties and equality, such as freedom of speech and freedom of assembly, which they hoped could be maintained in a society which would largely deprive people of their economic freedoms. The problems Orwell and other socialists had to grapple with were the lack of examples, past or present, of any countries successfully adopting democratic socialism. Even worse, any states that had turned to collectivism in the first half of the 20th century, such as Nazi Germany and Soviet Russia, were becoming increasingly totalitarian. They were adopting what Orwell called "oligarchical collectivism" not democratic socialism. In addition, he had no answer to the question of life under democratic socialism where individualism and unalienable rights were no longer considered important.

Oligarchical collectivism is a system wherein an elite few, under the guise of a certain collectivist ideology, centralized power using force and deception. Once in power these oligarchs crushed not only the economic freedoms of their citizens, a move which socialists like Orwell favored, but also their civil liberties. Orwell was concerned that following the death of capitalism the entire Western world would succumb to oligarchical collectivism. This fear was in part due to his perception that hedonism was on the rise in Western societies. Hedonism is an ethical position that maintains that life's ultimate goal should be the maximization of pleasure and the minimization of pain and discomfort.

Having come up during the 1920's, i.e., the Roarin' 20's, when hedonism was rampant in America due to high prosperity, I can understand why Orwell might think that; however, the 1929 stock market crash ended those "good times" and ushered in the Great Depression. So, Orwell had polar opposites to consider.

In an increasingly urban and consumerist West, Orwell believed that many people were structuring their lives in a hedonistic manner, and this did not bode well for the freedom of Western civilizations. Hedonistic lifestyle, according to Orwell, weakens people, it makes them feeble and incapable of mounting resistance to radical ideologues who desire to rule over society. Some believe that this fear has proven unfounded up to this point in time. While the West, since Orwell's death, has become more hedonistic, this has not yet led to totalitarian dictatorships taking over control. Unfortunately, Americans must admit that we have increasingly embraced hedonism as prosperity increases, despite economic inequality. Likewise, we have also seen a weakening of moral fiber as well as a mindset that perhaps it is best if the government 'runs the show' and takes "care" of us.

Aldous Huxley, the author of another famous dystopian novel, "Brave New World", may have had a better grasp of the ways Western societies would become enslaved in the late 20th and early 21st centuries. Huxley, like Orwell, was an anti-hedonist, but his aversion to hedonism was different from Orwell's.

Huxley's main concern was that hedonism could be used as an effective tool to oppress a society because people will willingly forgo freedom in exchange for sensory pleasure and endless consumption. If a society can be structured so that people can devote much of their time to pleasures gratifying material wants and even drugging themselves to escape from reality, then persuasion and conditioning rather than physical coercion will be sufficient to exert extreme control over a society. Neil Postman, in his book "Amusing Ourselves to Death", nicely contrasts the different fears of Orwell and Huxley, when he wrote:

> "What Orwell feared were those who would ban books. What Huxley feared was that there would be no reason to ban a book, for there would be no one who wanted to read one.... Orwell feared that the truth would be concealed from us. Huxley feared the truth would be drowned in a sea of irrelevance. Orwell feared we would become a captive culture. Huxley feared we would become a trivial culture.... In "1984", people are controlled by inflicting pain. In "Brave New World", they are controlled by inflicting pleasure. In short, Orwell feared that what we fear will ruin us. Huxley feared that what we desire will ruin us." (Neil Postman, Amusing Ourselves to Death: Public Discourse in the Age of Show Business.)

The West, it seems, finds itself in a situation somewhat analogous to what Huxley feared, for like the proverbial frog in boiling water, citizens in the West accept greater and greater intrusions into their freedoms and with little resistance. The overt physical coercion that Orwell thought to be required to enslave a society has so far proved unnecessary. Before dismissing Orwell's fears completely, however, it must be noted that Orwell was familiar with Huxley's position. And he did not deny that the hedonistic society Huxley feared was a possibility. But Orwell saw it as a temporary stage creating the ideal conditions for a more brutal regime to seize control and impose its will upon society.

Whether Orwell will be proven correct in the end remains to be seen. Yet, as was pointed out, Orwell did not believe that totalitarianism, which he feared, could emerge in a society without it first becoming collectivist. So perhaps what is preventing his fears from coming true thus far is that capitalism did not die as he believed it would. And collectivism has yet to emerge fully formed in the West. (Source for this material: Academy of Ideas, published 12-30-2017; http://academyofideas.com.) Note: In 1958, Mike Wallace interviewed Aldous Huxley on ABC, and opened with the statement, "This is Aldous Huxley, a man haunted by a vision of hell on earth. Searing social critic, Mr. Huxley, 27 years ago, wrote "Brave New World", a novel that predicted that someday the entire world will live under a frightful dictatorship."

Let us not forget the truth about the 60's, when the CIA experimented with the hallucinogenic LSD to see if it could be militarized, then released it into the general population to see what the effects would be. It was credibly alleged that certain parts of our own government were running opium, heroin, cocaine, and methamphetamines into our inner cities, with the results that neighborhoods broke down into crime ridden areas, where drugs, prostitution, and murder became a daily fare, especially in the African-American communities.

If we have lost our morality as a nation, especially in departments of our own government, legislators and congress included, we the people suffer the consequences, not them.

"He who studies books alone will know how things ought to be, and he who studies men will know how they are." Charles Caleb Colton.

PART 2: GEORGE ORWELL'S "1984"

In this Part, I want to explain what I have learned about the fictional works of George Orwell, who wrote the infamous book "1984." After we go over the highlights and their relevance, I will continue the top-down approach.

His quotations number 3,864, which anyone can find at www.goodreads.com. Some of them are:

> "Who controls the past controls the future. Who controls the present controls the past."

"Whoever controls the image and information of the past determines what and how future generations will think; whoever controls the information and images of the present determines how those same people will view the past." He who controls the past commands the future. He who commands the future conquers the past."

"In a time of deceit telling the truth is a revolutionary act."

"A liberal is a power worshipper without the power."

In doublespeak, "War is peace, freedom is slavery, ignorance is strength."

"Myths which are believed in tend to become true."

"Every generation imagines itself to be more intelligent than the one that went before it, and wiser than the one that comes after it."

"The most effective way to destroy people is to deny and obliterate their own understanding of their history."

"If you want a picture of the future, imagine a boot stamping on a human face – forever."

"But if thought corrupts language, language can also corrupt thought."

"Political language is designed to make lies sound truthful and murder respectable, and to give an appearance of solidity to pure wind."

"Doublethink means the power of holding two contradictory beliefs in one's mind simultaneously, and accepting both of them."

"If liberty means anything at all, it means the right to tell people what they do not want to hear."

"That rifle hanging on the wall of the working-class flat or labourer's cottage is the symbol of democracy. It is our job to see that it stays there."

Interestingly, his saw his books "Animal Farm" and "1984" as total failures which he wrote while he was very ill and dying. It would be 1956 before Hollywood would produce a loose version of "1984" in the movie so titled.

In his book "1984" he writes:

> "Now I will tell you the answer to my question. It is this. The Party seeks power entirely for its own sake. We are not interested in the good of others; we are interested solely in power, pure power. What pure power means you will understand presently. We are different from the oligarchies of the past in that we know what we are doing. All the others, even those who resembled ourselves, were cowards and hypocrites. The German Nazis and the Russian Communists came very close to us in their methods, but they never had the courage to recognize their own motives. They pretended, perhaps they even believed, that they had seized power unwillingly and for a limited time, and that just around the corner there lay a paradise where human beings would be free and equal. We are not like that. We know that no one ever seizes power with the intention of relinquishing it. Power is not a means; it is an end. One does not establish a dictatorship in order to safeguard a revolution; one makes the revolution in order to establish the dictatorship. The object of persecution is persecution. The object of torture is torture. The object of power is power. Now you begin to understand me."

And, "Power is in tearing human minds to pieces and putting them together again in new shapes of your own choosing."

Also: "Totalitarianism, however, does not so much promise an age of faith as an age of schizophrenia. A society becomes totalitarian when its structure becomes flagrantly artificial: that is, when its ruling class has lost its function but succeeds in clinging to power by force or fraud."

Although it is more likely, I assume, that less people today watched the movie "1984" (1956) than read the book, I ask you to remember the quotes, especially this one —- "The past was erased, the erasure was forgotten, the lie became the truth." – when you here read my description of what "1984" means in re-lation to the "Orwellian Factor" that is alive and well and growing in the world today, especially in the United States. This is what is going on today.

In Orwell's work of fiction, "1984", every record has been destroyed or falsified, every book has been rewritten, every picture has been repainted, every statue and street building has been renamed, every date has been altered. And that process is continuing day by day and minute by minute. History has stopped. Nothing exists except the endless present in which the party is always right.

What the ruling elite achieved was thought control, a masking of true reality with a false reality with its own language, its own changed history, and a pop-ulation which came to believe the great lie thought-control mandated.

Orwell correctly wrote, "From the totalitarian point of view, history is some-thing to be created rather than learned." He said, "So much of left-wing thought is a kind of playing with fire by people who don't even know that fire is hot." Socialism, communism, and totalitarianism each is a fire that consumes all that is good and leaves the population devastated, demeaned, confused, des-titute, and miserable." That is the truth and the reality. As Orwell said, "Ho-wever much you deny the truth, the truth goes on existing." Lies can be exposed and broken down. Truth stands firm on what it is.

In a letter to "The Tribune" (20 December 1940), later published in A Patriot After All", 1940-1941 (1999), it was written, "We are in a strange period of history, in which a revolutionary has to be a patriot, and a patriot has to be a revolutionary." In other words, in today's world, the pro-socialists are prom-ising Utopia by an ideology that has never been anything but a Dystopia of misery. They are promising the exact opposite of the reality of fact.

First, I am not alone in recognizing Orwellian traits in today's confused iden-tity and language crisis. According to moderator of a 2002 event featuring Christopher Hitchens on his popular book "Why Orwell Matters", (which speaking engagement was subsequently posted on YouTube April 24, 2013), there exists a growing sense among some that we are repeating history here, that "doublespeak" is growing across the globe, and Orwell was the one who asked us to think very critically of how those messages are sent by governments,. The moderator noted that colleges and universities across the nation were actually looking at Orwell's works, and that it was a good time to take such a look since there were many who are beginning to see that "doublethink" as Orwell described is rising, especially with regards to a rise in hostilities in Iraq and the continuing global hostilities and wars. He noted there was a need to examine language and the way we use language to represent events in the world.

Hitchens is an author of many books and articles, and, while often controversial, is renowned in the publishing and media industry; a query on YouTube will display numerous links about this author. I found it interesting, and somewhat refreshing, that after I independently learned about Orwellianism, I also discovered I was not alone in what I was seeing in the world today. In writing this book, I discovered Hitchens' take on the matter.

While it was somewhat clear that Hitchens exhibited some angst towards capitalism, he seemed to have clarity of insight about human behavior and cultures.

Orwell talked about the promised so-called "Stalinist Utopia", the false promise that (quoting Hitchens), "if the citizen would give up his freedom, or her freedom, for security, if you give the State your right to decide, if you give them all that and grant them the power then they will take care of his or her other needs. Such a bargain is fatal, because you will then end up with neither freedom nor security, with neither freedom nor food, neither freedom nor bread, you will be starved and bullied and told that you're being well-fed. And, you will not dare to point out the discrepancy between the reality and the promise because the Party says the promise is the reality and don't you dare go saying that you've confused the two and it's more than your life is worth." In Orwell's "1984" the reality set forth is terrifying, without hope, and leaving nothing left to live for. The citizen is property of the State and therefore disposable. Hitchens suggested that Orwell made it so frightening that it would mobilize people to resist it, but many simply found it so frightening that they believed it would be futile to resist it.

In the book "1984," the world is divided into three states: Oceania, Eastasia, and Eurasia. Oceania is constantly at war with one of these states while at peace with the other. For the majority of the book, Oceania is at war with Eastasia and is allied with Eurasia. Oceania covers the entire continents of America and Oceania and the British Isles, the main location for the novel, in which they are referred to as 'Airstrip One'. Eurasia covers Europe and (more or less) the entire Soviet Union. Eastasia covers Japan, Korea, China and northern India. Unfortunately, there's not much 'super' to these states except their size. All three are totalitarian dictatorships. Oceania's ideology is Ingsoc (English Socialism), Eurasia's Neo-Bolshevism and Eastasia's is the Obliteration of the Self (one imagines some kind of Buddhist-inspired fascism.). These ideologies are very similar, but the people are not informed of this.

The three states are in a perpetual state of warfare – sometimes two against one, sometimes all three against each other. These wars are fought in the disputed territories, running from North Africa over the Middle East and southern India to Southeast Asia. There has been a nuclear exchange, and the blocs seem to have agreed to perpetual conventional war, probably because constant warfare serves their shared interests in domestic control.

George Orwell's main character Winston Smith wrestles with oppression in Oceania, a place where the Party scrutinizes human actions with ever-watchful Big Brother. Defying a ban on individuality, Winston dares to express his thoughts in a diary and pursues a relationship with a woman named Julia.

Oceania regime's obvious form of total control was that the individual's every move was always watched, even in the home, and controlled every action and forms of speech that were obvious. The threat of stepping out of line was severe, including death.

Oceania demands total subservience. It is a police state, with helicopters monitoring people's activities, even watching through their windows. But Orwell emphasizes it is the "ThinkPol," the Thought Police, who really monitor the "Proles," the lowest 85 per cent of the population outside the party elite. The ThinkPol agents move invisibly among society seeking out, even encouraging, thought crimes so they can make the perpetrators disappear for reprogramming.

The other main way the party elite, symbolised in the mustached figurehead Big Brother, encourage and police "correct thought" is through the technology of the Telescreen. These "metal plaques" transmit things like frightening video of enemy armies and of course the wisdom of Big Brother. But the Telescreen can see you, too. During mandatory morning exercise, the Telescreen not only shows a young, wiry trainer leading cardio, it can see if you are keeping up. Telescreens are everywhere: They are in every room of people's homes, even monitor things said during one's sleep-dreams. At the office, people use them to do their jobs.

Other forms of control were not so obvious, including the concept that whoever controls the past controls the future, thus the government of Oceania engages in brainwashing techniques by overwhelming the people with a barrage of data and facts that are totally untrue and manufactured by a specific department known as the Ministry of Truth. All that it does is lie to the citizens of Oceania. The Ministry of Peace is the military. Hard labor camps were called Joy-camps.

Political prisoners are detained and tortured under the Ministry of Love. In the Ministry of Love is Room 101, introduced in the climax of the novel, and is the basement torture chamber, in which the Party attempts to subject a prisoner to his or her own worst nightmare, fear or phobia, with the object of breaking down their resistance.

As in each Ministry, the irony is that they are the opposite of what the title is. This deliberate irony is called "double-speak." Words are not used to convey meaning, but to undermine it, corrupting the very ideas they refer to.

The Oceania government removed words from the language, and rearranged words in such a manner that discouraged critical thought and deductive reasoning, thus dulling the brain and mental process resulting in a state known contemporarily as "cognitive dissonance." Orwell called this mental state "double-thinking", a hypnotic state of cognitive dissonance where one is compelled to disregard their own perception in place of the officially dictated version of events. This left the individual completely dependent upon the State's definition of reality itself. This created a world in which the very process and privacy of one's own thoughts are violated. A person may even be found guilty of a "thought crime" by talking in their sleep. Keeping a diary or even having a love affair is considered "subversive rebellion."

In "1984" there was a "Hate Week" which was a psychological operation designed to increase the hatred of the population for the current enemy of the totalitarian Party, as much as possible, whichever of the two opposing super-states that may be. This was reinforced by the "Two Minutes Hate" which is a daily period in which Party members of the society of Oceania must watch a film depicting the Party's enemies and express their hatred for them for exactly two minutes.

On May 1944, before "1984" went to publication in June 1949, Orwell replied to a letter from a Noel Wilmett answering his question about what Orwell's thoughts were about totalitarianism and current events. (This can be found at https://www.thedailybeast.com/george-orwells-letter-on-why-he-wrote-1984, References #2.) Quoting from this letter, he says:

> Many thanks for your letter. You ask whether totalitarianism, leader-worship etc. are really on the up-grade and instance the fact that they are not apparently growing in this country and the USA. I must say I believe, or fear, that taking the world as a whole these things are on the increase. Hitler, no doubt, will soon disappear, but only at the expense of strengthening (a) Stalin, (b) the Anglo-American millionaires and (c) all sorts of petty fuhrers of the type of de Gaulle.
>
> All the national movements everywhere, even those that originate in resistance to German domination, seem to take non-democratic forms, to group themselves round some superhuman fuhrer (Hitler, Stalin, Salazar, Franco, Gandhi, De Valera are all varying examples) and to adopt the theory that the end justifies the means. Everywhere the world movement seems to be in the direction of centralized economies which can be made to 'work' in an economic sense but which are not democratically organised and which tend to establish a caste system.

With this go the horrors of emotional nationalism and a tendency to disbelieve in the existence of objective truth because all the facts have to fit in with the words and prophecies of some infallible fuhrer. Already history has in a sense ceased to exist, ie. there is no such thing as a history of our own times which could be universally accepted, and the exact sciences are endangered as soon as military necessity ceases to keep people up to the mark. Hitler can say that the Jews started the war, and if he survives that will become official history. He can't say that two and two are five, because for the purposes of, say, ballistics they have to make four.

But if the sort of world that I am afraid of arrives, a world of two or three great super-states which are unable to conquer one another, two and two could become five if the fuhrer wished it. That, so far as I can see, is the direction in which we are actually moving, though, of course, the process is reversible.

As to the comparative immunity of Britain and the USA: Whatever the pacifists etc. may say, we have not gone totalitarian yet and this is a very hopeful symptom. I believe very deeply, as I explained in my book The Lion and the Unicorn, in the English people and in their capacity to centralise their economy without destroying freedom in doing so. But one must remember that Britain and the USA haven't been really tried, they haven't known defeat or severe suffering, and there are some bad symptoms to balance the good ones. To begin with there is the general indifference to the decay of democracy. Do you realise, for instance, that no one in England under 26 now has a vote and that, so far as one can see, the great mass of people of that age don't give a damn for this?

Secondly there is the fact that the intellectuals are more totalitarian in outlook than the common people. On the whole the English intelligentsia have opposed Hitler, but only at the price of accepting Stalin. Most of them are perfectly

ready for dictatorial methods, secret police, systematic falsi-
fication of history etc. so long as they feel that it is on 'our'
side. Indeed, the statement that we haven't a Fascist movement in England largely means that the young, at this moment, look for their fuhrer elsewhere. One can't be sure that
that won't change, nor can one be sure that the common
people won't think ten years hence as the intellectuals do
now. I hope they won't, I even trust they won't, but if so it
will be at the cost of a struggle. If one simply proclaims that
all is for the best and doesn't point to the sinister symptoms,
one is merely helping to bring totalitarianism nearer.

You also ask, if I think the world tendency is towards Fascism,
why do I support the war. It is a choice of evils—I fancy
nearly every war is that. I know enough of British imperialism
not to like it, but I would support it against Nazism or Japanese imperialism, as the lesser evil. Similarly, I would support
the USSR against Germany because I think the USSR cannot
altogether escape its past and retains enough of the original
ideas of the Revolution to make it a more hopeful phenomenon than Nazi Germany. I think, and have thought ever
since the war began, in 1936 or thereabouts, that our cause
is the better, but we have to keep on making it the better,
which involves constant criticism.

Yours sincerely, Geo. Orwell

PART 3: THE ORWELLIAN
FACTOR IN MODERN DAY AMERICA

In "1984" we can find how Orwell drew similarities for his work of fiction.
What similarities to Orwell's concerns about a totalitarian world do we see
today? We cannot ignore world affairs, the shadow government, and what is
really going on.

What we have seen more recently, is the attempt of the Islamic world to re-write history about the genocide of Jews, even saying it never happened at all, how in our own schools history is being taught to our children with a bias against the truth and a predilection for assigning guilt from that bias, and how our schools no longer teach to promote good thinking and principles.

Students are not being taught true history, or how to think, other than thinking about thinking (which is circular and achieves nothing), or what it takes in the real world to achieve and prosper. Why? Perhaps because teachers, by and large, went to school and became teachers, and never worked in the actual marketplace and thus know little about it. And there is innate racial discrimination, where "affirmative action" now is applied to not fail students who fail their tests so as to not 'damage' their 'fragile self-esteem'. It is work, struggle, and success that builds self-esteem, not catering to failure.

Blacks are being brainwashed by anti-white racist blacks who call for the "extermination" of all "white people" despite the very minority of whites who actually owned slaves, i.e., 4.9% of the Southern population, and despite the fact that Northern whites liberated the Southern blacks from slavery at a huge cost in white lives. But today, to many blacks, "white" lives don't matter at all. Although no one today ever owned slaves, one wonders if blacks expect some kind of personal apology by whites to blacks that slavery was a part of American history, and are angry when no apology is given. It is not given because it is not owed. Yet in our schools, white students are being bullied into a sense of guilt for a heritage that no longer applies. Blacks want financial reparations for that history, yet whites could just as easily seek financial reparations for the hundreds of thousands of whites who died to free the slaves. This in itself is misplaced thought. In merit-based market-economy, everyone, regardless of color, has opportunity to seek and achieve prosperity, if one qualifies by motivation, values, education, and skills. No one is held back based on race. Discrimination, if you will, in a market economy, is based on behavior, not skin color.

But they are being fed this anti-white hatred by non-black forces as well, the very forces that are now trying to destroy the ideology of the United States in order to usher in (step 1) socialism and (step 2) totalitarianism. Once again, blacks are being used for purposes that will not be kind to them in the end result.

Although the pro-socialist movement has been ongoing in America for about half-a-century, and has been quietly growing in schools where pro-socialist teachers and professors have managed to keep under the "radar", it has more recently manifested as follows, to name some of the more overt manifestations:

1. "Political Correctness" in speech and behavior.
2. The Feminist movement to effeminize men.
3. The LGBT movement to normalize the abnormal in re-gendering.
4. The growing attack against Christianity and beliefs in God.
5. The growing demand for open borders to allow foreigners into the country in order to radicalize politics towards socialism.
6. A growing demand by blacks seeking financial reparations from modern-day whites who never owned slaves to all blacks claiming ancestral ties to slaves.
7. Creating laws to eliminate anything and everything that might emit carbon dioxide (CO_2), including cows (just about anything that farts), gas vehicles, airplanes, trains, that list is endless.

It's only been a few years since "political correctness" has become a household word. It is a term emphasized by the Left and first permeated the political landscape. New words are created, like Islamophobe which, as I learned, is a term created by Islamists who hate America and have their own agenda for world domination. "Political correctness" is Orwellian, no doubt about it.

But this term trickled into the public domain and is stronger than ever. It has become a power against mainstream America. The Progressives push the idea that the First Amendment right to freedom of speech and expression manifests only as they interpret it, and does not exist for those whose beliefs and ideas differ from theirs. Republicans and Independents accept that everyone has the right to their own beliefs and opinions, and they don't attack or assault those whose opinion differs from theirs. But the Progressives do. Like their counterpart, the Nazis of old, we have seen the violence manifested in protests, in threats to public officials and their families, the vandalism during protests, the omniscient presence of violence as they push their pro-socialist agenda. I came to realize that "political correctness" was just another term used for "new-speak", "double-speak", and "double-think" terms described by George Orwell in "1984." While this was a piece of fiction, it was a warning by Orwell to us all, and I have begun to realize that what he warned us about was coming true right now, and growing.

So, what does this mean today? We might accept that this kind of Oceaniac control could only happen in totalitarian or authoritarian regimes. Certainly, we have seen the results of dictatorships in our own lifetimes across the globe. Genghis Khan, Adolf Hilter, Joseph Stalin, Mao Zedong, Pol Pot, the list is long.

We can even point to Islam as an example of a totalitarian ideology, masquerading as a religion of peace and love, where from birth to death, its emphasis on "religious ritual" requiring prayer 5-7 times each day at the risk of violent repercussions if missed, controls and shapes the minds until death. It mandates that anyone not a believer and devout adherent to the Quran is considered an "infidel" and may be killed under the authority of their "God". Islam may well be the most effective brainwashing ideologue the world has ever known, created for reasons that are not purely epistemic, and certainly questionable when one recognizes Islam's Holy Book has been "interpreted" by men over centuries to suit what men want.

Their reality is what the clerics and Imams say it is, based on their interpretation of the Quran, and is then enforced by the government and each other, just like in "1984." Right now, today, fundamentalist Islamists are committing genocide against Christians and other religions. Islamists are permitted to lie to non-Muslims, about anything and everything. Islam is an example of overt totalitarian Orwellian conditions. But we cannot say that this is the ONLY example of totalitarianism in the modern world. But it is the worst.

Orwell was warning us about how the Orwellian factors of double-speak and double-thinking could occur, and flourish, in contemporary democratic societies. This is why totalitarian or authoritarian alone does not Orwellian make. In other words, our own basic freedom of speech and expression can give rise to pre-authoritarian platforms by the enforcement of realities born from the minds of those seeking to control and indoctrinate others. And, once again, Colton warns us: *"Knowledge is two-fold, and consists not only in an affir-mation of what is true, but in the negation of that which is false."*

Despite the broad scope of our constitutional right to freedom of speech and expression, both the legislative and judicial bodies have determined that there are, and must be, limitations. For example, you can't scream out "FIRE!" in a crowded theater because people are likely to be seriously injured as everyone scrambles for the exits. You can't falsely besmirch one's character and do dam-age to his/her career by your lies. You can't lie in a court of law without con-sequences. You can't beat up people as if it was a protected right under freedom of "expression." You can't take overt seditious or treasonous actions against this country without consequences. Yet, this is what occurs today, and often overlooked under the power that "political correctness" has claimed. But se-ditious speech remains protected unless it actually results in violence by the speaker or by those who act, and are proven to have acted, upon his/her call to violence. The law requires an overt act against the government, including politically-driven terrorism. In the move to advance the Progressive's agenda, we are losing the rights that are God-given and embodied in our own Consti-tution, by the Progressives demanding only THEY have those rights.

But it's not only the "re-setting" of our nation to a socialist ideology that drives the radical Left. The Progressives are trying to force upon us all that gender identity at birth is not an absolute, that a girl might really be a boy and vice versa, where a child, nowhere near an adult and whose brain itself won't mature fully until the late teens or early 20's, and whose mind cannot mature until the brain is fully mature, should nonetheless be given the right, at 6 or 8 or 10 or 12 years old, to decide to change his/her sex in a permanent and unchangeable way. The Progressives push the idea that little children, even in kindergarten, should be required to engage in role reversal by wearing the opposite sex's clothing and playing with their toys, so that they can choose to be the other sex. In Sweden, there are children's playgrounds with large blow-up penises and vaginas that are like slides that the children go into and through. How crazy is that perverse curriculum? This is insanity manifested.

Political correctness says that it's no longer acceptable to protest or criticize if you don't believe as the Progressives do, and one can be sued or be charged with a crime, if a person is addressed as a him or her, she or he, Mr. or Mrs. or Miss. They are to be neutrally addressed as "hen." "Hen." Transgenderism now requires we all share the same bathroom, no longer separated by sex. Some non-compliant businesses have been boycotted, even vandalized.

The Progressives foster racial hatred, as I mentioned earlier, now specifically targeting "white people" and, particularly, "old white men." Blacks are taking up the racist banner and calling for the death of "all white men." (Not necessarily white women, either, do you understand the meaning of that?) The Black Panther movement, formerly a murderous group from the 60's and 70's, mostly wiped out by imprisonment for their crimes, is back and growing, and expressly calling for the death of "white people." The Progressive's intent is to divide and conquer, to vilify the opposition and convince their own supporters to commit violence.

This kind of insanity pushed by the Progressives is thus far unchecked, and it is a growing problem even now in the United States, imported from European countries. Even now, the European Court of Human Rights have submitted to the demands of Sharia blasphemy laws and decided not to allow criticism of Muhammad, lest Muslim feelings be hurt. The court actually chose hurt feelings (expressed by a totalitarian genocidal regime) over freedom of speech, expression and truth as a defense.

As Noah Tavlin succinctly pointed out, in Orwell's essay on Political Speech in 1946, Orwell said, *"Political language is designed to make lies sound truthful and murder respectable, and to give an appearance of solidity to pure wind."* (Politics and the English language, 1946.)

I have arrived at similar conclusions that our world today has gone Orwellian, which is why I named this article, World Beyond Reason: The Orwellian Factor.

At this precise point in this article, I took a break and asked myself, "I wonder what is online" about this, so I typed in "Modern Orwellianism" and found a long list of videos by people who have likewise arrived at conclusions that we are now facing Orwellian forces destroying not just our own country and values, but manifesting itself around the globe. These aren't random manifestations, but created by and funded by the globalist trillionaires. I wonder if George Orwell, in writing 1984, inadvertently gave rise to an articulated blueprint adopted by the modern-day globalists and those they control. Colton said, "*In life we find many men that are great, and some that are good, but very few men that are both great and good.*"

George Orwell understood how great noble ideals can turn into their opposite, a condition which currently seems lost on the alt-Left in America. Orwell understood that sometimes the government said just the opposite of what they intend – much like the alt-Left Progressives are doing here today – that War is Peace, Freedom is Slavery, such as what Orwell saw with Stalinism, where when Stalin said the situation of the country was extraordinary, and that when extraordinary measures were needed, that meant mass graves. No one had to tell Orwell that, he knew.

I would like to quote a view by author Christopher Hitchens (2005), which explains his viewpoint of Orwell's attempt to enlighten us all about the dangers of governing by an all-powerful government. Hitchens said:

> "How did he (Orwell) achieve this extraordinary achievement of being right when everybody else was wrong, to put it bluntly?
>
> Orwell achieved this in two ways: one, by life experience. He did know that power was not its own justification, the authority did not come from God, it did not come from tradition, it came from people who wanted power. He understood that (reality) and he felt that he should never stop criticizing them and exposing them. That's the first thing. Second, I think he realized that often this I 'trick' is masked in language. If you only read one essay of his, you must read, "Politics in the English Language" in which he exposes the fraud, the way in which euphemism is used to mask brutal reality. If I were to give you an example now, I suppose I would say, to take the most recent and the most obvious one, I don't

think now that any member of any American administration would use the world "collateral damage" again, to describe what it does describe, civilian casualties. Those of you who know that expression and have known how to see through it, have done – in your own way – an Orwellian job, and you probably, without knowing it, owe it to Orwell, this capacity that you have. But that's the trick, in effect, you find a nice name for a nasty thing, and you get it spread around by making it seem technical, or technological. If I could summarize (the meaning of euphemism), that would be it.

Orwell was on to that. He knew every time the Stalin regime said, "*Well, in extraordinary times we need extraordinary measures*" that meant mass graves, i.e., genocide. He knew without being told, by reading their own propaganda, that whatever the truth was, the propaganda was lying, and it was using nice words for disgraceful things. This is a trick that should never desert you. You can all do it yourself. There's no reason not to do it. Interrogate what you read and what you're given, in that spirit, and you'll find it all the time.

It's remarkable to me that he (Orwell) was able to do it and to be considered exceptional for it. But he did stick to it. And he did it by understanding that great noble ideals can turn into their opposite. And, in (his book) 1984, Freedom is Slavery, and Peace is War. And people live with negation because they believe the Party, or the Authority, or the Dictator who claimed it in the first place, and they didn't have the nerve to doubt it, because if they were wrong … if they themselves had been fooled, then what would it make them? (A fool?)

Power is only what YOU allow it to be. Very many people put up with political lying and political illusions, and political propaganda, because if they were to denounce it they would have to admit that for decades themselves they had been fooled, that they had been taken for granted, that they had allowed themselves, so to speak to be deceived. The con man's work is always done for him by the victim, the victim doesn't want to go to the police and say "I've been conned." "I was so stupid that I did this." They don't wish to admit it. So in a subtle and deadly way the dictator can dirty enough people up to make them all complicit in his rule, ... can make them the tortured and masochistic complicit element in his sadistic mania.

What you can necessarily do about power, about authority, you can do for yourself. You can resolve not to be a citizen like that, you can resolve not to do the work of power for it, you can resolve not to allow lies be told in your hearing, you can resolve not to use sloppy language that is euphemism.

You'll realize that your reading of Orwell is not an exercise in projecting blame on others, but is an exercise in accepting responsibility for yourself. And it's for that reason that he will always be honored and that he'll always be hated. Orwell wouldn't have had it any other way, and as a crony of his neither would I.

Hitchens said that the question of why Orwell seemingly did no essays on Nazism may be answered by saying it is likely he simply condemned Hitler as evil because he assumed no further explanation was needed. Hitchens noted Orwell wrote no essays against fascism; all he did was take up a rifle and fight against it. It was more like "vermin control" than an ideological fight. Whereas against communism you have to argue against the illusions of civilized people who think that there might be a higher synthesis, a better society available, by following a one-party initiative, and which would take guts and nerve, fascism itself was simply evil itself.

And, if you don't know it already, the Russian revolution, initiated by Lenin, was inspired by Karl Marx, the socialist. Leninism was the result, a failure, out of which Stalin and Stalinism arose that resulted in the genocide of tens of millions of Stalin's own populations.

In America today, with the rise of the alt-Left and their demand for socialism as our ideology, the illusions in their propaganda, are easily seen for the lies and misconceptions on which they are based, but the millennials, at least a great portion of them, have foolishly fallen into the trap of Orwellian propaganda, thinking that a market economy based on a capitalist democracy is evil and creates a caste system of have's and have not's, which is hardly the reality. What is reality is that a merit-based system where people are able to achieve or fail on their own merit is fundamentally a system where education and inspiration, or lack thereof, drives the outcomes. Once again, I quote Colton: *"The consequences of things are not always proportionate to the apparent magnitude of those events that have produced them. Thus, the American Revolution, from which little was expected, produced much; but the French Revolution, from which much was expected, produced little."*

Briefly, I would like to include a conversation on Tucker Carlson (Fox News) and Heather MacDonald, author of "The Diversity Delusion" in which she talks about the failure of diversity in America. In the following excerpt of the interview she explains how much in danger Americans are with regards to "political correctness" being used to shut down opposition to the socialist agenda. "Political correctness" is the new Orwellian term for "double-speak" et al.

Tucker asked Heather:

Are you surprised, having followed this whole line of argument for so many years, and closely, are you surprised that Pelosi, and Biden for that matter, are both being denounced as racists right now?

Heather:

No, Tucker, it's hilarious. Let's take a moment to savor this moment, when the Left turns on itself wielding the exact weapons it wields against everybody else, and accuses itself of racism. It's preposterous. But it's also a serious matter. I disagree slightly with you to say that people don't believe this. What we're witnessing, I believe, the most dangerous thing is the import from the academy into the real world. Students are taught from the moment they arrive on campus two things, and two things only reliably, which is that the most important thing about themselves is their own group identity, defined reductively as going after melanin, and that racism and sexism based on those characteristics are the defining features of American society. Taught to believe that, when they are faced with any kind of disagreement they reflexively accuse their ideological opponent of bigotry and hate, and that works wonderfully on a college campus. You accuse the president of racism and he immediately crumbles and orders another million dollars in diversity bureaucracy, you accuse a corporation of racism and it folds, as we saw with Nike and the preposterous claim that the Betsy Ross American flag was racist. It works with politicians, as with Biden repudiating his justified support for the 1994 federal crime bill which saved thousands of minority lives. The question is, is this going to work on the rest of us, and if it does, Tucker, civil society is over, because this is a totalitarian power play. It is an attempt to shut down any kind of dialectical search for truth, and to occupy the sole ideological ground, and that is a recipe for a society to halt dead in its tracks and go in reverse.

Tucker:

Because it is not really an argument. I mean, no one is making the case and, by the way, this eliminates the need to make the case, I mean, you don't need to actually have to convince anybody of anything, if you're doing it to fight racism it's a moral imperative and everyone else should just shut up and obey.

Heather:

You know, there's been political disagreements long before "identity politics." People disagree. That is what America is about, that we have to have the right, we have the freedom to debate our opinions. The alternative to debate is violence, it is an act of narcissism to think that everything is about yourself, to immediately say "It must be because of my gender and my race that I'm being disagreed with, and you must be a bigot to disagree with me." No, that is not the case; these are issues that deserve to be threshed out in the public forum and, again, if they are not, we are approaching a totalitarian state very quickly.

Tucker:

And so, this is a much longer conversation, but in the short time we have would you recommend, what is the course of action for normal people, ignore these racial slurs, kind of cynical politics that they are, how should the average person fight back against this totalitarianism?

Heather:

Well, the average person has to simply reject the racism charge. All of us have to start working on alternative explanations for our reality. Racism is no longer the predominant characteristic of America, if it ever was. It was a part of it, it was never the defining feature, but it is certainly not, this still remains the land of opportunity. The alternative explanation is that are profound behavioral differences, choices that individuals make that determine social outcomes, that we have to fight back against this narrative, Tucker, because if they win we lose our civilization, we lose meritocracy and we lose freedom.

End

Our youth of today, described as "millennials" have long been victimized in our schools and youth-related pro-socialist mainstream media to believe that a capitalist democracy is evil and based on pure greed. The goal is to brainwash American's young people so that when they enter the age of voting, politics, government and business they will vote for socialist politicians in order to destroy the meritocracy and usher in the "Utopia" they have been brainwashed into believing socialism is. Try to tell them how victimized they are, and they immediately reject it and turn against you.

But it is also worse than that, if possible. The curriculum and emphases in the schoolrooms of our nation do not teach students to think about the subject matter. It seems to teach a cyclic process of thinking about thinking that leads nowhere. It is no longer a matter of studiousness, deductive reasoning as a learning tool, or even achievement based on merit, but an official process to dumb down our children so that they always accept and not question authority, a theme they learn from the teacher's control of them.

Some may disagree with my use of the word "meritocracy" but the actual definition is: 1) system based on ability, i.e., a social system that gives opportunities and advantages to people on the basis of their ability rather than, e.g., their wealth or seniority; 2) elite group, i.e., an elite group of people who achieved their positions on the basis of ability and achievement; 3) leadership by elite, i.e., leadership by an elite group of people who are chosen on the basis of their abilities and achievements.

A plutocracy is rule by the extremely wealthy who believe they know best what is good for the "common" people. A plutocracy can easily degenerate into totalitarianism.

A "capitalist democracy" is a system whereby citizens can engage in any type of vocation they want, from business, to administrative agencies, to government bureaucracy positions, the arts, and so on, where their success is generally determined by their own merit. If they choose an income source, such as a small business they own or work in, and if they qualify for the tasks entailed in that business or vocation, they will get paid the common rate such businesses pay at, and at least the "minimum wage" (a living wage). The merit system is the fundamental basis of the "American Dream." Dream as you will to set your goals, pursue your goals, learn what is needed for that dream, and qualify to perform that vocation by your own efforts. If your dream has step-dreams, i.e., a first step, second step, third step, etc., for movement up the income ladder, that is your right.

I don't hate rich people. Other than those who inherited money, business(s), and status earned by their parents and/or grandparents, most of them worked to achieve their wealth. People who have invented things of use and value, from simple things like toothbrushes to high technology like electronic devices popular with the public, they have gotten very rich, so why should I hate them? These products may have made my life much better. One should not hate someone just because you envy them and their wealth. Authors of popular books, especially those on the list as "Bestsellers", can also become quite wealthy. Should I hate them even though I might really like their books?

What I distrust and view as enemies of us all are those in the all-powerful aristocracy who think they are above everyone else and never make decisions that should be made for the betterment of our society. What I distrust also are those who cannot seem to function successfully in a merit-based society because they were unable or too lazy to prepare properly for being a part of it. Lazy kids in school who do not study and who do not prepare, but when faced with life on their own complain they are somehow disenfranchised; so they want socialism with the belief they'll be taken care of without effort on their part.

The socialists tend to be morally- and socially-empathic failures, or snooty socialites or elites from a mindset of self-conceit that they are better than everyone else who should be ruled over, or both. Like today, recognizing they who support the socialist movement as the best form of government now believe a huge government will provide them with free food, free clothing, free medical care, free cars, free everything, yet they seem to fail to recognize that government can provide nothing free on its own. They have been and are being sold another false promise of actual equality of rights, conditions, and purse. That is not going to happen. What they will get, as bears saying over and over, is "equality" of poverty, destitution, degradation, and misery. Socialism always ends that way. Colton aptly cautions: "*There is a difference between happiness and wisdom: he that thinks himself the happiness man, really is so; but he that thinks himself the wisest, is generally the greatest fool.*" Progressives really need to get this point.

A country has to have an economy based on workers performing the many tasks that it takes to have a socialist country. If they are not total slaves, the Government will have to pay them a basic wage so they can survive. But what happens when a socialist country has little money or is in debt? So what happens to those people who cannot work and earn a wage, or who don't want or refuse to work, or who are simply too old to work? Government cannot give to anyone that which they did not take from someone else, and welfare seems something like the redistribution of wealth at the expense of the working class, much of whom are already struggling to make ends meet.

In a socialist, communist, or totalitarian ideology, the elderly have to rely on their grown children for survival; there is no welfare in such ideology. Those who refuse to work, or can't work, rely on hand-outs like our own homeless, because there is no welfare in the ideologies of socialism, communism, or totalitarianism. In mainland China, it is illegal to give a beggar anything.

It is the state which tells you where to work, how to work, and how many hours you work. (I recall it is North Korea, a totalitarian state, who has enslaved large portions of its own people in conditions resulting in starvation, disease, and death. This has been its ideology for many years, and the only accurate word for the mistreatment by Korean leaders of its own citizens is simply "grossly inhumane" as crimes against humanity itself.) Despite America's involvement in many countries to help free citizens from oppression, I can't help but wonder why America, and even the NATO countries, have not freed the North Koreans of the horrors they have endured for generations. Perhaps it is because NK has no resources that benefit America?

Crime? In a socialist or communist or totalitarian nation? What crime? Crime is usually punished in the most extreme ways, cutting off of hands and/or feet, torture, life imprisonment in ungodly conditions, and death by hanging, shooting, torture, beheading, chopping, drowning, thrown off a cliff or building, burning one alive, burning eyes out, choking, bludgeoning, the list is as long as the vile perpetrator can dream up to do. Utopia? Where, in Socialism? Communism? Totalitarianism? Is that a joke? Never happens. All of these ideologies share a common theme about equality: what life is like under such ideologies is equality of poverty and misery, because once that kind of government gets control, it is always the very worst who seem to climb to the top of the power ladder. Genocide is usually what actually occurs. Can you imagine what socialism would be like under a dictator like Alexandra Ocasio-Cortez, or Raschida Tlaib, Kamala Harris, or Linda Sarsour? These are not nice people; they are angry and driven to destroy, destroy and destroy. They are radical haters. They hate America and Americans, Christians, white people, and so on. They are the Ted Bundy's of politics.

In countries with free education and medical care, that some point to as successful socialist countries, like Sweden or Finland for example, these are not true socialist countries; their income base is capitalist, and the working class are taxed very high, at higher than 50% of citizen income, sometimes a lot higher. Their rights and freedoms are determined by the government.

In a meritocracy, a capitalist economy is what sustains freedoms and rights, and allows a nation to thrive based on freedom to choose and achievement by merit, i.e., choose your path and earn your way to whatever success goals you have in mind.

Has this worked In America? Yes. What Americans rightly complain about is that government, local, state, and national, has grown so obese with a steady stream of regulations, penalties, licenses, permits, etc., that it is difficult for business to remain health and profitable. This is the real complaint. This is a valid complaint. Our Founders expected we would have the common sense to keep government small and regulations at minimum, so that we could truly have the freedom to pursue, achieve, and enjoy the American dream. It is the bureaucrats in government who prey upon other Americans by over-regulation and mountains of paperwork, with unending fees for just about everything.

Who turned America into an obese "fat cat" government-run bureaucracy at the expense of the rights and freedoms of the American citizens? Greedy politicians, yes, from all political parties. But which are the States that have the worst economies, the lowest job growth, the highest numbers of welfare recipients, the highest number of terrible schools and colleges, and the worst crime levels? More to the point, for these states, which political party is the most dominant? Democrat states. Democrats. A Party now hi-jacked by a powerful movement of socialists whose goal is to destroy America and bring about socialism.

Now the supporters, like the millennials, think the end goal is socialism, and it will be a Utopia where everything is free and wonderful. But socialism is not the end goal at all. I repeat myself: The end goal is a totalitarian world being called the "New World Order" which will be a world controlled by the very snooty and wealthy elites of the type socialists actually hate. But they don't know the true end goal and don't seem to want to hear anything about what reality will actually be like during this process from socialism into totalitarianism. This is what is scary.

We Americans need to do some serious housecleaning in our own Parties and bureaucracies, so that we can return to America-the-Beautiful and the Land-of-Opportunity it was supposed to always be. If we continue to sit back and assume our elected officials will always do what is moral and ethical on all matters in our behalf, there will always be citizens left without hope or dreams. If we can fix the "people problem" in our Parties and government, we can have back the country where the American Dream is possible.

Shun "political correctness." Reject "double-speak" and "double-think" Orwellianism. Return to basic Christian principles of ethics and morality, and embrace the "Golden Rule." Shut down the brainwashing technology being practiced and controlled by social media like Twitter, Facebook, and others; they are deliberately helping to "dumb down" Americans and American children. We can't wait until it is too late to act. Get it?

PART 4: A WORD ABOUT "ANIMAL FARM"

In addition to "1984", Orwell wrote "Animal Farm" which was published on the heels of WWII, in England in 1945 and in the United States in 1946. He wrote this book during the war as a cautionary tale in order to expose the seriousness of the dangers posed by Stalinism and a totalitarian government. Due to initial difficulty getting this novel published, it was published only at the war's end, during the same month that the United States dropped atomic bombs on Hiroshima and Nagasaki. The tragically violent events of the war set the stage well for Orwell's fictional manifesto against totalitarianism. (Reference at https://www.gradesaver.com/animal-farm/) The reference Grade-Saver summed Animal Farm this way:

> Animal Farm is an allegory or fable, a fairy tale for adults. Orwell uses animal characters in order to draw the reader away from the world of current events into a fantasy space where the reader can grasp ideas and principles more crisply. At the same time, Orwell personifies the animals in the tradition of allegory so that they symbolize real historical figures. In their own universe, people can become desensitized even to terrible things like deception, mistreatment, and violence. By demonstrating how these things occur in an allegorical world, Orwell makes them more clearly understood in the real world. For instance, in Animal Farm's public execution, Orwell lays bare the matter of execution by having the dogs rip out the supposed traitor's throats. In these scenes, the reader is led to focus not as much on the means of execution as on the animalistic, atrocious reality of execution itself. Animal Farm is also a powerful satire. Orwell uses irony to undermine the tenets of totalitarianism, specifically that of Stalinism.

I also immediately noted similar irony in the matter of Islam, itself a totalitarian ideology proselytized as a "religion" of "peace and tolerance" when the facts show that for 1400 years Islamists have murdered millions of people whose only "crime" was they were not Muslims, and the Muslims genocide of Christians in particular is ongoing in current times. But, more about that later.

PART 5: HOW ORWELLIANISM CAN ALTER AND/O RE-WRITE HISTORY

To understand Orwellian activity today, we must look at things from the top down, not the bottom up. We know for a fact that the New World Order (NWO) is a fact, not a "conspiracy theory." We know that the NWO group are the extremely wealthy who 'own' many countries through their multi-national banking systems. These people believe that they, and only they, own the world and that they, and only they, have the privilege and right to exert control over all countries as to what the world is to become. President Kennedy was assassinated for threatening to reveal the NWO, the MIC (Military Industrial Complex) as he stated on live television. From what I've learned, it is my conclusion that James Earl Ray was a patsy; he did not fire the fatal shot. Will the truth ever be known? I don't know.

The Bush presidents both declared we should change to a NWO one-government world. Obama promised "fundamental change." He even said, while assuming he would be elected President, "In five days we are going to see fundamental change." He was prepared to accept his role in the NWO agenda, and I still wonder whether he actually knew how limited his role would be if he carried out his part. It appears he wanted Islam to play the ultimate role of world domination, insofar as he – as President – catered to Islamists to the point of putting them in his cabinet and in agencies like the FBI, CIA, and Homeland Security.

The factual evidence is known all over the globe this NWO group exists, and meets in closed meetings as the Bilderberg group. Author Daniel Estulin, over 14 years, has investigated and researched the Bilderberg Group's far-reaching influence on business and finance, global politics, war and peace, and control of the world's resources and its money. (https://www.globalresearch.ca/the-true-story-of-the-Bilderberg-group-and-what-they-may-be-planning-now/13808).

Summarized here, Estulin states that in 1954, "the most powerful men in the world met for the first time" in Oosterbeek, Netherlands, "debated the future of the world," and decided to meet annually in secret. They called themselves the Bilderberg Group with a membership representing a who's who of world power elites, mostly from America, Canada, and Western Europe with familiar names like David Rockefeller, Henry Kissinger, Bill Clinton, Gordon Brown, Angela Merkel, Alan Greenspan, Ben Bernanke, Larry Summers, Tim Geithner, Lloyd Blankfein, George Soros, Donald Rumsfeld, Rupert Murdoch, other heads of state, influential senators, congressmen and parliamentarians,

Pentagon and NATO brass, members of European royalty, selected media figures, and invited others – some quietly by some accounts like Barack Obama and many of his top officials.

Columnist Stephen Lindman, of the Global Research publication reviewing Estulin's book, *"The True Story of the Bilderberg Group,"* (published in 2005 and is now updated in a new 2009 edition), states:

> Whatever its early mission, the Group is now "a shadow world government….threaten(ing) to take away our right to direct our own destinies (by creating) a disturbing reality" very much harming the public's welfare. In short, Bilderbergs want to supplant individual nation-state sovereignty with an all-powerful global government, corporate controlled, and check-mated by militarized enforcement.

Early in its history, Bilderbergs decided "to create an 'Aristocracy of purpose' between Europe and the United States (to reach consensus to rule the world on matters of) policy, economics, and (overall) strategy." NATO was essential for their plans – to ensure "perpetual war (and) nuclear blackmail" to be used as necessary; then proceed to loot the planet, achieve fabulous wealth and power, and crush all challengers to keep it.

Along with military dominance, controlling the world's money is crucial, for with it comes absolute control as the powerful 19th century Rothschild family understood. As the patriarch Amschel Rothschild once said: *"Give me control of a nation's money and I care not who makes its laws."*

We now have a list of names of that group. The Group met in 2017 right here in the USA, in Virginia, not far from the Whitehouse. They never meet in the same hotel twice. Should we thus consider that the world agenda is a trickle-down manipulation as the means to achieve that NWO agenda? My research shows Bill Gates also attended one of their sessions, and possibly was invited to join, but that did not occur, either because he declined, or because after interview the Group declined. That is an open question.

Let us consider that possibility. How far have we gone these days suppressed by "political correctness?" Is modern reality being manufactured? Are we seeing an Orwellian system using social media to decide citizenship status? Are we being surveilled with every phone call and all that we do on the internet? Are we realizing that the tech-giants have already produced and marketed "smart phones" and televisions and computer-monitors that can track you and watch your every move?

Are you not aware that a new audio speaker has been developed and is now being marketed that has a tiny camera to watch you, and voice recognition that listens to all that you say while you are just thinking that it's nice to be able to turn on your radio by voice and tell it what to do? Are we now living in the emergence of "newspeak", "doublespeak", and "doublethink?" Are subsonic sounds being transmitted in that device that harms us? And, to this last question, what is going on with the "5G" internet system being set up all over the United States putting out frequencies now raising questions of harming the brain itself? There are cases where the proximity of a 5G transmitter has made people physically ill.

Are the so-called "vaccinations" actually a method for birth control, even genocide? What about the 500,000 African girls/women (ages 15-35) who have been sterilized under the auspices that it was a vaccine to prevent a serious contagious disease; why was it given to only birth-age women? My research shows it was Bill Gates, with the help of UNICEF, who brought that "vaccine" to Africa, a vaccine which contained a sterilizing ingredient.

Is the push for nano-chips inserted into our bodies for alleged purposes of "national identity" or "medical information" leading us to thought-control or government control itself? We have been told by experts on robotic technology that computers are at the stage where they are far smarter than humans, transmit data at light-speed, and can create software itself. Will intelligent robots take over someday, and will someday find humans, flawed as they are, obsolete?

Is "political correctness" a more dangerous form of totalitarianism? Are we being "brainwashed" by the electronic media daily? Is there going to be some kind of Orwellian "religion" that takes over?

Is Russia actually our enemy or is this Orwellian-type propaganda to keep citizens hating Russia as the "enemy" even if that may not be true? Are they fostering war between Russia and the USA to accomplish their NWO agenda? I personally believe Trump could have forged an alliance with Vladmir Putin that would have been greatly beneficial to both countries and, ultimately, to the rest of the world. But, the RINOs in Congress and the MIC pressured against that. One huge factor in indoctrination propaganda is distraction, and the notion of keeping Russia the perpetual "enemy" of America just because it is a communist country seems to me little more than distraction from the insidious agenda undermining our own country.

Do we have an Orwellian oligarchy focused on world control? These are legitimate questions we must ask and learn the answers to. There is no question that the Bilderberg group exists, and Estulin spent 14-years in their shadows learning all about them, much from insiders. It's hard to keep bad secrets, I imagine.

Orwell described a single-party system in which a tiny core of oligarchs, Oceania's "inner party," control all information. This is their chief means of controlling power. In the US today, information is wide open to those who can access the internet, at least 84 per cent of Americans use it daily. And while the US arguably might be an oligarchy, power exists somewhere in a formalized tight-knit formation including the electorate, constitution, the courts, bureaucracies and, inevitably, money. In other words, unlike in Oceania, both information and power are diffuse in 2017 America. But there is also no question that there is a focusing of information and disinformation rising by leaps and bounds by the very creators of the social media and public media to control the ideas and minds of the public in an untoward fashion.

Those who study the decline in standards of evidence and reasoning in the US electorate chiefly blame politicians' concerted efforts from the 1970s to discredit expertise, degrade trust in Congress and its members, even question the legitimacy of government itself. With those leaders, institutions and expertise delegitimized, the strategy has been to replace them with alternative authorities and realities to bring us closer to the NWO.

In 2004, a senior White House advisor suggested a reporter belonged to the *"reality-based community,"* a sort of quaint minority of people who *"believe that solutions emerge from your judicious study of discernible reality. That's not the way the world really works anymore."* Do you realize the magnitude of that Orwellian reference?

Orwell could not have imagined the internet and its role in distributing alternative "facts," nor that people would carry around Telescreens in their pockets in the form of smartphones, or mounted on our walls as our screen to the outside world of entertainment, news, and marketing. Our home environments are already Orwellianized. There is yet no Ministry of Truth distributing and policing information, but in a way, everyone is Big Brother.

I personally have found several times that Google has accessed and was using the personal camera plugged into my desktop computer, because a pop-up jumps out and tells me Google is using my camera (which I immediately unplug). Why is Google using my camera? Perhaps Google has been monitoring the websites I visit to gain the kind of information I am writing about here. I don't know, but I often wonder why my cursor jumps around my screen when my mouse is still.

It seems less a situation that people are incapable of seeing through Big Brother's big lies, than they embrace "alternative facts." Some researchers have found that when some people begin with a certain worldview – for example, that scientific experts and public officials are untrustworthy – they believe their misperceptions more strongly when given accurate but conflicting information. You see, oftentimes one's self-identity is based largely on the belief systems held; if you try to demonstrate the fallacy of the belief systems, the person is likely to fight back dismissively or aggressively because it inherently undermines or destroys one's self-identity. Again, Islam and Muslims are a prime example of core self-identity being intrinsically interwoven with the Islamic ideology that determines their way of life and perspective; it's virtually impossible to change that perspective when it is based on a lifetime of effective brainwashing.

In other words, arguing with facts can backfire. Having already decided what is more essentially true than the facts reported by experts or journalists, those brainwashed seek confirmation in alternative facts and distribute them themselves via

Facebook and Twitter, no Big Brother required. Caleb says, "*Nothing more completely baffles one who is full of trick and duplicity, than straightforward and simple integrity in another.*" And, thus, the pro-socialists hate those who do not embrace socialist at all because those who do not embrace socialism will not fall for the false narratives the socialists believe. And, unfortunately, we have seen the rise of violence from these "Progressives."

In Orwell's Oceania, there is no freedom to speak facts except those that are official. In 2017 America, at least among many of the powerful minority who selects its presidents, the more official the fact, the more dubious. For Winston, "Freedom is the freedom to say that two plus two make four." For this powerful minority, freedom is the power to say two plus two make five.

Does it not seem that "political correctness" spanning the globe, including here in America, shows strong similarities to "double-speak," "double-think," and "newspeak"?

The idea that none of this will be sufficient to actually destroy the United States poses the singular question: If we do nothing about it, and we are wrong in our tolerance, complacency, and acquiescence until it is too late to act against it, who will be to blame when our future generations have to suffer the horrors it will bring to this country?

A nation undergoing "fundamental change" (remember, these are the exact words Barack Obama used in his presidential campaign) while under the onslaught of "political correctness" and Orwellianism can, and likely will, end with a totalitarian authority using offensive brainwashing techniques to create a new reality for the citizenry. It will enforce that reality much like what Orwell showed us in the movie "1984." History will be re-written until all vestiges of our Christian capitalist democracy have disappeared and no one will remember what once was. It will be immediately demonized over and over, until all thought of what it really was is forever forgotten.

"Political correctness" is Orwellian; it is the modern term for Orwellianism. We must reject it. It is extremely dangerous, not funny. It is shutting down free speech and discussions from different viewpoints. The far-Left power-base is demanding that all those whose viewpoint differs must SHUT UP!, because anything different from theirs MUST be the result of racism, bigotry, or some phobia or other. They are nailing everyone in opposition to the cross of these terms and calling for violence to ensure they SHUT UP! They demand we speak the new language of "political correctness" they design, whether it makes sense or not, and they demand penalties against those who reject it or do not comply. They are engaging in Orwellian "double-speak" and "new-speak" and "thought control" using social and public media to reinforce this indoctrination. Already the immature minds of the millennials have fallen victim by 80%, already robotized to march-step in line with the Left's agenda.

As Orwellianism grows in America and across the world, if the world falls under the agenda of the New World Order, the one-government world that will take over will, like it did in the book "1984", engage in thought-control, thought-police, double-speak, and the other factors of Orwellianism. The government will likely re-write history, engage in book-burning and any other form of electronic books and information media. What history actually was will be changed over time to become what the NWO wants it to be, and eventually the United States and the world as we know it now will become a mere myth, and even that will eventually cease to be. Political Correctness is Orwellianism, and it is just plain dangerous to us all. We must fight back and shut it down.

PART 6: NIHILISM AND ITS ROLE IN ORWELLIANISM

One cannot view the millions of Islamic refugees migrating across Europe like a locust swarm epidemic without asking the question: Why is this happening? Just looking at the war-torn countries from which they come and seeing them as refugees seeking refuge is not answering that question at all. The problem goes far deeper than that. Or, far higher, I should say. We can look at the ongoing wars against Islamic terrorism, as well as the Islamic war against the rest of the world as it seeks total world control.

But we can also look at the global war machine and its industry, and acknowledge the Catch 22 position that we are in because of it. On the one hand, we are willing to war against those who threaten us and others, so we need the war machine to protect us. On the other hand, the war machine and its industrial complex need war to sustain the bottom financial line to remain in the black. There are great profits to be made in war, especially by the multinational/international banks who "bankroll" both sides, as well as the corporations that own the MIC businesses. If there is no war or conflict, how can the machine and industrial complex remain solvent? How can we defend ourselves and our country against enemies around the world who will not hesitate to strike a weakened America? Remember, Estulin identified how war and the military fit into the Bilderberg skillsets. But who are they and do they have any moral compassion for the world-at-large? The answer to that seems to be a resounding "NO!"

One cannot ignore the rise of "newspeak" (now known as "political correctness") and "double-speak" and "double-think" by the Leftist Progressives without wondering why they would push such an agenda. It spells doomsday for the vast majority of the populations, including those who push this Orwellianism yet lack a true understanding of what it means. Rather, they push forward on the offense under the assumption that the end result they seek, socialism, is somehow a Utopian world where we will all live as if in Heaven.

One might even question whether the mischief of "nihilism" is at play on a global scale and, if so, from where does it originate. What is nihilism?

Nihilism comes from the Latin "nihil," or "nothing." That which does not exist. It is the belief that values are falsely invented. The term 'nihilism' can also be used to describe the idea that life, or the world, has no distinct meaning or purpose. Nihilists believe that there are no true morals because they do not typically believe that an entity called "God" or places called "Heaven" and "Hell" even exist, that religious ideology is mere mythology.

Still, the puppetmasters have also been found to be Luciferians, and believe in God and Satan but worship Satan. Former members have informed us of the blood sacrifices these Luciferians use, such as killing babies and small children and drinking their blood.

The German philosopher, Friedrich Nietzsche (1844-1900), is most often associated with nihilism. In <u>Will to Power</u> [notes 1883-1888], he writes, "Every belief, every considering something true, is necessarily false because there is simply no true world." For Nietzsche, there is no objective order or structure in the world except what we give it. From this website I will quote: (https://www.allaboutphilosophy.org/nihilism.htm)

The objective of nihilism manifests itself in several perspectives:

> Epistemological nihilism denies the possibility of knowledge and truth, and is linked to extreme skepticism.
> Political nihilism advocates the prior destruction of all existing political, social, and religious orders as a prerequisite for any future improvement.
> Ethical nihilism (moral nihilism) rejects the possibility of absolute moral or ethical values. Good and evil are vague, and related values are simply the result of social and emotional pressures.
> Existential nihilism, the most well-known view, affirms that life has no intrinsic meaning or value.
> Nihilism – A Meaningless World

Shakespeare's <u>Macbeth</u> eloquently summarizes existential nihilism's perspective, disdaining life:

> Out, out, brief candle! Life's but a walking shadow, a poor player that struts and frets his hour upon the stage and then is heard no more; it is a tale told by an idiot, full of sound and fury, signifying nothing.

Philosophers' predictions of nihilism's impact on society are grim. Existentialist, Albert Camus (1913-1960), <u>labeled nihilism as the most disturbing problem of the 20th century</u>. His essay, The Rebel paints a terrifying picture of "how metaphysical collapse often ends in total negation and the victory of nihilism, characterized by profound hatred, pathological destruction, and incalculable death." Helmut Thielicke's, Nihilism: Its <u>Origin and Nature, with a Christian Answer</u> warns, "Nihilism literally has only one truth to declare, namely, that ultimately Nothingness prevails and the world is meaningless." In other words, if the belief in a God or gods is destroyed and negated, and nihilism becomes the norm, mankind is guided by no morality or ethics but by individual desire or greed, essentially an anarchy of death.

Yet, we are seeing a movement in the United States by the new harbingers of death known as the Leftist Progressives who seem to be aggressively pushing the idea that God is a purely man-made creation, not real, and that the so-called Word of God, the Bible, is also a man-made creation and not one inspired by an actual God. They believe that morality, insofar as it is rooted in the belief that God exists and that Jesus was the actual Son of God, is obsolete and invalid. They want to invalidate all facets of faith-based morality and free up all persons to do as they please without guilt or condemnation. In other words, total anarchy of the person. We are seeing nihilism in all its forms being manifested by the Leftist Progressives.

FOR EVIL TO PREVAIL, ALL IT TAKES IS FOR GOOD PEOPLE TO DO NOTHING AGAINST IT.

PART 7: POLITICAL CORRECTNESS IN SPEECH AND BEHAVIOR

Let's take a look at this subject. The thought police are watching you today. Back in the 90's, lots of jokes were made about "political correctness", and almost everybody thought they were really funny. Unfortunately, very few people are laughing now because political correctness has become an Orwellian way of life in America. If you say the "wrong thing" you could lose your job or you could rapidly end up in court. Every single day, the mainstream media bombards us with subtle messages that make it clear what is "appropriate" and what is "inappropriate", and most Americans quietly fall in line with this unwritten speech code. But just because it is not written down somewhere does not mean that it isn't real. In fact, this speech code becomes more restrictive and more suffocating with each passing year. The goal of the "thought Nazis" is to control what people say to one another, because eventually that will shape what most people think and what most people believe. If you don't think this is true, just try the following experiment some time. Go to a public place where a lot of people are gathered and yell out something horribly politically incorrect such as "I love Jesus" and watch people visibly cringe. The name of "Jesus" has become a curse word in our politically correct society, and we have been trained to have a negative reaction to it in public places. After that, yell out something politically correct such as "I support gay marriage" and watch what happens. You will probably get a bunch of smiles and quite a few people may even approach you to express their appreciation for what you just said. Of course, this is going to vary depending on what area of the country you live in, but hopefully you get the idea. Billions of dollars of media "programming" has changed the definitions of what people consider to be "acceptable" and what people consider to be "not acceptable". Political correctness shapes the way that we all communicate with each other every single day, and it is only going to get worse in the years ahead. Sadly, most people simply have no idea what is happening to them. (Info source: www.thetruthwins.com/archives/20-outrageous-examples-that-show-how-political-correctness-is-taking-over-America/.)

Political correctness today is very dangerous because it seems to be an extreme form of denial of reality. It has become increasingly difficult for even the most reasonable and careful of thinkers to say anything critical about socialism progression in the U.S., or about the true violent nature of Islam, or about the indoctrination of our children in the nation's pro-socialist schools, or against the false narrative of climate change, and so on. Efforts at fair criticism and sharing of facts which expose the false narratives have become unjust forms of censorship, and this is Orwellianism.

While the violence of Islam is very real, critics of those against the protestors of Islamization are characterized as "a new crop of far-right groups whose rise has paralleled the increasing use of anti-immigrant fears to buoy right-wing political parties in the West." (Quote from Denis MacEoin, July 28, 2019, in an article entitled "An Increasingly Dangerous Stand-off between Civilizations, published by the Gatestone Insitute.org.) This characterization of ordinary peoples who are trying to avoid or stop the Islamization of their countries after seeing the huge amount of crime and violence Muslims bring with them, is shameful and misleading, and to tie it directly to the Republican Party in the U.S. is just another Orwellian ploy to turn the gullible into haters of Republicans and believers that the Party is evil. It is more than just censorship; it sends the message that anyone who is anti-socialism is simply just evil.

MacEion's reference to "extreme right wing" groups in the West might not mean, to him, what the West – particularly in the U.S. – considers "right wing" because in the U.S., the characterization of "right wing" includes white supremists, new age Nazi party, and conservative Republicans, if you believe the alt-Left's narrative. But the reality is that "right wing extremist" designations more accurately depict the pro-Socialism movement because the truth about the movement is that they are actually pushing for authoritarianism and totalitarianism and fascism. Everything in the "war chest" of the alt-Left contains all of those ideological elements. For them, the individual be damned, it is about the collective, the nameless faces of a world society that serves the masters who control every aspect of the lives of its population. Those who have been indoctrinated in the Left's agenda are ignorant. They have bought the ideological lie, and their minds are closed to the reality of this socialist movement and all of its consequences once it moves past that into the New World Order's totalitarian, Orwellian world.

On November 29, 2019, Vladmir Putin referred to a law passed in France earlier this year which MANDATES that schools refrain from using "father" and "mother" but instead use "parent 1" and "parent 2" but it is unclear whether women will demand to be "parent 1." Putin said, "I hope we never have that (kind of nonsense) in Russia." Although officials attending the meeting of the Council for Interethnic Relations laughed, the reality is that for many in the West, who are told to accept such absurdities in silence lest they be punished for a myriad of potential thought crimes, it's not that funny. Journalist Robert Bridge noted that yet another crazy train from the West is on a collision course with Russia, and wonders whether Russia will be able to hold out forever against the globalists' ultra-liberal agenda now threatening the planet.

In Scotland, a boy was suspended from school for saying there are only two genders; this underscores how people in eastern Europe are completely bewildered by the West's obsession with identity politics. Back in June Putin commented on a similar topic, asserting that liberalism was in its death throws thanks to forced multiculturalism, adding that "so-called liberal idea has outlived its purpose." He is right. Political correctness is destroying human culture all around the globe.

The following examples of the new political correctness are not funny, but they are outrageous examples of the government, including the military, folding to the demands of the enemy. Some of these go back to the early Obama years too.

#1 According to a new Army manual, U.S. soldiers will now be instructed to avoid "any criticism of pedophilia" and to avoid criticizing "anything related to Islam". The following is from a recent Judicial Watch article…

> The draft leaked to the newspaper offers a list of "taboo conversation topics" that soldiers should avoid, including "making derogatory comments about the Taliban," "advocating women's rights," "any criticism of pedophilia," "directing any criticism towards Afghans," "mentioning homosexuality and homosexual conduct" or "anything related to Islam."

#2 The Obama administration banned all U.S. government agencies from producing any training materials that link Islam with terrorism. In fact, the Obama's FBI went back and purged references to Islam and terrorism from hundreds of old documents.

#3 Authorities are cracking down on public expressions of the Christian faith all over the nation, and yet atheists in New York City are allowed to put up an extremely offensive billboard in Time Square this holiday season that shows a picture of Jesus on the cross underneath a picture of Santa with the following tagline: "Keep the Merry! Dump the Myth!"

#4 According to the Equal Employment Opportunity Commission, it is illegal for employers to discriminate against criminals because it has a "disproportionate" impact on minorities.

#5 Down in California, former-Governor Jerry Brown has signed a bill that will allow large numbers of illegal immigrants to legally get California driver's licenses and to become registered voters although they are not citizens. Current Governor Newsom supports that.

#6 Should an illegal immigrant be able to get a law license and practice law in the United States? That is exactly what the State Bar of California argued earlier this year...

> An illegal immigrant applying for a law license in California should be allowed to receive it, the State Bar of California argues in a filing to the state Supreme Court.

> Sergio Garcia, 35, of Chico, Calif., has met the rules for admission, including passing the bar exam and the moral character review, and his lack of legal status in the United States should not automatically disqualify him, the Committee of Bar Examiners said Monday.

#7 More than 75 percent of the babies born in Detroit are born to unmarried women, yet it is considered to be "politically incorrect" to suggest that there is anything wrong with that.

#8 The University of Minnesota – Duluth (UMD) initiated an aggressive advertising campaign earlier this year that included online videos, billboards, and lectures that sought to raise awareness about "white privilege".

#9 At one high school down in California, five students were sent home from school for wearing shirts that displayed the American flag on the Mexican holiday of Cinco de Mayo.

#10 Chris Matthews of MSNBC recently suggested that it is "racist" for conservatives to use the word "Chicago".

#11 A judge down in North Carolina has ruled that it is unconstitutional for North Carolina to offer license plates that say "Choose Life" on them.

#12 The number of gay characters on television is at an all-time record high. Meanwhile, there are barely any strong Christian characters to be found anywhere on television or in the movies, and if they do happen to show up they are almost always portrayed in a very negative light.

#13 House Speaker John Boehner stripped key committee positions from four "rebellious" conservatives in the U.S. House of Representatives. It is believed that this "purge" happened in order to send a message that members of the party better fall in line and support Boehner in his negotiations with Barack Obama.

#14 There was a huge push to have a woman elected president in 2016. It doesn't appear that it even matters which woman is elected. There just seemed to be a feeling that "it is time" for a woman to be elected even if she doesn't happen to be the best candidate.

#15 Volunteer chaplains for the Charlotte-Mecklenburg Police Department have been banned from using the name of Jesus on government property.

#16 Chaplains in the U.S. military are being forced to perform gay marriages, even if it goes against their personal religious beliefs. The few chaplains that have refused to follow orders know that it means the end of their careers.

#17 All over the country, the term "manhole" is being replaced with the terms "utility hole" or "maintenance hole".

#18 In San Francisco, authorities have installed small plastic "privacy screens" on library computers so that perverts can continue to exercise their "right" to watch pornography at the library without children being exposed to it. Sick!

#19 You will never guess what is going on at one college up in Washington state…

> A Washington college said their non-discrimination policy prevents them from stopping a transgender man from exposing himself to young girls inside a women's locker room, according to a group of concerned parents.

#20 All over America, liberal commentators are now suggesting that football has become "too violent" and "too dangerous" and that it needs to be substantially toned down. In fact, one liberal columnist for the Boston Globe is even proposing that football should be banned for anyone under the age of 14.

#21 The Missouri State Fair permanently banned a rodeo clown from performing just because he wore an Obama mask, and now all of the other rodeo clowns are being required to take "sensitivity training." The Commission went even further, saying it will require that before the Rodeo Cowboy Association can take part in any future state fair, "they must provide evidence to the director of the Missouri State Fair that they have proof that all officials and subcontractors of the MRCA have successfully participated in sensitivity training."

#22 Government workers in Seattle have been told they should no longer use the words "citizen" and "brown bag" because they are potentially offensive.

#23 A Florida police officer was fired for calling Trayvon Martin a "thug" on Facebook (and he was a thug).

#24 "Climate change deniers" are definitely not wanted at the U.S. Department of the Interior. Interior Secretary Sally Jewell was quoted as making the following statement: "I hope there are no climate-change deniers in the Department of the Interior."

#25 A professor at Ball State University was banned from even mentioning the concept of intelligent design because it would supposedly "violate the academic integrity" of the course that he was teaching.

#26 The mayor of Washington D.C. asked singer Donnie McClurkin not to attend his own concert because of his views on homosexuality.

#27 U.S. Senator Chuck Shumer called on athletes marching in the opening ceremonies at the Winter Olympics in Sochi to "embarrass" Russian President Vladimir Putin by protesting for gay rights.

#28 In America today, there are many groups that are absolutely obsessed with eradicating every mention of God out of the public sphere. For example, an elementary school in North Carolina ordered a little six-year-old girl to remove the word "God" from a poem that she wrote to honor her two grandfathers who had served in the Vietnam War.

#29 A high school track team was disqualified because one of the runners "made a gesture thanking God" once he had crossed the finish line.

#30 A Florida Atlantic University student who refused to stomp on the name of Jesus was banned from class.

#31 A student at Sonoma State University was ordered to remove a cross she was wearing because someone "could be offended."

#32 A teacher in New Jersey was fired for giving his own Bible to a student that did not own one.

#33 Volunteer chaplains for the Charlotte-Mecklenburg Police Department have been banned from using the name Jesus on government property.

It would be hard to overstate the power that all of this relentless "thought training" has on all of us right here in the United States. Young people are particularly susceptible to the power of suggestion. One only need to look at the Sweden 16-year old, who actually has suffered from mental disease, who is now on the world stage with fans wanting her awarded with a Nobel Peace Prize for her refutable statements about climate change and the end of the world coming. Her parents are wealthy, they are actors, and this young lady, proven totally wrong, will suffer the public consequences and criticisms for her well-intentioned but totally wrong statements; she will become "that girl!" in a very negative way throughout her lifetime. Millennials who are also on the wrong side of history, who enter the public arena, will likewise become known as enemies of the state when the socialist effort fails and sanity is restored to our country. Our common goal should be the restoration of sanity in this country because, from all indications, we have drifted aimlessly in the other direction. Time to pull out the compass and set our sails for restoring our homeland.

The CATO Institute came out in 2017 with a poll showing that 71% of Americans say "political correctness" has silenced discussions society needs to have. 58% have political views they're afraid to share. (www.cato.org/poll-71-americans-say-political-correctness-has-silenced-discussions-society needs-have/.)

The poll showed a solid majority (59%) of Americans think people should be allowed to express unpopular opinions in public, even those deeply offensive to others. On the other hand, 40% think government should prevent hate speech. Despite this, the survey also found Americans willing to censor, regulate, or punish a wide variety of speech and expression they personally find offensive:

- 51% of staunch liberals say it's "morally acceptable" to punch Nazis.
- 53% of Republicans favor stripping U.S. citizenship from people who burn the American flag.
- 51% of Democrats support a law that requires Americans use transgender people's preferred gender pronouns.
- 65% of Republicans say NFL players should be fired if they refuse to stand for the anthem.
- 58% of Democrats say employers should punish employees for offensive Facebook posts.
- 47% of Republicans favor bans on building new mosques.
- Americans also can't agree what speech is hateful, offensive, or simply a political opinion:
- 59% of liberals say it's hate speech to say transgender people have a mental disorder; only 17% of conservatives agree.
- 39% of conservatives believe it's hate speech to say the police are racist; only 17% of liberals agree.
- 80% of liberals say it's hateful or offensive to say illegal immigrants should be deported; only 36% of conservatives agree.
- 87% of liberals say it's hateful or offensive to say women shouldn't fight in military combat roles, while 47% of conservatives agree.
- 90% of liberals say it's hateful or offensive to say homosexuality is a sin, while 47% of conservatives agree.

The full text of this poll, complete with graphs, are available at the website link listed above. It is well-worth a full review.

In an article by Leo Goldstein in the *American Thinker* dated September 17, 2019, Goldstein opens with the title "Google and Its Pals Are Worse Than Anyone Thought. The first question is: Is it true that Google suppresses conservative voices branding them as 'conspiracy theories'? Answer: No, this is a conspiracy theory (*an imaginary conversation with Google PR*).

Goldstein identifies the internet gatekeepers – Google, Facebook, Twitter, Microsoft, and Apple. He notes that the liberal anechoic [echoless] prison looks like an alternative reality (AR) created by these gatekeepers. He says, "This is not the same as an old-style echo chamber, in which inhabitants were still aware that there are people with other views outside the chamber. The prisoners of the AR are not aware of their status. After all, it is confirmed by all their information sources: all the news channels (except for the vilified Fox News), Google searches, anti-social media, Wikipedia, and the fact checkers. Ironically, all these outlets continually espouse that Trump supporters are the ones living in an alternative reality."

Goldstein argues that these gatekeepers cause polarization in the country, that they seem to be the main cause of liberal self-delusion and of mass confusion for everybody else, in addition to their hate-mongering. He also argues that these gatekeepers aid coup attempts. Certainly, it was like a coup when Infowars and Alex Jones were de-platformed by Apple, Google, Facebook, and followed by Twitter, two weeks later. This was done for political reasons in response to a third-party request. Goldstein also alleges that the gatekeepers target the central subjects of public debate when the targets are supportive of President Trump and opposing strong left-wing agendas. Goldstein notes that the "evidence of Spygate, the coup attempt (continuation of Spygate after Trump's inauguration), climate realism, the racism and anti-Semitism of the Democrat-Socialist party, and the evidence of this collusive tech suppression itself are among the most suppressed topics. These gatekeepers suppress conservative opinion and evidence, under the pretense of fighting conspiracy theories and false news. In addition to direct de-platforming of the opposition, the gatekeepers's behavior has a chilling effect on speech because speakers and publishers are afraid to associate themselves with people and views targeted by the gatekeepers.

So, on top of the millennials soaking in tons of false narratives and themes, without vetting the input for accuracy and truth, we find the social media, nearly all of them, supporting the pro-socialist movement and censoring, banning or de-platforming those who oppose this socialist movement.

Going back to Orwellianism, in his novel 1984 Orwell imagined a future world where speech was greatly restricted. He called that the language that the totalitarianism state in his novel created "Newspeak", and it bears a striking resemblance to the political correctness we see in American today.

According to Wikipedia, "Newspeak" is "a reduced language created by the totalitarian state as a tool to limit free thought, and concepts that pose a threat to the regime such as freedom, self-expression, individuality, peace, etcetera, any form of thought alternative to the Party's construct is classified as 'thoughtcrime.'"

Just as Britain and some EU countries have criminalized certain free speech and are hauling off to prison people for what are saying, we are in the early stages of that very thing here in the USA. Every single day, the elitist-owned mainstream media in the US bombards us with subtle messages about what we should believe and what "appropriate speech" consists of.

In the newsletter "Accuracy in Academia" by www.academia.org, in February 2000, a speech by Bill Lind entitled "The Origins of Political Correctness", was reduced to an article. (See, www.academia.org/the-origins-of-political-correctness/)

Lind says, essentially, that for the first time in our history Americans "have to be fearful of what they say, what they write, and of what they think. They have to be afraid of using the wrong word, a word denounced as offensive or insensitive, or racist, sexist, or homophobic", even though anyone can take offense about anything at all said, even if the same word or words would not be offensive to 99% of the entire population. He describes this as a disease.

He describes "political correctness" origin as "something of a joke, literally in a comic strip, and we tend still to think of it as only half-serious. In fact, it's deadly serious. It is the great disease of our century, the disease that has left tens of millions of people dead in Europe, in Russia, in China, indeed around the world. It is the disease of ideology. PC is not funny. PC is deadly serious."

From the historical perspective, political correctness is cultural Marxism. It is Marxism translated from economic into cultural terms. It is an effort that goes back not to the 1960's and the hippies and the peace movement, but back to World War I. If we then compare the basic tenets of Political Correctness with classical Marxism, the parallels are very obvious, so Lind describes.

> "First of all, both are totalitarian ideologies. The totalitarian nature of Political Correctness is revealed nowhere more clearly than on college campuses, many of which at this point are small ivy-covered North Koreas, where the student or faculty member who dares to cross any of the lines set up by the gender feminist or the homosexual-rights activists, or the local black or Hispanic group, or any of the other sainted "victims" groups that PC revolves around, quickly find themselves in judicial trouble. Within the small legal system of the college, they face formal charges – some star-chamber proceeding – and punishment. That is a little look into the future that Political Correctness intends for the nation as a whole."

And here it is, nine (9) years after Lind's speech, seeing how Political Correctness has begun to swallow the nation such that dialogue is harnessed by the bridles held by those promoting the disease or by those in power who fear to cross the disease by doing the right thing. Lind gives this example:

> "Indeed, all ideologies are totalitarian because the essence of an ideology (I would note that conservatism correctly understood is not an ideology) is to take some philosophy and say on the basis of this philosophy certain things must be true – such as the whole of the history of our culture is the history of the oppression of women. Since reality contradicts that, reality must be forbidden. It must become forbidden to acknowledge the reality of our history. People must be forced to live a lie, and since people are naturally reluctant to live a

lie, they naturally use their ears and eyes to look out and say, "Wait a minute. This isn't true. I can see it isn't true", the power of the state must be put behind the demand to live a lie. That is why ideology invariably creates a totalitarian state.

Second, the cultural Marxism of Political Correctness, like economic Marxism, has a single factor explanation of history. Economic Marxism says that all of history is determined by ownership of means of production. Cultural Marxism, or Political Correctness, says that all history is determined by power, by which groups defined in terms of race, sex, etc., have power over other groups. Nothing else matters. All literature, indeed, is about that. Everything in the past is about that one thing.

Third, just as in classical economic Marxism certain groups, i.e., workers and peasants, are a priori, good, and other groups, i.e., the bourgeoisie and capital owners, are evil. In the cultural Marxism of Political Correctness certain groups are not good – feminist women, (only feminist women, non-feminist women are deemed not to exist), blacks, Hispanics, homosexuals. These groups are determined to be "victims" and therefore automatically good regardless of what any of them do. Similarly, white males are determined automatically to be evil, thereby becoming the equivalent of the bourgeoisie in Economic Marxism.

Fourth, both economic and cultural Marxism rely on expropriation. When the classical Marxists, the communists, took over a country like Russia, they expropriated the bourgeoisie, they took away their property. Similarly, when the cultural Marxists take over a university campus, they expropriate through things like quotas for admissions. When a white student with superior qualifications is denied admittance to a college in favor of a black or Hispanic who isn't as well qualified, the white student is expropriated. And indeed, affirma-

tive actions, in our whole society today, is a system of expropriation. White-owned companies don't get a contract because the contract is reserved for a company owned by, say,
Hispanics or women. So expropriation is a principle tool for
both forms of Marxism.

And finally, both have a method of analysis that automatically
gives the answers they want. For the classical Marxist, it's
Marxist economics. For the cultural Marxist, it's deconstruction. Deconstruction essentially takes any text, removes all
meaning from it and re-inserts any meaning desired. So we
find, for example, that all of Shakespeare is about the suppression of women, or the Bible is really about race and
gender. All of these texts simply become grist for the mill,
which proves that "all history is about which groups have
power over which other groups." So the parallels are very ev-
ident between the classical Marxism that we're familiar with
in the old Soviet Union and the cultural Marxism that we see
today as Political Correctness.

But the parallels are not accidents. The parallels did not
come from nothing. The fact of the matter is that Political
Correctness has a history, a history that is much longer than
many people are aware of outside a small group of academics
who have studied this. And the history goes back, as I said,
to World War I, as do so many of the pathologies that are
today bringing our society, and indeed our culture, down.

Finally, Lind writes about a current form of Marxism that combines both economic and cultural Marxism, with a touch of Freudianism (the human conditions in individuals of repression), that became known as "Critical Theory."
Critical Theory is about simply criticizing. It calls for the most destructive
criticism possible, in every possible way, designed to bring the current order
down. This is what is happening today even in the media, and it is all coming
from the Frankfurt School here in the US, which essentially draws on both
Marx and Freud in the 1930's to create this Critical Theory. The theory is to

criticize. The theory is that the way to bring down Western culture and the capitalist order is not to lay down an alternative. Proponents expressly refuse to do that. They say it can't be done, that we can't imagine what a free society would look like (their definition of a free society). As long as we're living under repression – the repression of a capitalistic economic order which creates (in their theory) the Freudian condition, the conditions that Freud describes in individuals of repression.

Lind says, "In conclusion, America today is in the throes of the greatest and direst transformation in its history. We are becoming an ideological state, a country with an official state ideology enforced by the power of the state. In "hate crimes" we now have people serving jail sentences for political thoughts. And the Congress is now moving to expand that category even further. Affirmative action is part of it. The terror against anyone who dissents from Political Correctness on campus is part of it. It's exactly what we have seen happen in Russia, in Germany, in Italy, in China, and now it's coming here. And we don't recognize it because we call it Political Correctness and laugh it off. My message today is that it's not funny, it's here, it's growing and it will eventually destroy, as it seeks to destroy, everything that we have ever defined as our freedom and our culture."

PART 8: THE SOCIALIZATION OF THE UNITED STATES

What is now irrefutable fact is that the push for socialism takeover in the United States is primarily generated in the Democrat Party and also includes actors from the "shadow government." I do not believe that mainstream moderate or conservative Democrats support America becoming a socialist country and government. But for a moment, let's take a look at who are the principal proponents of the mountains of regulations imposed upon nearly every aspect of business and life in the United States. This is a topic that is or has been addressed in depth by other authors, but I'd like to throw one or two your way that should make you see red, certainly here in California.

In 2016, the *InstituteForJustice* published on 11/1/2016, a video entitled "Watch California Cops Steal Every Penny from an Innocent Family." The question that was subsequently addressed in court action was this: "Can the government take all of a family's money based on suspicion that one family member committed a crime?" That was exactly what occurred to the Slatic family earlier in 2016, when the San Diego County District Attorney seized over $100,000 in personal bank accounts belonging to James Slatic, his wife Annette, and their two teenage daughters, Lily and Penny, without charging anyone with a crime. (See www.youtube.com/watch?v=gl3hHVclcdY.)

California legislators passed Senate Bill 443 Forfeiture: assets: controlled substances (see leginfo.legislature.ca.gov/billNavClient.xhtml?bill+id=201520160SB433, approved by Governor Brown September 29, 2016, filed with Secretary of State September 29, 2016). The summary of the bill is as follows:

LEGISLATIVE COUNSEL'S DIGEST

SB 443, Mitchell. Forfeiture: assets: controlled substances. Existing law subjects certain property to forfeiture, such as controlled substances and equipment used to process controlled substances. Existing law allows peace officers, under specified circumstances, to seize property that is subject to forfeiture. Existing law authorizes specified public agencies to bring an action to recover expenses of seizing, eradicating, destroying, or taking remedial action with respect to any controlled substance. In a forfeiture action with regards to cash or negotiable instruments of a value of not less than $25,000, existing law requires the state or local agency to prove by clear and convincing evidence that the property is subject to forfeiture. Existing law requires seized property or the proceeds from the sale of that property to be distributed among specified entities. Existing law requires the Attorney General to publish an annual report on forfeiture within the state.

This bill would require a prosecuting agency to seek or obtain a criminal conviction for the unlawful manufacture or cultivation of any controlled substance or its precursors prior to an entry of judgment for recovery of expenses of seizing, eradicating, destroying, or taking remedial action with respect to any controlled substance. The bill would prohibit maintaining an action for recovery of expenses against a person who has been acquitted of the underlying criminal charges.

The bill would prohibit state or local law enforcement agencies from transferring seized property to a federal agency seeking adoption by the federal agency of the seized property. The bill would further prohibit state or local agencies from receiving an equitable share from a federal agency of specified seized property if a conviction for the underlying offenses is not obtained, except as specified. The bill would require notices of a forfeiture action to contain additional details, such as the rights of an interested party at a forfeiture hearing.

The bill would change the burden of proof that a state or local law enforcement agency must meet to succeed in a forfeiture action with regards to cash or negotiable instruments of a value not less than $25,000, but not more than $40,000, from a clear and convincing standard to beyond a reasonable doubt. The bill would require the Legislative Analyst's Office, on or before December 31, 2019, to submit a report to the Legislature on the economic impact of this change, and the above-described prohibition on receiving an equitable share from a federal agency, on state and local law enforcement budgets. The bill would make other related changes to court forfeiture proceedings. The bill would also require the Attorney General to include additional information on forfeiture actions in the annual report.

So let's see how that worked out for the Slatic family.

Using civil forfeiture, the District Attorney seized nearly every penny from the Slatic family following a January 2016 raid on Med-West Distribution—the legal medical marijuana business owned by James. Police accused Med-West of operating a "clandestine" drug lab, even though the business complied with state medical marijuana laws, operated publicly for two years, and paid its taxes. The police took everything from Med-West, including $324,000, and shut the business down. Then, a few days later, the District Attorney went after James' family, seizing nearly every penny in their personal bank accounts.

The seizure of the Slatic family's money has nothing to do with crime fighting; it has everything to do with policing for profit. In the nine months since the raid, the District Attorney has not brought criminal charges against the Slatics or anyone associated with Med-West. The District Attorney has instead left the Slatics' money in legal limbo, refusing even to begin legal proceedings in which the Slatics could prove their innocence.

Now the Slatics have teamed up with the Institute for Justice to demand their money back. The District Attorney's abuse of civil forfeiture takes the American principle of innocent until proven guilty and flips it on its head, treating innocent property owners like the Slatics worse than criminals. A victory in this case will not only mean the return of the Slatics' money, it will uphold the principle that no American should lose his or her property without being convicted of a crime. (Text by InstituteForJustice.)

But California is not the only state with Civil Forfeiture laws. In 1986, the Department of Justice's Asset Forfeiture Fund took in $93.7 million; in 2008 it took in $1 billion dollars. Much of this growth occurred in the past decade period from 2002 to 2012, suggesting that seizures had grown 600 percent from 2002 to 2012. From 2005 to 2010, government seizures of assets from both criminals as well as innocent citizens went from $1.25 billion to $2.50 billion. In 2010, there were 15,000 cases of forfeitures. Over 12 years, law enforcement agencies have taken $20 billion in cash, securities, other property from drug bosses and Wall Street tycoons as well as ordinary citizens who have not committed any crime at all. One estimate was that in 85% of civil forfeiture instances, the property owner was never charged with a crime. In 2010, there were 11,000 noncriminal forfeiture cases. In 2010, claimants challenged 1,800 civil forfeiture seizures in federal court, this small number may be because the claimants could not afford to hire an attorney. In some states there are few restrictions on how police use seized assets, while Missouri, for instance, puts seized funds into accounts earmarked for public education. In Vermont, seized funds go into "neutral" accounts, i.e., the general fund. In our Washington District of Columbia, victims seeking to get their seized property back may be charged up to $2500 for the right to challenge a police seizure in court, and it can take months or years for a decision to finally happen.

This is all coming from the unaccountable Fourth Branch of government, the Administrative State, in league with and approved by the State Legislature.

What about burden of proof? In criminal prosecutions, the standard is "proof beyond a reasonable doubt", yet in civil forfeiture cases, particularly in cases where no criminal charges were ever brought, some states have adopted the minimally-stringent "probable cause" standard, while other states adopted the "preponderance of evidence" standard, which is the arbitrary 51% level.

Proponents claim civil forfeiture laws help fight crime, but critics point to serious instances of abuse in which innocent owners have been victimized, like the Slatics. Critics are from both sides of the political spectrum, from left-leaning groups such as the American Civil Liberties Union and the right-leaning groups such as The Heritage Foundation.

Critics suggest that civil forfeitures are mostly "devoid of due process" despite the Constitution's due process clause when the issue of "life, liberty, and property" are involved. Critics see some seizures as assaults against individual and human rights. One only has to look at how the government seized all cash and all bank accounts of the entire Slatic family, leaving them without a means to live, eat, or pay bills. And they were never charged with any crime. In civil forfeiture cases, the burden of proof is shifted to victims to prove innocence, thus creating an air of guilt upon nothing more than an allegation of "probable cause." This turns the principle of innocent until proven guilty on its head.

In June 1996, Supreme Court Chief Justice William H. Rehnquist, a liberalist, ruled that federal forfeiture in drug-related cases was not a punishment
but served non-punitive purposes such as encouraging people to be careful
that their property is not used for something illegal. In the 1996 cases, the
only dissenting vote was Justice John Paul Stevens, said that it was an example of an excessive fine, and a violation of the Eighth Amendment's "cruel
and unusual punishment" clause, to permit civil forfeiture of a house, in
which marijuana had been illegally processed, leaving the tenants homeless.
People, a finding of "cruel and unusual punishment" requires a very high
standard of proof.

Proponents say civil forfeiture enable police forces to equip themselves further
for more effective crime prevention; for example, a $3.8 million drug bust let
officers equip their cars with a $1,700 video cameras and heat-sensing equip-
ment for a seven-member force.

There are no penalties for wrongful seizures, particularly when taxpayers pay
when ill-gotten gains from innocent citizens must be returned, so there is an
incentive to "find" a drug-related issue when police come across cash, i.e., to
make up a false charge.

Local and state police often cooperate with federal authorities in what has been
called "equitable sharing" agreements. Since many states have laws restricting
or limiting civil forfeitures, as well as requiring higher standards of proof before property can be taken, local police can sidestep these rules by treating the
suspecting criminal activity as a federal crime, and bringing in the federal authorities. As a result, after the seizure, local and federal agencies share the proceeds with 10% to 20% going to the federal agency and the remainder to the
local police force. Accordingly, "equitable sharing" effectively subverts the will
and intent of the statute legislatures as being a "complete violation" of the
principle of federalism.

The abuse is rampant, although proponents argue the extent of cases of innocent persons is a small number. The Baltimore Sun made reports that in 2012,
half of victims with seized assets were NOT convicted of a crime.

The USA Today described systemic abuse of civil forfeiture as *"an increasingly common – and utterly outrageous – practice that can amount to legalized theft by police."* The New Yorker, reporter Sarah Stillman, published a "sprawling investigation" about how cities abuse civil forfeiture to *"bolster their cash-strapped coffers by seizing the asserts of the poor, often on trumped up charges."* This is how Marxist or corrupt governments operate; is this what America has become?

In 2015, only New Mexico's legislature outlawed civil forfeiture.

As civil forfeiture challenges are considered by some legislatures, a new practice has emerged. By classifying valuables such as cars, cellphones, and wallets with cash as "evidence" the police can keep them and by making it very difficult and time-consuming to get them back. After 120 days the police can "sell" the items, therefore making it impossible to return. (https://www.theatlantic.com/technology/archive/2016/08/how-police-use-a-legal-way-to-rob-suspects-of-their-belongings/495740/) (Source: www.en.wikipedia.org/wiki/Civil_forfeiture_in_the_United_States)

I included this information not to single out the police force of America, because I do respect them, but this is but one glaring example of government abuse some politician and/or bureaucrat dreamed up to steal money and property from innocent citizens, by considering them "collateral damage" against the war on crime. If you think politicians and bureaucrats cannot and will not find ways to oppress and damage ordinary citizens in order to gain money and power, you're not paying attention. Can it be fixed? Of course. Just about anything can be fixed, but it takes the willpower of citizens to step up and say "No!" to these immoral and unethical "windows of opportunity" for government abuses.

Worse, it serves the concurrent purpose of increasing government coffers so they can spend more, including on the "free stuff" welfare system being given almost automatically to illegal migrants or new legal migrants, here despite the immigration laws that says immigrants must be and become self-sustaining, not a burden on the government (or taxpayers). It allows local governments and police agencies to purchase fancy equipment on the backs of innocent citizens they just stole money from. "Stole" money.

One recent example I have learned of, because it affects my own personal life, is the upstart but popular use of personal homes as short-term rentals by travelers, vacationers, and people needing a place to live for a short time while moving from one property to another. The recent star of the industry seems to be Airbnb.com, who has clear and ethical rules of conduct of this business for those who join its services.

Now these are not bed-and-breakfast rentals, because "transient rentals" as these personal home rentals of a bedroom or two are called, do not have to pay expensive permits to the local government if they are not serving food. Since Airbnb.com handles client requests through acceptance by a "host" including fees charged and payments made to the "host" by Airbnb, there is no need for the government to step in for "oversight."

But local governments in counties around the nation decide that ownership of a property does not mean that the government cannot require a tax for how it is used. So while they already get annual property tax income from every property, now they also want the property owner who runs a one or two bedroom availability as a short-term rental of "transient renters" as they are deemed (less than 30 days renting), to collect 10% from the renter on the aggregate amount of rent charged, and to then pay that total for each month to the County Tax Collector.

In California, as in Shasta County, I know for a fact that they passed an ordinance saying any owner allowing "transient rentals" for 30 days or less must pay a tax of 10% of the total fee paid to the "host", so if a renter stays for 5 days at, say, $40 a day, the county gets $40 tax. For what? For nothing other than on-going permission to use your personal property to make a little extra money. If this tax is not paid, the county can invoke "civil forfeiture" to seize the property for unpaid taxes and, if not paid, can sell the property at any price they choose, thus making a potentially huge profit on that unpaid $40 or whatever. This goes on all over the country these days, and local governments want their share of a share they are not entitled to.

Think about this kind of graft. The renters rent out bedrooms in their own houses to strangers for, say $20 a day, or $140 a week, small money per month, because THEY NEED THE EXTRA MONEY. But the Tax Collector must be given 10% directly from the renter to the landlord (making the landlord the on-site tax-collector), or else the landlord must pay the tax fee personally. Who needs the money the most?

California is a Democrat-controlled state, but even red counties like Shasta have local governments always seeking more ways to tax its own citizens. Many owners of houses where they rent out one or two bedrooms are people who need extra money for their families, to help with school expenses and college enrollments, and who don't need local government to simply find another way to dig into their pocketbooks.

The point of all of this focus is to remind you that when you give over control to local, state, and federal government, such that it keeps getting more and more obese, you are the one who ends up on the losing end because the government never stops growing and demanding more money from YOU. Understand that as the three "official" branches grow, so does the Fourth Branch, the Administrative branch. Our Founders warned us about large government becoming a government for the government and not for the People. These two things I write about here are just the tip of the iceberg.

One thing this above tells us, in the event of a "fundamental change" to socialism, these kinds of abuses and pick-pocketing described here will immediately blossom into total control of you and your property, even your livelihood. In fact, you will lose your property because private property ownership will be banned.

There will always be a "need" for government, even if the ideology changes from a capitalist democracy to a socialist ideology or to a totalitarian ideology. History has shown that during the transition from one to another, it only gets worse.

PART 9: THE SOCIALIST AGENDA
HAS BEEN UNDERWAY A LONG TIME

What research has shown is that the forces for socialism, communism, and totalitarianism has been with us a very long time. During the 50's, for example, post-war exuberance and prosperity brought some to believe "Let the good times roll!" and there was no need for anything more than a socialist democracy where everyone would be happy. But this notion was also exhibited after the First World War, in the 1920's, fondly known as the "Roarin' Twenties" because of the opportunity and wealth. But, this was a short-term party, primarily due to a single banker who plotted how to make money but ended up, after making him and his cohorts millions, crashing the economy nationwide in 1929, from which America got the "Great Depression" of the 30's where we nearly starved to death, where "soup lines" permeated every city and town in America.

When World War II occurred, the US was not really in a good shape militarily because of the depression years, but it entered it anyway when Japan provoked us by its Pearl Harbor attack, (after Japan and Germany reached a mutual ally agreement), and when we learned that Germany was seeking world domination and England asked for our help America stepped up. Apparently, Hitler was worried about the U.S. entering the war against him and figured if Japan attacked and got our limited military attention, he would be successful in his quest to conquer the world. Well, he was wrong. Japan, on the other, was planning to conquer the Philippines and perhaps other parts of Indonesia, and bombed the ships at Pearl Harbor to ensure the Western part of America had no ships to interfere with Japan's incursion. The attack merely slowed us down, but fired up the American people who came forward and worked in the factories to rebuild the navy. We punished Japan severely in the end. During all of this, the Marxists never wavered in their beliefs. After the war ended, and the world entered into the recovery stage, the Marxists came out of the woodwork, poised to take advantage of the weakened conditions around the world.

Senator McCarthy, in the 50's, viewed the socialist movement in America as the greatest treasonous crime for the nation, and the hunt and punishment of socialists became known as the Era of McCarthyism. When he died, and the anti-communism fervor generated by McCarthy died down somewhat, there were a few years when the Marxists laid low, but not for long.

After McCarthyism, and in the 60's, socialism began to be moved forward a little at a time. The "hippy generation" did a lot to support that agenda with their "peace and love" movement, and the song which contained the following lyrics, "C'mon people now, smile with your brother, we've got to love one another right now. Right now. Right now." As I talk about more in depth later, the Russian KGB funded new Marxist organizations around the world, as well as here in the United States, like the Weathermen.

Those who embrace an ideology may do so out of good intentions or personal benefit, but they may not always be right or wise. When it comes to America, our home, it is not in our best interests as individuals to mind our own individual business when there is good cause to look around at what others are doing that may affect us individually in a very bad way. We cannot ignore those who want a completely alien ideology for our home country, whether that be socialism, communism, or the totalitarianism guaranteed by the Illuminati's one-government world and their plan for the erasure of ethnic bloodlines into a single bloodline (by the Kalergi Plan). The NWO agenda has been ongoing since the early 1900's, and has been getting stronger and stronger. John F. Kennedy warned us about it. Herbert W. Bush was in favor of it, and so was George W. Bush and Barack Obama.

We are today at the strongest point in time that the push towards socialism has ever been, and had Hillary gotten elected and proceeded with the Obama "fundamental change" plan, we would by now been engaged in a civil war against each other, or martial law by now, and UN intervention and gun confiscation, and internment by the millions in the FEMA concentration camps, perhaps many executed already, but the socialism step would have been a very short stopping point to the totalitarian goal of a one-government world, thus making the destruction of America complete. Which would make George Soros one happy man. Remember, I told you he said publicly, in a video I downloaded, that destroying America would be his greatest achievement.

History has shown us quite clearly what socialism looks like in actual practice, and it is not an ideology I would like to live under. Socialism has been described as "soft communism" and, left alone, it usually turns into communism through a strong leadership by a single person.

For those of you who don't know the difference between Authoritarianism and Totalitarianism, it is as follows.

The Authoritarianism form of regime is characterized by the rule of one person or a committee that wields the entire power of governance. However, in authoritarianism, social and economic institutions that are not under government control exist. The single person in authoritarianism is called the Dictator, who creates a sense of fear in the minds of those who oppose him in that regime. He generally uses his power more than the totalitarian, and can be described as a power-hungry dictator.

On the other hand, Totalitarianism is a complete form or an extreme form of authoritarianism. Everything is totally under the control of a single person called the dictator in the totalitarianism form of governance. It can be said that both the social and economic aspects of the country are also under the control of the government, which the dictator himself handles. Such a dictator tends to maintain appreciation of the people by his personal charisma and virtue of his sheer prophetic leadership, but he or she will be no stranger to violence and oppression if the need arises.

It could be said that Islam is a totalitarian ideology because the teachings of Mohammed as interpreted in the Quran controls all aspects of Islamic life. It is re-enforced by Imams and policed by those in power of the government. Its sharia law is enforced by its courts according to the Quran, not by social justice concerns.

"Social justice" originated as primarily a religious concept by Catholics who wanted the thwart the socialist upheaval of the 1840s. Seeking an answer to social unrest, the first social justice activists looked to the past. In place of capitalism, they offered theism; in place of socialism, they offered charity. The Catholics saw socialism as "conscription, a disallowance of free will", arguing that "by legislating and forcing the distribution of wealth much of the good of helping our less fortunate brethren is lost."

Despite some conservatives' reservations and criticisms of "social justice" having "socialist" implications or overtures, it is an outlook that seeks to strengthen the identity of the individual because it sees that human dignity derives its meaning from being made in God's image (Genesis 1:26), which seems to correlate with the Constitution's "unalienable rights" provisions that conclude that such rights are God-given, not man-made. Obviously, such rights are not recognized in Islamic ideology, which focuses on the collective strictly-monitored supplication to Allah and sharia law rather than individual freedom of thought or expression.

Socialism is a threat to individual identity, while social justice is a call to honor the life and dignity of each individual and the emphasis on individual upward mobility in life.

Writer George Paulo, a Catholic, in 2009, on Social Justice and Socialism, wrote:

> Justice can be defined as the way we balance equality and freedom: equality: treating things the same and freedom: treating things differently. Social justice is a balance between the way we treat people equally and the way we allow them to be different (freedom: the right to be different). Constitutional law, which protects the bedrock of Democracy, our Constitution, assumes that all people are to be treated equally under the law unless there is a significant difference that must be taken into account. For example, all are treated equally but doctors have certain privileges that gives them certain rights to care for people medically due to their knowledge, education, and skill. The same might be said for policemen, politicians, and clergy, or the unborn and homosexuals.

> Socialism does not recognize differences except for the law and the police. As such it becomes tyrannical (same clothes, same houses, same cars, same education, same thought, same religious: tyranny). It forces all people to be the same which is unnatural and destructive to the will. Socialism treats people as ideas rather than as actual [persons], and ideology is blind to reality and tolerance for differences. Socialism cannot work because people are "actually" different, not the same. We treat them as though they are the same to preserve justice but justice cannot be served if we do not recognize the inherent "originality" of all people.

Scripturally we need only to look at 1 Cor. 2:13-31 to see Paul's treatment of social justice. We treat weaker members of the body with as much respect and dignity as the stronger ones though there is in fact a difference in function and power.

Socialism apart from redemption will be the worst form of tyranny the world has ever seen. We need only to look at Lenin and Stalin to see the consequences of socialism in the political arena.

Critics of "social justice" also make a point about how it is actually viewed and promoted, and I think I should include that as well.

The ideal of "social justice" is about protecting the rights and privileges of the individual and supporting or encouraging upward mobility, i.e., the "Be all that you can be" philosophy. An online post by Will Shetterly raise the following questions:

1. Why qualify "justice" [by the adjective modifier "social"]?

2. Who benefits when justice is qualified?

He came to those questions when he recognized four things:

1. "Social justice" is used by children of privilege, graduates of the U.S.'s most expensive private schools.

2. Social justice activists talk in quasi-religious terms about making a better world, but when you ask for their solutions, they only offer *bourgeoisie oblige*, the notion that the powerful should be generous towards people who are not white, male, heterosexual, Christian, able-bodied, upper-class, etc.

3. Social justice activists see infinitely divisible identity groups in conflict – people of color vs. white people, women vs. men, straight folks v. gay folks, the transgendered vs. the cisgendered, the disabled vs. the

physically or mentally able, etc. Socialists see sisters and brothers in the human family.

4. Social justice activists have a racial model for group identity: if you don't share a fundamental identity, you may be an ally, but you will always be an outsider. Socialists have a tribal model: what matters is your allegiance, not your class identity – a fact that baffles many capitalists, who shriek as though it matters that Marx and Engels were middle-class, as if people's social class matters more than their work.

Shetterly argues that the social justice activists are divisive when it creates models for correction that utilize a "superordinate identity" to reduce prejudice by creating the "common in-group identity model" the "in-group projection model," the "mutual intergroup differentiation model", and the "in-group identity model." Such group models that create identity models like this actually apply the divide and conquer concept. Shetterly argues that "incompatible concepts of freedom are the heart of the divide between socialism and social justice. To socialists, everyone should be free to share the wealth of others; to social justice activists, the rich should be free to be charitable when they please."

 Absent the fact that "social justice activists" are often the wealthy and privileged, the Christian concept of "charity" is not the distribution of wealth of the rich to everyone who are poor or not wealthy; rather, charity looks at the need and not at the cause. A capitalist democracy is a system where charity is applied to the need of other, regardless of the cause, and so should it be, in my opinion.

As for socialism being an Utopian ideal of people of color, it is not because they are people of color but because of the demographics of countries that have either not developed their country's economic systems to create jobs and opportunities for upward mobility, or because the ideology is socialist, or because their government is corrupt. In South America, we have seen a highly successful economy in Argentina and Venezuela to a point, then the opposite due to poor government, lack of focus on education, corruption, and/or foreign meddling.

A century ago, there were only seven countries in the world that were more prosperous than Argentina (Belgium, Britain, and four former English colonies including the United States). In 1909, per capita income was 50 percent higher than in Italy, 180 percent higher than Japan, and almost five times higher than in neighboring Brazil. Over the course of the 20th century, Argentina's relative standing in the world incomes fell sharply. By 2000, Argentina's income was less than half that of Italy or Japan. What happened?

In its pre-World War I heyday, Argentina thrived as a trading giant, shipping beef and grain abroad. After World War II, formerly poor countries including Japan, Korea and Italy followed an export-led model to wealth. A combination of external shocks (two world wars and the Great Depression) and protectionism caused Argentina to turn inward.

While Argentina had been wealthy, it was not that well-educated. Argentina, like most of South America, had been a recipient of the earlier slave trade, much of its exports were beef and grain, and the workforce reflected that earlier history. Education was not a major concern for its workers, since its long-run national success was built on human capital.

Argentina had been plagued with bad policies, and high levels of corruption. Much of the 19th century boom was financed by foreign investors, and Argentina also repeatedly felt the need to turn to a sectarian populism as a solution to grave inequalities from its slavery history. And, unfortunately, there was the matter of ideology, the Left's insistence on socialist interventionism, failing to realize that government was the source of corruption.

Venezuela is another example of prosperity crashing completely. There were several factors why Venezuela crashed. One was hyperinflation, where its inflation rate had been over 50 percent since 2014, and reached 536.2 percent in 2017 largely due to the rapid depreciation of the local currency on the black market, so said the opposition-controlled National Assembly. The International Money Fund, in 2017, estimated that inflation would reach 2,068.5 percent by 2018.

The government said it was the victim of an "economic war", including speculation and hoarding, by pro-opposition businessmen. Venezuela's currency weakened sharply on the black market.

There were food shortages. The government controlled the price of basic goods, but the black market had a powerful influence on prices. Prices on basic goods repeatedly changed in a matter of days, causing severe food shortages. The food shortages were reflected in the long lines of people inside and outside of supermarkets and the attempts to cross the border with Columbia to buy basic goods.

Venezuela's oil production, a major source on its former healthy status, continued to fall in 2017 by huge amounts, creating a major hole in its income. Venezuela also had a major foreign debt, but President Nicolas Madura dismissed the possibility of default, deciding instead to work on refinancing and restructuring that debt.

The economic crisis also hit Venezuela's public health system the hardest, and in the country's public hospitals, medicine and equipment became increasingly unavailable. Additionally, because of the food shortage crisis, people were out scouring for food and, by the time they brought family members to the hospital, they were already dying.

Crime and poverty go together. Crime and violence were widespread. In 2016 24,479 thousand people were killed in Venezuela, an all-time high.

Coalitions for change were also hit by internal power struggles as well as disagreements over ideology and policy.

In 2018, Venezuela officials launched the pre-sale of its new digital currency called the "petro." According to that government, the "petro" was backed by oil, gas, gold and diamonds, and was meant to help overcome U.S. and E.U. sanctions, but the U.S. barred any U.S.-based financial transactions involving that new currency as being nothing more than a "scam."

And then we, once again, see George Soros in that picture. Among other actions by Soros damaging the economic health of countries was the Asian financial crisis of 1997, where he reportedly played a part in undermining banks and currencies. Malaysian Prime Minister Mahathir directly named George Soros as behind it all.

In 2009, when elections were being held in Venezuela, the people were told basically that if they do not vote as the big powers wanted, they may be harmed in some way. But the people voted for Hugo Chavez, and right afterwards the price of oil was forced downward. On January 30, 2009, Soros said that "the main oil producing countries have been the enemies of the prevailing world order." The price drop hurt Russia, Iran, and Venezuela. Soros said, "*It's not so easy to finance a Bolivarian revolution with $40 oil*." Soros also said of Chavez that "*probably his days are numbered*" and gave the Chavez regime less than a year.

I include Soros here in this review of socialism because of his current influence in America in goading our youth into believing the idea that socialism is a good thing, inasmuch as he has publicly stated his ultimate success would be the destruction of the United States.

PART 10: THE INFILTRATION OF OUR SCHOOLS BY SOCIALISTS

Aristotle (384-322 BC) once said: "*Educated men are as much superior to uneducated men as the living are to the dead.*" It can be said of our schools over the last couple of decades that indoctrination by our schools and universities is what is bankrupting our nation and our children's minds. Schools have become places of socialization, not learning. Rather than encourage students to strive and achieve, it coddles under-achievers and rewards them by passing them to higher grades they did not earn because it was better to pass them than to damage their self-esteem by failing them. Achievers are not rewarded openly because that might damage another student's self-esteem. This is misguided teaching. In every other aspect of learning, whether a skill or trade, the best achiever is the one likely to rise to the top of the selection of candidates.

In its decades-long efforts to dismantle the load-bearing structures of traditional and classical liberal society, including democratic capitalism, Marxist dogma in its various forms – socialism, communism, neo-Marxism, Cultural Marxism – has embarked on a sustained campaign to weaken and ultimately to abolish the institution of marriage as it has been commonly understood since time immemorial. The dissolution or disruption of marriage, as a contract between a man and a woman committed to raising a family and recognizing its attendant responsibilities, is a prerequisite for the revolutionary socialist state in which the pivotal loyalty of the individual belongs to the sovereign collective, not to the family. This becomes a prelude to a two-party state, i.e., rulers and serfs, masters and slaves, the all-powerful and the oppressed. The life of the individual is subverted as only important to the degree deemed by the rulers.

There have been tribes and cultures in the past, and some even today, that are small and believe that raising a child was a communal responsibility. Small villages of people have often taken that view. Even in small-town America years ago, some – mostly of Christian faith – have taken that position as well. Quakers did. Certain, if not most, of the American-Indian tribes took that position as well. As I understand it, the Mormon community as well as the Amish still practice that communal idea of raising children. The importance of our next generations seems these days to take a lesser role of importance in the American society.

It seems like the MJ-clouded and the LSD-warped mindset of the 60s that children should grow on their own without parental or societal guidance is now showing up in our children today, even without the mind-muddling of drugs.

Even today, as a 60s product, I still like Pink Floyd, and his infamous song "The Wall" which talked about kids *"don't need no education, kids don't need no thought control"* and *"leave these kids alone,"* a message that children do not need guidance, that they should grow up open to the world around them and let them decide their own actions, reactions, and destiny. Otherwise, they would be mind-controlled robots. It was Pink Floyd's most loved and popular songs, so one might imagine the influence it had on the drug-cultured world of the Hippy Generation, and how that message influenced their evolving trek into adulthood and the future. What we do know today is that there was a spurt of interest in Marxism that found its way into our school system, supported in part by the Russian KGB. Yes, really.

Over the following decades, we have seen changes in the behaviours of our society, and a lessening of parental guidance in the homes, as well as an increase in divorces and single-parent households. What have we done? We have not done right by our children, and we are seeing the deleterious effects today in the decline in social and personal values and the rise in antisocial and rebellious behaviours. America remains an exceptional opportunity to those who want to be a virtuous person and set goals for achievement of that which would make them happy. But more and more are going in the opposite direction, without values, without purpose, without satisfaction, without happiness, quick to anger, quick to adopt the worst values and behaviours. What have we parents done to our children in their absence of parental supervision and guidance? Some 65% of Americans are rejecting faith-based religion, many rejecting the idea of God at all, and thus rejecting the Christian-based morality of America itself. Too many people, especially the millennials indoctrinated in our broken schools, are refusing to be cabined, as they see it, by the virtues and morality of Christianity and have embarked on doing whatever makes them feel good, regardless of how abnormal or how perverse.

And here we are today, watching an autistic teenager from Sweden, parroting nonsense about "climate change" to the young, to the establishment, to world leaders, and being treated like she is the new embodiment of Christ returned. The Church of Sweden even said so. Wow! Greta Thunberg, a mind-controlled enraged teenager who actually knows very little about her subject matter, a child who will grow into an adult and find herself wrong about the whole thing, and laughed at the rest of her life. Well, the old saying is true, you get what you pay for. The mistakes of the fool will be known to the world. Yet, she has garnered enough of a fan club even in the USA to help fuel the nonsense about climate change to the gullible.

What should be a major concern of all reasonably intelligent citizens is what is being allowed in our school systems, how socialism is being promoted alongside "gender identity" curriculum and why Republicans and capitalism are evil and greedy. Yes, there are lots of greedy people and they are certainly not limited to Republicans and capitalists. Greed cannot be defined by one's politics or ideology. It is expressed or manifested by what people do and what people want and how bad they want it. We are all driven by something, some are driven by money and power.

I was particularly intrigued by a conference entitled Socialism2019 in Chicago July 4-7, 2019, by a socialist organization that challenged the difference in education standards between private or charter schools and public schools. The emcee was Brian Jones, a teacher, actor and activist in New York, who contributed to the book *"Education and Capitalism: Struggles for Learning and Liberation."* It is a two hour and six-minute video which rails against capitalism and private/charter schools, where Jones's opening expressed a demand that public schools be of the same quality as the expensive charter and private schools. I don't have a problem with demanding and expecting better schools, but the push of this organization, despite talking about the pitfalls and short-comings of America's public education system, seems a bit of propaganda alleging if America were a socialist country, the education system for all would be the same quality. But of what quality? Do they somehow think that a socialist government is even interested in a high-quality public school system? If all businesses and banks are nationalized under socialism, exactly how will the school system benefit?

From the very beginnings of a socialist country, there will be a tendency of despotic-minded, power-hungry individuals to gravitate to each other. There are those who want power over others, and yet there is only a smaller number of opportunities compared the numbers wanting power. So, in a Marxist government, these despots gravitate into positions where they collaborate in gaining absolute control because only one can have the top position, but he or she will need like-minded people around him or her. In a Marxist ideology this tendency of despots to gravitate to the power seats cannot be avoided because the structure itself enables it, not intentionally but by the process of controls. Those in power, not just at the top, but along the ladder of power, enable each other to rise, and accept that there is only one top spot, so everyone on the ladder wants to be as close as possible to the top dog because that is where the power is, and that is where despotism can rear its ugly head, and usually does at some point.

I noted on their website are these words:

NO BORDERS – NO BOSSES – NO BINARIES
SOCIALISM2019
July 4-7 CHICAGO

In a moment of rising class struggle, resurgent social movements,
and the growing popular appeal of socialism, the Socialism 2019
Conference is an important gathering space for today's left.
Featuring dozens of panels, lectures, and workshops on topics like the
fight against racism, how to win gender justice, radical working-class struggle,
current debates on the left, and more, the Socialism Conference
brings together hundreds of activists from around the country
for four-days of organizing, learning and collaboration.

WHAT TO EXPECT
Over 50 meetings.
Covering debates on the left
today and the hidden history of working-class
and socialist struggles
Free, professional, on-site childcare.
Parents can fully participate in the conference
knowing their children are enjoying themselves.
Expand your political toolbox.
We are committed to fighting injustice and oppression
and building a socialist future. Join us!
Socializing with socialists.
You are not alone! Meet with comrades from
across the country and around the world.

I think I understand better why, in our public schools especially, and particularly in the colleges, there is a focus by teachers and management to promote
the socialist ideology as the answer to all the woes of society and public education. This is where racism of diversity gets born, with the propaganda that
the country's problems are correctly laid at the doorstep of "greedy capitalists"
and, especially, the "white establishment." Organizations like this seem to be
the birthplace of this kind of selective racism, despite the white people who
are a part of this movement.

Such organizations are using the education system's problems as proof that a
capitalist democracy will never work for people of color or, even, people in
the communities predominantly of people of color.

Marxist indoctrination happens through many channels – entertainment, speeches, censorship, double-speak, political correctness – but its main instrument in the Marxist playbook is the school system. Teachers have a captive audience of malleable young minds for several years, immature minds that tend to go with "feel good emotions and desires" rather than logic and deductive reasoning their minds are not mature enough for. While it may be difficult to determine the extent of indoctrination, we can now see by a survey of the nation's millennials that 70% to 80% believe that capitalism is "evil" and socialism is "utopian." Our education system is so infiltrated by Marxist teachers, many of whom embraced Marxism in the Hippy era of the 60's, that indoctrination apparently has been easy and effective. For about two decades, in the 70's and 80's, most students leaving school seemed content to remain disengaged from politics, even religion, and most ideas in general, content to allow the influence of mainstream media to think for them and tell them what to think.

The concept of indoctrination may not be clearly understood by many, and definitions from many people seem quite superficial. While indoctrination involves pushing a certain opinion, viewpoint, or theory, it is also much more; it is the comprehensive effort of passively disseminating a particular viewpoint, with passive being the key. We see this in the more simple environment of adolescents in the schools, where popular students tend to foster the narrative for other students who, through that peer pressure, adopt without analysis that narrative. People who are indoctrinated with a certain narrative or ideology do not arrive at the intended conclusions through their own thinking, but hear the same thing repeated in many different ways until they finally take it as unquestionable truth. Again, in the immature environment of students, the adoption of silly narratives after hearing it repeated by numerous students, all bouncing off of each other to arrive at the same perspective, even when it is totally incorrect.

Indoctrination tends to occur in the absence of thinking, in the absence of reason or analysis. In the schools, many teachers who engage in indoctrination may do so unconsciously. They themselves take what they're given to teach and pass it along without thinking. Ideologues often intervene at this level by writing the scripts for teachers, which is how LGBT advocacy and anti-Semitic fabrications and socialistic ideals become included, even embedded, in their lessons.

Thoughtlessness is essential. As the fictional demon Screwtape, from C.S. Lewis's "The Screwtape Letters," states in his letters to Wormwood, "It is funny how mortals always picture us as putting things into their minds: In reality our best work is done by keeping things out." A person who really thinks will eventually reason himself out of the things he heard in school.

Even changing curriculum will not prevent indoctrination, and while curriculum should help guide the teachers to create lessons and use materials that will train the students to think and function independently, most public schools curricula, either adopting the Common Core standards or initiating them, do just the opposite. The Common Core curricula neither teaches children in ways that build self-esteem or help them want to learn, but rather teaches *circular* reasoning that gets them nowhere at all, the premise being to teach kids about *thinking about thinking* which accomplishes nothing except a process that dumbs-down students. It is a Marxist technique.

All taught via the Common Core curricula damage our own children's ability to learn, to think, to reason, and to synthesize what they learn into a mature mental process promoting cognition and deductive reasoning. What Common Core does is assist the Marxist goal of indoctrination students to accept false narratives without thinking, without analysis, without objection, and it does so by focusing on their immature mental induction process based on their "feelings" rather than any "reasoning." Make students feel good about something, and all the logic-based arguments in the world against it will still meet resistance.

Because too many non-socialist Americans, who are the majority by far over socialists, are not stepping up to stop the socialist propaganda to our own children in the nation's schools, and are not suing school districts for hiring and supporting these pro-socialist teachers, and are not demanding legislation against the teaching of our children that they should be socialists in order to be happy, now we are seeing the result of our own inaction. Only clear thought will be the death of indoctrination, and we must teach our children how to think, how to reason, how to process and question information, before they enter school and while they are in school; keeping abreast of what our children are being taught is, in today's schools, purely self-defense. The way that our children are being taught over the last several decades has created huge problems that inevitably lead to what is commonly known as Attention Deficit Disorder (ADD) and, subsequently, drugging children with the powerful ADD drug Ritalin. We cannot just let our children hear this propaganda and make up their own minds; they are too immature and inexperienced to do so.

Well, you say, our First Amendment right to free speech and freedom of expression and association, protects us for our view that socialism is the ideal ideology for a country. To that I say, no, it doesn't. Discussions about socialism and capitalism with a biased and jaundiced view do not reveal the truth about the reality of either. To teach the impressionable young that socialism is about love and peace and friendships and life in a Utopia close to heavenly, is without doubt a bold lie told to our children in our schools. Evidently, no fair or correct historic representation is even engaged because if the truth were told about the horrors of socialism in countries around the world, and that no socialist country has ever been successful at anything other than oppression and equality of misery, even our immature children would be able to see the lie being told to them. These wanna-be socialists cannot point to a single country in history that went socialist at the desire of the people that did not turn out badly for that population. Power-mongers seeking control over populations gravitate to power positions and, if they are lucky, become part of the "top dog" fraternity with total control over the population and, if one of them gets total control, things always get really bad. Once pro-socialists become activists to indoctrinate America's children, this can aptly be characterized as sedition against the country itself, and is very close to treason itself which requires overt action against the country. In my view, indoctrinating our children is treasonous overt action against the country and should be severely punished.

I doubt that anyone in this socialist organization has even gone back through history and learned what is the real nature and reality of socialism, communism, fascism, and totalitarianism. If they had, they would not be accusing the United States and our government of being a fascist country or government. Incompetent sometimes, inept at times, unable to do right by the citizens oftentimes, and failing to observe correctly the Constitution's Bill of Rights when creating legislation, all that is true, but it doesn't create a "fascist" country or government. That is a false narrative.

Teaching kids they would like socialism so that they wouldn't have to work and support their own families, that they could engage in endless vacations, take up arts and crafts as they please without any regard for earning a salary because everything would be free, should be considered a crime of significant proportion, a sort of sedition to the futures of these kids, and certainly an act against this country as a whole in a treasonous manner.

Private or charter schools are not the problem of public schools. The very problems of public schools are why many parents want to avoid public schools so that their children have a safer environment where focus remains on the best education possible. Vilifying private or charter schools does not improve the public schools; it only creates an excuse by those who fail rather than try hard to shift blame from themselves to those who have the means for more expensive private or charter schools. This is not to say private or charter schools all teach as they should; some might teach Marxist thought. I don't know. Do you?

Do I wish the public schools were fixed and provide high levels of education to all students? Of course I do. But socialism is not the answer. The answer lies in funding, in teachers who teach what students come to learn for their futures and what parents expect them to learn. Socialism2019 does not do a positive service for their communities by encouraging them to promote socialism as the solution to all their problems.

Auguste Meyrat is an English teacher in the Dallas area. He holds an MA in humanities and a "MED" in educational leadership. He is the senior editor of The Everyman and has written essays for The Federalist, The American Conservative, and The Imaginative Conservative, as well as the Dallas Institute of Humanities and Culture. In an article in a 2018 issue of The Federalist, he addressed the problem of socialists infiltrating our school systems and curriculum and what it is going to take to save our children from being brainwashed and indoctrinated by our own teachers. The full article can be found at www.thefederalist.com/2018/10/26/public-schools-indoctrinate-kids-without-almost-anyone-noticing/ and I invite you to read this and act accordingly.

A few quotes will help set the stage of his article:

Many people have long suspected that governments sometimes attempt to indoctrinate their people to increase the
government's own power and influence. Unfortunately, ambitious governments will not stop at merely controlling what
their people can do; they must control their minds.

Indoctrination happens through many channels – entertainment, speeches, and censorship – but its main instrument is
the school system. Teachers have a captive audience of malleable young minds for several years. They may not have figured out how to make students smart and productive, but
they can at least make them submissive and obedient.

Judging by results and from most people's experience, indoctrination is not only a problem with rogue regimes, but also
a distinctly American problem. ...

Most [Americans] ... seem content to remain disengaged
from politics, religion, and most ideas in general, and allow
the mainstream media to think for them.

Far from resembling a unified collective, society has become
more polarized and tribal [via our emphasis on and definition
of "multiculturalism"]. Some might see this as evidence of
the failure of indoctrination, and the insuppressible human
desire for freedom and justice, but they are mistaken. Indoctrination does work, and it is one of the main reasons America is so divided.

[Indoctrination] is the comprehensive effort of passively disseminating a particular viewpoint. The passive aspect is the
key. People who are indoctrinated with a certain narrative or
ideology do not arrive at the intended conclusions through
their own thinking, but hear the same thing repeated in a
million different ways until they finally take it as unquestionable truth.

Because indoctrination happens in the absence of thinking, many teachers in indoctrination do so unconsciously. They themselves take what they're given and pass it along without thinking. Ideologues often intervene at this level by writing the scripts for teachers, which is how LGBT advocacy and anti-Semitic fabrications become included in their lessons.

Common Core has facilitated progressive indoctrination by smothering independent thought and stifling intellectual development. It effectively trains students not to think by emphasizing skills over content, process over product, and relative standards over absolute ones.

Meyrat identifies how Common Core's standards damage student development by focusing on supposedly practical skills rather than quality content, how history teachers teach their students "history skills" which "involve everything except remembering actual history and synthesizing information." Both literary and historical content is "drained of relevance or meaning." Meyrat describes how math and science are "hurt more by Common Core's obsession with the process over the product" by teaching students various arbitrary methods for computation at the expense of simply reaching the right answer. Meyrat emphasizes that Common Core's methodology causes students to stop thinking since it's all pointless, since in such a system *"thinking is only the articulation of opinion; it has no bearing on truth."* He writes:

> This means that people don't really need to think critically and understand why they believe what they do. They just need to have the right viewpoint and force others to conform like they've been forced to conform. They engage in arguments where the loudest voice wins because no one's points are better than another. They pressure instead of persuade.

> This in turns leads to tribalism – groups of people united in feeling and opinion, but not in reason and truth. The lack of thought makes all these groups vulnerable to mass media

and prevents any organized resistance to an encroaching state or lawless ideologue in power. Indoctrination is complete when perception (i.e., whatever is on the screen, whatever an "expert" says, whatever is popular) really does become reality for most people because they're too stupid or apathetic to respond rationally.

Only clear thought will be the death of foggy indoctrination. ...

At some point, indoctrination will always collapse on itself and leave mediocrity in its wake. Teaching [with good teachers], by contrast, is what will sustain our culture and bring out its virtues. It fosters the presence of active thought – no uniform thought – and it is what will ultimately mend and civilize our sorely divided country.

Another author, Charlotte Thomson Iserbyt, in 1999, wrote a "chronological paper trail" 738-page book entitled "*the deliberate dumbing down of America*" which was published by the Ohio-based Conscience Press. Iserbyt's book is "*a small tribute to the late Honorable John A. Ashbrook, 17th Congressional District of Ohio, whose work in Congress during the 1960s and 1970s exposed the treasonous plans which ultimately led to the internationalization and deliberate dumbing down of American education.*" She describes her book as "*a history book about another kind of war*" as opposed to conventional shooting wars. She notes that it is about a war "using psychological methods; a one-hundred year war; a different, more deadly war than any in which our country has ever been involved; and a war about which the average American hasn't the foggiest idea." She explains that "*[t]he reason Americans do not understand this war is because it has been fought in secret – in the schools of our nation, targeting our children who are captive in classrooms. The wagers of this war are using very sophisticated and effective tools: Hegelian Dialectic (common ground, consensus and compromise); Gradualism (two steps forward, one step backward); and Semantic deception (redefining terms to get agreement without understanding).*"

The Hegelian Dialectic is a process formulated by the German philosopher Georg Wilhelm Friedrich Hegel (1770-1831) and used by Karl Marx in codifying revolutionary Communism as dialectical materialism. The "Thesis" represents either an established practice or point of view which is pitted against the "Antithesis" – usually a crisis of opposition fabricated or created by change agents – causing the "Thesis" to compromise itself, incorporating some part of the "Antithesis" to produce the "Synthesis" – sometimes called consensus. This is the primary tool in the bag of tricks used by "change agents" who are trained to direct this process all over the country.

Remember Obama's promise of "fundamental change"? While he did not say it directly, it was about converting America into a socialist nation as the first step to an international totalitarian regime called the New World Order.

Aserbyt gives an example of Hegelian Dialectic in practice in America, using a Michigan example of property taxes for local schools. She writes:

> The internationalist change agents must abolish local control (the "Thesis") in order to restructure our schools from academics to global workforce training (the "Synthesis"). Funding of education with the property tax allows local control, but it also enables the change agents and teachers' unions to create higher and higher school budgets paid for with higher taxes, thus infuriating homeowners. Eventually, property owners accept the change agents' radical proposal (the "Antithesis") to reduce their property taxes by transferring education funding from the local property tax to the state income tax. Thus, the change agents accomplish their ultimate goal; the transfer of funding of education from the local level to the state level. When this transfer occurs it increases state/federal control and funding, leading to the federal/internationalist goal of implementing global workforce training through the schools (the "Synthesis").

Regarding the power of "gradualism" we only need to recall the story of the frog and how he didn't save himself because he didn't realize what was happening to him. He was thrown into cold water which, in turn, was gradually heated up until finally it reached the boiling point and he was dead. This is how "*gradualism*" works through a series of "created crises" which utilize Hegel's dialectical process, leading us to more radical change than we would ever otherwise accept.

Iserbyt explains "semantic deception" by example: "[d]o you remember your kindly principal telling you that the new decision-making program would help your child make better decisions" What good parent wouldn't want his or her child to learn how to make "good" decisions? Did you know that the decision-making program is the same controversial values clarification program recently rejected by your school board and against which you may have given repeated testimony? As I've said before, the wagers of this intellectual social war have employed very effective weapons to implement their changes."

Iserbyt warns: "This war has, in fact, become the war to end all wars. If citizens on this planet can be brainwashed or robotized, using dumbed-down Pavlovian/Skinnerian education, to accept what those in control want, there will be no more wars. If there are no rights or wrongs, there will be no wanting to "right" a "wrong." Robots have no conscience. The only permissible conscience will be the United Nations or a global conscience. Whether an action is good or bad will be decided by a "Global Government's Global Conscience," as recommended by Dr. Brock Chisholm, executive secretary of the World Health Organization, Interim Commission, in 1947 – and later in 1996 by current United States Secretary of State Madeline Albright."

And finally, Iserbyt says: "To withhold the tools of education can kill a person's spirit just as surely as a bullet to his body. The tragedy is that many Americans have died in other wars to protect the freedoms being taken away in this one. This war which produces the death of intellect and freedom is not waged by a foreign enemy but by the silent enemy in the ivory towers, in our own government, and in tax-exempt foundations – the enemy whose every move I have tried to document in this book, usually in his/her/its own words."

Much of Iserbyt's book contains quotes from government documents detailing the real purpose of American education, to wit:

- to use the schools to change America from a free, individual nation to a socialist, global "state," just one of many socialist states which will be subservient to the United Nations Charter, not the United States Constitution;
- to brainwash our children, starting at birth, to reject individualism in favor of collectivism;
- to reject high academic standards in favor of OBE/ISO 1400/90007 egalitarianism;
- to reject truth and absolutes in favor of tolerance, situational ethics and consensus;
- to reject American values in favor of internationalist values (globalism);
- to reject freedom to choose one's career in favor of the totalitarian K–12 school-work/ OBE process, aptly named "limited learning for life-long labor," coordinated through United Nations Educational, Scientific, and Cultural Organization.

In the Foreword to her book, we find:

> "Charlotte Iserbyt is to be greatly commended for having put together the most formidable and practical compilation of documentation describing the "deliberate dumbing down" of American children by their education system. Anyone interested in the truth will be shocked by the way American social engineers have systematically gone about destroying the intellect of millions of American children for the purpose of leading the American people into a socialist world government controlled by behavioral and social scientists. ... Mrs. Iserbyt has also documented the gradual transformation of our once academically successful education system into one devoted to training children to become compliant human resources to be used by government and industry for their own purposes. This is how fascist-socialist societies train their children to become servants of their government masters. The successful implementation of this new philosophy of education will spell the end of the American

dream of individual freedom and opportunity. The government will plan your life for you, and unless you comply with government restrictions and regulations your ability to pursue a career of your own choice will be severely limited. …
What is so mind-boggling is that all of this is being financed by the American people themselves through their own taxes. In other words, the American people are underwriting the destruction of their own freedom and way of life by lavishly financing through federal grants the very social scientists who are undermining our national sovereignty and preparing our children to become the dumbed-down vassals of the new world order. It reminds one of how the Nazis charged their victims train fare to their own doom."

Have I not warned you in this, my own book, about the New World Order agenda? The socialist/fascist global, one-government world is being implemented at this very moment. The next part of this chapter highlights this agenda, because it was the goal of Barack Obama and Hillary Clinton, who were and are backed by the globalists.

Further information about the presence of socialist tools being used in the school systems to "dumb-down" our children has a well-established quantifiable history.

The foreword to the video states: "We discuss the high levels of illiteracy in America and what Alex Newman sees as the progressive agenda taking over the American school system to promote a collectivist, socialist, atheist world view. And we look at what role individuals like John Dewey, Horace Mann, and Robert Owen played in transforming the US education system."

I also note that in listening to this video on my iPhone, I noticed that there were RECOMMENDED American Thought Leaders' videos listed, which I'll name here, because parents need to look more into this education system hijacking by socialists.

1) Fixing America's Education Crisis. (K12's Kevin Chavous.)

2) Fixing a Broken Education System & Giving Students More Choice. (Department of Education Secretary Betsy DeVos.

3) Yes, Parents Are Capable of Choosing How Their Children Should Be Educated. (Kerry McDonald)

4) Ideological Fascism is Prevailing in Higher Education. (Dr. Everett Piper.)

5) Deception, Espionage & Totalitarianism – The Communist Threat to US National Security. (Bill Gertz)

6) Brandon Straka: On the #Walkaway Campaign & Media's "Fabrication of Reality" [Eagle Council Special].

7) Parents Should Decide. (Tammy Nichols on Sex Ed., Vaccinations & Sex Change. [Eagle Council Special.]

The EPOCH TIME (www.theepochtimes.com) produced, with their *American Thought Leaders* division, both a telecast of an interview about the "dumbing down" process. At the 48th Phyllis Schlafly's Eagle Council, EPOCH sat down with Alex Newman, author of "Crimes of the Educators: How Utopians Are Using Government Schools to Destroy America's Children." All citizens, especially parents, should view this video at the EPOCH TIMES website. But I'll give you some of the details here. Quoting:

> "I think we should be worrying about the entire education system, not just what is going there. Look at the people who created it; almost to a man, they told us what their agenda is: to turn our children into little socialists, communists, and humanists, and away from traditional American values, away from Biblical morality, and really cornerstones on what America was founded on.
>
> And so I think the entire edifice is a threat to our freedom, to our nation, to our children, to our families, and when you look at what is happening there now, it would become even more clear to people.
>
> They're bringing in the LGBT indoctrination, they're bringing in *The Drag Queen Story Hour*, the stuff that's going on in

the public schools today would shock even the most liberal "progressive" parent.

Half of the children graduating can't even read, that's according to the government's own data which shows that 50% of adults are illiterate, this is mind-blowing.

In 1993 the government did a literacy study and they categorized Americans into five categories, #1 being completely illiterate, couldn't even read a STOP sign to save their lives; #2 being basically a functional illiterate, and #5 being a good reader. Half of the Americans tested were in the bottom two categories.

In another survey 10 years later, same result. In a Washington, D.C. survey, it showed that 2/3's of Americans are functionally illiterate. This is mind-blowing.

They spent 12 years in a government school, spending $150 thousand, $200 thousand dollars, and these kids are graduating and they can't even read their high school diploma.

Now anybody who tells you that's an accident doesn't know what they are talking about. This is absolutely deliberate, proven; we re-printed one of the essays here by John Dewey, the founding father of American's school system, explaining that basically they wanted to dumb down the children, they didn't need how to read and write, and do math, they just need to socialize them, but to do it without people noticing, otherwise there's going to be a violent reaction."

When asked how could people do that to the children, Newman said that the beginnings of the current quackery of teaching had its beginnings by a Reverend Goladecz (sp), who had found the problems with teaching deaf children reading needed a new way to do that because words must be phonetically made and heard and deaf children had no way to do that. So the Reverend looked at and developed the Chinese method of teaching children thousands of characters they use in China by memorization, and applied this to deaf children to teach them whole words as similes [a figure of speech that draws a comparison between two different things]. It worked fine for deaf children, and the better a child could remember the words and their meaning, the better he or she would be able to read books and such.

In the Prussian dictatorship, the education system experimented with the Goladecz model in their schools, but after a few years it was completely discarded as completely unworkable, even to the point that some students became dyslexic and couldn't read.

Newman explains:

> "Horace Mann, who was really the pioneer for setting up schools in America, he started off as the Education Commissioner in Massachusetts, he got this idea from the Prussian dictatorship — that the government ought to educate all the children, equalize all men, get the Bible out, etc. – and so he thought, why don't we try out this reading system in the new government schools they created in Boston. Well, they did, but within a few years all the headmasters of all the schools in Boston said, "We not going to do this anymore; it doesn't work. The kids were developing what we today call dyslexia because the kids could not read properly because that's not how you teach reading. Even the really smart kid cannot memorize 8000 words they would need to be able to properly understand the written language that we have. That was completely discredited. .... Well, John Dewey, who I mentioned, he was inspired by the Soviet Union, by the way, he went to the Soviet Union, he loved what Lenin was doing instilling a collectivist mentality into the children, he [Dewey] wanted to replicate that in the United States. He resurrected this quackery that Horace Mann had tried out, knowing full well that it wasn't going to work. So they set up an experiment school with Rockefeller money, and the

kids were unable graduate because they couldn't read or write. Dewey says this is perfect, let's do it all across the nation, so they put together readers like "*Dick and Jane*" which handicapped millions of Americans and became a big scandal back in 1955, when Rudolf Flesch wrote the book "Why Johnny Can't Read." [Can be found on Amazon or at www.goodreadscom.] Flesch blew the lid off of all this, he said this is ridiculous, this way of teaching reading flies in the face of all logic, all common sense, and it's being taught in every public school in America. So something is wrong. This caused a national uproar, they were exposed, they had to retreat slightly, they had to introduce phonics, at least a little bit. And, in 1973 Dr. Blumenfeld put out *The New Illiterates* and another scandal ensued. And yet, to this day, under Common Core, they have children in kindergarten memorizing "sight words." If anyone thinks that's an accident, or somehow "I forgot.", as in after years of teaching we forgot how to do it, I say that's preposterous, that's ludicrous.

When asked if perhaps this problem is well-intentioned, Newman responded that:

"Well, I don't think that it is well-intentioned. Robert Owen, he was one of the earliest socialists, in fact he was socialist before Karl Marx came along, and he come over from Scotland, he set a colony in Indiana he called the *New Harmony Colony*, and it was an absolute failure. They were going to set up a communist system here even before communism existed. They called it a "social system" where no one would have private property, where everything would be communal and collective; it was a miserable failure. So Robert Owen went back to the "drawing board" and said the problem is not the idea of communism, the problem is that people are raised in selfish environments, they are given an education that turns them into little individualists when they need to be collectivists, so his organization actually branched out, instead of focusing on founding a communist colony he said we need to set up a national system of government schools where we can prepare these children for a future of collectivism. And Horace Mann got his inspiration from Robert Owen, and the King of Prussian got his inspiration from Robert Owen, and should have written him a Thank You letter, and …, you could say Robert Owen was well-intentioned but he rejected Christianity, he rejected God, he rejected private property, he rejected all of the things that I would consider good. But, I think, clearly from his writings he believed that what he was doing was good; he thought human nature was actually good, whereas the traditional American ethos has always been Calvinistic, humans are innately depraved and our heart is desperately wicked. Well, Robert Owen didn't believe that, he thought our problem was definitely environmental, and if you could get the children when they were young you could train them to create what the Soviets call "new Soviet man" – one who wouldn't only think of themselves but of the collective. So he, in that sense, maybe you could say he was well-intentioned. I think the current crop of people who insist on teaching this quackery to our children masquerading as 'reading instruction' know what they are doing is wrong, they know full well the damage they are doing, and I think it's very deliberate. As a Christian I think it is almost self-evident. The first education law we ever had in what is today the United States was actually passed in the 1640s by the very religious people of what was then the Massachusetts Bay Colony, of the "Old Deluder Satan's act" … it was the first education-related act that was ever passed in the United States, … the premise of the law which was actually passed by their legislature, that Old Deluder Satan, one of the chief projects of Satan was to keep men from knowledge of the scriptures. They had in mind burning people at the stake for trying to translate the Bible into the common language of the people. But they said the main project was to teach everybody to read the scriptures so that Old Deluder Satan could not deceive them. And so, what happens if most of the population you have is illiterate? They haven't been reading their Bibles, they haven't been reading their Constitution, the Declaration of Independence, they're not reading genuine history books, or reading primary-source documents, they're turning to fake news, like CNN, or they'll be relying on government teachers in government schools to teach them, so this creates an enormous problem from the perspective from handing on our traditions, passing on our religious values, maintaining political institutions, and our freedoms. I think it almost self-evident that that's the goal, to quote a more recent public figure Barack Obama, "fundamentally transform the United States." They would never have been able to advance the socialist agenda, the size and scope of government as we've seen without having dumbed-down the American population.

As the host pointed out in the interview, this situation does make people more susceptible to indoctrination because it harder to find the alternate perspective that they can consider. Newman agreed, noting that there is no substitution for going back and reading the Constitution, reading the Bible, or reading the Declaration of Independence. He said it is a totally different thing to read it for yourself than it is to hear it from a Marxist political science professor. Newman said, "And if you look at America, it came out of a society that was overwhelmingly Christian and was overwhelmingly literate, far more Americans were literate at the time of our war for independence than are today."

But the people who set up our government school system since those times vehemently disagreed with that early system and they wanted to move more towards the Soviet system. Newman points out, in fairness to John Dewey, that the Soviets and Dewey had not yet seen the horrors that this century has seen in the socialist/communist system, like Cambodia, Stalinism, China, Vietnam, maybe they didn't know millions of people would be slaughtered under such systems, so someone might say he was "well-intentioned."

Newman's book contains a whole range of crimes being committed against our children in the schools, from the drugging of children, to the abuse of children, to the exposing of them to the obscene to the pornographic materials, to encouraging them to fornicate, and to get abortions, but he believes the most serious comes under child abuse, i.e., the deliberate handicapping a child to a life of illiteracy should be considered abusive, extremely, when children are handicapped literally for the rest of their lives, making the written word inaccessible to them, making their career prospects much dimmer. Newman also said this insidiousness is even larger, to wit:

> "When you're trying to subtly, through deception, through fraud, overthrow our political institutions, overthrow our freedom, not openly by saying like, 'Hey guys, my idea is that we should give up our freedom and live in a collectivist society", but surreptitiously by indoctrinating young people, ... you know, back in the 1980's Ronald Reagan put together a commission, the National Commission on Excellence in Education, and they came out with a report, "Nation at Risk", and they said ... that if a foreign power had done this through the educational system, we would consider it an act of war. And, what Dr. Blumenthal and I argued was that we should do it as an act of war. It was a calculated and strategic effort to overthrow our system of government and ... I consider collectivism to be slavery, and so, these people were trying to enslave us."

Again, government surveys have at least twice, perhaps several times over the years, confirmed that students are not achieving proper literacy, and the problem remains ongoing.

Another leader advocate for school choice and education reform is Kevin Chavous, president of a K12 company, a company that partners with U.S. schools to offer personalized education programs. EPOCH talked with him on video, pointing out that an estimated two-thirds of America's high school graduates are neither career- nor college-ready. Chavous noted that even the former Secretary of Education Arne Duncan said the picture of education in America is stagnation, with lots of kids who aren't getting what they deserve in the government's education system. He called it "shameful" that our schools are graduating a lot of kids who do not actually qualify to be graduated, and who are just not ready for entry into the world marketplace. He pointed out that Founding Father Thomas Jefferson believed that the only way citizens could survive and that democracy could survive is through an educated population.

He also noted America used to have a "can do" cultural spirit that said, "Pull yourself up by your bootstraps, get an education, you can receive your piece of the American Dream." He described our current educational condition as an "acceptance of mediocrity."

Dr. Samuel L. Blumenfeld is the author of nine books on education. His input includes the following:

> By now we know exactly what the progressives mean by "what reading really is." The word method is now called Whole Language, and in 1991 three Whole Language professors wrote a book, Whole Language: What's the Difference?, in which they defined what they mean by reading. They wrote:
>
>> From a whole language perspective, reading (and language use in general) is a process of generating hypotheses in a meaning-making transaction in a sociohistorical context. As a transactional process reading is not a matter of "getting the meaning" from text, as if that meaning were in the text waiting to be decoded by the reader. Rather, reading is a matter of readers using the cues print provide and the knowledge they bring with them to construct a unique interpretation....This view of reading implies that there is no single "correct" meaning for a given text, only plausible meanings.
>
> This is the kind of pedagogical insanity that now reigns in our colleges of education and has filtered down to the classroom

teacher. Most parents assume that our educators are sane human beings who use common sense in their classrooms. Unfortunately, few if any parents have access to the writings of these so-called professors of education, and so are totally ignorant of the kind of crackpots who are educating their children.

(Source: NewAmerican (www.thenewamerican.com), February 11, 2011.)

To close this Part 4, the idea that we've allowed, for years, to let our education system be crafted and administered by socialists is outrageous and shameful; we should have, long ago, created and passed legislation that would require proper education techniques and criminalize actions by teachers who veered from the ideological structure of the country and education system intentionally to undermine the proper education of our children. Today, all over America, we hear of political science and sociology professors who teach socialism is the Utopian ideal for a government to have, such as Berkeley, U.C. Davis, Contra Costa Community College, and others just in California, but we're seeing that across the nation and in some of the most previously-revered Universities, including the esteemed Yale. Right now, and for a long time now, the teachers in our classroom are deciding the futures of our children.

We need legislation that spells out what teachers can teach, and if socialism or communism or totalitarianism needs to be taught so that students know the various kinds of government, they should teach how those institutions operate based on historic documents, particularly those that show the oppression and subjugation citizens suffer under such regimes. We don't need a fair and academic look at the ideologues, because we already know the reality of such systems, and it is the reality that needs to be taught to our students. In my opinion.

So let's take a look at what the law says about proselytizing socialism to take down this country. I quote Title 18, United States Code, Section 2384, under Seditious Conspiracy, which makes it clear that pushing socialism, communism or totalitarianism in America by anyone is a felony crime:

If two or more persons in any State or Territory, or in any place subject to the jurisdiction of the United States, conspire to overthrow, put down, or to destroy by force the Government of the United States, or to levy wear against them, or to oppose by force the authority thereof, or by force to prevent, hinder, or delay the execution of any law of the United States, or by force to seize, take, or possess any property of the United States contrary to the authority thereof, they shall each be fined under this title or imprisoned not more than twenty years, or both.

Hmmm …. so why haven't the pro-socialists, including Antifa and presidential candidates and other organizations, been investigated with mass arrests under Section 2384 and prosecuted into prison? Why is the law not being enforced? Perhaps we can get this started in 2020.

For a seditious conspiracy charge to be effected, a crime need only be planned, it need not be actually attempted. According to Andres Torres and Jose E. Velazquez, (Temple University Press, 1998) the accusation of seditious conspiracy is of political nature and was used almost exclusively against Puerto Rican independentistas in the twentieth century. However, the act was also used in the twentieth century against communists and radicals (United Freedom Front, the Provisional IRA in Massachusetts), neo-Nazis, and Islamic terrorists including Omar Abdel-Rahman.

Yet, here we are, undergoing mass treason from the alt-Left, with publicly admitted socialists like B. Sanders and E. Warren running for President of the United States, while the mainstream media, owned and operated by the globalists pushing the New World Order Agenda, spew their hatred, false narratives, demands, and support for this socialism agenda. And our own government leaders, the ones who do NOT want socialism, seem to be overlooking the very law that could put an end to this socialism agenda.

As I have written this book, and continued to research these matters, I came across a TeaParty247 article entitled "Is a Civil War Coming? One Professor Believes This Group Is America's Next Revolutionaries". You can Google it at www.teaparty.247.org. It is another solid layer of proof against the agenda of the alt-Left; if anything going on today makes you patriots angry, this certainly will.

There has been a lot of talk about civil war coming to America. In my book I have pointed out how Marxist Obama spent 8 years setting it up, alongside Marxist Clinton, and how Clinton was supposed to be a "no-brainer shoe-in" as the next President. Her job was to engage Step 2 to create more racial division, civil war, martial law, and disarmament of Americas, i.e., the typical socialist game plan.

The TeaParty247 article discussed a very cogent warning by a college professor, C. Bradley Thompson, professor of political science at Clemson University and author of "America's Revolutionary Mind: A Moral History of the American Revolution and the Declaration That Defined it." In this book he discussed his concerns about the continuing fracture of American politics and culture in an interview on SiriusXM's Breitbart News Tonight with hosts Rebecca Mansour and Joe Pollack.

As I have explained throughout this book, connecting the dots, I also discussed the problem of socialist propaganda taught in out K-12 schools and universities. As the TeaParty247 rightly noted, "It's alarming just how inundated our public education system has become in such a short period of time" and noting in other countries that fell to socialism and communism, the Marxist theology began in the schools to convince those generations in favor of socialism or communism so as they grew into adults, entering the marketplace and political institutions, it would be they who brought about socialism or communism. Already 70-80% of the millennials favor socialism.

Who is to blame? Should it surprise you that WE are to blame? And not just for allowing our educational institutions to be overrun by Marxists either. Throughout America's history, there have been those who wanted a Marxist-based ideology, not democratic capitalism. But the current movement is precisely the same reiteration that began in the 1960's "hippy era" when Marxism was very popular with millions of hop-heads and pot-heads and LSD-stargazers. As they grew up into adults, THEY entered politics and the educational institutions, bringing their Marxist ideas with them, knowing full well that the educational institutions were the platform for Marxism in the future. This is WHY our educational institutions have become so permeated with socialism-teaching teachers/professors. Marxism is what they taught their children, and they too are entering the political and educational systems affirming a new generation seeking socialism. Our somewhat fondly-recalled "hippy era" set the initial stage for what is going on right now, today, in our political and educational systems. So, who makes it easier? Billionaires like George Soros and other wealthy Marxist funders help this socialist ideology gain ground. These teachers and professors are determining our children's future by indoctrinating their immature and malleable minds.

Professor Thompson's public interview deserves inclusion here. In his interview he pointed out that there are two factions that have formed in America. Conservatives represent one while the far-Left "progressives" represent the other. Thompson points out that the United States is not just a country but an ideology "associated with the principles of the Declaration of Independence", a Declaration which the Progressives are hell-bent on destroying.

Thompson notes that the Declaration used to be widely accepted by all Americans regardless of political leanings, but now the division in politics seems to boil down to ideological differences in the way in which the two factions view the words of the Declaration. Professor Thompson asked the obvious question:

> "So the question is: What is it, what ideas can Americans rally around? If we cannot rally around these words – We hold these truths to be self-evident, that all men are created equal, that they are endowed by their Creator with certain unalienable rights, among which are the rights to life, liberty, and the pursuit of happiness – then we can rally as a nation around no words."

> "The problem is, part of the United States – one group in the United States – they seem to despise the principles on which this country was founded, and so we find ourselves in

this very difficult position where one part of the nation really hates what this country has always stood for."

The TeaParty247 noted that Democrats seem to hate truth and reality and have found the best way to combat the principles they despise is to literally take over the very meaning of truth which results in confusion and the breaking down of America's moral fabric. Thompson pointed this out too.

"Those very simple but graceful words in the second paragraph of the Declaration," he started, "So, just go through them: 'We hold these truths to be self-evident.' The first thing to say is that in 2019, the intellectual class in the United States doesn't believe in the concept of truth. In 2016, the word of the year in the Oxford dictionary was '*post-truth*.' It said that we live in a post-truth society, that is to say, we live in a world where truth is allegedly subjective. Every person effectively has their truth, or every group has their truth, whereas the Founding Fathers believed in truth with a capital T, that truth is absolute, certain, permanent, and universal."

If then, if truth is subjective, is it thus so with morality? The answer is apparently. We know the Bible teaches against sexual perversion, against homosexuality, against theft, adultery, coveting another man's wife or vice-versa, and murder. The Ten Commandants are simple rules of morality and conduct. Yet, the Progressives want "truth" to be whatever the individual wants it to be, thus whatever morality is to the individual. So we have a growing LGBT movement to normalize abnormal behavior, and we've seen the Progressives promoting even worse: pedophilia and beastiality. As to the latter, we have heard on the talk show "Young Turks" Cenk Uygur talk with a female guest about the "rightness" of being able to have sex with animals; in particular, he pointed out that why not have sex with a horse if the horse obviously enjoys it. Sick, very sick! (To think that Cenk has announced he was going to run for Congress! Really?!) Is this the direction 'morality' is going? Thompson further noted:

"The reining intellectual and moral orthodoxy of American intellectual life, American universities would be the twin towers of moral relativism and nihilism, and the idea here, and the goal of the left over the last 50 or 60 years has been this long march through the institutions. What they've tried to do – and in fact, have done quite successfully – is to take over America's cultural institutions, particularly education, particularly K through 12 education, and colleges and universities, and that's where the real battle is. It's a battle of ideas. ... Unfortunately I think, too many libertarians and conservatives and classical liberals invest too much time in politics, whereas John Adams and Thomas Jefferson believed that – what really is the underpinning – the soul of a nation is how we educate our children. That's the core issue, and so whoever controls the schools, and now also the universities, will control the culture. ... As Andrew Breitbart once said, politics is downstream from culture, and culture is downstream from the universities, and so if we lose the battle for the universities – and our schools, K through 12 – then we find ourselves in a very difficult position."

Professor Thompson was very concerned about how to fight an ideological war because it is already fracturing America and could fracture it irreparably. A civil war as an ideological war might not involve violence, he wonders, but patriots must fight back now, and one of the more effective, albeit long-term ways, would be to "homeschool" your children, get them out of these Marxist-run institutions. He pointed out that the way in which our children are educated now will have a profound impact on the result of a future civil (ideological) war. He suggests homeschooling is the best way to combat the pervasiveness of the Progressive Left's agenda, which has invested government-run public schools all across the country.

So, parents, the question is: Are you going to take individual action to safeguard your own children from the Marxist culture in our educational systems? Ultimately, you are responsible for protecting your children. How you do that is up to you. Parents can also meet together and agree to investigate local schools for such Marxist propaganda, then file lawsuits against them demanding "cease and desist" orders and monetary damages for the damage of "brainwashing" the children.

Don't be complacent. As I say over and over, complacency ultimately is acquiescence, and both are fundamental enemies of freedom and morality.

I spend a lot of time, considering I am retired, thinking about things going on in the world and, in particular, right here in my home country America. I am aware that there will always be those pro-socialists who wrongly think that socialism is the best form of government, even though history shows definitely this belief is simply not true. Socialism, with rare exceptions in Europe where certain countries have a hybrid form of socialism supported by a capitalist market economy, has usually resulted in poverty and misery for its population. Genocide has often occurred in both socialist and communist countries.

I was born in 1949. My childhood was in the 50s and 60s. I saw my first television when I was seven years old. There was no risqué or overt sexuality on TV back then, and the violence was minimal, with the good guys always winning. There was always a clear line between right and wrong, all of which began to change in the later 60s and worsened over the following decades. Murderers somehow were made heroes. Murder for revenge became almost daily fare in the movies. Violent crime in our communities soared as a result. Crimes of rape and sexual assault, including pedophilia, rose dramatically as movies became more sexualized.

So I have a moral question many might have asked themselves: Is murdering someone you have reason to hate justifiable? If the answer is Yes, you might consider that human nature can be quite fickle and that line of justification varies in a major way between individuals. Killing is far easier for some than most.

The path to the future goes through the past. This is Psychology 101. We are what we've done, and what's been done to us. Inductive reasoning and lack of sound values, and a life bereft of rational thought, creates monsters amongst us. Oftentimes, a rough life can lead into dark pathways. While adversity and struggle might make someone stronger, there are usually consequences, often severe ones.

Being a product of our environment and how we respond to all the factors around us, a failure to think carefully about what information is coming our way, can easily led us to destructive behavior if our sense of moral values is not strong.

One might think that we are in the best era of our history, with social and information media literally at our fingertips in the schools and on the internet. Yet, we are at a more dangerous time than any time in our history and, in this country, facing a potential of a civil war that will make the previous civil war between the North and South seem like a walk in the park. Christianity and morality is under major attack by the social media itself, and the movies coming out of Hollywood illustrate that morality is waning in importance, i.e., if there is no God, then morality is man-made and no longer valid. This is what is happening.

The alt-Left socialist Progressives pose a real threat of civil insurrection and possibly civil war. Our own educational institutions, populated with socialist professors and teachers, have been creating a very large population of the millennial generation of our own children who believe that capitalism is evil and socialism is Utopian. One might think our children, having the best of the best educational institutions in the world, might know better, that they might actually research and learn about the horrors of socialism, communism, and fascism instead of accepting the false narrative that current American government is fascist, a notion taught by the alt-Left in an obvious _fascist_ manner. This is the blind leading the blind.

So I ask you, i.e., any pro-socialist reading this, who are YOU really? Can't you see that your efforts to shut down dialogue about these differences of opinion and ideology is the very foundation of <u>fascism</u> itself? You accuse others of fascism and you take the same approach as fascists to shut down free speech and free expression. What do you want? Why do you refuse to see that the cause and agenda for socialism is about destroying morality and right-thinking? How about engaging in deductive reasoning based on actual research?

I am sorry that our educational system has brainwashed you into believing that Marxism is Utopian. It is not. I am sorry that the masters of perversity in Hollywood have confused you about right and wrong, about daily virtues of right and moral conduct, about individual responsibility itself. I can see that you have been spoon fed the idea that you should not have to make an effort and work for what you want in life, that socialism would allow you the freedom to do nothing but acquire free stuff for everything you want from the government. I can see that you have somehow embraced an ethos of "anything goes" for all of the perverse things morally defined as evil thinking and conduct. I can see that you somehow think it is right for YOU and people like YOU to forbid any thought or opinion contrary to what you believe, and you're willing to forbid by violence.

There will come a time when we patriots route the socialist teachers and professors from our educational institutions. Personally, I think we should do it right now, and we can do it with local populations gathering together and demanding the expulsion of these traitors from our schools.

I wish I could send you pro-socialists to Venezuela, once the most prosperous market-economy country in South American, now a country where its people are starving and violence is out of control. All because of socialists deciding socialism is better. What would you say to them, when they know firsthand the empty promises of socialists?

How will you feel when you lose this Marxist agenda here in the USA, and when you and those who think and act like you are deemed by the winning side to be a "traitor" to your own country and countrymen? Our side will not likely go easy on you if this dark pathway results in serious violence like terrorist attacks or even civil war. We will NOT forgive you for that. You want to purge "white people" and "conservatives" from the population, perhaps send them to the hundreds of FEMA camps that were built to keep people in, like Russian gulags. Well, perhaps you'll get a first-hand view of those gulag internment facilities.

Even if you are simply convicted of treason and sent to prison, and someday lucky enough to get paroled, everyone will know you are a traitor. They will shun you, even spit on you and perhaps assault you. You will be an outcast. Do you not know that the winning side may choose to enact a special law to purge all traitors from American soil? Where will you go then? How will you live and survive? The seditious crimes you are even now committing against Americans intend the gravest of crimes against humanity itself, so why would patriots ever forgive you? Why should we not take the attitude, "God forgives! I don't!" against you? Your crimes and intentions are far greater than even first-degree murder. Your Marxist goals will result in death and poverty and devastation on a global scale and billions will surely die. Life and survival will get worse across the globe itself if you destroy the most successful market economy in the world.

Your plan, governance by Marxism, fixes nothing and destroys everything. Our Constitution's Bill of Rights and the unalienable rights embedded in the Amendments protect human beings from what you are actually trying to accomplish. Our Second Amendment gives patriots the right to bear arms and kill you if you decide to commit terrorist acts or create civil war, and we will. Piss off the patriots enough and you might as well jump in the water with a polar bear.

How could you want to destroy the freest country in the world, the place where anyone, with effort, can achieve a decent lifestyle, grow a family, enjoy the fruits of your own efforts. Unless you hate yourself and your life, or you are clinically insane, you better do a little more research about socialism and communism and totalitarianism and fascism before you continue on in this stupid Marxist goal of yours. If things go bad in this country because of what you and people like you cause, there will be no redemption for you.

One might wonder why the alt-Left has traded fact and truth for fantasy and false narratives. Perhaps they don't understand they are being manipulated by a totalitarian "shadow government" using them to bring America to the first step, socialism, which will then allow them to continue on to creating a totalitarian world. Perhaps the alt-Left doesn't want the truth or reality to interfere in their already meaningless and vacuous lives.

So many millennials have embraced the socialist notion and actually believe they are trying to accomplish a better way of life. I feel sorry for you buying into the rise of whatever feels good must be good mindset, embracing a feeling even if what causes it is not real, and joining with like-minded peers because they want to fit in to the group. So we get "group think" where people agree on something important without analytic thought as to whether the end goal is what they think it is.

It is cognitive dissonance reinforcing what they want to believe is true, not wanting to know if it has ever been as they believe. They are unknowingly preparing to initiate anarchy and violence, possibly even civil war where many thousands, even millions of citizens might die.

They do not know or realize that if we divide ourselves into warring factions in civil unrest or war that the United Nations can and will intervene with military troops from nations that do NOT like America or Americans. This will be an invasion. It could also create a weakened situation where our enemies in the Arab, Chinese, North Korean, or Russia, decide to invade as well, killing us off and carving up America into their "conquered" territories; after all, the history of the world has seen nations conquered by other nations.

Former President John Quincy Adams once said: "America does not go abroad in search of monsters; she only vindicates her own." Obvious, the warnings by Theodore Roosevelt about the expansion of the military industrial complex have gone unheeded where America is going abroad in search of monsters, and I do not doubt that the international bankers bankroll both sides of these small wars so the MIC can profit financially, as they do. We should protest that.

Our post-WW-II history seems to have increased the breadth of our world leadership, but with it came the evil of war-for-profit the MIC and bankers need and want. And so we engage in war after war in countries where tribal factions have historically warred against one another, and show no signs of ever achieving peace amongst themselves. We should leave them alone. But, there's the oil issue. Why do we not use our own vast oil reserves? Is it because the international bankers won't profit as much if we withdraw from the Arab world? Is it because the MIC would lose vast revenue affecting their economic bottom line? Is it because there are huge profits to be made at the expense of morality, where we war in countries killing soldiers and citizens alike? It is immoral to claim we are imposing "freedom" upon those to whom "freedom" is evil and the mischievous harbingers of evil? Islam is one of those ideologies which openly opposes "freedom" because it is diametrically opposite of Islamic ideology and rules. Why do Americans ignore this truth and still support Islam here in America, despite what we have seen in Europe over the past 20 years?

Islamists in America actively work to destroy our American ideology because Islamic ideology demands it. Is that simple truth too hard to comprehend? If so, what has happened to American sensibilities?

I have inserted this paragraph about international affairs, the MIC, and Islam because I too believe that American government needs fixing. I just don't believe socialism etc. is the way to do so. Because of the MIC and the international bankers, under socialism or totalitarianism, wars will only get worse as they vie for control of the world itself. The socialists are doing nothing more than helping that New World Order (one government world) to occur, and are failing to understand that the United Nations itself is at the heart of the NWO, and has been since its creation.

It is, for me, both saddening and outrageous, what the pro-socialists are doing. It is, for that reason, that I decided to do extensive research and write this book. Someone had to put together the pieces of the spiderweb-like puzzle of who is manipulating world affairs and out to destroy the joy of freedom and liberty for every person on this planet, except themselves. The rulers historically have been the ones that enjoyed whatever they wanted to be or do, while everyone else suffered.

One final thought on the matter of proper education systems. A century ago, there were only seven countries in the world that were more prosperous than Argentina (Belgium, Switzerland, Britain, and four former British colonies including the United States). In 1909, per capital income in Argentina was 50 percent higher than in Italy, 180 percent higher than Japan, and almost five times higher than in neighboring Brazil. Over the course of the 20th century, Argentina's relative standing in world incomes fell sharply; by 2000, Argentina's income was less than half that of Italy or Japan. Why? Notwithstanding that Argentina was plagued with bad policies, but Argentina's public sector was quite problematic. This was not about just bad luck. A major reason for its demise was avoiding focus on its educational institutions. Argentina did not invest well in education of its citizens. Schooling is measured by the share of relevant populations that were enrolled in primary, secondary, or tertiary schooling. Argentina may have been rich, but it was not that well-educated. In 2000, Argentina was doing about as well as would be expected based on its education levels in 1990. Long-run national success is built on human capital, both because of the link between schooling and technology and because of the link between education and well-functioning democracy.

Our education system nationwide is failing our children, failing them by a curricula and by teaching techniques that do not help build mature-thinking minds, but instead result in students leaving high school without an adequate mental maturity for sound thinking and without the mature mental skills to succeed in the marketplace. We have at least one entire generation who have been indoctrinated with nonsense, having been taught only to think about thinking instead of how to analyze, compare, and process information through cognitive reasoning. But for the Common Core curricula dominating through America's institutions of learning, the current batch of millennials would not be indoctrinated that Marxism is the road to Utopia.

One of Adolf Hitler's Nazi Party Officials, Gregor Strasser, spoke of National Socialism: "*We are socialists, enemies, mortal enemies of the present capitalist economic system with its exploitation of the economically weak, with its injustice in wages, with its immoral evaluation of individuals according to wealth and money instead of responsibility and achievement, and we are determined under all circumstances to abolish this system!*"

Hmmm! Is this not the mirror argument currently being set forth by the Progressives who are seeking socialism and the abolition of capitalism? Both Hitler and Italy's Benito Mussolini (fascist) started World War II, causing widespread destruction and the death of 70 to 80 million people. The Western capitalist democracies fought against them, but at its core the war was between communists and fascists. Their armies lost a combined total of 15 million soldiers on the Eastern front, and when the smoke cleared, only communism (under Stalin) was left standing, and just barely. With subsequent Soviet military gains, communism was imposed in Eastern Europe and North Korea, where the people of these new communist states became prisoners in their own countries. And when Mao Zedong took China to communism, promising a collective modern industrial economy within five years, Chairman Mao instead dragged China backwards with an estimated 30-40 million peasants dying of starvation. Only in the last 30 years has China found economic success by embracing elements of free-market capitalism.

How many Americans would die if socialism or communism take over, by murder as well as starvation as the economy collapses?

I have spoken of the Hippy generation being moved towards Marxism in the 60's where the drug culture met with opposition to the validity of the Vietnam war. Soviet Intelligence saw an opening in the new "counter-culture" movement of the Hippy Generation. These were young people motivated by Marxist principles who wanted to overthrow the capitalist establishment from within. The first large group of Hippies, pacifists and pro-socialists numbered over 50,000 protestors in San Francisco. The Russian KGB funded and manipulated these counter-culture groups and left-wing political organizations in the West to so dissent, while also helping to train and support Marxist terrorist groups, like the Red Army faction in Germany, the Red Brigade in Italy, and the Weathermen Underground in the United States, who wanted to overthrow Western governments and replace them with communism. Russian has been psychologically invading America for over three decades, and has focused on funding of organizations and associations that teach socialism and communism in our schools. These Marxists have grown up, entered the marketplace, corporate America, government agencies, the educational institutions., and the political process, and thereby slowly built up today's advocates of national socialism, as we are seeing today more openly than ever. Calling it "democratic" socialism is incorrect; it is more akin to "national socialism" as with the Nazi Party, once you understand the playbook of both.

Indoctrination or "brainwashing" is a grave, deliberate process that goes slowly along and is divided into four basic stages: demoralization, destabilization, insurgency, normalization.

Demoralization takes about some 15 to 50 years to educate one generation of students exposed to the ideology of the enemy, but Marxism is being pumped into the heads of at least three generations of students without being challenged or counter-balanced by the basic values of Americanism.

Destabilization takes 2-5 years to destabilize key factors of America: the economic, foreign relations, defense systems, by Marxist and Leninist influence, leading eventually to fascism.

The third factor is crisis, of creating a crisis touted as a violent change of power, or insurgency, or pandemic, as we see today with the uprising against President Donald Trump by false narratives and downright lies by the mainstream media and other questionable sources, including outspoken socialists and communists. The violence is increasing.

The fourth factor is "normalization" and while this encompasses an infinite span of time, it comes down to making it "normal" thinking that socialism is the answer to all of a society's ills, as if socialism was Utopian in reality. It includes the rise from the shadows demands for behavioral changes to "normalize" what has been and is, abnormal behaviors and ways of thinking. We see this in the move to mainstream homosexuality, of transgenderism – starting with small children – and even calls for pedophilia and beastiality as normal behaviors. We see this in the concept of "political correctness" the new term for Orwellian "double-speak" all of which causes mental chaos and social anarchy. Britain's Lord Action correctly said: "Socialism easily accepts despotism." We seem to be on the road to the crushing of free speech where freedom will be reduced to the dusty volumes of unread books that may survive the bookburnings that are inevitable in a society's demise by socialism, communism, or fascism.

The Progressives point to Denmark as a successful socialist nation. This Nordic socialist system is "far from a socialist planned economy. Denmark is a market economy. The Nordic model is an expanded welfare state which provides a high level of security for its citizens, but it is also a successful market economy with much freedom to pursue your dreams and live your life as you wish." Lars Ramussen, Danish Prime Minister. Even China now rides on a market economy. The tax rate on citizen incomes in Denmark is around 57% because this is what it takes to support its social programs. 57 percent.

But there is something more sinister about the Progressive's playbook that we need to know. The Progressives are neo-Nazis because they are using the same National Socialist playbook that Hitler and his inner circle used. I'll explain. Let me sub-title this explanation as follows.

The Nazi Plan: Volksgemeinschaft

The inner circle of Adolf Hitler fluctuated a bit as these members jockeyed for their own part of Nazi power, but the important ones to note are:

Adolf Hitler, rose to prominence with help of aristocrat Dietrich Eckart; became Chancellor of Germany after two failed attempts to establish the Nazi Party as top Party in Germany.

Adolf Eichmann, SS Commander in charge of the facilitation and transportation of Jews to ghettos and extermination camps. Fled to Argentina, captured there by Mossad operatives in 1960, tried in Israel and executed on June 1, 1962.

Hermann Goring, Hitler's German Air Force commander, highest-ranking military officer in the Third Reich; sole holder of the Grand Cross of the Iron Cross; sentenced to death by the Nurenberg Tribunal but committed suicide before his scheduled hanging.

Rudolf Hess, Deputy Fuhrer to Hitler until his flight to Scotland on the even of the German invasion of the Soviet Union in June 1941; intended betrayal for leniency.

Heinrich Himmler, Reichsfuhrer-SS. As head of the SS, Chief of the German Police and later the Minister of the Interior, one of the most powerful men in the Third Reich; he was the architect for the Jew extermination program.

Joseph Goebbels, anti-Semite; one of Hitler's closest associates and most devout followers, known to zealous oratory and antisemitism. Minister for Public Enlightenment and Propaganda; named Reich Chancellor in Hitler's will, just before he committed suicide, after which Goebbels also committed suicide.

Reinhardt Heydrich, came from nobody to Himmler's right-hand man. Principal architect of the Night of the Long Knives; considered total psychopath and killer; died from complications after assassination attempt with car bomb.

Martin Bormann, Head of the Party Chancellery and private secretary to Adolf Hitler.

Ernst Rohm, a co-founder of the Storm Battalion or SA, the Nazi Party militia and, later, was the SA commander. In 1934, as part of the Night of the Long Knives, he was executed on Hitler's orders as a potential rival. Many of the SA members were likewise executed on the Night of the Long Knives.

Albert Speer, architect for Nazi offices and residences, Party rallies and State buildings (1932-1942), Minister of Armaments and War Production (1942-45)

Recently, I began researching a little more in-depth about the rise of Nazism in Germany, and watched on Netflix ten (10) episodes about Nazism, its players, and its playbook. The documentary, Hitler's Circle of Evil, was quite illuminating because of its relevance to what is going on in the United States today. I was quite surprised to find that strong similarities exist today right here in the United States. I think there are readers who might find this brief trek quite enlightening.

I learned that Hitler had given an impassioned speech about the troubles of Germany after losing in WW-I. A journalist, Dietrich Eckhart, saw Hitler as a candidate for becoming the Chancellor of Germany and help in restoring it. Hitler was unpolished, table manners were somewhat missing, but Eckhart befriended him, encouraged him, introduced him to the "upper-crust" of German society, and polished his mannerisms so that he would fit in better. So Eckhart had a great deal of influence on Hitler's rise to power.

Eckhart was also a politician who was one of the founders of the German Worker's Party, the predecessor to the Nazi Party (NSDAP). He was the original publisher of the party newspaper, the *Volkischer Beobachter*, and became called the spiritual father of National Socialism.

Eckhart (1868-1923), on his deathbed around Christmas 1923, wrote: "*Follow Hitler. He will dance, but it is I who have written the music. ... Don't weep for me: I shall have had more influence on the course of history than any other German.*"

Eckhart was a prominent figure in Germany's Bohemian and occult subculture before World War I. A well-known playwright, poet and journalist, he was involved with the shadowy Baron Rudolf von Sebottendorff and the secretive Thule Society in Munich. After hearing Hitler speak at a political meeting in 1919, Eckhart recognized Hitler's talent as a demagogue and an organizer. He saw in Hitler someone who could translate the occult worldview of the Thule into action. He took Hitler under his wing and made him his protégé. Eckhart popularized the central tenet of the Thule Society, the belief in the coming of a "German Messiah" who would redeem the nation from its defeat in World War I.

Historians agree that Eckhart had considerable, unequaled influence on Hitler. Without his patronage and mentoring, Hitler would never have become the leader of the party that came to completely dominate Germany in the 1930's. It is also interest to note that after Eckhart's death, another journalist, a much younger one, became Hitler's Propaganda Minister and outspoken architect of the "Final Solution" for the Jews of Germany, Austria, and Poland. His name was Joseph Goebbels, an anti-Semite, eventually becoming as evil as Heinrich Himmler.

However, Hitler did not really believe in occultism, at least not to the same degree as Eckhart, although Eckhart's promotion of his to the Germans as a "messiah" come to save them, had a significant effect on Hitler himself. However, the only one of Hitler's inner circle who later became obsessed by occultism was Rudolf Hess, originally Hitler's right-hand man.

I would encourage all patriots to study these 10 episodes on Netflix and you will see the accuracy of the correlations I make here to the "alt-Left Progressives" because this pro-socialism faction called "Progressives" is an Orwellian double-speak for neo-Nazism in America. I have to wonder, however, if most of the members of the Progressives even realize that what they have been doing to destroy capitalism in the United States is actually from the Nazi playbook.

During the rise of Nazism, after several failed attempts, Joseph Goebbels, Propaganda Minister, a rabid anti-Semitic, created the *Volksgemeinschaft*, the People's Community, which is still known as an enormously successful social-engineering project of epic proportions. It was a Utopian kind of vision. Hitler envisioned the ideal German society as a racially-unified and hierarchically-organized body in which the interests of individuals would be strictly subordinate to those of the nation, or *Volk*.

Within this concept was *Gleichschaltung*, for the process of successively establishing a totalitarian control and coordination over all aspects of German society and societies occupied by Nazi Germany. Essentially, gleichschaltung meant stamping out unions and political-parties hostile to National Socialism, while other institutions like the church and education systems were co-opted into vehicles for Nazi ideology. The word literally means synchronization or "to bring into line," but it refers to the process in Nazi Germany that ensured political conformity "in all sectors, from the economy and trade associations to the media, culture, and education."

Under both of these concepts, this was the Nazis' attempt to create a Germanic Utopia as the supreme master state. This was the creation of the mastermind Propaganda Minister Joseph Goebbels, who sold it to Hitler. Hitler wanted Germany to be a National Socialist country, and he said the only way to subvert democracy would be through democracy and its systems. The Nazi Party would need to participate in the elections and gain power through the electoral process and not through an armed insurrection. It would take 10 years. In 1933 Hitler and the Nazi Party gained political power, and while he almost immediately turned Germany from a democracy into a dictatorship, he did so by persuading the government leaders to endorse that change; their vote was almost total in favor of Hitler taking ultimate control. I find it interesting a comparison between Hitler and Caligula, the Roman Emperor who went from nice guy who the Roman Senate quickly turned over absolute power to thinking he was a good guy, but it did not take Caligula long before becoming a ruthless killer, before he was finally assassinated by the Senators themselves 1400 days later.

Hitler was anti-semitic. There was an initial period when Hitler called for the boycotting of Jewish businesses, but for the most part, Germans ignored even the Brownshirts posted outside Jewish businesses who were supposed to deter citizens from shopping there. Coupled with that was the plain fact that many Germans had inter-married with Jews and thus had mixed bloodlines. This became a problem for the anti-Semites who wanted Germany to become the master race with only a Germanic bloodline. So, that initial People's Community plan did not work out too well.

Since the fall of Nazism in WW-II, nearly all the conversational focus has been on Hitler as being the architect of Nazism, the ultimate anti-Semitic, and all the evils that followed. But, this is not entirely true. He was anti-Semitic, but not rabidly so like Joseph Goebbels and Heinrich Himmler. Goebbels was out-front about it, welcomed street violence against Jews, whereas Himmler, more secretive and definitely more evil-minded, eventually gained control of the police, paramilitary, and the infamous Gestapo SS secret police. He became the administrator of the concentration camps generally and the architect of death for Jews and others not in line with the Nazi movement.

The rise of Hitler and the Nazi party had several failures and nearly went out of existence. Joseph Goebbels, made the Propaganda Minister, was a master at speaking and writing, and he was largely responsible for restoring support for Nazism when it faltered. Indeed, he was instrumental in the *Volksgemainschaft* creation.

Initially, the People's Community got major support, as the people were promised jobs and prosperity and vacations, but as it became clear the Nazi Party could not deliver on its promises to fix the economy, to bring jobs and prosperity, it began to falter. It reached the level where few considered the Nazi Party viable or supportable.

Ever the creative spirit, Goebbels began a campaign that blamed the problem on "outsiders," which meant the Jews. Using the Jews as the scapegoat, they were sold to the German public as an identifiable enemy for all their ills, and Goebbels called for systemic violence against the Jews and the confiscation of their wealth and properties. Hitler initially rejected the violence, but when it was clear his supporters agreed with Goebbels, he changed his mind. Immediately, a flurry of new laws and regulations were written against the Jews and their businesses.

Hermann Goring, himself of the aristocracy whose grandfather was a third-removed Jew, and owned a lavish estate in Austria, was anti-semitic but not rabidly so at all. He was given, by Hitler, control over Prussia and the Gestapo SS. Goebbels was one step beneath him in power, but he ordered Goebbels – who was quite prone to violence – not to destroy Jewish homes or businesses, or their goods, artwork, anything of value, or general looting, which assets would go to the State. Goebbels ignored this limitation, and encouraged German citizens to join hands in the streets and punish the Jews. Many were killed, houses and businesses were looted and burned to the ground. This horrific assault against the Jewish community in November 1938 became known as *Kristallnacht*, meaning the Night of Broken Glass, carried out by SA (*Sturmabteilung*) paramilitary forces and civilians. (The SA were later superceded by the Gestapa SS under Herman Goring, eventually taken over by Heinrich Himmler, who expanded it dramatically.) Goring subsequently sent squads of his underlings to confiscate Jewish valuables wherever they found it, and he hid this for what he envisioned as an opulent future for himself. This included money, jewelry, paintings, sculptures, furniture, etc.

Although one of Hitler's goals was to bring Poland back into the fold of Germany, of which many were Germans living in Poland, he was reluctant to invade Poland with power. After all, Goring had managed to persuade Czechoslovakia and Austria to become part of Germany without firing a shot, which Hitler admired. However, Goebbels proposed a pretext for invading Poland. It was all about fake news. He claimed Polish gangs and government were brutalizing and killing Germans in Poland, confiscating their property, and causing them to flee to refugee camps. Goebbels and Himmler staged incidents of violence, actually creating the means for the Nazi invasion of Poland and its destruction. Goebbels' tactics were strikingly similar to how Islam views the Jews and non-believers. Islamists for centuries have "dehumanized" Jews and non-believers by calling them "infidels" or demons and devils, not really human beings. Since Muslims are taught this almost from birth, this is what they become brainwashed to believe and, therefore, killing the infidels is a mandate from Allah. Goebbels likewise dehumanized the Jews not because they did anything wrong, but because, first, he was anti-Semitic, and two, because Germany needed an enemy, a villain, so the German people would come to agree with the propaganda and therefore help instill support for the Nazi Party and their goals. Goebbels gave the German people an identifiable enemy "responsible" for all the troubles of the German people, when the truth was, in fact, it was the Versailles Treaty.

Hermann Goring, in charge of the Gestapo SS, did not support Goebbels radicalism against the Jews. His grandfather, in Austria, was a third-generation Jew. While he was himself somewhat anti-Semitic, he was not rabidly so and did not agree with Goebbels or Himmler on how to deal with the Jews.

Goebbels then aligned with Heinrich Himmler, also avidly anti-Semitic, and together devised plans to get rid of the Jews. The rest is ugly history. While I do not attempt to whitewash Hitler by saying this, it is my belief that had not Goebbels and Himmler gotten into major positions of power, it is unlikely there would have been a Holocaust. Both of them were rabidly anti-Semitic and they are the true architects of the Holocaust.

Heinrich Himmler, unlike Goebbels, was more subtle in his goals about getting rid of the Jewish people in Germany. Himmler did not want the public violence that followed Goebbels methods, but in the end, Himmler's method was more subtle but diabolical, out of the public eye, as Jews were ushered into concentration camps where the true horror show began in earnest. And it wasn't just gas chambers, but also mass graves of Jews shot by the Nazis.

Also of note, Himmler brought in a young man by the name of Reinhardt Heydrich, who became Himmler's enforcer in the intelligence service. His instruction was to take down the Nazi SA police, which is the story that later was told in the publication "Night of the Long Knives." Heydrich became Himmler's top police officer. He was a psychopath, utterly ruthless, so Goring also tasked him to deal with the Jewish "problem." Heydrich interpreted that as the discretion to deal with it in any way he wanted. He first wanted to ship all Jews to Madagascar. He killed as he saw fit, without mercy. However, even Nazi Party members were growing uneasy with this psychopath. He was a victim of an assassination attempt by the Czech's Secret Service, and later died of his wounds. Had he remained around for the gas chambers and mass murders of Jews, there is no doubt but that he would have fully enjoyed his "work."

The Jews were not the economic problem they were accused of being. The economic problem that left Germans reeling economically and with 30% unemployment was the Versailles Treaty, following World War I, when the Germans were initially defeated for their aggression. The Treaty resulted in the annexation by foreign nations of a large sector of German industries, and a huge tax to repay those nations for their losses caused by Germany.

So how does this relate to the Progressive movement today? Well, first of all, they are using our own democracy to subvert democracy in this country. They are using the electoral system to install National Socialists into our Congress, as mayors, as Governors, as heads of government agencies, and as teachers and professors in our schools. They are using the right to free speech to proselytize "socialism" at the Utopian form of government to replace the "failure" of American capitalism and the capitalist marketplace. They are urging re-distribution of wealth, equality of wealth, and the elimination of private ownership of property and business all of which would go to the sole control of the Fourth Branch of Government, i.e., the Administrative State. The Progressives have chosen "white men" as the identifiable enemy for all of America's troubles, and they make their case over and over again, like the Nazi Goebbels did, to vilify "white people" who they believe should be killed off so that multiculturalism, diversity, and redistribution of wealth can occur. Just as Muslim radical Linda Sarsour, among the alt-Left folks, calls for violence against the Jews and tries to muster support from the American people, she is not immune from casting "white men" in an anti-White manner for extermination; after all, most "white people" are Christians and therefore, by Islam's standards, all infidels." (I saw this information about Sarsour in a 2020 article by the Clarion Project (www.clarionproject.org) which is an excellent media bearing the truth about Islam and Islam's migrants.)

While the Nazis may well have borrowed the "dehumanizing" technique from the Muslims, we now see the Progressives following that playbook, so it leads one to conclude that for Progressives to accuse the Right and white men of being Nazis is a deflection and false narrative because the new Nazis in the United States is actually the misnomer known as the Progressive Party.

In an article by alt-Left media QUARTZ, January 26, 2017, by Oliver Staley, Culture & lifestyle editor, he opens the article (https://qz.com/895436/gleich-schaltung-the-german-word-that-perfectly-encapsulates-the-start-of-trumps-presidency/) by stating, "For students of German history, the first week of Donald Trump's presidency summons a word fraught with dark meaning: *Gleichschaltung*." Staley claims that after only six days into the Trump administration, there are signs of *"the instinct for control and conformity across all the domains the White House touches,"* such as "clamping down on communications by federal employees, publishing weekly lists of the crimes committed by "aliens," *threatening to withhold federal money from so-called sanctuary cities, and reportedly telling the EPA to remove climate-change language from its website. It also extends to the White House promising launching an investigation into voter fraud – despite widespread agreement that none exists –* [which, as we now know, was a false narrative], *to explain why Trump didn't win the popular vote, attempts to delegitimize the media which challenges his version of the facts, even Trump's frantic tweeting about slights real and imagined. All of it is of a piece: Re-frame the political landscape around Trump's world view."*

I found this fallacious description completely nonsensical and twisted logic. As the years have since passed, we have come to see that under prior administrations, particularly under Barack Obama, Marxist and New World Order forces have formed a loose alliance to infiltrate and undermine government at all levels, of using voter fraud, illegal aliens, sanctuary states and cities, social and mainstream media, all to attack Donald Trump and America itself in order to destroy our capitalist republic and market-based economy and private ownership of property and businesses. So, let's go back over this a moment. As I have tried to do in this book, is to make connections, dot the i's and cross the t's, and show how there is a spiderweb of danger to America, and the world itself, linked to many different factions, but all orchestrated by a mere few.

Staley was right about one thing: there are neo-Nazi forces who are quite accurately following the *Volksgemeinschaft* and *Gleichschaltung* playbooks right here in America, but they call themselves "Progressives." So, let's explore that for a moment.

The Progressives today are the new Nazi Party, but they avoid being so labeled by accusing the conservative Right and Donald Trump of Nazism, a classic sleight-of-hand to accuse their enemy of being exactly what the accusers actually are.

The Progressives blame "white men" for the ills of America and the world, strikingly similar to the Nazis blaming the Jews and non-Germanic populations so as to create an identifiable enemy. The Progressives blame the monetary and employment problems on the wealthy elitists, and demand their wealth be extremely taxed or taken and spread down to ordinary citizens, despite the clear caution that socialism always fails because it blazes in on the platform of re-distribution of wealth but crashes when it runs out of other people's money. Very Nazism of the Progressives, don't you agree? As said, it was the Versailles Treaty after WW-I that plagued the German people, leaving them without jobs and income. So what is it that is the actual cause of the problems, social and economic, that plagues America? For that, we can point to the New Deal begun by former President Woodrow Wilson and subsequently endorsed by Delano Roosevelt. The socialist-style programs arising from the New Deal eventually came to make life less prosperous for working-class Americans but great for the significant expansion of the Fourth Branch of government, i.e., the bureaucracy known as the Administrative State. While the welfare system was designed to be a temporary fix for post-Depression/Recession times of the 1930's, it has been expanded out-of-control to allow non-citizens (illegal aliens) to gain access to the welfare system and to the Social Security (even though they never paid a dime into the SS). This expansion of socialist-style programs upon the backs of the working-class is a problem, and it isn't caused by "white people" or "old white men." It is caused by Democrats; if there is an identifiable culprit, one need only to look at Democrat-controlled states, cities, policies and legislation.

The Progressives have also organized terrorist groups, the one best known being Antifa, a cadre of thugs much like the Nazi Brownshirts under Goebbels and Himmler. These thugs are flown around America to various events, especially those put on by conservatives, to disrupt those events with violence against those in attendance and destruction of property. Again, just like the Nazi Brownshirts. Who funds them? George Soros funds them, through his own organizations, which include Organizing For Action (OFA), which is run by Barack Obama these days. Antifa, like the SA and the SS, are becoming symbols of terror and, like the Nazis, the Progressives are using Antifa to terrify their opposition into subordination, slowly eliminate them entirely, or scare people into supporting them. And they also have invigorated a small come-back by the 60's/70's Black Panther Party, who are openly calling for the extermination of white people, openly creating an "identifiable enemy" subject to direct terrorist activity in the future.

As in Nazi Germany, where Joseph Goebbels ultimately got control of all public media (radio and newspapers), including the German state of Prussia (controlled by Hermann Goring), any opposition to the Nazi position was suppressed and disallowed, what we see today is a mainstream media owned by the extremely wealthy (Facebook, Twitter, YouTube, Google, ABC, CBS, NBC, CNN, etcetera), all censoring conservative thought and expression. We are also seeing legislation in Marxist-controlled states to create new language and words under the Orwellian concept now called "political correctness." Why would the "wealthy" do that, if they are the ones who benefit most from a capitalist democracy and market-economy? First, they don't think they'll be the losers; after all, achieving socialism is but a stepping stone to the totalitarian Utopia now called the New World Order where they, the very wealthy, will become the ruling class over everyone else. Besides, the owners of the social and mainstream media is a very small number, comparatively speaking.

Also, as in Nazi Germany, where Hitler began using German youth by militarizing them, the Progressives include Marxist teachers in our K-12 schools and universities, for generations now, who have indoctrinated our own children into the Marxist Utopian concept of "democratic socialism." Our own children are being made into the enemy of our Constitution, Bill of Rights, and of God and Christianity. The Progressives are calling for an end of religion and its rules of morality; if successful, without such rules society itself will break down into anarchy and starvation, disease, violence and murder, out of which will be borne a single power that takes absolute control and power over what is left. Think what the world would become, where the moral laws of the Ten Commandments no longer exist.

The Progressives should be called for what they are: the New Nazi Party. They are not here to rebuild America, but to re-create it by killing off "white people" who are analogous to the Jews in Nazi Germany demonized as scapegoats for the failings of Germany's economy. We are seeing a developing hierarchy in the Progressive Party, and I do not doubt but that some really evil people are rising through the ranks, much as they did in Hitler's inner circle. Without doubt there are psychopathic wanna-be killers vying for positions of power, hoping that in the end they will be in charge of what to do with America's patriots who disagree with "fundamental change" of the United States into the United States National Socialist State. You think about that.

If we patriots continue to treat the Progressive movement as a blemish that will go away on its own, this will be a very bad decision. While we are complacent, we acquiesce to their growth by default, and they grow more and more powerful. Already, in various cities, counties, and states, they have managed to get laws and regulations passed in direct contravention of the Second Amendment right to buy, own, and carry firearms. They have so far won the indoctrination battle in our schools, similar to what occurred in Nazi Germany, and they were successful, if only temporarily, in getting national healthcare legislation called Obamacare which turned out to be really bad for Americans and, more insidiously, contained innocuous provisions giving the President dictatorial powers in time of crisis. These innocuous provisions were intentional to hide what they meant, much like Nancy Pelosi attempting to hide one-billion dollars to Planned Parenthood in the law Trump wanted to distribute money to Americans suffering under the coronavirus "social distancing" recommendation.

Disarming Americans is a necessary step before initiating more widespread violence against the patriots of this country who, once disarmed, will be relatively defenseless against the violence these new Nazis will bring to our communities. "White people" must not allow themselves to become the new "Jews" destined for genocide by the Progressive Nazis. And that is what they are, Nazis, following the same playbook Hitler and his inner circle used, the same playbook by which the Muslims have committed genocide for some 1400 years against non-believers and other Muslims who were not as conservative as another.

Being a patriot is a non-partisan condition, and rightly so. We can agree or disagree in the politics of our nation, but a direct or indirect threat to our nation is a threat to us all, and only collective patriotism will prevent the Progressives Nazism from achieving victory over us. Let's not let our nation down, fellow patriots.

PART 11: THE FEMINIST MOVEMENT TO EFFEMINIZE MEN

Bill Lind opines that the radical feminism movement is an extension of Critical Theory. A fundamental element of this movement is based on something said in the 1930s by Erich Fromm and Herbert Marcuse. It is the sexual element. Particularly Marcuse, who in his own writings calls for a society of "polymorphous perversity." That is his definition of the future of the world that they want to create. Marcuse in particular, by the 1930s is writing some very extreme stuff on the need for sexual liberation; in his view, masculinity and femininity were not reflections of 'essential' sexual differences, as the Romantics had thought. They were derived instead from differences in life functions, which were in part socially determined, that sex is a construct, and sexual differences are a construct.

One of Marcuse's books was the key book. It virtually became the bible of the SDS and the student rebels of the 60s. That book was Eros and Civilization. Marcuse argues that under a capitalistic order (he downplays the Marxism very strongly here, it is subtitled "A Philosophical Inquiry into Freud", but the framework is Marxist), repression is the essence of that order and that gives us the person Freud describes – the person with all the hang-ups, the neuroses, because his sexual instincts are repressed. He argues that we can envision a future, if we only destroy this existing oppressive order, in which we liberate eros, we liberate libido, in which we have a world of "polymorphous perversity" in which you can "do your own thing." And, by the way, in that world there will no longer be work, only play. What a wonderful message for the radicals of the mid-60s! They're students, they're baby boomers, and they've grown up never having to worry about anything except eventually having to get a job. And here is a guy writing in a way they can easily follow. He doesn't require them to read a lot of heavy Marxism and tells them everything they want to hear which is essentially, "Do your own thing", if it feels good do it", and "You never have to go to work." Marcuse is also the man who creates the phrase we from the 60s know quite well, "Make love, not war." With regards to the situation people face on campus, Marcuse defines "liberating tolerance" as intolerance for anything coming from the Right and tolerance for anything coming from the Left. Marcuse joined the Frankfurt School in 1932, so all this goes back to the 1930s.

The Feminists today, in a remarkable show of stupidity, actually aligned themselves with the Muslims despite the reality that Muslim is dominated exclusively by men and their view of women is that they lesser than men, they are "things", i.e., chattel of men, and if the women are not Muslim women they are fair game for rape and violence because they are not just women, they are infidel women. So why are women finding comradery with a culture like Islam? Have they lost their mind?

The answer might be found in gamesmanship strategies, i.e., the women hold lots of influence and power as females in America, they are energetic and fervent in their movement, but Muslim men can cry victimization by Christians, the Right, and racism. An 'alliance' can further both of their goals.

But the feminist movement wants to cancel out the enculturation of men whose roles are socially determined by history and tradition. The warrior nature of men they want to neutralize and then browbeat men into a more feminine "nurturing" disposition. This is another form of expropriation Lind talks about, of rendering men from wolf to sheep, of 'breeding out' their male protectiveness towards women and the family unit. This may be why the Feminist strongly support transgenderism as a means of encouraging young boys to play with dolls and girl things so that they might want to change their sex from male to female.

I find it ironic that some feminists make the point that women should simply reject relationships with men, that women do not need men; such a narrative seems silly in light of the fact that without men there would be no baby girls either.

Tradition tends to tell us all what is socially accepted, and what is normal versus abnormal behavior. We have traditionally accepted the roles that history long describes for men and women, roles that see men going off to war facing danger and death, while women remain safe at home, perhaps working in munitions and ordnance factories for the war, like my own mother did in WW-II. Men were drafted into the military post-WW-II, making service mandatory. Women were homemakers mostly. Men did not change that dynamic, women did. In the search for equality women began to demand access to traditionally male roles, like police and military, and it was true that men resisted letting women get involved with such dangerous roles. They did not believe women could handle the level of mental stress, the physical demands, or the violence inherent in war.

But now the feminists simply want men to buckle to their demands and become more like women, abandoning their male nature to be politically correct as seen by the feminists.

Although some men will abandon their male roles, I doubt that most men will do more than give lip service if at all, and more likely just laugh it off as just stupidity.

However, however unlikely it is that feminists will make much of a dent in the roles and nature of men, the damage feminists can do against the nature and ideology of this country might be great, particularly as they have formed a coalition with Muslims and the pro-Socialist Left.

But we will see how that plays out soon enough.

However, I cannot rest on just the above because what the feminists are doing finds its origins in Marxist dogma too. I mentioned earlier how a prerequisite of socialism is the destruction or dissolution of marriage to establish that the pivotal loyalty of the individual belongs to the sovereign collective, not to the family.

In a 2018 article by David Solway, in the AmericanThinker, titled "Marxism and Marriage" he explains how feminists and the Leftists are hard at work to destroy marriage and the family. He writes:

> "Advocacy and legislation that sunder the intimate love between a man and a woman, that deprive children of male and female parental role models, that compromise the integrity of the family and that dissolve the purpose of marriage as a guarantor of cultural longevity are indispensable strategies essential to realizing the left's master plan. Dismissing the nuclear family as an archaic and repressive arrangement whose time has passed, the state would then operate in loco parentis [as the acting parent].

> The problem for the left is that the family is a traditional dynamic that precedes and eclipses the tenure of the authoritarian state, not only because it encourages a prior allegiance, but because it allows for the retention of inheritance and property rights within the generational unit. This is anathema to the Marxist vision of, in historian Jacob Talmon's phrase from <u>The Origins of Totalitarian Democracy</u>, the "all-property-owning state," a function of "political Messianism." [Note: This currently out-of-print classic covers the battle between liberal democracy and "social democracy" after 1800. Basically those who wanted progressive change were divided between two opinions: (1) the revolutionary vanguard knows best what the people want and so should implement authoritarian "people's democracy," versus (2) just let people have individual freedom, i.e., universal suffrage, free speech, human rights, etc., and people will implement themselves what they want. Almost everybody thought that only #1 could solve the "social question" of poverty, yet almost everybody hoped or feared that universal suffrage [a vote or right to vote] would lead to massive redistribution and confiscation of the private property of the rich. Almost everybody was wrong on both counts: #1 was a disaster per se,

while #2 led to moderation, i.e., capitalism with social protection and gradual reform, and also #2 made more progress on the "social question" than #1 ever did.] The Marxist offensive against marriage may be seen, in part, as the ideological version of a corporate takeover.

An effective way to destroy marriage and the family was advanced by communist theorist Georg Lukacs, who introduced the concept of "cultural terrorism," which involved the liquidation of religion, monogamy, and the ostensibly male-dominated family. Lukacs advocated the introduction in the schools of – and as a minister in the 1919 Hungarian Bolshevik government of Bela Kun actually installed – courses on free love, sexual liberation, and Freud's notion of "polymorphous perversity," which he believed a revolutionary necessity.

We see his pernicious influence at work today in the cultural obsession with sex, the zeal for so-called sex re-assignment, and the insensate proliferation of pronominal "genders" into a Heinz 57 omnium-gatherum [miscellaneous collection: a collection of many different, often unsorted ideas or items]. (Canada's Supreme Court whiffling [indecisive or unpredictable in thought or action] is another variant of this rubbish.) It is also a cardinal value in the education establishment, for example in my home province of Ontario, where under the direction of former premier Kathleen Wynne, an avowed lesbian, sex-ed classes exposed young children to varieties of sexual practices far beyond their level of emotional development.

Leftist attempts to dismantle conventional society by unleashing a multi-pronged assault against it, including rewriting history, undermining religious observance and subverting traditional morality, a program sedulously [painstakingly] advanced by the pseudo-discipline of "Critical Theory." This pedantic and ostentatious schematism was promoted by clique of salon provocateurs known as the Frankfurt School [in the U.S.] in their effort to develop what they called "social emancipatory strategies." They were the answer to the rhetorical question Lukacs asked in his 1916 study "The Theory of the Novel" : "Who will save us from Western civilization?"

As noted, the left has many weapons in its incendiary arsenal, but perhaps its most piercing labret [ornament worn on the lip pierced through the lower lip] in its war against the traditional family is the penetration of the institution of marriage and its replacement by an indiscriminate caricature of its original purpose. Its advocacy for pseudo-marriage is therefore not surprising. It is true that communism may once have purged gays and, as Hoyt [PJ Media columnist Sarah Hoyt] implies, will do so again, but in its assault on the family structure, its socialist epigones [mediocre imitators] have long jumped on the redefining marriage bandwagon. As Paul Kengor writes in Takedown: From Communists to Progressives, How the Left Has Sabotaged Family and Marriage, "[a]s long as the traditional family is reversed, Marxism is advanced." Marriage redefined, he continues, is "an ideal, handy device to destroy the family."

Lest I be misunderstood, I do not endorse civil restrictions on or repression of homosexuality. So long as common law remains in force (e.g., proscribing pedophilia or polygamy), couples should be free to follow their passions and desires. They are free to enjoy recreational sex or to love whomever they wish. As the late Canadian prime minister Pierre Trudeau famously said, "there's no place for the state in the bedrooms of the nation." But when same-sex couples usurp the fiscal, estate, and legal privileges of productive procreant families – truly an unearned increment – and certainly when the right to marry can be claimed by any category of individuals and any cosplay group with no relation to the traditional armature of Western civilization, the disintegration of social norms and usages must inevitably follow. As Engels and company knew, marriage and the family constitute the ground on which the battle is most auspiciously fought.

Armed with both the theoretical and empirical power of sexual license, the left now appears unassailable, cresting with self-assurance. Its campaign against the institution of marriage seems close to fulfillment. There can be little doubt that once the traditional institution of marriage, or even binding common law (sui iuris) arrangements within heterosexual couples, has been disabled, when forms of sexual deviance are encouraged, when men embrace MGTOW (Men Going Their Own Way) and women are regarded as victims of the so-called patriarchal family, and when marriage distorted beyond its definition has been ordained and consecrated as normal, the new dialectic of Marxist inversion may well have won the day."

(By David Solway, Marxism and Marriage, American-Thinker.com.)

PART 12: THE LGBT MOVEMENT TO NORMALIZE THE ABNORMAL

Much of the preceding section (Part 2) likewise apply to the LGBT movement to normalize the abnormal behaviors.

It is now politically incorrect to criticize homosexuality, or to refer to the Bible's scriptures that condemn homosexual behaviors.

As a simple matter of nature, a male is designed to have sexual relations with a female, and vice versus.

With a growing demand for abolition of the Bible and the concept of God, the rise of "Political Correctness" now forms and advances a protective shield around abnormal relationships like homosexuality. The gay community demands that heterosexuals must accept and not criticize or otherwise speak against homosexuality and, if they do, they can be liable at law for hurting the feelings of the gay person.

This is carrying freedom of expression to a level of intolerance, thus effectively shutting down the right to freedom of expression by the heterosexual. The homosexual says, "I want my freedom of expression" while also saying to the heterosexual, "You have no right to freedom of expression if that means you can criticize me, or if you do not believe as I do."

Heterosexuals tend to believe that homosexual behavior is abnormal, particularly when they see males running around in female clothing or dollied up with make-up and acting with the mannerisms of a woman. But, even among heterosexuals homosexuality is generally tolerated under the old doctrine of "Live and let live." Just don't expect that tolerance constitutes change in beliefs. Heterosexuals are entitled to believe as they want. Nor will the LGBT movement alter the beliefs of devout Christians who believe the Bible's condemnation of homosexuality is and will always be the last word on that subject.

It bears repeating that this demand by the gay community for acceptance across the board may be why many homosexuals are against the Christian doctrine because the Bible condemns homosexuality.

It is one thing to give tolerance to someone who does not believe as you do; it is quite another to attack someone because they do not believe as you do.

The rule of law in the United States is that one's belief in one's religious doctrines is inviolate, and Congress shall make no laws with regards to religion and religious freedom.

However, Congress may make laws that expose so-called religions as covers for criminal enterprises, not true religions, and when it comes to Islam, by the way, immigration laws already indicate that Congress should act against the advocacy of Islam imams in the U.S. to convert to the totalitarian structure of Islamic sharia law, and simply deport them.

PART 13: THE ATTACK ON
CHRISTIANITY AND THE BELIEF IN GOD

Around the world we see violent and deadly attacks on Christians. History shows us that Islamists have been murdering Christians for some 1400 years, and want to wipe out Christians completely even now. Thousands are murdered every year now. But, then again, the Muslims want to kill all "infidels" which means demon to them.

And these days we see China's President Xi clamping down on Christians in China too, brutally and including long-term prison sentences. Are we concerned? Not today. We have atheists all over America trying to shut down Christianity, trying to force the government to take out all mention of Christ/God in books, in public places, and in government buildings. This country was founded as a Christian nation, and it has done quite well under the Bible's teachings. But God and Jesus is being taken down in places like Canada, Australia, European countries, and many other places. But what are they being replaced with? Nothing.

What will rise if Christianity is taken down will be nothing short of satanic and pagan, devoid entirely of a moral compass that defines civility and social contract. Such a condition leads to endless violence and murder, of a "dog eat dog" daily fare.

Quadriplegic Steven Hawkins, a renowned and respected scientist, posited that there was no evidence of God's existence or that He created the Earth and all that is in it. Other scientists tend to support Darwinism, that all life is a creature of eons of evolution. Yet none of them can explain the marvel of individual DNA, which could not have been the result of randomness; randomness creates nothing.

Only a higher life form could create DNA as we know it here on Earth.

Why are the atheists and the current pro-socialists so aggressively trying to blame religion for all the troubles of the world and discounting the validity of religions doctrines and dogma?

The Bible gives Christians ten (10) simple commandments, and it is difficult for Christians to understand why anyone could disagree with the wisdom of these commandments.

The Ten Commandments (Exodus 20:2-17 NKJV)

1 "I am the Lord your God, who brought you out of the land of Egypt, out of the house of bondage. You shall have no other gods before Me.

2 "You shall not make for yourself a carved image, or any likeness of anything that is in heaven above, or that is in the earth beneath, or that is in the water under the earth; you shall not bow down to them nor serve them. For I, the Lord your God, am a jealous God, visiting the iniquity of the fathers on the children to the third and fourth generations of those who hate Me, but showing mercy to thousands, to those who love Me and keep My Commandments.

3 "You shall not take the name of the Lord your God in vain, for the Lord will not hold him guiltless who takes His name in vain.

4 "Remember the Sabbath day, to keep it holy. Six days you shall labor and do all your work, but the seventh day is the Sabbath of the Lord your God. In it you shall do no work: you, nor your son, nor your daughter, nor your male servant, nor your female servant, nor your cattle, nor your stranger who is within your gates. For in six days the Lord made the heavens and the earth, the sea, and all that is in them, and rested the seventh day. Therefore, the Lord blessed the Sabbath day and hallowed it.

5 "Honor your father and your mother, that your days may be long upon the land which the Lord your God is giving you.

6 "You shall not murder.

7 "You shall not commit adultery.

8 "You shall not steal.

9 "You shall not bear false witness against your neighbor.

10 "You shall not covet your neighbor's house; you shall not covet your neighbor's wife, nor his male servant, nor his female servant, nor his ox, nor his donkey, nor anything that is your neighbor's."

Granted, this was written many years ago and translated, but they are simple to help achieve and sustain a peaceful social order. They embody the Golden Rule, which has a couple of constructs:

1. Do unto others what ye would have done unto you; or,

2. Do not do unto others what ye would not want done unto you.

In a September 2019 edition of the American Thinker, by Anthony J. DeBlasi (article entitled New World Odor [not an error in spelling]), he wrote the following excerpt from his article, in which he notes that the "claim of superiority of modern over traditional order that lacks objectivity is suspect to begin with" and explains:

> "My own experience tells me that what Gospel lacks in intellectual prowess they make up for in purity of heart, acceptance of the real world, and an upbeat spirit, which accounts for their general decency, good sense, and fair play, in addition to solid morals, without which justice fumbles and ultimately vanishes. …. Calls for governance and social order derived from traditional religion, because they are allegedly not backed by science or are not endorsed by intelligent secularists, are to be banished from human thought and action.

This now over objective of New World Order activism is grounded in the smug assumption that might does make right, after all. But how does anyone reconcile this idea with the enormous number of senseless deaths that have occurred in the wake of "enlightened" might?

Personally, for most of my life and despite my own mistakes along the way, the Golden Rule was how I lived my life. I did not find that too difficult, so why does it seem the atheists and socialists want to cast all that aside?

While the first purpose of government is to protect citizens from foreign and domestic threats, it must also undertake other essential actions in order to secure natural rights. These include the protection of property rights, the defense of religious liberty, and the promotion of the moral character necessary to sustain free government and freedom itself. The basic notion is that people should be "decent" in order to respect others around them as well as their own country. A free community of people can be harmonious only when morality and virtue are strong amongst them.

Establishing morality is a means of securing our natural rights, such as the right to possess and acquire property. Promotion of morality is necessary for citizens in a free society. We see this truth manifested in socialist and communist countries which do not believe in a "God" nor allow religion at all. China is a good example, where it has recently begun a tough crackdown on both Islam and Christian, where churches are being destroyed, ministers imprisoned, and believers are imprisoned or sanctioned from publicly gathering to practice their faith.

Individual morality means a disposition of the character and the heart of the individual. Our Founders thought that too was a duty of government to be concerned with in order to establish and maintain harmony and law among the people and thus protect their natural rights. In the Virginia Constitution, established in 1776, we find: "*No free government, or the blessings of liberty, can be preserved to any people, but by a firm adherence to justice, moderation, temperance, frugality, and virtue.*"

Being a Christian nation, everyone accepted the view that schools are going to promote a generic version of Christianity. That became the concensus that emerged out of the founding, and by the time of the 1840s it was being done everywhere. That lasted up until the 1960s. Schools had prayers starting school, schools routinely called the children to the front of the school building where the America flag flew, where they learned the Pledge of Allegiance, right hand over their hearts, and said that pledge every day. Schools had some discussion of religion, basic teachings of morality and virtue, because the Founders believed that without morality and virtue a nation could not be properly protective of basic human rights. As a Christian nation, the Founders thought that morality was a basic foundation that schools should promote. In every state there were government-funded educational institutions that promoted morality, such as Christian colleges and universities.

There is also another consideration. The Founders encouraged morality that included sexual conduct. Unfettered sexual conduct often produced children, and children are a special responsibility because they need to be protected and raised so that they would become responsible human beings too. Early government thought that the best avenue was to promote marriage as an institution for two people to remain married when children were involved, that the best condition for children was to be raised by both biological parents. This belief was promoted in the early family laws, but over time, especially in more recent times, family laws are being ground down in ways the Founders never intended. Back then, it was expected that a marriage would be sustained, especially if there were children, and while divorce was permitted it had to be for an important cause, not on whim. Legitimate causes were those things that caused real harm, like domestic violence, adultery, or abandonment. The family structure of the earlier days, and into the 1960s, was the father was the family figurehead and provider, with the responsibility of supporting his family. The wife was the keeper of the household, the nurturer of the children, the companion of the husband. This was an important structure so that father and mother each had their own duties that contributed to the whole of the family. Divorce inherently breaks down that structure, divides the family, and undermines the proper training and care of the children they are responsible for.

In modern times, post-1960s, this structure came under growing criticism by women who condemned the patriarchal structure as a violation of the constitutional notion of equality, i.e., that all people, men and women, are created equal, and under the law, the family structure should practice total equality. And, of course, we have witnessed the disintegration of the preferred family unit as both wife and husband took on individual careers that left the children without the quality of parental involvement in their daily lives that reinforced the nurturing and guidance children need as they grow. The modern family unit has become an institution of separation, not unity, where social media and media technology have taken over family life. Children are constantly on the iPhones or playing computer games, even parents head for the computer after work, little communication exists between each other, and the family unit is almost anarchistic, i.e., do your own thing.

The changes in our educational systems of not requiring diligence and excellence from students, of passing students to higher grades who have actually failed, of eliminating tests for fear that a student who fails a test or the ability to go to a higher grade next school year might have his/her "self-esteem" damaged, is destroying the kind of outcome required for students in preparing to enter to job market with solid tools. Instead, they are being trained to fail, to lack the character and courage to achieve, to believe that capitalism and the market-economy is evil and that socialism would allow them to live happily without working at all. This situation is, or should be, a crime against humanity itself, not just a crime against our children by such schools, teachers, and professors.

Also, looking beyond the schools to immigrants, if one considers that immigration laws require that immigrants from any foreign country "assimilate" into the American ideology and culture, this too would mean assimilation into the basic morality and virtues upon which this country was founded. This meant that even if immigrants were from another religion entirely, the practice of their religion would be permitted so long as it did not grossly conflict with the Christian morals and virtues embedded in the American ideology. In other words, a Muslim whose culture permitted the family from murdering a wayward daughter because she "dishonored" the family would not be permitted to do so in America without serious criminal consequences. This is why there have been instances where a family of another culture in Arabia, Pakistan or India would send their daughter back to their family in the country of origin for punishment according to that culture, which may include the death of the daughter.

We are losing the moral platform to a dearth of migrants from other cultures who are demanding "freedom" to practice all aspects of the culture or religion here, regardless of America's criminal laws and prohibitions. We have a growing chorus of atheists who do not believe in a supernatural "god" at all, and want to destroy the basic tenets of morality and virtues that have guided and protected the rights of the people from the beginnings of America. Without rules of morality and virtue, only anarchy can be the result. Non-believers of any form of religion, in this country, can so exist without sanction, but the manifestation of their beliefs cannot operate to destroy the foundational beliefs, practices, and protections of the believers. But, atheists too have an interest in religious principles, where testimony in court, or oaths given in court, are sworn with one hand on the Bible and the oath given "under God."

In his farewell address in 1796, George Washington said: "Reason and experience both forbid us to expect that national morality can prevail in exclusion of religious principle."

And so must America return to its Christian roots and eschew the demands of the non-believers and those of cultures and religions that are diametrically inapposite to Christianity? Across the world, and across history, Christianity has been the basis for human growth and evolution into a gentler, kinder world, notwithstanding some atrocities that have historically been committed under the guise of Christian doctrine, such as the Spanish conquering of Central and parts of Northwestern America by the Catholic Papacy in its quest for gold, jewels and conquest. We might acknowledge the Christian Crusades of long ago, but if one compares the lands of conquest from the Crusades to the lands of conquest by Islamists, what the Crusades acquired is miniscule compared to the vastness of Muslim conquests. Christianity under the teachings of Jesus has enabled more peace, prosperity, and harmony across the world than any other religion, while Islam's conquests produced little more than genocidal conduct and enslavement of women for sexual reasons. So, who would you rather have living next door, or running your country?

Morality and virtue necessarily establish a sort of paragon that requires a balancing between those whose beliefs are different from others, in order to maintain the natural rights and freedoms of everyone. This has proven a most difficult task that continues to be debated today, particularly here in the USA where atheism is growing, where Islam's influences are spreading, and where socialism is infecting our own children being so taught in our own schools as a Utopian ideology. Political correctness itself is undermining morality and virtue in America, moving us along to the path of Orwellianism and criminalizing free thought and free speech.

Morality is a responsibility of the individual if we are to have a responsible government and maintain our natural rights and freedoms. Without morality a people, a society, devolves into "anything goes" which ushers in abject anarchy and societal suicide itself. Instead of vigilance and courage to act against government intrusion and oppression, we now see a pro-socialist movement for a government historically renowned for oppression of the people and the almost total dismantling of human and natural rights. These are misguided beliefs wrought by a failure to investigate the history and reality of what socialism is and always becomes. It is like holding a revolver to one's head, knowing there are six chambers for bullets, and only one of them is empty, yet playing "Russian roulette" anyway. One must be prudent in their lives and their viewpoints.

PART 14: THE CALL FOR EXTERMINATION OF "WHITE PEOPLE"

At a time in our history, when socialists are demanding an end to our capitalist democracy, we are seeing a commensurate rise in anti-white reverse racism, and it has already turned violent.

The Democrat-controlled Washington Post claims that the "war on whites" is a core concern of Trump's base, and is just a myth. Really? Yeah, I expect that is just what the alt-Left want white people to think. The WP claims white people, especially white males, still have a huge advantage in American society. In an article by a William Saltan in the SLATE News (2016), Saltan argues

James C. Lewis

and concludes that the issue is really more about "tribal enmity and vengeance" rather than racism and ideology.

The problem with his conclusion is that he seems to ignore the reality of Islam's agenda of world domination and killing "infidels" (non-Muslims), as well as the reality that a growing number of people of color have adopted the espoused narrative that all "white people" are evil and greedy and are the prime reason people of color can't get ahead in life and so must be exterminated.

Saltan reduces the reality to this: "These visions of mortal struggle between a white West and its dark-skinned enemies mirror, almost precisely, the ideology of Islamic jihad. Look at Osama bin Laden's pronouncements over the years, and you'll see a striking resemblance to the rhetoric of Newt Gingrich and Donald Trump. Both sides describe and promote a clash of religions, and this unites them in a global alliance against Christians and Muslims – including President Obama, former President George W. Bush, and King Abdullah of Jordan – who argue that the real enemy, terrorism, belongs to no religion."

So here we find a distraction in the form of debate using the premise that both viewpoints are inherently flawed because they overlook that they are just manipulated into the strategy of religious polarization outlined by ISIS. Hmph! Really? So we are supposed to believe that what is being described as "racism, bigotry, and ethnic-defense" is just a misunderstood dynamic that is really nothing more than a disagreement about different ideologies?

I don't think the sniper in Dallas who shot five law enforcement officers (white ones) and stating afterwards that "he wanted to kill white people, especially white officers" was mulling over religious ideologies.

And so what if some blacks who targeted whites are fundamentally allied with white people who target blacks, i.e., on the same race war team, just opposite sides? There are racists on both sides. But to say that blacks are the ones who suffer victimhood from whites in class-hood and are justified in hating and attacking whites, but that whites who suffer victimhood from violent blacks must simply suffer the justified consequences of black victimization generally, in no argument to the dynamic.

Nor is the argument justified when a white blames blacks for the highest rates of crimes, and then says that is because blacks hate white people or because they simply uneducated and ignorant or low IQ. These kinds of generalizations back and forth defeat any gesture of tolerance or insight or resolution or understanding. They simply create wider chasms of bias and prejudice, the breeding grounds of separatism and racism.

But, it cannot be refuted that the very highest numbers of violent crimes in America are committed by people of color, particularly blacks and Hispanics. And it is also noteworthy to understand the dynamics of upbringing that poised them for an unwise lifestyle of crime, violence, and prison. They didn't just wake one day and say, "I think I'll be a criminal and hurt people." We are influenced by or indoctrinated by our upbringing and environment dynamics.

Once lost in the criminal lifestyle, accepting interruptive or potential violence as consequences, the indoctrination is difficult to back-track, or perhaps I should say, roll-back, but I see back-track and roll-back as different from the other; back-track is a reflective activity, and roll-back is a reformative activity. Notwithstanding, the highest crime neighborhoods are a statistical fact to be predominantly populated by people of color. I do not believe their high crime propensity is race-based at all. It is a behavior that is learned, from conditions they endure or accept, from lifestyles and interactions with others similarly enculturated.

So, the topic is, is there a race-based dynamic from an indoctrinated culture that just happens to be black and/or Hispanic populations who simply hate white people and feel the need to "exterminate" them like the Nazis did to the Jews? Interesting analogy.

The recent resurgence of "anti-white" hatred is racism when the hater generalizes a race or culture as the oppressor just because they are white, yet while there are racist whites it cannot be accurately said that ALL whites are racists or inherently racists. The truth is that most whites don't trip on the race thing, unless they are laughing at or complaining about blacks "always playing the race card." Affirmative Action was supposed to equal the employment and educational field, which the Republicans set forth. But it didn't work out too well after the Democrats, who voted against it, decided to modify it not in the black community's favor.

Let's look at the statistical record of this violence today. In an article written by Heather MacDonald entitled "A Platform of Urban Decline", September 23, 2019, she notes that "Democratic presidential candidates believe America is racist, yet they ignore the evidence on crime and ensure that racial disparities persist." In their zeal to vilify Republicans so they can win elections, they blame Republican whites for all the violence. So let's see what the truth is. MacDonald says:

> Democratic accusations that America is endemically racist are becoming ever more frequent and strident. At the last presidential debate, Pete Buttigieg announced that "systemic racism" will "be with us" regardless of who wins the presidency; Beto O'Rourke claimed that racism in America is "foundational" and that people of color were under "mortal threat" from the "white supremacist in the White House"; Julian Castro denounced the growing threat of "white supremacy"; and Cory Booker called for "attacking systemic racism," especially in the "racially biased" criminal justice system.

> At the same time, the allowable explanations for racial disparities have shrunk to one: that self-same racism. During this month's debate, Joe Biden tried to suggest that some poor parents could benefit from instruction regarding optimal child-rearing practices: "We [should] bring social workers into homes of parents to help them deal with how to raise their children. It's not that they don't want to help, they don't want – they don't know quite what to do," he said. Biden was invoking one of the Obama administration's key anti-poverty initiatives. Home-visiting programs pair nurses and other social service workers with pregnant women and new mothers to teach them parenting skills. Progressive activists have demanded and won hundreds of millions of federal dollars for such programs, yet pundits have denounced Bidens "horrifying racist answer," in the words of *The Inter-*

cept, and called for him to pull out of the presidential primary because of it [or was it to just prevent another "white man" from becoming president?]. Buttigieg sniffed that Biden's statement was "well-intentioned" but "bad", since it ignored the fact that "racial inequity" in this country was "put into place on purpose."

In today's political climate, Barack Obama's 2008 Father's Day Speech in Chicago would be deemed an unforgivable outburst of white supremacy. "If we are honest with ourselves," Obama told his audience in a South Side church, Americans will admit that too many fathers are "missing – missing from too many lives and too many homes. They have abandoned their responsibilities, acting like boys instead of men." In the current frenzy of intersectional rhetoric, any such reference to personal responsibility brands the speaker as irredeemably bigoted.

Yet key parts of the intersectional narrative are not born out by data. It is now a standard trope, implanted in freshmen summer reading lists through the works of Ta-Nehesi Coates and others, that whites pose a severe, if not mortal, threat to blacks. That may have once been true, but it is no longer so today. Just this month, the Bureau of Justice Statistics released its 2018 survey of criminal victimization. According to the study, there were 593,598 interracial violent victimizations (excluding homicide) between blacks and whites last year, including white-on-black and black-on-white attacks. Blacks committed 537,204 of those interracial felonies, or 90 percent, and whites committed 56,394 of them, or less than 10 percent. That ration is becoming more skewed, despite the Democratic claim of Trump-inspired white violence. In 2012-13, blacks committed 85 percent of all interracial victimizations between blacks and whites; whites committed 15 percent. From 2015 to 2018, the total number of white victims and the incidence of white victimization have grown as well.

Blacks are also overrepresented among perpetrators of hate crimes – by 50 percent – according to the most recent Justice Department data from 2017; whites are under represented by 24 percent. This is particularly true for anti-gay and anti-Semitic hate crimes.

You would never know such facts from the media or from Democratic talking points. This summer, three shockingly violent mob attacks on white victims in downtown Minneapolis were captured by surveillance video. On August 3, in broad daylight, a dozen black assailants, some as young as 15, tried to take a man's cellphone, viciously beating and kicking him as he lay on the ground. They jumped on his torso like a trampoline, stripped his shoes and pants off as they riffled through his pockets, smashed a planter pot on his head, and rode a bike over his prostrate body. On August 17, another large group kicked and punched their victim until he was unconscious, stealing his phone, wallet, keys, and cash. In July, two men were set upon in similar fashion. Such attacks have risen more than 50 percent in downtown Minneapolis this year.

Racist blacks have been demanding monetary reparations from white people for the slavery that occurred over 200 years ago, and for the Jim Crow years after 1940 to 1964, and for the failure of the Affirmative Action programs (initiated by Republicans, opposed and subsequently undermined by Democrat "tinkering"), yet these blacks seem to have no real knowledge about the actual scope of slavery during slavery years.

In a September 26, 2019 article by Doug Petrikat, published in the *American Thinker*, he noted that there is a rise in claims that American prosperity resulted from slavery, and he then explains what the falsity of that narrative is:

> If we consider the historical experience of other nations involved in the slave trade, it could help our understanding of the issue. The transatlantic slave trade that took place from the 16th to the 19th centuries was a system in which Africans

sold members of other tribes, often prisoners, as slaves to Europeans, who then shipped them to the Americas. During this time period only 5% of the total number of slaves sent across the Atlantic went to the U.S., with the other 95% going mostly to South America and the Caribbean.

If American prosperity is based on slavery, then we would expect other nations that participated in the transatlantic slave trade to also be prosperous. If we take Brazil, for example, that nation took about 20 times more slaves than the U.S. So, if slavery leads to greater prosperity one would expect Brazil to be much more prosperous than the U.S., since they took many more slaves. However, the U.S.'s GDP per capital is about four times greater than Brazil's. Although the standard of living in Brazil is significantly lower than that of the U.S., other nations in South America are even worse off and among the poorest in the world, despite their historical experience with slavery.

Now if we consider a sample of other prosperous nations that have a standard of living comparable to that of the U.S., would we find that their prosperity resulted from slavery? In Europe, let's take Switzerland, Germany, and Norway; in Asia, Singapore, Japan, and South Korea; and let's also consider some other former British colonies, such as Canada, Australia, and New Zealand. None of these prosperous nations participated in the transatlantic slave trade.

If American prosperity were based on slavery, then we would expect to learn that in the 1800s the Southern States were wealthier than the Northern States, where slavery was illegal. However, this was simply not the case. The Industrial Revolution, which included new mechanized manufacturing techniques along with innovations in transportation and communication, such as the railroads, steamboats, and the telegraph, dramatically increased production. This was the driving force of the North's economy, and in 1860, 90% of the nation's manufacturing output came from the North.

In the Southern States that became the Confederacy during the Civil War, 85% percent of the population worked in agriculture in contrast to 40% in the North. Although the South had an agricultural-based economy, through mechanized techniques the North also surpassed the South in some areas of agriculture. For example, in 1860 80% of the U.S.'s wheat was produced in the North. Southern plantation owners had less motivation to invest in modern farm machinery since they owned slaves, so Southern agriculture remained more dependent on labor, which hindered progress and economic growth as the North became more mechanized and productive. In 1860 per capita income in the South was only 72% of the U.S. average, so there is no evidence that slavery made the South wealthy, let alone the entire U.S.

While it is true that a small elite group in the South did become wealthy from growing cotton through the use of slave labor, we also need to take into account the impact this had on the U.S. economy as a whole. At the outbreak of the Civil War the Confederate States of the South had a population of 9 million as opposed to 23 million in the Union. The overwhelming majority of people in the South were poor farmers who did not own slaves. The 4.9% of Southerners who did own slaves had most of them working on plantations to produce cotton, which was the South's biggest cash crop. Almost all was sold to the British market. Cotton made up 59% of exports from the U.S. at the outbreak of the Civil War, but in 1860 cotton production represented just 5% of the U.S. economy. It is also worth noting that in the years after the war cotton production increased dramatically without the use of slave labor.

We also need to be aware that during the war, wealth that had accumulated in the South was wiped out. The physical devastation that was experienced by the Confederacy left it in ruins. As Union soldiers marched through, buildings were burned, crops destroyed, and livestock killed. Southern cities such as Atlanta, Savannah, and Richmond were burned. At times, Confederate troops also contributed to the destruction of their own territory when they burned anything that could be used by advancing Union troops. And by the end of the Civil War, the currency of the Southern States had become worthless.

By any objective measure, American prosperity is not based on slavery. [In actual measure, slavery inhibited prosperity, because it was limited to just a small percentage of land owners.] The industrial revolution set the stage for people such as Thomas Edison and Henry Ford and, later, Boeing and Apply. It set the stage for all the American entrepreneurs, small businesses, and workers that contributed to American economic growth and prosperity. This, along with a developed legal system, property rights, a high literacy rate, and a market economy, is what led to a prosperous nation. To deny this and distort history to further a political agenda only creates more conflict and division at a time that has already become one of the most divisive in the U.S. since the Civil War.

The low literacy rate of modern schools, and the twisting of facts by the socialists and elites, creates a very unfair condition for blacks because it literally creates a history that emphasizes to blacks their ancestry was not only victimized by (all) "white people" but they are "entitled" to "reparations" today because the "white people" have not only kept them down economically and educationally, but the "white people" have "prospered" on that slavery history today. Educated blacks, who actually know the dynamics of American history, as explained here by Doug Petrikat who obviously has done his homework, will be able to put 2 and 2 together and realize how the socialist-Left is skewing historic facts to create racial division and violence, which is currently working. These socialists know that a race war will result in "martial law" and martial law will result in invasion by the UN who will confiscate firearms from all Americans, thus making it inevitable that the result will be a change from our capitalist democracy to a full-blown socialist ideology (where all of us will suffer the same poverty and misery socialism always brings).

So, anyway, generalizing doesn't get anyone anywhere. Nonetheless, here we are, with the people of color community hating, and calling for violence against, all white people. So what is to be done about that? Surely, this carries all the hallmarks of fascist mindset against white people, which was how Hitler groomed Germans to accepting the genocide of some six million Jews and even participating in it. But the result in Germany occurred after Hitler had already disarmed all Jewish people.

What does it look like here? Is it not fact that the Alt-Left Progressives, out front in their socialist agenda, are calling for full and complete disarmament of all Americans. So what happens if that occurs and "white people" become marginalized and subsequently victimized when they are no longer in power?

After all, the mass movement, disregarding the immature and unwise millennials, is comprised predominantly by people of color, many of which also espouse the banner of protest that the "whites" stole America from the "Hispanics", the latter being the narrative of many the Central and South American migrants illegally challenging or crossing our southern border. So, it seems an 'alliance' of sorts is being created that will, in fact, begin to marginalize "white people" by greater powers in the political arenas of local, state, and national politics by people of color. We are already seeing what that looks like with the Squad of 4 women of color in Congress.

Will the anti-white genocide be America's Germany under Hitler? The same elements that created the genocide dynamic in Germany (that spanned over nearly a decade) is also at work here (which also has spanned over more than a decade).

The re-emergence of the New Black Panthers demonstrates that anti-white sentiment is growing in the black neighborhoods, but how far across America has it reached. Fifty years ago spreading that sentiment would have taken a bit longer, since the media was not that sophisticated, nor was the technology. Today, sentiment can be spread across the country, even the globe, in just seconds or minutes. A tiny match of sentiment can create a huge wall of sentiment in a very short time across the Internet and phones. As we are seeing now, blacks are being indoctrinated by a skewed narrative about their own ancestral slavery history, and are being indoctrinated now that "white" America still has its slavery foot on their necks, which is only true to them, not in actual fact. Increasing one's sense of victimhood is a recipe for hate speech and violence, which we are seeing now.

There is a re-newed demand by blacks for reparations to them for their black history. This demand is that white people, today, who never owned slaves, must give money to the black people, today, who were never enslaved. This is especially true when one considers that the Civil War was primarily between "white people" – the 4.9% wealthy slave-owning Democrats and the poor whites of the South, and the anti-slavery Republicans of the North. Thousands of thousands died killing each other over this difference of opinion and belief. Should whites be able to seek reparations from blacks today on behalf of all those "white people" who died in combat to free them from slavery? Perhaps if that dynamic were considered, we could say, "OK, we're even then." Far less of blacks died in the Civil War than whites; a number comparison is miniscule. Even if reparations were justified, and they're not, in my opinion they should demand reparations from the Democrats only, because there were no Republicans at the time who owned slaves. After all, aren't Democrats now largely populated by blacks who have forgotten who originally enslaved them? So, asking the Democrats for reparations should be easy, right? Get them to pay reparations. And, after all, Republicans wrote and voted in the Affirmative Action program in the 60s, opposed by Democrats. And it was the Democrats who kept tinkering over time with the Affirmative Action program that has caused it to be ineffective and a failure, never achieving the goals set by its original authors. In effect, the tinkering has, for one thing, created a financial situation where a black woman with children on welfare does financially better than if the father was around, which is why some 13% or higher black families are fatherless in America, and why the crime rate is so high among that fatherless population.

I'd like to digress just slightly with a review of a recent video.

I recently watched a June 2019 video made by a young black man who calls himself RizzaIslam, who starts off agreeing that current white people should not have to pay reparations for the deeds of the white ancestors who were slave owners. But he then characterizes white people as "the devil." I guess that's his Islamist beliefs talking. (And he talks extremely fast, like a speed freak on cocaine or meth.) He particularly singled out Mitch McConnell and John Connors.

However, he goes on to say that current white people SHOULD pay reparations to black people because white people "inherited" all the good things that resulted from slavery while the black people "inherited" all the bad things, and since white people were enjoying the "good life" of this inheritance and black people were "suffering" the bad inheritance they got, whites were thus responsible and should pay. He says because there were at least 250 years of slavery, and 90 years of "Jim Crow", and at least 60 years of separate-but-equal-ism. He goes on to figure that anyone born during the "Jim Crow" era, before the 1964-5 Civil Rights movement, partook of the "white privilege" of that era. He continues to justify reparations as characterizing the slavery era as the black holocaust requiring reparations in the same way that the United States gave "reparations" to the Jews after the German holocaust and Jews of that holocaust were not even on American soil, like the American slaves were. Comparing slavery to the genocide of six million Jews grossly conflates the matter.

He argued that all banks and institutions that were built on the backs of slavery still circulated that wealth through their business dealings – which is not true at all – and thus, reparations were in order there too because blacks still suffer the negative effects of slavery and Jim Crow. Thusly, he generalizes ALL white people as responsible for this reparation debt owed to all black people today.

He went on to argue that the U.S. government has, over many years, given native Americans multi-million dollars in financial and land reparations and thus blacks today are also entitled to reparations for ancestral slavery. This simplistic viewpoint overlooks the fact that the North fought for an end to slavery, and it was mostly "white people", and the banks and other institutions of wealth were formed primarily in the North by the same "white people" that freed the slaves, and that the United States government in the North was the government in control AFTER the Civil War and subsequently took upon itself to give reparations to the tribes that were indigenous people who populated the land before European conquest. Blacks lost no land, they were slaves, and the North freed them so they would have the opportunity to advance under their own merit. Further, while the South remained primarily Democrat, it was the Republicans who created and passed the Civil Rights Act of 1964, along with some Democrats, and who created Affirmative Action so that blacks could become better educated with greater opportunities through education. It was all well-intentioned, but when Democrats, claiming good intentions, got to tinkering with the Affirmative Action program to expand welfare systems with "incentives" for fatherless homes, the black community overall was cubbyholed and disadvantaged because an emphasis on self-motivation and excellence in achievement gave way to institutional reliance. In the Democrat's "good intentions" effort to "give" blacks their own schools or advantages in public schools in their neighborhoods, the schools remained underfunded, good teachers were hard to find, and the economics of "black neighborhoods" saw a rise in black-on-black crime. The result, high crime neighborhoods like Minneapolis, Chicago, New Orleans, Baltimore, and Detroit, to name the worst.

This demand for reparations is separatism any way you look at it, and singling out "white people" as the reparation-responsible party constitutes, any way you look at it, racism itself. Blacks like RizzaIslam continue dividing America along racial lines and build the fires of violence from his own community. Why is he really so divisive and racist?

His Islamic allegiance finally surfaces at the end, when he acknowledges that the $50 trillion dollars black folks are entitled to in reparations will never happen because America is in debt for $60 trillion and is broke, BUT, he says, blacks should be able to get "back" LAND and businesses from the Jim Crow era, and then emphasizes his Islamic allegiance tells him "we can get it.", meaning these claimed reparations. He says blacks deserve to be given 8 to 10 states. Given entire States.

He closes with: "We are owed it, we will get it, *one way or another*. On the way, let's continue to build for ourselves until the government comes around, *one way or another.*" Racial violence is what he is after. He is a Muslim, fundamentally hating "infidels" and, especially, "white infidels." His agenda, to divide and then conquer, is the foundation for all the tripe that he advocates.

RizzaIslam lists contact information to book him for speaking engagements, and I could conclude it is likely he'll monetize his nonsense because it sounds so good to those who are already disenfranchised and/or willing to listen to pay him for more "get free stuff" reparations dialogue. Crazy. This dialogue is divisive and nothing more than a recipe for more anti-white protests and demands. He says, "one way or another." I ask: Or what? Violence? I don't doubt but that he'll be able to persuade a lot of blacks to join his anti-white, Islamic-driven, narrative.

Let me talk about another, very different point of view, from another black man who once held viewpoints similar to Malcom X. His name is Walter Williams, who is now one of America's most important and provocative thinkers on the major social and political issues of our time. He is black, yet he opposes affirmative action. He believes that the Civil Rights Act was a major error, that the minimum wage actually creates unemployment and that occupational and business licensure and industry work against minorities and others in American business. Perhaps most importantly he has come to believe that it has been the welfare state that has done to black Americans what slavery could never do: destroy the black family unit. Walter Williams expresses all of these provocative ideas in a public television documentary by Free to Choose Network in 2015. Williams' criticisms and reservations find factual support in the dynamics of the disenfranchised black communities in America. Before Affirmative Action and the welfare state, black families included a father figure, a complete family unit. During that earlier time, blacks were very demanding of their children about getting an education. He talked about how there were different values then, of hard work and sacrifice and respect, and how many of those values are absent today among Americans in general, and often, even more so, among young Americans who are black. De-spiriting change occurred under the welfare state system. Williams has also talked about a "spiritual poverty" the system has produced. He defines it as a poverty of spirit where black people have lost the vision of what constitutes the "good life." Williams says, "spiritual poverty is where people lack the ambition [because] they've developed the idea of dependency, and they are engaging in all kinds of pathological behavior, such as the high illegitimacy rate where 70% of black kids are born out of wedlock and, in 1930, it was only 13%. And now, once that stage has been reached, changing the culture is the only way to solve that problem." Williams opines that the welfare system simply subsidizes "slovenly" behavior and dependency mindsets. This is a basic economic principle: if you tax something, you get less of it; if you subsidize it, you get more of it. In the 1940's despite Jim Crow, any youngster, black or white, who wanted a job could get a job. Williams went from shining shoes at age 10, high school he delivered mail and packed shipping orders for the Sears and Roebuck company. He later worked for one of the largest restaurant chains at the time, the Automat, America's original "fast food" enterprise. As time passed, after the Civil Rights movement, and after the Affirmative Action Act, things began to change; by 1985, Williams, in his first televised documentary "Good Intentions" revealed that "70% of black children, who look for jobs, cannot find them." This was due to Democrat "child labor laws." He explained how these basic entry level jobs were more than "pocket change" but were the opportunity of young blacks to enter into the greater job market for their own futures. He argued that the Democrat's "minimum wage" laws actually held young people out of the job market at entry-level jobs they needed to experience in the market itself.

Fast forward to 2012, where crime statistics show that blacks made up 38.5% of all persons arrested for violent crimes (mostly males) and 51.5% of those under 18 arrested for such crimes, but blacks only constituted 13% of the population. When looking at violent crime demography, when the race of the person committing homicide was known, blacks committed 51% of the homicides. What happened? The racially-focused Civil Rights Act and Affirmative Action plan, along with the new "welfare state" system, was simply debilitating to the black community. Williams argued that affirmative action in the educational institutions, by not requiring excellence from under-performing black students and instead giving them "passes" they hadn't earned were "racial preferences" is simply one of the most effective means of reinforcing racial stereotyping.

Democrat President Johnson's called for <u>equality as a fact</u> and <u>equality as a result</u> did little more than increase the racial stereotyping and lower the standards for excellence based on racial profiling. The resulting plethora of "good intentions" for "equality" simply undermined the emphasis the black community would most benefit from, i.e., encouraging excellence over racial condition. A "hands-up" call is far more effective for future success than a "hands-out" delivery system because the latter creates "enchainment" and <u>dependence</u> rather than self-motivations for achievement through excellence. Where will the black man be in the future without freedom and opportunity? What will it look like under a socialist ideology?

As to the "reparations" movement, on his website Williams offers people of European descent a proclamation of amnesty about slavery. Williams says this:

> "I, Walter Williams, do declare full and general amnesty and pardon to all persons of European ancestry for both their own grievances and those of their forebears against my people. Therefore, from this day forward, Americans of European ancestry stand straight and proud and know they are without guilt and thus obliged not to act like damn fools in their relationships with Americans of African ancestry."

A recent book by Jason Riley entitled *Please Stop Helping Us: How Liberals Make It Harder for Blacks to Succeed*, discusses why these depressing statistics stem not simply from poverty or prejudice, but from cultural changes that have occurred in the black community and the unintended consequences of liberal efforts to blame everything on poverty and prejudice. Riley looks to this and found that the major problem in the black community that accounts for so much of the disparity in achievement and criminal behavior is that more than seven in 10 black children are born to single women and will spend much of their lives with no father present. Riley emphasizes the need for a male role model in the home, but not one fully engaged in the criminal element outside the home. It is this lack of a father of virtue and goodness in the home environment, regardless of the race of the father, that is the single most important factor in the development of a decent child-to-man person. It is NOT because of "white people" per se, but the fault of "liberals" of all colors who think in simple terms about complex components of behavior, and then issue "fixes" that are either ineffective band-aids or cause worse problems. Lay it at the door of the Democrats whose do-gooder intentions do little more than making things worse for the black community.

Riley, a black man, says there is something very bad happening in our inner cities, and it has nothing to do with racism, even if it manifests and is perceived as racism. So what might that be? I suggest it is a divisive move to further a political agenda, and it is not about who gets elected. It is much larger than that, although the Progressives have become, knowingly or unknowingly, pawns in the agenda process.

If we factor in the growing recognition that the Kalergi Plan is alive and well, i.e., that the goal of the New World Order is to eliminate racial diversity by interbreeding, merging all bloodlines over time, it's easier to question whether the anti-white agenda is part of that Plan. Already, people of color are already saying the way to get rid of "white people" is to marry them and have children of color who are not "ALL" white. But it goes both ways. The Kalergi Plan does not intend to exempt any race. There will be no Africans, Asians, South Americans, Mexican-Americans, none of that. The intent of the Kalergi Plan is to interbreed until there is no predominant bloodline at all. A wholesale change in genetics by interbreeding does not result in a gene more dominant than the rest. Granted, for a time, new generations will see some who are lighter or darker than others, perhaps, but all that will disappear over future generations. If we of different ethnicities are currently proud of our genetics/race, and don't want to see it disappear altogether, then we must reject the Kalergi Plan because it is already underway.

If whites are to face this "anti-white" sentiment that might turn into a "race war", it has to first be recognized WHY does this sentiment exist, and what all the elements that drive it. It is not enough for whites to rest on the assurance that blacks only represent 13% of the overall population and far out-gunned. America cannot afford a civil war, whether it is racial or ideological. Too many enemies, like the U.N. countries, waiting like vultures to take advantage of our division and weakness, especially if we have a race war or civil war.

But, more so, blacks and Hispanics are predominantly Democrat, and the difference between capitalism and socialism, to them, is that socialism will make their lives better because there would be no class divisions or wars, and everyone will be on equal terms. Historically, they are dead wrong, but pro-socialists always seem like their goal is always well-intentioned; of course, they are totally ignorant of what inevitably occurs when a small few at the power controls of a socialist ideology decide to begin making decisions and policies that bleed and oppress the population *because they can*. Power always begets abuse of power in such ideologies.

Populations around the world consists of human beings, people, as like or different from us as anywhere else. They generalize foreign or racially or culturally different people, just like we do. There is no sense of homogeneity or assimilation with foreign, racially, or culturally different peoples. Fundamental assimilation could be interpreted as the core component of the Kalergi Plan. Create a single bloodline from the many, and all the world's problems will go away. We should be smart enough to know that a Utopia can never exist, unless it is Heaven. There will always be conflicts between people, even if they are victims of an Orwellian transformation to a world where every second of your life is monitored and regulated and used by the government. Which is also underway.

"White Americans" should not be shamed into "white guilt" about anything in the past. This is what occurred post-WW-II with Germans, once their genocide was exposed to the world. Over time, and inclusion into the European Union (EU), Germany developed into a world economic power, but their embracing of open borders and accepting migrants from all countries indiscriminately was the result of "German guilt" or "holocaust guilt." As a result, it is now failing as a nation, and Germans have now essentially lost their nation to Islam and Orwellian thought controls. It is now a crime for Germans to protest Muslim crime, which has been overwhelming as the North African hordes swarmed over European countries. Thousands upon thousands of rapes of young girls and women, even boys, and assaults upon German men, did not result in prosecutions, but it did result in laws passed making it a crime for Germans to complain. This government action spread to other European countries as well. Why? Because the U.N. said that low birth rates and low fertility rates were depleting the workforce and needed to be kick-started from the outside, so they brought in many thousands of rapists and pedophiles from North African Muslim countries to fix that problem.

Americans must not fall for this U.N. lie, because the U.N., in its report also named the United States as having "low" fertility and birth rates. We know that is a lie. The U.N. has already gotten the U.S. to accept many thousands of Muslim migrants from North African countries under the "war refugees" designation. Why have Americans fallen for this scandalous lie? And why do Americans sit back in acquiescence while the government continues to "obey" the U.N.? At least did under Obama. Donald Trump? Well, that's another story. He is all that stands between a continuation of the Obama legacy and the next step in the NWO/UN agenda Hillary was supposed to enable.

While I have not dwelled much on the more difficult factor, i.e., the criminal cartel that has invaded politics, our legislatures, big business, and even in our most sacred agencies, we must realize that those puppeteers are the ones or-chestrating much of what is going on in the world, and particularly here in the United States. We must recognize that the criminal gangs of the "Roarin' 20's" began the cartel movement, today's criminal cartels are far more sophisticated than ever and have infiltrated all levels of power on a global scale. I have tried to show that by tying together various people and groups throughout this book. They are using tried-and-true methods to fool us, to mis-direct us, to cause us to fight amongst us and blame each other for all our ills, all the while they are laughing at their success in getting away with crimes against humanity. Fortunately, there are forces in power directing their attention to bringing these cartels and members to justice. It will not be easy, and the alt-Left is not helping that endeavor at all.

Modern racists talk about discrimination, about inequality, about people of color being disadvantaged by "white people." They talk about multiculturalism and diversity as being the ideal way, yet diversity has done nothing but <u>divide</u> us more and multiculturalism has turned into a separation of cultures rather than an assimilation of cultures into the one-culture intent of the American ideology. America was intended for assimilation as Americans, not Black Amer-icans, not Asian Americans, not African Americans, not Arab Americans, not

Irish or Italian or Norwegian or Chinese or Russian Americans, none of that. All of that origin history became irrelevant to the idea that we should drop that hyphenation and be a country of Americans, one nation, under God, indivisible, with liberty and justice for all. Theodore Roosevelt made that very clear.

Who do you think has acted against that? Not "whites". The vast majority of "white people" in this country like to see "non-whites" become successful and happy and a participating part of this country. It is many among the "non-whites" that seek separatism through "diversity" and "multiculturalism." You can't blame "white people" for that. When you bring animus against "white people" and practice separatism, it is YOU who is the "racist." If you don't get a proper education in school because you don't pay attention and/or don't bother with your homework, whose fault is that? It is YOUR fault. If you failed to PREPARE for life as an adult, it is YOUR fault, not some "white guy." The same goes for everyone, regardless of race. Mess up your education, mess up your life. If the educational institution is sub-standard, that is a government problem, not a "white person" causation.

Today it is people of color who have become racists against white people although the vast majority of white people are not racists at all. But if a white person walking down a darkened street, or even in broad daylight, and a group of young people, dressed like hoodlums and acting like trouble-makers, are coming towards you, and are a race other than your own, and you cross the street to not encounter them, that is hardly a "racist" action; it is good sense these days. Act and dress like a hoodlum, you'll be seen as a hoodlum.

PART 15: THE IMPEACHMENT MOVEMENT

The fear of the Left that they will lose the elections and their agenda of socialism is seen in their obsessive use of Critical Theory, i.e., the never-ending criticism tool. Over time, Nancy Pelosi, Maxine Waters, and others on the Left in Congress, are ganging up on Donald Trump on "trumped up" impeachment charges, demanding his impeachment so that he can't run for President. Fortunately, that impeachment movement failed miserably, but it will still be promoted by the Left to keep Trump from being re-elected.

So I ask you patriots who are not pro-socialists to set aside your political partisanship views, and look only to the end result of what the hijacked Democrat Party socialist radicals (called Progressives) are trying to accomplish. If these Progressives achieve their socialist goals, it is only a heartbeat away to communism to totalitarianism. From that, the New World Order one-government world, there will be no return to what we know as American lifestyle and prosperity and happiness. This was never about Trump; his election just got in the way of this socialism movement, and they vilified him for it with lies upon lies.

Democrats Nancy Pelosi, Maxine Waters, Bernie Sanders. the list of these caterers for socialism is long. There are even a few of the RINOs against Trump because he upset their free ride and applecart of graft income. If the patriots of America, Democrat, Republicans, Independents, Libertarians, do not protect Trump with your vote for him, we're done. You may not like Trump's tweets, but he is John Q. Citizen even if he is wealthy far beyond the common man (but he earned that in our merit-based economic system). You've seen what he has done, rolling back some of the Obama socialist nonsense, fighting for our sovereignty at the borders, expanding employment opportunities, standing up for Christianity and the Constitution, negotiating for fair treatment on the world stage markets and trade agreements, bringing back corporations from foreign countries so American can have jobs, standing against the United Nations who wants the one-government world of the New World Order, and always putting America first. This is his track record. Obama didn't do that. Clinton would not have done that, but would have carried out the rest of Obama's plan towards the New World Order.

The Democrats called for the impeachment of Trump and accused him of being a "criminal", and demanded impeachment right away, i.e., rush it through and ignore due process. Pressure the Judiciary Committee into acting before the evidence, if any, is even heard. Bully, bully, bully the impeachment through. Protect the socialist agenda at any cost. That is what we face.

When Pelosi announced moving forward with impeachment, the Hollywood Left exploded with joy. *Westworld* star Jeffery Wright said:

"Not a perfect country, but one thing is inarguable: America wasn't founded to be an authoritarian state. Impeach Trump. We're accountable to the law. He must be. Hammer him. Trump and any other Americans who favor authoritarianism can find another country."

What a laugh. How misguided can this guy be? It is the Left, the Democrat Progressives, who are pushing socialism and disarmament and repeal of the Constitution, who are calling for the New World Order which is ultimately a totalitarian ideology. He doesn't want authoritarianism, yet he's in bed with those pushing a socialist agenda which, if successful, will eventually get far more than they bargained for, since socialism is but a stepping stone to the totalitarian state of the New World Order. It is Trump who told the UN, which pushes for the NWO, that it should not be vying for the globalist New World Order. That message to the UN was a clear statement of where Trump stood on the subject of socialism, communism, and totalitarianism. These movie stars are not experts on people or politics or even economics and history. They are just actors. Why do people even listen to them about such matters and politics?

And we know the lead Democrat candidates for presidency are following destructive agendas towards socialism, depopulation masked as climate change mitigation, spending trillions for some Green New Deal or whatever the term is, eliminating CO_2 emissions to 0%, eliminating fossil fuel for electricity and relying solely on solar, tearing down houses and other structures and building new ones based on unreasonable energy-efficiency goals, and so on, all a mish-mash of unattainable fantasies but willing to waste trillions of dollars that will result in inflation so bad that the country will effectively be destroyed.

David Limbaugh, brother of radio host Rush Limbaugh, is an accomplished author of several books. Just today, I read a brief message that I'd like to quote at least in part, because he, like me, sees clearly the danger the Left is creating for the future of America. David Limbaugh writes:

> The left is becoming more unapologetically totalitarian every day. Every freedom-loving American should be alarmed.

From hounding conservatives out of restaurants to spitting on Trump supporters at rallies, from firing employees for politically incorrect statements to fining people for "misgendering" a person, the left is on a path toward absolutism.

Even some former and current leftists have recognized this intolerant trend and broken from their colleagues, lamenting their intolerance of opposing ideas and disturbing mission to suppress dissenting opinion.

In the most recent Democratic presidential debate, Sen. Kamala Harris pushed for the suspension of President Trump's Twitter, speciously alleging that he is trying to obstruct justice and intimidate and threaten witnesses. You see, the left always has some urgent rationale to smother conservative speech — whether it's to prevent the incitement of violence or obstruction of justice. But it just wants to shut us up.

Those who would silence the other side are the very definition of dangerous. Don't take Harris' musings lightly, even if she is mostly posturing to gin up more support from the Trump-hating Democratic base. It is instructive that efforts to muzzle speech almost always come from the left, not the right, because the left is insecure about the popularity of its kooky ideas.

The third incident involved demagogue and former Rep. Beto O'Rourke, who said in a CNN forum on LGBT issues that churches and religious organizations should lose their tax-exempt status if they oppose same-sex marriage. If I have to explain how outrageous this is, the country is in even greater danger than I imagined.

America was founded on the idea of claiming and preserving our God-given liberties. The illiberal left, which believes our rights and freedoms come from government, is hell-bent on destroying our liberties and forcibly imposing its thoughts and ideas on all of us.

God save us. (https://www.bizpacreview.com/2019/10/18/david-limbaugh-the-totalitarian-american-left-840837)

-End Quote –

These crazy folks are trying to impeach President Trump with as many lies and falsifications they can come up with. They have endlessly attacked President Trump from the day he won the election, and yet he trudges on against this morass with dignity, despite his tweets some supporters don't like. Has he been incompetent? No. Has he achieved all of his promises? No, and not his fault either. Is he a patriot? I believe he is, and I'll be voting for him again. If I thought otherwise, I'd vote for someone else because I care only for competency and honesty and patriotism. He was never a politician. He was just Donald Trump, successful businessman. It is this successful businessman we supporters voted for to fix a government that seems to know little about solid business practices. He tackled a bureaucracy we often complain about, and it has pushed back, but I believe he is making inroads into that bureaucratic fraternity. Much of the problems we complain about are correctable, if only we would vote the RINOs or DINOs out who are the problem children. We should find legitimate reasons to impeach the likes of Pelosi, Waters, and Sanders. Find someone honest and ask them to run for office. Might help a lot, don't you think?

Political experts have long-argued that House Democrats don't have the requisite votes to pass articles of impeachment against President Trump. Democrats need 218 votes for impeachment in the House. They face an even steeper 67-vote threshold in the U.S. Senate to convict and remove the President from office. As Pelosi announced an impeachment inquiry, Democrats have just about 175 votes despite their 235-seat majority. The move by Pelosi may help encourage Democrats in her caucus who fear the political backlash a vote to impeach Trump might bring; on the other hand, on the fence Democrats who are NOT pro-socialist just might decide to do the right thing and vote NO on any impeachment proceedings. We all need to call our Congressperson and let them know you don't support impeachment. I've been told that for every person who calls in, that one person represents the opinion of about a thousand voters, so Yes, your vote counts. If 1,000 people call in, that represents about one million voters.

Kamala Harris, former California Attorney General, promoted absolutism and loss of freedom of speech. If she is elected, no one will escape the suffering that her regime will bring upon America. Fortunately, she dropped out.

We are at the crossroads of citizen accountability. Either we again vote for the one who loves our country like we do, or we must accept accountability for the results when our own children later ask us what happened and why is life suddenly so bad. Will you look at the floor in shame and regret, or will you honestly say, "Honey, I tried very hard for this not to happen. But the bully won." Or would you rather vote for Trump once again so that one day, in the future, your children will still have a chance at the American Dream?

PART 16: THE ORWELLIAN FACTOR
AND PRESIDENT DONALD TRUMP

Some sources on the Internet who have spoken about the Orwellian factor in the United States have tried to associate or blame the push towards socialism through socialism to totalitarianism on Trump. This is a prime example of double-speak and double-think, since Trump is not even close to the NWO's Orwellian scheme. (See, for instance, the liberalist's Guardian, at https://www.theguardian.com/ commentisfree/2017/jan/25/george-orwell-donald-trump-kellyanne-conway-1984. (Reference #3.) The New Yorker magazine, a fine source of fake news, is doing the same thing. See, https://www.newyorker.com/news/daily-comment/orwells-1984-and-trumps-america (Reference #4).

Another anti-Trump dissident, the Los Angeles Review of Books, also accused Trump of ushering in an Orwellian future. (See, https://lareviewofbooks.org/article/big-brother-is-watching-you-is-america-at-risk-of-becoming-orwells-nightmare/#!, Reference #5.) The Orwellian factor was already well in place long before Trump came along as a candidate.

The extent to which the anti-Trump movement will go to thwart Trump from restoring America is almost frightening. This attack and criticism is an important element in Marxism, called "Critical Theory" as I also talk about further herein. Critical Theory is all about criticism, never-ending criticism, no alternatives, just criticism. Which is what the Left is doing to Trump. Lies upon lies, never-ending criticism.

This movement ascribes lies upon lies to Donald Trump, but all of their accusations are based upon lies upon lies. The reality of the Left's Progressives is that their insistence and enforcement of "political correctness" is a mere rewording of "double-speak" and "double-thinking" in Orwell's 1984 scenario. The agenda on the lower levels of this movement is in fact socialism, and through their power of "double-speak" approximately 80% of American students in both high schools and colleges think that socialism is Utopia and want it here in the USA. They are drowning out freedom of speech, thought and expression if you do NOT agree with them. They are resorting to violence, destruction of historic property and statutes in their frenzy to re-write history to achieve their socialist Utopia. Obama's "Rules for Revolution" adopting the Saul Alinsky Marxist model were in full swing by the time Trump got elected, which model already had the Orwellian factors embedded.

In addition, radical liberal Hollywood, is doing its movie-making magic by producing violent action movies where the bad guys are the good guys and the law enforcement community and the Republican Right are the enemies, and the script of these movies are that the citizens should take the fight to their "enemies" and violently overthrow and kill everyone in their path. Young people are walking out of these theaters finding similarities and anger-points in the world around them, and thus "buy in" to the actual message intended by the movie-makers: start trouble, commit violence, create racial hatred and violence against "white people", and overthrow the "white" government, such as "The Hate U Give" (2018), "Blindspotting" (2018), "Black Panther" (2018), "BlackkKlansman" (2018), and, the worst of all, the "Purge" series (2013, 2014, 2016, 2018), with buckets of unrestricted gore.

The problem, notwithstanding that a capitalist republic is the closest a country will ever get to a Utopian world, the globalist elites at the top orchestrating all the way down to the socialist movement, are using that movement to achieve civil unrest, create civil war, and, in the end, a takeover and destruction of the United States as a democracy/republic so that the elites can establish a one-government Orwellian world aligned with their occult systems.

Obama was their front-man, his handler was and is George Soros, and Hillary Clinton was next in line to finish the job Obama started. Both are masters of deception and double-speak, with millions of Americans still under their spell. We were an election away from racial war, civil war, anarchy, martial law, disarmament, and invasion by the United Nations and other countries bent on America's destruction. Remember, the U.N. has about 36 countries governed by Islamists pushing the sharia agenda, including blasphemy laws.

The Interpol Police is an international police force with 192 member countries, whose mission (ideally) is to assist law enforcement agencies around the world in combating all forms of transnational crime and terrorism. How many of those 192 countries are Muslim-governed? What would that mean for Americans if the U.N. military and Interpol police entered the USA for so-called "peace-keeping" purposes. It was Obama who spoke to the U.N. about disarming Americans in the event of martial law, and it was Obama who made an agreement to allow Interpol, in such times, to take control over all local, state, and federal law enforcement agencies during martial law event. Yes, that is true.

Trump was the wrench in that gearbox of our pending destruction, and we should all be thanking him for that alone. The Left is so far enamored by the barrage of brainwashing affecting them daily that they seem unable to awaken from the hypnotic trance in which they exist when it comes to what is really going on in the world. Again, we all need to realize that we're not just squabbling among ourselves and hating on each other; we are being manipulated by forces high up on the international stage who have agendas not in our favor. If we can't come to see that reality, then we're all going to lose in the end, because the world "they" seek is NOT one any of us are going to like. These are occultists wanting total and absolute, and despotic, control of the planet.

Even with the currently ongoing destruction of European countries, our own citizens are mumbling the mantra, "Oh, that will never happen here!", even as it is already occurring. So blinded against facts and truth, they stumble along with their ears folded over to shut out any utterings at all that do not fit their beliefs. The old adage, "We are our own worst enemy" is true today. Those who refuse to see represent the three monkeys of <u>See No Evil, Hear No Evil, and Speak No Evil</u>.

Sometimes we need the Word of God as our trumpeter, like this,

but sometimes we need other means of communication, like this:

Remember, as I have said, "new world order" had two meanings.

Anti-trump columnists like Frank Vogl of the Globalist publication, appeared in January 23, 2018, article in the JapanTimes, which I am copying here to show you just how far such columnists will go to try and convince the reader that Trump is the new Stalin. Much of the allegations he sets forth are more akin to what Obama was engaged in than resembling anything Trump has done. In his article, "Trump Is Pushing For U.S. Authoritarianism", Vogl writes:

Trump Is Pushing For U.S. Authoritarianism

(Vogl) His act is familiar to all by now: Donald Trump diverts public attention with clownish acts, outrageous statements and headline-making Tweets. But the U.S. president's agenda is sinister. He is moving consistently, persistently and successfully to undermine American democracy and enhance his power.

> [My Analysis: Trump inherited a country with an already sinister force trying to destroy America for the globalist elites known by several names: New World Order, multinational bankers, Illuminati, the Bilderberg Group, the Shadow Government, generally the wickedly wealthy who want to rule the world and depopulate it down to one billion total persons by any means necessary. Their paid minions have been elected politicians, mayors, heads of government agencies, a veritable spiderweb of players carrying out the single purpose of the New World Order controllers, to own and control the world by any means necessary.]

(Vogl) There has never before been such a forceful effort to replace democracy in the land of George Washington, Thomas Jefferson and Abraham Lincoln with dictatorship. The reason is simple: Trump is driven by a lust for personal power and for accumulating still greater personal wealth that such power can yield.

> [My Analysis: There is no credible information that Donald Trump is interested in turning American into an Authoritarian government or Dictatorship. Not a single item that he is "mad" with a lust for power or accumulating greater personal wealth. That he is a powerful and wealthy businessman does not automatically translate to the Vogl belief.]

(Vogl) Any honest assessment of the current political situation would find that Trump's assault on democracy is graver than the Watergate scandal.

> [My Analysis: The Watergate Scandal was overblown. All countries use spies to gain information, whether as police "undercover" investigators or CIA spies on the world stage, all countries spy on each other. Trump has done nothing that could be equated with an "assault on democracy" but what he has done is acknowledge the extent to which the Democrat Party has leaned towards turning America into a Socialist country. Socialism is not a right embodied in the Freedom of Speech range for overt action to achieve it.]

(Vogl) That episode was a combination of illegal dirty tricks, obstruction of justice and lies directed by the nation's top public officials. Their first goal was to secure the re-election of President Richard Nixon and their second goal was to cover up the crimes committed in the pursuit of the first goal.

> [My Analysis: The reference Vogl makes to Watergate and Nixon is misdirection. It would not be misdirection if attributed to the Obama administration.]

(Vogl) The United States' constitutional system strives to check absolute power by a system that established three co-equal branches of government (the judicial branch consisting of the Supreme Court and lower federal courts, the legislative branch and the executive branch). Plus, the U.S. Constitution's First Amendment, which enshrines freedom of the press.

Trump is now, ever more brazenly, diminishing the influence and, in time, the independence, of the Congress, the courts and the press.

[My Analysis: From the time Trump agreed to run for President, mainstream media, owned by the NWO group, exploded with frenzied character attacks against Trump, uncaring whether anything they said was true or not, where they even manufactured what they alleged was true and facts. It was about lies and endless criticisms, i.e., the Marxist tool of Critical Theory. Why? For the Left, Trump running for President was a joke, something to sneer at, but for the elitists it was no joke at all, since Hillary was already groomed to be the next President who would finish the takedown-America agenda Obama already started. No one on that side believed Trump could win, and when he did that anti-American side had a meltdown, which translated into an all-out media attack against his character. He interfered with the NWO agenda, and they felt they were so close to a world takeover had Hillary gotten elected. Supporters of Obama and Hillary had no clue of what was in store for them too, because they believed the lies of a Utopian life.]

(Vogl) **Sycophancy rules**:
Trump frequently derides Republican Party leaders in the Senate and the House of Representatives, but — like lap dogs — they remain loyal to him.

[My Analysis: As said, Trump inherited an America already infiltrated by minions of the NWO, including Republicans who are part of the "Deep State" in Washington (RINOS). Yes, he called them out when they opposed his efforts to fulfill campaign promises, and he made it known they better get in line for what is best for Americans or he would continue to expose them. Facing this, they better fall in line, or we'll vote them out, as we should anyway.]

(Vogl) Trump, for example, has frequently humiliated Congressman Paul Ryan, the speaker of the House of Representatives, yet as the new tax legislation was signed in December, Ryan declared: "Something this big, something this generational, something this profound, could not have been done without exquisite presidential leadership." That is quite an amazing act of sycophantism.

[My Analysis: Paul Ryan may have significantly influenced Donald Trump in Trump's acclimation to political life, but Trump was elected precisely because he was NOT a career politician but rather a champion of the working class. His tweets resonated with the people who only wanted jobs, the ability to have a good life, and a government that rolled back from the idea that the People are servants of the Government to the Government is the servant of the People, as it is supposed to be. Trump may have pushed some of the career politicians to retire; good for him. They are the ones who perpetuate the growth and power of the Government over the People. Good riddance.]

(Vogl) **De-basing political system**
Trump's assault on the courts and the legal system is persistent and vicious. When judges rule against Trump's executive

orders, be it on immigration or repealing environmental regulations, then he blasts the courts as corrupt and opponents of the executive branch.

[My Analysis: Judges are required by their oath of office to be non-partisan, to handle all matters according to the law, not to make law, yet for the past half-century we have seen a rise in law-making from the judicial bench as well as partisanship in decision-making. If Trump blasts a judge for such misconduct, he is doing the right thing. In California, we see Left-leaning judges refusing to uphold Federal immigration law against the State's Sanctuary Law and handling of illegal migrants. If Trump attacks that, who is right, he or the judge? He emphasizes to the judiciary to stay strictly within the Constitution, as the law requires. Do NOT make law, which is the jurisdiction of the Legislatures. Interpret and adhere to the law according to the fair import of its terms, is the judicial mandate.]

(Vogl) Trump compounds this assault by regularly attacking the professional lawyers and investigators at the U.S. Department of Justice, the Federal Bureau of Investigation and the intelligence agencies. Rarely does a week go by without Trump turning to Twitter, or giving campaign speeches, to attack the whole system of law enforcement.

[My Analysis: Trump was and is faced with the infiltration of the DOJ, FBI, CIA, HS, and other agencies by persons placed there by Obama to render those agencies powerless or in line with the NWO agenda. It is absolute fact that Obama placed members of the terrorist-supporting Muslim Brotherhood in all of the agencies, knowing that the MB has been banned in numerous countries for their open support of radical Islam jihadists.]

(Vogl) At the same time, Trump has proposed hosts of new judicial appointments, almost all of which have strong conservative credentials and/or have been large financial contributors to the Republican Party.

[My Analysis: Trump has indeed proposed new judicial appointments of conservative judges, but they are judges who are conservative in interpreting constitutional provisions and law. Trump's view of judgeships is that they should act strictly in accord to the power given them in the Constitution and its provisions rather than interpret them in a way that serves to undermine our ultimate law.]

(Vogl) As The Guardian reported: "The makeup of America's judges is quietly becoming the site of one of Trump's most unequivocal successes: Nominating and installing judges who reflect his own worldview at a speed and volume unseen in recent memory."

[My Analysis: I would hardly call the Guardian an unbiased, impartial publication or source for even-handed politics. The Guardian has long known as the world's most liberal media.]

(Vogl) **Most media are intimidated**
Then there are his constant tirades against "fake news" and the media that opposes him, plus his calls for legislation to introduce tough new libel laws. His deliberate and cunning acts of intimidation are having an effect.

[My Analysis: Tirades? Cunning acts of intimidation? How about the truth, here, something like Self-Defense? The world now knows the mainstream media giants and even most downstream outlets are owned by the globalist elites, and must keep

lockstep with what "the bosses" want them to say
and do. Their attack against Trump from the beginning was biased tirades as well as "deliberate and
cunning acts of intimidation." If he calls for legislation to attach consequences for the media for lying
and "fake news" then so be it; they deserve it.]

(Vogl) The mainstream media, be it The New York Times,
CNN or MSNBC, which all have commentators who regularly attack Trump (unlike his favorite, Fox News), now all
go to considerable lengths to give space to Trump's supporters and defenders. They have become more cautious,
quite often, in their reporting because of the persistent attacks on them from the White House.

[My Analysis: " have become more cautious…"?
That's an interesting interpretation for being put in
check for lying to the entire American public on a
worsening scale.]

(Vogl) Republican Sen. Jeff Flake of Arizona stated on the
Senate floor that Trump reminds us of Joseph Stalin when
calling the press "the enemy of the people." Flake said: "Of
course, the president has it precisely backward. Despotism is
the enemy of the people. The free press is the despot's enemy,
which makes the free press the guardian of democracy."

[My Analysis: If the mainstream media has under-
taken a policy of lying with false news on an ever-
increasing scale in order to influence elections or an
agenda for impeaching the President, is that not illegal seditious speech, or even treasonous action itself? Whatever the legal level of severity it is, lying
to the American public is hardly cause to accuse
Trump of Stalinist despotism. Even if Stalin called
the USSR press "the enemy of the people," here in

the USA the press has in fact become the enemy of
the people by unashamedly lying to them.]

(Vogl) **Unbalancing political system**

The constant efforts by Trump from his first day in office to
diminish Congress, the courts and the press have a gradual
cumulative impact. There has rarely been a U.S. president
who so dominates the news, and inevitably this provides less
media space for good coverage of the courts and Congress.

The unbalancing of the political system in favor of an ever-
stronger White House has been fortified by the consistent
Trump effort to make the rich still richer and American business still more ruthless.

The termination of environmental regulations has been one
of the central pillars of this strategy. Another has related to
the strengthening of financial institutions, from the hollow-
ing out of consumer protection in this sector, to attacks on
financial regulation to tax benefits.

The excessive income and wealth inequality in the U.S. produces an ever greater number of citizens who feel that their
government is not treating them fairly. So far, in what is the
most bizarre act of American shortsightedness, they continue
to see Trump as their champion.

They do so, in sheep-like manner, despite the fact that so
many of his actions have damaged the lower-middle class.
There is no American public figure who is as masterful a
media manipulator as Trump.

[My Analysis: This entire section is precisely why
Trump called the media the "enemy of the people."
Here is Vogl, anti-Trump, explaining his narrative
about Trump's actions based on nothing more than

Vogl's personal perspective of what it looks like to him and/or what he is told to believe. Everything that Trump has accomplished and is trying to accomplish is despite the resistance against him of the trickle-down NWO agenda folks. Has Vogl been brainwashed too, or he deliberately trying to destroy Trump with his eloquent lies?]

(Vogl) **Conclusion**

There is one effective way out of the current conundrum since Trump feeds off public attention, like moths fly to any source of light.

The one way to cool his heels would be to stop responding to whatever his latest attention-craving, headline-grabbing outrageous Trump tweet is. We should understand by now their ultimately almost always sinister purpose.

By the same token, rather than all the vapid and self-glorifying talking about the "resilience" of U.S. civil society, we Americans ought to prove to ourselves and the world that we can stop the slide into authoritarianism.

This matters all the more given that we have been world champions in telling others around the globe how to run their own affairs, a lot is at stake for America's standing in the world.

To succeed, we will need to focus far more forcefully on the unprecedented attack by the U.S. president on a constitutional system that has been designed — and historically succeeded in the mission — to guard against the rise of authoritarianism.

At the end of Trump's first year in office, the U.S. faces graver challenges than in many generations.

[My Analysis: Vogl mentions not a single thing about the rise of socialism from the Left, nor the fact that polls show that 80% of our own children today have been brainwashed to think that socialism is the best form of government. He mentions nothing about Obama's ties to George Soros, or what Soros does, or who he is a part of. Instead, Vogl tries to rally support for his proposition that Americans need to wake up against Trump and fight him because he is nothing more than another egalitarian power-monger who wants to become our first American dictator. Rubbish, all rubbish. He accuses all supporters of Trump to be asleep or brainwashed, yet we can at least see the actual outcomes of Trumps accomplishments that are, in fact, restoring America to what it should be, a place where people can be free, and become able to thrive in a market-economy. There is no abuse of power here, except from the Leftist masters at the NWO top. Once we all learn that the world today, including what goes on in the USA, has to be viewed from the TOP down, not the BOTTOM up, because it is at the top, where the "shadow government" lives, that America is so divided today, so confused, and so taken by the Top's propaganda machine they are lost, certainly on the Left. At least Republicans and conservative Democrats are finally understanding who runs the propaganda machine. And here, Vogl seems to be a part of that machine.]

Finally, the problem with this piece of journalism is that the author, while very eloquent in his presentation, is citing a list of false reasons why Trump is allegedly creating an Authoritarian government. It is the same kind of eloquence that distinguished Obama both in his campaigns and in his presentations as president to the country. People were mesmerized by Obama's charm and eloquence, reaffirmed by all the good things he said he was going to accomplish in making his "fundamental change" in America. They substituted Obama for Jesus in their Christian churches. They prayed to him at bedside and had their children pray to Obama too. Women's eyes sparkled all goo-goo in his presence or while watching him on television. It was sickening, this blind reverence to a man whose very Birth Certificate was, in fact, a fake, whose children were NOT even his or Michele's, a man without any background in business or the legal profession, nothing at all before being selected by George Soros, who he had come to know, to mentor/sponsor him for public office. Everything Obama said he was doing or going to do was the opposite of what he was actually doing and going to do. Obama was President with the goal of destroying America. He claimed to be Christian, yet bowed to the Saudi Kings and assured them he was Muslim.

Obama's eloquence in his lies finds similarity with Frank Vogl's diatribe against Trump. What Vogl sounds like is one of Obama's "mesmerized" minions still hanging on to his every word and falsely accusing Trump for things that are simply untrue. Despite all the dirt on the Clinton's, as factual events, it is left totally ignored by the Vogl's in the journalistic world.

I have focused here on Vogl, but there have been many anti-Trump writers who have declared war on Donald Trump, a self-man billionaire businessman. Why? All because the NWO handlers ordered it and the mandate spread through the Left community.

PART 17: CALIFORNIA'S GOVERNOR GAVIN NEWSOM

There are MANY people in the U.S., likely millions, who have simply bought in to the viewpoints of those around him/her, without actually doing any research on which those viewpoints were based, or even being curious about the validity of those viewpoints. They come to form who THEY are around a belief system that could very well be invalid and little more than perception and bias. Anything outside that viewpoint is automatically rejected; unfortunately, like me, it is likely many patriot Americans have lost friendships merely because the ideological conditions have become diametrically opposed, based on ideas and viewpoints that may have been "unvetted" and inaccurate on many core points.

I think this is why it is so difficult to change the course of a movement, especially from someone in the "enemy camp." The divisiveness over ideological politics has created this hardline rejection of each other, where both sides are emotionally involved and angry that someone else disagrees with them. Friendships become lost in the mix, in some ways like the families of the North and the South often fought and killed each other in the Civil War.

I am in California, in a state crippled by years of Democrat control. We have a large crime problem, 42 state prisons plus contracts with private prisons, very high welfare numbers, voter fraud, high taxes, low morality, and a Hollywood movie industry that caters to the most evil aspects of human debauchery. California is one of the most regulated states in the Union, demands open border and sanctuary cities and state, and has growing angst against conservatives of any party. Morality here is almost becoming a crime.

For some 80 years the Brown, Newsom, Pelosi, and Getty families have ruled over the State of California, effectively turning it into the economic, social, and political disaster that we see and, as Californians, endure today. Other prominent Democrat players are the two senators, Barbara Boxer (at 73), and Diane Feinstein (at 81), have held their jobs since the early 1980's.

These wealthy families, in league with other prominent wealthy families and organizations, have basically controlled California in politics throughout these decades, yet California, the world's 5th largest economy, has an estimated $2-trillion dollars in debt with the highest taxes in the country, while homelessness is extremely high and ignored – with some 8 blocks in downtown San Francisco literally being the toilet for drug users, prostitutes, the mentally challenged, and the homeless – with state government-spending out of control. Many Californians today are struggling to make ends meet, while those on top of the food chain are profiting from its demise.

Pat Brown was Governor, son Jerry was Governor (2x), Gavin Newsom now Governor, the Getty's (Paul, Gordon, Billy, William Jr., and Tessa) all interconnected over time to keep the "family business" (California) under their control. John Pelosi (Nancy Pelosi's brother-in-law) ended up marrying Belinda Barbara Newsom, William Newsom Sr.'s daughter. Between the Newsom's,

Getty's, Brown's, and the Pelosi's, they have, for generations, been playing ping-pong with positions of power, keeping it all in the family, i.e., the "You scratch my back, I scratch yours" type of situation.

Right now, as of Monday, September 30th, Democrat Governor Gavin Newsom, will likely sign a bill into law that requires all groups of electors to possibly change their names. Here is the text. This is a clear fascist move against non-Democrat political parties and affiliates. It is carefully couched as a benefit and problem-solver; it is more dangerous than that.

> **SB696, Umberg. Elections: political parties**.
> Under existing law, a group of electors may qualify for a new political party by holding a caucus or convention at which temporary party officers are elected, by designating a party name, or by filing notice with the Secretary of State that the party has organized, elected temporary officers, and has declared its intent to qualify in a primary election. Existing law prohibits the name of a new party from being so similar to the name of an existing party so as to mislead the voters or from conflicting with the name of an existing political body that has previously filed notice with the Secretary of State.
>
> This bill would prohibit the name of a party from including the phrase "no party reference" or "decline to state" or the word "independent" or a variation of that word or those phrases. The bill would require a party that is qualified on the effective date of the bill, but whose name includes a variation of the phrase "no party preference" or "decline to state" or the word "independent", to file a change of name notice with the Secretary of State by October 29, 2019. The Secretary of State would be required to disqualify, by October 30, 2019, any party that fails to so submit an appropriate change of name notice. The Secretary of State would be required to send related notices, as provided.

This bill would declare that it is to take effectively immediately as an urgency statute.

This Democrat action is nothing more than a political tool to move people into the "no party preference" category, which move could and likely would create confusion for the voters. This legislation removes Parties with the word "independent" in it; the Left can get rid of existing political parties over descriptive words, they can tell citizens in this legislation that the government can tell them what they can name their Party, and if they don't immediately comply, they will be moved into the "no party preference" category, a condition that could unlawfully and certainly unethically influence the elections by creating confusion of process. They started this in February 2019, and it is being enacted right now, just before the 2020 elections. It is a political ploy, done by those who control California politics, the Democrats. A recall petition is underway against new Democrat Governor Gavin Newsom, for reasons that include this SB696.

What will be next from the California socialist lawmakers, more direct indoctrination of the public towards re-creating California as a full-blown socialist state? It is definitely heading that direction in fact, because to those in power, it is or will be a fact done eventually.

But in September, 2019, the newly-convened Democrat-controlled House of Representatives introduced a bill to eliminate the electoral college. It seems that, since they didn't win the last presidential election under the rules that have existed for almost 250 years, they now want to change the rules. Here is why.

In their infinite wisdom, the Founders of the United States created the Electoral College to ensure all states were fairly represented. Let's be clear: the Electoral College is not a "college", it is NOT a place, it IS a PROCESS to protect Americans. The premise was and is this: Why should one or two densely-populated areas speak for the whole of the nation?

The following list of statistics has been making the rounds on the Internet. I am simply bringing it forward. It should finally put an end to the argument as to why the Electoral College makes sense. This needs to be widely known and understood.

There are 3,141 counties in the United States. Trump won 3,084 of them. Clinton won 57. There are 62 counties in New York State. Trump won 46 of them. Clinton won 16. Clinton won the "popular vote" by approximately 1.5 million votes. In the 5 counties that encompass NYC, (Bronx, Brooklyn, Manhattan, Richmond & Queens), Clinton received well over 2 million more votes than Trump. Clinton only won 4 of these counties; Trump won Richmond. Therefore, these 5 counties alone more than accounted for Clinton winning the popular vote of the entire country. The United States is comprised of 3,797,000 square miles. When you have a country that encompasses almost 4 million square miles of territory, it would be ludicrous to even suggest that the votes of those who inhabit a mere 319 square miles should dictate the outcome of a national election. Large, densely-populated Democrat cities (NYC, Chicago, Los Angeles, Detroit, San Francisco, etc., DO NOT and SHOULD NOT speak dispositively for the rest of the nation. And, it's been documented and verified that those 319 square miles are where the majority of our nation's problems foment, especially extremely high rates of felony crimes. Democrat States like California, for instance, where the crimes in its "sanctuary cities" have skyrocketed, where its regulations strangled business and the economy, where its homeless problem is unbelievably high, where its employment rate is unbelievably low, and where its population on welfare is reaching 50% and promise to go higher, is nearly accomplishing full-blown socialism. The most densely populated of its cities are Democrat-controlled; should they dominate voter outcomes despite the many Republicans in the more rural counties?

At the national level, the 2020 elections are now critical. We must not allow the Electoral College to be taken down so that a few can ruin an entire country. This fact is the very reason why Democrats, especially the alt-Left Progressives, are trying to eliminate the Electoral College system.

We patriots are at war. Regardless of political party, if you are a patriot and believe in the Bill of Rights and our Constitution, then we patriots all have common ground to unite together on to fight back this alt-Left effort to destroy our country. Right now it's just a war of propaganda. But it is packed with problems of refugee migrants, increasing violence from pro-socialist advocates, the fight against open debate, and political-gerrymandering. Will it remain so?

Americans are facing many dangers. The enemies of our ideology are not going to stop, until we stop them. Hoping they just get tired and go away is NOT going to happen. They are well-organized and well-funded. They are out there active against us. Their propaganda is working successfully; just look at what they have already convinced the millennials of, i.e., that socialism is Utopia. And too, they are attacking us violently. We have to be rational and pragmatic, but we have to push back firmly; if in doing so we hurt their feelings, we can always offer them a boat ride to somewhere else.

So, the question is: how do we organize against this madness before us?

As a simple man, I don't think it is too complicated to figure out a plan. I suggest that we can alter the future, but the conservatives of Democrat, Republican, Libertarian, or Independent Parties need to help us out; if we lose this war, we all will lose too. The wealthy will lose all their wealth, just as did wealthy people in other countries where socialism or communism prevailed, i.e., China and Chairman Mao, Russia and Stalin, Germany and Hitler, Italy and Mussolini, Cambodia and Pol Pot. Need I say more?

Local Republican, Independent, and Democrat Committees should start organizing and meeting together on these common ground matters, work out an agreeable plan, network with other Committees of the State, form networks with Committees in other states, plan public rallies at their State Capitols, plan rallies in Washington DC, create "safe zones" for all meetings and events, put pressure on their lawmakers, kick out lawmakers who are supporting socialism, elect new ones who will fight as we want them to fight in state and federal legislatures, establish a strong central media, television, internet, and radio, and get these message out to as many people as possible. Demand legislation against the social media giants and technological corporations to force them to cease censorship of conservative voices. Go door to door, and let people know we are fighting against the destruction of our country and our homes and how they can help, if only by their votes. Tell them what socialism is actually about in reality.

I recently watch a video on YouTube entitled "Milton Friedman Speaks: Is Capitalism Humane." Dr. Friedman spoke on the morality of capitalism. He concluded the question was irrelevant. According to him, it comes down to this: capitalism per se is not humane or inhumane; neither is socialism. If we compare the two in terms of results, it is clear that only capitalism fosters equality and works toward social justice. The one is based on the principle of voluntary cooperation and free exchange, the other on force of position and power. In a free economy, it is hard to do good; you either have to use your own hard-earned money to do it or work hard to persuade others to your course. But by the same token, it is difficult to do harm because, by preventing a concentration of power, capitalism prevents people from committing sustained, serious harm. Is capitalism humane or inhumane? It is neither. But it tends to give free rein to the human values of human beings. That is not how socialism works at all. (See, www.youtube.com/watch?v=27Tf8RN3uiM.) I urge you all to listen to what Milton Friedman had to say in his 45.18 minute speech to a college group. He also quoted Thoreau, *"Philanthropy is an over-rated virtue. Sincerity is also an over-rated virtue. Heaven preserve us from the sincere reformer who knows what is good for you, and by Heaven he's going to make you do it whether you like it or not."*

The essence of the Progressive movement is that they have increasingly accepted the tyrannical ideas of reduced private property rights and reduced rights to profits, and have become enamored with restrictions on personal liberty and control by the government.

We can't be lazy. But we can alter the future that we are facing right now. I recall, as the two planes crashed into the Twin Towers of the World Trade Center, what occurred in the hijacked Flight 93. Passengers were hearing on their phones what was going on, and realized their plane was likely headed for another large building target. Some realized they had to do something. We heard, on one of their phones, a determined man, say to others, "Let's roll!" as they attacked the hijackers. I'm sure they hoped to save themselves and the passengers on the plane as well as preventing it from being crashed into a populated building somewhere, but it is likely that they were too late from saving it from crashing into the rural ground. But, they gave their lives trying. What are you willing to do to save America? All it takes is to get up out of your chair, join your local political party, and grow it in numbers and financing, and network with others, and network with parties in other states, grow, grow and grow. If you are a patriot, regardless of political party, then come together as patriots first and foremost. I know patriotism by the millions exists in every American Party except the Socialist Party. Survival of America supercedes Party lines. Bear in mind that we are SHORT OF TIME to do all this.

When our soldiers, white, black, brown, and so on, are sent into combat, they fight the enemy as a team, as brothers trusting each other, giving their life for one another in the battlefield. And our soldiers, in the battlefield under fire, they don't create politically-biased strategies independent to each other. They form a team, non-partisan, a fighting force against a common enemy.

But at home, it's a different story. Divisive forces reinforce racist narratives, promoting angst towards others races, primarily against the "white people" these days, even to the point of calling for white extermination. It makes me angry that the pro-socialists are using the race card, the fascist card, and "white privilege" card to instigate hate and violence for no other reason than to achieve their socialist and Islamic agendas. "Divide and Conquer" is exactly what these people are doing, and right now they seem to having a growing influence on people of color. I hesitate to believe people of color are just not smart and are just incapable of reasonable discernment. But, they seem to be falling for the socialists' Utopian false promises.

Should we patriots ignore all this, should we remain complacent? No, we shouldn't. This socialist agenda is an act of war against Americans, if only through their propaganda and, thus far, limited violence. But we are already seeing their violence is growing. Antifa is no different than the Nazi SA Brownshirts.

Conservative and moderate patriots should put aside Party-bias and work together to win this war being fought against all of us right now. We've let it go on too long and it's only getting stronger and gaining ground with our younger people being brainwashed in our own schools by pro-socialist professors and teachers. Shut that down! We must somehow declare that our school system is ideologically-corrupted, that it has failed our own children over the last 20-30 years, and that legislation is needed to criminalize schools and teachers when they promote socialism or communism or fascism to our children. We must call for remedial education to try to roll-back the indoctrination damage that has already been done to our children, with re-education programs set forth in the public media domain that cannot be taken down by the social media platforms who have been banning conservative thought and ideas, programs that our current and past students can watch and understand the brainwashing they have received thus far.

The main thing is network with each other, call everyone, use your Party's online state political data banks and call everyone on the list that you can call. Phone bank. Create a brief narrative about the future if the socialists win, then argue why President Trump will not allow that to happen if we just vote him back in. He's already fighting against it.

There are very dark pathologies affecting and even undermining American, and we must block them and destroy them. There is a growing sickness, and there is a need for a 'healing' by the best and most effective means available.

As said by American journalist and lecturer Chris Hedges about America's condition, he said, and I think this is accurate: "*When national and political discourse is no longer rooted in verifiable facts, then facts are interchangeable with opinions. Truth is whatever you want it to be.*" Expedient lying is whatever one wants to achieve something in the most expedient way. The permanent lie is the most ominous because reality and facts don't matter. When the institutions like mainstream media, politics, the courts, ignore the verifiable facts about reality, those institutions have become corrupted, weakened, even irreparably destroyed, or replaced by systems masked by false narratives claiming to be pronouncements of truth.

While I agree with his reasoning, Hedges, however, takes issue with the "right wing" and conservative media, while completely ignoring media streams like Washington Post, New York Times, CNN, and others who seem to have lost the ability to discern truth and facts at all. One only needs to consider who owns mainstream media outlets. He is anti-Trump and seems to lay the blame for America's decline at the feet of what he describes as right-wing conservatives, i.e., the millions of people who are Republicans and constitutionalists. While he identifies many of America's problems, including on the world stage, it appears to me that he has mis-identified the culprits who have undermined Christian and social values, who are on the Left, not the Right. It mystifies me how such a scholar overlooks the radical Left's demand for socialism and an end to democratic capitalism.

PART 18: TAMING THE BEAST

I want to begin this chapter with an unpublished article I wrote June 4, 2002. It is called "The Beast Within Us: Eradicating The Osama bin Laden Syndrome.

> There is no doubt but that Americans were shocked to the core by the tragic deed orchestrated by Osama bin Laden on September 11, 2001. Osama had his own spin, that this is a holy war on immoral, capitalist people. Yet he does not explain how living in dirt holes in a dirt-poor country is any better. Nor has he explained his hypocrisy; don't his millions (to finance terrorism) come from capitalism, i.e., the family fortune, arms sales, and the opium industry?

> This was a hate crime, this act of murder, rendered by extremists whose backward existence, murderous conditioning, and fundamentalist notions of "good and evil" are so warped and twisted as to be psychopathic. Are these Islamic notions?

> We cannot, in this country, or from this country, control ideas and opinions, or muzzle religious beliefs of others. But we can, and must, inhibit, restrain and prevent radicalism or extremism in any form from being carried forth into deed that deprives others of lie, liberty, and the pursuit of happiness.

> That said, I was not one of those shocked by the attack of September 11th. I asked myself why that was so. First off, it doesn't take a rocket scientist to figure out that this act, or an act like it, was a certain eventuality. This is a violent planet, always has been. Second, I was not shocked because

this was an act from the beast that lurks to some degree in far too many people all over the world. For Osama bin Laden, he just had the money and followers to carry out the hatred manifested from his own beast. Perhaps we can even name it now: the Osama bin Laden Syndrome.

This is the beast of unreasonable hatred. This is not to say that this beast manifests in the same way or to the same degree as the events of September 11th. It is simply that ugly force that manifests by an unreasonable hatred towards any race, nationality, or class of people that is different from another. It is the beast of unreasonable hatred of ideas that may be different from one's own, the force that results in book-burning, ostracizing, and violence.

The beast within is no stranger in this country. Unreasonable hatreds have been the cornerstone of American life, from the conquests of European pilgrims, explorers, settlers, immigrants, and colonialists as they conquered and settled the new continent called America. The beast was there in the era of indentured servants, of slavery, later in KKK rallies and lynchings, and civil war. It is there in the way gang fight against other gangs or act against anyone not of their gang. The beast is alive and well in our ongoing racist and separatist attitudes, with many people who falsely accuse others of racism when that is how they themselves are acting. The beast infects all strata of society. It lives in the dark places of our prejudices and biases, impairing our sense of understanding, acceptance, and compassion for the misfortunes of others, and in the differences of race, class, or social standing or stigma, and in religion itself. As a species, we seem to have hundreds of types of prejudices that at times manifest in unreasonable hatreds. By these prejudices and hatreds we declare others worthless; this is a method of dehumanization.

I often have wondered how such haters, from any walk of life, can live with themselves so full of hatred. Yes, there are things that are unacceptable in a civilized world, and even the morally sound amongst us must confront evil forces. But confrontation of evil must be by the highest moral indignation and standards if only to show others that evil can be effectively confronted without becoming evil too.

Whatever bin Laden did, his motives are important only to the degree that we learn from them so that we can more effectively face others of his ilk.

But what we must learn is this: we must recognize that centuries of 'civilization' have not eradicated the beast within, and that we must confront that dark force inside of us, eradicate it, control it, dismiss it, emasculate its power, in other words, to do what is necessary to prevent it from rising and ruining our lives and our character. We must learn how to fight evil from the "high ground" of moral standards and commitment to true justice.

The ability to hate seems to be an intrinsic part of human nature, but it is often our weakness, and not always a source of strength. It can be invoked in just about anyone under the right circumstances, but lives within most of us to some degree under ordinary circumstances. It is our internal yin/yang. Recognition of it acts as an illumination of the dark place in which it lurks and breeds. It cannot survive in the sunlight of illumination nor against the power of compassion for the less fortunate nor against the wisdom of reasoned tolerance.

We need to return to or embrace a better objective and learn how to extend a helping hand to the fallen and disenfranchised to help return them to the family fold, not as a permanent "hand out" of free stuff, but as a "hands up" so that they may achieve self-determination on their own merit. If we continue to provide the fish and bread those in need will never learn to fish or bake for themselves.

So here it is, some 17 years later, and I find that the beast within seems to have grown by leaps and bounds, among the world populations at large, and within America's own citizens. We are nearly at the place where Americans were, many years ago, when the Civil War began, where neighbors and brothers fought each other and so very many died in a needless war. Only this time, a civil war will not be a skirmish between the long-established ideology and the demand for a historic-failure called socialism; rather, it will become an invasion by enemies from outside or now hiding within, while we are fighting each other, and none of us will get what we want as America itself is destroyed.

What most people do not seem to understand is that this is all a manipulation by forces against the United States, and those Progressives who push for socialism are too brainwashed to realize that manipulation and that are puppets.

What America faces today and ahead is the conversion of our merit-based capitalist democracy into a free-stuff, hands-out gimme-gimme illegal migrant population, socialist government while the puppeteers continue the conversion of our nation into an oppressive totalitarian ideology they call the New World Order. Totalitarianism is hardly something new, and labeling it as such doesn't change it into a Utopian world.

Chapter II:

The Globalist Agenda and the Aristocracy

After the World War I and World War II, history shows a world in chaos that resulted in many millions of people, soldiers and civilians, killed off in various countries. Since then, we saw the horrors of the Korean War, the Vietnam War (characterized as a "police action" and not a war), The Iraqi War, and the "wars" still ongoing in North African Arab countries. Not all of the campaigns of horror involve the United States. North Korea's treatment of its own citizens is and has been a daily horror show for many of its citizens. Somali and countries next to it suffer from the genocidal atrocities of the Boko Haram group. The Phillippines suffer from its growing hardline Muslim invasion and indoctrination. The list is long. It seems the governments of the world learned little from the results of war. What many of us believe, here in the United States, is that "war" has become nothing more than "Big Business" where the "War Machine" can only be profitably sustained by having some kind of war going on throughout the world. What we do know, also, is that the multinational banks bankroll all sides of these wars, nonetheless ensuring that certain countries are favored over others.

Yet, other than the profits of war-mongering the banks and "war machine" corporations make, there are other factors at play. For many years there have been those powerful entities who have tried to manipulate all countries, particularly those holding the deciding power, to join together to create a one-government world. This agenda is under the auspices of uniting the world into a single Utopian world where peace and harmony rules. Yet, there is the sinister element at play as well: how to control the people and the Earth's population. So let's take a look at these entities and understand the roles they play as the secret "shadow government." We'll begin with those we call the aristocracy or the elitists or the "nobility."

PART 1: THE ARISTOCRACY: A HISTORIC LOOK

Aryan is "A ry an" meaning Aristocracy, and those who come from sun and their "blue blood" and all their "right to rule" aristocracy. The adoption of the Nazis of the word "Aryan" as the highest race comes from the belief in the aristocracy's right to rule over all lesser people. The aristocracy considers themselves "nobility." They always were, and still some today, believers and practitioners of Satanism, and other dark mystical practices, including blood sacrifices, and even using children for blood sacrifices.

Historically, the parasitic aristocracy often claimed "first rights" to females, even requiring that a woman on her wedding night had to sleep with an aristocrat. Over the centuries the aristocracy lived at the highest level of luxury, taking from the "lower class" their work, the food they produced, often leaving the people with little to eat and starving to death. An aristocrat could choose a child from the family; if the family resisted, they simply killed the entire family and still took the child they wanted. Aristocrat men used their authority to have sex with whomever they wanted, often getting the women pregnant and spreading their eugenics all over.

Just as the "pharaohs" never disappeared entirely (though bloodlines), neither has the aristocracy disappeared either. The word "aristocracy" means those who come from the sun. Over the centuries they have always been protected, generally, by whatever "government" existed at the times, including their police, whether by czars, kings, queens, noblemen, because they had the power to do so. There were some notable exceptions.

The Marquis de Sade, the torturer (1700s to1800's) is where the word "sadism" begins, since the Marquis was very fond of all kinds of torture.

Eventually, Napoleon Bonapart locked him in prison for 10 years after his arrest in 1801. He died in 1814.

England's Prince Charles disclosed publicly in 2011 that he was a descendent of the Prince of Alakia (sp), i.e., Vlad Dracula, the Impaler of Transylvania (1431-1476). His favorite pastime was torture and impaling. Impaling victims was forcing a round stake through the anus up and out of the mouth and then staked vertically into the ground. The 8-pointed star Vlad wore on his crown (octagon) represented "nobility." He is known to have impaled more than 100,000 people, mostly Saxons. Even the Ottomans Muslim Army turned around and went back when they came to a forest of some 20,000 impaled bodies.

From 1730 to 1801 there was the Russian nobility under the czar with Darian Nicoli Leyevna Zhaltikova (sp). A "noble-woman", she tortured and murdered at least 200 people.

From 1560 to 1614, the Countess Esti Beit Baettori of the Hungarian "nobility" was called the "Blood Court Countess" tortured and murdered some 650 virgins from the local community because she believed that bathing in the blood of the virgins would keep her young forever. She and her fellow aristocrats even constructed an ingenious metal structure at which the victims could bleed to death while still alive and tortured sadistically on the way to their death. Ex-president Osarrah (sp) (Coozi of France?) comes from the Hungarian aristrocracy and the family line of Baettori, as the pharaoh part of his name means "king." The Countess was imprisoned in her own castle after an uprising of 650 families who suffered losses from their families to the Blood Countess. Note that it took 650 deaths before the people rose up against the Countess.

Baron Zeudina was an aristocrat, Franc serial killer, who lived from 1404 to 1440, who sodomized, tortured and murdered at least 600 boys and girls from the ages of 6 to 18, together with his accomplices Watu and Oenya. He used to laugh watching his victims dying, as he opened up their stomachs admiring their intestines, which he was fascinated with. His gold seal carried a Knights Templar cross, the same one as on the Swiss Army Knife we see today.

These examples are just the tip of the iceberg of horrors committed by the "nobility" over the centuries. And, as we'll see, with the example of Illuminati rituals, the arrest of Harvey Weinstein and the sexual predation that continues to this day, also by those who consider themselves the aristocracy. Over the centuries, only the so-called nobility could read or write, but not those beneath them, so there was no way of keeping a historic track of these abuses by the "ruling class" except by stories/legends passed down through the ages.

The two parasitic evils, the aristocracy and the Ecclesiastical Order of the Priests of Amun, who continue to exist here in modern times, have never worked and always lived on the blood of others, in some cases, literally. Over the centuries these parasites grew fat, never hungered, threw great parties with music and troubadours, and reproducing like rabbits between the parties. All descendants wanted to be king or queen and have the castles.

At times, wars broke out between them as their vied for these fortunes and powers. Of course, the people (the "peasants") had to fight and die for the nobility. Eventually, the aristocrats finally came together to elect a King. But the uprisings by the people continued due to the same "policies" of ignoring the slave-like conditions their existence imposed. Eventually, the aristocrats decided to go "underground" in Freemason lodges divided in 33-degrees to indicate the degree of "pharaonic" genes of the noble bloodline in their veins.

Prince Bernhard of the Netherlands was a Dutch prince who was the consort of Queen Juliana of the Netherlands. He belonged to the princely House of Lippe. He held the title of Count of Biesterfeld, and his aristocrat uncle raised him to princely rank with the Style of Serene Highness in 1916. He became the Prince of the Netherlands after he married Princess Juliana of the Netherlands, and was thereafter given the "rank" of Royal Highness. He was one of three key figures who created the Bilderberg Group; the other two were Joseph Retinger and Sir Colin Gubbing.

Joseph Retinger (1888-1960) was a Polish diplomat, international political adviser and activist, and writer. He was a Freemason, and after the World War II, his actions to co-found the European Movement (a lobbying association that coordinated the efforts of associations and national councils with the goal of promoting European integration, and dissemination about it) lead to the establishment of the European Union. He was instrumental in the formation of the Bilderberg Group.

Sir Collin V. Gubbins (1896-1976) had been a Major-General in the Second World War, of British aristocracy. He had served in the First World War, commissioned into the Royal Field Artillery in 1914. After he retired, he was invited by Prince Bernhard to join the Bilderberg Group.

The Bilderberg meeting is an annual conference established in 1954 to foster dialogue between Europe and North America. The group's agenda, originally to prevent another world war, is now defined as bolstering a consensus around free market Western capitalism and its interests around the globe. Participants include political leaders, experts from industry, finance, academia, and the media, numbering between 120 and 150.

The group's original goal of promoting Atlanticism, of strengthening U.S.– European relations and preventing another world war has grown; according to Andrew Kakabadse the Bilderberg Group's theme is to "bolster a consensus around free market Western capitalism and its interests around the globe".[1] In 2001, Denis Healey, a Bilderberg group founder and a steering committee member for 30 years, said, "To say we were striving for a one-world government is exaggerated, but not wholly unfair. Those of us in Bilderberg felt we couldn't go on forever fighting one another for nothing and killing people and rendering millions homeless. So we felt that a single community throughout the world would be a good thing."

In the Bilderberg Group are people in the aristocracy who believe in their pure strand of pharaonic blood even over the usual 33-degrees of pharaonic genetics, i.e., like alcohol has a certain percentage of alcohol. They believe that a one-government world run by the aristocracy would create a single, peaceful community throughout the world. Hence, the New World Order.

There are many of these "pharaonic bloodlines" among us today, all looking to get into positions of ease where they can live like nobility. So, the pharaohs of the past have never really gone away, they just evolved into an ongoing aristocracy that continues to prey upon the common people today. The "nobility" today exists and many 'rule' as politicians and elected officials, in some cases, and this is precisely why the Deep State/Illuminati/Bilderbergs have admitted that few candidates ever get elected to high office without their "permission" and support. Even the "Skull and Bones" of Yale University is a gateway where such candidates are screened and indoctrinated for future positions. Although the Freemasons publicly claim they do not, as an organization, involve themselves into politics, throughout this organization are those already indoctrinated.

Across the centuries of recorded history, there has been no greater enemy of open competition than collusive, wealth-centered aristocracy because there are more and more of them who have descended from the pharaonic bloodline who want to do nothing except live in the plushness of aristocratic lifestyle. There is a pendant for women claiming "nobility" called the Fleur de Lis" or the "Lotus of the Nile", which is a symbol of the Pharaohs.

What we have is not just the "nobility" populating the Legislative and Executive political positions, perhaps even the Judicial system as well, but particularly in the shadowy branch now becoming known as the Fourth Branch of government, the so-called bureaucratic Administrative Branch, who carry out the various controls by rules and regulations over the everyday lives of the citizenry. We don't really know of their bloodline because they don't advertise it, except perhaps amongst themselves.

I admit I have been unable to find credible lists of this "pharaonic" bloodline but one can reasonably conclude their involvement in national and world politics in various Western countries.

When the government's boot is on your throat, whether it is a Left boot or a Right boot, it is still a boot, and it generally manifests as the government's hand in your pocketbook, in the same way that the "nobility" of old "taxed" the locals by taking most of the food they produced on their farms to feed the "fat cats" who controlled them.

The place known as Octagon Switzerland is a "base" where current "pharaonic" bloodlines congregate. Part of their icon array includes the 666 mark of the Beast. The pharaonic bloodline of the global elite all send their children to the Octagonic school.

What is important to understand about the history of the "nobility" are the horrors and cruelties they always imposed upon the peoples of the world. Differentiating this from other genocidal campaigns is Hitler's treatment of dissenters and Jews, Stalin's campaign of genocide by direct murder and indirect starvation of millions of his own countrymen. and Mao Zedong's communist reign that also killed millions of Chinese. Neither Hitler, Stalin or Zedong were aristocrats or from any special class, but they rose to power, took on the role of aristocrats, and murdered people once they got there.

But throughout recorded history, we do see in Europe how the aristocracy always exploited, oppressed and murdered the "commoners" for any reason or purpose such actions might have served the aristocracy.

The current attack on Christians around the world, primarily done by the haters of Christians by the Muslims, is not fought against by the world governments precisely because their leaders are innately descendants of the pharaonic bloodlines who are occultists and Satanists, who all are anti-Christian. Do they believe in God? Yes, they do, because they believe in Satan. The anti-Christian genocide currently occurring by Muslims is playing into the plan of the "Nobility" itself. Razing the planet of Christians is what they want, so they let the Muslims do the job for them. Will the Muslims take over the world? No. Once the Christians are done, the Muslims will be next, if the "Nobility" has their way.

Another consideration is America's War of Independence. Our ancestors and Founders fought against the British aristocracy, and won. But only for a short time. Over time, the descendants of the European aristocracy infiltrated the new government, and played the Republicans against the Democrats, thus instigating the Civil War over ideology and status, creating a hardline divisiveness first between the North and the South, and following that, between the Republicans against the Democrats, which exists to this day. The New World Order playbook is just another chapter, with this current pro-socialist movement orchestrated quietly in our schools since the 1960's and strengthened since then. Achieving a change from capitalism to socialism is not an end-all, it is just the next step towards the totalitarianism envisioned by the globalist elites under the rubric of a utopian New World Order. This is all a plot by the descendants of pharaonic aristocracy which has been protected over centuries.

Who are these people? Can they be identified? Those are good questions. Some we know, like the Rothschilds, Warburgs, those in the Bilderberg group, Rockefellers, but a complete pharaonic bloodline chart is likely only to be found within this demonic league itself, and they are unlikely to disclose it anytime soon.

What we should recognize is that the people of this planet have been victimized from one generation to another, for hundreds of years, by the pharaonic aristocracy of Satanists and occultists, and they play behind the scenes. In America, their efforts have resulted in the most insidious form of government called the Fourth Branch of government, the administrative bureaucracy which through rules and regulations, licenses, permits, fines and penalties, rule our everyday lives and take money from our pockets. America began as a small government to be controlled by the people, but has become a hugely intrusive government which pretty much controls the people and is unaccountable to any other branch of government.

Interestingly, who have we seen here recently who wanted to be queen or king, even under another title, i.e., "President", if not Hillary Clinton (demanding "It's my turn!", and Barack Obama, even John McCain).

PART 2: THE HOUSE OF THE ILLUMINATI

I would like to note from the outset that the existence of the Illuminati today is controversial. One article online I found was by a Phil Edwards who claimed that he consulted a variety of experts who say that the ongoing discussion about the Illuminati and belief that it exists is absurd on its face. My research tells me different, and I do not agree with Edwards or his alleged "experts." Secret societies like deniability, because they work better in the dark.

The Illuminati are a supposed secret order that governs the world since the time of the Enlightenment. If you don't know what the Enlightenment Period is, here it is. The Enlightenment Period is also referred to as the Age of Reason and the "long 18th century." It stretched from 1685 to 1815. The period is characterized by thinkers and philosophers throughout Europe and the United States that believed that humanity could be changed and improved through science and reason. Thinkers looked back to the Classical period, and forward to the future, to try and create a trajectory for Europe and America during the 18th century. It was a volatile time marked by art, scientific discoveries, reformation, essays, and poetry. It began with the America War for Independence and ended with a bang when the French Revolution shook the world, causing many to question whether ideas of egalitarianism and pure reason were at all safe or beneficial to society. Opposing schools of thought, new doctrines and scientific theories, and a belief in the good of humankind would eventually give way to the Romantic Period in the 19th century. The Enlightenment expired as the victim of its own excesses. The Enlightenment was so focused on abstract reason and stoicism, above all other virtues, that some people grew tired of it and began to seek its opposite: emotion, sensationalism, and the softening of every moral value such as what we had in the "Roarin' Twenties".

The one enduring philosophical thread that remained was the idea that the human race was, as a whole, moving forward. The idea of progress. These beliefs and factors combined with the scientific leaps made during the Enlightenment would drive the world forward toward the Industrial Period and, to the philosophical, artistic, and literary period known as the Romantic Era. Out of this conflict of thought came new organizations, such as the Illuminati, which also toyed with the occult and powers that lay therein. It is believed that the Illuminati, which tries to remain secret, still engages in the "black arts" of occultism, and there is testimony by insiders to that effect. It is claimed that the Illuminati was originally a branch of Freemasons that started off in 1776, and its influence has been attributed to historical events such as the defeat of Napoleon, the assassination of John Kennedy or, in modern times, the triumph of Barack Obama in the presidential elections.

More recently, I have learned that the Illuminati is a part of the Deep State in both national and transnational affairs. They want a one-government world.

The beginning of the Illuminati had little influence and few members. However, as it grew, and changed leaders, there was an attempt to shift the pro-monarchy catholic movement into a more scientific and secular movement. Since the knowledge of this group would have adverse consequences, the leader of the group gave the other members and himself nicknames and shrouded the group with symbols and rituals. In the 19ᵗʰ century, the Illuminati joined forces with the Freemasons in order to expand its membership. The early group got shut down by the Bavarian government which banned all secret societies, but subsequently, the Illuminati was resurrected. As it grew to even greater numbers and influence, they became involved in world affairs and are alleged to have infiltrated governments by masterminding events and planting agents in governments and corporations in order to gain political power and influence and to establish a New World Order. Central to some of the most widely known and elaborate conspiracy theories, the Illuminati have been depicted as lurking in the shadows and pulling the levers of power to achieve their goals.

Perhaps I should have begun this essay with the introduction of the elusive Illuminati organization that many people have dismissed as "conspiracy theory" nuts. Yet, it is funny that even Wikipedia, which I generally respect, gives a history but concludes with a discussion of its demise many years ago. Illuminati is an organization that is so secretive there is no documented track record of who they are and what they do. But that it doesn't exist is simply not true. So let's take a look at the Illuminati. I have done considerable research on this, and there are at least three article by David J. Smith which I'll reference in this section of my essay.

THE HOUSE OF THE ILLUMINATI:
13 BLOODLINES OF THE ILLUMINATI
- THE ROTHCHILDS –
Article by David J. Smith

The Rothschilds are one of the most well-known of the thirteen Illuminati families. There are several bloodlines derived from occultist rituals, the most powerful being the Springs, (original name was the Springsteins when they came to America in the mid-1700s and settled in NY and NJ). They later changed their name to Springs to hide their identity. Leroy Springs was later hired by a L.C. Payseur, one of the most secret and most powerful families in North America at the time, so powerful they could hide their wealth and power, and use other Satanic families as proxies. The Payseurs are part of the 13 top Illuminati families. For more information, see Smith's book, "Be Wise As Serpents".

Some of the men who worked for the Paysuers, according to Smith, were Andrew Carnegie, J.P. Morgan, the Vanderbilts, Giftord Pinnchot, and John D. Rockefeller. These men were selected to run Payseur companies because they belonged to the satanic elite.

I mention this history because the power that came to be under the control of the Illuminati was globally immense. As Smith said, "*If one looked on the backstage of history, he would find the House of Rothschild. They have indebted Kings, manipulated kingdoms, created wars and molded the very shape of the international world. Among the hierarchy of the Illuminati they are revered as a powerful satanic bloodline. They are "living legends.""*

If you read Smith's articles, which you can read without cost at the link below in References, you'll find the history of the origins and events of the Illuminati fascinating. Make no mistake, it exists today by numerous parts of the original bloodlines.

I did locate a "New World Order Organizational Chart" although I could not find who was the creator/author of it. There are numerous pictures depicting it, easily found by typing in Illuminati Pyramid.

It is a pyramidic structure, which seems interesting in itself because the pharaonic aristocracy bloodline passed down through the ages came originally from Egypt's pharaohs. The Illuminating "Royal" bloodlines are: Rothschild, Astor, Bundy, Collins, DuPont, Freeman, Kennedy, Li, Onassi, Rockefeller, Disney, Russell, Van Duyn, Merovinglan, Reynolds. The chart lists as Foundation nations of the New World Order in America, England, Israel, Australia, and China as:

Financial Groups:
>IMF, World Bank, Central Banks, Federal Reserve, Bank of International Settlement.

Research Institutions:
>Institute For Policy Studies, Stanford Research Institute, Brookings Institute, Tavislock Institute, Committee of 300, Aspen Institute, Jason Society.

Secret Societies:
>P2/Opus Dei, Rosicrucians, Freemasonry, Skull & Bones, Bohemian Club, The Knights of Malta.

Political:
>Council on Foreign Relations, Trilateral Colmmission, Governmental Leaders, U.S. Supreme Court & Electoral College, NATO, EU, EEC, United Nations, Bilderbergs, Club of Rome.

Intelligence:
>MI-5, CIA, INSA/FBI, Interpol, Drug Cartels, Homeland Security, Military Intelligence.

Religious:
>UNESCO, Lucis Trust, World Union, World Goodwill, Esalen Instiitute, Planetary Congress, Media Establishment, World Federalist Assc., World Constitution Association.

Corporations, Multinationals and Banking Supporting the NWO:
>Bechtel, Carlyle Group, TRW, Raytheon, Rand, Walmart, Texas Utilities-Atlantic Richfield-Arco, Exxon-Esso-Mobil, Texaco, Shell Oil, Tenneco,Corning, Dow Jones, MBNA Citigroup, Chase Manhattan, Bank America, Bankers Trust, Glaxo-Smith-Kline, Archer Daniels Midland, Chemical Banking, Schering Plough, Goldman Sachs, American Express, AT&T, Phillip Morris, Boeing, Amtrak, Northwest Airlines, American Airlines, Ford Motors, Chrysler, General Motors, John Deere, Nabisco, Coca Cola, Pepsi Co, Anheuser Busch, McDonalds, Burger King, Etna (Phillip Morris/Kraft), Blackstone Group, Chevron-Texaco (Caltex), Motorola, Dell, Levi Strauss, Motorola, Johnson & Johnson,

Bristol Myers, Squibb, Eli Lily, Pfizer, Kissinger Assoc., Amway, Monsanto/Solutia, Dow Chemical, News Corp Limited Inc., Time-Warner/AOL, Disney, CBS, NBC, ABC, PBS AP, CNN, Reuters, Washington Times, Children's TV Workshop, U.S. News & W.R., New York Times, Time, Inc., Newsweek, Washington Post, Wall Street Journal.

All of these folks, groups, organizations, banks, et al, support the "internationalism", as Richard Nixon termed it (meaning the New World Order), as, for them, "good for business." The aristocracy would rule, the banks and corporations would be expanded, and the common folks would bear the burden, the vice, all that which flows downhill from the "nobility" in total charge of the world. But, despite the fact that the NWO has not yet been achieved does not mean that it lacks influence on the planet itself, because the supporters and designers do use their influence to control the world to the extent possible. As I talk about here, the Bilderberg Group meets once a year as undisclosed locations that change every year, to review their planning, progress, and outcomes on what occurs around the globe.

I do not purport, as the author here, to claim all of my information is without some error, but I try to base my findings on as many legitimate sources as I can, under the belief that "where there's smoke, there must be fire." One such source is author/journalist Fritz Springeier (1995) who wrote the book "Bloodlines of Illuminati", a 292-page volume chock full of details about the modern Illuminati as well as its history. Note, this comes from the CIA's library.

(See, download at https://www.cia.gov/library/abbottabad-compound/FC/FC2F5371043C48FDD95AEDE7B8A49624_Springmeier.-.Bloodlines.of.the.Illuminati.R.pdf)

In his Introduction, Springmeier writes he is not a conspiracy theorist, and says about the Illuminati, "*I do not fear the Illuminati taking over this country and doing away with the Constitution, because they took over this country long ago, and the Constitution has not technically been in effect due to Presidential emergency decrees since W.W. II. … Don't think for a moment you are going to vote the Illuminati out of office. They control the major and minor political parties. They control the process of government, they control the process of information flow, they control the process of creating money and family, they control Christendom."* He adds, *"However, God controls the hearts of His people."*

Springmeier describes the Illuminati as *"generational Satanic bloodlines which have gained the most power."* The Illuminati is "Satan's elite." He characterizes his intent to expose the Illuminati as the head of *"the secret occult oligarchies which rule the world"* and urges the reader to investigate for yourself.

As I too have noted here from other research, Springmeier talks about the history of the dark forces of Satan who still exist and who greatly affect the world, noting that God Himself told us that the whole world lies in the power of the wicked one. Springmeier writes: *"Long ago in the dark unwritten pages of human history, powerful kings discovered how they could control other men by torture, magical practices, wars, politics, religion and interest taking. These elite families designed strategies and tactics to perpetuate their occult practices. Layers upon layers of secrecy have hidden these families from the profane masses, but many an author has touched upon their existence."* He says that in mockery and imitation of God's 12 tribes, Satan "blessed" 12 bloodlines: Ishmaeli, Egyptian/Celtic/Druidic, Canaanites/Astarte/Astorga,Ashdor, and then Astor. Another was the tribe of Dan later used as a Judas Iscariot type seed, subsequently descending through history as a powerful Satanic bloodline. Another bloodline (13th) was considered the direct seed of Satan (both Christ's blood and Lucifer's blood). Another bloodline goes back to Babylon and are descendent from Nimrod. In short, these bloodlines were shepherded and protected down through history to today as generational Satanic bloodlines of the Illuminati. The Illuminati has 13 bloodlines, but they include the Mellons, Carnegies, Rothschilds, Rockefellers, Dukes, Astors, Reynoldses, Stilimans, Bakers, Pynes, Cuilmans, Watsons, Tukes, Kleinworts, DuPonts, Warburgs, Phippes, Graces, Guggenheims, Milners, Drexels, Winthrops, Vanderbilts, Whitneys, Harknesses, and other super-rich Illuminated families who generally get along quite well with Communists.

Springmeier posits that "there is a delusion that Communists are the enemies of all Capitalists. But the Communists, like the super-rich families, are not the enemies of monopoly capitalism, they are the foes of free enterprise (i.e., American-style).

Of the Illuminati bloodlines, Springmeier actually identifies 17 Illuminati bloodlines, and writes separate chapters, and I will not infringe upon the details, which you can easily find by downloading his book; it's free. Here are the families he identifies and discusses:

1. The Astor bloodline.
2. The Bundy bloodline.
3. The Collins bloodline.
4. The DuPont bloodline.
5. The Freeman bloodline.
6. The Kennedy bloodline.
7. The Li bloodline.
8. The Onassis bloodline.
9. The Rockefeller bloodline.
10. The Rothschild bloodline.
11. The Russell bloodline.
12. The Van Duyn bloodline.
13. The Merovingian bloodline.
14. The Disney bloodline.
15. The Reynolds bloodline.
16. The McDonald bloodline.
17. The Krupps bloodline.

All of these bloodlines are extremely wealthy, have immense influence and power, and are all connected to and members of the Illuminati and some of the secret societies therein. The common thread seems to be their allegiance to occultism, or Satanism, or mysticism, and all of this. Family members have been in big business, world affairs, international and American politics and organizations, and have been in positions of significant influence and control to politicians and some of our Presidents. Springmeier's account of all these spans 292 pages, at times a bit tedious, but definitely informative.

PART 3: ROTHSCHILD INFLUENCE IN AMERICA

According to David J. Smith:

> This subject is so massive that it will only be touched on. In 1837 August Belmont came to the U.S., during the Panic of 1837. August Belmont appears to have been a Rothschild proxy. Belmont bought up government bonds in this Panic and his success eventually led him to the White House where he became the "financial advisor to the President of the United States". His policies helped pit the North against the South for the Civil War. Judah P. Benjamin, who according to A. Ralph Epperson was the Civil War campaign strategist for the House of Rothschild held many key positions in the Confederacy. He was apparently connected to John Wilkes Booth. J.P. Morgan has been called a Rothschild agent. His father was one of the many elite who made their fortunes by shipping supplies past the North's blockade and into the Confederacy. J.P. was a major supporter of an American central bank (Interestingly enough, he is reported to be related to Alexander Hamilton). In 1869, J.P. Morgan went to the House of England and formed Northern Securities as an agent for New Court in the U.S. Then, in 1907 J.P. Morgan shuttled back and forth between London and Paris, presumably getting orders from the Rothschilds. He returned to America and instigated the Panic of 1907, which led to the need" for a central bank. Another man who appears to be connected to the Rothschilds was Thomas House, who also made his fortune slipping supplies past the North and into the South. His son, Colonel Edward M. House was one of the main Illuminati figures to control America during the early 20th Century.

Smith talks about other players, such as J.P. Morgan, the railroad tycoon, a member of the Illuminati house, and how in 1907 Morgan started a rumor that the Knickerbocker Bank in New York was insolvent. That rumor started a run on the bank, and then on other banks, thus bringing about the Panic of 1907. He brought in Harold Stanley, creating Morgan, Stanley, and Co. Harold Stanley was a member of the infamous "Skull and Bones" that apparently is connected with the S&K "club" at Yale. Morgan killed off rival banks, and consolidated the pre-eminence of the banks within the Morgan banking orbit. Out of this grew the idea of a "central bank" from which we now have as the "Federal Reserve," an Illuminati bank still operating.[FN3.]

Smith also talks about WWII's outcome:

> World War II facilitated the American acceptance of a global 'peacekeeping" institution - the United Nations. After the U.S. had rejected the first attempt to create such an institution in the League of Nations, the Illuminati decided to create an arm of the Rothschild funded Round Table groups which could help influence western society towards the embracement of Globalism. The original idea was to create an international special interest group of advisors that would promote a New World Order, called the Institute on International Affairs. The plan eventually changed; the Institute was split up so that separate groups could influence separate governments without having the appearance of a conspiracy. These groups were formed at what are called the Hotel Majestic meetings. The Rothschild network had significant influence in the creation of the foreign relation groups. This influence continues today. The Rothschild's power within the secret "Society of the Elect" and the Round Table Groups extended to the semi-public CFR, RIIA, etc. The House of Rothschild was up in arms with their fellow elites; managing the creation of the New World Order.

[FN3.] George W. Bush was and is "Skull and Bones," even gave the sign on live TV once (crossed arms, 332 sign, and head bow). In fact, insofar as former President George H.W. Bush spoke out on public television that he wanted us to embrace the idea of America becoming a part of a "New World Order", it is likely that he too was of "Skull and Bones" and thereby a member of the Illuminati. The Skull and Bones fraternity at Yale is a recruiting ground for future members. More on the "Skull and Bones" upcoming. President Nixon spoke approvingly of "internationalism" to avoid using the name New World Order which was evolving some negative implications.

There is a Part 3 of this Smith report, that investigates individual Rothschilds from the world war era up into the modern-day world, and their continuing involvement in the Illuminati. See, (http://www.lovethetruth.com/books/ 13_bloodlines/rothschild_02.htm), from which you'll find the 3 books by David J. Smith.

Suffice it to say here that this "secret" society is not altogether secret, and there have been detractors who were once members who have spoken out about modern day Illuminati, including a former wife of one of the members who did several interviews on video, which I downloaded and watched.

Let's talk some more about the Illuminati which are represented in the Bilderberg group, but who is higher in power than the Bilderbergs, the Bilderberg group being a world planning group.

I learned through Lindsey Williams the reason. For you who do not know Lindsey Williams nor have watched his videos or read his books, he was a pastor for twelve (12) years before the Alaskan Pipeline project began in 1975. Construction began with the first pipe laid on March 27, 1975, and was completed May 31, 1977. But pre-construction set-up and preparation began in 1967 by Atlantic-Richfield Oil when it began a survey for oil in Pruhdoe Bay. A discovery well was hit in March 1968, and others hit later. Too slow to ship or truck, they began to focus on creating a pipeline. Transporting oil by tanker ship proved too risky in ice-berg laden and violent sea storms. Obviously, a shipwreck filled with oil would have been an ecological disaster back then too.

With full-time teams now in the area planning the pipeline and clearing the path, Lindsey Williams became the pastor of the labor crews there for the next three years. During that time, management observed how he helped keep peace and order with the crews. They subsequently inducted him into the level of management as advisor and the advocate for the crews, which proved successful for everyone. A great part of the pipeline crew lived on the pipeline as it was being built, far from their families and homes. Thirty-one pipeline camps were built for 28,000 workers, but due to the high turnover, over 70,000 people actually worked on the pipeline. As you might imagine, weather conditions could make working conditions horrible.

Williams began to be invited into the top boardrooms, and soon learned that the men at the very top of the pipeline project were directly connected to the top funders, the bankers of the Illuminati and, on occasion, he actually met some of them from the very top. Two of them became his close friends, and often told him things that were occurring, often reminding him to keep it to himself. Lindsey Williams said that he directly heard things going on, and also got information from those two members that he could barely believe. He heard them talk about controlling the nations and people, and manipulating currency.

Lindsey remained for 3 years until the pipeline was completed, and afterwards he kept in touch with the two friends he had made, and who continued to tell him things that were going on. Pastor Williams began to write books about things he knew, and after the second friend died he began to tell things and gave their names. His second friend died recently.

Before he died, this is what he conveyed to Pastor Williams. First, the elitist said that their person for President (Hillary Clinton) was already determined, that Trump had no chance whatsoever of winning, and then mentioned that Soros's company builds the voting machines.

Initially, the elites were bound and determined to bring President Trump down, one way or the other, and even Soros, in public media, said that Trump would be stopped by 2020, or sooner. He had interrupted their plans against America to crash the economy, which would result in food shortages, civil unrest, civil war, martial law, and UN intervention and control. After all that, the New World Order.

After Trump actually won, Lindsey's Illuminati friend called him, saying first two words, "God intervened." Lindsey said the elitists do believe in the existence of God, although they are occultists and view the spiritual world far differently. Pastor Williams's friend said, "they" said "God intervened." He said the "New World Order" was set-back about 20-25 years and was going to have to create a new agenda.

After Trump's announcement about job growth and opening our own oil deposits, the Illuminati suspended their agenda to crash the economy.

Pastor Williams's friend told him clearly that their president (Hillary Clinton), when she gets elected, that within 4-5 months we would have a major financial crisis, because they wanted to bring in the "new world order" in a massive way. (The meaning of the "new world order" does not only talk about a one-government world, NWO's Illuminati meaning is more occult than that, as I will explain later.) They decided to wait and profit from Trump's renewal of America's oil industry. The outlier of this is not just financial, of course, but the "cycle" these occultists believe in that required a suspension of their immediate push to destroy the USA.

His friend told him, "Chaplain, we know we cannot have a financial crash under Donald Trump because we have too much to lose. Donald Trump would not initiate a quantitative easing[FN4.] as George Bush did and as a result, we don't dare have a financial crash under Donald Trump."

Back to the oil issue. My research has revealed that Obama had shut down oil exploration offshore and north, further damaging the oil industry in the U.S. and keeping us relying on Saudi oil, thus continuing to enrich his "Muslim brothers" as he once referred to them.

An option of using the increasing oil from Venezuela hit a snag when it began to collapse, also orchestrated, which is another story of elitist involvement to keep the U.S. from obtaining cheaper oil elsewhere. Oil prices continued to rise, and in many states, if not most, a gallon of gas, for a while, was around $5.00, whereas now it fluctuates between slightly under and a little over $4.00 per gallon. (On this, I admit there is more to be said that I have verified information about, but the point here is Obama's actions were against the best interests of the U.S.)

[FN4.] Quantitative easing (QE), also known as large-scale asset purchases, is an expansionary monetary policy whereby a central bank buys predetermined amounts of government bonds or other financial assets in order to stimulate the economy and increase liquidity. An unconventional form of monetary policy, it is usually used when inflation is very low or negative, and standard expansionary monetary policy has become ineffective. A central bank implements quantitative easing by buying specified amounts of financial assets from commercial banks and other financial institutions, thus raising the prices of those financial assets and lowering their yield, while simultaneously increasing the money supply. This differs from the more usual policy of buying or selling short-term government bonds to keep interbank interest rates at a specified target value.

Trump, on the other hand, rescinded Obama's restrictions and began to approve oil production from closed wells, oil exploration and drilling offshore and up north. Pastor Lindsey was told by his friend that Trump will survive as President at least to the 2020 elections because the elitists decided to let Trump continue to open up the American oil industry, and to cause the OPEC nations like Saudi Arabia to lose that grip by letting the USA become the world's leading exporter of oil. (Note that the Emirate nations like Saudi Arabia don't use this money to help anyone but themselves, and to further the spread of Islam across the world. And, they would rather squander its super-riches on expensive trinkets like gold plated and diamond-encrusted automobiles or outrageously castle-like mosques to keep its Muslim populations devoted Islamists; but those riches don't trickle down to the citizenry either.)

Trump's opening of the oil industry should result in a major drop in fuel prices for Americans. For the elitists, this was a win-win situation worth several trillion dollars over the next two years. What happens after that?

Well, let's go back to the 1970's, when states had a thriving oil industry based on our own oil wells. Under the Tehran Agreement in 1971, oil import prices were reasonable, and a gallon of gas cost American drivers about $0.30 cents. Low gas prices in the 50's and 60's helped drive the "muscle car" industry of big engines burning lots of gasoline. It was hot-rodder's dream come true and the creation of custom cars became an industry that still exists, even after oil prices arose.

But the Muslim oil-producing nations came together in 1973 against world support of Israel, and we had the Oil Producing Exporting Countries (OPEC) and the Organization of Arab Petroleum Exporting Countries (OAPEC), create what was termed an "embargo" that reduced oil production and raised prices on exported oil and fuels drastically, as a means to punish nations who supported Israel. It had no effect on their goal, but did cause a slowing of economic activities in the industrial market. What it did was cause a cessation in America's oil industry. States like Louisiana, Texas, and Oklahoma thrived from that industry. After the OPEC agreement, that industry nearly died out, and little more than refineries remained. Many people with jobs in or connected to the oil industry lost their jobs and even their homes. I recall driving through Oklahoma and seeing what once were beautiful homes completely abandoned, lots of them.

As the USA's oil industry returns, there will be an upsurge in the industrial marketplace. Stocks will rise, particularly in the ancillary support industry of the oil producers.

Most importantly, since Trump's move on the oil matter, America has seen a lessening of protests and violence by groups originally funded through George Soros. Why? Because it was in the best interests of the elitists. While it has not stopped, the radicals' activities seem more like a hold-over activity by those previously brainwashed.

Pastor Williams's friend, before his death, told him that they were going to leave Trump alone for the next 2 years for sure, but perhaps not oppose his re-election in 2020. Williams said there was going to be a "panic up" in the stock market by thousands of points (where the elitist will also make money), thus making the economy flourish and where investors can make a lot of money. Williams's friend noted that the oil industry stock will sky-rocket, including the ancillary support industries on the stock market (as I mentioned earlier.).

But make no mistake, the elitist "new world order" agenda has only been postponed. And please, don't try to connect Trump to actively helping the Illuminati/Bilderberg's agenda. You alt-Leftists, give that false narrative a rest. Turn off your Marxist Critical Theory criticism mode. No one believes you.

Throughout their history, the Rothschild family has created "golems" like George Soros, whom I will dissect further along, to do their dirty work for them. One of the major sources of funds for the founding of Soros's Quantum Fund N.V. was George Karlweiss, who was then Edmund de Rothschild's Banque Privée. Only a few years earlier, Karlweiss was busy launching the business career of the "Detroit Kid," Robert Vesco, who, with Rothschild assistance, would soon take over *Investors Overseas Services (IOS)* and milk it for a fortune, before becoming a fugitive.

Given that Soros, in 1996, spent millions in a campaign to legalize drugs, it is interesting that Vesco, flush with over $100 million capital from looting IOS, helped the Medellin drug cartel set up its finances, finally settling in Havana, Cuba, where he operated as part of the "Silver Triangle" cocaine trade. It appears there was more going on than just making huge profits from drug money; rather, the goal was more insidious, to get as many Americans hooked on powerful drugs. The Illuminati folks knows from America's history that Americans like mind-altering alcoholic spirits, and that until its becoming unlawful in the early 1900's, they also liked marijuana. Drugging down millions of Americans makes it easier for the shadow forces to manipulate a country's population. In other words, Americans can become their own worst enemy when they weaken themselves with recreational drug use.

As I quote from later, in the EIR report on Soros, Soros's relation with the Rothschild finance circle represents no ordinary or casual banking connection. It goes a long way to explain the extraordinary success of a mere private speculator, and Soros's uncanny ability to "gamble right" so many times in such high-risk markets. Soros has access to the "inside track" in some of the most important government and private channels in the world, and the Rothschild family is always somewhere in "the mix."

So, don't forget, Soros is the money-man behind Barack Obama and the Organization for Action.org organization.

Finally, I want to note that both the Council on Foreign Affairs and the International Council on Foreign Affairs are a creation of the folks in the Illuminati, created with the express purpose of influencing countries to continue to move towards a one-government world. These committees have had significant influence on the United Nations which also was intended to bring the world together as a one-government world. In Springmeier's book, he talks about this as well.

PART 4: THE FEDERAL RESERVE (FED) BANKERS

So, let's take a look at the Federal Reserve. At its website, www.federalreserve.gov, note the ".gov", it declares, "*The Federal Reserve, the central bank of the United States, provides the nation with a safe, flexible, and stable monetary and financial system.*" But, the Federal Reserve bank was an Illuminati-created bank designed to take control of the country's money and, thereby, have major control over the country and its political infrastructure and policies.

It was created December 23, 1913, with the enactment of the Federal Reserve Act, after a series of financial panics (particularly the panic of 1907) led to the desire for central control of the monetary system in order to alleviate financial crises. Over the years, events such as the Great Depression in the 1930s and the Great Recession during the 2000s have led to the expansion of the roles and responsibilities of the Federal Reserve System, according to Wikipedia. There are twelve Federal Reserve Banks, each of which is responsible for member banks located in its district. They are located in Boston, New York, Philadelphia, Cleveland, Richmond, Atlanta, Chicago, St. Louis, Minneapolis, Kansas City, Dallas, and San Francisco. But like the Federal Reserve, these are all private banks.

Although Article 1, Section 8 of the Constitution states that Congress shall have the power to coin (create) money and regulate the value thereof, today, since 1913, the Federal Reserve Bank (FED) which is a privately owned company, controls and profits by printing money through the US Treasury, and regulating its value.

The FED began with approximately 300 people or banks that became owners in the Federal Reserve Banking System. This group make up an international banking cartel of wealth beyond comparison. Although originally the ownership of the 12 Central banks was a very well-kept secret, the names are now public.

Rothschild Bank of London, Warburg Bank of Hamburg Germany, Rothschild Bank of Berlin, Lehmann Brothers of New York, Lazard Brothers of Paris, Kuhn Loeb Bank of New York, Israel Moses Seif Banks of Italy, Goldman-Sachs of New York, Warburg Bank of Amsterdam, Chase Manhattan Bank of

New York, all connected to London Banking Houses which ultimately control the FED. Also, private owned banks who own shares in the FED are partly foreign-owned, as follows:

> First National Bank of New York, James Stillman; National City Bank, New York, Mary W. Harnman; National Bank of Commerce, New York, A.D. Jiullard; Hanover National Bank, New York, Jacob Schiff; Chase National Bank, New York, Thomas P. Ryan, Paul Warburg, William Rockefeller, Levi P. Morgan, M.T. Pyne, George F. Baker, Percy Pyne, Mrs. G.F. St.George, J.W. Sterling. Katherine St.George, H.P. Davidson, J.P. Morgan (Equitable Life/Mutual Life), Edith Brevour, T. Baker.

We know the Federal Reserve is a private bank owned by multinational banks, like the Rothschilds, Rockefellers and Warburgs. Ultimately, who gets your money is the unbelievably wealthy and powerful bankers who "call the shots" around the globe in just about every country.

Who did this? Former President Woodrow Wilson, whose campaign for president was funded and staffed by a group of these bankers. Wilson committed to the Federal Reserve Act and signed it in 1913. He later was remorseful and said, "*I have unwittingly ruined my country.*"

These bankers have continually financially backed sympathetic candidates, most of which get elected. In the 1930's the FED began buying up the media and now, today, owns or significantly influences most of it.

Notwithstanding that the Kennedy family had significant ties to the Illuminati bloodlines, it is noteworthy that President Kennedy tried to stop this family of bankers by printing U.S. dollars without charging the taxpayers interest. He also warned us publicly about the insidious New World Order movement. We know what happened to JFK. Today, if the government runs a deficit, the FED prints dollars through the U.S. Treasury, buys the debt, and the dollars are circulated into the economy. In 1992, taxpayers paid the FED banking system $286 billion in interest on debt the FED purchased by printing money virtually cost free. Forty percent of our personal federal income taxes goes to pay this interest. The FED's books are not open to the public, and Congress has never audited it. Repeatedly, over the years, various Congressmen has attempted to repeal the Federal Reserve Act, without success. It was always defeated, and the public never learned of it because the media remained totally silent.

Rep. Louis T. McFadden (R. PA), serving 12 years as Chairman of the Committee on Banking and Currency, becoming one of the foremost financial authorities in America, characterized the FED thusly:

> "The Federal Reserve Board, a government board, has cheated the government of the United States and the people of the United States out of enough money to pay the national debt." He also said, "They are private credit monopolies which prey upon the people of the United States for the benefit of themselves and their foreign customers; foreign and domestic speculators and swindlers; the rich and predatory money lenders. This is an era of economic misery and for the reasons that caused that misery, the Federal Reserve banks are fully liable." Another quote is: "Every effort has been made by the Federal Reserve Board to conceal its power but the truth is the Federal Reserve Board has usurped the government of the United States. It controls everything here and it controls all our foreign relations. It makes and breaks governments at will. No man and no body of men is more entrenched in power than the arrogant credit monopoly which operates the federal reserve board and the federal reserve banks. These evil-doers have robbed this country of more than enough money to pay the national debt. What the government has permitted the federal reserve board to steal from the people should now be restored to the people. Our people's money to the extent of $1,200,000,000 has within the last few months been shipped abroad to redeem Federal Reserve Notes and to pay other gambling debts of the traitorous Federal Reserve Board and the Federal Reserve banks. The greater part of our monetary stock has been shipped to

foreigners. Why should we promise to pay the debts of foreigners to foreigners? Why should American Farmers and
wage earners add millions of foreigners to the number of their
dependents? Why should the Federal Reserve Board and the
Federal Reserve banks be permitted to finance our competitors
in all parts of the world?" Rep. McFadden asked. "The Federal
Reserve Act should be repealed and the Federal Reserve banks,
having violated their charters, should be liquidated immediately. Faithless government officers who have violated their
oaths should be impeached and brought to trial."

But, aside from their role in the Federal Reserve, and their influence on major
politics, they are also the bankers of the world, alongside a few others. Multinational or transnational banks bankroll the world's countries, affecting their
economic systems, but also they benefit from both sides of a war, large or small
because they essentially bankroll all parties. In point of fact, these bloodline
of family bankers who own the FED funded both sides of major wars. They
created fake colonial money to destroy the Americans during the Revolutionary War and tried to finance both sides in the American Civil War. Wars create
more debt which means more profit to the bankers. These bankers planned
three world wars so people would welcome United Nations intervention to
govern the world in peace, not war.

More recently, they publicly announced the plan to force us into a cashless society by 1997; fortunately, this has not yet occurred, although most of us rely
on credit and debit cards for nearly all purchases.

Furthermore, if you wonder who is behind this "New World Order" look no
further; the bankers planned the creation of a one-world government, (or a
one government world as I like to say), through the United Nations headed
by the FED, Tri-laterals, the Council on Foreign Affairs, and the International
Council on Foreign Affairs (European). By the definition of treason, this is
treason! If they were successful, and the plan is still underway, Americans
would lose their rights under the Constitution and Bill of Rights. Think this
is conspiracy theory? Already, twenty-four U.S. Senators (two of them presidential candidates, Harkin and Tsongas) and 80 Representatives, have signed

a "Declaration of Independence." This Declaration, designed to make a one world government, is treason to the oath of office they took. The media has remained totally silent on this. The FED announced publicly that their first objective was to get nationalism out of the heads of the American people because patriotism to a country would not be of value in the future. The media makes us think that the U.N. has all the answers, and to "think globally." Congress passed a law stopping individuals from being tried for this treason. Why pass this law if no treason was committed? State Department document 7277 calls for the disarming of America, thus turning our sovereignty over to a one-world government. Again, the media is pushing to eliminate guns. Our forefathers believed that the right to bear arms would prevent a takeover of our country. History shows that before any government took over, they disarmed citizens. Hitler did it, and before our Revolutionary War, King George told us to disarm – good thing we didn't!

In the past 30 years, Congress has raised our taxes 56 times or more, and balanced the budget only once. Right now, our income taxes go only to pay the interest on the national debt, and not a dime on the principal.

Such banks have the power to manipulate a country's currency, like George Soros does, funding a struggling country to become socialist, or crashes a country's economy to wreak havoc (Venezuela, Guatemala, Honduras, African and other countries), and then help them with the requirement they establish socialism, which we can watch as these countries began to make a comeback. But, always, we see millions of people suffer, and many of them die in the processes of change.

Our Constitution, Article 1, Section 8, allows America to buy back the FED for 450 million dollars and have the U.S. Government collect all profits. This could soon eliminate the national debt. The 18th century banker Amshell Rothschild said: "*Allow me to control the issue and the nation's money and I care not who makes its laws!*" Thomas Jefferson, one of our Founding Fathers, said, "*I believe that banking institutions are more dangerous to our liberties than standing armies…*." The American Revolution was a struggle to wrest control of wealth from the Bank of England and to restore the centers of power to the People where it properly belongs. The Constitution is specific about the authority of the

People, through their elected officials, to control the money, and thus, the affairs of their government.

Thomas Jefferson also said, *"If the American people ever allow private banks to control the issue of currency, first by inflation, then by deflation, the banks and corporations that will grow up around them will deprive the people of all property until their children will wake up homeless on the continent their fathers conquered."* Even Napoleon, formerly a sympathizer of the banks, turned against them in the last years of his rule: *"When a government is dependent upon bankers for money, they and not the leaders of the government control the situation, since the hand that gives is above the hand that takes... Money has no motherland; financiers are without patriotism and without decency; their sole object is gain."*

By controlling Congress, the FED has been able to control the nominating conventions of both political parties. In this way, it has been able to hand-pick the presidential nominees so that no matter which party wins, their nominee for President is under definite obligations to the FED.

In 1975, the Rockefeller Foundation Report discussed the "interdependence" of the countries of the world on each other. It stated we are one world and America shall become a nation-state under one government. They also say we must reach a zero-state population growth. The Rockefeller Foundation stated that they have in excess of 747 million dollars to achieve this with. Again, that was 1975; in today's money 747-million would be a LOT more today, i.e., in the billions.

Former Congressman John R. Rarick stated that the Council on Foreign Relations (CFR) is dedicated to a one-world government. The media remained conspicuously quiet. The CFR wants to convert the U.S. from a sovereign, constitutional republic into a servile member state of a one-world dictatorship. On February 17, 1950, CFR member James Warburg (banker, and architect of the Federal Reserve System) stated before a Senate Foreign Relations Committee, "We shall have one world government whether or not you like it, by conquest or consent." Again, the media remained silent. In the April 1974 issue of the CFR journal, "Foreign Affairs", page 558, Richard Gardener states that the new world order "will be built... but an end run around national sovereignty, eroding it piece by piece, will accomplish much more than the old-fashioned frontal assault." Congressman McDonald, Heinz and Tower stated that this is a conspiracy. This goal is also on the agenda of the International Council on Foreign Affairs (Europe) and the United Nations. Again, the media remains silent.

The late Thomas A. Edison explained the matter of issuing currency this way: "If our nation can issue a dollar bond (interest bearing) it can issue a dollar bill (interest-free). The element that makes the bond good makes a bill good also. The difference between the bond and the bill is that the bond lets money brokers collect twice the amount of the bond and an additional 20 percent, whereas the currency pays nobody but those who contribute directly in some useful way. It is absurd to say that our country can issue $30 million in bonds and not $30 million in currency. Both are promises to pay: But one promise fattens the usurers (interest collectors) and the other helps the people."

The FED is owned largely by foreign banks that control our economy and Congress through the power of money and the media which they bought with profits generated with profits generated by artificial debt.

If we can convert U.S. dollars that are debt and interest-free to interest bearing currency, we can change it back just as easily.

Without the Federal Reserve System, there can be no continuing march towards socialism, and with it there can be no free economy.

All of the above about the Federal Reserve I excerpted from the November 28,1998 report entitled "The Federal Reserve Is A PRIVATELY OWNED Corporation" by Thomas D. Schauf, originally released in 1992. This is an amazing report that should wake us all to the very real threat America faces from these bankers who are focused on eliminating sovereign governments on this planet, especially the United States of America. This treatise is available at www.rense.com/ufo2/fedrez.htm. The references are at the end of this book.

The following represents more about the push for socialism in America. As I set about writing this book, it was to expose who are the puppeteers creating the problems, over many years, that keep this planet called Earth from achieving utopian status for all its citizens, a status that includes nation sovereignty, basic, fundamental, unalienable human rights and freedoms from Earth from oppression, and the right of free thought, expression, and association. Now you know. It has nothing to do with whether the country's political parties are in disagreement over policies, politics, or ideology. Over generations, we have all suffered by policies, practices, and power-mongering and greed from a small community of the top 1% of the top 1% of the wealthiest people, particularly bankers, in the world. Over those years, billions of people have died because of them. They have bought many, if not most, of our politicians in office. Isn't it time for us to fix what former presidents and patriots have warned us about many years ago?

For those elders who remember and believed in Franklin D. Roosevelt, listen to what Mr. Schauf has learned:

> For the secret owners of the FED to control the volume of money and become our absolute masters, they had to get the Gold away from our grandparents. This was accomplished in 1933 with the threats of fines and imprisonments by their President Franklin D. Roosevelt with aide Harry Hopkins, who said… *"Elect, elect, elect, tax, tax, tax, spend, spend, spend, for the people are too damned stupid to understand"*. By the way, Roosevelt was an international Banker. (See Fool's Gold is Green by Winston Smith.)

So I looked up "Fool's Gold is Green" which is a booklet by Winston Smith sub-headed as "An Encyclopedia of Banksterese, Economic Euphemisms and Reality" some 36 pages long. It opens with:

> *"There is no surer, more subtler means of over-turning the existing basis of society than to debauch the currency. The process (of inflating) engages all of the hidden forces of economics on the side of destruction and does it in a manner that not one man in a million can diagnose it."*

> — John Maynard Keynes
> in Economic Consequence of the Peace

The booklet is dedicated in memory of that one man in a million who was one-year old when the above statement was written in 1920, Merrill M.E. Jenkins, Sr. (1919-1979), the First Monetary Realist. He authored 7 books on the subject of economics with the first being "Money", the Greatest Hoax On Earth. In his view, economics is the art of convincing people that paper is money while plundering them with it and eventually enslaving them. Economists are those who are skilled at keeping the sheep calm while they are being shorn.

The booklet here was written as a test of someone's Cognitive Dissonance. The theory of cognitive dissonance, as explained by the great writer on mind control, K.M. Heaton, is a theory that the mind involuntarily rejects information not in line or cognizant with previous beliefs or actions. That is, people believe what they like to believe or things similar to other things they believed before. As noted in the booklet, "*There was a time when they believed the Earth was flat and those who knew the truth were punished or ostracized for expressing a different view.*" The Bible says, at 2 Tim, 4:3, "*The time will come when people won't listen to the truth, they will seek out teachers who teach them what they want to hear.*" Are we not there yet?

An interesting tidbit about Jimmy Carter: one of the first acts Jimmy Carter did as president was to sign a treaty with the United Nations authorizing them to abolish all private property. Can you imagine that? How could he do such a thing? Though many weekly papers printed this, it is not known if any daily papers did, and it is believed that the daily papers did not carry this huge boondoggle. Some interesting quotes are:

> "The world is governed by far different personages than what is imagined by those not behind the scenes"
> — Benjamin Disraeli

> "Those who issue and control money and credit determine the policies of government and hold the destinies of the people in the hollow of their hands"
> — Sir Reginald McKenna

"The money-power preys upon the nation in times of peace and conspires against it in times of adversity. It denounces, as public enemies, all who question its methods or throw light upon its crimes"

— Abraham Lincoln

History shows that the money changers have used every form of abuse, intrigue, deceit and violent means possible to maintain control over governments by controlling the money and its issuance"

— President James Madison

"Banking institutions are like standing armies"

— Thomas Jefferson

"Our monetary system would not work if all of the world's bankers were not in collusion"

— Merrill M.E. Jenkins

"In fact, evil men and false teachers will get worse and worse deceiving many, they themselves having been deceived by Satan."

– 2 Tim. 3:13.

"When plunder becomes a way of life for a group of men living together in society, they create for themselves in the course of time, a legal system that authorizes it and a moral code that glorifies it."

– Economic Sophisms by Frederic Bastia (1801-1850)

Although our money is supposed to be backed by the gold standard, the fact is that the United States has no gold at all, not even in the Federal Reserve. The bankers own it all.

I learned in the booklet the following, which I share with you here:

In 1848, bankers hired a man by the name of Karl Marx to draw up a plan to perpetuate their plunder with non-redeemable notes. It is known today as the "Communist Manifesto". The 5th plank called for the establishment of a central bank which would legalize what bankers in the past were hung for, the process known as "fractional reserve banking". The 1st, 2nd and 3rd planks call for real estate tax, income tax and inheritance tax to get their fraudulent notes out of circulation after they plunder us with them. Rebel against these taxes and you learn about the 4th plank which calls for "confiscation of property of rebels!" The 10th plank calls for "free education in public schools" so that acceptance for this system of plunder is gained at an early age.

As the years in our lives have gone by, and we wondered why personal financials are not getting better in the consumer market even though monthly income has risen (due to your own effort), perhaps we can begin to see that we are getting ever closer, due to these bankers and corporations amongst us, to a two party existence, the rulers and the serfs.

On December 23, 1913, when Congress passed the Federal Reserve Act and, in implementing this 5th plank of Karl Marx's communist manifesto, they legalized what bankers in the past had been hung for. Then, to control the volume of counterfeit used by its victims, the 16th Amendment was passed in the same year, i.e., Marx's 2nd plank, a progressive income tax. Congress could not have passed such an Act unless it had already been infiltrated or controlled by the Illuminati.

One thing the mendacious 16th Amendment DID NOT DO was to authorize compulsory filing of income tax returns! It could not do so without repealing our 1st amendment right to remain silent; our 4th amendment rights to privacy and our 5th amendment right not to be a witness against ourselves. These rights as well as rights guaranteed by the 9th and 13th amendments are waived when any person files a tax return. If Congress could pass a law that requires us to waive our rights, then we have no rights! Is THAT right? No such law has ever been passed. So what would happen if everyone simply did not file a tax return? Would the government panic? Would the bankers panic? What would happen?

I learned in the booklet another thing: There can be no modern wars and no communism without bank credit and legal tender. Communism is just sophisticated theft.

Finally, I'll close this topic with the following quotes:

> "We are in a time of distorted words and phrases. Meanings have been twisted and reversed. It is the day of "doublethink". Money no longer means money. Income no longer means income. Voluntary no longer means voluntary. I could go on and on with the government's game of doublethink, exchanging means and perpetuating a system of lies and deception that is as old as Satan himself. The purpose of keeping the public confused and causing them to question their own common sense is to trick them into doubting the truth, no matter how evident it is. Once we have doubted the truth that we see and know in our hearts, it is easy to get us to accept a lie"—The Sentinel.

See the reference to Orwellianism the Sentinel made? And. as Winston Smith, from the booklet, said:

> "Skillful use of words is vital in getting the people to believe what isn't so. Control people's words and you control their thinking. Control their thinking and you control their minds. Control their minds and you control their bodies. Words are used for communications. Control of Communications is part of 6th plank of Communist Manifesto.

In closing, *"Those unaware are unaware of being unaware."* – Merrill M.E. Jenkins, Sr. M.R. *"All that is necessary for evil to triumph is for good men to do nothing."* Sir Edmund Burke. The longer you take to join the fight for liberty, the harder the battle will be for your children and the less chance they will have of winning.

PART 5: THE BILDERBERG GROUP:

In 1954, the most influential figures of the world met in a hotel to discuss and plan the global agenda for the following year. Since then, they have continued to meet annually, but the content of their conversations remains a closely guarded secret. The Bilderberg is not exactly a secret society, but many people in the know worry about the influence their annual meetings have, and some say they are behind the New World Order. My research strongly indicates they are the global planning arm of the New World Order.

What we have seen throughout history is that those of large wealth and elite status always seem to think they know better than anyone how to run the world, and when they are able to run a country, they tend to be authoritarian at the very least. Notwithstanding, it is interesting that revolutions that begin with a commoner who challenges the existing ruling class or leader and succeed, tend to commit outright genocide of intellectuals, religious people, and anyone who does not fit within their new control narrative, burn books, and generally reduce everyone to the common level of poverty and sameness. It is goal of collectivism to indoctrinate out individualism so that all individuals see only their service to the collective. For the power-crazed despot dictators, power comes by killing all opposers or who might be opposers so that the rest of the population fall in line and lets themselves be subjugated.

I do not see the Bilderberg Group in a genocidal mode, but they have been involved in efforts to unite nations in "treaty" alliances, but it also appears they either support or do not oppose the globalists' agenda for the New World Order one-government world effort. In my opinion, helping to create alliances for mutual protection, defense, and economics is one thing. Uniting countries of dissimilar cultures and/or ideologies with the goal of fitting them all into a borderless world and expecting multiculturalism and diversity to achieve assimilation and compatibility is quite another, which I would not support. Cultures with diametrically oppositional ideologies, where one or both refuses to recognize the existence of the other, cannot be assimilated under the rubric of multiculturalism, pluralism, or a banner of compromise and tolerance.

Originally, the Bilderberg group was formed in 1954 in the Netherlands for the express purpose of promoting Atlanticism, i.e., which was basically a cooperative movement between the United States and Europe to promote financial prosperity, as well as to pool defense and international influence.

Unsurprisingly, this meeting in 1954 came into existence just as the Cold War ramped up into second gear and countries around the world chose their side of the Russia/U.S. conflict.

One of the founders of the Bilderberg group was Jozef Retinger, who was the first Secretary General for the European Movement, which led directly to the modern-day European Union. So, effectively, the original intention of the Bilderberg Group was to join all the Westernized countries in Europe with the hyper-western United States. Not only did this union work, it followed the stability of the North American Treaty Organization, or NATO. The defense network against the Soviet Union provided a solid backing for Western leaders to work together.

The defense network against the Soviet Union provided a solid backing for Western leaders to work together. Today, although almost no details of what is specifically discussed behind closed doors are ever openly shared, a list of broad topics are provided to the public.

As we have seen, the bankers comprising the Federal Reserve Bank, along with other banking institutions outside of the FED bank, all comprise a cartel that collaborates on world affairs. However, while this can be based on deductive reasoning, I have been unable to tie other world banking institutions directly to the FED cartel. This is a very secretive situation, but some major banks might be ruled out, such as the Chinese banks at the top of the 100 banks list, and who hold the most assets. It is highly unlikely that the Chinese government and its banks, being communist, are aligned with the New World Order, one-government world agenda. The same may be said of Arab, Russian, and certain other countries who have banks not a subset of the American/European banking cartel. But an exact list of the NWO cartel is not necessary to address the problem they pose.

From what I have been able to discern, the combined planning arm is the Bilderberg Group, of which the Rothschild family has long been a part.

While the Bilderberg Group is quite secretive, it holds a conference once yearly at different locations. The Group is made up of some of the wealthiest people on Earth, including bankers and CEOs from some of the largest corporations in the world, and including some "delegates" there by invitation.

Although secretive, they do publish an agenda that lists topics they would be discussing, but the topics are so vague as to give no indication whatsoever any details or concerns they will be discussing. Further herein, I will list the topics on the 2016 agenda. From all that I have learned over the past five years, I think I can safely speculate on what is discussed about some of those topics, as I will do further herein.

Nonetheless, it is believed that they discuss prior agendas and goals to see how they are doing, as well as current items and concerns and how they want to deal with them upcoming. Former President Bill Clinton was, in fact, invited to one of their annual meetings, Bill Gates's name has appeared on a leaked membership list (I do not have a copy of that; learned it from a journalist's investigation). Among the banking institutions, of course there are the Rotchschilds, the Rockefellers, the Warburgs, and numerous others.

During the last presidential elections, the Bilderbergs did not want to see Donald Trump elected. His actual election came as a surprise to both the Illuminati and the Bilderberg Group, and one can discern from this the link to why the mainstream media —- all owned by these folks – became so intensely critical of Trump.

Totally unsurprisingly, this meeting came into existence just as the Cold War ramped into second gear, and countries around the world chose their side of the Russian/US conflict.

Today, although almost no details of what is specifically discussed behind closed doors are ever openly shared, a list of broad topics are provided to the public.

The June 2016 meeting in Germany, included points about cyber-security, energy and commodity prices, Russian and China, and the term "precariat", which describes workers in jobs with no future security or long-term goals.

In 2016, these issues were seen as those most likely going to be the most relevant for the global economy and security in the near future. In reality, perhaps there was discussion about how to move forward with the New World Order agenda.

We also know who attends these conferences. It is invite-only and varies from about 120 to 150 attendees, and the 2016 guest list was publicly revealed to include powerful figures such as former secretary of state Henry Kissinger, former CIA head David Petraeus, Senator Lindsey Graham, billionaire Peter Thiel, and a large number of CEOs from companies as diverse as LinkedIn to Royal Dutch Shell.

What few things members of the conference ARE allowed to discuss publicly, are bound to what is called the Chatham House Rule. No information shared from the meeting can be attributed to the person who said it, or their affiliation; allowing controversial opinions to come through without fear of public repercussion.

Of course, such secrecy is prone to conspiracy theories, from both sides of the political spectrum. Some conservatives suggest that the group intends to take over the world, imposing a single government and a sort of "socialist economy", while those on the liberal side fear a strip-down of regulation, and unbridled free market capitalism. The distinction shows that nobody actually knows what the meeting is about, besides those who attend.

One thing is clear, however: such a large grouping of the most powerful people in the world is not a simple "sit-and-chat", and it is likely that world events are influenced by the results of the Bilderberg Group.

But at least the Bilderbergs have a publicized meeting, other secretive conspiratorial groups like, say, the Illuminati, barely exist on paper. But, does the Illuminati have more influence than most people think? With the Illuminati, there is no proof on paper that they even exist, but isn't that what they want you to think?

Things to know:

1. The current chairman of the Bilderberg Group is the French CEO of AXA, Henri de la Croix Castries, a multinational insurance firm. Significant members have always been members of their country's Parliament.

2. The Bilderberg Group releases the agenda for their meetings, but that's it. The topics on the agenda are always hugely broad topics making it impossible to know exactly what they discussed. For example, the 2016 agenda listed its key topics as:

   1. Current events
   2. China
   3. Europe: migration, growth, reform, vision, unity
   4. Middle East
   5. Russia
   6. US political landscape, economy: growth, debt, reform
   7. Cyber security
   8. Geo-politics of energy and commodity prices
   9. Precariat and middle class
   10. Technological innovation

3. The Bilderberg Group did not want Donald Trump to win the presidential election.

4. Hillary Clinton has never been a Bilderberg Delegate, but Bill Clinton allegedly appeared before the Bilderbergs. Many believe that they were behind Hillary for President. The Group is cited as the way Presidents and Prime Ministers are "chosen." Bill Clinton first attended the Bilderberg Conference in 1991 and became the US President just a year later. Tony Blair was fairly insignificant in his own political party when he was invited in 1993. By 1997 his election as

Prime Minister was being celebrated. Every year political figures are invited who may be relatively unknown but who are about to become very famous.

5. Theory claims that the Group planned to increase oil prices in 1973. It is true that the Group has a very serious say in oil prices. Many of the delegates represent major oil companies, such as Shell and British Petroleum (BP). In 1973, leaked information was that the Group managed to increase the price of oil by 400% to manage the increase in incoming oil dollars.

6. In 1955, the Group wanted to merge North America, Canada and Mexico. Leaked transcripts have shown how the Bilderbergs openly discussed how they could influence the merging of Canada, the United States and Mexico to create a North American Union. The Group allegedly are pro-America and pro-Europe, and anything that binds them and brings them together is greatly encouraged, according to them.

7. David Rockefeller openly admitted that he's part of a "secret cabal" and he was one of the oldest members of the Bilderberg Group. He publicly and proudly admitted he was part of a group seeking to establish a "New World Order."

8. Britain's Margaret Thatcher was also a delegate of the Bilderberg Group, but a former Washington Post journalist who resigned specifically to investigate the Bilderberg Group learned that Thatcher did not like what she heard at the Bilderberg Group and she was replaced by a new delegate the following year.

Regardless of what the true function of the Bilderberg Group is, it is strongly rumored that the goal of the Group is to establish a world with only two class groups, rulers and serfs. There is also the accusation that the Group's long-term goal is sinister, that they want to create a welfare state, a world military, and absolute control of education. Again, the Group is Illuminati populated according to the various sources I researched.

My addition: There are, however, those who were engaged with the Illuminati who have spoken out, including a former wife of an Illuminati member, confirming their existence as a Luciferian-driven organization. As I mentioned earlier, I downloaded that three-part video series for posterity.

This secrecy of the Illuminati has begged the question of whether the Bilderberg group was and is a sub-group of the Illuminati. However, deductive reasoning leads to the conclusion that if well-established members of the Bilderberg Group are also members or delegates of the banking cartel or the Illuminati, it can be assumed that the Bilderberg Group is the planning arm of the Illuminati.

Other than the concern about who constitutes the membership of the Bilderberg Group, the primary concern citizens of the world should have, is how this small group of extremely powerful people exert that power in the political arena as well as in the market economies of the world and the budgets of those countries. This concern could be characterized similarly to the political power dynamics of countries in their central planning in that the Bilderberg group identifies in their agenda matters that are clearly global, and what does it imply when such an organization has to concentrate power, and how they will end up using that power to achieve their goals. If those goals are the same as the globalists who want to destroy all governments except one, and that would be the one they create, then in the end we can expect a totalitarian government ruling with an iron fist and a society without any of the freedoms Americans now enjoy.

PART 6: SKULL & BONES SOCIETY

Skull and Bones was founded in 1832 after a dispute between Yale debating societies Linonia, Brothers in Unity, and the Calliopean Society over that season's Phi Beta Kappa awards. It was co-founded by William Huntington Russell and Alphonso Taft as "the Order of the Scull [sic] and Bones". The Skull and Bones Society has long promoted the idea of a New World Order, i.e., one-government world. The intent behind post-war creation of the United Nations and the European Union was to eventually achieve that New

World Order goal, which remains alive today. It had and has a great influence in politics, business, education, just about every aspect of government and the bureaucracy.

The society's assets are managed by the society's alumni organization, the Russell Trust Association, incorporated in 1856 and named after the Bones co-founder. The association was founded by Russell and Daniel Coit Gilman, a Skull and Bones member, and later president of the University of California, first president of Johns Hopkins University, and the founding president of the Carnegie Institution.

The first extended description of Skull and Bones, published in 1871 by Lyman Bagg in his book Four Years at Yale, noted that *"the mystery now attending its existence forms the one great enigma which college gossip never tires of discussing."* Brooks Mather Kelley attributed the interest in Yale senior societies to the fact that underclassmen members of then freshman, sophomore, and junior class societies returned to campus the following years and could share information about society rituals, while graduating seniors were, with their knowledge of such, at least a step removed from campus life.

It is a "recruiting" organization. Skull and Bones selects new members among students every spring as part of Yale University's "Tap Day", and has done so since 1879. Since the society's inclusion of women in the early 1990s, Skull and Bones selects fifteen men and women of the junior class to join the society. Skull and Bones "taps" those that it views as campus leaders and other notable figures for its membership.

Once in the society, it appears to be a given that its members will rise to positions of power in government and in business, including banking.

I note here that Wall Street, along with Great Britain, helped finance Hitler, subsequently financed Stalin who created communism rule in Russia. They (Wall Street, and international bankers) financed the build-up of three kinds of socialism: Bolshevik socialism in Russia, what we might call welfare socialism in the United States, and Hitler with national socialism. It is a little-known fact that Adolf Hitler, in his earlier years, spent some time in England as an agent, where he received training in the means of achieving leadership back in Germany. He learned how to talk persuasively at which he became quite good, as we know, since he united his countrymen as never before. (Of course, this was with the help of Propaganda Minister Joseph Goebbels.)

I learned that Hitler's original goal was not to kill Jews, but to invade and conquer Poland. He met with Stalin, and made an alliance, reaching an agreement not to attack Russia and that Russia could have the Eastern half of Poland. Of course, Hitler reneged on that agreement and attacked Russia, who was relatively weak, starting that war. It was this invasion of Russia, along with the Japanese attack, that prompted the United States to become involved in what became World War II.

At the end of the book, in the References section, are links about the Skull and Bones fraternity.

PART 7: OTHER INSTITUTIONS

A. The United Nations

The United Nations (UN) is an intergovernmental organization tasked with maintaining international peace and security, developing friendly relations among nations, achieving international co-operation, and being a centre for harmonizing the actions of nations. It was established after World War II, with the aim of preventing future wars, and succeeded the ineffective League of Nations. Its charter, which began in April 1945, was adopted in June 1945 in San Francisco in the Herbst Theatre auditorium in the Veterans War Memorial Building. It took effect October 1945 when the UN began operations. The UN has six principal organs: the General Assembly; the Security Council; the Economic and Social Council; the Trusteeship Council; the International Court of Justice; and the UN Secretariat. The UN system agencies include the World Bank Group, the World Health Organization, the World Food Programme, UNESCO, and UNICEF.

With the addition of South Sudan in 2011, there are now 193 UN member states, including all undisputed independent states apart from Vatican City. The "Group of 77" (G77) at the UN is a loose coalition of developing nations, designed to promote its members' collective economic interests and create an enhanced joint negotiating capacity in the UN. Seventy-seven nations founded the organization, but by November 2013 the organization had since expanded to 133 countries. One of the UN's primary purposes is "promoting and encouraging respect for human rights and for fundamental freedoms for all without distinction as to race, sex, language, or religion", and member states pledge to undertake "joint and separate action" to protect these rights.

While the UN has heretofore presented as a stellar organization that carried out its charter functions commendably, even winning multiple Nobel Peace Prize awards, what is happening now? Why is the UN now pushing an old agenda about creating a one-world government?

Let me say first, one must assume that the multinational bankers and power-brokers in the Illuminati, including the Bilderberg Group, have substantial influence with the United Nations. When you have a group of people, some of whom are trillionaires, who basically control the budgets of nearly every country on the planet, if not all countries, having influence over a country's policies and operations is a given. We have seen George Soros, for example, an unabashed front-man for the Illuminati (although you won't hear him mention that), who brags how his Jewish father got a friendly German family to take him in as their son during Hitler's genocidal campaign, and how he made his fortune during and after the war selling property formerly owned by Jews who went to the gas chambers. Soros goes around the world messing with the economies of target countries, causing them to fail, then buys up their currency so they crash, after which the Illuminati banks loan them money to recuperate but only if they agree to become socialist. Why? The short answer to that is that in order to pressure countries around the world into joining the New World Order (of a one-government world) they must first weaken them by socialism.

How does the United Nations fit into that scenario? The essence of the United Nations's long-term agenda has always been to create an organization that would be the governing body over all countries, including the United States.

This is the one-government world envisioned by the globalists as the New World Order program. You might be interested to take your dollar bill out and look at the back, at the bottom of the Masonic pyramid at the Latin words, "Novus Ordo Seclorum" which means in English, "New World Order." Again, this is further affirmation of the goal of the globalists.

The idea of the New World Order has actually been around at least since the turn of the century. It can be traced back to scholar Cecil Rhodes of the Rhodes Scholarship fame. He was one of the first who dreamed up and believed the entire world should be under one government. For him, it would be the British Empire. In 1891, Rhodes created an organization called "The Society of the Elect", a secret society. Later, it became the Chatham House gang and it was where the idea of the global governance movement was born in Europe. In America, there was a man named Colonel Mandell House. He was President Woodrow Wilson's advisor and the chief negotiator for the Versailles Treaty (1919), the most important of the treaties that ended the state of war between Germany and the Allied Powers. Like Rhodes, House had somewhat of a like-minded following for one-world governance. His group named themselves "The Inquiry." This group later met with the Chatham House group and formed a sort of alliance. Out of that meeting was formed two organizations for globalization. The Chatham House gang called their group "The Royal Institute for International Affairs" and the American group called their group "The Council on Foreign Relations."

President Roosevelt, about two weeks after Pearl Harbor, issued a "Declaration of United Nations" which contained Roosevelt's thoughts and political ammunition, but which were mostly created by the CFR, and was for establishing a one-world money group. It didn't go through. But in 1961 the United States introduced a program calling for all military nations to transfer their military power to the control of the United Nations, thus making the U.N. the global entity. This would have been a major accomplishment in the globalists one-government world goal. What did occur was a weakened version where the U.N. would control the international police (Interpol) and also would be able to draw upon member nations for military insertion where countries so requested intervention assistance.

Without belaboring the point, American presidents have not all believed that America's market-economy democratic capitalist ideology was adequate or best, and some believed in, as Nixon favorably called it, "internationalism" and the Bush's called it, New World Order. So the push for a one-government world, run through the United Nations, has been around awhile, and while it might have begun as a democratic socialist ideology, history has shown that such ideologies that make government the all-powerful parent always ends up the tyrant of the people.

As I mentioned earlier about the Islamization of Europe, it is without question that the United Nations played the primary role in the migrant swarm that basically spiraled European countries into self-destruction. Here is why.

In a U.N. publication dated March 27, 2000, entitled, Replacement Migration: Is It A Solution To Declining And Ageing Populations? The summary of that publication states very clearly:

> United Nations projections indicate that over the next 50 years, the populations of virtually all countries of Europe as well as Japan will face population decline and population ageing. The new challenges of declining and ageing populations will require comprehensive reassessments of many established policies and programmes, including those relating to international migration.

> Focusing on these two striking and critical population trends, the report considers replacement migration for eight low-fertility countries (France, Germany, Italy, Japan, Republic of Korea, Russian Federation, United Kingdom and United States) and two regions (Europe and the European Union). Replacement migration refers to the international migration that a country would need to offset population decline and population ageing resulting from low fertility and mortality rates.

So, I wonder, with the U.N. currently discussing "OVERpopulation" of the planet, why would they have been encouraging "replacement" migration to kick-start new birthrates in Western countries? Do you see any conflict here?

Having a member population including 36 Muslim-dominated countries, the U.N. somehow chose a means to destroy the primarily "white" populations of the West by bringing in millions of migrants from Arab and African nations, and Hispanic migrants into the United States. But how to accomplish that?

First of all, "replacement populations" are nearly ALL primarily "white" populations. The U.N. has acknowledged the planet is really over-populated, but the U.N. was formed alongside and in consideration of the Kalergi Plan, as I show in another chapter. This is the plan to interbreed different racial bloodlines to achieve a world in which there was only one bloodline by merging all others over time. This would effectively eliminate individual races and, particularly, the white race. This is notwithstanding the irrebuttable facts that it has been the Caucasian race that has lead the world in innovations, in industry, in agriculture, in medicine, in inventions, in the study of space, every aspect of major achievements have been done primarily by the Caucasian race. And it is also a fact that the bloodlines that have scarred their own populations with violence, oppression, starvation, poor education, lack of innovation and achievement have been people of color. I do NOT say this as a statement of racism; I too am a person of color, at least insofar as I am mostly Caucasian but part American-Choctaw blood.

Facts are indisputable, and if the facts hurt, find out why they hurt. I also admit here that IQ testing taken around the world by two different social scientists have revealed that the Asian race has very high IQs, the "white" race is slightly lower, the Jews are fairly high, and other bloodlines are lower. For example, Somalians were tested twice at an average IQ of 70. A couple of islands in Indonesia were tested with an average IQ of 60-65. Persons testing over 140 IQ are considered to be in the top five-percent of the highest on the planet. I tested at 142 when I was 25 years old, and was a Mensa Intl. member for several years. To demand equality of intelligence is simply not possible, so those who test lower than others should not feel angst towards those whose higher IQ has enabled them to have better-paying vocations and skills. Besides, a high IQ doesn't automatically render someone wise; I should know. Wisdom, regardless of IQ, comes with experience and perception and responses.

To avoid the accusation of "racist" one might consider that some countries developed over time better than others in all aspects of their lives and communities, leaving others to catch up or some that did not develop at all until the more developed countries, through greater means of travel, found them and brought new ideas aboard. Of course, many such countries were simply exploited for their resources too. (The world is not perfect.) But, the fact that the Caucasian bloodline did better than most should not be grounds for hating them either. China did better than most until Mao Zedong nearly destroyed China, but modern Chinese remains high IQ and studious. So did Japan. While tribal, both races had extraordinary advances, including artistic beauty as shown in their buildings, furniture, and weapons.

Secondly, the ageing population of Europe provided a prime opportunity for the U.N. to act on the Kalergi Plan by justifying "replacement migration" on the problem of ageing ethnic populations with low birth rates that eventually would disappear, as the narrative goes. Since most of the Western countries were identified as having ageing and declining populations from low fertility and birth rates, the only malleable countries left were, as for Europe, Northern African Black and Arab countries. Obviously the Islamic world liked this "replacement migration" idea as working right alongside Islam's world domination agenda by making it a cakewalk for Islamics to waltz into European countries, tear them up, rape all the girls and women (to create new generations of what would be both European white and Arab/Black children) all across Europe, which is exactly what occurred. Wars in the Middle East became an ongoing norm, creating thousands and thousands of refugee "migrants" who then swarmed over Europe, the majority of which were military-aged men who, again, raped the girls and women along the way. With impunity, by the way. Including Great Britain, Ireland, Scotland, and Greenland. In Britain, Muslim gangs engaged in raping girls and women, even enslaving some to work in the sex-trade. British government called them "grooming" gangs; what an insult!

In addition, (remember the United States was on the U.N.'s "replacement population" list?), the step to achieving "replacement populations" in the U.S.

would have the actual effect of, over time, breeding out the "white race" altogether. Europe would accomplish that, having started it already, and the U.S. would be next. But how? Why do you think the best capitalist democracy in South America, Venezuela, was crashed, along with Guatemala and El Salvador? The globalists needed refugee migrants. Lots of them. Send swarms of brown-skilled Hispanics across the borders, encourage the weak Democrats to protest for open borders to all these illegal migrants, and get millions of Central and South American Hispanics into the U.S., and in a few generations interbreeding, the U.S.-based Kalergi Plan would have accomplished its goal.

Hispanic-and Portugese-dominated countries in Central and South America did quite well in modern times, but failed for reasons of corruption, inadequate focus on education institutions, and outside interference. Hispanic countries today tend to be economically-challenged with socialist leanings, and my research indicates this might be due to socialist/communist/globalist interference undermining what were democratic nations. Create problems in those countries, encourage and help them come to the U.S. as refugees (U.N. sent people to help with the caravans), let them infiltrate over the entire country, and into the politics where, on plan, socialism would be ushered in, and the New World Order, having accomplished all the steps necessary to control various populations, could now establish the one-government totalitarian New World Order of rulers and serfs. But the USA has to be destroyed first. At that point, major depopulation of the planet could far more easily occur. (This, of course, does not mean that other forms of genocide would not also take place along the way, such as "vaccines" that kill people, escalating wars, race-baiting for the purpose of more people killing each other, and so on.) Conspiracy theory? I don't think so.

So, you see, what is going on today is all just a part of the NWO plan, and this is the reason why after Trump got elected the relentless criticism and false accusations escalated and have never ended. Trump interrupted the plan. Hillary was part of that plan. Obama was part of that plan. Hillary was to continue the plan already engaged by Obama. But for Trump, we might have already lost America to the Kalergi Plan and the NWO plan.

Yet, there are those in America who like the Kalergi Plan. One New York professor Jessie Daniels, a white woman, wrote that having "white nuclear families" *promotes* white supremacy, and argues that white women should *stop* having white babies, but choose a non-white to father her baby. She specifically threw this criticism at the women of Europe who were being raped by the black and Arab Muslim migrants. White women are guilt-tripped by allegations of racist if they want to, and do, marry a white man and have a white baby, and white women are acting weakly by acquiescing to this criticism and accusation. Is this not racism against the "white" race? Is the "white" race becoming the identified "enemy" like the Jews of Germany and Poland?

The United Nations is a wolf in sheep clothing, run by elitists from the globalist sectors who don't want more white people, who want to "replace" all white people in all nations by breeding out their bloodlines. This is part of why you don't see the United Nations protecting Christians around the world from assaults and murder by Islamists. Thirty-six countries represented in the U.N. are Islamist countries, i.e., haters of Christians and endorsers of Christian genocide (like the Nazis were towards Jews).

The U.N. targets "white people" for several reasons, other than the Kalergi Plan. The globalists who are driving the NWO agenda, even if many are white, are extremely wealthy and powerful elitists, who see themselves as "entitled" and "gifted" to rule over those beneath them (mostly everyone else). They want to control the world according to their standards, which are all about power and control. Some of them either do not believe in God or do believe in God but worship Satan instead as Luciferians, so their view of good and evil are skewed towards evil. They do not like white people because they believe:

1) White people are defense #1 because they are generally against globalism and open borders.
2) White people are #1 for fighting for free speech, liberty, prosperity, and limited government rather than having a welfare state.
3) White people are #1 for holding politicians accountable, for having rules and laws about accountability, and a process for removing those who need to be removed.
4) White people are inventors, innovative, successful business people, and problem solvers.

5) White people in America will not be enslaved without a fight to the death.

6) White people in general believe in God in the Christian context.

7) White people are fighters and have established the most successful military systems on the face of the Earth, and have shed their blood upon the land again and again across the globe to defend other lands and peoples.

Globalists want a dependent, docile population that is easy to control, and that isn't white people. We have seen other races/ethnicities fall subservient to socialist, communist, and totalitarian regimes, but whites will not go "quietly into the night".

Not all white people are good people, but for the large part, they are decent people who believe in live and let live, but don't rock the boat too much.

I suspect that some whites and perhaps more non-whites will accuse me of being a white supremist (did you know this word is not even in the dictionary, but it sure gets bandied about). I assure you I am not, but I will defend whites when unfairly accused and criticized. Then again, I would equally defend unfair and untrue criticisms and accusations of another race or culture as well. In fact, I heard a guy talking one day, saying, "Look at that damn Muslim raghead!" pointing to a Middle Eastern person. I looked but saw not a Muslim but a Sikhs, which is NOT a Muslim at all and believes in a loving and peaceloving God. He wore a large turban and had a beard, but Muslims do NOT wear those large turbans. I told him that, as well as the fact that Sikhs soldiers fought hard and well alongside American soldiers during one of the "wars" in the Middle East. He muttered something about the "rags" they wore on their heads, and I explained those served a survival purpose in their desert countries of old when they lived in the deserts and rode camels, that the turbans served to keep their heads cooler, as well as provided a cloth to sleep on or cover up with on the sands. So, I educated him and he ultimately thanked me for telling him what I did. I have done so numerous times since then. I have engaged conversation with Sikh's I've met in parking lots or stores. I am not a racist, but I am proud of my bloodlines (Scottish, French, and Native American (Choctaw, my grandmother told me)), and I see no reason why I, listed as "white" cannot, under the political correctness regime, be proud of who and what I am while, at the same time, non-white races can all publicly express pride in their racial heritage. The anti-white pressure to guilt-trip white people is childish and unfair. And, most importantly, I do not dislike or disrespect non-whites just because they are not white. I've made and have good friends who are black, Hispanic, Asian, Filipino, Jews, Russian, and so on. I discriminate on the basis of behavior. And treating "whites" as a race to be exterminated by breeding or genocide is the epitome of racism, no different that the Final Solution Nazi Himmler had for the Jews.

The globalists want white people gone because we are fighters against authoritarianism and dictatorships, and they fear white people the most as the only ones who can bring them down when push comes to a shove. They believe non-whites will not put up much of a fight, but will go quietly into the night accepting the fate that faces them. In fact, they believe non-whites will go easily because non-whites tend to be easily convinced that socialism will take care of them.

Personally, I will not submit to guilt-tripping tactics by non-whites or other whites just because I am legally white. When I was born, there was no such thing as a birth designation as "binary" or whatever is the term for mixed bloodlines. I will not give credence to race-baiters who accuse me of racism or demand I submit to reparations for ancestral past deeds. I will not bend my knees and kneel so that someone can cut off my head.

I do think that the approach by some whites about "white supremacy" is not going in the right direction because the messages they are sending is not acceptable to mainstream white Americans who are both patriots, are proud of their racial heritage, and who believe they have a constitutional right to be proud of who they are. Whites flying Nazi and Confederate flags, promoting fascism as an ideal for America, are not helping the legitimacy of white people who are pushing back against non-whites who simply hate them because they are white.

If patriots of this country do not all act in unison to confront and take down the globalists, jihadists, and racists who want us dead, we could lose the battle before us, whether in the political arena or in a civil war in the streets. Patriots should stand together as Christian soldiers, and engage in God's work. I believe the globalists are setting up a Satanic caliphate as their end agenda, and that Islamists are planning the way to subjugate and kill all the Christians of the world. As Christian soldiers, we do God's work and battle this evil before us. We do not let the evil-doers guilt-trip us into thinking we are the problem and they are the solution. We can fight the easy way (through the electoral system) or the hard way (full-fledge battles), but the alternative – doing nothing at all – ensures our fate in the end will not be very nice.

President Donald Trump has threatened to pull the U.S. out of the UN because so many member countries are paying either not their share at all, but only an amount less than what they are obliged to pay, and Trump has said no longer will the USA fund the greatest portion especially when all other payees pay far, far less than the United States. I think Trump realizes very clearly the U.N. is up to no good because of their globalist leanings and "replacement population" policies.

B. The North Atlantic Treaty Organizations (NATO)

NATO is an alliance between North America and Europe that was born out of World War II, and it was signed into effect in 1949. Its main aim back then was to push back against any future aggression from the Soviet Union. This became particularly important in 1955 when the Soviet Union and seven other European countries signed the Warsaw Pact. Communism was spreading across Eastern and Central Europe and the Pact promised support for several Soviet satellite states. There were twelve original NATO countries, but today there are 28. Seven of those are former Warsaw Pact countries. Each member of NATO has an equal say in discussions and decisions. One of the most important principles of the NATO treaty is Article V; it states that an attack on one country is, in theory, an attack against all members.

Like the UN, NATO's budget comes from an aggregate of funds of all member countries, but there are only five member countries that pay more than 2% of that budget, an unfair situation which caused Trump to threaten withdrawal of the U.S. from NATO unless all member countries agree to and pay their fair share. Trump has called the Treaty obsolete. As with the UN, Trump said that the U.S. would only help those member countries who pay their fair share.

Thus, transatlantic relations are under pressure from disputes over NATO commitment, and the unfairness of member countries to fail to pay their fair share while expecting the U.S. to always "foot the bill." There was talk of a European "army" and even hostile gestures on trade, sanctions, and cyberattacks. If the U.S. pulled out of NATO, and NATO countries sought to retaliate, we could see NATO countries turning against America. NATO may be, in the future, more supportive of the UN goal of a New World Order, it has a lot of soldiers and equipment they can draw from, but all that potential is based on the fact that the U.S. has consistently provided the major part of NATO's budget and hardware.

However, in fairness, immediately after 9-1-1, NATO stood up in support of the U.S. and on the rising war against terrorism anywhere in the world. NATO members are sworn to an alliance of mutual support for each other. The question is what is their position on the New World Order agenda, do they support the idea, or do they recognize the very real danger of the totalitarian agenda the NWO intends?

There are demagogue forces at work around the world today. Many of those are member countries of the UN and/or NATO. Some of them just want total control of countries, and some of them have set their sights on the United States. There are spearheads pointing in our direction from numerous directions; how are we going to challenge them all successfully?

C. The European Union

The European Union (EU) is a political and economic union of 28 member states that are located primarily in Europe. Its members have an estimated population of about 513 million people. The EU developed an internal single market through a standardized system of laws that apply in all member states in those matters, and only those matters, where members have agreed to act as one. EU policies aim to ensure the free movement of people, goods, services and capital within the internal market, enact legislation in justice and home affairs and maintain common policies on trade, agriculture, fisheries, and regional development. For travel within the Shenghen Area, passport controls have been abolished. A monetary union was established in 1999 and came into full force in 2002 and is composed of 19 EU member states which use the euro currency. The states are:

Country	Capital	Country	Capital
Austria	Vienna	Belgium	Brussels
Bulgaria	Sofia	Croatia	Zagreb
Cyprus	Nicosia	Czech Republic	Prague
Denmark	Copenhagen	Estonia	Tallinn
Finland	Helsinki	France	Paris
Germany	Berlin	Greece	Athens
Hungary	Budapest	Ireland	Dublin
Italy	Rome	Latvia	Riga
Lithuania	Vilnius	Luxembourg	Luxemborg City
Malta	Valletta	Netherlands	Amsterdam
Poland	Warsaw	Portugal	Lisbon
Romania	Bucharest	Slovakia	Bratislava
Slovenia	Ljubljana	Spain	Madrid
Sweden	Stockholm	United Kingdom	London

The EU member states retain all powers not explicitly handed to the European Union. Member states can withdraw from the EU for cause.

The treaties declare that the EU itself is "founded on the values of respect for human dignity, freedom, democracy, equality, the rule of law and respect for human rights, including the rights of persons belonging to minorities, and in a society in which pluralism, non-discrimination, tolerance, justice, solidarity and equality between women and men prevail.

Since the creation of the EU in 1993, it has developed its competencies in the area of justice and home affairs; initially at an intergovernmental level and later by "supra-nationalism." Accordingly, the Union has legislated in areas such as extradition, family law, asylum law, and criminal justice. Prohibitions against sexual and nationality discrimination have a long standing in the treaties. In more recent years, these have been supplemented by powers to legislate against discrimination based on race, religion, disability, age, and sexual orientation. By virtue of these powers, the EU has enacted legislation on sexual discrimination in the work-place, age discrimination, and racial discrimination. The Union has also established agencies to co-ordinate police, prosecutorial, and immigration controls across the member states. This cooperation had to particularly be developed with the advent of open borders through the Schengen Agreement and the associated cross border crime. Twenty-two EU member states are members of NATO as NATO was seen as appropriate and sufficient militarily for member state defense purposes.

I give this information assuming a great portion of Americans have not been interested in the European Union to learn anything about it, and what I have given here is the truncated version of information readily available on Wikipedia. I included this information because it gives a better understanding of why the EU states (countries) allowed the swarm of Muslim migrants from African and Arab countries to invade their countries demanding free stuff, and it explains why the governments looked the other way and even downplayed the huge crime problem of robberies, assaults, and rapes these migrants committed, while at the same time using its own laws and policies to create laws, to formulate new laws making it a crime for its own citizens to identify Muslims as the criminals committing these crimes or to openly protest against the invasions. It also explains why Sweden is one of the most sexually degenerate countries because its laws do not control sexual behavior or preferences, which itself explains why schools are allowed to engage in gender education that encourages small male and female children to play with opposite gender toys and clothing so that they can choose which sexual orientation they want to be – in which case transgender medical procedures are then available. It also explains why school and public playgrounds have mammoth plastic, blow-up penises and vaginas that children can use as slides to slide through. Yes, I've seen them.

When the EU was formed, the UN supported that union because the EU placed itself under the auspices of the UN in large portion, relying on the UN for military and intra-state policing protections. At the same time, the UN urged the United States to form its own union with Canada, Central and South America in the same manner as the EU. This must be seen as the attempt to create another step in the UN's goal of helping to bring about a one-government world under the New World Order. The United States, fortunately, declined. That might change, however, if the Democrats win the 2020 elections.

A Western union between the U.S., Canada, and Mexico, would soon encompass all of Central and South America, and if its new treaties, policies and laws are similar to or mirror those of the current EU, Americans will lose the unalienable rights enumerated in our Constitution for the subjective policies and practices we see in the EU states now. We will see laws that criminalizes freedom of speech and expression, laws that criminalizes identification by one race the race of another who commits a crime, like EU countries have done to "forgive" the cultural differences Muslims brought to their countries. Remember, in Great Britain, Muslim street gangs raping British girls and women are not identified as Muslim gangs, they are simply identified as youth "grooming gangs" and given slaps on the wrists and vacuous warnings not to do that again.

The perhaps well-intentioned (by some) efforts to unite the world under a single banner, despite religious and cultural differences, may be a noble goal, but it overlooks what local indoctrination means for individual countries and their peoples, and what conflicts would occur which incompatible cultures collide. Like Islam with the rest of the world.

The 2020 elections are critical, because the alt-Left, now controlling the Democratic Party, is moving in the direction of the NWO, whether they know it or not. I believe the top drivers know exactly what they are doing, while the ill-informed minions are lost in the fantasy of a Utopian world.

D. The Military Industrial Complex (MIC)

I mention the Military Industrial Complex because it is an amalgam of corporations and militaries that fight the wars. Generally speaking, the MIC builds weapons and ordnance, and all ancillary products that are needed. By its very nature, all of the industries and services involved must remain profitable to sustain them. That means a war is needed somewhere all the time. That's the reality of the "war machine." It does not care that to remain profitable means that soldiers and civilians alike must die; after all, the business of the war machine is to kill people, often in the name of "peacekeeping." In fact, the role of the UN's military branch is designated as "peacekeepers."

What is relevant here is simply the ongoing fact that American soldiers, and civilians around the world, die in wars that are created for the sole reason of keeping the "war machine" in the black, i.e., profitable. I can imagine a boardroom of the companies and government agencies of the "war machine" meeting to discuss what is the next country to get militarily-involved with because the profit margin was beginning to reach the red zone. Seems quite pathological somehow to determine economic health knowing the direct and collateral deaths of human beings beforehand. "Collateral damage" is politically correct speech for "Well, we're probably going to have to kill X-thousands of people, and that will include many of our soldiers." I can imagine the members in that boardroom saying, "*Well, that's the price of business.*"

There is no doubt that the world is a dangerous and deadly place, always has been. There is no doubt but that there are cultures in the world whose entire history has been one of violence and death, like Islam. But also, African tribes, and even American natives – before Europeans arrived, killed and enslaved each other. Killing is common to humankind, all over, and it seems it is only increasing with "civilization".

For Americans, who live on a scale higher than most of the world, the "war machine" is a self-preservation must. Perhaps someday we'll have the technology advanced enough that neither soldiers nor civilians need to die. Right now, we simply are saddled with a necessary 'evil' of a killing machine.

Having said that, I admit that I nonetheless highly respect the soldiers and personnel of our military, and I have to accept that somehow, we have to protect ourselves from those who would kill us all if they just have the chance. The "war machine" is that mechanism, like it or not. Perhaps we can figure out how to make it profitable without needing to actually use it just to maintain the profit margin.

We could have simply conquered Iraq and Saudi Arabia, considering SA helps fund terrorists, and then Iran, Libya, Sudan, Yemen, and other Arab countries and nationalized their oil under American control. We could have shut down the ideological enemy of the world, Islam, which flourishes solely because they are backed by huge oil-production profits. Without that revenue, Islamists would be unable to subjugate other countries. We could have used their oil to pay for the "war machine" sustainability. Americans wouldn't have to pay $4.00 per gallon or more for gasoline anymore. Crazy? No, not when you consider 1400 years of genocide and a goal to take over the entire world and make it an Islamist caliphate. Islam is no friend of the rest of humanity. Why should the West give them such huge powers by oil-generated wealth? The West would have been much better off by conquering those oil-producing nations. It certainly would have been safer for the rest of the world today.

E. The Role of the Media in the Globalist NWO Plan

We have seen an unbelievable growth in mainstream media engaging in totally false narratives in order to achieve political and globalist goals. On October 19, 2019, talk show host Rush Limbaugh described the new narrative the New York Times (owned by the globalists) is pushing, and intends to get it in the schools in their history curriculum to teach to our children. This false narrative, which reframes history as to the beginnings of America, claims that before the United States was ever formed, slaves came to America in the 1600s, and it is they who created America and built it before the "white" European Americans came and stole it from the African blacks. This is another attempt at the globalists, using the power of THEIR media companies, to create not only more racial division and anger from Blacks, but also to create expectations from Blacks and non-Black supporters that they are rightly due reparations for the theft of the land they built. The NYT admits they only rediscovered this historic "truth" and they want history changed that is taught in America's schools.

It is clear to me, and it should be clear to all rational-thinking people that this false narrative is just another attempt to keep President Trump from winning again in 2020, as well as to reinforce the globalists' agenda to destroy America in their quest to create a New World Order, as I've described further in this book.

Everyone must realize that the globalists' NWO agenda overrides anything else and they care not what lies they have to tell to achieve that goal. Remember, former President George H.W. Bush, publicly told America that we were heading forward into a new utopian world, the New World Order.

Remember too, that Obama's two terms was to set up for the downfall of the USA, using Orwellian double-speak, telling Americans exactly the opposite of what he intended. Hillary Clinton was to win the presidency, bring about civil unrest, increase the racial divide and violence, create civil war, implement martial law, allow the UN to come in and disarm Americans (which Obama personally set up when he went to the UN), and take the USA into socialism. Again, one might question is my conclusion nothing more than false conspiracy theory? I can only say, this is what my research told me, and any conclusions I drew were based upon the facts and leading information.

Remember that once into socialism, the next step planned was communism just before it would go into the totalitarian mode using the deceptive description, the New World Order.

Remember too, that Herbert Walker Bush supported Adolf Hitler in Hitler's beginnings, and only pulled back when word of Hitler's genocidal campaign came out and the United States finally decided to step into the war.

Wake up Americans, moderate and conservative Democrats too. Wake up.

What is going on here, with regards to President Trump and conservative Americans, is the form of Marxism known at Critical Theory. Critical Theory is criticism, just criticism, endless criticism, no alternative, just criticism. It is not about truth, skewing truth, bald-face lying, it is about criticism, which is exactly what President Trump got from the moment of the election. It has not stopped. Endless criticism is a Marxist tool under Critical Theory. It cares not about truth or facts, it doesn't care about any response or argument is given, the result will continue to be the same: endless criticism. It's like the Orwellian rule: say it enough, emphasize it enough, force it down the throats of everyone you can, brainwash them with it, and undermine their ability to think and reason. What has been going on with this Marxist tool applied to our President is unforgivably shameful and immoral. The Southern Poverty Law Center engages this Marxist tool as well.

F. The Southern Poverty Law Center

The Southern Poverty Law Center was founded by civil rights lawyers Morris Dees and Joseph J. Levin Jr. in August 1971 as a law firm originally focused on issues such as fighting poverty, racial discrimination and the death penalty in the United States. In 1979 the SPLC began filing lawsuits against Ku Klux Klan chapters and similar organizations for monetary damages on behalf of their victims. The favorable verdicts from these suits served to bankrupt the KKK and other targeted organizations. In 1981, the Center began its Klan-watch project to monitor the activities of the KKK. That project, now called Hatewatch, was later expanded to include seven other types of "hate" organizations. In 1986, the entire legal staff of the SPLC, excluding Dees, resigned as the organization shifted from traditional civil rights work toward fighting what they deemed as "right-wing extremism" meaning just about everything Republicans believed, thought, or did.

Reverse racism reared its head with a vengeance. Couched as "hate groups" were just about anything predominantly or exclusively white, despite the historic facts to date that the SPLC has never classified, characterized, or challenged any other ethnic group that created organizations whose members were exclusively of that ethnicity or face; only white groups were targeted. Whites could not have a Caucasian-American party, group, or organization; that was racist. But none of the non-white groups were racist even they identified as

Hispanic-American, Chinese-American, Vietnamese-American, Japanese-American, Arab-American, African-American, Puerto Rican-American, Cuban-American, and on and on and on. Any of these could segregated themselves by culture or spoken language (being no longer required to learn English as required by Immigration Laws), but they were not viewed as "racists." Only "whites" were disallowed to form such a group. Whites increasingly became the new "Jews" of an anti-white population; now, more so than any other time in our history.

For instance, in their study of the white separatist movement in the United States, sociologists Betty A. Dobratz and Stephanie L. Shanks-Meile referred to the SPLC's Klanwatch Intelligence Reports in saying, "we relied on the SPLC and ADL (Anti-Defamation League) for general information, but we have noted differences between the way events have been reported and what we saw at rallies. For instance, events were sometimes portrayed in Klanwatch Intelligence Reports as more militant and dangerous with higher turnouts than we observed. In 2013, J.M. Berger wrote in Foreign Policy that media organizations should be more cautious when citing the SPLC and ADL, arguing that they are "not objective purveyors of data." The SPLC's identification and listings of hate groups and extremists has been the subject of controversy. Critics of the SPLC say that it chooses its causes with funding and donations in mind, and argue that people and groups designated as 'hate groups' are targeted by protests or violence that prevent them from speaking. In 2018, David A. Graham wrote in The Atlantic that while criticism of the SPLC had long existed, the sources of such criticism have expanded recently to include "sympathetic observers and fellow researchers on hate groups" concerned about its research and activist strains.

In 2009, the Federation for American Immigration Report (FAIR) argued that allies of America's Voice and Media Matters had used the SPLC designation of FAIR as a hate group to *"engage in unsubstantiated, invidious name-calling, smearing millions of people in this movement."* FAIR and its leadership have been criticized by the SPLC as being sympathetic to, or overtly supportive of, white supremacist and identitarian ideologies, as the group's founder has stated his goal as ensuring that the United States remains a majority-white country.

In 2010, a group of Republican politicians and conservative organizations criticized the SPLC in full-page advertisements in two Washington D.C. newspapers for what they described as "character assassination" because the SPLC had listed the Family Research Council (FRC) as a hate group for alleged "defaming of gays and lesbians." In essence, the new-speak promoting "Adam and Steve" and vilifying the original Godly view of "Adam and Eve" became increasingly prominent under "political correctness."

The criticisms continued over the ensuing years, but the SPLC became more adept in evading judicial libel actions.

In an 2019 article published by USA Today, a victim of the SPLC's 'hate group' smear, who was almost a victim of a shooter who invaded the building of the Family Research Council with a gun, the shooter later admitting that he attached the FRC because the SPLC labeled it as a 'hate group." Jessica Prol Smith wrote:

> "I wrote and edited for the Family Research Council, a public advocacy organization that promoted the principles I have cared about since childhood: protecting the family, promoting the dignity of every human life and advocating for religious liberty. It reads like a tagline, but it's also just what I believed and the way I chose to match my career with my convictions. ... My daughter thinks she's transgender. Her public school undermined my efforts to help her. ... I never expected that everyone would celebrate or share my beliefs. But I did expect to be able to discuss and debate these differences without becoming a political target in an act of terrorism, the first conviction under Washington, D.C.'s 2002 Anti-Terrorism Act.
>
> It was the type of violent incident that one could expect a group that purportedly monitors "hate," like the Southern Poverty Law Center, to notice, research and decry. In fact, we were in the center's radar but for all the wrong reasons. The assailant acknowledged later in FBI testimony that he

had selected our office precisely because the SPLC had labeled my employer a "hate group."

It has always been easier to smear people rather than wrestle with their ideas. It's a bully who calls names and spreads lies rather than thoroughly reading a brief's legal arguments or challenging the rationale underlying a policy proposal. The SPLC has chosen to take the easy path — to intimidate and mislead for raw political power and financial benefit.

Hate groups in America: I grew up a white nationalist. We never blamed ourselves for mass shootings like El Paso.

For years, former employees revealed, local journalists reported and commentators have lamented: The Southern Poverty Law Center is not what it claims to be. Not a pure-hearted, clear-headed legal advocate for the vulnerable, but rather an obscenely wealthy marketing scheme.

For years, the left-wing interest group has used its "hate group" list to promote the fiction that violent neo-Nazis and Christian nonprofits peacefully promoting orthodox beliefs about marriage and sex are indistinguishable. Sometimes, it has apologized to public figures it has smeared, and it recently paid out millions to settle a threatened defamation lawsuit.

The SPLC has its own troubles. These shameful secrets are no longer hidden in shadows. The New York Times, Politico, NPR and a host of other mainstream publications are reporting on the corruption and widening credibility gap. The SPLC dismissed its co-founder in March, and its president has resigned amidst numerous claims of sexual harassment, gender discrimination and racism within the organization — a parade of disgraces that vividly force the conclusion: The SPLC is hollow, rotten and failing at the very virtues it pretends to celebrate.

Fifty-one years ago, Dr. Martin Luther King Jr. fell to an assassin's bullet. The SPLC pretends to carry his legacy but weaponizes hate labels instead. Unlike SPLC's name-calling, Dr. King's words and vision stand the test of time. "Injustice anywhere," he warned, "is a threat to justice everywhere."

The SPLC, as an institution, has thoroughly disqualified itself as an arbiter of justice. But this country would be a better place if the center's donors, lawyers and friends would truly believe and apply Dr. King's legacy – his peaceful pursuit of justice and his love of neighbor.

In May 2017, The Federalist published an article entitled "12 Ways The Southern Poverty Law Center Is A Scam To Profit From Hate-Mongering.", written by Stella Morabito. She writes:

> That makes the hate list of the Southern Poverty Law Center different from the "burn book" a high school queen bee keeps in the 2004 movie "Mean Girls"? Answer: not much. The burn book was a compilation of insults, gossip, and rumors intended to repel the diva's "enemies," label everybody, and keep herself on top of the heap.

> The SPLC uses its lists of designated hate groups in much the same way: to manipulate the lives of others, smear reputations, control personal relationships, and reap the spoils. The dynamic is the same, whether played on the adolescent scene or in the political arena. Both lists serve as power-mongering tools.

> In civilized societies, we supposedly grow out of that sort of tribalism. But look around and you'll see such behaviors proliferating in every sphere: politics, journalism, education. A recent headline in the Washington Examiner nailed it: "The Bret Stephens Freak-Out is a Reminder that the Media Is Basically a Massive High School Clique."

Why do so many folks treat the SPLC with underserved reverence, the way too many high school kids treat a self-appointed nasty queen bee? Why do they accept the Southern Poverty Law Center as the nation's Grand Inquisitor dictating who may speak and who must shut up? And why are its smears and caricatures so often blindly accepted at face value? What qualifies the SPLC to act as judge, jury, and social executioner of any human being who is not their blind supporter?

Those questions have been hanging in the air for decades. As with all vilification campaigns, the SPLC plays a dangerous and cruel game under the guise of defending victims. So let's take a closer look at some of the SPLC's history and behavior. Let's count some ways it's a con game.

1. It's a Big-Money Smear Machine
2. The Center's Work Has Incited Violence
3. SPLC Uses Emotion-Laden Images to Spread Innuendo
4. The FBI Stopped Citing SPLC as a Resource
5. People On Its Political Team See the Problems too.
6. Its Nonprofit Status Masks Highly Political Fundraising
7. Its Public Activities Are a Ruse for Fundraising
8. Its Founder Is a Direct Marketing Guru
9. Civil Rights Activists Say Its Founder Is 'A Con Man'
10. The Center Is Advertising For New Revenue-Raisers
11. SPLC Propaganda Seems to Encourage Hoax Hate Crimes
12. Its Blacklist Foments the Campus Anti-Speech Movement

The full text of this article can be found online at www.thefederalist.com/2017 /05/17/12-ways-southern-poverty-law-center-scam-profit-hate-mongering/.

Just for clarity, the SPLC is a cash-collecting machine. In 2015 it collected $50 million in contributions and foundation grants, in addition to its $334 million holdings of cash and securities and its headquarters worth $34 million. Its founder Morris Dees was actually inducted into the Direct Marketing Hall of Fame in 1998. Perhaps he employed those skills while working on George Wallace's 1958 gubernatorial campaign in Alabama and as finance director for George McGovern's 1972 presidential bid, as well as campaigns of Jimmy Carter and Ted Kennedy. With the SPLC he created a "poverty palace" in the SPLC building.

In 2019 Morris Dees was fired for allegations of *"mistreatment, sexual harassment, gender discrimination, and racism"* that threatened the *"moral authority and our integrity"* of the SPLC.

Perhaps the SPLC has earned the allegation of a "scam" organization that markets itself as a leader in values and justice. Certainly that claim has earned it great power and wealth.

But make no mistake, the SPLC is highly involved in the education system as it currently stands, with its brainwashing and indoctrination policies and curriculum aimed at dumbing-down our youth in preparation for the socialism agenda pushed by the Left's Progressives and the "shadow government".

Even worse, the SPLC's name-calling has a clear goal. They wish to silence anyone who disagrees with them on a variety of subjects, including same-sex marriage and related LGBT issues.

In August 2018, U.S. Attorney General Jeff Sessions spoke at the Alliance Defending Freedom Summit on Religious Liberty, where he reiterated the Trump administration's commitment to upholding the first freedoms of every American. Confronting the troubling smear of ADF as a "hate group" by the SPLC said that such slander, clearly untrue, was no way to describe a well-respected legal-advocacy organization that had won nine cases at the Supreme Court in the past seven years, including three victories *after* the SPLC tagged ADL with its erroneous and vicious "hate group" label in early 2017. Sessions said the SPLC has *"used this designation as a weapon, and they have wielded it against conservative organizations that refuse to accept their orthodoxy and choose instead to speak their conscience. They have used it to bully and intimidate groups like yours, which fight for the religious freedom, the civil rights, and the constitutional rights of the American people."*

Sessions also said that, at his direction, the Department of Justice is reviewing partner organizations to make sure they no longer work with groups that, like the SPLC, *"unfairly defame Americans for standing up for the Constitution or their faith."*

National Review journalist Michael Farris said it clearly:

> "Our nation has a choice. Will we stand up for free speech for all, or will we give in to the growing impulse to harass, vilify, and coerce every person who disagrees with our views? Will we stand for freedom of the press, even when we don't like its viewpoint? These rights travel together and must both be defended. Defending the right of those with other viewpoints to speak and publish is an absolute prerequisite for a society that embraces a truly civil discourse. Force homogeneity of thinking never results in civility.
>
> ADJ seeks to cultivate a society that is typified by the free exchange of ideas and respect and tolerance for those with different views. These uniquely American and constitutional principles are essential in a diverse society like ours. They enable us to peacefully coexist with each other. They are the best way to ensure human flourishing."

Farris noted how some in our country have given up on American values, including ... surprise! surprise! ... Georgetown University law professor Louis Michael Seidman, who commented to the New York Times that what he has *"come to see is that it's a mistake to think free speech as an effective means to accomplish a more just society."* A law professor, of all people, one who should clearly understand the vast constitutional and other legal protections American society is given over those of nearly every other country. In fact, twice in 2017 the U.S. Supreme Court ruled that *"Neither waving the white flag on free speech nor harassing political opponents into silence has a place in our society."*

In both cases, *MasterpieceCakeshop v. Colorado Civil Rights Commission*, and *National Institute for Family and Life Advocates v. Becerra*, the state was merely acting on the same philosophical premises of the SPCL and Professor Seidman. In *Masterpiece*, Colorado forced a man of faith to create artistic expression that violated his religious beliefs about marriage rather than letting all views on marriage flourish. In *NIFLA*, pro-abortion California passed a law that compelled pro-life pregnancy centers to provide free advertising for the abortion industry rather than respecting these groups' life-affirming views. The Court rightly rebuked these states' attempts to commandeer conscience and coerce speech in the name of *"forward thinking"* (a new term for Orwellian "thought control").

Farris also noted that outgoing Justice Anthony Kennedy got it right in his concurrence in *NIFLA* when he wrote, *"It is forward thinking to begin by reading the First Amendment as ratified in 1791; to understand the history of authoritarian government as the Founders knew it; to confirm that history since then shows how relentless authoritarian regimes are in their attempts to stifle free speech."*

Courts of constitutional authority can, and should, uphold the First Amendment without twisting it around in a partisan manner. The Sixth Circuit Court of Appeals in Michigan, recently pounded another nail in the coffin of the University of Michigan, which was accused of having a bullying and harassment police against free speech that did not align with the University's partisan view, and as it acted only in behalf of the alt-Left students. But the day when universities are forced to rediscover their historic role as guardians of open inquiry and debate is coming, whether they like it or not. Many universities have, for years, restrictive campus speech regulations which, for years, have been ruled unconstitutional speech codes.

Between 2009 and 2019, the portion of surveyed American universities - with what the Foundation for Individual Rights in Education classifies as "red light" speech codes - has shrunk from 74.2 percent to a mere 28.5 percent, and a total of 17 states have enacted some form of campus free-speech legislation. But the impulse to censor dies hard, and some schools have been nothing if not creative in their efforts to control speech without explicitly and clearly running afoul of the law. Witness, for example, the phenomenon of the "bias-response team."

While this system varies from university to university, in general a "bias-response team" represents an institutional effort to identify *alleged* student bias and bigotry and eliminate it through some form of "*reeducation.*" Students report speech they find discriminatory or otherwise problematic, a university team investigates the "*incident*" – including meeting with the alleged offender – and then often creates a report describing the events. Sometimes a bias-response team can and will refer conduct to university disciplinary officials or university police if they feel more substantial punishment is warranted. In other words, criminalizing "*free speech*" they don't agree with.

The "Speech First" group filed the lawsuit against the University of Michigan challenging the content of the university's bullying and harassment policy and its bias-response team's procedures. The district court denied Speech First's request for an injunction, holding in part that the group lacked *standing* (right to sue) to challenge the policy. The court required that there be an "injury in fact" for *standing* and held Speech First would have to show it suffered an "*objective chill*" to their free-speech rights or a mere "*subjective chill*," thus requiring a "concrete harm" (enforcement of a statute or regulation) "occurred or is imminent."

I see this reasoning quite troubling and, to be sure, hypocritical. If an "injury in fact" must be shown to be an "objective chill" and not a mere "subjective chill", then why is it that in the new "woke" language realm of transgenderism or feminist demands all that it takes in a "subjective chill" is to have someone found guilty of committing an "injury in fact"?

Basically, Michigan argued that the courts should move along, that there was nothing to see. However, the Sixth Circuit Court of Appeals did not agree with the district court and, instead, sided with Speech First, reversed the district court and ordered it to reconsider the group's request for an injunction. Its ruling recognized the power of the bias-response team, to wit:

> The Response Team's ability to make referrals – i.e., to inform OSCR or the police about reported conduct – is a real consequence that objectively chills speech. The referral itself does not punish a student – the referral is not, for example, a criminal conviction or expulsion. But the referral subjects

students to processes which could lead to those punishments. The referral initiates the formal investigative process, which itself is chilling even if it does not result in a finding of responsibility or criminality.

It should be obvious to anyone that there isn't a student who wouldn't find the bias-response team's investigative process intimidating. But the problem extends beyond the team's ability to refer students for punishments; it reaches to the team's power to request a meeting with the accused student, as the court went on to explain:

> Additionally, the invitation from the Response Team to meet could carry an implicit threat of consequence should a student decline the invitation. Although there is no indication that the invitation to meet contains overt threats, the referral power lurks in the background of the invitation. It is possible that, for example, a student who knows that reported conduct might be referred to police or OSCR could understand the invitation to carry the threat: "meet or we will refer your case." Additionally, the very name "Bias Response Team" suggest that the accused student's actions have been prejudged to be biased. The name is not "Alleged Bias Response Team" or "Possible Bias Investigatory Team." It is the "Bias Response Team."

Should the University appeal that action, it will now be required to defend its response team on the merits, and it is highly likely to lose. If there are other similar cases in the Circuit Courts, the matter will eventually find its way before the United States Supreme Court, which is the highest court for the application of constitutional law. There, free speech without government or institutional restraints will prevail.

Perhaps the vast majority of Americans could defeat the demands of the LGBT community that everyone must use the new pronouns created by any individual as to how he or she may be addressed by arguing any perceived "injury" is a mere "subjective chill" that has no legal standing under the law.

G. The "Fourth" Branch of Government

In our civics classes, students are taught there are only three branches of government, the Judiciary, Legislative, and Executive. The reason for this split is because a separation of powers is necessary to keep any one branch from usurping complete control of the government and country, and thus this prevents any branch from shredding our individual rights and liberties set forth in the Constitution.

However, over the years another "silent branch" has emerged, essentially a hidden branch that may correctly be called the *"administrative state."* Tea-Party247 reports (see, www.teaparty247.org/is-the-deep-state-attempting-be-come-the-secret-fourth-branch-of-the-goverenment/) that as early as 1937, in a "Report of the President's Committee on Administrative Management", the authors wrote:

> Without plan or intent, there has grown up a headless,
> "fourth branch" of government, responsible to no one, and
> impossible of coordination with the general policy work of
> the government as determined by the people through their
> duly elected representatives."

In my book, I have touched on the problems of local governments finding new ways of taxing the tax-payers as a means of expanding an already bloated bureaucratic system. But the problem is far worse than that. As early as 1937, *"the problem of waste and lack of accountability in this fourth branch, has been clearly recognized for generations and has been growing steadily worse decade by decade."* Yet, in these earlier times, when America was still in its growing stages, and while we citizens were focused, if at all, on the three branches of recognized government, this fourth branch called the "civil service" administrative branch grew quietly and established a *"bureaucratic class"* which see its interests and loyalties as separate from the *elected* civilian government. As this article explains, *"This detachment from elected policymakers meant the administrative state was not terribly concerned with either efficiency or responsiveness to the public. It became an interest group all its own, but with far more power than any ordinary interest group. ... [T]his new non-political bureaucracy was anything but unbiased. Over time, the bureaucracy became self-consciously devoted to the "merit" system under which bureaucrats imagined they gained and retained their offices by virtue of their own excellence."* In other words, rule from self-conceit, i.e., nihilism.

Within this bureaucracy are the "regulatory agencies" which came to assume all the powers that were supposed to be reserved to the three branches of government that were given specific powers in the federal Constitution. In his book "Ex America" (aka The People's Pottage), Garet Garrett described this transformation.

> These agencies have built up a large body of administrative law which the people are obliged to obey, and not only do they make their own laws, they enforce their own laws, acting as prosecutor, jury and judge. An appeal from their decision in the regular courts is difficult; thus, the constitutional separation of the three governmental powers, namely, the legislative, the executive, and the judicial is entirely lost.

All of us citizens have had the stress and often displeasure having to deal with one administrative agency or another, and we have all seen the occasional dismissive attitude of the person you have to deal with, i.e., the apparent self-importance of the bureaucrat. American citizens, now awash in a menagerie of bureaucracies governing just about every aspect of our lives, are nonetheless subject to laws not passed by any Congress, and subject to judicial punishments not commanded by any court of law, because it is all done "administratively" by agencies able to "make and execute their own laws."

The TeaParty247 article questions what portions of this administrative state are involved or constitutes the "deep state", a question that remains the subject of debate. As I have mentioned herein, "forfeiture laws" are created and administered by this bureaucracy.

But it may be more serious than that. As the article suggested, the term "deep state" carries connotations beyond just regulatory agencies, but tends to point toward those agencies that can – by invoking national security and the need for secrecy – stifle efforts and oversight of the organizations in question.

One commenter noted that some 50 years ago, he heard a bureaucrat saying, *"Elected officials come and go, [but] we run the government."*

I question, then, where heads of some of these bureaucracies are "appointed" by elected politicians or heads of higher agencies, how deeply goes the "administrative" branch in support of the current socialist agenda, if at all? I do not doubt but that a bureaucracy led by a socialist can make life difficult or miserable for citizens over which they can exert control or punishments.

More recently, book author Craig Huey wrote a book entitled "The Deep State" where he identifies the "Deep State" as the government bureaucracy and private agencies. But, we now have sources identify the Deep State as a government bureaucracy and others identifying the Deep State as something on an international level beyond mere bureaucracies. Different sources subjectively naming the Deep State being one thing while another names it to different factions need not confuse us nor contradict the other. In other words, you might say, Deep State 1 and Deep State 2. With Huey, he has the right to name what he has identified to us any title he wants, although I would think his faction might be more accurately identified as the "Fourth Branch" of government or, perhaps, the "Shadow State."

Another faction identified as the Deep State by Craig Huey in his recent book "The Deep State" is described as

> "The traditional bureaucrats who think they can control and manipulate because in a bureaucracy there are two things: one is to expand your money, expand your power, and number two, to protect yourself. But the second part is the ideology. President Obama had brought into the bureaucracy where ideologically-driven people wanted to transform America into a socialist society. And that is the difference; and with that we find that the Deep State is at war with liberty. It is the bureaucratic, administrative state that is a threat

to individual freedom. ... The Government is so big, and it wants to keep getting bigger. They may be in charge of departments or administrative tasks that are no longer needed. They're a waste of money. They're a duplication. But a bureaucracy continues on and on and on, always wanting to grow and protect itself. That is one of the enemies. They see the policies of President Trump, the policies that have come out from Congress, that are disrupting the bureaucracy. It is deregulation. That takes away their jobs, that takes away their influence, their power, they see downsizing of the government as the enemy, and they got to fight back. Then when you add the ideology of all the Obama appointees where you have – in the EPA itself, at least one third of those in the EPA is an army of resistance against change – abusive power by the EPA. They're fighting an ideological war along with the bureaucrats, they're fighting to protect themselves. ... There is an abuse of power that has gone on, and they have the power. You have 18 agencies that are able to cause great harm, not only to overseas, but to America, and we saw that in the FISA abuse that has taken place under the Obama administration. We see that we have the FBI, the CIA, we have these intelligence agencies that are also becoming enemies of liberty, enemies of the people in the sense that they are abusing their power. And, the only way to stop this is to be able to put more restrictions on the ability of the bureaucrats to use their power."

In another radio interview, Craig Huey gave another example of the abuse of power by the government surrounding the "Mueller Report" and noting the report was done by highly skilled lawyers who were also haters of President Trump. In this interview on the "Bottom Line" show, he points out that the Deep State include both private entities and the government. He notes that in the government are career bureaucrats in some of the most powerful agencies of all, like the intelligence agencies, who have been at war with Trump since he began running for office on the platform of "draining the swamp" because they were his target as well. Huey warns that the very nature of this Deep

State is to keep the bureaucracy growing at the expense of the liberty rights and freedoms of the American people.

Huey pointed out that Obama became President on the platform of "fundamental change" but did not tell his voters what that meant. Obama installed lots of young people – whose ideological leanings were toward socialism – into numerous government agencies at the top or high levels, all of whom were there to help transform America to a socialist state. When Trump got elected, many of those appointees could not be fired, and were there supporting and pushing the anti-Trump agenda. These subversive young socialists are still in office at these numerous government agencies.

There is much for America's patriots to recognize and fix as we step up to impose oversight measures in taking back our country from those who are hell-bent on destroying it for a socialist or NWO result.

Watching water boil one sees transparent movement as the water heats up, and then we begin to see the tiny bubbles. If we stick our fingers in, it is already hot even though it might not "look" hot. We know it is hot when it begins to boil and we take measures not to get splashed and burned by boiling water. We Americans must recognize we are past the tiny bubbles stage of this socialist movement; it is heating up into a dangerous cauldron and we cannot afford to allow it boiling over onto us. It is up to us to turn the heat down and off.

H. The Deep State: Another Version

Over the years the term "shadow government" and the "deep state" have been bandied about, sometimes indicating they are one and the same, and sometimes indicating they are separate. To put a dispositive finger on who it is and what it is seems to be hard to identify, hence the term "shadow" government.

Recent research I found made me add this information at this part of the book. Since it makes a lot of sense, I'll talk about it here, but also leave you with an online link to see it for yourselves. If it is no longer available, I downloaded a copy.

This analysis appeared in a publication called Zero Hedge (*www.zerohedge.com/geopolitical/understanding-deep-states-propaganda*), and authored by a Eric Zuesse via the Strategic Culture Foundation. I can't identify what political leaning Zero Hedge has, but it appears that the information about the Deep State pervades the USA at a very powerful level but is actually an international 'organization' if that is even a proper term to use. The information might also place into another perspective the information I am providing in this book, thus tying yet another strand to the world-wide net of the "shadow" government called the Deep State. I had first thought it was only American politicians and interests by powerful corporations and those of extreme wealth, but it goes way beyond that.

In this book, I have noted what both the Rothschild and Rockefeller once said, in a slightly different way, *"It does not matter who the American people elect, we already own them."* And so what I found here about the "Deep State" re-confirms that, as you will see.

Here is small part of what Eric Zuesse says:

> The Deep State is the small number of people who control the organizations that donate the majority of the funds which finance the political careers of national officials, such as Presidents, Prime Ministers, and members of the national legislature. Almost always, the members of the Deep State are the controlling stockholders in the international corporations that are headquartered in the given nation; and, therefore, the Deep State is more intensely interested in international than in purely national matters. Since most of its members derive a large portion of their wealth from abroad, they need to control their nation's foreign domestic policies even more than they need to control its domestic policies. Indeed, if they don't like their nation's domestic policies, they can simply relocate abroad. But relocating the operations of their corporations would be far more difficult and costly to them. Furthermore, a nation's public know and care far less about the nation's foreign than about

its domestic policies; and, so, the Deep State reigns virtually alone on the nation's international issues, such as: which nations will be treated as "allies" and which nations will instead be treated as "enemies." Such designations are virtually never determined by a nation's public. The public just trust what the Government says about such matters, like, for example, the US regime's standard allegation, for decades, that "Iran is the leading state sponsor of terrorism", which is clearly a blatant lie.

The above might explain why George Soros, a frontline member of the Deep State, has the task of helping to crash the economies of various nations to bring them in line with whatever policies the Deep State wants; e.g., Venezuela, Guatemala, and others, including the crash of European countries due to hordes of migrants invading.

Zuesse talks about how the Deep State has mis-labeled North African countries as terrorists for its own purposes, and that the Deep State controls at least these three countries: United States, Saudi Arabia, and Israel.

Zuesse goes on:

> The Deep State here is the US-anatallied Deep State, not merely national organizations. It consists mainly of America's billionaires, plus many of the billionaires in US-allied countries such as UK, France, Saudi Arabia, UAE, and Israel – but many more (including, for example, in Honduras, Brazil, [and other South American countries]). These people number fewer than 2,000 in total, and they do deals together, and their contracts with one another are both person-to-person, and indirect by means of representatives or agents. However, America's billionaires lead the US-and-allied Deep States. That's to say, the leaders are among the 607 US billionaires, the people who mainly fund American national political campaigns and candidates – and these 607 individuals determine who

will get an opportunity to become a US President or member of Congress, and who won't. For example: these individuals don't necessarily select the politicians who will become America's President, but they do select who will get the opportunity to be among the serious contenders for that position.

Although an anti-Trump person might use this as ammunition to say that Donald Trump is one of those Deep State billionaires, I suggest this is easily contested by the point that I have also made in this book. In the part on the Illuminati and Lindsey Williams, Lindsey Williams, a pastor on the Alaskan Pipeline project, became a "fly on the wall" of board meetings with the funders of the pipeline, i.e., members of the Deep State he knew as members of the Illuminati. Having since been long away from the Illuminati, but keeping in touch with two Illuminati who had become his friends and conveyed information to him about what the Illuminati was doing, Lindsey remained in contact and learned much about the Illuminati. Just before the second friend passed away, but just after the elections, the man called Lindsey, and said just these words: "God intervened!" about Trump getting elected. It thus is my belief that Trump never made it into the Deep State membership, which may explain a few things: One, his accepting a nomination to run was to almost everyone (but the American people) a joke and not one of the Deep State took his candidacy seriously. Two, the mainstream media automatically went into gear during his campaign, once the Deep State began to take him seriously after the surge in conservative voter support, to vilify him in every way they could. Once his election, the media went crazy, throwing everything at him including the proverbial "kitchen sink" and, every allegation against him had no evidence to support it, to try to derail his election. It was Trump's election that thwarted the next step planned for America's destruction.

Who owns the mainstream media? Well, looks like it is the Deep State, and/or the Illuminati, who - it appears to me – to be one and the same or, at the least, tied together by – as AOC put it – the "Benjamins." So, Zuesse puts another nail in the coffin answering the big question many of American citizens have as to WHY the mainstream media became a monstrous fake news machine against not only Donald Trump, but conservative America itself.

Zuesse talks about George Soros:

> One [member of the Deep State], in particular, is George
> Soros, and this article will detail the views of one of his many
> beneficiaries. Another of these billionaires is Charles Koch,
> but he will not be discussed here, and inside the United
> States he is popularly considered to be an enemy of George
> Soros, only because the two men oppose each other on do-
> mestic issues. (Billionaires tend to be much more concerned
> with, and united about, foreign affairs than about domestic
> affairs, though they do oppose both their taxation and other
> regulation – they are for 'free markets', both domestically
> and abroad, and yet they also favor imposition of economic
> sanctions against countries which resist becoming controlled
> by them [i.e., Ukraine, Venezuela, Guatemala, and so on],
> and so they don't really favor free markets except to the ex-
> tent that free markets favor their own increase in power and
> thus tend toward oligopoly [*Oligopoly is a market structure with
> a small number of firms, none of which can keep the others from
> having significant influence. The concentration ratio measures the
> market share of the largest firms. A monopoly is one firm, duopoly
> is two firms and oligopoly is two or more firms. There is no precise
> upper limit to the number of firms in an oligopoly, but the number
> must be low enough that the actions of one firm significantly in-
> fluence the others*], and away from competition. Both men are
> much more alike than different, and both represent what's
> called "*neoliberalism*," which is the universal ideology of bil-
> lionaires, or at least of all billionaires who donate to (i.e., in-
> vest in) politicians. Only a few billionaires don't invest in
> politicians; and, though politicians disagree with one another,
> almost all of them are neoliberals, because politicians who
> aren't, they are not funded by the Deep State (the billion-
> aires). The *foreign* policies of neoliberals are called "*neocon-
> servative*" and this means supporting regime-change in any
> country that's labeled by billionaires and their government
> as an "enemy" nation. So, "neoconservatives" is merely an

extension of "neoliberal"; it favors extending neoliberalism to other nations, it is internationally aggressive neoliberalism, it is imperialistic neoliberalism. It is fascism, but so is neoliberalism itself fascist; the difference between the two is that neoconservatism is the imperialistic extension of fascism. It is the imperialistic fascism that, in World War II, was represented by the three Axis powers: Germany, Italy, and Japan, not by the purely domestic fascism that was represented by Spain. Whereas Spain was merely neoliberal, the Axis were also neoconservative (*expansionist neoliberal*), and the latter is what the Allies in WWII were warring against. But now the US has emerged as the world's leading neoconservative regime, invading and occupying country after country, none of which had ever invaded or threatened to invade the United States. Propaganda is necessary in order to "justify" doing that. This article will describe how that's done.

The Deep State doesn't concern [itself with] domestic issues because virtually all of its members control international corporations, and the Deep State is almost entirely about international issues: foreign policies, diplomacy, military issues, and international spying agencies called "intelligence agencies", [thereby] extending the empire. ...

The dictatorship of the US Deep State really is more international than national; it provides the continuity in international relations, when it chooses and defines which nations (which foreign governments) are "allies" (meaning "we sell arms to them") and which are instead "enemies" (meaning "we should sanction them and maybe even bomb them'). Both allies and enemies are essential in order for the military-industrial-press-government complex ... to thrive, and the Deep State controls the entire MIPGC. In other words, the Deep State is an international empire and, as such, its supreme aspiration is to conquer (via subversion, sanctions, coups, and/or invasions) all countries that it labels as "enemies."

The way that the Deep State views things, there is no need for an "enemy" to threaten or invade the United States in order for it to *be* an "enemy," but, instead, the United States and its allies possess a God-given right to impose sanctions against, or coups overthrowing, or invasions of, any country they choose, so long as they can criticize that other country for being a "dictatorship", or for "violating human rights," or for otherwise doing what the Deep State itself actually does more than any other government on this planet does (and particularly does it to *its selected 'enemies'* – such as were Iraq, Libya, Syria, Iran, Venezuela, and any other country that's either friend toward, or else an ally of, Russia, which is the *other* nuclear super-power, and the Deep State's central target).

So now we know who and what the Deep State is and all about. One might recall that in the early days of the Trump administration, there was a potential for a United States and Russia alliance. Trump was willing to extend his hand for peace and fellowship with Russia under Vladmir Putin, and Putin was hopeful for such an alliance because it would benefit both countries economically and politically on the international levels. But then all went quiet. Why? Information filtering out was that Trump had a "talking to" by someone, someone very powerful. A lot of us thought this was from the RINOs who were so entrenched in their hatred for Russia that they would not idly sit by and let this alliance occur. We were partly right, insofar as the Deep State members undoubtedly include some of these RINOs. And DINOs too. No one knows what kind of threat was made to Trump, but he let go of that idea, and I don't think he liked doing that.

In addition, George Soros helped to fund the overthrow of the democratically elected and internationally non-aligned President of Ukraine in 2014 and to replace him with an Nazi Anti-Russian regime which serves as a terrific asset for the US-and-allied Deep State, because of Ukraine's having a 1,625-mile border with the country that the US-installed regime in Ukraine hates: Russia (hates it because the Deep State craves, above all, to control also the *other* nuclear super-power, so this is hatred-on-command).

What Zuesse reveals, which I have referenced for additional research should the reader be so inclined, is that Russia, with Putin at the helm, is trying to rebuild the country for his people after the collapse of the USSR, and he is not interested in world domination but in an alliance with the freedom-loving America. The Deep State does not find this acceptable, and so we keep hearing about Russia doing nuclear testing and preparing for another world war; this is simply another propaganda lie. During the "Grom-2019" military exercise, with the personal guidance of Putin, the nuclear submarine cruiser K-44 "Ryazan" fired only one ballistic intercontinental missile R-29R. The other missile just didn't come out. This is not the first time that the Russian army has failed. So the question arises, is Russia really a threat to peace, or is all this just propaganda by the Deep State? Russia does not yet have the money nor the technology to do more than build self-protection.

Having said that, I have recently had a long conversation with a Russian about Vladmir Putin. Despite the positive side where Putin has taken control and the country is stabilizing and becoming wealthier and, by and large, the citizenry are experiencing a reasonable economic life, there is a negative side as well. The old saying that power is a corrupting force and absolute power corrupts absolutely does apply in some ways with Putin. Putin's KGB experience resulted in a perspective that under communist rule the "President" was essentially the same as a King, an absolute ruler who for all intents and purposes the "owner" of everything in the country. There are no big corporate businesses in Russia that are independent. All of the major businesses exist in a "circle" around Putin, from which he benefits personally along with the country. The average citizen is allowed to have a small business but if it gets too big, the government will come knocking and gives the owner one of two choices: cut the government in or close down. Putin's administration has, in fact, helped the people and they are doing much better than ever since the collapse, and are generally happy. But, unlike America where citizens can visit or tour any government building, that doesn't happen in Russia. Also, citizens cannot criticize Putin or the government; any instance of that results in jail time. As long as the citizen goes about his/her daily affairs and takes advantage of the freedoms they have, they can do reasonably well. Russia's educational system is also reasonably fair, and Russians are getting good educations if they want it. I mention these things because socialism is often referred to as "soft communism" because there is not that much difference. Under a socialist regime, criticism of the government is also frowned upon or forbidden, sometimes with censorship and sometimes with brute violence, or death. The freedom in America to criticize government will end if the pro-socialists win and take control; already, we are seeing the beginnings of thought and speech control under the rubric of "political correctness" fostered by these pro-socialists.

Let me ask you this: Who would you rather America have an alliance with, Russia or China? Now, we do lots of business with China. Nearly everything we buy is made in China. The tariff differentiation is totally one-sided, but Trump has forced China into capitulating to a large degree on equalizing the tariff issue. But what is China doing today?

China has already begun imprisoning Muslims who have pushed their sharia law agenda now that their population has grown. China is having none of that nonsense. I agree with China about that. But China's regime does not believe in the concept of a God in Heaven at all. China is now moving against its growing Christian population, even imprisoning some and forbidding Christian churches and meetings, bibles or brochures, etc. While China has laws, they are not based on morality, and "morality" in China is what its leaders say it is, but not based in Christianity or any other religion.

But that is not the worst thing about China. China is now heavily engaged in surveillance technology. Already there are cameras everywhere using "facial recognition" technology. China is installing intrusive technology everywhere in a very Orwellian way so that every citizen can be tracked everywhere. In China today a citizen can be denied the ability to work, to buy anything, to have medical care, to travel, etc., and can be left to starve to death by the use of this surveillance technology and micro-chipping. This same technology is already here in America and is in its infancy for application to all Americans as well. Under socialist rule, Americans will be subject to this same Orwellian surveillance and consequences.

It is my opinion that an alliance with Russia would create a global power that can control China's spread. If you are not already aware, China has already taken over a large part of Africa and continues to grow a Chinese population there. Remember, Africa has great natural wealth, particularly in gemstones, and China is quietly taking that continent over.

But, back to Russia. It was the Deep State's influence that created the Russia-Syria problem. Why? Seems all Putin wanted from Syria was an oil pipeline for his own economy and people. It was the Deep State's influence, via Soros, that crashed the most democratic and economically successful country in South America, Venezuela, all because Putin had tried to make an oil deal with Venezuela. So, the Deep State has put Russia on its "enemy" list and punishes any country that is considering doing business with Russia.

The Deep State says that *"Russia has an extremely powerful nuclear arsenal."* Does it really? The Deep State says, *"The Kremlin has promised to develop short- and medium-range missiles and deploy them to confront the West."* Did he really? Or is Putin looking toward self-defense, and recognizing the true enemy is nothing more than the Deep State? The Deep State claims that the *"security situation in Europe is very difficult and relations with Russia deteriorate. The absence of signs that this deterioration is coming to an end is worrying. There are no very effective ways to improve relations with Russia."* More propaganda? Is it really a bad attitude from Russia, or is it the Deep State which is fostering that deterioration in order to bring harm to Russia, or, perhaps, to create a war with Russia so the Deep States military industrial complex can be extraordinarily profitable in another war? The Deep State claims Russia's military exercises are an indication Russia is preparing an attack on the West. It lists those exercises locales and points it out as a potential or imminent attack by Russia. This, I am convinced, is far from the truth and Russia may become a scapegoat for reasons only the Deep State knows.

The Deep State claims that Russia is helping Syria. If so, why should he not? Syria became embroiled in war-conflict over reasons that went beyond what was simply Russia trying to get a deal with Syria for oil. If the truth is merely about that, but the Deep State is pushing false propaganda, then it is not Russia aggressively preparing for war against the West, it is the "West" Deep State that has already *selected* Russia as one of its *"enemies."*

As Zuesse explains, *"As can be clearly seen …, the basic method of the Deep State's propagandists is to ask questions which have assumptions that are the reverse of reality, and to answer these questions in ways that confirm those falsehoods. This is what many millions of people get paid to do. And it creates "Big Brother" or the Deep State here, just as, in 1948, George Orwell might have been thinking it would do in 1984."*

In the research I have been doing, the "world" has become a scarier place, not just because of backward cultures and undeveloped or criminally-corrupt cartels and governments, but because in great part because of the small number of extremely wealthy people who decide world affairs. Whether they are called the Deep State, the Illuminati, the Bilderbergs, international bankers, or transnational corporations, the "shadow government", they are all the same and all involved in controlling world affairs to become more wealthy and powerful. There is little consideration, if any, about the needs of the populations of the world. Profit and power are what they crave and get. The sufferings of those whose country has been crashed by these people are not an issue for them. The current destruction of European culture by the UN's "replacement population" ignores the rapes, violence, homicides and horrors of that "replacement population" bringing to these nations, factors which the Deep State care nothing about even as they make it happen through their agencies and organizations. They lie to the American people to distract them from the actual facts that they manipulate countries for their own economic gain; the Deep State folks are the true enemies of mankind.

America is on that list. It's already begun. It is of no significance to the members of the Deep State that most are domiciled in America. They have a plan, and the citizenry be damned, come what may.

I. The "Progressive" Movement

The word *"progressive"* first comes to mind as "making progress" to "achieve" something of value, like moving forward to something better. Reminding you of the "double-speak" of Orwellianism, the "Progressive" movement of our history, particularly in the 20s and 30s, and which has been rejuvenated quite recently, is believed by its believers to be "progressive" to "achieve" something "better" as a form of government. I decided to go back and review the history of this "Progressivism" to understand how they could arrive at a conclusion that a market-economy of democratic capitalism is somehow "evil" enough to be replaced by what traditionally has been oppressive ideologies, i.e., socialism and communism. Since I had earlier made assumptions on the literal definition of the word "progressive" as an attachment to the current socialist movement, I was left with questions. I here have those answers I am going to pass on to you.

We hear a lot these days about the pro-socialist "Progressive" movement. At first, I just thought it was just a bunch of poorly-informed lazy idiots who thought equality, multiculturalism, diversity, and Marxist thought were somehow brilliant and the cure for their animus against the merit-based capitalist economic model of America. I took this view mainly because the concept of the American dream was that if you wanted to achieve in this country, greatly or not, you bore the ultimate responsibility for preparing to achieve your goals (dreams) through education and action. To me it looked like children growing into adulthood today must have been disadvantaged in homes where there was little parental guidance, perhaps only one parent who had to work, where there were few demands on the children to do chores, to do well in school, to do anything beyond being lazy and on their iPhones, computers and the social media/internet most of their lives, and now finding themselves old enough to enter the marketplace without decent employable skills and knowledge. I lack sympathy for this group whose numbers seem to reflect the majority of young people today. They don't want a job; they just want the free stuff life they had as children.

But the term "Progressive" is not new, not at all. And the reasons it was at one time popular is eye-opening, and now that history lines up perfectly with the promise of Obama that he was going to bring about "fundamental change" because the Bible of this nation, the Constitution, he claimed, was out-of-date and out-of-touch with contemporary times. It was, they posit, supposed to be a "living" document that evolved as America evolved, or which makes the original worthless today as a guiding instrument.

So, I want to talk about that a little for those of you who do not know this history. I learned this from a (12 lecture) course at the Hillsdale College on the

Constitution. It is relevant to what is occurring today. What makes it relevant is that if we look around at what is going on today in this country and government, it does not look much like what was created and intended by our Founding Fathers, so studying the Progressive Era might be the most important history study Americans can make to understand historic and current events and status. What we can see is that the country has taken on various forms of socialism, such as the politics of welfare and government subsidies, we can see they are built on a direct rejection of the principles of the Constitution, the Declaration of Independence, and the rights and protections of the individual expressed therein.

The "Progressive Era" began at the turn of the century, a time of Theodore Roosevelt and Woodrow Wilson, the Presidents at the time. Even Franklin D. Roosevelt, in his 1932 campaign speech about the "New Deal" being proposed, referred back to Theodore Roosevelt and Woodrow Wilson and the ideas proffered by the Progressives; in other words, the "New Deal" was inclusive of the foundations proposed earlier by the Progressives. Thus, the Progressives have played a role, perhaps the most significant role, in the development of our government and ideology from what we got from the Founding Fathers and the Constitution and Bill of Rights to the government we have today, which is a huge government pretty much in control of America and not controlled by the People, as originally envisioned. Progressives then, as now, advocated a complete repudiation of our Constitution and Bill of Rights, and were far less concerned about our unalienable individual rights as the demands of a socialized community would be where individual rights are no longer important or protected. This is also the basis of "collectivism".

The general thought of the Progressives was that the growth of America and its issues and conditions could not have been envisioned by the Founding Fathers and, therefore, repudiate the abiding validity of the Constitution because their principles and institutions were about what existed at the time that may not or do not exist in contemporary times. This is what Progressives of today are saying. This is also what Obama said, that the Constitution is "outdated" and should be discarded.

There are several main points: 1) Why is progressivism important, and why do we need to talk about the Constitution as seen from that Progressive Era?

2) Once it is established how important is the question; we need to understand who are they and what are the core ideas of progressivism. 3) How did, and do, the Progressives criticize the Constitution and the American founding? 4) What are the main points of progressive thought? 5) What are the sources of progressive thought?

The Founders had a clear and permanent understanding of a "just" government, meaning a "fair" government that prioritizes the value of the individual's basic rights and standing (legitimacy). When they talk about a "just" government in the Declaration of Independence, what Jefferson meant by that is not only government right then and there, what he is talking about is a government that transcends time, one that evolves with the growing nation, but remains constrained by basic principles of governance where the people remain in control and the government serves the people, not the other way around.

By contrast, the Progressives argue that the ends of government, the scope of government, is going to change and evolve, contingent and relative to circumstances of new events and new times. The individual would be subsumed under the concepts and demands of "collectivism."

This position finds a bit of support in decisions from the United States Supreme Court where it interpreted the cruel and/or unusual punishment clause of the Eighth Amendment of the Constitution, where it said that the interpretation of what is or is not cruel and/or unusual punishment is determined by the evolving standards of decency recognized by a given society. While the Court did not use the term "devolving" (meaning going backwards), it clearly intended the meaning to mean that evolving standards of decency in our Christian society would rely less and less on harsh punishments and conditions in the punishment of criminal offenders. (See, *Trop v. Dulles*, 356 U.S. 86 (1958), Chief Justice Earl Warren, stating, "The [Eighth] Amendment must draw its meaning from the evolving standards of decency that mark the progress of a maturing society," thus looking, in subsequent decisions, to societal developments, as well as looking to its own independent judgment, in determining what are those "evolving standards of decency." Some of these cases had to do with property as well. "Decency" involves how we interact with others, how we respect other's feelings, thoughts, expressions, and behavior in a nurturing way, a society that "matures" away from tribalism, nihilism, racism, and all those negative-oriented "ism's," because *decency* inherently flows from the concept of the preeminent Golden Rule, to treat others as you would like to be treated, or to not treat others in a way you would not like to be treated. A "maturing society" learns from its mistakes and weaknesses and moves forward to wisdom and inner strength for the individual and for society as a whole. Socialism, communism, totalitarianism, fascism, all auger towards the worst evils of mankind. The "ruling class" always ends up in oppression of the masses. Despots always have an easier time rising to the top of such ideologies.

However, originalists like Justice Antonin Scalia argue that societies may rot instead of maturing, and may decrease in virtue or wisdom instead of increasing. Thus, they say, the framers of the Constitution and Bill of Rights wanted the amendment understood as it was written and ratified, instead of morphing as times change and, in any event, legislators are more competent than judges to take the pulse of the public as to changing standards of decency.

A similar concern with the Progressive's belief that the Constitution is outdated and must be discarded in favor of whatever standards for a new ideology they promote, generally socialism, comes down to the fact that challenging long-standing principles and precedents upon which the country was built cannot be left to the dangerously shifting and nebulous notions of "societal consensus" and contemporary "standards of decency." If our Constitution *et al* is left upon to current "societal concensus" and contemporary "standards of decency", or prevailing demands for "collectivism," we as a nation are in dire trouble, considering that Progressives are demanding socialism; equally bad, they are moving for normalizing behavior which, until just recently, has formerly been flatly rejected as "normal" behavior, such as homosexuality, transgendering, beastiality (which Cenk Uygur of the Young Turks promoted), open borders, non-white racism against white people, disarming Americans, Orwellian-style "political correctness" of thought and speech, the list is long and, as Justice Scalia correctly cautioned against, would constitute "*rotting*" by an overt *decrease* in morality, virtues, and wisdom. This would be devolution, not evolution.

Contrary to the Progressive belief, government should not be contingent upon the circumstances at the time, because circumstances change. Progressives seem to believe that history shows that governments evolve, that they have changed from horridly oppressive governments to governments that are better at achieving things the People want and better able to solve problems of human history. The conditions around the world today repudiate that baseless notion. The socialist nations are failing on their own, finding that they need some sort of market-economy and some element of capitalism in order to afford the expense of socialism. Plus, the pro-socialist, pro-globalist, and Muslim powers in the UN, and the European Union (EU), have virtually destroyed European countries with mayhem, violence, and chaos coming from a single source: Muslim refugees.

Progressives argue that the major problems our nation's Founders were most concerned with at the time, i.e., the tyranny of the British rule, no longer exists in our time, and thus the need to constrict the growth of government to ensure rule by the People is no longer necessary or desirable. In some ways, our government has manifested fringes of tyrannical behavior, if only through the Fourth Branch of government itself, the administrative bureaucracy, which creates rules and regulations without oversight from the three Branches set forth in our Constitution (Judicial, Legislative, Executive).

Historically, the ideas of the Progressives have formed a kind of common thread among the most important political figures, and most important intellectuals going back to the 1880's, and well into the 1920's and beyond. They have manifested in speeches and lectures of prominent national figures like Presidents Theodore Roosevelt and Woodrow Wilson, John Dewey (socialist educator who was instrumental in setting our school systems up), and other less important scholars and intellectuals.

The view of the Constitution by the Progressives is this: The Progressive Era is the first time in American history that featured a strong criticism of the Constitution unlike earlier criticisms. These were ideas of some of the most important political people and scholars dominating the political domain at the time. These new ideas came as a reaction to the old system. The basic idea was that the Constitution is old, that it was written to deal with circumstances that are now well in the past, and that it needed to be replaced so that they could deal with the new set of social and economic problems.

The original Progressives were educated men and women who understood the Constitution, its structure, and its intention. They knew that the intent of the Constitution was to limit government, to channel consent, and they understood they needed to be careful about changes and how quickly and immediate public opinion could be translated into an actual policy. They recognized the "checks and balances (or restraints)" could be substantial obstacles to the desired policies of the Progressives, who wanted to do new things. But they knew the Constitution limited their ability to make new changes and policy. They had a variety of legislative programs in view, such as to redistribute wealth, to regulate in ways that had not been done before, or to intervene in private economic matters, in matters of property in ways that had not been done before. Some of this legislative agenda were clearly socialist in nature, and the Constitution stood firmly in their way.

Original Progressives believed the Constitution was enacted only as a means to an end, a structure that aimed at something higher and more fundamental, being rooted in the Christian principles of God. However, the Constitution was written and enacted to elucidate and protect the natural rights of human beings, as written in the Declaration of Independence.

Original Progressives believed if they were to make an effective argument against the sustainability of the Constitution, they would have to move beyond that enumerated by the Founding Fathers. They would have to look at and critique the structure of the Constitution, but also those deeper, fundamental principles that the Constitution was founded upon, and they would have to go after the Declaration of Independence itself. Progressives know that their argument must demonstrate why those original principles and structure no longer apply in today's circumstances.

What are these principles? First is the "social compact" which is to say the Founders had the belief that mankind as individuals have certain rights, not ones given by men, but ones given by God the Creator and bestowed long before the creation of governments. Thus, because of these inherent rights, human beings generally will only consent to government if those human, natural rights are protected. Progressives believed that if government were limited only to the protection of these human rights, government would be limited, and not broad-based enough to provide for the population, so they had to attack the "social compact" theory and the Declaration theory. Therefore, the regulatory and redistribution aims of Progressivism would be on a collision course with the Constitution. Devaluing Biblical values and even the concept of God became a focal part, where they argued there was no God, God is a myth created by man, and there are no "God-given" inherent rights of mankind. With the rise in atheism, which is causing American flags and Christian crosses to be removed, or ending prayer in the schools, the Progressives are focusing on this anti-God narrative to argue since morality evolved around the concept of God, and there is no such thing as God, the Constitution is inherently invalid, and it is the rights of the "collective" that surpass any individual "rights" of the American people.

Woodrow Wilson, a strong Progressive, stated that "*If you want to understand the real Declaration of Independence, do not repeat the preface.*" What he meant was that in the preface to this document, which informed the British of their grievances, the most potent and consequential words in American History, i.e., "*We hold these truths to be self-evident, that all men are created equal, that they are endowed by their Creator with certain unalienable Rights, that among these are Life, Liberty, and the pursuit of Happiness,*" that if you ignored that preface, the entire remainder of the Declaration was merely a list of grievances against the British government. However, Presidents, educators, scholars, jurists, and even politicians, throughout history, considered the Declaration to be the foundation of political philosophy because it is a statement of principles through which the United States Constitution should be interpreted. And that is correct. If we removed "by their Creator", it will still articulate clearly the value of the individual. Let's try it: *We hold these truths to be self-evidence, that all men are created equal, that they are endowed with certain unalienable rights, that among these are Life, Liberty, and the pursuit of Happiness.* So, to the Progressive's argument, is flaccid and immaterial.

Notably, our Declaration was modeled, in pertinent part, after the British Bill of Rights of 1689, a landmark Act in the constitutional law of England that set out certain basic civil rights. It was supplemented with the Act of Settlement in 1701, with later rights extended in the Magna Carta, the Petition of Right, the Habeas Corpus Act of 1679, and the Parliament Acts 1911 and

1949. The British Bill of Rights applies in England and Wales. It was incorporated into Australian law, also in Canada, New Zealand, and the Republic of Ireland.

Furthermore, our Declaration has inspired many similar documents in other countries, the first being the 1789 Declaration of United Belgian States issued during the Brabant Revolution in the Austrian Netherlands. It also served as the primary model for numerous declarations of independence in Europe, Latin America, Africa (Liberia) and Oceania (New Zealand) during the first half of the 19th century. It inspired the content of the French Declaration of Rights of Man and Citizen (1789), the Venezuelan Declaration of Independence (1811), the Liberian Declaration of Independence (1847), the Vietnamese Proclamation of Independence (1945). Some countries have copied statements directly from it, including the Haitian Declaration (1804), the United Provinces of New Granada (1811), the Argentine Declaration of Independence (1816), the Chilean Declaration of Independence (1818), Costa Rica (1821), El Salvador (1821), Guatemala (1821), Honduras (1821), Mexico (1821), Nicaragua (1821), Peru (1821) Bolivian War of Independence (1825), Uruguay (1825), Ecuador (1830), Columbia (1831), Paraguay (1842), Dominican Republic (1844), Texas Declaration of Independence (1836), California Republic (1836), Hungarian Declaration of Independence (1849), New Zealand Declaration of Independence (1835), and the Czechoslovakian Declaration of Independence (1918). The Rhodesian Declaration of Independence is based on the American one, as well, ratified in 1965, although it omits the phrases "all men are created equal" and "the consent of the governed".

With so many countries and so many peoples believing in and wanting to be acknowledged and respected of their natural rights, and following the high standards set forth in America's Declaration and its Constitution, why should Americans give any credence to this stubborn attempt by these "Progressives" who want to destroy the Constitution, change our market-economy to socialism, and declare that individual rights must be subsumed to the whim of the collective governed by an all-powerful government?

To ignore the preface of the Declaration of Independence and consider only the list of grievances made to the British government is to fail to understand how those grievances relate to the numerous violations of the human rights of Americans. The preface is inseparable from those violations. Despite these grievances were limited to King George at the time, the preface provisions are not so limited because they are a declaration of timeless natural rights of human beings. If one does not ignore the perverse goings-on today, in America and around the world, any intelligent person would embrace the Declaration and the Constitution today because that is all that stands in the way of the anarchy that would result in the transition from capitalism to socialism, and that stands in the way of the arbitrariness of social constructs that now cater to the basest desires of the human condition. With them, morality is a concept deserving of fading into history.

A more recent expression seeming aligned with Progressive thought was made by Herbert Walker Bush, as President, when he smoothly promised Americans that what was needed and coming was a "New World Order" and a one-government utopian world, the same NWO that John F. Kennedy tried to warn us against and which got him assassinated for doing so. "*Oh, it was Lee Harvey Oswald who killed him!*" Really? You still believe that?

An academic, Frank Goodnow, in 1916, contrasted the theory of the Constitution and the rights it embodies with the current position of the Progressive theory. Goodnow is a Progressive who believes that other countries have begun to move toward the theory behind the Progressive agenda, the new ideas believed to be more appropriate for circumstances today, and he believes that America is stuck behind this "progress" in social ideology. Goodnow's essay is called "The American Conception of Liberty and Government." His essay contrasts with what the Founders thought about rights and the way Progressives wanted to think about rights, and still do. (Again, this is an old failed agenda rejuvenated by today's Progressives.)

Goodnow said, in part, "*The end of the eighteenth century was marked by the formulation and general acceptance by thinking men in Europe of a political philosophy which laid great emphasis on individual private rights. Man was, by this philosophy, conceived of as endowed at the time of his birth with certain inalienable rights.*" He goes on to talk about man as an individual first and as a member of society second. "*At the time of making this contract these individuals were deemed to have reserved certain rights spoken of as "natural" rights. These rights could neither be taken away nor be limited without the consent of the individual affected."* In other words, the rights a person has comes from God and nature, and one has them first, and government is only legitimate if it respects those rights, and that's a permanent limit on government. That's the theory of the Founding Fathers.

Goodnow wrote that this theory was not the theory in Europe, that Europe has gotten beyond this. He said, *"In a word, man is regarded now throughout Europe, contrary to the view expressed by Rousseau, as primarily a member of society and secondarily as an individual. The rights which he possesses are, it is believed, conferred upon him, not by his Creator, but rather by the society to which he belongs."*

At this point, one might consider, apart from Europe, how Arab countries based in Islam and sharia law, regard the issue of individual rights and freedoms we Americans consider important. Islam holds that all men and women who are Muslim do not have "freedom" as America thinks of it. Rather, they are a society bound by the extreme strictures of their Quran and sharia law, such that the ideology controls every aspect of their lives, and "freedom" is considered an evil to forever be banned. Strict control of individual behavior is laid out to every citizen with severe punishments for even the slightest infraction, particularly towards females who are totally subjugated to the men much like slaves. In Islam, it seems the goal is neither for the community nor the individual, but focused only on the perpetuation of Allah as God, and Muhammad as Allah's chosen prophet. Now you start getting an understanding why Muslims are intolerant and dangerous; Allah demands it.

Goodnow writes, *"What they [your rights] are is to be determined by the legislative authority in view of the needs of that society. Social expediency, rather than natural rights, is thus to determine the sphere of individual freedom of actions."*

Thus, the Progressive thought is that in this society where circumstances and societal needs have changed, we need to adjust our principles, we need to think about the society as a whole first and the individual second. From the point of view of Goodnow and the Progressives, the problem with the Founding was not so much about its principles per se, but rather than the Founders assumed the principles ought not to apply just to them, not just to their own time, but for everybody at all times. So that was the problem the Progressives found disputable about the theory of natural rights.

Yet it was this very feature that Abraham Lincoln recognized and celebrated. So, when Lincoln was making his great speeches about the abolition of slavery, he was always referring back to those principles, and believing their value was timeless. In fact, in 1859, Lincoln wrote in a letter, *"All honor to Jefferson – to the man who, in the concrete pressure of a struggle for national independence by a single people – had the coolness, forecast, and capacity to introduce into a merely revolutionary document, an abstract truth, applicable to all men and all times."* For Lincoln, this was the great virtue of that Declaration, not just the principles it laid out, because Lincoln recognized to a certain extent those principles of equality were still not fully realized at the time, so not just then and there but that those principles were laid down as the permanent principles of the regime.

His comments, however, contrasted with Progressive Woodrow Wilson, who said to *"disregard those very things that Lincoln points out as the most important part."*

Lincoln's comments were also contrasted by those of John Dewey, one of the most public philosophers in the first half of the 20th century. John Dewey, who subsequently was responsible for creating America's educational system, also took issue with Lincoln's message. Dewey did not support the idea that the virtues and principles set forth by the Founders, which he considered were contingent upon circumstances of that time, did not transcend all time. He believed that that way of thinking about the permanence of those principles were the thinking of the old "liberalism" and were no longer applicable.

One has to wonder how a consensus to keep natural law individual rights close and inviolate, and God-given, could be construed as "liberalism" is a bit puzzling. Dewey believed there was a crisis in his time, and they were stuck in the old liberalism and unable to move forward as a society and its government. He believed that "liberalism" was progressing in other countries, like Europe and Canada, but America was stuck with an obsolete ideology. Dewey wrote in 1915, that *"It blinded the eyes of liberals to the fact that their own special interpretations of liberty, individuality, and intelligence were themselves historically conditioned, and were relevant only to their own time. They put forth their ideas as immutable truths good at all times and places; they had no idea of historic relativity, either in general or in its application to themselves."* This was the benchmark argument of the Progressives during that time.

Where did this type of argument come from? The initial pedigree of the argument adopted/adapted by the Progressives originated in Germany in the 19th century. Hopkins University also brought to America this Progressive thought, as well as the idea that the Constitution was a "living thing" that had to be understood according to organic life. Other colleges and universities since that time have likewise pushed the Progressive's argument. Woodrow Wilson, a Progressive, did not believe the Constitution was a mechanistic thing, and he said: *"The trouble with the theory is that government is not a machine, but a living thing. It falls, not under the theory of the universe, but under the theory of organic life. It is accountable to Darwin, not to Newton"* (law of gravitation mechanics). He argued that *"It is modified by its environment, necessitated by its tasks, shaped to its functions by the sheer pressure of life. No living thing can have its organs offset against each other, as checks, and live."* (1913) In an essay, Wilson addressed his view of the relationship between the individual and state: *"It [socialism] proposes that all idea of a limitation of public authority by individual rights be put out of view, and that the State consider itself bound to stop only at what is unwise or futile in its universal superintendence alike of individual and or public interests. The thesis of the state socialist is that no line can be drawn between private and public affairs which the State may not cross at will."* So, he argued that the power of the state trumps the rights of the individual. He pointed out that that is pretty much how the Progressives view democracy. He said, *"In fundamental theory socialism and democracy are almost if not quite one and the same."* He explains that they are one and the same because the Progressives believe that democracy is not limited to individual rights, because *"They both rest at bottom upon the absolute right of the community to determine its own destiny and that of its members. Men as communities are supreme over men as individuals. Limits of wisdom and convenience to the public control there may be: limits of principle there are, upon strict analysis, none."* (Wilson, Socialism and Democracy (1887).)

So, the Progressives believe and argue that government is a "living" entity that has to respond the circumstances in a changing societal environment, and to adapt as it goes, that it cannot be rigidly fixed or constrained, and perform its tasks. This argument on its face sounds rational, but yet as it is made it also is undermined by historical events, not just in America but throughout the ages where governments have risen, small at first, then grown, and generally have been populated by the aristocracy of the times or despots who have simply taken control. Take socialism, for example, where the intent is to have a government that takes care of the people in all ways, but which always seems to become communistic and even totalitarian. The claim that successful democracies never last more than 200 years belies the claim that socialist countries tend to end up in abject misery and abiding poverty, oppressed by the government, and converted into communism or totalitarian regimes.

Giving complete control to a government of men/women who relish the prestige and the benefits leaves the population unarmed against further intrusions and oppressive control by the same government, because it is fact and natural that giving power always result in the empowered becoming more powerful and less concerned about those who have no power to resist. The Progressives do not seem to understand this irrefutable fact. What protects America is that old, faded, but still vibrant document called the Constitution of America. This wise document circumscribes the powers of the government, because the Founders were concerned that the new government, then or as it evolves as the country grew, would overstep its boundaries and become a regime acting for the aristocracy and not for the people of this nation.

Only the aristocracy, the elitists, want the Constitution destroyed because they want to bring in the New World Order which will be a totalitarian government over the entire world. Never forget, power corrupts and absolute power corrupts absolutely. If you think that egomaniacs and evil people cannot achieve the supreme leader position in a communist or totalitarian regime, you'd be wrong. And if you think that smile, personable, smooth-talking person who plays to the people's good feelings can't also be an evil person, you would do well to watch the Netflix video on Roman Emperor Caligula, who was assassinated after only 1400 days because he was absolutely bloodthirsty and loved gore-and-violence. He started off at a young age a smiling, easy-going, playful young man but, after quickly arising to the top spot and having total power, his hidden face emerged and he reveled in the violence and the gore. The Roman Senators killed him, as a group, each stabbing Caligula until he died.

History since has told similar stories time and again (Kahn, Hitler, Stalin, Mao Zedong, Pol Pot) and we can even throw a nod to Ted Bundy the Charmer who loved murdering people. Evil people exist, always will. When they are wealthy and powerful, they can make life miserable for others.

These earlier Progressive arguments are the same ideas and argument and the basis for the current rise of Progressives in America, with tweaking according to the increasing devolution of virtues and values as the belief in God the Creator lessens in America. The essential argument is that our government poses no threat to the liberties and values of Americans, so that government can be given greater controls and power over the people so that the problems and ills in our society today can be overcome and fixed – by the government. The Progressives are also about the redistribution of wealth, against ownership of private property, but for businesses owned by government and not individuals. Socialism. Collectivism.

It is true that a small cadre of "economic oligarchs" have used their vast property and business holdings to prey upon the upper, middle, and lower-class persons, with impunity by the government officials who are on the take, who receive money to look the other way. Should they be reined in? Certainly, but by laws that do not emasculate the rights of the people or that give the government total control. The ongoing problem with the "nobility" in high places is that they are some of these "economic oligarchs" too, and they too are in high places in the government and private sector. A general plan of redistribution of wealth that goes beyond curbing in these pharaonic aristocrats and suppresses the rights of the common people to better their own financial circumstances, as does socialism or communism, is not the answer to fixing America. We see major corporations doing "buy outs" of their competition, thereby consolidating companies into one umbrella corporation that controls the market in hands of a single Board and a CEO (who makes millions in salaries and stock options, etc.). If there are to be controls through law, the law should address this problem of cabining economic power in the hands of the very few "aristocrats." These monolithic corporations use their power to control politicians who serve them, not the people. Is that really true, one might ask? Good question. The real question that answers that question is how is it that elected officials, whose prior income was perhaps high but in line with their job, suddenly become wealthy during their first term of office and continue to higher wealth the longer they remain in office? The investigative solution is transparency of income of the politicians. Follow the money trail.

I am not for redistribution of wealth as the low-income class wants it to be, considering they seem have the audacity to expect the "wealthy" as inclusive of the middle-class working folks too. To them I say, get a job, get an education, join the merit-based system and set goals to achieve the income level at which you'll be satisfied and comfortable. But I do think that the hoarding of billion-dollar incomes by a few oligarchs, relatively speaking, should be taxed, not given tax loopholes, so that this excess can go to upgrading our infrastructure of schools, medical services, and welfare programs to those who truly need welfare after booting out those who are just too lazy to get a job and work.

There is little difference between the cry of America's poor for the redistribution of wealth and the Muslim migrants who came by the thousands across European borders loudly demanding "GIMME MONEY" while vandalizing, assaulting, and robbing citizens and businesses alike. The only difference is how the cry of redistribution is manifested. Ultimately, it is about being forced to give money to those who haven't earned it and don't deserve it because they won't work for it.

Today's Progressives also want to ignore the preface in the Declaration for the reason that they believe a socialist form of government will protect the people and serve the people even if that means undermining the legitimacy of the natural rights of human beings as a factor in government administration.

As I have discussed before, there has become what is now being called by some to be the silent Fourth Branch of government, or the "Administrative State", which is the bureaucracy of the nation. Our Founders did not envision that America would have a huge government in control of the people, but a small government represented by persons elected by the people. In socialist countries the government is all-seeing and all-controlling, where the people serve the functions and demands of government, and individual rights are simply not recognized because the bureaucracy is the parent.

No one in this country today can say they are not directly or indirectly affected by demands and controls of the current bureaucracy. The bureaucracy of the Administrative State is comprised of "satellite" departments and institutions, but they coalesce as a force that decides everything about business, private matters, the marketplace, real estate, medical, and so on and on and on. They create rules and regulations, unfettered by the legislative process which creates laws through discussion and consent of the members. The Administrative State decides what they want to do, and then devise and implement the means to accomplish their objective. Sometimes politics are involved, sometimes the Congress gets involved, but the end result is that the application of law, rules and regulations is by the Administrative State, federal, state, and local.

Turning America's ideology upside down and throwing out the Constitution to enable total control by the government in a new socialist government, having viewed the massive intrusion we already have, is nothing short of suicide in terms of our rights, protections, property, and dreams.

Originally, the administrative bureaucracy's purpose and job was to take the general laws passed by the legislatures and translate those into particular solutions to the problems that the people wanted solved, to the delivery of services, to the concrete devising of means to accomplish the goals that are set out in legislation.

Under the Progressives governance, Congress will continue to enact laws that the Administrative State will apply, but markedly different from the way our current government operated. The things that a "Progressive" legislature will enact as laws will be more in the nature of a "vision statement" than actually making what Alexander Hamilton called in Federalist 75 (publication) as rules for the regulation of society. It was Congress's job to reflect and express the will of the community in broad legislation that laid out goals for the administrative system to accomplish. So legislative, regardless of its incredible verbiage today, will boil down to things like clean air, we want safe workplaces, we want quality, affordable health care. It would then become the task of administrative agencies, or the administrative apparatus, to translate those goals into actual rules, into actual policy, in order to bring about the good that the people said that they want through the laws that their elected representatives passed. So, instead of issuing instructions to citizens, Progressive legislation is going to issue instructions to "regulators" and those regulators will devise rules that issue instructions to citizens. The essence of this process is like Nancy Pelosi saying they had to pass Obamacare to find out what was in it, because that will be true. The citizenry will not know what is in the legislation or how the legislation will work until they are notified by a regulator of the new law. So, the legislature passes a law, then sends it to the hands of "administrators" who tells regulators what is in it, who then let the citizenry know how it will affect them. These administrators are thus charged with making the rules on the legislation, and enforcing them. This puts administrative agencies, at times, in direct violation of the separation of powers restriction on government, because they will be carrying out legislative, judicial, and executive functions.

The Progressives' response to this conundrum is that is not a problem, that the Administrative State should be given broad powers to carrying out the tasks caused by legislative as well as jurisdictional matters. Progressives do not consider this power a problem because they anticipate an administrative agency for every problem, i.e., a never-ending expansion of government bureaucracy.

A most interesting question is who are these people who run the Administrative State and all its agencies? These are not elected persons. Progressives say there are three basic requirements: 1) that they be experts, people who are qualified for that particular agency; 2) they have to be independent, outside the normal process of politics; and 3) they have to be progressives. Yet, while the Progressives claim this is what they want and expect, they do not make the same demands for qualifications of elected officials. For instance, President Obama had no education in business economics, had never held a job, and got elected senator without any credentials at all except for being in college. Yet he was elected on the platform of "fundamental change" with a smirk, not telling the electorate that his view of fundamental change was to destroy the "colonialist America" he believed it to be; he wanted to usher in socialism and, if we consider his indications of Muslim leanings, to turn America into one big mosque for Muslims. Obama was about elected officials who might be fresh out of college and having never worked for a living. They should be elected for the skills they can bring to the negotiating and voting tables of

Congress. After all, Obama never held a job, never ran a business. He went from college to a senator to President, totally unqualified and markedly biased against "colonialist" America.

Franklin D. Roosevelt (1882-1945) was another Progressive who became President. He served as the 32nd president from 1933 until his death in 1945. Officially he was a member of the Democrat Party, and he won a record of four presidential elections. He introduced the "New Deal" as a platform for his belief that redistribution of wealth was the key to relieving economic hardship for many. Remember, this was the 30s, during the Great Depression (brought on by the top banks and wall street), where millions of people were suffering greatly. Roosevelt's view was that if one was constrained by economic necessity, he was not really free. Roosevelt believed that government should be the instrument liberating people from economic necessity; otherwise those same people were at the mercy of economic royalists. The situation in the 30's was that America was, in fact, moving towards an economic oligarchy where wealth was in the hands of a very few, like the Rothschilds, Rockefellers, J.P. Morgan, and the like. Employment opportunities were almost non-existent during the Great Depression, and there were people who literally starved to death, while fewer and fewer corporations were gaining more and more wealth of the country.

Roosevelt felt that what America needed was a reorientation of government, and an enlightened administration that served the needs of the people instead of catering to the oligarchy. The New Deal he proposed was to remedy the fact that economic growth in America had somehow come to an end, and what was needed was a means of stimulating economic growth and employment. FDR wanted to administer resources and plans already in hand, that the country needed to adjust production to consumption, so essentially FDR put the burden of changing the way things are done to ways that fixes the problems of the nation and restores prosperity. Remember, prior to the economic collapse of 1929, the Roarin' Twenties were a time of high prosperity because Wall Street had propped up a fallacious stock market system where everyone bought and sold stocks with great profits but which was not sustainable over time, and that time ended in 1929, after which America endured the Great Depression that lasted up to the Second World War. It is also claimed, however, that the biggest problem of the Roarin' Twenties is that the economic system was producing far more than was consumed, and FDR believed that the fix was returning to a system where what was produced was consumed in the marketplace. A sort of quid pro quo, i.e., we produce, you buy.

The FDR plan was to realign and task government to help achieve a balance between production and consumption. An example of this is found in John Steinbeck's Grapes of Wrath where there is scene where firemen are burning oranges on the side of the road. That was mandated by FDR's "farm program" where the point was to reduce supply until supply was even with demand in order to prevent over-supply, over-production, and therefore economic collapse. This act of destroying oranges and other over-supplies of foods was both shameful and controversial considering the hordes of starving people too poor to even buy the oranges or destroyed foods at any price, but these over-supplies were not distributed to those starving to death despite FDR's belief that wealth should be redistributed more fairly and equitably, and despite his belief that America should adapt existing economic organizations to the service of the people. FDR wanted to shift to a more planned economic system to reduce what he saw as "so much waste" in the free market. He believed that for every success there were ten failures, thereby creating new burdens on government. He wanted to stop the cycle of "boom and bust" to a more steady and sustainable capacity and prosperity.

FDR had economic advisors he called his "Brain Trust" which was a group of Columbia University academics who helped develop policy recommendations leading up to Roosevelt's New Deal. One of them that rose above the others was an economist named Rexford Tugwell who was later forced out in 1936. Tugwell was a specialist on planning and believed the government should have large-scale plans to move the economy out of the Great Depression because private businesses were too frozen in place to do the job. Tugwell helped design the New Deal farm program and the Resettlement Administration that moved subsistence farmers into small rented farms under close supervision. (This relocation plan raised accusations that these measures were similar to Stalinism and Stalin's attack on farmers, an attack that saw many thousands murdered and resulted in starvation of millions of Russians.) Tugwell's ideas on suburban planning resulted in the construction of Greenbelt, Maryland, with low-cost rents for relief families. He was denounced by conservatives for advocating state-directed economic planning to overcome the Great Depression. Tugwell said that planning would create order and regularity but planning would actually involve huge dislocation of the established ways in which people operate. He said that if you have a planned economy that would mean "the abolition of business." In other words, the obliteration of private, unregulated, unsupervised businesses and economic activity would require the government taking control of planning and operating marketplace business; no longer would there be private ownership and upstart business by private citizens but, if there were, the owner would lack incentive to expand because his income would still be limited. Government would have to control the markets, production, and profit margins. While Tugwell was not calling for socialism, he was referencing all the earmarks of socialism as the means for market stability. The idea of profit and loss would disappear, the idea of limiting profits would result in more mundane responses and lack of incentives to do better, all would result in a workforce that would have to be personally motivated by fervor and a sense of service if quality of product and production were to be maintained. This problem is one we see in American companies today which have transferred their production facilities overseas to workers paid very little who have only supervisory threats as an incentive to keep the manufacturing and assembly lines moving.

A Supreme Court case in 1942 supports what Tugwell was saying. In the case of *Wicker v. Filburn*, where the Court said that there cannot be any economic activity outside of the control of the central planners of the federal government. Filburn was a farmer who was told he could only plant 11.1 acres of wheat. Instead, he planted 23 acres. Although the surplus never left his farm, he used it for fodder, food for his own family, for seed for next year's crop, yet the federal government descended upon him and fined him. The Supreme sided with the federal government 9-0, saying if the Court allowed Filburn to do this, then every small farm was going to engage in this "pseudo-legal activity" and if they do that then there is all of this economic activity out of our sight and therefore we cannot plan the economy. This was the argument of the government, and this was the argument the Court accepted.

To avoid confusion about the New Deal history, let me point out there were two "New Deals", the first (1933-1934) dealt with the pressing banking crisis through the Emergency Banking Act, which was designed to prevent a re-peated stock market crash that ushered in the Great Depression. It provided huge funds to relief operations by states and cities during the crisis, money to locals to operate "Make-work" projects in 1933-1934.

The Second new deal in 1935-1936 included the National Labor Relations Act to protect labor organizing, The *Works Progress Administration* relief pro-gram which made the government by far the largest employer in the nation, i.e., the rise of the Administrative State, the Social Security Act and new pro-grams to aid tenant farmers and migrant workers. The final major items of New Deal legislation were the creation of the United States Housing Au-thority and the FSA (Farm Security Administration), which both occurred in 1937; and the Fair Labor Standards Act of 1938, which set maximum hours and minimum wages for most categories of workers. There were numerous problems with the expansion and application of these liberal programs, and after 1974 a call for deregulation of the economy gained bipartisan support and the New Deal regulation of banking (Glass-Steagall Act) lasted until it was suspended in the 1990s. While some New Deal programs remain active, others fell by the wayside as unworkable. In fact, the Supreme Court abolished some New Deal programs as unconstitutional in the 1930s.

It is noteworthy to add that Democrats under President Lyndon B. Johnson won a massive landslide and Johnson's "Great Society" programs extended the New Deal temporarily. But in 1980, former New Deal supporter Ronald Reagan won the presidency and turned against the New Deal, viewing government as the problem rather than the solution, and he moved the nation away from the New Deal model of government activism, shifting greater emphasis to the pri-vate sector. The New Deal (1 and 2) may have had some beneficial aspects but their evolution to a more controlling government caused them to resemble a socialist form of government that was oppositional to the Constitution itself.

Notwithstanding, in 1934, in one of Roosevelt's "Fireside Chats" to the Amer-ican people over the radio, he said, "[Some] will try to give you new and strange names for what we are doing. Sometimes they will call it "Fascism", sometimes "Communism", sometimes "Regimentation", sometimes "Social-ism." But, in so doing, they are trying to make very complex and theoretical something that is really very simple and very practical. … Plausible self-seekers and theoretical die-hards will tell you of the loss of individual liberty. Answer this question out of the facts of your own life: Have you lost any of your rights or liberty or constitutional freedom of action and choice?"

The New Deal did not die a natural death; it was killed off in the 1970s by a business coalition mobilized by such groups as the Business Roundtable, the Chamber of Commerce, trade organizations, conservative think tanks and decades of legal and political challenges. Historians generally agree that during Roosevelt's 12 years in office there was a dramatic increase in the size and power of the federal government as a whole.

It was World War II that accounted for the end of the Great Depression begun in 1929 to 1933; American began a recovery until the recession in 1937-1938. The war effort resulted in factories hiring everyone they could find regardless of their lack of skills. As the military grew, new labor sources were needed to replace the 12 million men serving in the military. Prior barriers for married women, the old, the unskilled, for race minorities, were lowered as the workplace was desperate for workers. Unfortunately, neither New Deal programs nor limited employment by the military industrial complex served the needs of blacks, who suffered greatly during the depression and recession.

There were charges by some that the New Deal was "fascist" so let's take a quick look at that. Worldwide, the Great Depression had the most profound impact in the German Reich and the United States. In both countries the pressure to reform and the perception of the economic crisis were strikingly similar. When Hitler came to power, he was faced with exactly the same task that faced Roosevelt, overcoming mass unemployment and the global Depression. The political responses to the crises were essentially different: while American democracy remained strong, Germany replaced democracy with national socialism, but later gave Hitler a Nazi dictatorship. Germany was economically burdened by the Versailles Treaty after WW-I, which imposed significant reparations upon Germany to victim countries, and then imposed a major fine on Germany. Hitler could do nothing about the Versailles Treaty, although Germany appealed it, but was denied. The Nazi Party needed a scapegoat, someone they could identify as the nation's problem, and the Jews were chosen because of Aryan supremacy notions viewed Jews as lesser than they, kind of like Muslims towards "infidels." So that is what the Nazis did to build a new government for Germany. Hitler was about national socialism, not "fascism" which is what Italy's Mussolini was all about. One must not confuse Hitler as a fascist too early, but he did become absolute ruler.

It is noted that there were communists in the government during the New Deal years, before they were purged in 1935. They denounced the New Deal as fascist in the sense that it was under the control of big business, but they dropped that line of thought when Stalin switched to the "Popular Front" plan of cooperation with liberals. Communism is about helping the working class to take government power out of the hands of capitalists and establishing a workers' government, which takes the means of production away from the capitalists and organizes them on a new socialist basis, as the common property of all, i.e., the banishment of private ownership and the subjugation to the government.

So, having taken an excursion into the New Deal as it relates to the expansion of government, let's return to the issue of the Administrative State.

There are two basic tenets for building the Administrative State. The first is the delegation of legislative power as a legislative principle to guide administrative agencies or executive actions. In other words, this provision allowed Congress to transfer legislative power to both administrative and executive forums, where rules and regulations and laws would be created not directly from Congress but by the Administrative State or the President, i.e., the power to make rules for the regulation of society which is necessary to build a model state. From that time, there have been a number of significant decisions from the Office of the President and the Administrative State, none of which came from Congress. I will not belabor the point with these examples, but the point is that as the Administrative State bureaucracy expanded, and continues to expand today, the power to create rules and regulations to government America's population and livelihoods is virtually absolute. We are not ruled by Congress or a despotic President or czar, but by the Administrative branch of government at the federal, state, and local levels. This is the Progressive way.

Nonetheless, at this time of history, Americans can still participate fully in the free market, since the New Deal way did not become fully parasitic or controlling of the free market. Notwithstanding, the socialist and communist argument for redistribution of wealth is based on the view that monopoly capitalists hope to close the door against all social legislation at the expense of the living standards of the toiling people. Even though there are supposed laws and barriers to monopolistic corporate takeovers, there remains the fact that there are US-based transnational corporate buy-outs and takeovers that tend to eliminate competition and monopolize the market, and thereby increase corporate wealth unfairly, thus making some incredibly rich while doing little economically for Americans. If some controls are needed for the health of America, perhaps it is this venue of business that should be looked at.

Communists and socialists believe, were one to look only at the ideal, that the working class comprises some 90% or more of the population of any given country, and that this class does not benefit equitably as it should in a free market economy where private ownership of big business siphons off the profits to enlarge their businesses and profits for themselves. Redistribution of wealth is an argument that says that any given society should have an economy that works to the benefit of societal needs and the masses, and not just for the monopolistic bourgeoisie folks who conduct themselves as aristocratic elites, i.e., the pharaonic syndrome.

The eternal struggle seems to be how to have a government where individual rights are valued and protected, yet where the masses are not left with wage and income levels that keep them at levels where, as here in America today, both parents have to work in order to have the "good life" at the expense of properly raising their children with an at-home parent. In the 20s and 30s the family unit was encouraged by law which viewed the separate roles of spouses, i.e., the man was the breadwinner, the wife was the at-home raiser of children, and employment was restricted against women with children unless there was no husband in the family unit. In that scenario of roles, the government and society recognized the value and importance of a family unit being responsible for the proper raising and education of children so they too could enter the marketplace and have their own jobs and family unit. In today's world, we are seeing the results of the fracturing of the family unit, of the rise in crime and

James C. Lewis

imprisonment by children where no father figure is at home, of the denigration of family and spiritual values to help people grow into "good" people. And, that problem is getting worse year by year.

There must be a way to focus on the family unit needs of the individual without resulting in subsuming families to the control of the "State" as in a socialist or communist environment. The further we fall in controlling our own destiny, our own values and principles, the closer we get to either anarchy or social-ism/communism as the means of establishing an "ordered" society.

Almost from its inception, America has had those who believe that socialism or communism is the perfect ideology for mankind. There have been both so-cialist and communist organizations in America, most notably in the 20s and 30s, and while the 1950s saw a major suppression of both by Senator Joseph McCarthy and that era of McCarthyism, as it was called, where imprisonment was used against them, in the 1960s "Hippy" era there was a new rise in em-bracing Marxist thought and ideology. As I have said elsewhere, those Marxists from the 60s often ended up as teachers and professors, business people, elected politicians, and workers in the Administrative State. In the 1970s and 1980s we did not see much about them, but what we have seen of late are the millennials coming out of our own schools with Marxist beliefs and calling for the abolition of the democratic capitalism completely so that socialism can take over and rule the nation. What has been going on while we patriots "slept" if not a quiet takeover of our school curriculum dumbing down students and brainwashing them about Marxist thought and ideals.

We as a nation are in trouble because socialist thought is definitely strong in America right now. If we don't learn how to harness the few nihilist oligarchs who have unfairly taken control of our government, the argument about re-distribution of wealth from these monopolistic oligarchs grows in validity and justification. We either rein them in or they will reign over us all.

Perhaps if there can be developed price controls on products that would im-prove the economy while limiting excessive profits. Producers might argue that there are no such thing as "excessive" profits. But let's say that a manufac-turer makes a product that only costs $2.00 to make, but then sells it for

302

$20.00, or a product that costs $15,000 to make but sells for $30,000 dollars, say an automobile. If there were limitations of profit margins making a product more affordable, more people would buy it, thus offsetting previous prices and profits lost by profit caps. Of course, monitoring companies to prevent cheating would be difficult or even costly, initially, and there would need to be a "sliding" rule for different businesses, but a review system would smooth itself out in time and penalties for violations would soon keep companies playing by the rules. Profit caps would not be a means to stifle production or expansion or innovation, and provisions would need to be made to ensure the health and growth of new businesses and corporations is reasonably unfettered. But there needs to be some controls and benefits for societal health itself.

The idea of "profit caps" could result in more prosperity at the working class level, and even create incentives to the so-called disenfranchised class to find employment, insofar as a healthy and prosperity population would obviously bring more money in and, thereby, improve the federal and state coffers by additional tax revenue. The oligarchy might cry it is discriminatory, but perhaps it would help the top earners to remember as members of our nation they too have a responsibility to help our nation stay economically healthy. There are no real losers, the rich will remain rich, and it will be to their benefit to support measures that will also enrich more people in the middle- and upper-classes, while helping the poor enrich their lives and help them find employment if they can work, or help them if public assistance is validated for them. America would be able to stop the siphoning off of the Social Security fund so that its purpose is restored to health and intent.

This method of control would not be direct "redistribution" of wealth, but it would result in the masses having products they could more reasonably afford and, perhaps, even help restore the family unit to having a breadwinner and an at-home parent raising the children.

Finally, as to this section, there are non-apologetic Marxist organizations in America on the rise. In November 2018, the New York City "comrades" of the International Marxist Tendency (IMT) hosted the "2018 Northeast Marxist School." In the 50s they would have all been arrested and sent to prison.

The IMT stated their weekend with the launch of their new book, "*The Revolutionary Philosophy of Marxism*, led off by its author Alan Woods. He quoted Lenin's paper "*What Is to Be Done?*" which included "without revolutionary theory, there can be no revolutionary movement." The general idea is to unite the "working class" to begin a revolution in America and around the world by training a new generation of revolutionaries to rise up and crush the so-called "ruling class" and usher in Marxist socialism.

What is known by history, including here in America, is that labor unions tend to be Marxist-leaners (and I did not misspell that), and have been pro-socialist in the past. But IMT, as author Woods explained, argues, they need to focus on the working class to show them a reference point they can embrace in the initiation of a revolution. Woods claimed that in modern times today, "*[i]t is clear that old and formerly respected institutions of capitalist rule – from the Constitution to the President, Congress, and the Supreme Court – are losing their grip on the minds of the masses and people can see how undemocratic they really are.*" (Remember now, this is an opinion.) Woods goes on to opine that "*The working class is starting to view these institutions as those of the ruling class and this is a big step forward in class consciousness.*"

Woods concluded by opining that capitalism today is in a downward spiral that is causing social, economic, and political instability across the board, and that the Marxist labor-class can change America through the elections, with the ultimate goal of changing the entire structure of government, of eliminating the non-workable "checks and balances" from the three branches of government, and to nationalize the top banking institutions and the top 500 corporations in America. What he does not say is how the labor-class will perform the duties needed in actually operating government, of understanding economics, of administrating America's infrastructures, and representing America world-wide.

The IMT is an affiliate of the Democratic Socialists of America. The DSA represents that it is the largest socialist organization in the United States with (as of 2018) some 6,000 members. The DSA believes that "working people should run both the economy and society democratically to meet human needs, not to make profits for a few. We are a political and activist organization, not a party; through campus and community-based chapters, DSA members use a variety of tactics, from legislative to direct action, to fight for reforms that empower working people." The DSA is for the "Green New Deal" and are organizing in their workplaces, communities and schools to build the working-class movement it will take to win the Green New Deal. The DSA supports Bernie Sanders for President "so we can beat back Trumpism and the Wall Street Democrats, while also building the grassroots pressure and infrastructure we will need to keep fighting long after election day, so we can transform our economy and politics into a true democracy."

The DSA wants to eliminate the Electoral College because, as they see it, protects the aristocracy and not the voters (yet their explanation via Woods is factually misguided). The DSA is promoting a "strong labor movement" to destroy "authoritarian" capitalism. The DSA is for free medicare for all. The DSA supports the movement for Palestinian Rights and the Adalah project, two of the largest U.S.-based Palestine solidarity organizations (which are all about anti-Semitism). The DSA appears to promote protectionism for Yemen which is extremely violent not because of American aggression, but from within and from other Arab Muslims, but the DSA still supports Muslims.

The DSA supports abortion rights, the LGBT community, transgendering, etc. The DSA strongly supports teachers teaching socialism in our schools and wants to enable their union to take on socialism as a goal in America, thus the DSA is very active in supporting and converting teachers for that purpose. The DSA supports and is trying to organized federal workers (those working in the Administrative State, the Fourth 'silent' Branch of government). The DSA endorsed California's Proposition 10, the "Affordable Housing Act", which would allow communities to expand and strengthen tenant protections, rent control, and preventing evictions (of those who stop paying rent?). The DSA stands with illegal immigrants and open borders. The DSA supports banning firearms.

So we have a growing Marxist movement no longer in the shadows in America, and is networking with similar groups around the world to create democratic socialist regimes across the globe. While they call it "democratic" socialism, I fail to see the difference when such socialism comes into fruition, particularly in light of the history of failure and that they merely create a different kind of aristocracy at the leadership level, most often where despots climb and take over. They openly recruit teachers who, by the Common Core curricula, teach to indoctrinate our children that socialism is a good thing.

But there is another factor I ask you to consider about the Progressives. The playbook the use today has striking similarities to the playbook Hitler and his inner circle used to rise to power and to use that power to commit genocidal atrocities. The Progressives are the neo-Nazis of our time.

PART 8. THE KALERGI PLAN

I have said and written that humankind itself is under attack by the globalist elites who have decided they own so much of the world currently, and real estate, as well as control of most governments, that they have the right to decide the future of mankind itself. "Conspiracy theorist!" is the response by some. My response is do your own research.

Local people in my county with whom I have conversed, including complete strangers, have admitted great concern, even fear, about what is going politically, locally in our governments and schools, about the illegal migrant issue, the Second Amendment attacks, the push for infanticide policies, increased assisted suicide policies for the elderly, and about the world stage in general. So, I am not alone. We have a crisis looming and if you're just crying "conspiracy theory!" you're a part of the problem itself.

There are possible explanations if one diligently investigates. For instance, born in the year 1894, Richard von Coudenhove-Kalergi, was an Austrian-Japanese politician, philosopher, who died in 1972. He is considered the pioneer and founder of European integration for a united Europe, which became the EU (European Union).

Aristocratic in his origins and elitist in his ideas, Coudenhove-Kalergi strove to replace the nationalist German ideal of racial community with Aryan bloodlines, with the goal of an ethnically heterogeneous and inclusive European union based on a commonality of culture, a nation whose geniuses were the "great Europeans" in a world he envisioned would be divided into only five states, with English serving as the world language, spoken by everyone in addition to their native tongue, and where individualism and socialism would cooperate instead of compete, and where capitalism and communism cross-fertilize each other. With the rise of fascism in the 1930's, the project of ethnic integration was abandoned, until its revival by Winston Churchill after the Second World War. Kalergie's plan was rejected by the Nazis. But, Kalergi managed to gain acceptance for his plan, post-WWII, by the United States government and later the CIA became involved in driving the plan towards completion. It was not meant to be anything more than an idea for reducing wars between countries.

Kalergi's elitist vision about miscegenation was the mixing of ethnicities by interbreeding the peoples of Europe with Asians and other non-White races, to create a multi-racial population, with no clear sense of tradition or identity, and therefore easily controlled by the ruling elite. Kalergi proclaimed the need to abolish the right of nations to self-determination and outlined the break-up of nation states through the use of ethnic separatist movements and the destruction of the nations themselves through *mass migration*. His goal of a homogeneous mixed-breed population, was expressed thusly: "*The man of the future will be of mixed race. The races and classes of today will gradually disappear due to the elimination of space, time, and prejudice. The Eurasian-Negroid race of the future, similar in appearance to the Ancient Egyptians, will replace the current diversity of peoples and the diversity of individuals.*"

Kalergi's ideas found acceptance with the United Nations and underlie some of the guiding principles of the European Union today, although you will find no direct reference to Kalergi. The belief that the peoples of Europe should be mixed with Africans and Asians, to destroy their identity, is the reason for community policies now promoting minority interests. The underlying motives are not at all humanitarian, because the driving power behind the ruthless regime dominating the EU, plans the greatest genocide in history. The globalists intend to reduce the world population to a stable one billion people, killing some five billion. There will be two classes of humans. (That plan might now be in effect with the "new" coronavirus spreading around the world killing off the old and weak.)

Just look around the world. The Kalergi Plan seems to be advancing. The USA faces Europe's inter-breeding fusion with the Third World. Just look south. Those who applaud it as extinguishing the "white race" don't seem to understand; all ethnicities, except the "homogeneous" one, face extinction. Like it? There will be no "pure" bloodline at all. Racial purity of any race will not be allowed to exist.

I will quote some authors who have taken a close look at the Kalergi Plan, as referenced below.

References:
Europe In Crisis: Intellectuals and the European Idea (1917-1957)
Authors: Mark Hewitson, Matthew D'Auria
The Austrian Mind: An Intellectual and Social History (1848-1938)
Author: William M. Johnston (University of California Press)
Also: www.westernspring.co.uk/the-coudenhove-kalergi-plan

One of the intellectual founding fathers of the European Union, the Austrian diplomat and Freemason Richard Coudenhove-Kalergi outlined his plans for the overall future implications of the EU in his book 'Practical Idealism'. Looking back at this text many years after it was initially penned by Kalergi it is interesting to note how many of his peculiar and often disturbing plans might be coming to fruition in contemporary Europe. The English translation version is a very difficult read because in translation there are words that are out of context and do not make any sense at all. But one is still able to discern what this is all about.

Kalergi described his dreams for a One World Government with its foundations in the European Union. He hoped that the European project would go on to become the blueprint for a society run entirely by the global *elite* over a completely powerless population. He wrote that he wished to see the end of national sovereignty and self-determination and he believed that nationalism, and indeed the very concept of nations, could be demolished through multiculturalism which itself would have to be redefined once miscegenation was complete. He wrote that a society that was racially and ethnically diverse was one which was easily controllable by the political elite. Clearly, he seemed to be talking in self-conflicting terms, on the one hand arguing for a merging of bloodlines, while on the other arguing for a world society that was racially and ethnically diverse.

According to Kalergi, a diverse and multi-cultural people were easy to control as they had no common identity to rally behind in the event of a political crisis. In addition to that, a diverse population would be easy to conquer by the means of divide and rule. The newly arrived immigrants would be pitted against the native people with both sides believing that they were a persecuted minority languishing under a system of law that was rigged against their favor.

Since the last world war, the European Union has gradually eroded aspects of national sovereignty for nation states, often making national law subordinate to that decided by unelected figures at the head of the international organization. What seems to have stuck about the Kalergi Plan was the idea of melding blood-lines to eliminate racial (and cultural) diversity in a one-government world.

There has also been a concerted attempt to chip away at nationalist sentiments and nation-orientated social projects by such policy decisions as freedom of movement as part of the European integration and Angela Merkel's open-door policy towards displaced migrant Syrian refugees.

Kalergi prize, otherwise known as the Charlemagne Prize

While Kalergi's text might seem to be a relic of a more authoritarian and in-tellectually warped era for the people of Europe, it is notable that he is still celebrated and honoured among key members of the European Union today. The Kalergi prize, otherwise known as the Charlemagne Prize, was created in his honour to be awarded to European figures who have helped to promote his plan. Among those awarded this prize in recent years are Angela Merkel, Herman Van Rompuy (the former Prime Minister of Belgium and first Pres-ident of the European Council) and Pope Francis.

The fact that Kalergi is still apparently alive in the minds of many prominent Europeans has led to the suggestion that this is what lies at the obvious antip-athy towards the president-elect Donald Trump by European leaders. Kalergi hoped that the United States would be the next region to fall under the One World Government he envisaged and perhaps many people still nourished that dream until Trump's shock election.

Trump has proven himself to be openly hostile to the idea of multiculturalism and further immigration to the United States, in stark contrast to any of his recent predecessors. He has also preached an isolationist foreign policy and appears to be drawing the lines of the classic nation state in much darker shades than previous presidents. Perhaps it is the case that he is seen as a potential fly in the ointment when it comes to pursuing Kalergi's bizarre plan for world domination.

But there is a larger consideration. Statistical projections are that the world is reaching an unsustainable population, now at 7.6 billion people. By 2050 it is expected to be 9.8 billion, and by 2100 it is estimated to be 11.2 billion. Not a single expert has said that Earth's resources can sustain such a population. In fact, it is believed that the Earth can only sustain something short of 10 billion. India is now overtaking China as the most populated, and Nigeria has the fastest growth in population anywhere on the planet and is expected to surpass the United States by 2050. (Terrorist group Boko Haram is committing unchecked genocide in Nigeria as well as the enslavement of girls while the world at large ignores it.)

Despite the exponential population growth, European indigenous populations are growing smaller. According to the British publication The Guardian (see, https://www.theguardian.com/world/2015/aug/23/baby-crisis-europe-brink-depopulation-disaster), low ethnic birthrates across European countries are causing what may be a population disaster in indigenous populations. If they reach a certain point, typically 1.5, their sustainability as an ethnic group is in serious trouble, and if goes to 1.3 or below, their race will not be able to make a come-back. Italy is at 1.3. This is causing an economic problem across Europe. With a low birthrate and an aging population, costs soar for this aging population without a younger working population to sustain it. Fertility rates are going down, and birth deaths are increasing. Without migration populations, to generate a population growth, many of the European countries face shrinking populations and eventually loss of ethnic populations itself. So why were the North African Islamic countries chosen to fix Europe's problems? In America, birthrates within the family unit is decreasing while out-of-wedlock pregnancies are common but "checked" somewhat by abortionists. One might wonder whether the increase in America's population occurs mostly from birthrates or actually by illegal migrants from our southern border.

With that European problem in mind, let's take another <u>higher</u> look. Who bankrolls the European countries? Who profits from a healthy nation and population with all its industry and businesses? Who loses trillions of dollars when populations decline through lower-fertility rates and small birthrates? Yes, that's right. The globalist bankers.

Which brings us back to *nihilism*. A small group of extremely wealthy people, with a lineage of occultism, supposed descendants of "pharaonic bloodlines", running the world through their banks, without conscience, without ordinary moral values as we Christians know them, are making decisions that affect the lives of world populations. Nihilists. All the earmarks of *nihilism*.

They foster war among populations they don't like anyway, particularly the Islamists, even though they know they are going to use these same people, made refugees of war, to re-populate European countries. Sounds crazy, right? Yet we see the governments of these countries all in lockstep with this migrant movement into their countries, passing laws making it criminal for their own citizens to protest or speak against Islam or the crimes they rampantly commit. Why would their own governments do that to their own citizens, if not controlled by the EU and UN and those who control both?

The elites surely know that at some point the indigenous populations may rise up against the violence of the Islamic migrants, and may even eventually kick most of them out, but the damage has been done. Their women and young girls have been raped and impregnated, and a surge in population after several years of this abuse will still occur. Did the controllers ask these young girls and women if they objected to being impregnated by violent rapes, sometimes by many men at a time? A resurgence in population is the goal, to create population sustainability, and to the elites it doesn't matter how it is accomplished.

The worst migrant abusers have been from Yemen and Somalia. Yemen is war-torn and its men are brutally violent. Somalia, whose population has been twice tested with an average low IQ of 70 are likewise extremely violent and literally mutilate and dismember women they rape in ways so horrendous it is inhuman, more animalistic that any other. Still, Somalian refugees flowed into Europe and America. The last count I saw was some 30,000 Somalian refugees are here.

Then there is also the Kalergi Plan's goal of integrating all races so that the result is but one bloodline on the planet, thus eliminating racial conflict itself. Yet, was it not God who struck down the Tower of Babel and created people of different languages, resulting in different cultures and spiritual beliefs? Did God not do this for a reason?

Chapter III:

The World Stage

PART 1. THE WORLD'S POLICEMAN.

On the world stage, the United States has, since WW-II, risen to the level of the world's "policeman" in the effort to avert war if possible and to prevent rogue nations from building nuclear bombs and missiles. But, as said earlier, the military branches, including the Pentagon, require billions of dollars each year to sustain them. Many billions. But, the "war machine" has not demonstrated a stellar commitment to business ethics, as I've pointed out earlier herein. It has become a source of major profiteering, often with those with financial investments in the offending companies having worked for or lead or were someway "in bed" with those companies/corporations having control over the contracts for the government. Not a very ethical practice, and a practice that should cease or have independent oversight of, including secondary oversight over the actual operations of these companies/corporations to ensure they are not "cheating" in some way, i.e., like padding the books, inflating the costs of materiel or labor, you know, "discretionary" decisions.

President Trump has been working on strategies to get America out of wars we never should have become involved in. Those heavily invested in the "war machine" – including some at the Pentagon – are not in favor of the USA backing up and taking care of its own citizens and country FIRST, but Trump does.

Fortunes are being made by those in the "war machine" including enablers of contracts, process, and operations. Are we the world's policeman, or are we provocateurs, or worse? If the goal of the "war machine" is never-ending war for profit FROM the UNITED STATES coffers, this is off-track from any benefit to Americans, especially those families whose sons or daughters have been maimed or killed in battle, or run the risk of being maimed or killed.

There's no benefit to the taxpayers who cannot consent or reject any direction their tax money is going, even if they believe or know there is graft going on. I suggest there is a need for reflection, correction, and resurrection of what Americans should expect, i.e., honesty, forthrightness, accountability, ethical administration and practices. Citizens should be entitled to injunctive relief when they learn something is legally, ethically, morally, and/or constitutionally amiss. Our dismissive, "But what I can do about it?" must become a collective voice of "I can, and I will, speak out against wrongdoing by my government or those it does business with." If Mr. Ordinary Citizen embezzles from his company, he commits a crime and can be sent to jail with a hefty fine. If Mr. Big Corporation conflates prices and labor services well beyond anything reasonable with the government, or charges for things never done, Mr. Ordinary Citizen should be able to protest, i.e., he should have "standing" to complain and/or sue because he has a right to honesty in government doing business on both sides. President Trump tries but cannot fight "the System" that is more powerful than he is. Yes, there is a need for reformation in our government and in who controls it.

The biggest complaint I've heard nearly all of my 70 years is this one: all politicians are crooked. I personally won't generalize like that because I know that many, hopefully most, are basically honest and ethical in their service to America. Still, there are far too many politicians, local, state or federal, who serve the masters of money, i.e., parties with whom money will be forthcoming in return for favorable legislative considerations. It is saddening to see a political condition where "trust" is a cautious consideration across-the-board. It should not be that way in America's political institutions. I've heard someone say that there are no honest politicians anymore, there are only opportunists. The elitists Rothschild and Rockefeller would agree, since they've bragged they already own those candidates who seek public office. Trump, however, was the "wild card" which is why he was so opposed and subsequently vilified. The elites got trumped!

Perhaps we could create educational institutions that do one thing: educate and train future politicians for the job they must do, and instill in them what they must NOT do, with ETHICS being the watchword. We need "statesmen" not malleable politicians who sell us out for money and power.

PART 2. WHO HATES THE UNITED STATES?

In part, perhaps in large part, because of the role as world policeman and its readiness to intervene anywhere around the world, with force if necessary, some countries have come to view the United States as the "bully on the block." Indeed, some countries accuse the United States of being the biggest "terrorist" on the planet. While some countries align themselves with the USA for economic reasons or for the umbrella protection offered, that doesn't mean they like the USA, and some downright hate us. There have been countries that have received foreign aid in commodities and money, only to turn them over to their own anti-American fighters we characterize as "terrorists." Iran is one of those countries, and their leaders have vowed to launch a nuclear attack on the USA if and when they obtain or are able to build a nuclear device and deliver it onto US soil. And they will do so. Even if the US pulled out of the Arab nations like Iran, Syria and so forth, and left those countries alone, those countries would use that cease-fire to forge ahead on ways to "take revenge" (as they see it) on America itself, including nuclear weapons. And who helped Iran get the uranium they needed? That's right, Hillary herself.

Although Turkey has been an ally, and where we have a military base, Turkey is being taken over by fundamentalist Muslims. Already, we are seeing Muslims in Turkey attacking and killing off Christians, or driving them out of Turkey. Muslims are the largest and fastest growing population today, and they have spread across the globe into many countries, mostly often coming with a smile and assurances they are peaceful and tolerant. Yet, as their population swells (birthing from 4 or more wives), they become more demanding and less hospitable, working their way into positions of power, and eventually gaining a

Muslim majority. Once accomplished, sharia law takes over, and the blood-baths begin against non-Muslim populations.

But aside from the Muslim countries that hate America, there are other Western counties like some European countries, including France, who have turned against and roundly criticized the United States. France, by the way, has welcomed sharia law Muslims into the country in such numbers that violence has become a daily fare for Frenchmen, and its government is considering dividing France into two countries and allowing Muslims to have half of that country. Let us recall that Hitler had taken France, and thousands of American and ally lives were lost on the Normandy coast as they tried to find an entrance into France to fight against the Germans. The Nazis had already built heavily-fortified concrete and steel bunkers with machines guns all along the coastline, placed barbed wire to prevent an invasion by sea. We gave thousands of lives taking the beach at Normandy, and freeing the French from the clutches of the Nazis. Yet here we are, many years later, and the French have turned against the United States. Why? What has happened over the years that turned France against the US? This has also occurred with citizens of other European countries. Why? Could it be our own fault? The fault of a steady stream of American tourists to Europe, many of which manifested a holier-than-though attitude towards Europeans, like they were just servants for tourists? Did Americans shoot themselves in the foot by their own attitudes towards the residents of Europe?

When the European Union (EU) was formed to create a unified coalition of countries against future invasions like they experienced with Germany and Russia, also pushed at the time was a unification of Canada, the United States, and Mexico, where advocates promoted making one country out of three, as nation states, I think the correct term is. But that didn't happen, as the United States wanted and needed to protect its sovereignty. That goal, if achieved, would have one country out of three, and thus more easily moved into the one-government world plan.

WW-I and WW-II thrust America into a world war we did not want. I do not believe we really had any choice about that. The results were freeing from tyranny the nations being threatened and warred against by countries seeking domination and exploitation on a world scale. In the Second World War, Japan wanted the Philippines and, I believe, some of Indonesia, thus expanding its tiny empire. Nazi Germany wanted the entire world. They both lost because of America and its allies.

But subsequent wars, like Korea, Vietnam, Iraq, Libya, Afghanistan, Yemen, etc., may not have been necessary, but rather were conducted with the sole purpose of feeding the "war machine" and some political agenda. Vietnam was about politics, that's it, not about China getting control of Vietnam. Our leaders claimed is was to prevent communist take-over, which may have been part of it, but the political decision was about keeping our "word" to the allies, under the concept that if we can't keep our "word" to the allies, we can't be trusted at all.

About Vietnam, here is what happened, according to an analysis by George Friedman. In an interview by GeoPolitical Futures (GPF), Jonathan Roth interviewing, entitled "The Truth Behind the Vietnam War", the following in a relevant quote:

> The United States entered the Vietnam War for multiple reasons, but the basic reason was Charles DeGaulle. The American strategy at the time was to contain the Soviet Union with a string of alliances swinging from Norway all the way through Iran and block them from expanding. Charles DeGaulle came along and said you can't trust the Americans because if they ever attacked, the Americans wouldn't come and they were not going to fight for you; you're going to be left alone. We have to form our own NATO independent of the United States. During the Vietnam War there's a word that became incredibly important, "credibility". Credibility meant that how credible were the American guarantees to this all-important structure of containment. How credible was it that we would come to Germany's aid or Japan's aid with everything we had if there were a war, and a terrible fear at that time was that these people would lose confidence in us. So, part of the reason we went

to Vietnam had nothing to do with Vietnam. The fear was that if we didn't go to Vietnam, our credibility with our other allies would be gone and the entire American strategy will collapse. On that basis there was no expectation we would wind up with 50,000 dead. On that basis the expectation was that we would go into it as a small "police action," we may win it, we may lose it, but the Germans would know that our guarantee means something. And to a very great extent in my opinion, worrying about how the Europeans react if we didn't go in it's important. Now the fact was the Europeans criticized the United States for going in, but if we hadn't gone in they would have really panicked. They would have really potentially said is NATO worth anything, is Japan's guarantees worth anything. And so we went in based on something that was repeated over and over again, *credibility*.

It's really hard to be a superpower because it's one thing to fight for your life in a World War II, but to go to war for an abstract political consideration having to do with strategy elsewhere, and send your kids to fight in a war like that is agonizing, particularly when you're thinking this is about winning in Vietnam, and it really isn't. So, when we look at the war, we wonder why did we fight this war this way, half-heartedly, not seriously; well, it got out of hand but the reason basically was, this was a political war. It had as its end not protecting Vietnam from the Communists, that was important, but it was a side issue. It had to do with maintaining the entire American 'lion structure' and keeping the Soviets from using this as a basis for unraveling our position.

We made a decision to demonstrate to our allies that we were prepared to go to war on behalf of another ally even if it was dumb.

The attack on Libya, framed as a kind of police action, was based on a false narrative that Omar Gaddafi was a Stalinist-type leader oppressing and brutalizing and killing his own people. What I've learned is that Gaddafi actually decided that it was not in his country's best interests, given its massive oil reserves, to continue with the world "petro-dollar" the US created much earlier. To Gaddafi, a "petro-dollar" was just paper, not backed by anything, such as gold. (Many years ago, after the Federal Reserve was created, what billions of dollars in actual gold America had went to the Federal Reserve, which is, as any American probably knows, or should know, a private bank, not our government bank, and became the property of the bankers to which our government had increasing gotten deeper and deeper into debt).

Gaddafi intended to take Libya out of the "petro-dollar" and go to something more substantial, gold, and to sell its oil only to those nations who could pay in gold. This act would have had a huge financial disaster for the United States and other countries without any gold reserves, because the US had no gold at all and would be unable to buy gold if the North African oil cartel countries also rejected the "petro-dollar." This is what I've learned, and how I understood that information. An economist or geopolitical professional might describe it differently, but I am an intelligent person and can understand basic facts even if I don't know all the innuendos involved in such a shift in oil sales and purchases. In essence, we got Gaddafi in a very brutal way over a decision he made that would have had dire economic and political consequences for America.

With further research, I suppose I could find out more wars to talk about, but I don't want too many details to distract readers from the mission of this book on how Orwellianism exists and why it is hugely dangerous to allow it to continue. What I'm doing is tying things together that connect back to us all, i.e., building the picture of the "spiderweb."

Although I believe that America is heading for a violent confrontation with pro-Socialist Leftists, I also think that, at some point, we may end up in a fight here in America against the Islamists already here who have already begun their own campaign to take down the United States (which they believe is the Mystery Babylon). Already they are leading in slowly with lots of propaganda but with only small acts of violence against Americans thus far; fortunately, the violent actions of one or two anti-socialists or anti-Islamists do not frame the will of the majority of Americans, at least not at this time, about a violent pushback. But it only takes a small match of violence to stir the angst and anger of patriot Americans who are the majority, whether Democrat or Republicans or Independents, such that they feel enough is enough and push back forcefully against the factions seen to be set on taking down America. The Marine motto, "Don't Tread On Me!" is a motto patriot America takes to heart. "Don't mess with my country!" is a good interpretation of what that motto means. This is why we need to protect the Second Amendment; these anti-America forces are very real.

We should step back into a moment of self-reflection. Much of the world sees Americans as full of self-conceit and arrogance, thinking ourselves uppity and better than everyone else. We often treat those in other countries, that we visit and vacation to, as less than ourselves, as merely parts of the tourist *service* industry. Our multiculturalism and diversity have only heightened this social problem, where we all seem to want to be seen as better than others here in our own land. Even now, people of color are doing all they can to create and push the anti-white narrative to marginalize whites and thereby to raise themselves higher in social and political status. It is the idea that by bringing down someone "higher" that means the "underlings" somehow elevate themselves which, of course, is not true. It simply increases the lower level population.

We should try to be ourselves as ordinary human beings in a country many people have died defending, and add that, as a sobering factor, we are really no better than everybody else, and we should conduct ourselves with grace, pride, humility, and dignity rather than conceit and arrogance. We can do these things that will better serve ourselves and restore a world view that Americans are nice people who care about others in the world. Quite frankly, I don't like the view of many around the world that America has become the new terrorists of the world. There is a fine line between being the world's policemen and terrorists; we must not cross that line. We must not allow the "war machine" to do so either.

Before I close this section, I think it relevant to talk briefly about the San Francisco based "Democratic World Federalists", an organization created in 2005, and is affiliated with the Coalition for Democratic World Government, the Community of World Citizens, and the World Federalist Movement, the latter begun in 1938-1939. The goal of these world-minded enthusiasts includes the creation of a single Democratic Socialist World Government without any borders at all, a world where all citizens could move around the world freely and without restraint, live where they want, do what they want.

The idea began after the devastation of countries in World War I, creating horror around the world. Post-war, in the 1930s and 1940s, numerous attempts were made locally, nationally, and regionally by activists to prevent the outbreak and spread of war and to mobilize initiatives and forces favoring a World Federation. In 1938-1939 the World Federalist Movement was begun by two women, and such organizations for world peace and civility of nations grew around the world.

A preliminary draft of the World Constitution by the World Federalist Movement reads, in its Preamble:

> The people of the earth, having agreed that the advancement
> of man in spiritual excellence and physical welfare is the com-
> mon goal of mankind, that universal peace is the prerequisite
> for the pursuit of that goal, that justice in turn is the prereq-
> uisite of peace, and peace and justice stand or fall together
> that iniquity and war inseparably spring from the competitive
> anarchy of the national states, that therefore the age of na-
> tions must end, and the era of humanity begin, the govern-
> ments of the nations have decided to order their separate
> sovereignties in one government of justice, to which they sur-
> render their arms, and to establish, as they do establish, this
> Constitution as the covenant and fundamental law of the
> Federal Republic of the World.

These goals for world peace are commendable, and the proposed Articles in its Constitution reveal quite a bit of thought and reason in its covenants. But while these one-world advocates do strive to believe in the innate goodness of all mankind, and believe that the institutions of power that rule can ultimately determine and suppress various conflicts and criminal activities around the world because citizens will all be disarmed, history has shown us that efforts to assimilate various cultures into one have failed, that efforts to promote multiculturalism anywhere in the world results in cultural conflicts and even divisiveness in mixed communities, and that always there will be despots vying for the power seats.

The European Union was one of the first organizations post-war that was amenable to this idea, and years later, we have seen the EU promote the migration of millions of Muslims into Europe, with devastating results due precisely to cultural and ideological reasons. Nowhere in the world's various countries have Muslims "assimilated" because their religious ideology and culture expressly prohibit it.

We who would love world peace and tolerance in the world cannot achieve those goals with open arms of welcome and expecting the same in return from cultures entrenched in separatism. We who would love to travel the world in the extraordinarily beautiful places all over this jewel among the stars must resist the temptation to embrace those who hate us and war against us because of ideology or inequality perceptions and would do us harm if we tried to vacation in their nation, as has happened to a man/wife team brutally murdered during a "peace and love" trip into Afghanistan recently.

A kind and peaceful world, where happiness, civility, and kindness flourishes must start, unfortunately, with the sequestering of cultures who are horribly violent and combative to anyone else. We have to face the facts that there are some cultures that cannot and will not change, no matter what good-hearted advances the rest of the world might make, and inclusion and assimilation is simply not an option because those cultures will flatly reject it. We have to recognize that some cultures exist without any morality at all, thus rendering them untrustworthy in social or political interactions with other cultures.

We also have to face the fact that the world is likewise infected with an aristocracy from pharaonic bloodlines who think they are more "special" that everyone else and that they are entitled by lineage to remain the "rulers" of the world; they must be put in their place and mocked for the self-conceit. So, at both ends of the scale we find problems, but both have solutions, and both of them have to be taken down in some way, by sequestering, by laws that prohibit their infestation, or by something of more permanence.

But, as it stands now, considering who has control of the world, and who are the violent ones as of culture or nation, uniting the world as one people, i.e., the citizens of Planet Earth, is a fantasy, a mere hope for Utopia here on Earth, that we can only dream about. Even now, around the Western world in particular, we are seeing a devolution of virtue, morality, values, and a slide into godless anarchy without limits. Orwellianism is alive and well in the Western world, and certainly growing here in the North American continent. We will never reach Utopia when we are plummeting into Dystopia. Until the Babel Tower Syndrome becomes non-existent, the world will remain unable to assimilate conflicting cultures or reach mutual agreements for peaceful co-existence. In my opinion.

Both the violent zealots at the bottom, and the self-appointed "nobility" at the top are the direct cause of strife and war and oppression. History have shown their bloody record and millions of needless deaths by their genocidal policies or campaigns. Eliminate them, and work towards civility and cooperation with other countries so that they will come to agree that universal peace and alliance with the other, and we might just achieve a much safer and friendlier planet.

PART 3: WHAT WILL HAPPEN IF WE HAVE CIVIL WAR?

A civil war in the United States will weaken us as a nation. A divided nation, as we were many years ago in the Civil War, pits American against American, bottom line, brother against brother, with losses of life that may be staggering. On our own, and in the end, we might recover as a nation, depending upon who wins. If the Left wins, the Constitution falls, Christianity falls, the belief in God falls, and within several years the Left's socialist result will crash as well, with the end result being the creation of a totalitarian government of the New World Order. The NWO has been characterized as a "one world government" but I think the correct name should be "one government world", perhaps a minor distinction to some, but I think my distinction leans more to the oppressive nature of what it will be. It will not be the new Utopia at all, but Dystopia is more likely. I come to that conclusion because the rulers are already chosen from the aristocracy.

I will speak more to that in Chapter V.

However, if Americans end up fighting and shooting each other, I suggest it highly probable that nation states that do not like America, and even wealthy and powerful criminal cartels, will attack us directly also, killing us off as quickly as they can and carving out new nations or territories on American soil. We have already seen what happens when Muslims come in; they separate themselves, take over parts of cities and real estate, declare them NoGo Zones to non-Muslims and act like where they have settled is no longer American property.

But, it is this latter probability of attacks from outside our borders that the NWO globalists may not foresee in their own plans to take control. I think, human nature being what it is, that in a weakened state of civil war our enemies will be happy to take advantage and bring with them what may be described as a new holocaust intent. The United Nations, which will likely invade as a "police action", is not our friend.

As I will say repeatedly in this book, moderate and conservative Democrats and Independents, and there are millions, better recognize what the Democrat Leftist Progressives are really after. The Democratic Socialists of America might be hoping for a lovely democratic socialist ideology blessed with nice labor-class people, but that's unlikely. If you, the reader, are among that American patriot group of moderate and conservative Democrats, Independents, and Republicans, you all need to step up and find others like you, organize against these radical Leftists, and shut them down. Right now, Democrats have two choices; fix your party, or join the patriot Right and fight to take back from these Progressives what has already been lost so as to avoid civil war. I do not doubt but that are millions of American patriots among the Democrat Party, people who believe in the value of the Constitution, who believe in law-and-order, who believe in the Christian ideology that has provided a higher level of morality in our social construct and system of laws than any other country on this planet. We lose that, and we lose this nation's ideology, and if the NWO totalitarianism prevails, we have gained nothing more than true

Hell on Earth forever. Patriots of all parties should find the "common ground" that to fix what ails America and the world can and must be fixed, but not by throwing our ideology away; our ideology has long been subverted by Marxists and even those Presidents who believed in "internationalism" and a one-government world; from them, we find ourselves suffering the pains of the socialist programs they put in place already.

Most critical, the NWO agenda of planetary depopulation intends to commit mass murder. By viruses or by other means of extermination, they intend a genocidal campaign until not more than one billion people populate the Earth, and it will be the rulers who decide what ethnicities will remain. But regardless, there will remain only two classes: rulers and serfs. History has shown that the aristocrats, i.e., the "nobility", have always been the most selfish and self-centered, the most cruel and perversely violent, and the most oppressive of rulers throughout history, regardless of their race or culture.

Is the possibility of such a future acceptable to you? Read Orwell's book. Watch "1984."

Chapter IV:

The New World Order

PART 1: THE HISTORY OF GREED

I call this section the History of Greed because the never-ending struggle of some over eons of time to control everything on this planet continues to haunt us to this day. Over time millions, perhaps billions, have died by the efforts of one or a few to take over the planet so they could rule it as if they were gods. The aristocracy arising from pharaohs – who were supposedly gods – have been the one class of human beings responsible for the deaths of more people than all but the worst of plagues the earth has endured over time. In their own right, they have been like plagues.

In 1990, an author by the name of Will T. Still wrote a book entitled "NEW WORLD ORDER: The Ancient Plan of Secret Societies." This book described how an ancient plan had been hidden for centuries deep within secret societies, revealing a scheme designed to bring all of mankind under a single world government – a New World Order. This plan is of such antiquity it is even mentioned in the Bible – the rule of the Antichrist mentioned in the Revelation of Saint John the Divine.

The Illuminati actually goes back to 1776, as a German secret society, but among those discussed by Still are the Freemasons or Masons, because it is the largest of those groups. Still does not characterize Freemasonry as "evil" in any way, but it was very secret although not so much in these modern times.

But the book also exposed recent plots by the Rockefellers on behalf on the Illuminati to support Richard Nixon for the Presidency and, in 1960 he did run for that office but was defeated by John F. Kennedy. While awaiting another chance for the Presidency, Nixon lived in a posh $100,000-a-year Manhattan apartment owned by Nelson Rockefeller, earning an annual $200,000-a-year salary, spending most of his time touring the country and the world, eventually rebuilding his political reputation and then campaigning to get the 1968 Republican nomination. Nixon campaigned as the arch-enemy of Communism, but flipped over after the elections, taking just about everyone by surprise. Even during his campaign he said if elected he would pursue what would be a fundamental change (to borrow Obama's term) for a "new internationalism" which was but a prelude to the real goal of some of these secret societies, particularly the Illuminati, which the termed the "New Atlantis" or the "New World Order." Remember, we heard this same NWO term from Herbert W. Bush and George W. Bush in favorable context, contrary to John F. Kennedy who tried to warn Americans about the NWO.

Nixon appointed Dr. Henry Kissinger, another Rockefeller confidant, as his national security advisor. Kissinger was Rockefeller's personal advisor on foreign affairs and a paid staff member of the pro-socialist Council on Foreign Affairs. The shadow forces were trying to create a coup, but that effort crashed with Nixon's resignation (due to Watergate) in August 1974. Unable to eliminate government by the Constitution, the strategy changed to eliminate it by legislative means. Subsequently, 34 state legislatures called for a Constitutional Convention, but failed to get more aboard after the scheme leaked into the public domain.

Rexford Guy Tugwell, which I mention elsewhere herein as a member of Franklin D. Roosevelt's "Brain Trust" (remember, Roosevelt was pushing socialist-type programs), published in 1974 the proposed Constitution for the New States of America, which proposed, *"The government will be empowered to abridge freedom of expression, communication, movement and assembly in a "declared emergency." The practice of religion would be considered a "privilege."*

Secret societies like the German Thule society, who was interested in mysticism, and the Illuminati, who was also invested in matters of the occult, were anti-God, so the goal of "new internationalism" intended to exclude religion except by permission. They want nationalism where all power is vested in the government. Nationalism would be a terrible system for managing world affairs. Besides being wasteful it has been the direct cause of countless wars, death, and poverty. Were a New World Order run by these secret societies, it can only lead to corrupt and absolute dictatorships mankind has ever known. These are not people who are virtuous and kind. Our way of life in America, whatever the criticism, is still far above the world norm. It is an aberration in the best way in world history. The rest of the world both envies us and hates us, and would rather we become like them subjugated to an oppressive regime. They are like crabs in a bowl, the few trying to climb out are pulled back down by the many.

There are those among us on this planet who greedily seek power, control, and wealth at the expense of everyone else. Many are banned together in some cult or organization all focused on their own schemes for power, control, and wealth, and if people die in large numbers, they don't care.

The greatest dangers to a peaceful world today is not just Islam; it is the pharaonic lineage from the days of the pharaohs. They dominate the aristocracy, the nobility, the privileged few, around the world, and many of them are operating right here in the United States, busy trying to take control.

The origin of Freemasonry, for example, began in Egypt. Essential to that history of ancient Masonry are the Egypt gods Osiris and Isis. Masonic literature still abounds with references to both figures. Isis is seen as the guiding light of the profession of prostitution, while Osiris is the chief evil god. Osiris was the god of the Egyptian underworld, the prince of the dead.

Masonry advocated a "religion" they termed Illuminism, or Luciferians. Illuminism teaches that man can become a god, and this belief seems to be what drives the pharaonic aristocracy lineage today, i.e., believing they "deserve" to rule, that they "deserve" to have control over everyone else, and so on. The Masons say today they do not engage in politics or mysticisms like

Luciferianism. They deny any dark intentions or behaviours, and lament that they are just a social club. Perhaps they are. Perhaps not.

PART 2. THE OBAMA/CLINTON SOCIALIST EFFORT

A. Barack Obama (Barry Soetero)

Barack Obama was an enigma to American politics. A former card-carrying member of the Democratic Socialists of America (DSA) as late as 1996, the year he was elected to state senator, he was also, as he states himself in his book, Dreams From My Father, anti-colonialist, and he had no love for America because, in his view, it began as a colonialist structure and remains in many ways the same.

Obama grew up in what researcher Max Friedman described as a "Marxist-rich environment" and that Obama's original mentor, Frank Marshall Davis, was a member of the Communist Party USA (CPUSA), a fact that Obama took pains to conceal in his book. State Senator Alice Palmer, who hand-picked Obama as her successor in the Illinois legislature, was herself a member of the U.S. Peace Council, a CPUSA front group.

This bit of information about Obama and the DSA was not discovered by any major U.S. newspapers, but it was discovered by a New Zealand libertarian Trevor Loudon (newzeal.blogspot.com/), who stumbled upon the Spring 1996 "New Party News" while researching far-left groups in the land down under. DSA, he says, was set up in Chicago by Trotskyites and former members of the Students for a Democratic Society (SDS) after a feud with the old-line CPUSA, which explains Obama's close friendship with former SDS leaders Bill Ayers and Bernadine Dohrn, in whose home he announced his Senate campaign. DSA had stressed that its chief goal was to "work within the Democratic Party and remove the stigma attached to 'socialism' in the eyes of most Americans."

There is a stigma because socialism is incompatible with private property and free enterprise. Ask any of the millions of immigrants who fled to this country because they could no longer stand to live in a socialist "worker's paradise."

The unresolved question, however, about Obama, is whether he had already become a Muslim in secret and masqueraded as a Christian while aligning himself with Islamic fundamentalists. After all, he was caught bowing to the Saudi Arabian King and promising that if push comes to a shove, he would "roll" with his Muslim brothers.

Other events occurred under the Obama administration. In a 2017 Pew Research Center report on How America Changed During Barack Obama's Presidency, we find the following:

> Barack Obama campaigned for the U.S. Presidency on a platform of change. As he prepares to leave office, the country he led for eight years is undeniably different. Profound social, demographic and technological changes have swept across the United States during Obama's tenure, as have important shifts in government policy and public opinion

Noting that the election of the nation's first black president raised hopes that race relations in the U.S. would improve, especially among black voters, by 2016, following a spate of high-profile deaths of Black Americans during encounters with police and protests by the Black Lives Matter movement and other groups, many Americans – especially blacks – described race relations as generally bad. And what we have seen since that time is a corresponding growth in white hatred by blacks manifesting in attacks on white people, especially white men. In a recent video I watched, a group of a dozen or so black youths mercilessly beat a helpless white man, kicking and punching him, jumping on him while on the ground, even riding a bicycle over his head area. While city cameras caught this event, allowing the police to arrest most of them, this only highlights the growing anti-white sentiment by people of color.

The Great Recession of 2008 cost millions of Americans their homes and jobs, leading Obama to push through a roughly $800 million stimulus package as one of his first orders of business, resulting in a lowering of unemployment, but by some measures, the country faced serious economic challenges from the Great Recession, including a steady hollowing of the middle class, and income inequality reaching its highest point since 1928.

Views on some high-profile social issues shifted rapidly, for example, eight states and the District of Columbia legalized marijuana for recreational purposes, a shift subsequently accompanied a striking reversal of public opinion, where a majority of Americans came to support legalization of the drug.

In 2015 the Supreme Court overturned longstanding bans on same-sex marriages, effectively legalizing such unions nationwide. A majority of Americans said for the first time they favored same-sex marriage.

With Millennials approaching the Baby Boomers as the nation's largest living adult generation and the largest generation of eligible voters, they are revealing – through the brainwashing in schools and colleges – that they favor socialism as the ideal form of government.

In 2013, for the first time, the majority of newborn babies in the U.S. were racial or ethnic minorities. The same year, a record-high 12% of newlyweds married someone of a difference race, thus helping to fulfill the Kalergi Plan of achieving a single bloodline of Earth's population by interbreeding ethnicities.

In addition, when it comes to the nation's religious identity as Christian, the biggest trend to rise during Obama's administration was those who claimed no religion at all. Those who self-identify as atheists or agnostics, as well as those who say their religion is "nothing in particular," now make up nearly a quarter of the U.S. adult population, up from 16% in 2007.

Finally, during and since Obama's administration, we have seen a significant rise in gender politics, where laws are being passed to allow and even require parents to acquiesce to their young child's wish – fostered by school teachers – to change their sexuality identity, or face criminal or civil charges. Consequently, among this gender identity situation there has been a spike in the number of suicides by transgender persons who matured enough later to realize they really wanted to be the sex they were born with, but are too late because the sex change was permanent. Did we do any favors by allowing them to make such choices before they were old enough and mature enough to understand what a sex change meant in the short and long run? I don't think so.

Obama will go down, in my opinion, as the worst president America has ever had. He promised a lot, but delivered almost nothing outside of Obamacare, which itself was a failure. In point of fact, only 20% of Americans trusted the federal government at the end of Obama's reign. The mistakes of fools become known to the world, and Obama's legacy will be as a traitor to his own country, and to humanity as well, in my opinion.

Obama was groomed for politics with the help of George Soros, a frontline member of the Deep State, who found a candidate for public office and even the Presidency. Obama's Senate time was simply a "training ground" where the "shadow government" of which Soros is a part could observe and evaluate him for candidacy to the Presidency. He proved himself a worthy candidate for their own twisted agenda and, like a true-Muslim, lied to the American people, convincing them that he was the new Jesus incarnate. Supporters even prayed to him, even inserted his name for Jesus in religious songs. Children saying their nightly prayers prayed to Obama, not God. Yep, his supporters were truly mesmerized, and I wonder what it feels like to have been such a patsy? Or is he still Jesus to them? It was a disgraceful thing to do to their own children, to confuse them about God and man. How sickening is that brainwashing?

So, what is he doing these days? His "Organizing for Action" organizations, well-funded by George Soros, is quietly making headway to continue the globalist agenda. Still thinking he is a "good guy"?

So, let's see what Obama has been up to. In the 2017 New York Post, in an article by Paul Sperry, the headline reads, "How Obama is scheming to sabotage Trump's presidency." Well, a lot of people figured that after the elections Obama would not "go quietly into the right."

Sperry noted that *"When former President Barack Obama said he was "heartened" by anti-Trump protests; he was sending a message of approval to his troops. Troops? Yes, Obama has an army of agitators – numbering more than 30,000 – who will fight his Republican successor at every turn of his historic presidency. And Obama will command them from a bunker less than two miles from the White House."*

Sperry writes:

> In what's shaping up to be a highly unusual post-presidency, Obama isn't just staying behind in Washington. He's working behind the scenes to set up what will effectively be a shadow government to not only protect his threatened legacy, but to sabotage the incoming administration and its popular "America First" agenda.

> He's doing it through a network of leftist nonprofits led by Organizing for Action. Normally you'd expect an organization set up to support a politician and his agenda to close up shop after that candidate leaves office, but not Obama's OFA. Rather, it's gearing up for battle, with a growing war chest and more than 250 offices across the country.

> Since Donald Trump's election, this little-known but well-funded protesting arm has beefed up staff and ramped up recruitment of young liberal activists, declaring on its website, "We're not backing down." Determined to salvage Obama's legacy, it's drawing battle lines on immigration, ObamaCare, race relations and climate change.

> Obama is intimately involved in OFA operations and even tweets from the group's account. In fact, he gave marching orders to OFA foot soldiers following Trump's upset victory.

> "It is fine for everybody to feel stressed, sad, discouraged," he said in a conference call from the White House. "But get over it." He demanded they "move forward to protect what we've accomplished."

> "Now is the time for some organizing," he said. "So, don't mope."

> "Far from sulking, OFA activists helped organize anti-Trump marches across US cities, some of which turned into riots.

After Trump issued a temporary ban on immigration from seven terror-prone Muslim nations, the demonstrators jammed airports, chanting: "No ban, no wall, sanctuary for all!"

Run by old Obama aides and campaign workers, federal tax records show "nonpartisan" OFA marshals 32,525 volunteers nationwide. Registered as a 501(c)(4), it doesn't have to disclose its donors, but they've been generous. OFA has raised more than $40 million in contributions and grants since evolving from Obama's campaign organization Obama for America in 2013.

OFA, in IRS filings, says it trains young activists to develop "organizing skills." Armed with Obama's 2012 campaign database, OFA plans to get out the vote for Democratic candidates it's grooming to win back Congress and erect a wall of resistance to Trump at the other end of Pennsylvania Avenue.

It will be aided in that effort by the Obama Foundation, run by Obama's former political director, and the National Democratic Redistricting Committee, launched last month by Obama pal Eric Holder to end what he and Obama call GOP "gerrymandering" of congressional districts.

Obama will be overseeing it all from a shadow White House located within two miles of Trump. It features a mansion, which he's fortifying with construction of a tall brick perimeter, and a nearby taxpayer-funded office with his own chief of staff and press secretary. Michelle Obama will also open an office there, along with the Obama Foundation.

The 55-year-old Obama is not content to go quietly into the night like other ex-presidents.

Critical to the fight is rebuilding the ravaged Democratic Party. Obama hopes to install his former civil rights chief

Tom Perez at the helm of the Democratic National Committee.

Perez is running for the vacant DNC chairmanship, vowing, "It's time to organize and fight ... We must stand up to protect President Obama's accomplishments," while also promising, "We're going to build the strongest grassroots organizing force this country has ever seen."

"You're going to see me early next year," he told his OFA troops after the election, "and we're going to be in a position where we can start cooking up all kinds of great stuff."

Added the ex-president: "Point is, I'm still fired up and ready to go."

The shameful Left's attack on the election institution and process merely highlights the dangers now apparent in our nation from what can only be accurately described as "enemies of the State."

According to a 2017 article in the AmericanThinker.com, entitled "Obama, Organizing for Action, and the Death Throes of the Democratic Party", journalist Scott S. Powell wrote:

"If you think you're going crazy from nonstop news coverage of unruly behavior and disruptive protests across the country since Donald Trump was elected president, rest assured there are veiled reasons for the current madness. Pulitzer Prize-winning journalist Michael Goodwin asserts the 'Trump Derangement Syndrome,' is no temporarily insane reaction, but rather "a calculated plan to wreck the presidency, whatever the cost to the country."

The beginnings of this "rolling coup" happened in broad daylight in the taking down of Lieutenant General Michael Flynn as Director of National Security by residual players within the Obama intelligence community — including the CIA and the NSA.

Political correctness remains so dominant in language and culture in the U.S., that no one dares utter the word "sedition." Unbeknownst to most Americans, Barack Obama is the first ex-president in 228 years of U.S. history to structure and lead a political organization, a shadow government, for the explicit purpose of sabotaging his successor — duly elected President Donald Trump. The primary vehicle of this campaign is Organizing for Action (OFA), legally founded in January 2013 by First Lady Michelle Obama and her husband's 2012 campaign manager Jim Messina, with input from David Axelrod."

Powell noted that the *modus operandi* comes right out of Obama's support and sympathy for Marxism and his background as a left-wing community organizer, and that it is a "combination of agitation and propaganda – much like old-style Soviet *agitprop*, and Saul Alinsky's *Rules for Radicals*. Powell explains the definition of "*agitprop*" as "*synonymous with community organizing in that both focus on stirring up public grievance over an issue for the purpose of mobilizing that constituency to join like-minded people to protest and demonstrate, which provides for made-for-TV drama scenes portraying "extemporaneous" mass protests that in turn get transmitted to millions through the media. This feedback loop is a key driver of fake news.*"

OFA in just two years took in over $40 million, according to IRS filings, and OFA's donors are also members of George Soros's Democracy Alliance, which is a donors' consortium of the left-wing super-rich aristocracy devoted to radical political change (i.e., New World Order). OFA has three-million donors and two-million active participants, so one should not underestimate OFA's potential influence, especially, as Powell cautions, "*with an uncritical media covering it up.*"

Powell did have some good news, however. He notes that "*the majority of Americans are not easily fooled. Their common sense was the key factor in electing Donald*

Trump ....." Powell notes that "*Obama has singlehandedly done more to damage the Democratic Party in eight years than the GOP could have ever hoped or planned – an unprecedented staggering net loss of 1,042 state and federal Democratic seats, among congressional and state legislatures, governorships and the presidency. Many state-level Democratic Party leaders are now in open revolt against Obama's OFA, which they see as a shadow party without coordination or accountability, and funded from the controversial "end of America" extremist sources like George Soros."*

We see media sources like the *"Young Turks"* (Cenk Uygur, who publicly promoted beastiality (sex with animals) on one of his daily broadcasts, with a women guest who must have been quite speechless at Uygur's admission and argument.) Cenk is planning to run against George Papadopoulos for Congress, organizing through the organization called "Justice Democrat" an ambitious and seditious plan to undermine the 2020 mid-term and general elections by holding auditions for political candidates, which is from where we got bubble-head Barbie Alexandra Oscasio-Cortez (AOC), a former bartender. Her handler, the JD's Director Saikat Chakrabarti, who is one of the founders along with Kyle Kulinski, and Zack Exley, created Justice Democrats in 2017. Zack Exley, however, is the real "brains" behind Justice Democrat. (Google it, it all shows up on YouTube.)

JD claims to be for solutions to skyrocketing inequality, catastrophic climate change, deepening structural racism as the country becomes more diverse, and the corporate takeover of our democracy. At their website, they state, *"We're looking for candidates who will actively build a movement around solutions that match the scale of the crisis."* So, JD, with the help of the Young Turks host Cenk Uygur, as a very popular media with some 4.5 million followers, has been canvassing for candidates whose mindset is either anti-America or pro-socialist or both. They hold actual auditions, which is how Cortez got picked. Her brother told her about the auditions and suggested she might do better than bartending if she got selected; obviously that turned out well for her, but now she's finding herself more in the spotlight for her stupidity than for her pre-scripted "concerns" and promises.

Cortez did not "run" for Congress on her own volition. She is an "actor" auditioned recruited by JD who got her elected and who writes her entire script;

she makes no decisions on her own but is directed what to say and what to do by JD handlers. What you may not have heard about is AOC's sinister "living wage rule." AOC announced she would be capping the salaries of her congressional staff at $80 thousand per year and giving lower staff a raise to a "living wage" and her interns $15 per hour. But AOC's "living wage" rule allows her staff to dodge financial disclosure laws. Under federal laws, congressional employees who earn over $126 thousand dollars per year must disclose all of the outside money that they earn. Because AOC's top staff will not be making over $126 thousand dollars per year, they will not be subject to this law. Who came up with this brilliant scheme? It wasn't the bartender. It was none other than Chakrabarti. This team of guys who got AOC elected and who are now pulling the strings for her congressional seat, declared at the outset that they were trying to bring "integrity" into government, to bring in transparency, to flush out the corruption. Yet it looks like they are trying in every way they can to hide their own corrupt and insidious plans and activities. AOC, as a congressperson, is a fake, she is a fraud, she's not real. None of her tweets are actually her tweets, none of her speeches are actually her speeches, her answers to questions in interviews – she was coached to give those, she is not a real congresswoman, she is an actress.

Rashida Tlaib, Ilhan Omar, and Ayanna Pressley, Raul Grijalva, Ro Khanna, and Pramila Jayapal, are all recruited candidates of JD who are now incumbent Congresspersons controlled by JD handlers. New "challengers" for 2020 are Marie Newman, Alex Morse, Betsy Sweet, Cori Bush, Kara Eastman, Jamaal Bowman, Morgan Harper, Jessica Cisneros, all controlled by JD handlers.

Justice Democrats is affiliated with *Brand New Congress*, a political action committee that endeavors, according to the group's website, *"recruit over 400 extraordinary ordinary Americans to challenge both Democrats and Republicans in congressional primary races across the country in order to replace almost all of Congress in one fell swoop."* Replacement of Congress in both Parties would set the stage for ushering in Obama's "fundamental change" which is socialism first, disarmament of Americans, and finally, the transition to the New World Order totalitarian system.

Cenk Uygur, in a video, admits that the goal of Justice Democrats intends to canvas for candidates not for their political savvy but for their malleability, i.e., who will serve the handlers in JD by making decisions in Congress based solely on what Justice Democrats want them to do and say. The goal is complete replacement of Congress with only Justice Democrats puppets.

Current candidates are listed in very positive terms that many Americans can get aboard with, as is shown on their Candidate page of the website (justicedemocrats.com), but this is all "double-speak" since the goal is not to improve American life but to push the agenda for socialism. Once again, the alt-Left is trying to fool us all. Despite the webpage statements about JD's current incumbents, we have already seen the anti-Semitic rage that defines Muslim Rashida Tlaib, and the outrageous agenda of Cortez, a Puerto Rican, as well as the anti-American and anti-Semitic rhetoric and direct lies of Ilhan Omar, another Muslim. JD's aggressive recruitment is the brainchild of Cenk Uygur, who seeks to install radical Leftists and socialists in all seats of Democrats, and, he hopes, all seats of Republicans by infiltration.

Among these radicals is Zach Exley, who is a radical Leftist and "open borders" advocate, who was a fellow at the "Open Borders Foundation" which is George Soros's organization. As radical as Soros is characterized, he is the least radical of the entire JD, OFA (Organizing For Action) and BNC (Brand New Congress) groups, and other affiliate groups. Obama's "fundamental transformation" of the U.S. is now, in large part, in the hand of admitted socialists JD, OFA, BNC, and other affiliates.

It is also interesting to note that Cenk Uygur's "The Young Turks" is a take-off from a group called "The Young Turks" which was a group of revolutionaries formed in 1911 who slaughtered 1.5 million in the Armenian genocide campaign. So, we know where Cenk's influence and allegiance is.

Saikat Chakrabarti is influenced by Subhas Chandra Bose who was the *violent* complement to the non-violent Mahatma Ghandi. While Ghandi was trying to expel the British from India non-violently, Bose thought it best to start a war and just kill all the British. Bose was quoted as saying, "*Our philosophy should be a synthesis of Nazism and Communism.*" And this is Chakrabarti's hero whose face is on the T-shirt he wears in all of his videos. Subhas is an anti-colonialist and, in India, early British colonialism causes deep resentment to this day. To the anti-colonialists, the U.S. is an evil empire whose roots were colonialist. Chakrabarti himself is an anti-colonialist Indian, which plays right into the hands of George Soros who simply wants to destroy America itself. So we have anti-America people in the JD, OFA, and BNC who are actively engaged in taking over or destroying America at any cost, whether through the political and/or economic system, or by violence, but rest assured if they ever win the control they seek, another round of genocide is certain to occur.

I'm sure we'll be hearing from Obama and that JD tribe more around the 2020 elections. My recommendation is, don't buy anything their candidates say. Like Obama, who said one thing when he meant the opposite, these candidates and incumbents are cut from the same cloth.

My recommendation is before voting in the 2020 and mid-term elections, check JD's website and the BNC's website, and do NOT vote for ANY of the candidates they list. Voting for any of them is dangerous and could spell complete disaster for the future of the United States if they actually achieve their "take over" agenda of Congress. Of the 66 candidates they brought forth in 2018, all lost except 7. Make sure that number does not get reversed in 2020.

B. Hillary Clinton

Hillary Clinton was Secretary of State destined to become the first woman President and, as she put it, it was "my turn." Her turn? Very telling, don't you think?

The amount of information about the corruption by the Clintons includes money and political corruption, war-mongering, and murders of people who opposed them and people who were close to them but knew too much. While there has not been sufficient proof to charge the Clintons with numerous murders, there is information that indicates the Clinton body account is around 54-55, most of whose deaths were 'officially' determined to be "suicides" even though at least one victim, officially deemed a suicide, died from three gunshots to the back of the head. No charges have ever been brought because there was simply no direct evidence linking them to the deaths, especially when a large portion were deemed "suicides" including a victim who shot himself three times in the back of the head.

In her rise through the political ranks, millions of women adored her for no other reason than she was the "strong" woman successfully "competing" with her male counterparts. Women believed the propaganda in their worship of her, and never knew just how nihilistic Clinton was/is.

So, let's explore Hillary Clinton in this section. I will draw this information from teleSUR.com, a media funded in whole or in part by multiple Latin American governments. Commentator Abby Martin did the honors in a broadcast entitled, "Empire Files: Abby Martin Exposes What Hillary Clinton Really Represents, published on April 17, 2016. (https://www.youtube. com/watch?v=PV_PLCC6jeI)

As the circus of the 2016 elections ground on, Hillary Clinton posited herself as a "candidate of the people." In hindsight, that should bring a belly laugh. Not many people have a vacation home in the Hamptons that cost $200,000 per month, or hang out with the world's billionaires. Admittedly, it's hard knowing who she really is, once being a proponent of Donald Trump-type positions, like building a wall at the Mexican border (which she may have done if elected President). She supported torture and opposing same-sex marriages until 2013. In 2016 she presented herself as the anti-Trump, anti-Republican candidate. There was a lot of outrage at the impression that the "Establishment" had already anointed her as the Democratic nominee, and had carved out her path to the Presidency. But in 2008 her 'guaranteed' ascendance to the throne was derailed by the masses and millions of young "Progressive" voters. She continued to play "shape-shifting" games to try to capture support from her opponent, but the real Hillary was still inside fuming. In fact, every layer of Hillary's career showed why. Far from being a candidate of the people, she was the top pick by the corporate world to do their bidding and do their real job of any U.S. President: be the CEO of the Empire. While Americans may not view past Presidents in that manner, further analysis would show that criticism has merit.

For example, the Bush family, the patriarch Herbert Walker Bush being a supporter of Hitler until it became politically-incorrect just prior to the US entering the War against Japan and Germany. Later, George H.W. Bush, being elected President, he too advocated for the US to enter the New World Order utopian one-government world agenda (being pushed by the Illuminati globalists and the United Nations), a call similarly taken up by George W. Bush who proved himself to be a member of the Illuminati's "Skull and Bones" fraternity as was his father. George W. was as a Yale graduate and Illuminati choice for inclusion into that society. I personally saw him on television giving the slight crossed arm bow and the 3-2 salute of the S&B.

Further back, Franklin D. Roosevelt, himself a powerful banker, was the one who pushed and signed the bill to create the Federal Reserve, a private bank owned by the top bankers of the world. Yes, there is history upon history of Presidents supported by the banking conglomerates getting ushered into the Presidency.

The banking and corporate powers both worked hard to keep Hillary on the path to the Presidency because they already knew she would be working for them.

Having been Party insiders for decades already, the Clintons knew how to manipulate DC media reporters, mastered the media spin, and they have a well-oiled Public Relations machine at their beck-and-call.

During the 2016 campaign, undisclosed was the fact that many of Hillary's supporters, including media supporters, worked at corporations employed by the Clintons and Super PACs. So, they had financial ties to the candidates they praise on the air. It was not just paid pundits, but reporters and owners themselves, including the head of the New York Times, all of which had personal and financial ties to the Clintons themselves.

But here's what may be a surprise to most citizens: Even with Citizens United and unfettered corporate funding, the "Establishment" cannot prevent an insurgent candidate like Bernie Sanders from winning with the votes, which is why back in 1984 the Democratic Party created a Super-Delegate process to further undermine democracy.

Here is how it works. There are about 4000 pledge Delegates divided by primary and caucus results. But there is an additional 700 Super-Delegates who remain "unpledged" meaning they CAN vote against the People's will to ensure nominees are hand-picked Party insiders. The single vote of a Super-Delegate is worth a thousand of ours. Many of these people are current and former members of Congress. But dozens more are literally corporate lobbyists working on behalf of every industry from healthcare to private prisons. Examples:

Talio Burgos: Pfizer lobbyist and Clinton fundraiser.

Jill Alter, M. Moore, and Maria Cardona: Dewey Square Group (DSG), a lobbying group that worked directly with the Clinton campaign on behalf of healthcare corporations to craft Obamacare for their own benefit.

Jeff Berman, top lobbyist at Briancave, and a former lobbyist for the Keystone pipeline, and the GEO Group (private prisons). Berman was even paid by the Clintons to round up other Super-Delegate votes.

This unelected "nobility" comprised one-third of all the delegates needed to secure the Democrat nomination. The Clintons were surrounded by a flock of Democrat Party politicians who knew the career benefits of hitching their wagon to the most powerful family in Washington.

With Bill Clinton's conjoining, Hillary had at least 500 Super-Delegate pledges under her belt months before the elections had even begun, a 45-1 delegate lead over Sanders.

This insane Democrat inversion played out every time Sanders campaigned a state, like in Wyoming where Sanders won by double digits but walked out with only the same number of delegates. (Dem Caucus, 18 delegates, 7 awarded to Sanders).

It wasn't just Super-Delegates that invested in Hillary. Every arm of the "corporatocracy" has been hedging their bets on Hillary for almost twenty years. For example: Media conglomerates Cablevision, Time Warner Cable.

Five of Hillary's top ten political donors since 1999 were some of the most powerful banks: Citigroup; Goldman Sachs; Morgan Stanley; JPMorganChase; Lehman Brothers.

But those members pale in comparison to how much the Wall Street donors have donated into Hillary's SuperPac, to the tune of $15 million dollars.

Beyond banks, nearly every other industry bought into another Clinton presidency, like lobbyists for prison groups like GEO and Correctional Corporation of America (CCA), who bundled dollars to the Ready Hillary PAC. Hillary was also given more money from Big Pharma than any other candidate and received a third of the total contributions given out by pharmaceutical giants.

Also, the defense industry (read Military Industrial Complex) thought Hillary would be a good candidate too. Defense contractors and employees gave her more cash than any other candidate. Fossil fuel lobbyists gave a lot of money too. Her 2016 campaign received more than four-and-one-half million dollars from lobbyists, bundlers and donors connected to the world's biggest polluters. Their investment was set to profit ten-fold. Hillary was also at the forefront for fracking, considered a dangerous and destructive method of natural gas extraction. She was much more than a supporter of fracking. She personally created the Bureau of Energy Resources to spread fracking around the world. One of her major sponsors was Chevron.

Throughout their rise to power, the Clintons have sold their "friendship" through other avenues, such as for huge honorariums for speaking fees. Much like George H.W. Bush's motivational speaking tours, Bill and Hillary are quick to exploit themselves for corporate loot, but they don't come cheap. Averaging 211,000 a pop, Bill and Hillary made more than 153 million dollars in paid speeches to elite "think tanks" and closed-door boardrooms since 2001.

In 2013, after leaving the State Department, Hillary made three million dollars giving just 12 speeches to Wall Street banks and institutions. This calculates to earning $5000 per minute. Good honest work? Yeah, right. Demands to release the speech transcripts have been laughed off by Hillary, saying, "We don't really need to see the transcripts, we already know what is in them." Her praising banks and committing to their prosperity, although Hillary appeared during the 2016 campaign to be critical of Wall Street to pander to Sanders' supporters, her banker donors were not worried in the slightest. They knew talking points about equality were just politics.

One has to wonder how Hillary became such a political force that the nation's biggest powerhouses and Establishment elites just flocked to her with money and support?

Hillary was born in 1947 to a wealthy textile wholesaler who unsuccessfully ran for public office. She has two brothers, one a failed businessman, the other a failed politician. Both have their own history of public scandals. Lack of ethics and manipulating "the System" appears to have been a core 'value' in the family.

Hillary's first campaign involvement was campaigning for the 60's household name, Barry Goldwater (1964), often considered a far-Right Republican. Since then, Hillary has tried to distance herself from the Right by saying she was just a foolish schoolgirl. However, that doesn't appear to be the case at all. The timing tells a different story, i.e., she is a master schemer.

This was in 1964 when the Civil Rights Act was passed, after the Freedom Rides, after Martin Luther King's "I have a dream." civil rights speech after the historic march on Washington. Goldwater's campaign was a reaction to that. Later, Hillary became president of the Young Republicans club at her elite university. She claims, however, that she later transformed. But her conservative past is more tied to her rise in recognition and power than she would like her current democrat base to know.

The Clinton's claim to prominence had everything to do with what was going on in the country at that time. Democrats, long at the forefront of racism and segregation in the South, decided it was time for a change in policy as a reaction to Ronald Reagan winning the Presidency for two terms. A new party of younger Democrats formed a new party to win back the southern votes by making a more conservative shift, cancelling out hallmark economic policies and appealing to anti-Black attitudes, and distancing themselves from prominent Black democrats, targeting the growth in perceived welfare queens, and pushing so-called criminal reforms that targeted African Americans.

Subsequently, this manifested in prison farms like Mississippi's notorious Parchman prison increasing its black population and continuing its resemblance to a slave plantation, and Louisiana's infamous Angola prison, with its 80% Black population and immense farm, as well as similar prisons in other southern states.

Remember, as said here, Hillary got major support from the private prison industry which has grown wildly lucrative in the 1980's into major political powerhouses and who have lobbied in every state they are in to pass harsher laws reducing paroles, lengthening prison sentences, and new laws criminalizing behavior previously handled as misdemeanors, all designed to create a new slave-class called prisoners. Their contracts with the states are based on body count. The Black and Hispanic communities are their best "customers."

This new generation of Democrats, led by Al Gore and Bill Clinton, did not think the way the former Party did. They focused on calling an end to welfare as we knew it, calling it a "second chance, not a way of life." They sent a strong signal to criminals by supporting the death penalty. Bill Clinton swept the white Democrat vote by his position on welfare and crime, also claiming he had balanced twelve budgets. He pushed the Crime Bill of 1964 to success. Hillary talked about this more recently at the Keene State College, in Keene Massachusetts, trying to rationalize the stiff measures of the Crime Bill, pointing out that the young people committing crimes were not just kids anymore, but rather were the kinds of "kids" called "super-predators" with no conscience about their crimes or empathy for their victims. Yet, the provisions of the Crime Bill precisely targeted African-Americans. At the helm of the "Right" turn, Democrat politicians flocked to the Clintons, applauding a new area of Democrat politics.

Subsequently, neo-liberalism enacted NAFTA, allowing American corporations to set up production in third world countries where the labor was cheap and the working conditions virtually slave-like. NAFTA decimated the United States economy and the economy of other countries abroad, as industries closed on American soil to take to foreign countries.

Massive de-regulation of Wall Street, and the repeal of the Glass-Steagal Act[FN5.] was signed by President Clinton in 1999, called the Financial Services

[FN5.] The Glass-Steagall Act, part of the Banking Act of 1933, was landmark banking legislation that separated Wall Street from Main Street by offering protection to people who entrust their savings to commercial banks. Millions of Americans lost their jobs in the Great Depression, and one in four lost their life savings after more than 4,000 U.S. banks shut down between 1929 and 1933, leaving depositors

Modernization Act, commonly known as the Gramm-Leach-Bliley Act, which effectively neutralized Glass-Steagall by repealing key components of the Act. It seems noteworthy that Alan Greenspan, the former Federal Reserve Chairman, embraced the pushback against the Glass-Steagall Act by arguing that if banks were permitted to engage in investment strategies, they could increase the return for their banking customers while avoiding risk by diversifying their businesses.

Some economists point to the repeal of the Glass-Steagall Act as a key factor leading to the housing market bubble (sub-prime market) and the subsequent Great Recession, the financial crisis of 2007-2008. In 1999, Joseph E. Stiglitz, a Nobel laureate in economics and a professor at Columbia University, wrote that by bringing "*investment and commercial banks together, the investment bank culture came out on top. There was a demand for the kind of high returns that could be obtained only through high leverage and risk-taking.*"

What many of us already know, during the subprime era and since, loans taken for home purchases by one institution were almost immediately sold to another institution who then sold to yet another. I reckon this was like a monetized "shell game."

In any case, less than 10 years following the gutting of the Glass-Steagall Act, America suffered through the Great Recession, the largest meltdown since the 1929 stock market crash that had originally inspired the act. It bears repeating, Bill Clinton signed the act repealing the Glass-Steagall Act. How many of you lost property and money in the 2007-2008 crash? Blame Bill Clinton.

Having reviewed this Clinton act that caused millions of Americans to suffer grievous losses in 2007-2008, we find Hillary and the Wall Street and corporate community flocking to her as she ran for President in 2016. It only takes a review of what that family is all about to realize that their connections and influence is not based in what is good and right for Americans, but in simple corruption and greed.

---

with nearly $400 million in losses. The Glass-Steagall Act prohibited bankers from using depositors' money to pursue high-risk investments, but the act was effectively undercut by looser restrictions in the deregulatory environment of the 1980s and 1990s.

Returning to Bill Clinton's 1964 Crime Bill, what occurred was an explosion in mass incarceration, with large part being African-Americans and Hispanics. Prisons swelled all over the country to over-crowded conditions, prompting subsequent litigations in various courts against the inhumane conditions prisoners were forced to endure. Unfortunately, only cosmetic changes ever occurred in numerous litigations that spanned two decades thereafter.

When the Clintons left the Whitehouse in 1999, their rise to power was just beginning, despite Bill's numerous sexual harassment cases. With a plan to put Hillary in the Oval Office next, they moved their home to the state of New York where Hillary, with huge money backing, was elected as State Senator the following year.

While wealthy at the time, that is no comparison to what they made thereafter. On their 1999 tax returns they showed $417,567.00 income. By 2014, they were making 15 times that amount, showing $28,336,212.00 income.

While Hillary went to work crafting a Presidential resume in the Senate, Bill capitalized on his former super-elite status as former President. The Clinton's way of cashing in on that status was exploiting human misery and disaster. Note its marketing sign said: Clinton *Global* Initiative.

In 2001, in response to a major earthquake in India, the Clintons joined the heads of Goldman-Sachs and Citi Bank and embarked on a phony philanthropy model which would define their Clinton Foundation. These "*development and relief charities*" acted as insertion venue for Western businesses. For example, some of the Clinton Foundation's development projects in India, Africa, and Central America included for-profit farming corporations to exploit small farmers. The donations typically ended up back in the pockets of donors, the companies getting so-called "*development contracts*" to build up mobile networks in real estate. In the past 15 years prior to 2016, the Clinton Foundation has grown into a lucrative fraternity of the rich and powerful which boasted of having projects in 180 different countries. Including its numerous spin-off divisions, it reported total assets of over 351 million dollars in 2013. The sources of cash for this political machine say everything about the true nature of this so-called "charity."

Other than a 25-million-dollar partnership with Microsoft's Bill Gates, the Clinton Foundation is a motley crew of criminal organizations and police-state monarchies. Giving the Foundation ten million dollars was the brutal theocratic kingdom of Saudi Arabia. A matching ten million dollars was the Victor Pinchuk Foundation, a Ukrainian billionaire oligarch who pledged tens of millions more to the Clinton Global Initiative to modernize Ukraine while Hillary was Secretary of State. Donations in the one to five million dollar range were the Gulf State monarchy Oman, the United Emirates, Khatar, and Kuwait, Saudi billionaire Asheer al Rasheed, Exxon Mobile, Dow Chemical, Walmart, Coca-Cola, Phizer, Barclays Capital, Goldman-Sachs, and Boeing (the number two defense contractor in the country). In the less than a million-dollar range are Monsanto (pharmaceutical), Chevron, General Electric, and banks: Bank of America, Citigroup, Morgan-Stanley, UBS, Banc of California, then media giants Fox News, News Corporation, and even George Soros' Open Society Foundation (who is determined to destroy America).

For the Clintons and comrades, it is a win-win relationship, one that continued to grow. The Clintons get massive financial support to run their machine, and their contributors get the perks of a loyal advocate in a position of power. Hillary, destined to ascend off of this relationship, grew the expectation that she would have greater power to grant more favors, leading to more contributions and so on. While Hillary was in the Senate these favors for her donors were numerous indeed.

Manufacturing giant Corning gave the Clinton Foundation hundreds of thousands in speaking fees. In return Hillary introduced legislation to allot hundreds of millions in federal aid to purchase Corning products. Notorious enterprises like FreddieMac and FannieMae were all Clinton Foundation sponsors who won big by investing in Senator Clinton. She played a key role in blocking measures to regulate them, helping them to reap huge profits before facilitating the crash of the economy (2007-2008). The art of the deal was always good for business while Hillary was in the Senate, but the plan was always something bigger going on in the shadows. Having created a major financial and power base, in 2006 Hillary announced her intention to run for President shortly after she was elected to the Senate for her second term. She was supposed to be a shoe-in. She believed it was her time, as she said, taking the position that she was entitled to win as it was her turn.

But everything blew up in her face. Mass protests against the Iraq war marginalized her as a candidate. A little known, grossly experienced, young Senator by the name of Barack Obama, admittedly a fine orator, was flung to the front for his opposition to the Iraq War. Hillary ardently defended her support for the war throughout her campaign. Knocked off a presumed right to the Whitehouse, she failed at trying to capture the Democrat Party base. Her campaign was criticized for its slew of dirty tricks, including an array of voter tactics mainly aimed at the youth. Considered a pathetic move, the release of a photo of Obama in a turban pandered to Islamophobia and thinly veiled racism the Clintons employed in the 60's.

None of Clinton campaign schemes worked, but she refused to give in and rode it out to the end despite Obama being the clear winner. She only acquiesced and backed Obama after a closed-door negotiation where she was promised a promotion and a path to succeed him. As Secretary of State her rewards to her sponsors grew to a new level, and so too were the donations to the Clintons. Her corruption is exemplified and became obvious when 181 Clinton Foundation donors lobbied the State Department simultaneously. She used her position to allocate out re-payment favors in a variety of ways. She funneled money from the State Department to Clinton friends and sponsors, like securing millions in government grants, like for a friend and owner of the for-profit education firm Laureate Education, Inc., whose call sign is Laureate's International Higher Education Network.

She also used her new title to help negotiate business deals with donor friends and heads of state. For example, she brought billionaire and mining magnate Frank Giustra to meet the President of Columbia, scoring him access to lush forests and pristine coastlines to be mined and drilled by his company. She did the same in Kazakhstan and beyond. Hillary convinced other countries to give up permits and be pillaged. In one incident, she convinced the Haitian government to issue a mining permit. The contract went out to a mining company that not only shells out millions to the Clinton Foundation, but her brother sits on its Board of Directors.

She also flew around the world on the taxpayers' 'dime' to act as a saleswoman for American corporations. For her sponsor Boeing, she made a personal pitch to the Russian government to purchase their jets. The result was a 3.7-billion-dollar contract to Boeing. The Clintons got a $900,000 bonus from Boeing for her contribution.

But none of these deals compare to her role as an international arms dealer. Her State Department approved a whopping $160 billion dollars in commercial arms sales to almost 20 nations who are also Clinton Foundation sponsors, doubling the arms sales previously made to those countries by President Bush. The lucrative deals are undeniably rewards paying off the Clintons. The amount of the rewards directly corresponded to the amount of the donation.

Beyond the obvious step-up from her corporate shilling as Senator and Secretary of State, wreaking economic and environmental havoc to line the pockets of Clinton coffers, a President Hillary would have put us in danger of catastrophic war, another fact she's proven time and again over the entirety of her career.

Perhaps Clinton's war record is most exemplified by her endorsement from Henry Kissinger, seen by many as a war criminal and the butcher of Cambodia. On the campaign trail she bragged, *"I was very flattered when Henry Kissinger said I ran the State Department better than anybody had run it for a long time. So, I have an idea about what it's going to take to make our government work more efficiently."* The relationship between Kissinger and Clinton was very close. Not only did she consult with him regularly as Secretary of State, her and Bill frequently vacationed with the Kissingers.

Her other foreign policy advisers were quite similar, including neo-conservative Robert Kagan. Kagan was a senior fellow at the Brookings Institution and a contributing columnist for The Washington Post, as well as a writer of books, and who has vilified Trump repeatedly. She shares public advisors like Ted Cruz. Her support for the war in Iraq came back to haunt her in her presidential bid.

In 2008 Senator Clinton made the chilling admission that, if President, she would not rule out using nuclear weapons on Afghanistan and Pakistan. After her promotion as Secretary of State, she boldly planted a flag in the Obama administration to establish the Hillary Doctrine. Accordingly, two dozen current and former administration officials, foreign diplomats, friends and outside analysts described Mrs. Clinton as almost always the advocate of the most aggressive actions considered by Obama's national security team.

Of course, she joined the Obama team in creating and leading the terrible affronts to human life and rights in what some have described as a murderous campaign in Yemen, Pakistan, and Somalia. The program's mass civilian casualties she took with a grain of salt.

However, on other issues she took the lead, showing how she would steer America's ship as she aimed for the Presidency. In her book, the Honduras Coup, she bragged about her leading role in the 2009 coup in the ouster of its democratically-elected president, further plunging the country into violence and instability.

Also that year, when it was long clear that the Afghan war was unwinnable, she lobbied for sending more troops, and when the time had come to bring home those troops, then Secretary of Defense Robert Gates said that Hillary argued forcefully against withdrawing the troops. She continued lobbying for more troops to be sent on a permanent basis. She did the same thing in Iraq, arguing that troops should be stationed there permanently and advocating for more troops to be sent there. Once again, it must be said her ties to the war machine and as a weapons dealer created a predisposition to the machine rather than to the purpose for being there in the first place.

And then there was Hillary's War, in Libya, an oil-soaked nation where she sought to showcase her military doctrine. She is known for leading the plan to attack the Libyan state to overthrow President Gaddafi. In an interview, she laughed about the torture and lynching of Gaddafi on television, laughingly saying, *"We came, we saw, he died."* Libya was tossed into an era of imaginable pain and suffering, a decimated infrastructure, and US-armed rebel fighters, turned Libya into a new nation crisis.

The scandal of Benghazi is not that Hillary allowed Americans to die, but that the Americans were there funneling weapons to extremists in a country she had just helped to destroy. What did Hillary take away from that Benghazi incident? That there should have been more American troops. Hillary said, in defense of the invasion, *"We have learned the hard way, when America is absent, especially from unstable places, there are consequences."*

But, was it because America was absent, or because the DOD had just carpet-bombed the country and ejected the sitting President and its entire government? The propaganda told the American people was that Gadhafi was abusing, torturing and killing his own people, yet videos of the country did not show that at all. What Gaddafi was doing that caused the US to invade was his plan to close down the petro-dollar and replace it with a gold standard, where all countries wanting oil from Libya would have to pay in gold. Why America reared for war was because America has no gold, no gold at all, and what gold there may have been has long went to the top bankers to pay our growing debts. Yes, had Gadhafi been able to achieve his gold standard, it would have had major financial repercussions under the US economy.

On Syria, Hillary led the push for war there too. She pushed hard, despite rejection by Obama, to establish a No Fly Zone over Syria, which would mean war. It was believed that it would undoubtedly create a conflict that could involve nuclear powers, like Russia, for the US to start a war conflict with Syria. Attacking Syria meant bombing all Syrian anti-aircraft and other defense systems, and the actual result, we have seen, is that Syria's cities have been decimated since then. We have accused Syria of collaborating with Islamic terrorists, and when that was determined not the case, we stayed to fight ISIS. What was the real reason though? Could it have been that Russian President Vladimir Putin was trying to achieve an oil pipeline from Syria to help build the health of his own country? Have we actually seen Putin invading countries other than wanting to re-unite Armenia with Russia? No, we haven't. In fact, we did see an early offer by Putin to President Trump about achieving an alliance.

The greatest risk of having Hillary elected President of the United States is her record of war-mongering, of starting new and lasting wars. Already, she has a record, as Senator, of wanting war with Iran. When asked who her greatest enemy was, she proudly stated it would be Iran. She stated that if Iran gained nuclear weapons and decided to strike with them at Israel, that we would then use our nuclear weapons and *"completely obliterate them."* Her words. But it's not just Iran. In every part of the world from Latin America to Asia, Hillary Clinton has made clear she would choose the path of death and destruction every time, no matter the consequences.

But there was another job for Hillary she helped establish as Secretary of State. She was a Saul Kaminsky student in college, and she found favor towards socialism. Her history shows she would be inclined to help in the new Left Progressive agenda for bringing down America as a capitalist democracy and establishing a socialist state with her at the helm. With her disposition, and her apparent psychopathic nature, how long would it be before she became a despotic dictator? We have already seen what she is capable of.

Obama was a fine orator who understood Orwellian "double-speak", the art of lying to your face by telling you he is going to do one thing but actually plans something the opposite of that. He got elected on his "Fundamental Change" platform, presenting it on a socialist-style platform of free medical care, free education, all promised as a Utopian system under his administration. The public loved it. He never used the word socialism or communism in that context, but that was precisely what he meant. He was driven by his anti-colonialism hatred, a system he alleges his father was caught up in, and he hated America precisely because he viewed it as having a colonialist beginning that included slavery of Blacks. His mentor was George Soros who took him under his wing and helped him, fresh out of college, never having held a job in America's marketplace at all, to win a Senator seat in Congress.

Obama's plan was to destroy America as a colonialist, capitalist country that deprived everyone of color of the promised American Dream. Soros funded him. "Fundamental change" was his logo, and his many supporters believed that meant almost messianic utopian results. They were misled, and Obama had far different results in mind. In his two terms, he did not accomplish as much as he wanted, but with Hillary destined for the Presidency after him, the next steps in their agenda was her responsibility as President.

Hillary was to play a role in that NWO goal. She had no trouble selling out America for profit, and she demonstrated that repeatedly. Her lack of ethics and patriotism was missing, even as she masked that vacuum with wit and oratory skills, like Obama. At the 2016 elections, she was a shoe-in, and Donald Trump was viewed as a joke and that Trump could never win. So, he was ignored, and no one on the Left ever expected Donald Trump could win. His winning was simply not possible.

This over-confidence of the Left and the globalists made his election a total shock and they were left was frozen in disbelief. Immediately, the Illuminati-owned media went into high gear, as we saw and still see, trying to overthrow the elections, then to impeach him, then to charge him with tax or other crimes, and when all that didn't have any credibility, to mount an overwhelming campaign to skew the upcoming 2020 elections. So why were the elites so crazy with shock? What was their plan?

What was Hillary supposed to? Hillary was supposed to create the racial division that Obama began, to instigate violent confrontations between both Party members and racists, and to fire that violence such that a civil war could begin, at which time Hillary could invoke Martial Law.

Obama set it up with the United Nations. If martial law is declared, the U.N. would send armies of troops to quell the civil war, to disarm all American citizens and kill anyone who resisted. He signed an Executive Order that in times of Emergency, the UN would take over, and Interpol (the UN's international police) would take control of all federal, state, and local police departments. We all saw all the UN vehicles on the streets and on rail cars going everywhere, miles of vehicles. We all saw military armament like tanks and troop carriers and such crisscrossing America. We saw urban warfare training in Los Angeles, going so far as to section off entire neighborhoods in an undeclared martial law scenario and invading unsuspecting citizen homes as armed soldiers entered their homes without probable cause about anything.

Was Hillary active in that? She was Secretary of State. She had to be. She had to approve every scenario. She had to approve the Norwegian UN military commander who brought Muslim troops to one of our communities to engage in door-to-door training for the confiscation of American weapons. When asked what he was doing, he said training for weapons confiscations. When asked what if a resident refused, he said he was under orders to shoot to kill. There was a video made of this incident that was later taken down from You-Tube. (I saw it before it was taken down. I would have copied it had I had the software to do so at the time.)

I'll reiterate: Hillary's job was to finish what Obama started, if she were elected President. Her job was to instigate more racial division, incite racial violence, incite civil war, all behind the scenes of course, and then to declare martial law so the UN could disarm Americans, send all dissenters into the new concentration camps set up by FEMA and Walmart (closing doors to create internment processing centers), and take America down to a socialist governance while the globalists, including the UN and EU, continued the agenda of establishing their one-government world. In the meantime, it is highly probable that millions of Americans would die in these concentration camps; hence, the millions of plastic, multi-body coffins that were discovered and made public.

And finally, it does concern me some that if I expose her here, I might wind up deemed a "suicide." I assure you now that it will NOT be a "suicide." Fact is, my information is simply the result of good research of information already in the public media.

C. FEMA Camps As American Concentration Camps

It is true that on the Left anything of major concern to the welfare of America, even backed by clear facts, is readily dismissed as "conspiracy theory" because it serves the radical Left's agenda. Repeatedly, the term "conspiracy theory" dismissal has been used to delegitimize facts about "chemtrails" (the spraying of poisonous material not just across America but also around the world disguised as nothing more than harmless vapor trails), or about the billions of rounds of hollow-point ammunition by FEMA itself, or the sudden building of hundreds of FEMA camps around the nation with prison-like barbed wire and fences surrounding them and designed to keep people in rather than keeping people out, or about the closure of many Walmart stores that have been converted into processing centers and militarized, or about the millions of plastic coffins stored around the country (oh, they say, that is just in case of national emergency like earthquakes and such), or about the use of vaccines supposedly to cure that were found to cause deaths instead, or the use of RFID chips implanted for "medical reasons" but in reality are to be to totally control the individual (quite similar to what China is now doing). And so on. We have been lied to many times.

Let's take a look at FEMA as a hijacked arm of the New World Order agenda.

First of all, as I have mentioned about Hillary Clinton, had she been elected President, her job was to complete America's devastation. The role that FEMA would play in all this, inasmuch as there are over 600 FEMA camps across the nation, would be internment of Americans rounded up after the civil war created by higher forces of the NWO.

Here is what I have learned about FEMA.

FEMA was created to have government involvement in major emergencies, like earthquakes, floods, fires, and even wartime events. Their facilities are large multi-person rooms with military-type cot, common area eating, communal bathrooms and showers. These are general things one would expect in an emergency shelter. But, the fences that surround the FEMA camps have prison-type fences with barbed wire and razor wire to keep people inside from leaving. And, like prisons, have gun towers. That should raise high concerns. Why do they need such prison wire and gun towers to prevent Americans from leaving, unless they serve the insidious purpose of internment for American citizens during the conversion of America's ideology to socialism? Or worse. And I say, "Or worse" because I have seen videos of the millions of multi-body plastic coffins, and I have also seen the videos taken by a couple of teenagers who entered an Off Limits area and took pictures of hundreds or more concrete coffins, already half-buried in the ground. They were all big enough to contain perhaps six (6) bodies.

In 2016, Stan Jones, U.S. Senate Candidate, Libertarian-Montana, came out and publicly stated the following:

"What I am about to say is fact. It is no longer a theory. A secret organization of the power elite are no longer secret. They are planning and are now leading us into a one world communist government."

Also, in 2016, RT News reported the following:

"An Executive Order by President Obama has sparked controversy on both sides of the political aisle. The National Defense Resource Preparedness executive order was signed quietly Friday night and gives the President the power to control US resources ...."

Fox News's Bret Baier, host of "Special Report" also weighed in:

The Senate Rules Committee is going to meet in the House and they are going to come up with a rule that makes it OK for them to do a "same day bill" so they'll pass this rule ... believe it or not it's called "Martial Law" ...."

Fox News Sean Hannity said:

"... This will give the President of the United States to declare, basically, martial law during times of peace."

In a subsequent broadcast, Hannity said:

"... There are new disturbing elements out of Washington tonight regarding the President's [Obama] belief that he has the legal authority to assassinate U.S. citizens; incredibly enough, it appears that the Commander in Chief actually believes that the authority exists not only on foreign but on American soil as well. ..."

In an interview on Fox News of Judge Andrew Napolitano, host of "Freedom Watch", Judge Napolitano said:

"...Senators McCain and Levin are at the head of this legislation which would authorize the President to declare the entire United States of America, all fifty states and all territories, to be a "battlefield" ... There is no battle going on here ... That would authorize him to use Commander in Chief authority in the United States to use the military to arrest people in the United States who are, in the President's opinion, enemies of the country...."

MSNBC's news host (name not given on the downloaded broadcast), said:

"To hear President Obama to claim the authority to keep people in prison indefinitely, with no charges against them, with no conviction, no sentence, just imprisonment ...."

Tucker Carlson, Fox News, introduced former Secret Service Agent Dan Bongino, and asked him a question about a statement he had made, i.e., *There is no such thing as gun control, there is only people control* ....? Bongino said:

"Tucker, this is part of an ideological ploy by this administration. They are not being authentic with America, whether it's with sequester, or health care, or the gun control issue. What they do is the manipulate an emotional crisis, a national emotional crisis, to further an ideological agenda, which involves the evaporation, a slow disintegration of your civil rights, your liberties, your ability to live and let live, and it's a disturbing pattern which, frankly, is really starting to get under my skin. ..."

RT News reported the following:

"The US is funneling money into tracking systems that are making the very concept of privacy a thing of the past. It could mean people's every move could be used against them to keep them under surveillance. ..."

As to FEMA, RT News in Washington asked:

> "David, why does the DHS [Department of Homeland Security] need 450 million hollow-point bullets?" ... and was answered .... *"That kind of ammo that they purchased is from ATK, hollow-point ammunition, as you explained, is designed to tear through human flesh and then expand. It is designed to kill people. ..."* He was also asked, "Do you think this is a sign of civil unrest?" ... to which David responded, *"They at DHS have an open bid for even more ammunition, for 175 million rounds of .223 caliber rifle ammo almost identical to the ammunition used by the NATO "peace-keeping" forces. So that's very interesting, are they planning for some kind of widespread economic unrest in the US, that would require NATO forces to help us out"* ....?

Max Blumenthal, Writing Fellow, the Nation Institute, interviewed on RT News, said:

> "... Half a billion dollars in surplus military weaponry from the Pentagon, which was authorized through the Pentagon's 1033 program [giving these weapons to local police departments].... During the late 70's, Congress passed legislation called *"posse comitatus"* barring the military from operating on American soil; in the early 80's there was an effort to circumvent that in Congress by arming police with military-grade weaponry, and now we're seeing that play out in the streets. People in the inner cities are experiencing this, so civilians in the West are now up against this. They are basically military-style policing. ..."

Then, on Christianity, we find that Christianity is becoming a target by government labeling conservative Christian extremists:

> "The battle against tyrannism involves all of us. Everybody in this country is a potential terrorist. ..."

Fox News reported:

> "The Department of Homeland Security sent to law enforcement agencies across the country warning about the potential for an increase in "right-wing extremist activity." It warns about groups and individuals dedicated to single issues like abortion, immigration, and gun rights. ...

Kimberly Guilfoyle, Fox News "The Five", reported:

> "Tonight, our focus is on our right to freedom of expression and freedom of religion. It is Christians who are under siege by government officials and anti-religion groups who believe that Christmas and Christianity have no business in the public arena. ..."

Her guest said: "The Department of Defense just issued a new list of "extremists" who should be watched, and on that, in fact, Number One, past the Muslim Brotherhood, past Hamas and the Hezbollah, Number One is Evangelical Christians...."

On InfoWars, it was reported:

> We begin tonight with a newly leaked U.S. Army military police training manual for what they're calling "Civil Disturbance Operations." The Army manual outlines the plan to kill rioters and demonstrators in America. That's right, they have plans to confiscate our firearms and kill U.S. citizens on U.S. soil. This during a mass civil unrest. I guess shooting innocent civilians, perhaps. And it goes on to describe how prisoners will be processed through internment camps. Wow! So, there you have it, our own military being trained for armed conflict with U.S. citizens, they're being trained to confiscate our guns, and preparations to process us into camps during civil unrest. ..."

In making the deal with the U.N. to invade the US in the event martial law was declared, Obama not only authorized the use of the UN's military force, but also authorized Interpol (the U.N.'s international police) to take control of ALL of America's federal, state, and local police forces and use them for the purposes of so-called "peace-keeping" and disarming Americans.

I also saw from a couple of sources, which included photos, that some 30,000 guillotines had been contracted for and delivered, with 15,000 in one place and 15,000 in another. I'm hesitant to list this, but in one of Obama's Presidential Orders about martial law, there was a reference to approved forms of executions; right at the top of that list was the execution method of "beheading." Beheading, like the Muslims do? Get it? (I had a copy of that document on my computer, but after the crash and repair, it appears many of my documents, including that one, did not get saved by the repair squad.)

So, our own government approved the distribution of military surplus weaponry to all federal, state, and local police departments, but FEMA gets some 8-billion rounds of hollow-point ammunition, and then contracts for 175-million rounds of .223 ammunition which is high-powered rifle ammunition. To top that off, the government purchases millions of plastic coffins that hold multiple bodies, and have concrete coffins in unknown numbers already set into the ground, most likely around the United States. And, Obama gave the U.N. the authority to "shoot to kill" any citizen that resisted gun confiscation.

During that time, all across America in the Obama era, we saw military training exercises, including a major urban warfare, gun confiscation exercises in Los Angeles and in the state of Washington, where citizens homes were invaded by the military without any notice at all, and citizens were told it was an exercise. What must those citizens have felt when masked, helmeted, armed military officers barged into their homes with guns drawn and focused on the family members, while multiple Blackhawk helicopters flew overhead and in downtown Los Angeles, just like in downtown Miami? But these exercises were not just military; they were a joint exercise with local police agencies. The same occurred in downtown Houston, where actual gunshots were heard from these military and police units. Most people there thought that they were firing real live rounds.

In Louisiana, at the time of Hurricane Katrina, which I talk about elsewhere herein, law enforcement entered homes of citizens who had remained during Katrina, with firearms drawn and trained on every household, and requiring all citizens with firearms to turn them over to the police. (www.youtube.com/watch?v=taU9d26wT4, by the National Rifle Association (NRA), published March 7, 2007.)

These exercises were called "anti-terrorism" exercises, but conducted around and in the homes of citizens.

All over America, we saw miles of military vehicles, tanks, troop carriers, and tanks, both U.S. military and U.N. vehicles, on railways, hundreds, perhaps thousands of them.

Consider this: Obama placed his own people in the DHS, FBI, CIA, retired Generals who, when asked if they would fire on U.S. citizens said "No," he then promoted Generals who said they would. Obama had Muslim Brotherhood in government positions, while Hillary Clinton's closest advisor (Huma Abedin) was a Muslim woman whose family members were tied to terrorist Islamic organizations.

We have seen none of this going on since the election of Donald Trump. If these were just "routine" exercises, don't you think they would have continued? Perhaps to this day? But they haven't. If that is not proof enough for you to realize what nearly happened to all of us in this country, I don't know what else it would take.

I have said, in this book, that Hillary's job, had she been elected President, was to carry out the "Destroy America" agenda Obama began. Now can you see the connections? Had Hillary gotten elected, today we would already be in internment camps, and many thousands of us would already have been murdered.

The FEMA camps were greatly expanded under Obama, while he also sent most of our military out of the country, and made his deal with NATO and the UN. He sent most of the military out of the country so that they would not be on American soil if there was civil unrest or the beginnings of civil war amongst ourselves, so that when martial law was declared, the U.N. would intervene, not our own military.

Guess what? Obama is still active in helping to build the Leftist movement towards socialism. He is not going away in his Soros-backed plot to destroy America.

The question for the 2020 election is this: What happens to the Left's agenda if President Trump is re-elected? Answer: They will have to re-group once again during the next four years. They will get more exposed, and more subject to getting shut down.

The second question for the 2020 election is this: What happens to Americans if the so-called "Progressive" Socialists win the elections and take over Congress as well? Answer: We may see a civil war begun by the patriots or even the Left. And/or we'll see what socialism is all about on our way to a totalitarian one-government world. We'll come to understand and endure the rigors of oppression and misery. We'll become broken by the genocide of so many people murdered to serve the depopulation agenda of the New World Order. We'll never know freedom again, or democracy, or even religion. We'll likely see the inner workings of the FEMA camps enclosed by prison barbed-wire to keep people in, and we'll come to know why FEMA bought so many millions of plastic coffins, and why FEMA bought millions of hollow-point firearm ammunition, and why the government bought 175 rounds of .223 bullets. We'll be at the single point of praying for deliverance from this evil empire by God's return as prophesied in the Book of Revelation to save his children. We will be on the road to perdition.

Someday, when Revelation is fulfilled, God (or St. Peter) will be asking us all if, at the end, we fought the good fight as Christian soldiers to protect His Word, or did we let Him down? Remember, if we lose this war raging even now, Jesus and God will fade away over time, book-burning, 're-education propaganda', and oppression until it becomes a mere myth, and then it will fade into oblivion never to be heard again. Or until Revelation begins and is fulfilled.

What will be YOUR 'report card' before St. Peter? Personally, if I had children or grandchildren, I'd prefer the world got fixed so that they would have a happy future and dreams to fulfill. I think responsible parents owe their children that much. But it is our generation that has to do the fixing. 80% of their generation already is fooled into believing that socialism is a good thing. If we don't fix it for them, before they take over as adults, their mistake in helping to usher in socialism will result in ruination of all that is and all that will be. There is no return from Perdition.

D. The Depopulation Plan Is Real.

The globalists have talked about how overcrowded the world has become, saying the planet's resources cannot sustain an ever-expanding population. It is estimated that in 40-50 years, with population growth being exponentially rapid, that the world population could become well over the current 7.7 billion people, and the planet simply could not provide the resources such a population would require. Wikipedia shows projections of about 10 billion by 2050, and more than 11 billion by 2100. North America (United States and Canada) has a population of around 363 million.

China experienced very rapid birth rates, rising from 430 million in 1850 to 580 million in 1953, and now stands at over 1.3 billion. The population of the Indian subcontinent, which was about 125 million in 1750, increased to389 million in 1941; today, India, Pakistan and Bangladesh are collectively home to about 1.63 billion people. Java had about 5 million inhabitants in 1815; its present-day successor, Indonesia, now has a population of over 140 million. Mexico's population grew from 13.6 million in 1900 to about 112 million in 2010. Between the 1920s and 2000s, Kenya's population grew from 2.9 million to 37 million.

Statistical tables show most rapid population growths have been in Third World countries where birth control simply does not exist and several children to a household is not uncommon. It should be noted that in such countries, having numerous children is cultural, oftentimes religious, or both, and children are expected to take care of their parents in their elder years, unlike America where the elders are often shuttled off to "senior citizen" communities or care agencies. I also note that in the USA it appears that the concept of "elders" being respected for the wisdom of their experiences hardly exists while the younger generation of teenagers and young adults seem to think they already know everything about everything.

The globalists, including the Bilderberg group, appears to have acknowledged that no growth in population is better than unchecked growth. Bill Gates of Microsoft has already engaged in the discussion of reducing the population of the planet; he thinks that it should be no higher than One Billion people. He has talked openly in speeches, one of which I downloaded, where he talks about using vaccines for population control. There are numerous videos featuring Bill Gates talking about vaccines and birth control, but he also says there is a need to REDUCE the current population; this is coming from one of the richest men on Earth, a man who was invited to the Bilderberg Group who is also 'concerned' about reducing the populations.

In a September 2019 edition of NewsTarget.com, article by Mike Adams, I learned that Bill Gate has an organization called *Project SCoPEx* which is his plan to carry out planetary genocide under the guise of halting "climate change." SCoPEx is an acronym for "Stratospheric Controlled Perturbation Experiment, and it's designed to eliminate most living humans by collapsing the biosphere. Adams writes:

> The dangerous SCoPEx plan, which is masterminded by mad scientists at Harvard, falls right in line with the genocidal dreams of communist Democrat presidential candidate Bernie Sanders, who recently announced his endorsement for expanding mass abortions across Third World nations in order to achieve accelerated depopulation of brown and black people.
>
> Both SCoPEx and Bernie Sander's eugenics population control scheme are being packaged under the label of halting "climate change," a false, manufactured crisis invented by globalists to spread mass hysteria and convince the people of the world to surrender all remaining liberties.

James C. Lewis

"This is not the crackpot plan of a garden-shed inventor," wrote the *UK Daily Mail*. "The project is being funding by billionaire and Microsoft founder Bill Gates and pioneered by scientists at Harvard University."

Recreating Massive Volcanic Eruptions That Caused a Global Collapse Of Food Crops.

The SCoPEx project seeks to duplicate the effects of an apocalyptic volcano disaster such as the 1815 eruption of Mount Tambora, which ejected so much particulate matter into the atmosphere that it produced what was called, "the year without a summer." Food crops failed across the planet, leading to mass starvation and disease. This is what Bill Gates and today's mad scientists are working to replicate through artificial means. And, Yes, it's all about unleashing mass starvation, genocide and depopulation on a global scale.

The mechanism by which this is achieved is rather straight-forward. By ejecting millions of tons of particulate matter (i.e., pollution) into the stratosphere, a measurable amount of sunlight is blocked and prevented from reaching the surface of the Earth, where plants grow. All plants need sunlight and carbon dioxide for photosynthesis, so reducing sunlight – even a little – would devastate plant-based food webs, food crops, and ecosystems across the planet. Because marine ecosystems also depend on the photosynthesis that takes place in phytoplankton, this pillar of marine food webs, much of ocean life as we know it today, would also collapse, leading to a cascading ecological nightmare that would destroy global food supplies and lead to the mass starvation of humans, land animals and sea creatures. (Of course, it would not affect the globalists who all have access to the huge food bank reserves already stockpiled in the Arctic circle.)

368

We aren't the only ones concerned about the implications of planetary-scale geoengineering and deliberate mass pollution of the skies. Even the *UK Daily Mail* admits the project generates *"fears that it could trigger a disastrous series of chain reactions, creating climate havoc in the form of serious droughts and hurricanes, and bring death to millions of people around the world."* The *UK Daily Mail* writes:

> *One fear is that spreading dust into the stratosphere may damage the ozone layer that protects us from hazardous ultraviolet radiation which can damage human DNA and cause cancers. Climatologists are also concerned that such tinkering could unintentionally disrupt the circulation of ocean currents that regulate our weather. This itself could unleash a global outbreak of extreme climatic events that might devastate farmland, wipe out entire species and foster disease epidemics… This dream 'fix' seems to have plenty of potential to become a global nightmare.*

Note that this is all being deliberately rolled out in the name of "climate change," which has become the cry of genocidal maniacs like Bill Gates, Elizabeth Warren and Bernie Sanders, people who now openly talk about global-scale eugenics and depopulation as *"the only way to save the planet."* Warren even claims that humanity only has 11 years remaining on planet Earth before a climate apocalypse destroys everything. So, they use this fabricated fear to justify mass murder, essentially telling the world that billions of humans are going to have to die in order to prevent the planet from collapsing. Yet **the real collapse is being engineered by these same people** who actively seek to carry out planet-scale genocide. I no longer doubt that the Deep State people are also supporting these depopulation agendas.

If successful, they will kill 1000 times more people than the Holocaust. We're talking about roughly six billion humans being annihilated by globalists, all in the name of "saving the planet." It's difficult to out-Hitler Hitler, but Bill Gates may yet go down in history as the man who spearheaded a global pollution program that murdered six *billion* humans. (All in the name of caring about the environment, of course.)

No longer a theory; these programs are funded and being rolled out right now.

It's no longer a conspiracy theory that the world's political and science leaders want to mass murder humanity: It's now admitted and right out in the open. The experiments are already funded and under way at this very moment. All voices of reason who are sounding the alarm on this issue are censored, silenced, de-platformed and ridiculed. Yet the experiments are under way right now to systematically pollute the atmosphere. Now, thanks to the lunacy of the climate change cult, **the goal is to pollute the planet and block the sun**, then collapse global food webs and starve out billions of people.

Climate change has been a topic of controversy for years now. Recently, a renowned Swedish scientist, said that climate change might lead to cannibalism as the planet grew hotter on its own. The scientist Magnus Soederlin of the Stockholm School of Economics made the comment during his talk at the Gastro Summit on climate change. Indeed, during the starvation caused by Joseph Stalin to his own people, there were reports of cannibalism as people starved to death.

But, over eons of time, there have always been cycles of climate changes, but they are cycles. Bill Gates and friends want to instigate a major climate change which will indeed starve out millions of people around the globe, including Americans, and, as in Russia, and other places throughout history, cannibalism may well occur. But this time, by Gates own hand, it is his global plan that will usher in this genocide and cannibalism.

As said, Bill Gates believes that the problem with global warming and climate change is tied directly to too many humans breathing out carbon dioxide, thus the need to depopulate the planet. He claims that 26 billion tons of CO_2 emissions by humans occur each year. (I wonder, by that number, perhaps Bill might want to eliminate all animals who also breathe out CO_2, or like Alexandra Osario-Cortez's pet peeve, cow farts.)

In recent years, further research on global climate change has led more scientists to doubt that global warming is upon us or that it would bring disaster. Yet these doubts are characteristically downplayed by the U.N. Intergovernmental Panel on Climate Change (IPCC). While the announced goal of the Global Climate Treaty is to avoid "dangerous interference with the climate system", this goal is entirely arbitrary because there is no irrefutable scientific evidence for determining what constitutes "dangerous interference." Nor is there compelling evidence that human activity has had much effect on world climate. It appears much of this "climate change" dogma has been the result of certain cities having major "smog" problems at certain heights of the year, and since then certain factions have run wild with the idea of "climate change" being a certainty beyond a reasonable doubt such that only a globalist government like the United Nations should have the ultimate power to restructure the entire world.

A closing thought about "climate change." I hadn't planned on addressing that matter, but recent escalation of that issue as being like a "truck barreling towards us" seems more to demonstrate the extent to which the globalists are prepared to go to win. While there are scientists who claim the evidence shows a warming "climate change" due to CO_2 emissions by humans (and cows, if you listen to Alexandra Osario-Cortez), there is a much larger body of scientists who say different. More recently, astrophysicist S. Fred Singer probed the literature on climate change and laid out the likelihood of an imminent, catastrophic global warming. He says that even if were to occur, the evidence suggests that it would be largely benign and may even improve human well-being.

The Left and its "scientists" rail that the Earth's population, animal and plant life, everything could come to an end in 15 years; our own children are being told this in school. They are creating a false narrative as a panic scenario to scare impressionable and gullible people into believing that the world will come to an end unless they vote the story-tellers into office so they can "fix" the problems.

While there is agreement that there has been some warming overall, changes in the world climate has been going on since time began. But even if climate change as the result of too much CO_2 emissions in the air, scientific literature also supports the view that such increases might actually improve human well-being. Some benefits include a CO_2-enriched biosphere being more conducive to plant growth, longer frost-free growing seasons, greater water efficiency for plants, and more available farmland at higher latitudes. Scientists suggest that a reduction in severe storms might likely be another benefit if global warming were to occur, since a global warming would probably mostly warm the latitudes farther north and south, the temperature gradient between the equator and the poles would fall, thereby reducing the severity of stores. Rising sea levels, another alleged consequence of a global warming, may also be a phantom problem, some scientists agree. It seems likely that a global warming would lower, rather than raise sea levels, because more evaporation from the oceans would increase precipitation and thereby thicken the ice caps of Greenland and Antarctica. This possibility, according to the scientists, is supported by an observed correlation between the rate of rise of the sea level and tropical sea surface temperature.

The actual problem, as I have suggested, is the correlation between the goals of the New World Order and its politics, with the pro-socialist Dems and media who are doing their best to convince Americans that "the sky is falling" and only a socialist policy and ideology can protect everyone. Politicizing alleged climate change for political advantage must be recognized for the Orwellian manipulation that it presents: say it over and over enough times until the gullible – of which there are now many – accept the lie as the truth.

And now, what do we have? We have a "new" virus spreading, called the "coronavirus" supposedly caught by Chinese who eat bats. Bats have been a delicacy in China and other Asian countries forever, so why a "new" virus that is spreading? Perhaps it was not caused by eating bats at all. Perhaps it is man-made, which is what I think. A few years ago I learned that the ebola virus had been created in a lab in Florida and let go in Africa, and that the HIV virus of years before, supposedly originated in Africa from monkeys, was also created in a lab and taken to Africa. Globalists have been wanting world dominion for a long time, and they do not like the amount of humans populating and destroying the planet, particularly in the Third World nations. It has come to my attention that the Coronavirus has some unusual properties normally not seen in viruses, almost like they were created and/or joined in some way. If we consider that we can no longer trust Big Pharma, transnational corporations, and many others, then we might ask ourselves if those in control with the greatest power and money are engaged in projects against the human populations. What if there are people who look at this planet, its filth and destruction caused by humans ruining the beautiful landscapes across the globe with trash, who had the power to decide they had enough money to fix the problems caused by over-populations and careless humankind?

Bill's Obsession With Vaccines

Bill Gates of Microsoft is perhaps the richest man in the world, outside of the Rotchschilds. In his old age he has developed an obsession with vaccines. One might think this is great and shows he cares about the world at large. But does he? Bill also believes that vaccines can be used to reduce childhood mortality and ultimately reduce population growth through associated social changes, not as an agent of death (so he says). Yet, Bill Gates has admitted the vaccines are for human depopulation. According to him, to stabilize the world population, 350,000 people must be eliminated per day. Interestingly enough, he refused to vaccinate his own children when they were growing up, even while he promoted toxic jabs all over the world, especially in third world countries. (Source: www.healthfreedoms.org) I downloaded and have the video of him before a large audience talking about vaccines, and how they can be used to help reduce world population.

Also, Bill likes microchip implants. In the "thesleuthjournal.com" it was noted that Gates was due to launch his new population control chip in 2018, which is a microchip he developed along with researchers at MIT, that will allow for adjustments to be made to a person's hormone level via remote control, as a means for reducing the planet's population. This is a chip that is medically inserted by your caregiver under the auspices that it carries all of your personal medical information plus it monitors your bodily systems 24/7; therefore, one would no longer need a plastic medical ID card or other physical forms of identification. This hasn't yet occurred, and perhaps it is being resisted, but the technology exists to engage this Orwellian plan. By the way, China has plans to microchip its population now, and it already has cameras everywhere capable of "face recognition."

In his presentation on vaccines Gates stated to the audience of supporters that, "If we do a really great job on new vaccines, health care, reproductive health services (abortion), we could lower that (world population) by perhaps 10 or 14 percent." I found it amusing that it said only "10 or 14 percent" when his actual intention is far greater than that, considering he publicly stated the planet should only have one-billion people, not the 6.5 – 7-billion it now has.

According to India's NTAGI (National Technical Advisory Group on Immunisation), its announcement that it was cutting all ties with the B&M Gates Foundation was followed by an explanation after it was shown that Gates's so-called vaccine "campaigns" conducted on tens of thousands of young girls throughout India back in 2009-2010, (that were meant to help protect them from cervical cancer), were actually cloaked vaccine trials involving two highly controversial vaccines known to injure and kill.

The vaccines in question were Cervarix by GlaxoSmithKline (GSK) and Gardasil by Merck & Co., both of which were marketed as protecting against the human papillomavirus (HPV), which is claimed to have a risk of cervical cancer. Both vaccines come with extreme side effects, and evidence shows that GSK and Merck essentially teamed up with the Gates Foundation to take advantage of young Indian girls and use them as human guinea pigs in trials of the two vaccines.

At the time of the first report, at least ten females died and dozens more were reported in critical condition after this "state-run" sterilization program designed to control the country's billion-plus population went badly wrong. (www.youtube.com/watch?v=C5VBkN_dCiE, at "At least 10 Indian women died after mass sterilization", AFP News Agency, published Nov. 11, 2014.)

There were also vaccines experimented with on little children, with the results that many actually died and many more became autistic. This also was in India.

Subsequent reports, according to independent journalists, these trials resulted in thousands of injuries and hundreds of deaths that were eventually traced back to the two vaccines. Once news of this got back to Indian authorities, an investigation was launched that landed the Gates Foundation in court for serious ethical violations.

In Africa some four years ago (2015), Kenyan Bishops discovered mass sterilization from Bill's 'anti-tetanus' vaccine. Although the Kenyan government (who were again paid by Bill to carry out the vaccinations also) said there was nothing wrong with the vaccines, the Bishops Kenyan Catholic Doctors Association found evidence to the contrary. They had six different samples of the 'anti-tetanus' vaccine sent to an independent laboratory in South Africa for testing. The results confirmed their worst fears, all tested positive for the ATC antigen. The ATC antigens are used in anti-fertility vaccines but was found present in tetanus vaccines targeted to young girls and women of child-bearing age. A doctor and spokesman for the Kenyan Association said that these tests confirmed their worst fears, that this vaccination campaign was not for tetanus at all, but a well-coordinated forced population control by mass sterilization exercised by using a proven fertility-regulating vaccine. This evidence was presented to the Ministry of Health before the third round of immunization, but was ignored. Doctor Ungari (sp) brought up several points about the vaccination program in Kenya that caused the Catholic doctors to become suspicious.

It should be noted that WHO (World Health Organization) and UNICEF distributed these vaccines among Kenyan hospitals and health centers for free, and that there were significant financial 'incentives' for the Kenyan government officials who participated in these programs.

Another video confirmed that Gates went to Africa and talked to a number of the governments of various states there. He convinced them, with money, to carry out vaccinations by their medical resources, which the government did. Some 500,000 women between the ages of 15 and 35 were vaccinated with what was supposedly a drug to help prevent diseases; what actually occurred was 500,000 females were rendered permanently sterile and unable to have children. (See, www.youtube.com/watch?v=it1HJq7zUeg, at **Odinga: Vaccination was a targeted mass sterilization program**, published 9/11/2017.)

But note this: When funds from the U.N. were not enough for a years' allotment of the vaccines, an organization started and funded by the Bill & Melinda Gates Foundation provided extra funding for many of the vaccination programs in poor countries. Interesting enough, there was no outbreak in tetanus in Kenya, thus no need for the "vaccine."

In addition, it should also be noted that UNICEF began a mass vaccination program with 500,000 doses of live oral polio vaccines in the Philippines after a super-typhoon devastated one of its cities; this program was in spite of the fact there were no reported cases of polio at all since 1993, and people given the live polio vaccine can spread actual cases of polio through the sewage system. Another 'request' from money-bags Vaccine-Bill? Or shall we call him Bill the Vaccinator?

Another mass vaccination in Syria occurred in 2013 when 1.7 million polio vaccines were purchased also by UNICEF in spite of the fact that no cases of polio had been reported since 1999. After mass vaccination occurred, new cases of polio began to appear in Syria. It seems apparent that UNICEF and the World Health Organization used these vaccines without cause on young children and women. Mass propaganda campaigns were needed and used to convince the populations that these vaccines were necessary to prevent disease and death. It was all a lie. People died. Was the Vaccinator involved in that too?

Worse, the CDC posted, then deleted, an article on the Gates' polio vaccine and how the SV40 virus may have been responsible for 10-30 million cancer deaths! A 2018 video shows that 98 million Americans were given cancer virus via the polio shot. That video showed this was a report from the CDC. Both the CDC and Google quickly removed it.

To further confirm this unbelievable admission, Assistant Professor of Pathology at Loyola University in Chicago, Dr. Michele Carbone was able to independently verify the presence of the SV40 virus in tissue and bone samples from patients who died during that era. He found 33% of the samples with osteosarcoma bone cancers, 40% of other bone cancers, and 60% of the mesothelioma's lung cancers all contained this obscure virus. This leaves the postulation that upwards of 10-30 million actually contracted and were adversely affected by this virus, to be deadly accurate.

In 2010 Gates spoke before the Bilderberg Group on how to lower populations through vaccines. His said he loves vaccines. He blamed the planet's problem with high carbon emissions on too many humans exhaling CO_2.

Bill the Vaccinator Gates is a self-proclaimed "humanitarian" and teamed with a new protégé, Facebook CEO Mark Zuckerberg. According to reports, Zuckerberg, in 2017 was in the process of opening up his own $600 million "biohub" in Silicon Valley, California, that aims to procure $3 billion in capital to "*cure, prevent and manage*" all disease throughout the entire world in just one generation, through *vaccines*. Zuckerberg was apparently inspired by Gates' ambitious goal to vaccinate every man, woman, and child on the planet with as many vaccines as possible in order to reduce the global population. Just like Gates, Zuckerberg couched his latest endeavors in faux benevolence, particularly when it comes to the vaccination agenda that is being branded as "*humanitarian aid.*" If one seeks to create actual "vaccines" one must know how viruses actually work; inherent in this knowledge and skill comes the ability to create a virus. If someone wanted to create a virus for a specific purpose, like depopulation, it seems reasonable that in creating the virus they also created its anti-virus vaccine to control the results, one might think.

The ultimate goal of Zuckerberg's biohub, as reported by the UK's "The Guardian" publication, is to usher in a "*new era of accelerated progress in science and health.*" In plain speak, the plan is to roll out all sorts of new vaccines, genetically-modified organisms (GMOs), crop chemicals, and other things to centralize control over the basic necessities of the world and its populations.

Several large universities have already partnered with Zuckerberg's biohub, including the University of California, San Francisco (UCSF), the University of California, Berkeley (UCB), and Stanford University. Together, these academic institutions partner with Zuckerberg and his various investors and project managers to begin the world's *"most bold and innovative and most risky work"* to bring the plan to fruition. Risky? Seems this glorious goal to help humanity would only be "risky" if they were working on viruses, wouldn't you think? It is easy to guess their marketing ploy will not be about the reality of what they are doing, but some Utopian claim of saving the world from hunger and disease. Perhaps through depopulation?

The vaccine focus of Gates is not new. Seven years ago, the B&M Gates Foundation and GlaxoSmithKline pharmaceutical teamed up and announced that they had discovered a new vaccine, ATSS, to combat mosquito-borne malaria. Now every year, some 800,000 people, mostly children, and most of them in Africa, die of malaria. It was actually a 30-year old vaccine that worked mostly on adults, and Glaxo claimed it had been successfully modified to work on children. Glaxo said they were going to only charge for the costs of production plus 5% profit because they didn't want to set a bad precedent by just giving it away. Yet studies showed that it was not a successful vaccine at all, and only 30% of those vaccinated were 'cured'.

Since the "renewed" fight against malaria unfolded, and since Gates got involved, there was 10 *billion* dollars donated in the fight against malaria. However, it had also been shown that mosquito control was increasingly ineffective as mosquitos developed resistance to the chemicals used to destroy their populations, noting too that the historic pattern for youngsters in central Africa, near the equator where malaria is concentrated, is to suffer repeated bouts of infections through childhood which, provided they survived them, gradually build up their immunity against malaria.

Thus, the 'seasonal concept' being applied to vaccines, the vaccines are done each year, resulting in massive profits for "Big Pharma."

It is also noteworthy that Bill Gates is heavily involved with Monsanto which has the "terminator seeds" (GMOs) which can't produce after the first planting, thus requiring that farmers, for each growing season, have to purchase new seeds from Monsanto, which ultimate raises the cost of the produce from these seeds. Monsanto has essentially created a monopoly on seed-growing, even to the passing of regulations (laws) that no longer allows farmers to use non-GMO seeds for their crops.

So, what does this review of Bill Gates have to do with the FEMA camps? Maybe nothing, maybe a lot. Bill Gates is only one of many in the topography of the New World Order, where depopulation is a topic and there is an intention, when they gain control, to depopulate the planet and regulate all birth thereafter, so only one billion people will remain at that number in perpetuity until the ruling elite says otherwise. But look at what just one very rich and powerful person can do to wreak havoc and death, and then multiply that by only a factor of 100 of similarly rich and powerful oligarchic elites, and it is easy to see how easy it can be to take control of the longevity issue of the world's population.

In closing this topic, understand the issue of coming climate change is not absolute fact and, in fact, it is being refuted. More than 500 scientists and professionals in climate and related fields sent a "European Climate Declaration" to the Secretary-General of the United Nations asking for a long-overdue, high-level, open debate on climate change. They were begging the United Nations to keep hysteria from obscuring facts. The declaration states:

> "Climate science should be less political, while climate policies should be more scientific. Scientists should openly address the uncertainties and exaggerations in their predictions of global warming, while politicians should dispassionately count the real benefits as well as the imagined costs of adaptation to global warming, and the real costs as well as the imagined benefits of mitigation.

The scientists underscored the importance of not rushing into enormously expensive and unproven climate action before fully ascertaining the facts.

> "Three is no statistical evidence that global warming is intensifying hurricanes, floods, droughts and suchlike natural disasters, or making them more frequent. However, CO_2 – mitigation measures are as damaging as they are costly. For

instance, wind turbines kill birds and bats, and palm-oil plantations destroy the biodiversity of the rainforests."

The signatories of the declaration also insist that public policy must respect scientific and economic realities, and not just reflect the most fashionable frenzy of the day.

"There is no climate emergency. Therefore, there is no cause for panic or alarm. We strongly oppose the harmful and unrealistic net-zero CO_2 policy proposed for 2050."

In particular, the scientists criticized the general-circulation models of climate on which international policy is currently founded as "unfit for their purpose."

"Therefore, it is cruel as well as imprudent to advocate the squandering of trillions on the basis of results from such immature models. Current climate policies pointlessly, grievously undermine the economic system, putting lives at risk in countries denied access to affordable, continuous electrical power. We urge you to follow a climate policy based on sound science, realistic economics and genuine concern for those harmed by costly but unnecessary attempts at mitigation."

(Source: Breitbart, Thomas D. Williams, Ph.D., 09-24-2019.)

In closing of this section, we have seen what has been going on with the proliferation of FEMA camps during the Obama era, coupled with many millions of multi-person plastic coffins (the manufacturers described as merely "grave liners"), stacked up in rural properties around the United States.

We have seen that Obama made a deal with the U.N. for invasion and disarmament of U.S. citizens if martial law was declared, and we have seen that during Katrina federal and local law enforcement entered people's homes in New Orleans and confiscated their guns, and I'm not talking about identified criminals either, just plain, ordinary citizens in a dangerous time needing their own firearms for self-protection in the post-storm chaos that was New Orleans. Some of those citizens were murdered.

We have seen the urban-warfare training that was done in the night in Los Angeles, with military helicopters and SWAT teams entering citizens houses without notice or permission, putting them in handcuffs, and using them without their consent for troop training purposes. And many of us watched the citizen-taken video of the U.N. Commando team in Washington, commanded by a Norwegian Colonel, conducting urban training on how to confiscate American's firearms; in fact, when asked on camera, the Colonel admitted that is what they were doing, and even said that those who resisted would be shot, as authorized by the U.N. (and as agreed upon by Obama). And there is no question but that Obama retired some military generals who, when asked if they could kill Americans and they said no, he replaced them with the generals who said they could. All under Obama. Again, we have seen none of this under Trump.

We have seen the long trains and roadways packed with U.N. vehicles and U.S. military vehicles being moved around to critical parts of the United States during that same Obama era. We have seen the closure of quite a few Walmart stores around the country, and seen the reports of citizens online showing how the buildings were stripped and remodeled inside, and how local and military presence guarded these buildings during that reconstruction. Processing centers, that's what they were turned into. We saw credible reports from citizens who talked about the underground work being done at Walmart sites, indicating underground rooms and even tunnels. We have seen videos of people complaining about heavy rumblings underground that sounded like very heavy equipment, at times out in the middle of nowhere, and at other times around the closed-down Walmarts. Was this equipment huge underground boring machines building tunnel-style roadways?

We have even seen videos of 18-wheelers delivering load after load of something inside government hollowed-out mountains, with curious people in cars actually sneaking into them and filming miles of rooms dug into the mountains.

We are seeing the new "5g" transmitters being installed all over the country, in cities and country-sides, supposedly to be for internet access, but we are also warned by experts that this "5g" frequency can result in brain damage and cancers, and we've heard from people complaining the one in their neighborhood actually made them sick or disoriented. So what is that all about?

And we still can't get a clear admission about the spraying across not just America but around the globe, of the "chemtrails" which have been identified as NOT being ordinary "contrails" from jet exhausts and which have been admittedly containing several chemicals, including nano-particles of aluminum, known to cause cancer. There is even a video, which I have, of California's Shasta County Board of Supervisors from 2013 holding a public hearing with one of the manufacturers of the chemicals for spraying. This representative admitted the chemicals being sprayed, and heard the testimony from the county about birds falling out of the sky, about fish and plant vegetation dying, about people getting sick with lung problems, all after a continued spraying over that county. The representative denied any wrongdoing or that there was any problem with the chemtrail ingredients. He claimed this was for fighting global warming, that the aluminum was so that when the sun hit this cloud the sun's heat would be reflected and help keep the planet cooler. This is a matter of local record. Anyone who has worked with aluminum knows that aluminum gets very hot very quickly, and it will radiate that heat in ALL directions, not reflect in one direction.

Nanoparticles of aluminum, breathed in, can be absorbed into the nasal passages and into the bloodstream, and on into the brain where they can wreak havoc on the electrical mental function, thus "dumbing down" the recipient and causing other physical and/or mental problems. They have been spraying for at least 18 years across the globe, including the United States. I have personally watched them here in California, and these were "chemtrails" and not "contrails" (water vapors that soon dissipate). Chemtrails don't "dissipate" like evaporation, rather they spread out like a cloud and dissipate as it spreads, but the ingredients do NOT go away, they just drift down to the Earth and the air that we breathe, and find its way into the soil or waterways.

To those who cry "conspiracy theory" let them cry. To those of us who pay closer attention, and recognize the central core agenda about the New World

Order, it is far easier for us to investigate enough to "connect the dots" about all this ancillary stuff, and to recognize that common humanity is facing a very dangerous future if we don't pay attention. A lot is going on against humanity itself, not just in the political arena.

PART 3. GEORGE SOROS: BILLIONAIRE WHO WANTS TO DESTROY AMERICA

George Soros is a multi-billionaire. He is a member of the Deep State (shadow government). He is a Jew from Hungary, and was 13 years old when the Nazis invaded and took Hungary. He is best known as "the man who broke the bank of England" because of his billion-dollar short sale during the UK's Black Wednesday currency crisis. He is now predicting that if the UK exits the EU (Brexit movement), the Sterling is almost certain to fall steeply and quickly, which is why, in 2016, he engaged in buying up gold and other precious metals. This is interesting because he already had a fortune in gold which, in 2011, he dumped his entire gold investment of US$800 million, possibly helping trigger a significant slide in the commodities market.

George Soros is also known for his manipulation of a country's economic system, causing a crash, at which time he buys up their currency and makes a fortune while the country suffers.

Soros claims his dream is to change the world for "the better" and he has the means to do it. He has critics, considering his views are often controversial. Politically, he was instrumental in the collapse of the Soviet Union and worked tirelessly to block President Bush from gaining re-election.

In an interview with Mike Wallace on 60 Minutes, he openly says that his greatest achievement would be destroying the United States.

He claims to be for democracy, yet expresses that his view that one Party, he did not expressly identify, is endangering the entire country. He claims America went wrong in engaging the war on terror. (See, www.youtube.com/watch?v= P_0rL8KKglc, entitled George SOROS on InnerVIEWS with Ernie Manouse.)

In interview, he admitted that he funds an organization (OpenSociety Foundation) to the tune of $400 million a year.

In the newspaper BREITBART, on September 7, 2016, a news outlet conceived in 2007 by two Jewish-American friends Andrew Breitbart and Larry Solov, with offices located in Washington DC, Los Angeles, London, Jerusalem, and Rome, journalist Aaron Klein, wrote about George Soros. The following is that article:

> NEW YORK – Just prior to the November 2014 midterm elections, George Soros's Open Society Foundations held a board meeting at which the organization discussed how it could further the use of President Obama's executive action authority to bypass Congress during Obama's final two years in office.
>
> Notably, the event featured a lunch session with Cecilia Muñoz, director of the White House Domestic Policy Council.
>
> The details were contained in a 67-page hacked file detailing the September 29-30, 2014 Open Society U.S. Programs board meeting in New York. The file was reviewed in full by Breitbart News.
>
> States the document: "Confident that open society goals can be advanced despite the political forecast for the remainder of the president's term, our grantees are actively involved in exploring the possibilities of executive action in areas of USP (Open Society Foundations' U.S. Programs) concern, including racial profiling, the census, and voter registration."
>
> The board meeting's minutes state outright that Soros's organization was seeking ways to "further" the use of potential executive actions by Obama:
>
> > There are two years remaining in the Obama Administration, and it is projected by all that the

anticipated results of the fall elections will make legislative accomplishments of significance nearly impossible. U.S. Programs (USP) grantees, and the OSF (Open Society Foundations) network more broadly, are thinking about how the administration can cement progress on key priorities through executive actions, while also minimizing problematic developments with long-term consequences.

Using three anchor grantees and a former senior administration official as discussants to detail their views of priorities and constraints, we will consider both the most promising substantive areas for executive action (in areas from transparency to criminal justice to wage and labor rules) as well how OSF might effectively further these.

Foundation grantees are "actively involved" in exploring the use of presidential executive actions, the document related:

Confident that open society goals can be advanced despite the political forecast for the remainder of the president's term, our grantees are actively involved in exploring the possibilities of executive action in areas of USP concern, including racial profiling, the census, and voter registration.

The Foundations' U.S. Programs had already begun to influence Obama's executive action efforts, the document relates:

Whatever the outcome of next month's elections, analysts expect continued gridlock in Congress, making any policy reforms that require legislation extremely unlikely. The President has telegraphed his determination to make progress on his priorities through administrative regulations and procedures; as he put it, "I've got a pen and I've got a phone."

USP has begun to influence the administration's efforts, as evidenced by our central role in launching the philanthropic partnership to the White House's My Brother's Keeper Initiative to promote opportunity for boys and men of color, as well as our ongoing efforts to encourage broad administrative relief to some segment of the undocumented population following the elections.

The Foundations' memo discussed areas of possible executive action that could fundamentally impact the U.S. political system.

There are some areas of executive action that have especially long-lasting consequences (e.g., nominations) and other steps which would be critical to framing issues for the 2016 election and the next president. How do we balance the relative merits of each approach?

The document notes the public pays less attention to executive decisions during a president's final two years, believing the president's powers are on the decline.

"Some of the most significant achievements of the Reagan, Clinton and Bush presidencies took place in their final two years. The public may pay less attention to the Executive then, and the president's perceived power may be on the wane, but he continues to possess the same, significant constitutional authority."

Muñoz, who served on the Foundations' U.S. Programs board in 2008, joined the September 2014 board meeting to "discuss the Obama administration's approach to select issues (criminal justice, immigration) and the remainder of his term," according to a summary provided by the hacked memo.

The possible executive actions being pushed are "sophisticated in their approaches, which range from broad and large-scale proposals to ideas more likely to fly under the radar," the hacked file states. "Our anchor partners, in particular, are thinking about how best to leverage the last two years, during which the President will have to adjust to 'lame duck' status."

The Open Society, together with partner grantees, assembled a general list of potential presidential executive actions on numerous issues, such as the following:

Voter registration, including pushing online voting:

Direct Health and Human Services to ensure that the federally facilitated health-care exchanges created as part of the Affordable Care Act ("Obamacare") incorporate voter registration opportunities as required by the National Voter Registration Act (NVRA, or "Motor Voter Act"), and direct federal agencies to find ways to increase voter participation nationwide.

Issue guidance interpreting the Americans with Disabilities Act with respect to accessibility of polling places, privacy when voting, and competence requirements.

Assist states with voter registration modernization efforts, including statewide database improvements, vote by mail, online registration and voting, and same-day registration.

Direct the Election Assistance Commission (EAC) to develop new data collection points that provide greater insight into county-based Election Administration and the ways in which voters interact with election systems (i.e., number of votes cast, type of voting machines used, provisional ballot statistics, etc.)

It should be noted that in January 2014, Obama's 10-person Presidential Commission on Election Administration released its recommendations for reforming the U.S. election process, including transitioning to voting via tablet computers and other technologies.

The commission recommended:

> Software-only products can be integrated with off-the-shelf commercial hardware components such as computers, laptops, tablets, scanners, printers, and even machine-readable code scanners and signature pad products.

> Tablet computers such as iPads are common components of these new technologies. They can be integrated into the check-in, voting, and verification processes in the polling place.

The commission highlighted new technologies in which the voter can "pre-fill" sample ballots at home to be scanned later at the polling place.

Obama's presidential panel dismissed concerns about hacking. The commission stated: "The fact that a tablet or off-the-shelf computer can be hacked or can break down does not mean such technology is inherently less secure than existing ballot marking methods if proper precautions are taken."

Meanwhile, other executive actions recommended by the Foundations include the following on judicial nominations: Continue to prioritize racial, ethnic, and gender diversity of federal judicial nominees, and focus on nominating lawyers with a diverse professional background as well.

Encourage Senate leadership to continue to support simple majority votes for cloture on judicial nominees and a reduction in the number of debate hours on judicial nominees.

Reform the Senate Judiciary Committee deference to the "blue slip" procedure when there is inaction/obstruction by home-state senators that lead to lengthy delays in the nomination process.

On so-called criminal justice reform, Soros's group drafted the following possible executive action ideas:

> Direct the Justice Department to identify federal prisoners to whom the Fair Sentencing Act would retroactively apply, and recommend commutations for all those eligible, barring exceptional circumstances.

> Issue an executive order to "ban the box" on federal agency job applications, except for law enforcement positions.

> Direct the Attorney General to issue new guidance banning discriminatory law enforcement techniques.

Aaron Klein is Breitbart's Jerusalem bureau chief and senior investigative reporter. He is a New York Times bestselling author and hosts the popular weekend talk radio program, "Aaron Klein Investigative Radio." (Source: www.breitbart. com/politics/2016/09/07/leaked-soros-memo-advance-obamas-use-executive-actions/)

What we can see from this article is the power and (implied) authority Soros had over his favorite presidential candidate, having been Obama's mentor during his college and senator days. So, Obama was, in fact, a puppet of Soros.

The question is what should be done to people who actively seek the destruction of America's ideology so they can replace it with socialism? I reckon we can look to the Federal Code, at 18 U.S. Code Section 2384 – Seditious Conspiracy, where we find:

> If two or more persons in any State or Territory, or in any place subject to the jurisdiction of the United States, conspire to overthrow, put down, or to destroy by force the Government of the United States, or to levy war against them, or to oppose by force the authority thereof, or by force to prevent, hinder, or delay the execution of any law of the United States contrary to the authority thereof, they shall each be fined under this title or imprisoned not more than twenty years, or both.

The next question is why are these pro-Socialists and their organizations allowed to get away with the sedition they are involved with for the dismantling of our capitalist democracy ideology and all the unalienable rights and freedoms embodied in our sacred Constitution?

And, obviously, there is the abiding question of why our government continues to allow Soros to be the puppeteer behind this Progressive Socialist movement?

The answer to that question might be related to what old man Rothschild once said about it doesn't matter who the President is or who the members of Congress are, so long as he (Rothschild) controls the money. Or, the comment by John D. Rockefeller that it doesn't matter who we elect to the Presidency because both candidates are already owned by the "shadow government" of transnational bankers and the Illuminati.

The exception to that latter comment was Donald Trump who, to them, was just a joke candidate who couldn't possibly win the election. Oh yeah?

But, let's review who George Soros is. I'm using as source material an EIR Investigation Executive Intelligence Review (EIR), dated 1996, a dossier based upon a report released on Oct. 1, 1996, by EIR's bureau in Wiesbaden, Germany, titled, "A Profile of Mega-Speculator George Soros."

> Time magazine has characterized financier George Soros as a "modern-day Robin Hood," who robs from the rich to give to the poor countries of eastern Europe and Russia. It claimed that Soros makes huge financial gains by speculating against western central banks, in order to use his profits to help the emerging post-communist economies of eastern Europe and former Soviet Union, to assist them to create what he calls an "Open Society." The Time statement is entirely accurate in the first part, and entirely inaccurate in the second. He robs from rich western countries, and uses his profits to rob even more savagely from the East, under the cloak of "philanthropy." His goal is to loot wherever and however he can. Soros has been called the master manipulator of "hit-and-run capitalism."

> As we shall see, what Soros means by "open," is a society that allows him and his financial predator friends to loot the resources and precious assets of former Warsaw Pact economies. By bringing people like Jeffrey Sachs or Sweden's Anders Aslund and their economic shock therapy into these economies, Soros lays the groundwork for buying up the assets of whole regions of the world at dirt-cheap prices.

> The man who broke the Bank of England?

> An examination of Soros's secretive financial network is vital to understand the true dimension of the "Soros problem" in eastern Europe and other nations.

> Following the crisis of the European Exchange Rate Mechanism of September 1992, when the Bank of England was

forced to abandon efforts to stabilize the pound sterling, a little-known financial figure emerged from the shadows, to boast that he had personally made over $1 billion in speculation against the British pound. The speculator was the Hungarian-born George Soros, who spent the war in Hungary under false papers working for the Nazi government, identifying and expropriating the property of wealthy fellow Jews. Soros left Hungary after the war, and established American citizenship after some years in London. Today, Soros is based in New York, but that tells little, if anything, of who and what he is.

Following his impressive claims to possession of a "Midas touch," Soros has let his name be publicly used in a blatant attempt to influence world financial markets—-an out-of-character act for most financial investors, who prefer to take advantage of situations not yet discovered by rivals, and keep them secret. Soros the financier is as much a political animal, as a financial speculator.

Soros proclaimed in March 1993, with great publicity, that the price of gold was about to rise sharply; he said that he had just gotten "inside information" that China was about to buy huge sums of gold for its booming economy. Soros was able to trigger a rush into buying gold, which caused prices to rise more than 20% over four months, to the highest level since 1991. Typically for Soros, once the fools rushed in to push prices higher, Soros and his friend Sir James Goldsmith secretly began selling their gold at a huge profit.

Then, in early June 1993, Soros proclaimed his intent to force a sell-off in German government bonds in favor of the French, in an open letter to London Times Financial Editor Anatole Kaletsky, in which Soros proclaimed, "Down with the D-Mark!" Soros has at various times attacked the currencies of Thailand, Malaysia, Indonesia, and

Mexico, coming into newly opened financial markets which have little experience with foreign investors, let alone ones with large funds like Soros. Soros begins buying stocks or bonds in the local market, leading others to naively suppose that he knows something they do not. As with gold, when the smaller investors begin to follow Soros, driving prices of stocks or whatever higher, Soros begins to sell to the eager new buyers, cashing in his 40% or 100% profits, then exiting the market, and often, the entire country, to seek another target for his speculation. This technique gave rise to the term "hit and run." What Soros always leaves behind, is a collapsed local market and financial ruin of national investors.

The Secret of the Quantum Fund NV

Soros is the visible side of a vast and nasty secret network of private financial interests, controlled by the leading aristocratic and royal families of Europe, centered in the British House of Windsor. This network, called by its members the Club of Isles, was built upon the wreckage of the British Empire after World War II.

Rather than use the powers of the state to achieve their geopolitical goals, a secret cross-linked holding of private financial interests, tied to the old aristocratic oligarchy of western Europe, was developed. It was in many ways modeled on the 17th-century British and Dutch East India Companies. The heart of this Club of the Isles is the financial center of the old British Empire, the City of London. Soros is one of what in medieval days were called Hofjuden, the "Court Jews," who were deployed by the aristocratic families.

The most important of such "Jews who are not Jews," are the Rothschilds, who launched Soros's career. They are members of the Club of the Isles and retainers of the British royal family. This has been true since Amschel Rothschild sold the

British Hessian troops to fight against George Washington during the American Revolution.

Soros is American only in his passport. He is a global financial operator, who happens to be in New York, simply because "that's where the money is," as the bank robber Willy Sutton once quipped, when asked why he always robbed banks. Soros speculates in world financial markets through his offshore company, Quantum Fund NV, a private investment fund, or "hedge fund." His hedge fund reportedly manages some $11-14 billion of funds on behalf of its clients, or investors—-one of the most prominent of whom is, according to Soros, Britain's Queen Elizabeth, the wealthiest person in Europe.

The Quantum Fund is registered in the tax haven of the Netherlands Antilles, in the Caribbean. This is to avoid paying taxes, as well as to hide the true nature of his investors and what he does with their money.

In order to avoid U.S. government supervision of his financial activities, something normal U.S.-based investment funds must by law agree to in order to operate, Soros moved his legal headquarters to the Caribbean tax haven of Curacao. The Netherlands Antilles has repeatedly been cited by the Task Force on Money Laundering of the Organization for Economic Cooperation and Development (OECD) as one of the world's most important centers for laundering illegal proceeds of the Latin American cocaine and other drug traffic. It is a possession of the Netherlands.

Soros has taken care that the none of the 99 individual investors who participate in his various funds is an American national. By U.S. securities law, a hedge fund is limited to no more than 99 highly wealthy individuals, so-called "sophisticated investors." By structuring his investment company as an offshore hedge fund, Soros avoids public scrutiny.

Soros himself is not even on the board of Quantum Fund. Instead, for legal reasons, he serves the Quantum Fund as official "investment adviser," through another company, Soros Fund Management, of New York City. If any demand were to be made of Soros to reveal the details of Quantum Fund's operations, he is able to claim he is "merely its investment adviser." Any competent police investigator looking at the complex legal structure of Soros's businesses would conclude that there is prima facie evidence of either vast money laundering of illicit funds, or massive illegal tax evasion. Both may be true.

To make it impossible for U.S. tax authorities or other officials to look into the financial dealings of his web of businesses, the board of directors of Quantum Fund NV also includes no American citizens. His directors are Swiss, Italian, and British financiers.

George Soros is part of a tightly knit financial mafia—-"mafia," in the sense of a closed masonic-like fraternity of families pursuing common aims. Anyone who dares to criticize Soros or any of his associates, is immediately hit with the charge of being "anti-Semitic"——a criticism which often silences or intimidates genuine critics of Soros's unscrupulous operations. The Anti-Defamation League of B'nai B'rith considers it a top priority to "protect" Soros from the charges of "anti-Semites" in Hungary and elsewhere in Central Europe, according to ADL National Director Abraham Foxman. The ADL's record of service to the British oligarchy has been amply documented by EIR (e.g. The Ugly Truth About the Anti-Defamation League [Washington, D.C., Executive Intelligence Review: 1992]).

According to knowledgeable U.S. and European investigators, Soros's circle includes indicted metals and commodity speculator and fugitive Marc Rich of Zug, Switzerland and Tel Aviv; secretive Israeli arms and commodity dealer Shaul

Eisenberg, and "Dirty Rafi" Eytan, both linked to the financial side of the Israeli Mossad; and, the family of

Jacob Lord Rothschild.

Understandably, Soros and the Rothschild interests prefer to keep their connection hidden far from public view, so as to obscure the well-connected friends Soros enjoys in the City of London, the British Foreign Office, Israel, and the U.S. financial establishment. The myth, therefore, has been created, that Soros is a lone financial investment "genius" who, through his sheer personal brilliance in detecting shifts in markets, has become one of the world's most successful speculators. According to those who have done business with him, Soros never makes a major investment move without sensitive insider information.

On the board of directors of Soros's Quantum Fund N.V. is Richard Katz, a Rothschild man who is also on the board of the London N.M. Rothschild and Sons merchant bank, and the head of Rothschild Italia S.p.A. of Milan. Another Rothschild family link to Soros's Quantum Fund is Quantum board member Nils O. Taube, the partner of the London investment group St. James Place Capital, whose major partner is Lord Rothschild. London Times columnist Lord William Rees-Mogg is also on the board of Rothschild's St. James Place Capital.

A frequent business partner of Soros in various speculative deals, including in the 1993 gold manipulation, although not on the Quantum Fund directly, is the Anglo-French speculator Sir James Goldsmith, a cousin of the Rothschild family.

From the very first days when Soros created his own investment fund in 1969, he owed his success to his relation to the Rothschild family banking network. Soros worked in New

York in the 1960s for a small private bank close to the Rothschilds, Arnhold & S. Bleichroeder, Inc., a banking family
which represented Rothschild interests in Germany during
Bismarck's time. To this day, A. & S. Bleichroeder, Inc. remains the Principal Custodian, along with Citibank, of funds
of Soros's Quantum Fund. George C. Karlweiss, of Edmond
de Rothschild's Switzerland-based Banque Privee SA in Lugano, as well as of the scandal-tainted Rothschild Bank AG
of Zurich, gave Soros financial backing. Karlweiss provided
some of the vital initial capital and investors for Soros's
Quantum Fund.

Union Banque Privee and the 'Swiss connection'

Another member of the board of Soros's Quantum Fund is
the head of one of the most controversial Swiss private banks,
Edgar de Picciotto, who has been called "one of the cleverest
bankers in Geneva"—-and is one of the most scandal-tainted.
De Picciotto, from an old Portuguese Jewish trading family,
who was born in Lebanon, is head of the Geneva private bank
CBI-TDB Union Bancaire Privee, a major player in the gold
and offshore hedge funds business. Hedge funds have been
identified by international police agencies as the fastest-
growing outlet for illegal money laundering today.

De Picciotto is a longtime friend and business associate of
banker Edmond Safra, also born in Lebanon, whose family
came from Aleppo, Syria, and who now controls the Republic
Bank of New York. Republic Bank has been identified in U.S.
investigations into Russian organized crime, as the bank involved in transferring billions of U.S. Federal Reserve notes
from New York to organized crime-controlled Moscow
banks, on behalf of Russian organized crime figures. Safra is
under investigation by U.S. and Swiss authorities for laundering Turkish and Columbian drug money. In 1990, Safra's
Trade Development Bank (TDB) of Geneva was merged

with de Picciotto's CBI to create the CBI-TDB Union Banque Privee. The details of the merger are shrouded in secrecy to this day. As part of the deal, de Picciotto became a board member of American Express Bank (Switzerland) SA of Geneva, and two American Express Bank of New York executives sit on the board of de Picciotto's Union Banque Privee. Safra had sold his Trade Development Bank to American Express, Inc. in the 1980s. Henry Kissinger sits on the board of American Express, Inc., which has repeatedly been implicated in international money-laundering scandals.

De Picciotto's start as a Geneva banker came from Nicholas Baring of the London Barings Bank, who tapped de Picciotto to run the bank's secret Swiss bank business. Barings has for centuries been private banker to the British royal family, and since the bank's collapse in March 1995, has been overhauled by the Dutch ING Bank, which is reported to be a major money-laundering institution.

De Picciotto is also a longtime business partner of Venetian businessman Carlo De Benedetti, who recently was forced to resign as head of Olivetti Corp. Both persons sit on the board of the Societe Financiere de Geneve investment holding company in Geneva. De Benedetti is under investigation in Italy for suspicion of triggering the collapse of Italy's Banco Ambrosiano in the early 1980s. The head of that bank, Roberto Calvi, was later found hanging from the London Blackfriar's Bridge, in what police believe was a masonic ritual murder.

De Picciotto and his Union Banque Privee have been implicated in numerous drug and illegal money-laundering operations. In November 1994, U.S. federal agents arrested a senior official of de Picciotto's Geneva bank, Jean-Jacques Handali, along with two other UBP officials, on charges of leading a multimillion-dollar drug-money-laundering ring.

According to the U.S. Attorney's Office in Miami, Handali and Union Banque Privee were the "Swiss connection" in an international drug-money-laundering ring tied to Colombian and Turkish cocaine and heroin organizations. A close business and political associate of de Picciotto is a mysterious arm dealer, Helmut Raiser, who is linked in business dealings with reputed Russian organized crime kingpin Grigori Luchansky, who controls the Russian and Swiss holding company Nordex Group.

Another director of Soros's Quantum Fund is Isodoro Albertini, owner of the Milan stock brokerage firm Albertini and Co. Beat Notz of the Geneva Banque Worms is another private banker on the board of Soros's Quantum Fund, as is Alberto Foglia, who is chief of the Lugano, Switzerland Banca del Ceresio. Lugano, just across the Swiss border from Milan, is notorious as the financial secret bank haven for Italian organized crime families, including the heroin mafia behind the 1980s "Pizza Connection" case. The Banca del Ceresio has been one of the secret Swiss banks identified in the recent Italian political corruption scandals as the repository of bribe funds of several Italian politicians now in prison.

The Sponsorship of the Rothschilds

Soros's relation to the Rothschild finance circle represents no ordinary or casual banking connection. It goes a long way to explain the extraordinary success of a mere private speculator, and Soros's uncanny ability to "gamble right" so many times in such high-risk markets. Soros has access to the "insider track" in some of the most important government and private channels in the world.

Since World War II, the Rothschild family, at the heart of the financial apparatus of the Club of the Isles, has gone to great lengths to create a public myth about its own insignificance.

The family has spent significant sums cultivating a public image as a family of wealthy, but quiet, "gentlemen," some of whom prefer to cultivate fine French wines, some of whom are devoted to charity.

Since British Foreign Secretary Arthur Balfour wrote his famous November 1917 letter to Lord Rothschild, expressing official British government backing for establishment of a Palestinian national home for the Jewish people, the Rothschilds were intimately involved in the creation of Israel. But behind their public facade of a family donating money for projects such as planting trees in the deserts of Israel, N.M. Rothschild of London is at the center of various intelligence operations, and more than once has been linked to the more unsavory elements of international organized crime. The family prefers to keep such links at arm's length, and away from its London headquarters, via its lesser-known outposts such as their Zurich Rothschild Bank AG and Rothschild Italia of Milan, the bank of Soros partner Richard Katz.

N.M. Rothschild is considered by City of London sources to be one of the most influential parts of the British intelligence establishment, tied to the Thatcher "free market" wing of the Tory Party. Rothschild and Sons made huge sums managing for Thatcher the privatization of billions of dollars of British state industry holdings during the 1980s, and today, for John Major's government. Rothschilds is also at the very heart of the world gold trade, being the bank at which twice daily the London Gold Fix is struck by a group of the five most influential gold trade banks. Gold constitutes a major part of the economy of drug dealings globally.

N.M. Rothschild and Sons is also implicated in some of the filthiest drugs-for-weapons secret intelligence operations. Because it is connected to the highest levels of the British intelligence establishment, Rothschilds managed to evade any prominent mention of its complicity in one of the more sordid black covert intelligence networks, that of the Bank of Credit and Commerce International (BCCI). Rothschilds was at the center of the international web of money-laundering banks used during the 1970s and 1980s by Britain's MI-6 and the networks of Col. Oliver North and George Bush, to finance such projects as the Nicaraguan Contras.

On June 8, 1993 the chairman of the U.S. House of Representatives' Committee on Banking, Rep. Henry Gonzalez (D-Tex.), made a speech charging that the U.S. government, under the previous Bush and Reagan administrations, had systematically refused to prosecute the BCCI, and that the Department of Justice had repeatedly refused to cooperate with Congressional investigations of both the BCCI scandal and what Gonzalez claims is the closely related scandal of the Atlanta, Georgia Banca Nationale del Lavoro, which was alleged to have secured billions in loans from the Bush administration to Saddam Hussein, just prior to the Gulf War of 1990-91.

Gonzalez charged that the Bush administration had "a Justice Department that I say, and I repeat, has been the most corrupt, most unbelievably corrupt justice system that I have seen in the 32 years I have been in the Congress."

The BCCI violated countless laws, including laundering drug money, financing illegal arms traffic, and falsifying bank records. In July 1991, New York District Attorney Robert Morgenthau announced a grand jury indictment against BCCI, charging it with having committed "the largest bank fraud in world financial history. BCCI operated as a corrupt criminal organization throughout its entire 19-year history."

The BCCI had links directly into the Bush White House. Saudi Sheik Kamal Adham, a BCCI director and former head of Saudi Arabian intelligence when George Bush was head of the CIA, was one of the BCCI shareholders indicted in the United States. Days after his indictment, former top Bush White House aide Edward Rogers went to Saudi Arabia as a private citizen to sign a contract to represent Sheikh Adham in the United States.

But what has never been identified in a single major Western press investigation, was that the Rothschild group was at the heart of the vast illegal web of BCCI. The key figure was Dr. Alfred Hartmann, the managing director of the BCCI Swiss subsidiary, Banque de Commerce et de Placement SA; at the same time, he ran the Zurich Rothschild Bank AG, and sat in London as a member of the board of N.M. Rothschild and Sons, Hartmann was also a business partner of Helmut Raiser, friend of de Picciotto, and linked to Nordex.

Hartmann was also chairman of the Swiss affiliate of the Italian BNL bank, which was implicated in the Bush administration illegal transfers to Iraq prior to the 1990 Iraqi invasion of Kuwait. The Atlanta branch of BNL, with the knowledge of George Bush when he was vice president, conduited funds to Helmut Raiser's Zug, Switzerland company, Consen, for development of the CondorII missile program by Iraq, Egypt, and Argentina, during the Iran-Iraq War. Hartmann was vice-chairman of another secretive private Geneva bank, the Bank of NY-Inter-Maritime Bank, a bank whose chairman, Bruce Rappaport, was one of the illegal financial conduits for Col. Oliver North's Contra drugs-for-weapons network during the late 1980. North also used the BCCI as one of his preferred banks to hide his illegal funds.

Rich, Reichmann, and Soros's Israeli links

According to reports of former U.S. State Department intelligence officers familiar with the Soros case, Soros's Quantum Fund amassed a war chest of well over $10 billion, with the help of a powerful group of "silent" investors who let Soros deploy the capital to demolish European monetary stability in September 1992.

Among Soros's silent investors, these sources say, are the fugitive metals and oil trader Marc Rich, based in Zug, Switzerland; and Shaul Eisenberg, a decades-long member of Israeli Mossad intelligence, who functions as a major arms merchant throughout Asia and the Near East. Eisenberg was recently banned from doing business in Uzbekistan, where he had been accused by the government of massive fraud and corruption. A third Soros partner is Israel's "Dirty Rafi" Eytan, who served in London previously as Mossad liaison to British intelligence.

Rich was one of the most active western traders in oil, aluminum, and other commodities in the Soviet Union and Russia between 1989 and 1993. This, not coincidentally, is just the period when Grigori Luchansky's Nordex Group became a multibillion-dollar company selling Russian oil, aluminum, and other commodities.

Canadian real estate entrepreneur Paul Reichmann, formerly of Olympia and York notoriety, a Hungarian-born Jew like Soros, is a business partner in Soros's Quantum Realty, a $525-million real estate investment fund.

The Reichmann tie links Soros as well with Henry Kissinger and former Tory Foreign Minister Lord Carrington (who is also a member of Kissinger Associates, Inc. of New York). Reichmann sits with both Kissinger and Carrington on the board of the influential British-Canadian publishing group, Hollinger, Inc. Hollinger owns a large number of newspapers in Canada and the United States, the London Daily Telegraph, and the largest English-language daily in Israel, the Jerusalem Post. Hollinger has been attacking President

Clinton and the Middle East peace process ever since Clinton's election in November 1992.

Soros and Geopolitics

Soros is little more than one of several significant vehicles for economic and financial warfare by the Club of the Isles faction. Because his affiliations to these interests have not previously been spotlighted, he serves extremely useful functions for the oligarchy, as in 1992 and 1993, when he launched his attack on the European Rate Mechanism.

Although Soros's speculation played a role in finally taking the British pound out of the ERM currency group entirely, it would be a mistake to view that action as "anti-British." Soros went for the first time to London, where he studied under Karl Popper and Friedrich von Hayek at the London School of Economics.

Soros's business ties to Sir James Goldsmith and Lord Rothschild place him in the inner circles of the Thatcher wing of the British establishment. By helping the "anti-Europe" Thatcherites pull Britain out of the ERM in September 1992 (and making more than $1 billion in the process at British taxpayer expense), Soros helped the long-term goal of the Thatcherites in weakening continental Europe's economic stability. Since 1904, it has been British geopolitical strategy to prevent by all means any successful economic linkage between western continental European economies, especially that of Germany, with Russia and the countries of eastern Europe.

Soros's personal outlook is consonant with that of the Thatcher wing of the Tory Party, those who three years ago launched the "Germany, the Fourth Reich" hate campaign against unified Germany, comparing Chancellor Helmut Kohl with Adolf Hitler. Soros is personally extremely anti-German. In his 1991 autobiography, "Underwriting Democracy," Soros warned that a reunited Germany would *"upset the balance of Europe .... It is easy to see how the interwar scenario could be replayed. A united Germany becomes the strongest economic power and develops Eastern Europe as its Lebensraum ... a potent witches' brew."* Soros's recent public attacks on the German economy and the deutsche mark are fundamentally motivated by this geo-political view.

Soros is quite close to the circles of George Bush in the U.S. intelligence community and finance. His principal bank cus-todian, and reputed major lender in the 1992 assault on Eu-rope's ERM, is Citicorp NA, the nation's largest bank. Citicorp is more than a lending institution; it is a core part of the Amer-ican liberal establishment. In 1989, as it became clear that Ger-man unification was a real possibility, a senior official at Citicorp, a former adviser to Michael Dukakis's Presidential campaign, told a European business associate that "German unity will be a disaster for our interests; we must take measures to ensure a sharp D-Mark collapse on the order of 30%, so that she will not have the capability to reconstruct East Ger-many into the economic engine of a new Europe."

While Soros was calling on world investors to pull down the deutsche mark in 1993, he had been making a strong play in the French media, since late 1992, to portray himself as a "friend of French interests." Soros is reported to be close to senior figures of the French establishment, the Treasury, and in particular, Bank of France head Jean-Claude Trichet. In effect, Soros is echoing the old Entente Cordiale alliance against Germany, which helped precipitate World War 1.

Soros admits that he survived in Nazi Hungary during the war, as a Jew, by adopting what he calls a double personality. "I have lived with a double personality practically all my life," Soros recently stated. "It started at age fourteen in Hungary, when I assumed a false identity in order to escape persecution as a Jew." Soros admitted in a radio interview that his father gave him Nazi credentials in Hungary during the war, and he looted wealthy Jewish estates. Further research showed that this operation was probably run by the SS.

Soros did not leave the country until two years after the war. Though he and his friends in the media are quick to attack any policy opponent of Soros, especially in eastern Europe, as being "anti-Semitic," Soros's Jewish identity apparently has only utilitarian value for him, rather than providing moral foundations. In short, the young Soros was a cynical, ambitious person, the ideal recruit for the British postwar intelligence network.

Soros Savages Eastern Europe

Soros has established no fewer than 19 "charitable" foundations across eastern Europe and the former Soviet Union. He has sponsored "peace" concerts in former Yugoslavia with such performers as Joan Baez. He is helping send young east Europeans to Oxford University. A model citizen, is the image he broadcasts.

The reality is something else. Soros has been personally responsible for introducing shock therapy into the emerging economies of eastern Europe since 1989. He has deliberately fostered on fragile new governments in the east the most draconian economic madness, policies which have allowed Soros and his financial predator friends, such as Marc Rich and Shaul Eisenberg, to loot the resources of large parts of eastern Europe at dirt-cheap prices. Here are illustrative case histories of Soros's eastern "charity":

Poland: In late 1989, Soros organized a secret meeting between the "reform" communist government of Prime Minister

Mieczyslaw Rakowski and the leaders of the then-illegal Sol-idarnosc trade union organization. According to well-in-formed Polish sources, at that 1989 meeting, Soros unveiled his "plan" for Poland: The communists must let Solidarnosc take over the government, so as to gain the confidence of the population. Then, said Soros, the state must act to bankrupt its own industrial and agricultural enterprises, using astro-nomical interest rates, withholding state credits, and burden-ing firms with unpayable debt. Once these were done, Soros promised that he would encourage his wealthy international business friends to come into Poland, as prospective buyers of the privatized state enterprises. A recent example of this privatization plan is the case of the large steel facility Huta Warsawa. According to steel experts, this modern complex would cost $3-4 billion for a western company to build new. Several months ago, the Polish government agreed to assume the debts of Huta Warsawa, and to sell the debt-free enter-prise to a Milan company, Lucchini, for $30 million!

Soros recruited his friend, Harvard University economist Jef-fery Sachs, who had previously advised the Bolivian govern-ment in economic policy, leading to the takeover of that nation's economy by the cocaine trade. To further his plan in Poland, Soros set up one of his numerous foundations, the Stefan Batory Foundation, the official sponsor of Sach's work in Poland in 1989-90.

Soros boasts, "*I established close personal contact with Walesa's chief adviser, Bronislaw Geremek. I was also received by [President Gen Wojciech] Jaruzelski, the head of State, to obtain his blessing for my foundation.*" He worked closely with the eminence gris of Polish shock therapy, Witold Trzeciakowski, a shadow ad-viser to Finance Minister Leszek Balcerowicz. Soros also cul-tivated relations with Balcerowicz, the man who would first impose Sach's shock therapy on Poland. Soros says when Walesa was elected President, that "*largely because of western pressure, Walesa retained Balcerowicz as minister.*" Balcerowicz imposed a freeze on wages while industry was to be bankrupted by a cutoff of state credits. Industrial output fell by more than 30% over two years.

Soros admits he knew in advance that his shock therapy would cause huge unemployment, closing of factories, and social unrest. For this reason, he insisted that Solidarnosc be brought into the government, to help deal with the unrest. Through the Batory Foundation, Soros coopted key media opinion makers such as Adam Michnik, and through cooperation with the U.S. Embassy in Warsaw, imposed a media censorship favorable to Soros's shock therapy, and hostile to all critics.

Russia and the Community of Independent States (CIS): Soros headed a delegation to Russia, where he had worked together with Raisa Gorbachova since the late 1980s, to establish the Cultural Initiative Foundation. As with his other "charitable foundations," this was a tax-free vehicle for Soros and his influential Western friends to enter the top policymaking levels of the country, and for tiny sums of scarce hard currency, but up important political and intellectual figures. After a false start under Mikhail Gorbachov in 1988-91, Soros shifted to the new Yeltsin circle. It was Soros who introduced Jeffery Sachs and shock therapy into Russia, in late 1991. Soros describes his effort: "*I started mobilizing a group of economists to take to the Soviet Union (July 1990). Professor Jeffery Sachs, with whom I had worked in Poland, was ready and eager to participate. He suggested a number of other participants: Romano Prodi from Italy; David Finch, a retired official from the IMF [International Monetary Fund]. I wanted to include Stanley Fischer and Jacob Frenkel, heads of research of the World Bank and IMF, respectively; Larry Summers from Harvard and Michael Bruno of the Central Bank of Israel.*"

Since Jan. 2, 1992, shock therapy has introduced chaos and hyperinflation into Russia. Irreplaceable groups from advanced scientific research institutes have fled in pursuit of jobs in the West. Yegor Gaidar and the Yeltsin government imposed draconian cuts in state spending to industry and agriculture, even though the entire economy was state-owned. A goal of a zero-deficit budget within three months was announced. Credit to industry was ended, and enterprises piled up astronomical debts, as inflation of the ruble went out of control.

The friends of Soros lost no time in capitalizing on this situation. Marc Rich began buying Russian aluminum at absurdly cheap prices, with his hard currency. Rich then dumped the aluminum onto western industrial markets last year, causing a 30% collapse in the price of the metal, as western industry had no way to compete. There was such an outflow of aluminum last year from Russia, that there were shortages of aluminum for Russian fish canneries. At the same time, Rich reportedly moved in to secure export control over the supply of most West Siberian crude oil to western markets. Rich's companies have been under investigation for fraud in Russia, according to a report in the Wall Street Journal of May 13, 1993.

Another Soros silent partner who has moved in to exploit the chaos in the former Soviet Union, is Shaul Eisenberg. Eisenberg, reportedly with a letter of introduction from then-European Bank chief Jacques Attali, managed to secure an exclusive concession for textiles and other trade in Uzbekistan. When Uzbek officials confirmed defrauding of the government by Eisenberg, his concessions were summarily abrogated. The incident has reportedly caused a major loss for Israeli Mossad strategic interests throughout the Central Asian republics.

Soros has extensive influence in Hungary. When nationalist opposition parliamentarian Istvan Csurka tried to protest what was being done to ruin the Hungarian economy, under the policies of Soros and friends, Csurka was labeled an "anti-Semite," and in June 1993, he was forced out of the governing Democratic Forum, as a result of pressure from Soros-linked circles in Hungary and abroad, including Soros's close friend, U.S. Rep. Tom Lantos.

Lighting the Balkan Fuse

In early 1990, in what was then still Yugoslavia, Soros's intervention with shock therapy, in cooperation with the IMF, helped light the economic fuse that led to the outbreak of war in June 1991. Soros boasted at that time, "Yugoslavia is a particularly interesting case. Even as national rivalries have brought the country to the verge of a breakup, a radical monetary stabilization program, which was introduced on the same date as in Poland—-January 1, 1990——-has begun to change the political landscape. The program is very much along the Polish lines, and it had greater initial success. By the middle of the year, people were beginning to think Yugoslav again."

Soros is friends with former Deputy Secretary of State Lawrence Eagleburger, the former U.S. ambassador to Belgrade and the patron of Serbian Communist leader Slobodan Milosevic. Eagleburger is a past president of Kissinger Associates, on whose board sits Lord Carrington, whose Balkan mediations supported Serbian aggression into Croatia and Bosnia.

Today, Soros has established his Foundation centers in Bosnia, Croatia, Slovenia, and a Soros Yugoslavia Foundation in Belgrade, Serbia. In Croatia, he has tried to use his foundation monies to woo influential journalists or to slander opponents of his shock therapy, by labeling them variously "anti-Semitic" or "neo-Nazi." The head of Soros's Open Society Fund—-Croatia, Prof. Zarko Puhovski, is a man who has reportedly made a recent dramatic conversion from orthodox Marxism to Soros's radical free market. Only seven years ago, according to one of his former students, as professor of philosophy at the University of Zagreb, Puhovski attacked students trying to articulate a critique of communism, by insisting, "It is unprincipled to criticize Marxism from a liberal standpoint." His work for the Soros Foundation in Zagreb has promoted an anti-nationalist "global culture," hiring a network of anti-Croatian journalists to propagandize, in effect, for the Serbian cause.

These examples can be elaborated for each of the other 19 locations across eastern Europe where George Soros operates. The political agenda of Soros and this group of financial "globalists" will create the conditions for a new outbreak of war, even world war, if it continues to be tolerated.

So, now you know who George Soros is; if you didn't know before how dangerous he is, you should know now. How does he get away with all that he does? He is protected by the aristocracy.

PART 4. THE CENTRAL AND
SOUTH AMERICAN MIGRANT CRISIS

A. The Puppetmasters

I have been increasingly following for years now since 2003 the growing threats in this word, many of which are pointedly aimed at the United States. As I became alarmed at the global insanity our future might hold, from all appearances now, I spent more and more time looking at events occurring around the globe. I have come to the conclusion that we, people of the world, are in dire trouble from a small group of unbelievably wealthy and powerful people;

they are bankers, big business folks, including generations of several families. They are rightly called the "shadow government." I have spoken of them earlier.

Some of them are members of the "conspiracy theory" group, the Illuminati, and also members of the Deep State, and also sit on the global secret council called the "Bilderberg Group." This group meets in once a year at different locations, known only at the very last minute, and never the same location twice. They are, in fact, the global puppetmasters who "cause things to happen", things like bad things to chosen countries. George Soros, as I've mentioned earlier, is connected with the Illuminati, or Deep State. He helps to crash countries for his own enrichment and/or to aid the Deep State in the disposal of their *"selected enemies"* and to further the globalists' agenda of a New World Order, i.e., a one government world with only two classes of people: rulers and slaves, by helping to crash the economies of target countries and force the resulting order out of the chaos to be socialist.

Ask just about anyone on the street or in your social circle what happened to cause the crash of so many North African countries, particularly Iraq, Yemen, Afghanistan, Somalia, Iran, Zimbabwe, Congo, Nigeria, and others, with endless wars and deaths, and they'll likely end their response with the conclusion that the wars caused the "refugee" migration north into Europe, and this migration consisted of families with children fleeing the horrors of those wars.

But this conclusion is only partly true. I can understand that someone can point to the effects of the wars as justification in itself for the "refugee crisis." Were these wars earlier planned and orchestrated and, if so, by whom? Was the U.S. a part in that and, if so, why were we engaged in these wars? Was our government manipulated and thus blind to why things were happening, or why we had to become involved? Did our government even know they too were being manipulated? Or did the U.S. government know exactly what part they were playing? Don't you think these are legitimate questions that should be asked by We the People? A mere deferential *"Well, that's the business of the government and the military and I have to trust they make the best decisions for America"* is not the response that protects all of us. Not in today's times.

Don't forget how many of Obama's pro-socialist appointees into our government there were, and how many "conservative" Muslims (some or all belonging to or linked in some way to terrorist organizations against America). President Trump has been weeding them out, you know, but how many remain? When people are "hired" or "appointed" to government positions, it is not easy to just remove them because you think they shouldn't have been hired or appointed. It is hard to remove a "civil servant."

So, anyway, who started these wars? I mean, did the shadow government play a role in getting these wars started? Did we attack Libya because Omar Gaddafi was going to back out of the petro-dollar and introduce its own money, the gold dinar, an African currency made of gold, a true sharing of the wealth to all its citizens, as well as selling oil to African countries and the world only for actual gold? That wasn't the reason given the public, was it? Would that action have hurt American and banker financial interests? The Deep State? What do you think? Yes, in a big way. Some say it was about the Gaddafi regime using military violence on its citizens, others say it is about the oil, but do you think we'd be in Iraq if the major export was sand? It was all about Gaddafi's move to bury the US petro-dollar in favor of a gold standard for its oil sales. But, if that is the truth, well I suppose telling the American public the government was going to assassinate Gaddafi for that actual reason might not have gone over so well with the American public.

Gaddafi's move would shift the economic balance of the world, and depend upon how much gold a country actually had, not how many dollars they have. Remember this, our dollar continues to have less and less spending value, due to inflation. We work the same, get the same salary, but our income, after taxes, is increasingly smaller and buys less.

The Federal Reserve, a private bank, sent its representative to tell the House Financial Services Subcommittee on Domestic Monetary Policy that it owned no gold at all, and hasn't owned actual gold since 1934. So, had Gaddafi managed to convince African, and perhaps other, countries to leave the petro-dollar in favor of the Libyan dinar gold standard, America would be unable to buy oil from African countries at all. But it would have affected the entire global banking and financial community. Did the shadow government demand the assassination of Gaddafi? Well, we got him killed, gave a bogus excuse to the public, and intimated by Gaddafi's assassination that the USA, its allies, and its financial institutions will not tolerate a withdrawal from the petro-dollar or go to the euro dollar instead.

Thus continued an ever-widening war in the Arab countries like Afghanistan, Syria, Iraq, and soon, perhaps, with Iran.

Do I personally agree with that decision to kill Gaddafi? I accept that his actions, as a Muslim who did not like America and the infidel West, would have rendered a major blow to the financial institutions of the West with a possible trickle-down effect on the entire economy of many countries. Did Gaddafi kill his own people, or did Al Qaeda fighters supported by the USA carry out violence against Libyans so Gaddafi could be blamed on the world stage for doing that? After all, Osama bin Laden, never coined the name Al Qaeda at all, but accepted it as the name the U.S. coined for 9-1-1. The U.S. declared Al Qaeda a terrorist organization run by bin Ladin. Photos of weapons given to Al Qaeda shows American-made military weapons of all types. Most of Al Qaeda in the beginning were young men hired to attack wherever they were directed. The argument given about Libya is the same excuse given about Iraq. Actual films about public appearances of Gaddafi among his own people clearly showed how much the people loved and respected Gaddafi. An hour and 40-minute speech before the UN accused the UN of non-democratic policies and actions, as well as allowing the so-called UN Security Council to act like a terrorist organization. Did we assassinate Gaddafi for legitimate reasons?

So, having raised this incident, as one example of justifying or rationalizing war, we must ask, who benefits the most, the individual countries or the global financial institutions? Through the U.N., does America do little more than follow the lead of these globalist masters? Did America's leaders, in the effort to carry out the agenda against Gaddafi for financial reasons, simply make him the "boogy-man" to vilify him before a world prone to acquiescence of government propaganda? Also, Gaddafi was fighting against the New World Order, the same movement by the globalists, a movement endorsed by George H. and George W. Bush in public commentary, a movement John F. Kennedy tried to warn Americans against and who was assassinated for making that attempt. In one of his most famous speeches to the American people, JFK warned us about the New World Order. Gaddafi didn't like the idea of a "New World Order" run by the super-wealthy non-Muslims. Is the Bush family one of the members of the Deep State?

So many events seem to all be traced back to the shadow government (Illuminati/Deep State/Bilderberg group), all who believe they own the entire planet and have the right to control every country.

So, what is it that we believe, or that we are willing to believe, for no other reason than failure to actually investigate on our own? Are we Americans going to acquiesce to our children, the millennials, believing (polls show 80%) that socialism is the best form of government, and that they are taught this in our colleges and universities by socialist professors? This propaganda has been ongoing for years now in our schools, and this will endanger the entire future of America. Are we going to sit back and grow old while our Marxist children enter the marketplace and vote out our capitalist market economy to vote in national socialism? Are we going to ignore that the pro-socialist Progressives are actually the neo-Nazis pushing national socialism the Nazi Party ushered in under Hitler?

If there is a rumor going around that there is a radical Muslim in the Whitehouse elected as President, and that if it is true, would you settle for a deferential, "*Oh, well, them darn politicians all lie anyway, so what's new?*"? I wouldn't, and I didn't. I looked and learned, and it looks like the facts are indisputable that Obama was not citizen-borne, yet that got "sanitized" and he remained in the Whitehouse as President with a promise of "*fundamental change*" that was NOT at all, the "*fundamental change*" the supporters understood it to be. I talk more about that in another chapter.

What happened to Europe? The "*shadow government*" are very wealthy globalists, people who are so rich and self-righteous that their noses are held so high in the air looking down at everyone else that you can see through their nostrils the evil being that exists. So, here's what I learned.

Taking into consideration that the majority of the European nations are predominantly white by large margins, let's take that fact back 10 or 20 years. In fact, let's go back to the end of World War II, where millions of people engaging in that war or caught in it got killed.

Statistics show that approximately 22-million to 30-million soldiers were killed during WWII. This includes soldiers missing in action, fatalities due to disease, accidents and prisoner of war deaths, along with battle deaths. Including civilians, approximations of all deaths, including civilians, vary between 50-million and 80-million. These numbers include all persons who died as a result of that war.

What made WWII so deadly, at an unforeseen scale, was the targeted extermination of civilian populations. Ethnic cleansing was "alive and well" in WWII, even though it was not unheard of in previous wars, but ethnic cleansing had never before been carried out with the full power of an industrialized society as had Germany against its Jewish, Roma, and disabled populations. Civilian deaths, including Holocaust victims and those killed through crimes against humanity, strategic bombing and population transfers are estimated to total between 19-million and 30-million. Civilians killed by war-related diseases and famine counted between 19-million and 25-million.

Stalinism murdered, many by starvation, between 20 and 40 million people; these vast differences in genocidal volume is because it was very difficult to find the actual numbers, but in Russia, Stalin's personal focus for genocide was because he hated farmers, which constituted a large portion of those he murdered. When there was no more food, having killed the farmers, Russian people were starved to death, and there were even reports of cannibalism, including parents killing young children.

Even China, during Chairman Mao's reign, may be second in the total number of deaths with between 10-million and 20-million (although some say that the civilian toll might have been much higher). (Source: www.historyonthenet.com/how-many-people-died-in-world-war-2.)

Horrible figures, huh?

So, after the war, like in America, war-torn European countries saw millions of their men-folk killed, not counting the women. (It has proven very difficult to get exact numbers between the men, women, and children victims of that war.) Creating new families and thereby renewing future generations of the citizenry was limited by the shortage of men. Over the years, statisticians showed that once the birthrates got as low as 1.3 on their scales, that affected population would eventually be gone forever and there would not be an ability for recovery. Too late.

A high number of the European countries were suffering a post-war low birthrate. The multinational bankers do business with all countries, and a smaller population in any country means less profits for the banks. And who owns most of the banks on this planet? Yeessss, that's right: The Deep State.

Which countries are producers of wealth that are still a large investment for the bankers, war or no war? We can point to Africa, primarily its countries of Somalia, Nigeria, Iraq, Iran, Libya, Saudi Arabia, Yemen, all with oil riches, and some with wealth in diamonds and other precious gems and metals, such as the Congo. For instance, the biggest oil producers in Africa are this: the African continent is home to five of the top oil-producing countries in the world, accounting for more than 8.7 million barrels per day (2014 stats). Nigeria, which is the 13th largest producer in the world, is state run by the Nigerian National Petroleum Corporation (NNPC) and relies heavily on international companies to fund development and provide expertise, companies such as the Chevron Corporation, Exxon Mobil Corporation, Royal Dutch Shell plc, Total S.A., and Eni S.p.A. In Angola, you see the same corporations, as well as Statoil ASA, and China National Offshore Oil Corporation (CNOOC). Algeria, Egypt, Libya, Saudi Arabia, Kuwait, Iran, Iraq, UAE (United Arab Emirates), Algeria, Syria, Uganda, Kenya, Mozambique, Tanzania, Ghana, South Sudan, Congo, Equatorial Guinea, Chad, Gabon, Tunisia, Cameroon, Ivory Coast, South Africa, and Mauritania, all have oil. The global oil companies are likely involved with all of those producing oil.

Chevron, founded in 1906, has an annual revenue of $129.9 billion. Exxon Mobil, founded in 1999, has an annual revenue of $236.8 billion.

I did not mention South Africa because, although originally conquered and created by Europeans and Australians (generally-speaking), the "white" regime has been taken out by the South African indigenous people (and whites continue to be killed off by the now-ruling "class" of indigenous people).

So, what happens to the income of the big banks when countries are rendered ungoverned and disorganized by war? Can we say the big banks lose billions in revenue? Perhaps. Can we also say that the big banks never lose in war because they fund all sides? War is money to the bankers. Do you think the banks are not funding all of the countries involved in the North African wars?

But, while these banks will also invest in the reconstruction of war-torn countries and make billions, a low GDP (gross domestic product) is not good for the banks either. An increase in population is what is needed, and citizens of low birthrate countries are not stepping up to that challenge. This is what has been happening to many of the European Union countries.

For approximately 20 years, immigration was encouraged in some of these countries. But, not enough to cure the problem. The banks needed these countries to have higher numbers of citizens for a larger workforce. Take Finland, for instance; some people think that Finland is a model example for what pure socialism is. But the Finnish pay something like 57% or higher in taxes each year, which is what pays for the socialist programs like free schools, free medical, stuff like that. Where do Finnish get their money? From the _capitalist economy_ system, that's where. It is NOT a true socialist country.

But lest I digress too much, the point is that in a non-war or post-war country, the banks thrive when the country is doing well.

Which brings us back to the problem, i.e., the low birthrate of these EU countries.

I can just imagine the "shadow government" planners sitting around, discussing this problem, and posing ideas on ways to increase birthrates.

One of those ways was chosen. I suggest to you, that in a world stage scenario run by a few, helping to push the North African wars in Iraq, Afghanistan, Libya, Somalia, Yemen, Iran, and others, does two things: one, the war itself makes money for the Deep State; two, it creates a likelihood of high numbers of refugees trying to escape the horrible deaths of Islamic radicals, compared to the non-torture deaths of Western military war means. By that I mean, American soldiers do not torture, behead, stone to death, set on fire, shoot prisoners for target practice, the kind of atrocities well-known to ISIS and Taliban factions, and other Islamic factions.

So, now we have a refugee crisis. Already, the UN and its puppetmasters have achieved acquiescence of the EU countries to accept these refugees, that it would be the "kind" thing to do to help these "poor people" escaping from the horrors of war in their home country. Thousands upon thousands have been migrating to Europe over many years, but in more recent the swarms of groups in the thousands are seen overrunning borders and choosing what country they want to remain in. And, these countries are giving them all "free stuff" which costs are born by the taxes on the working class and business.

But, of particular interest is that a very large percentage of the swarm are from non-Arab Muslim countries, such as Somalia, where Muslim-extremist Somalians are known over every other Muslim country for the sheet level of torture and violent abuse to their victims, especially women and children. Gangs like Boko Haram are not less than diabolical in their torturing of men, women and children.

Videos have been posted on media like YouTube showing the swarms of blacks, nearly all military age men running over borders into towns breaking store windows, vandalizing, robbing, assaulting citizens, and, raping women and girls, even young boys, and demanding "Give me money!!!" But then, we also see the videos of Arab Muslims, and there again is a large portion of military age men without families with them, doing the same things, including surrounding helpless European women by the hundreds, and sexually assaulting them repeatedly. One victim said that the rapists were trying to pull out her hair and tear her breasts from her body. I saw that video too. You could see the men swarming over something, but the woman was barely visible, and the men were like hungry rats on a sugar cookie.

So why would the shadow government choose such people to whom raping women and sexually enslaving them is a normal part of their culture ideology? I ask you: Do you think the puppetmasters give a whit about what happens to these women? The end result, a pregnancy from the rapes, happening to thousands of women, produces children unless aborted, a new generation. Does it matter that the ethnicity is changed, so that the child is no longer just Swedish, but binary with one parent an African black or Arab, and the other Swedish? No, it doesn't matter to the global elites. The elimination of many ethnicities, including the "white" race, has been a goal for many years by the globalists, who are in agreement with the Kalergi Plan, which I've described in this book. Even the U.N. and the EU agree with the Kalergi Plan tenets. Having a single race, dumbed down by interbreeding and brainwashing, produces a more docile race more easily controlled by those running a one-government world, which is the ultimate globalist agenda.

Which brings me to the direct matter at hand, which is the question of whether the Hispanic swarms of thousands from Central and South American countries were just pure happenstance, or just another swarm migration orchestrated by the shadow government? George Soros undoubtedly had a major hand in the crash of Venezuela, which was the most successful and prosperous democratic capitalist country in South America, even beyond the heydays of Argentina. Just like he had a hand in crashing Honduras.

In addition, we should not overlook that among the Hispanic caravans have been extremely violent criminals and drug-cartel members, as well as Arab men coming from through South America as terrorists, some of whom were caught by Border Patrol. There are also Chinese trying to come through with these Caravans; are they communist infiltrators or trying to have a better life in the USA? I do know that for Chinese from Mainland China, a communist regime, getting a visa to immigrate to the USA may take two or more years to get approved. But we must not ignore the criminal danger that unvetted and unapproved migrants can bring upon US citizens if there are open borders. Do not forget that when Fidel Castro took control, he emptied his prisons of all criminals and put them on boats to Florida's shores, and we took them in. Crime rates soared. Just look at what Miami has been turned into as a result. It's like another Cuba.

Based on all that I have researched, it is my conclusion and opinion that this south-of-the-border swarm is our Europe-swarm event. Even though there are millions of migrants here illegally already due to porous borders in the past, one cannot overlook that a great deal of the "caravans" are also young and military-age men, without families with them, all alleging they were escaping the horrible conditions in their home country. Why? We're not suffering from an irreversible decline in birthrates, although we should pay attention to what that rate is. But what we have seen from illegals in the past is a high crime problem and a high rate of imprisonment, sometimes higher than the American-born prison populations. This is not insignificant.

But the USA is also suffering from a different kind of problem. There is a growing movement from former "minority" groups calling for the death of all white people, blaming white people for all of the problems of the world and failing to consider that white people are the ones who have created wealth and the individual opportunity for income advancement for anyone who is willing to work for it. Their birthrate will eventually outnumber "white" births, and whites will become "minority" in America. I wonder if the new "majority" will treat "whites" well, or will they resort to genocide instead, or just mix their blood and eliminate the "white" bloodline altogether. This kind of undermining of America and "white people" does not have to result in sudden changes, but will likely spread out over time. But, make no mistake about, "white people" will become marginalized over time, and ultimately disenfranchised in perhaps the same way as the Jews in Nazi Germany.

Having Hispanic migrants pour in while demanding open borders for everyone is part of the "ethnic cleansing" agenda the Kalergi Plan allows for so as to meld the cultures so as to achieve one ethnicity over time. Whites and Hispanics will continue to intermarry, their children will likely be designated Hispanic if the father is Hispanic, or White if the father is White. Or, the government will devise a system, which the Left is already pushing for, that recognizes the binary outcomes and creates a name according to the mix. In other words, for example, whites/Hispanic bloodlines might be something like "Caucaspanish" and whites/blacks like "AfriCauscas", and so on. But the long-term goal of the Kalergi Plan is when all bloodlines have been merged into one.

Now some people might think that is a good idea, but is it? There is no doubt but that the "white" race has led the world in innovation and morality and inspiring rules to live and flourish by. Yes, we have also had the opposite folks, the criminals, the self-absorbed, the psychopaths in power, the mentally dysfunctional, the Satanists, and the impoverished. Overall, how do we compare with other countries? To answer that, one would have to consider the curve that we are on today, where the high point was WWII where we entered the war when it was clear that we could no longer sit that war out against an entire globalist movement by Germany and a direct attack by Japan.

Yet, here we are, are on a moral decline today, but that is also being orchestrated by the alt-Left, the Marxists, the atheists, the mainstream media services, also owned by the shadow government folks. But if we overlook that the majority of Americans are basically good-hearted people with strong moral convictions, should we let the other part distract us and bully us to their way of thinking? I think not.

Americans cannot afford to have open borders. From the financial burden, and with numbers of people on the government dole, the working class is growing smaller (isn't that an oxymoron?). The government is supported by taxes, from individuals and from business. If the working class is taxed so heavily they cannot afford to pay their bills and living costs, a major loss in tax revenue means there will be no money for the social services that give money to those on welfare and other public aid. So, who will fund this growing socialization of the American marketplace? Not these illegal, uneducated migrants, that's for sure. As free-stuff for them dries up, we'll just see a commensurate rise in crimes. We cannot afford this kind of open migration because most of them can't support themselves after they are here.

B. Why Thousands of Illegal Migrants Pose
An Economic Crisis for America and Americans

With millions of illegal migrants already in the United States, the majority are on government programs like Medicare, Medi-Cal, welfare, social security, and the like, these handouts are in fact paid by the working class of the nation. With many thousands more illegal migrants streaming through porous borders, and with an ideological conflict ongoing between the political Left and the Right, this addition to the welfare rolls mean an ever-increasing financial burden to an already burdened middle-class and business-class through higher taxes.

Already these two classes are becoming smaller than the free-stuff population demands. For example, in California, which Democrat-controlled government wants open borders and as many migrants who wish to come, and is willing to take care of them on the hand-out programs, businesses and middle-class citizens are leaving California by the thousands each year, unable to survive financially in this State. Here, and nationwide, already the working class consists, in high numbers, of both parents having to work to make ends meet, leaving children less and less supervised and guided.

When Americans realize, over time, that they are becoming a sort of "slave class" to support the welfare states as well as billions going to support other countries while the homeless population at home increases along with the national debt, what happens then? Once they realize that things are not going to get better for them, that this increasing burden is not ending, that it is not a cyclical thing, that it is not temporary, what then? What we have seen is the growth of divisiveness through multiculturalism, where the illegal migrant population does not assimilate with the American culture and ideology, but rather segregates themselves into their own communities or associations. What we have seen is the takeover of many of the small businesses or franchises by these non-citizens as well as legal migrants from various countries, thus resulting in the loss of employment opportunities for American-born citizens, especially the younger folk trying to enter into the job market.

How does this rising loss of employment opportunities impact our own younger citizens? At what stage of this drain and burden on Americans create a push-back, a flashpoint perhaps, where anger coalesces into civil unrest by millions of Americans? When the American Dream ceases to be a reality for most Americans, what will Americans do to reverse what has been done to them by our own politicians? Perhaps the correct question is, what can they do?

When the American political system realizes that their failure to attend to Americans, particularly the working class, has been realized by that class of citizens, the backlash from that class could jeopardize the entire economic system as well as the political system. When millions of Americans awaken to the devastation foisted upon them by political leaders, the "System" will be unable to "keep" this class in "their place" and they will emerge from these shackles with focused and unfocused anger, and likely, violence. The Constitution's Second Amendment gives Americans the right to rise against a political and government leadership that harms them; by birthright, all Americans are "militia" with the right to "bear arms" against a government that no longer serves the citizenry, or against another organized entity trying to overthrow the government.

In our times, we have the Progressives pushing socialism through propaganda, mainstream media, the school systems, and by infiltrating the government with legislators and congresspersons. And we have hordes of illegal migrants already in the USA with many thousands slipping through our porous borders while our politicians "debate" the matter.

But there is also another economic factor involved in illegal migrants entering our country: the crime and violence many bring. Aside from the threat to Americans on a personal safety matter, there are the costs of arrests, jail and prison time, the medical care the criminal element receives while in custody, plus the costs of violence to the victims and their families. To estimate these costs is difficult to ascertain but common sense should inform us that they are in the millions, even billions of dollars each year. The evidence shows that the drug cartels not only collect money through the coyotes working for them smuggling the poor and disenfranchised from mother countries, but the cartels also smuggle drugs and guns into America to sell to buyers in gangland and to provide their own members in the USA who are running marijuana farms, meth factories, and other drug-related and sex-related operations. In rural areas of America are cartel farms/operations, but also Muslim enclaves that are training camps for terrorists, all populated by illegal migrants. In the case of Muslim enclaves, they may even by legal migrants who disappear into the enclaves to train for future terrorism in the USA.

Americans must not ignore the growing threats against us by illegal migrants because the actual violence they unleash when the "green light" is given will be horrendous. In the gang world, the term "brothers and others" means that those not in the "brotherhood" are ripe for "victimhood." In Islam, it means all non-Muslims are "infidels" (devils) who must be enslaved or killed off. The Muslims' entire lives consist in daily brainwashing by ideology and its regimented demands. If we choose to ignore these problems, socialist and Islamist alike, we may lose the United States altogether; once it is gone, it may take hundreds of years, and likely not ever, to recover or rebuild. Once the countries go globalist under a single government, freedom as we Americans know it will cease forever. As Pink Floyd's song the Wall goes, we'll all be just "another brick in the wall." No individuality, no creativity, nothing beyond survival, enslaved forever by the global masters.

All of the "open borders" buttercups might want to consider some actual facts about Mexico. Open arms and hugs to thousands, perhaps millions of south-of-the-border Mexicans and Latinos without them going through any legal and formal immigration process at all ensures the destruction and downfall of this country, and you will NOT like what a cesspool of corruption, violence, rape and murder it will become. Central and South American countries always end up with corrupt governments and gang cartels.

So, let's just take a quick look at what happens if an American wants to immigrate to beautiful Mexico. First, if he/she gets caught coming in illegally, it is instant prison in some of the most vile and deadly prisons on this side of the globe. Second, if he/she goes through the legal immigration process, this is how it goes: The following was written by a Tom O'Malley, who was a Director with S.W. BELL in Mexico City:

> "I spent five years working in Mexico. I worked under a tourist Visa for three months and could legally renew it for three more months. After that you were working illegally. I was technically illegal for three weeks waiting on the FM3 approval.

> "During that six months our Mexican and U.S. attorneys were working to secure a permanent work visa called a 'FM3'. It was in addition to my U.S. passport that I had to show each time I entered and left the country. Barbara's was the same, except hers did not permit her to work.

"To apply for the FM3, I needed to submit the following no-tarized originals (not copies):

1. Birth certificate for Barbara and me.
2. Marriage certificate.
3. High school transcripts and proof of gradu-ation.
4. College transcripts for every college I attended and proof of graduation.
5. Two letters of recommendation from super-visors I had worked for at least one year.
6. A letter from the St. Louis Chief of Police indi-cating that I had no arrest record in the U.S. and no outstanding warrants and, was "a citizen in good standing".
7. Finally, I had to write a letter about myself that clearly stated why there was no Mexican citizen with my skills and why my skills were important to Mexico. We called it our 'I am the greatest person on Earth' letter. It was fun to write.

`"All of the above were in English that had to be translated into Spanish and be certified as legal translations, and our signatures notarized. It produced a folder about 1.5 inches thick with English on the left side & Spanish on the right."

"Once they were completed, Barbara and I spent about five hours, accompanied by a Mexican attorney, touring Mexican government office locations and being photographed and fin-gerprinted at least three times at each location, and we re-member at least four locations where we were instructed on Mexican tax, labor, housing, and criminal law and that we were required to obey their laws or face the consequences. **We could not protest any of the government's actions or we would be committing a felony**. We paid out four thou-sand dollars in fees and bribes to complete the process. When this was done, we could legally bring in our household goods that were held by U.S. Customs in Laredo, Texas.

This meant we had rented furniture in Mexico while awaiting our goods. There were extensive fees involved here that the company paid."

"We could not buy a home and were required to rent at very high rates and under contract and compliance with Mexican law."

"We were required to get a Mexican driver's license. This was an amazing process. The company arranged for the licensing agency to come to our headquarters location with their photography and fingerprint equipment and the laminating machine. We showed our U.S. license, were photographed and fingerprinted again and issued the license instantly after paying out a six-dollar fee. We did not take a written or driving test and never received instructions on the rules of the road. Our only instruction was to never give a policeman your license, if stopped and asked. We were instructed to hold it against the inside window away from his grasp. If he got his hands on it you, would have to pay ransom to get it back."

"We then had to pay and file Mexican income tax annually using the number of our FM3 as our ID number. The company's Mexican accountants did this for us and we just signed what they prepared. It was about twenty legal size pages annually."

"The FM3 was good for three years and renewable for two more after paying more fees."

"Leaving the country meant turning in the FM3 and certifying we were leaving no debts behind and no outstanding legal affairs (warrants, tickets or liens) before our household goods were released to customs."

"It was a real adventure and if any of our Senators or Congressmen went through it once, they would have a different attitude toward Mexico."

"The Mexican government uses its vast military and police forces to keep its citizens intimidated and compliant. They never protest at their capitol or government offices, but do protest daily in front of the United States Embassy. The U.S. Embassy looks like a strongly reinforced fortress and during most protests the Mexican military surrounds the block with their men standing shoulder to shoulder in full riot gear to protect the Embassy. These protests are never shown on U.S. or Mexican TV. There is a large public park across the street where they do their protesting. Anything can cause a protest such as proposed law changes in California or Texas."

Please feel free to share this with everyone who thinks we are being hard on the illegals.

VERIFIED!:
http://americandigest.org/mt-archives/issues_episodes /_the_following.php

Now, if you cannot understand why real patriots of America are against "open borders" and "sanctuary cities" or "sanctuary states" I feel sorry for you. Self-blindness to facts will never get you to the right place mentally or physically.

What is readily apparent to those who understand the underlying cultural and behavioral norms of Central and South America citizens and officials, it comes down to this: They have lived so long in harsh, often brutal, corrupt systems that corruption and avarice becomes the everyday fare of just about everyone. Honesty is a virtue, but it is a luxury that such citizens in that entire region simply cannot afford. Desperate times call for desperate measures, and when subjected to desperate times for many years, even a lifetime, is a brainwashing condition, and the result is manifested in the lack of concern for others and the lack of individual honesty overall. Why do such migrants care nothing about America's immigration laws? Because they believe we are weak fat-cats, and they will come here because it is better than what they left.

That does not mean that they will conform to our laws or assimilate into our ideology and culture. To the contrary, they will find their own neighborhoods and those neighborhoods always turn out the same: crime and gang infested, drugs, robberies, assaults, murders. By analogy, it is like throwing up the gates of all of our prisons and letting them all out with nothing, and expecting they'll willfully join the marketplace and earn their way honestly and without violence. Try it, protest for opening the doors of America's prisons, let them all out, and see what happens. No? Of course not, unless you're really stupid. Yet here you are, and of course I'm talking to the "open borders" pro-socialist folks, wanting to let anyone from anywhere in the world waltz right on in and take over our country and destroy it. And somehow you think the end result will actually be Utopian. What you WILL get – after the civil war – will be one of two results: either good patriot Americans will win and re-establish this nation as the Republic it was intended to be and remain, or, if they lose, there will be anarchy, Dystopia, and a totalitarian state, assigned to a line, one which might lead to enforced work areas, another to re-education camps, and another to the death camps that will inevitably follow. Think about that.

A final example: Today, as I add information, I saw an article from December 22, yesterday, that talked about a sex-trafficking ring exposed in Wisconsin. The Green Lake County Sheriff's Office arrested six ILLEGAL ALIENS from Guatemala on December 11th on charges related to sex trafficking. The Sheriff's Office had been contacted by a juvenile girl on the run saying she had just escaped from a residence where she was being sex trafficked; she was able to provide information that allowed the police to start an investigation, obtain a search warrant, and executed that warrant at a house in Manchester,

Wisconsin, where they seized multiple items of evidence connected to the sexual assault of the juvenile.

This is not an isolated incident; rather, it is the reality of illegal immigration. The people who come here illegally and live in the shadows are generally not well-intentioned. Conversely, the kind of immigrants we want to adopt as citizens are the ones with enough integrity, determination and skills to go through our legal immigration process and bring to the table a mindset and skills to add to our greater society, not burden it. We are seeing crimes rising across the nation every new swarm of illegal infiltration, yet the Left is obsessed with open borders regardless of what it costing the American people in terms of our safety, well-being, and quality of life.

You can walk into any Post Office and find Missing Person photos lining the bulletin boards. What are they? Kidnappings, especially if they are children and young women. Where are the ransom demands? There are no ransom demands when the kidnapped person is taken for sex-trafficking or, worse, organ donor trafficking. These kidnapped persons are American citizens, our children, and it is highly likely that they are being trafficked by foreign cartels. Recently the news had an article and video about China engaging in a huge organ replacement "factory", charging huge sums to non-Chinese for organ transplants, thousands of them, yet there were less than a hundred of organ donors who were Chinese. Instead, China is using its prisons, and particularly its political prisoners, for this organ replacement business. From my research I learned that organ harvesting is also being performed by Muslim cartels in South America, along with drug smuggling, arms smuggling, money laundering, and sex-slave trafficking. I suspect that many of our own who come up missing have been kidnapped and destined for one or more of these human-trafficking "industries."

We cannot be a world without borders. The Left's vision of one happy dystopia where everyone coexists peacefully is simply not attainable and never will be. Where we are born and the cultures in which we are raised dramatically and profoundly affect who we become, and some cultures are better than others. Our culture, committed and centered on freedom and personal liberties, as are some others in the West, are now being hammered by cultures like those of the Middle East and south of our own borders who are full of violence, oppression, and hate. America did not create those cultures, and we don't have a moral responsibility to welcome them into America just because the Left and the United Nations say we "should" help these poor, downtrodden peoples.

We have to stop with the self-conceit notion that America is the "world's savior" and are therefore obliged to sacrifice our own self-interests, freedoms, and safety in doing so.

Chapter V:

The Attack on the United States Constitution

Our first job is to protect and secure our Constitution, especially the First and Second Amendments, but we must also determine whether the First Amendment protects sedition and active traitors promoting the overthrow of the American ideology. I say the right to freedom of speech and expression does not intend that the First Amendment allows for its overthrow or application only to socialists as promoted today by those who believe our Constitution is archaic and out of touch with the modern world. It is not, and we must protect it now more than ever.

The First Amendment says:

> Congress shall make no law respecting an establishment of religion, or prohibiting the exercise thereof; or abridging the freedom of speech, or of the press; or the right of the people peaceably to assemble, and to petition the government for a redress of grievances. (Proposed September 25, 1789; ratified December 15, 1791.)

The Second Amendment tells us that patriots are the militia as our birthright, and the right to bear firearms is unassailable and absolute to protect us from the very kind of attempt occurring right now by the pro-Socialists to disarm

Americans so socialism can follow unimpeded like in other countries where
socialists disarmed its citizens before taking over and then killing off millions
of citizens.

The Second Amendment says:

> A well-regulated militia, being necessary to the security of a
> free state, the right of the people to keep and bear arms, shall
> not be infringed. (Proposed September 25, 1789; ratified De-
> cember 15, 1791.)

The Fifth Amendment is also important to Americans:

> No person shall be held to answer for a capital, or otherwise
> infamous crime, unless on a presentment or indictment of a
> grand jury, except in cases arising in the land or naval forces,
> or in the militia, when in actual service in time of war or pub-
> lic danger; nor shall any person be subject for the same of-
> fense to be twice put in jeopardy of life or limb; nor shall be
> compelled in any criminal case to be a witness against him-
> self, nor be deprived of life, liberty, or property, without due
> process of law; nor shall private property be taken for public
> use without just compensation. (Proposed September 25,
> 1789; ratified December 15, 1791.)

The Ninth Amendment is more important than you might think:

> The *enumeration* in the Constitution of *certain rights* shall not
> be construed to deny or disparage *others* retained by the
> people. (Proposed September 25, 1789; ratified December
> 15, 1791.)

The Thirteen Amendment is also broader in scope too:

> Neither slavery nor *involuntary servitude*, except as a pun-
> ishment for crime whereof the party shall have been duly

convicted, shall exist within the United States, or any place subject to their jurisdiction.

The Fourteenth Amendment is very important, as it relates to citizenship, representation, and Payment of Public Debt. I will quote the part about citizenship.

All persons born or naturalized in the United States and subject to the jurisdiction thereof, are citizens of the United States and of the state wherein they reside. No state shall make or enforce any law which shall abridge the privileges or immunities of citizens of the United States; nor shall any state deprive any person of life, liberty, or property, without due process of law; nor deny to any person within its jurisdiction the equal protection of the laws.

So, with all these rights and protections set forth in the "stone" of our Constitution, there for all times and all conditions, why would any person living in the United States or one of its holdings want to destroy this document for the sake of a false narrative about the Utopian ideal of socialism? This Constitution is the offspring of the Articles of Confederation of 1778. Article I of the Articles stated: "The style of this Confederacy shall be "The United States of America." Our country was officially named in 1778.

It was in 1987, in Convention dated September 17th, that the Constitution of the United States became the law of the land. In its Preamble, it begins with:

We the people of the United States, in order to form a more perfect union, establish justice, insure domestic tranquility, provide for the common defense, promote the general welfare, and secure the blessings of liberty to ourselves and our posterity, do ordain and establish this Constitution for the United States of America.

How can anyone fault or criticize the Founders for such a wonderful document set forth with such clarity of purpose in its Preamble?

Let us understand one thing clearly: In our demand that our basic unalienable rights be protected is the inherent requirement of our taking responsibility for those rights. Rights and responsibility go hand in hand, because you cannot have one without the other. We who demand our rights be protected have the responsibility to protect them ourselves, directly and indirectly. We cannot merely leave them to those politicians who have an agenda that is not a part of the responsibilities we vest in them to carry out.

An unalienable right is not an ethereal thing that we pray to or give lip service to. It is a right of passage that lives through us, that makes us the protectors who bear the responsibility for maintaining them against the forces of anarchy and chaos. Political correctness insidiously undermines those rights by redefining them in the most abnormal and unreasonable ways, and insinuating that any other definition or interpretation is evil, abnormal, fascist, or invalid. The carnage of our freedoms is already underway, and gaining ground. If we want to protect those freedoms, it is our responsibility to take whatever steps are necessary to do that. If the State of Virginia is anything, it an example of what patriots must do, at the very least, to protect those unalienable rights set forth in the Bill of Rights and the Constitution.

PART 1. BARACK OBAMA'S INTENT TO DESTROY THE CONSTITUTION

I do not doubt but that hundreds of millions of Americans saw and heard Barack Obama, whose platform promise was "fundamental change" in America, said that the United States Constitution was no longer useful, outdated, and needed to be scrapped. Of course, he never said what "fundamental change" it was going to be.

Despite his college education, he may have acquired political knowledge, but his focus, along the lines of his hatred of anything "colonialism" (like his view of America), was anti-colonialism married to Saul Alinsky's handbook for socialism. Who was his mentor? Who else but George Soros, who found in Barry Soetoro, aka Barack Obama, a willing candidate for infiltrating Congress and the Halls of Power. Now well-funded and guided by the one billionaire (front man for 'higher powers') who has said publicly he wants to destroy the United States as his greatest achievement (having helped destroy other countries already). Obama, hating America because it was founded on colonialism, was certainly willing to 'disguise' himself as a Christian, a good American, and simply wanting to lead the country into better and better times, a Utopia, where equality and tolerance and cooperation among all peoples would rule (isn't that pretty much what the Constitution is also about?). Everything Obama said he stood for was a lie, but it swayed millions, especially women who fawned over him breathlessly like he was Jesus returned to Earth. Churches sang his praises, substituting "Jesus" for "Obama", even little children praying to "Obama" before going to bed. All this was disgusting to me and millions who knew better.

Obama was a con-man, a consummate liar, a polished orator for sure with plenty of con-man charisma. He made lots of promises, but his goal was not for the welfare of Americans, it was to take down what he saw as the result of a "colonial hierarchy" and its residual colonialism elements.

PART 2. THE FIRST AMENDMENT

What we do know these days, is that "political correctness" is merely a new word for Orwellian "double-speak" and "thought control" conducted by the radical Leftist Progressives, including mainstream media and talk shows like "The View." What we know is that the unalienable right to freedom of speech and freedom of expression exists only if citizens conform to the "political correctness" by these Leftists, which includes the LGBT and Feminist movements. As in Europe, places like Sweden, for example, where a male or female child is not male or female anymore, and are not referred to as a him or her, she or he, but some other stupid word – and there are now many – this new language is fast-growing right here on American soil. In Europe, some countries are even passing laws to enforce this new language, and criminalizing those who do not agree. Sweden, Denmark, even Germany.

And freedom of religion is freedom to practice Satanism, or pedophilia, Islamism (diametrically opposed to US ideology), and other forms of immorality, such as beastiality as Cenk Uygur of the Young Turks advocates. But NOT Christianity, because a growing number of people dis-believe that there is a God or that Jesus was God's Son. Scientists like Steven Hawkins said there is no "proof" of God as a matter of science, so the disbelievers have come to believe there is no God because the scientific community says so. Clearly, they do not understand that the building blocks of all like, DNA, could not possibly have been created through the Darwinist thought of randomness. Randomness produces nothing, and DNA could not have been produced by randomness over time. Not possible.

All over the world, as it has been for some 1400 years, Islamists have been murdering Christians, and still do, as they try to stamp out Christianity altogether so that they can impose Islamism on the entire world, which is a unquestionably violent, murderous, perverted ideology that only a Satanist could dream up. And Islamists are using the First Amendment to insinuate Islam into America, and are rapidly building mosques all over this country. And we let them and, in so doing, we are committing future suicide. Islam is not a religion, as I have said earlier, it is a way of life, an ideology masquerading as a religion, a totalitarian-type governance, where women are just "things" for subjugation, sexual perversion, and making babies.

Our immigration laws clearly do NOT allow active socialists, communists, or totalitarians to immigrate into the United States, so why are we allowing Islamists to come here and proliferate and proselytize? Have we gotten comfortable with shooting ourselves in the foot?

The First Amendment identified rights are unalienable rights, not created by man but God bestowed, but that unalienable status does not mean being totally stupid either; it is there so that we might protect ourselves in a peaceful and tolerant manner, so that we might worship a God who is all about peace and love and tolerance, so that we might associate with those who are of the same mind about the First Amendment, despite our various differences and beliefs and cultures. The Ninth Amendment makes clear that the limited enumeration of rights in the First Amendment are not the only rights protected by the Constitution.

A country based originally and through many decades on immigration had, and has, as its foundation, the demand that all immigrants, regardless of culture or country, learn English, assimilate not as an African-American, or Asian-American, or Irish-American, or Hispanic-American, none of that divisive doctrine, but as an American who does not come here as a burden to anyone but who brings something of value, skills, a profession, a desire to achieve, and then go forward in this new land that applauds and awards by a merit-based work ethic, not demanding a hand-out, free stuff, or a sense of entitlement that they should receive Social Security (they paid nary a dime into) and welfare (to be supported by America's working class).

Our First Amendment is not an "open season" to live without any rules or ethics or contributions and with a misguided sense of entitlement.

This is what America and true Americans should NOT stand for or tolerate. We patriots, Republicans, Democrats, Independents, or Libertarians, should all be willing to carry signs in protest and say to all those freeloaders arriving here to "GET YOUR HANDS OUT OF MY POCKETS!!" and "WORK FOR A LIVING LIKE WE DO!!"

But let us delve further into the right to free speech, freedom of expression, and freedom of religion, and take a look at what that means to Islamists.

Going back a few years further than the migrant Muslim swarm that has created unprecedented crime rates, especially rape, as they crossed from country to country, England for a number of years had been allowing Muslims to immigrate into England. The crime rates from Muslims skyrocketed, and English citizens cried out for justice against these immigrants. Muslim gangs cornered English girls and raped them, often taking them from their homes and keeping them prisoner for sex and prostitution. As the outcry got louder, what did the government do? Did it let its police force drop the hammer on these perverted criminals? No. Did it allow the news media to report on crime by Muslims and actually identify them? No. Did it even identify the crime of rape? No. Instead, they called it a cultural problem because of the Muslim ideology that allows Muslims to rape any non-Muslim girl of any age. So, the British government identified these gangs as "grooming" gangs. Grooming! They're not 'grooming' their hair, for Christ's sake, they're committing RAPE.

The British government so wanted to welcome Muslims into the country and show how nice and tolerant and open the British are to immigrants, they allowed their own citizens to be victimized without recourse. For years, and even today, Great Britain rarely allows Christians from other countries where they are being persecuted and murdered to immigrate to England, but they welcome Muslims from an ideology of terror and death to flood in.

So, what next? In April 2018, Britain's All-Party Parliamentary Group on British Muslims began work on establishing a "working definition of Islamophobia that can be widely accepted by Muslims, political parties and the government". How well do you think that went? Muslims demanded, the Brits caved, no middle ground, no compromise, that's how it went.

In December 2018, the group concluded its work with a "Report on the inquiry into a working definition of Islamophobia / anti-Muslim hatred." The report defines "Islamophobia" as a form of racism, conflating religion with ethnic origin or nationality: "Islamophobia is rooted in racism and is a type of racism that targets expressions of Muslimness or perceived Muslimness." What?! Expressions of Muslimness?! Does that mean the rape gangs are free to rape because that is their Islamic expression validated by their Quran? Does that mean that it is OK for Muslims to express hatred for all Christians and, for that matter, all non-Muslims because Muslims consider them "infidels" (demons) according to the Quran?

The report, furthermore, claimed that a definition of Islamophobia is "instrumental" to "the political will and institutional determination to tackle it." What?!

The National Police Chiefs' Council, which represents the leaders of law enforcement in England and Wales, have also expressed concern with the broadened definition. Its chair, Martin Hewitt, said:

> "We take all reports of hate crime very seriously and will investigate them thoroughly. However, we have some concerns

about the proposed definition of Islamophobia made by the all-party parliamentary group on British Muslims. We are concerned that the definition is too broad as currently drafted, could cause confusion for officers enforcing it and could be used to challenge legitimate free speech on the historical or theological actions of Islamic states. There is also a risk it could also undermine counter-terrorism powers, which seek to tackle extremism or prevent terrorism".

Richard Walton, a former head of Counter-Terrorism Command of the Metropolitan Police, wrote:

"Adopting the definition would hand the initiative to those who have been trying to dismantle the Government's Countering Violent Extremism programme for years; it is no surprise to see many of those same campaigners and radical groups have been closely involved in the APPG's work in developing the definition (as authors or sources)... how could the police or anyone else disprove that they had targeted an expression of 'perceived Muslimness'?...

"If the Government accepts the APPG definition of Islamophobia, all of these [anti-terrorism] powers are more likely to be challenged by anti-Prevent campaigners and their supporters who would seek to label police officers 'Islamophobic' (and, therefore, racist)...

"... Whole government departments, the entire police service, intelligence agencies, the Crown Prosecution Service (CPS), judiciary and HM Prison and Probation Service could be branded and labelled 'institutionally Islamophobic' by anti-Prevent campaign groups. It would be an allegation that would be impossible to refute, owing to the indistinct and imprecise nature of the APPG definition..."

Similarly, the UK government, according to a Buzzfeed report, is concerned that defining Islamophobia as a form of racism "could mean people who criticise aspects of Islam might be prosecuted under discrimination laws."

.

The UK government is right, of course. Islam represents an idea, not a nationality or an ethnicity. The conventional purpose of most hate-speech laws is to protect people from hatred, not ideas. The new proposed definition would criminalize criticism of Islam.

Considering the origins of the All-Party Parliamentary Group (APPG) on British Muslims, that is probably the whole point. The APPG on British Muslims, according to its website, was established in July 2017. The organization is chaired by MPs Anna Soubry and Wes Streeting and is meant to build on the work of a former APPG: the APPG on Islamophobia. That came into existence as the result of a meeting at the House of Commons in March 2010, hosted by, among others, the Muslim Council of Britain (MCB) — the largest Muslim organization in the UK, and that claims to be representative of British Muslims. It is linked to the Muslim Brotherhood [2]. By November 2010, after the APPG on Islamophobia had been formed, it quickly ran into trouble. The Muslim organization that was appointed as its secretariat turned out to be the Muslim extremist organization iENGAGE, which has since changed its name to MEND [3]. Both MEND and the Muslim Council of Britain are among the many organizations and individuals that contributed written evidence [4] to the report on a definition of Islamophobia.

Wes Streeting, co-chair of the All-Party Parliamentary Group on British Muslims, recently criticized the government's refusal to adopt the new definition:

> "What we're up against goes wider than anti-Muslim hatred. It is structural, often unconscious, bias... It is particularly disappointing to see a noisy chorus of vocal opposition making arguments in bad faith that accuse us of trying to use the term Islamophobia to shut down criticism of Islam and introduce blasphemy laws by the back door. In fact, our report makes it crystal clear that our definition does not preclude criticism

of Islam or Islamic theology. God, if you believe in such a thing, doesn't need protection from criticism."

Streeting appears to pretend that Islam allows either criticism of Allah and Mohammed, or free choice of religion.

That is not the case: Sharia law prohibits questioning, seeming to regard it as a form of blasphemy:

> "O you who have believed, do not ask about things which, if they are shown to you, will distress you. But if you ask about them while the Qur'an is being revealed, they will be shown to you. Allah has pardoned that which is past; and Allah is Forgiving and Forbearing." [Qur'an 5:101, Sahih International translation]

> "A people asked such [questions] before you; then they became thereby disbelievers." [Qur'an 5:102, Sahih International translation]

The prohibition against questioning also seems why several Muslim organizations, such as the Organisation of Islamic Cooperation (OIC), fight for the introduction of blasphemy laws in the West, to prevent questioning Islam.

The proposed definition also does not take into account the threats ex-Muslims receive from Muslims (here, here, here and here), and how the definition would only make life more difficult for those Muslims who dare to leave or speak out. According to Nikita Malik, writing in Forbes:

> "The term Islamophobia has a broad meaning that can easily be used to restrict free and fair discussion about the Islamic religion and Islamist extremism. Instead, an alternative definition of Anti-Muslim Hatred should be specific and narrow. It should focus on addressing bigotry directed at individuals, and avoid censoring debate or freedom of expression on religion. Finally, a comprehensive definition of

Anti-Muslim Hatred must take intra-Muslim hatred into account to protect those who want to speak freely or express themselves differently."

Whether that will happen remains to be seen.

(Source: www.gatestoneinstitute.com, by Judith Bergman, a columnist, lawyer and political analyst, is a Distinguished Senior Fellow at Gatestone Institute, in New York, New York.)

So, what does all that mean for America? As I have shown in various sections of this book, Christianity is under attack by Muslims all over the world, and genocide is what it can be called. In England, and in other European countries like France, Sweden, Spain, and others, the migrant swarm of North African Muslims can only be described accurately as an "invasion." The imams have openly proclaimed Islam will someday rule the world, and everywhere they end up they over-populate with multiple wives to take the "take road" of birthing new populations that eventually overwhelm a country's indigent population. But, in the meantime, they rant and rail against non-Muslims and caste themselves as victims of racial and religious discrimination, demanding justice from the United Nations and so on, pushing false narratives to cow governments and populations into giving in to their demands.

America is doing the same thing, on an ever-broadening scale. Look at Alexandra Ocasio-Cortez and her Muslim cohorts, already making a mockery of our culture and political system, but no one wants to kick them down the road as inept, incompetent, racist, and anti-American, which they are, but instead they are tolerated.

We are losing the right to criticize enemies of the State by the instrument called "political correctness" or Orwellian thought control. We are giving in to a people and an ideology that seeks nothing more than to destroy anyone who does not believe as they do.

Instead, our own government, under Obama, put Christian fundamentalists, whatever that means, on its own terrorist lists, as well as Constitutionalists and patriots. And we allowed it with little more than a whimper in protest. Why? I haven't seen any news where President Trump has intervened and removed Christians, Constitutionalists and patriots off the DOJ's, DHS's, FBI's, and the CIA's terrorist watch lists. If he has done so, I would surely like to know, and I would certainly not want to think that our own government is turning against our own ideology in favor of the pro-Socialists and Islamists's world takeover agenda. Although I haven't heard anything about Trump removing patriots et al. from these terrorist lists, I suspect that he will do so or has already done so.

We see and hear our own youthful Millennials, already brainwashed towards Socialism in our own schools and colleges, aligning themselves with the pro-Socialist Progressives, and actually believing the false narrative that socialism is the path to Utopianism.

The First Amendment, in my humble opinion, is not designed as an open "vehicle" for enemies of the State and haters of the ideology on which the United States was founded. Free speech, and freedom of expression, was never meant to confer anything more than the right to protest against a government that had become inept and oppressive in a way that totally undermines the founding ideology of our Republic. If we call it a capitalist democracy, that's acceptable because we're talking only about a merit-based ideology where the American Dream can be achieved by anyone who takes the time and makes the effort to earn their way along the path to goals set along the way to ultimate achievement. Just because some folks aren't willing to make the effort, and instead complain about racial discrimination as the watchword typically used by them, doesn't mean we should cater to their disgruntlement and failures and tear down the entire system so we can all rot in misery and poverty with them.

There is, without doubt, a growing danger with misinformed Millennials. Journalist Lloyd Marcus, on July 30, 2019, wrote an article in The American-Thinker magazine, in which Marcus, self-titled "The Unhyphenated American", showed an excerpt from an email of a misinformed white millennial:

> Mr. Marcus, as a black man, if you don't agree in part with
> Mr. Kaepernick, I feel bad for you. I am white, and feel that
> the issues facing the black community in the US from the

police, legal elements, property, education are skewed, and need to be rectified. I am concerned that someone with your pulpit isn't out there helping out.

Marcus concluded that,

"This well-intentioned young emailer is infected with anti-Americanism via public education and casual contact with Democrats, Hollywood, social media, and fake news media. He is a prime candidate for recruitment into a terrorist hate group like Antifa.

Everything he thinks he knows is wrong. For example: Blacks are not persecuted by police. Research data confirms that police are the greatest defenders of black lives. A Harvard study said there is zero evidence of police racial bias. The greatest threat to black lives are black criminals.

Haters of America and Trump had a cow, accusing Trump of racism, for daring to tweet the ugly truth about Baltimore which is a hellhole of crime and record black-on-black homicides. I praise God for our president's courage. Trump is making Democrats accountable for the pain, suffering, and lawlessness in cities they have controlled for decades. I say, "Right on, brother Trump. Right on!"

My young emailer believes education is skewed against blacks. The opposite is true. K-8 white students are outrageously taught they were born racist and should feel guilty for their "white privilege." The fact that blacks drop out of school in epidemic numbers has nothing to do with white America. It has everything to do with fatherless households and an abandonment of biblical morality.

Because millennials have a different news feed than us older folks, my young emailer is probably clueless about numerous important cultural and political issues. I suspect he does not know San Francisco is so overrun with homeless people leaving piles of human excrement on the streets that maps are provided to help tourists avoid them. Dangerous diseases are resurfacing.

He probably supports Planned Parenthood not knowing that it was founded by a racist largely for the purpose of exterminating blacks. My emailer doesn't know Planned Parenthood was caught selling dead baby body parts for profit. He does not know a majority of Planned Parenthood chop shops are located in black neighborhoods.

He is probably pro-choice, not knowing that Democrats seek to extend a woman's choice to murder her baby even after the child is born.

Filling the minds of our youths with lies and hatred for our country, traditions, institutions, Trump, conservatives, and Republicans has gotten dangerously out of hand. The viral videos of angry mobs boldly attacking police with impunity places the lives of all Americans at risk. If anarchists can get away with assaulting police, it is only a matter of time before a MAGA cap wearer is killed. A while ago, radical homosexuals disrespectfully entered a Catholic church and wreaked havoc. The next step will be assassinating preachers in the pulpit for preaching the Bible. A frighteningly high number of college students believe they have the moral high ground to physically beat up people for speaking conservatism.

Anti-American progressives' tactic of hijacking the hearts and minds of youths is not new. Hitler dehumanized Jews in the minds of Germany's youths. Police and Trump supporters have been dehumanized in the minds of far too many millennials.

Progressives' domination of public education has successfully created a generation clueless to the evils of socialism. An alarming 49% of millennials favor socialism over capitalism. Youths do not know socialism has failed everywhere it has been tried. Socialism always leads to wealthy dictators living high on the hog while the people barely survive on crumbs.

Socialism kills the incentive to strive for excellence. It spreads mediocrity equally. A professor gave a great example of the unfairness of socialism. You're an "A" student. A classmate is an "F" student. The teacher gives both of you a "C." That's socialism.

A few years ago, the waiter of Mary's and my wedding anniversary dinner was outstanding. I tipped him generously. Rather than rewarding him for his hard work and professionalism, socialism would force him to put his tips into a jar to be distributed between waiters who don't care, take long smoke breaks and keep their heads buried in their iPhone. In a nutshell, socialism punishes achievers to benefit irresponsible non-achievers.

Marcus cites the following quotes, and asks us all to spread the truth.

> "The problem with socialism is that you eventually run out of other people's money." — Margaret Thatcher

Please tell your representative to oppose socialism by signing the petition at DJKM.org/Liberty.

I bet my young emailer does not know progressives always promote their radical initiatives as the polar opposite of what they truly are. When progressives say free healthcare for all, they really mean outrageously expensive and rationed healthcare. Progressive bureaucrats will dictate behavior and decide who lives or dies. A caller on the Rush Limbaugh radio show said he pays $3000 a month for ObamaCare and his deductible is $12,000.

Bottom line, folks — we must stop allowing progressives to own the hearts and minds of our youths. Speak up!

> "Silence in the face of evil is itself evil. God will not hold us guiltless. Not to speak is to speak. Not to act is to act." — Dietrich Bonhoeffer

American patriots cannot just ignore the problems and the wickedness that drives those who hate America, its ideology, its religion, and its system. If we remain complacent, ignoring this anti-American movement, and we lost it, we'll never get it back. There are too many forces against us who will likely, at some point along the way, act against us, either by invasion, or some other way, but they will act when we are weakened.

Step up, Americans. Whatever Party ties you have, put them aside. This is a matter of common ground that adversely affects all of us. We can't play politics with this mess.

PART 3. THE SECOND AMENDMENT

The following is a direct quote from the United Nations:

> "States should work toward the introduction of appropriate national legislation, administrative regulations and licensing requirements that define conditions under which firearms can be acquired, used and traded by private persons. In particular, they should consider the prohibition of unrestricted trade and private ownership of small arms and light weapons." — The United Nations' Report of the Group of Government Experts on Small Arms, August 19, 1999.

American patriots who support the Bill of Rights and Constitution of the United States should do all that is possible to protect the Second Amendment's guarantees to be militiamen and owners of firearms without restrictions designed to suppress ownership or to disarm Americans completely. Let's take a look at relatively recent events.

In 2012, the government of Great Britain initiated a new policy restricting gun ownership which included a "buy back" program. Despite their reservations, gun owners turned in all firearms, including collections of antique firearms, all of which went to the metal grinders for destruction. Apparently having some hindsight regrets, British citizens by the thousands took to the streets in silent protest, like at a funeral, and let their government know they had betrayed the people of Great Britain.

The history of disarmament in various countries around the world has always been a prelude to a tyrannical government. A disarmed citizenry is a citizenry helpless against the despots who always arrive to take over and oppressively control the citizens, typically resulting in hunger, violence, and loss of all human freedoms. A citizen become the property of the State, meaning that one's life becomes meaningless should the government so choose. Rulers-and-serfs is always the result of disarmament and tyranny.

One senior interviewed during the protest said it simply: "Our livelihood, our way of life, employment, we're finished. It's as serious as that."

The narrator of the video said this: "This is what a disarmed country looks like. This is how little is left once free men and women surrender their right to own a firearm. The silence was deafening, marching like a defeated people, thousands of shooters and sportsmen grabbing at one last chance to resist, fighting for a freedom they had already lost" ... "Gun owners were shamed into silence while politicians and the anti-gun forces moved swiftly, turning two tragic shootings into legislative opportunity."

A proponent of confiscation was female Gill Marshall-Andrews, Chairperson of the Gun Control Network, who said: "It becomes quite clear, if you want a safer society with lower gun violence, then you've got to reduce your gun ownership."

Albie Fox, Director of the Sportsman's Association, said: "The main thing that's been destroyed in the U.K. is democracy. The simplistic-minority has hoodwinked the media and the public into believing what they've done is right."

And then there is Australia. It took just two winks for an all-out ban on firearms to occur. The government issued a deadline to turn in all weapons, and made gun owners instant criminals on the day after that deadline if they had turned in their firearms. One police officer characterized the loss as follows: "It's the feeling of being a second-rate citizen. It's the feeling of being a Jew in Nazi Germany. It's the same feeling." Another gun collector, with a collection of antique and unique firearms worth thousands of dollars, said this: "My family fought for this country, for his rights, for my rights, and I did it for nothing, because what we've got now is, I believe we're heading for close to a dictatorship."

Gun owners in Great Britain and Australia admit that it is they who have only themselves to blame for not standing up when they should have and fight back against the proponents of gun confiscation. Gun dealers and shops in both countries lost their livelihood, including dealerships that went back generations. One owner warns, "The biggest mistakes gun owners could make is disunity, ... and the media and the politicians will exploit that lack of unity." Australians were shamed and brow-beaten into not only giving up the firearms on the government's list by the politicians and media but also by public confiscation proponents, but all their guns, giving in to a complete loss of their freedom to own firearms.

This "gesture policy" created by the government resulted in a complete loss of rights for the government's false promise of safer communities. In fact, in the years that followed, criminal cartels were emboldened because they retained their (illegal) firearms and the robberies and assaults rose dramatically. So much for "safer" communities.

It must be said that the loudest proponents of gun control and disarmament are women who lack perspective on the truism that a community rich in firearms is in fact a safer community because law-abiding citizens can, will, and do intervene in crimes committed before the police are even able to arrive and intervene. If crimes go up in a disarmed society, is that the price law-abiding citizens must pay for this knee-jerk reaction by gun control proponents? Are their lives and abilities for self-defense just "collateral damage" for a disarmament policy? Would it be better to say that if there is "collateral damage" in either direction, then it should be smaller numbers when the citizens are armed and can intervene in criminal incidents than when they are unarmed and can do nothing at all until the police arrive? We have seen how much damage a lone shooter can do in "Gun Free" zones where law-abiding citizens are unarmed and helpless to intervene. Why should we suffer that condition because proponents of gun control seem to lack logical perspective?

As Australian Chief Inspector of Police (RET) Gary Fleetwood pointed out very clearly and prophetically: "The crime rates not going to drop. The use of firearms by criminals will still be there and they will obtain their firearms on the black market, and the black market in Australia is booming at the moment." Another official concurred: "I think the criminals are absolutely rejoicing in the fact that the legal guns are taken out of circulation."

In fact, one British criminal interviewed said this about gun confiscation: "It's a crock! It's made no difference whatsoever. I mean, the people on the street they're going to get their guns anyway. No problem."

Another British gun-owner said: "As soon as they (gun control proponents) suggest a ban on one type of weapon, say "NO!", do everything you can to oppose it, because it's just the beginning of a broader ban."

The Left's claim that disarmament will make us all safe overlooks several facts that refute that. First of all, criminals will use the black market to get theirs. So, I'm going to tell you a little about that black market.

Islamic jihadis have migrated into the Triple Frontier area of South America (Paraguay, Brazil, Argentina) and established major criminal activities, and, as well, have also aligned themselves with three major drug cartels. There are two major Islamic factions there, one, the Barakat family, who are also in Australia but who originate from the Middle East. The other is Nader Mohammad Farhat, a top Hezbollah financier recently extradited to the US from Paraguay to face drug money laundering charges. Both of them are top financiers for both Hamas and Hezbollah jihadis, who are being stationed and trained in the Triple Frontier area, and then are being smuggled into the US and who infiltrate into the Hispanic caravans trying to overrun our southern border. These Islamic terrorism-funders are also engaged in drug smuggling, human and sex trafficking, as well as **weapons trafficking**. They are selling all manner of weapons, including explosives, to the street gangs and Islamic sleeper cells here in this country. Many of these weapons are military-style automatic weapons, and huge amounts of ammunition, all of which is readily available in America's own underground marketplace. Furthermore, Islamists have been immigrating to Mexico for years now, and have their own communities, and they are proselytizing to the natives and getting Hispanics to join them. This is why in the Hispanic caravans you see Hispanics carrying their signs of "F**K America!" and signs that boast how they are going to take back "their" country. They're not coming here on vacation; they are coming here to destroy.

The idea that disarming American citizens will make the US safer is not just bogus on its face, it is extremely dangerous to all citizens because to criminals and jihadis, a disarmed America is prime victim **terror-tory** (my term for territory of terror) at which point we will experience the "killing fields" of Cambodia right here throughout the United States. Our ability to fight off the numerous factions that want to destroy America and turn it into the "killing fields" like Cambodia is tied directly to not just preserving the Second Amendment but in rolling back ALL of the nit-picking gun regulations imposed by the gun-grabbers thus far, and I mean every single one. The Second Amendment does NOT need to be open to "interpretation"; it was written clear and simple so the basest of idiots could understand what it says. If we wind up in a civil war, which the alt-Left is definitely pushing, we will find ourselves facing factions who are armed with military-grade weapons, and our little .22 or .38 pistols or .40 Glocks, or hunting rifles and shotguns are not what we will need the most. We will need the so-called "assault" rifles the Left seems determined to ban with all their restrictions on these rifles as well as on ammunition. We will be, without question, in the fight of our lives.

In America, we have seen the successful efforts by anti-gun proponents chip away little by little at the Second Amendment gun rights, from mandatory registration (so law enforcement has a record of where all guns are in the event of confiscation mandates), to types of firearms, pistols, rifles and shotguns with certain features, even to types of ammunition. The National Rifle Association (NRA) is the one powerful organization that has thus far prevented the destruction of the Second Amendment and the disarmament of Americans. But the NRA is not fully supported as it should be, even by those who do not own guns but who believe in the sanctity of the Second Amendment, and it is the only national organization standing between the Second Amendment and the gun-grabbers. Yet too many citizens who are pro-Second Amendment simply do not help the NRA in any way to keep that Amendment safe. It's like Superman standing up to the villains of the world while the People stand around holding Kryptonite to weaken him.

Women in particular, who are not typically interested in guns at all, seem to think they know best on the issue of disarmament as a "public safety" policy, yet they do NOT consider or understand why public safety would be greatly enhanced if there were no restrictions against firearms in the hands of law-abiding citizens, and open carry and concealed carry were the rule, not the exceptions. Gun free zones are an open invitation to criminals and wackos who do not have to purchase firearms through gun shops/dealers.

Quite frankly, because women typically do NOT enter the military, and do NOT fight on the frontlines of WAR, and who stay home while the MEN go into battle, women should NOT have a say in what the Second Amendment is for, what it says, or what it means, unless they can simply agree that it IS clear and needs no re-interpretation. I like women, but except for a few, they are not warriors. Their very nature is maternal, which instinct can cloud discussion about things that should be left to the male gender whose very nature has always been protective, i.e., a warrior. Their very upbringing has been as the giver, the nurturer, the weaker sex. Even the Bible recognizes the male gender as the head of the household. Equality of opportunity is one thing, and both genders deserve to be treated equally in the marketplace, but in matters of violence, like war and fighting for one's safety and country, it is in the male gender's DNA to take that warrior role. I don't say this to denigrate women, but if the male gender continues to cater to women about firearm controls and disarmament, we'll lose everything men have already died for, our freedom, our country, everything.

In a speech on Civilian Disarmament, William Norman Grigg quoted Sir Walter Raleigh warning that the first goal of any would-be tyrant is "to unarm his people of weapons, money and all means whereby they could resist his power."

But could this happen in the US? Yes, it happened in New Orleans after Hurricane Katrina. The DEA targeted people who looked like they had packed belongings and were exiting New Orleans. This profile resulted in numerous cars being pulled over by the DEA and New Orleans police, and asked if they had any firearms. When there were firearms, the DEA confiscated them, often breaking them against the sidewalk curbs. Were they deterring criminals, or were they deterring law-abiding citizens exiting that hurricane area from defending themselves against looters and predators? During Katrina there were a large number of thugs who did not leave New Orleans but who remained behind looting, robbing, and assaulting in what became a lawless area. But the police instead targeted families with belongings, figuring if there were guns to be found it would be in cars with families exiting the area.

Citizens who were stopped and subsequently interviewed by the NRA described how when stopped by the police the police were several people at once, all pointing military-style weapons at them, not just pointing them but aiming them, fully prepared to fire upon any provocation or perceived provocation, all ready to slaughter citizens. The police took their guns, refused to give receipts, and sent the citizens on their way. The police recognized no "due process rights" at all.

As I have written about elsewhere in this book, the United Nations has long been after countries to disarm their citizens. Great Britain did so. But the UN has long been critical of the USA for not criminalizing all firearm ownership. When I realized how Obama vis-à-vis Soros vis-a-vis the Illuminati had set in motion an active agenda for destroying the US for the NWO folks, which agenda included race war, civil unrest and violence, civil war even, and worked out a deal with the UN to enter the US and confiscate all firearms, and then to put Interpol in charge of all federal, state, and local police agencies, it occurred to me that Obama not only committed a crime of treason, but also there is the question of whether

America's law enforcement agencies would agree to be subjugated under the UN when its agenda includes gun confiscation.

History shows that the UN supported socialist Chavez's disarmament of civilians in Venezuela, leaving its citizens no means to fight back against what became an oppressive, murderous regime, destroying one of the most successful democracy's South or Central America. Let's not forget how Argentina had risen to a very successful democracy until the UN got involved there as well, again supporting a socialist takeover. The UN also sponsored civilian disarmament in Brazil, which became another socialist country at the expense of the citizenry.

President Obama promised not to come after American's guns. Instead, he broke his promise and began speaking up against the right to keep firearms by U.S. citizens.

On September 25, 2013, Secretary of State John Kerry signed the United Nations Arms Treaty (Arms Trade Treaty) as a multilateral treaty that regulates the international trade in conventional weapons. Kerry did so on behalf of the Obama administration. In October of that year, a bipartisan group of 50 senators and 181 representatives released concurrent letters to President Obama pledging their opposition to ratification of the ATT. Four Democratic senators sent a separate letter to the President stating that "because of unaddressed concerns that this Treaty's obligations could undermine our nation's sovereignty and the Second Amendment rights of law-abiding Americans [they] would oppose the Treaty if it were to come before the U.S. Senate. Even today, as former President, he actively speaks up for firearm restrictions.

In 2014, after the Newtown shooting, President Obama indeed called for gun control. On December 14, 2014, Obama announced new executive orders on gun control, requiring all firearms dealers to obtain licenses, new funding for mental health treatment, and exploring ways to increase gun safety. In 2018, Obama threw his support behind the teenagers vocally advocating for stricter gun control after the Florida school shooting.

But just for perspective, did you know the impact of the Swiss Civilian Militia on Hitler's war plans? Every citizen is expected to have a firearm, that the citizen receive training in its use, and every citizen is a militia person (as in America's Second Amendment). This is an excerpt from Dave Kopel's review of Target Switzerland by Stephen P. Halbrook, entitled "The Impact of the Swiss Civilian on Hitler's War Plans."

"By the summer of 1940, there was only one country on Germany's borders whose free press and rights of assembly allowed the Third Reich to be publicly and lawfully denounced as the evil empire that he was. In every country on Germany's borders–except Switzerland–Jews, Gypsies, homosexuals and other targets of Hitler's hate were sent to extermination camps. But there was no Holocaust on Swiss soil. Switzerland protected her own Jews, and sheltered many more refugees of all religious backgrounds. Had America sheltered refugees at the same per capita rate as Switzerland, the United States would have taken in over three million refugees. Instead America accepted hardly any.

In all the countries that Hitler conquered, the economy was plundered for use in the Nazi war machine. As a neutral, Switzerland did trade with Germany and Italy, and with the Allies. (For the Allied trade, the Swiss smuggled out precision ball bearings and other military equipment disguised in consumer products like watches.) But unlike in the countries which Hitler conquered, the only products that Hitler could get from Switzerland were what he could buy at full price.

Target Switzerland includes the maps of the evolving Germans invasion plans for "Case Switzerland." Yet although the Germans several times massed troops on the Swiss border for an invasion, the invasion never went forward. With so many reasons to invade Switzerland, why did the Nazis desist?

The Nazis could have eventually conquered Switzerland, but at a fearful price. The Wehrmacht expected 200,000 German casualties; it would have taken a very long time to remove the

Swiss military from the Alpine "Reduit" to which they planned to make a stand. And by the time the Swiss were defeated, every bridge and train track and everything else of value to the conquerors would have been destroyed.

The reason that Switzerland was too difficult to invade—in contrast to all the other nations which Hitler conquered in a matter of weeks—was the Swiss militia system. Unlike all the other nations of Europe, which relied on a standing army, Switzerland was (and still is) defended by a universal militia. Every man was trained in war, had his rifle at home, was encouraged to practice frequently, and could be mobilized almost instantly. The Swiss militiaman was under orders to fight to the last bullet, and after that, with his bayonet, and after that, with his bare hands. Rather than having to defeat an army, Hitler would have had to defeat a whole people.

Conversely, the Swiss citizen militia, with its extensive network of fortifications, had no offensive capability. The Swiss militia was not going to sweep into Berlin; modern Swiss-bashers who condemn the nation for not declaring war fail to understand that by keeping the Axis out of Switzerland, the Swiss were already doing everything they could for the Allied cause.

From the Anschluss of Austria to the Fall of France, Hitler swallowed nation after nation where cowardly ruling elites surrendered the country to the Nazis—either before the shooting began, or a few weeks afterward. But such a surrender would have been impossible in Switzerland, explains Halbrook. The Swiss governmental system was decentralized, with the separate 26 cantons, not the federal government, having the authority. The federal government did notify the Swiss people that in case of a German invasion, any claim that there had been a Swiss surrender should be disregarded as Nazi propaganda. And because the military power was in the hands of every Swiss man, the federal government would have been unable to surrender had it ever wanted to. Nothing could stop the Swiss militiamen from fighting to the very end.

America's Founders admired Switzerland as a "Sister Republic" amidst the despotisms of Europe. The American Founders—like the Swiss—understood the moral implications of a universal militia system: a people who are trained to self-reliance and responsibility will defend their freedom to the utmost. But a people who rely on a professional standing army may not have the nerve to resist tyranny.

When, as William Shirer wrote from Berlin, the lamps of freedom were going out all over Europe, they burned brighter than ever in Switzerland, as the Swiss people maintained their democracy, their right to assemble, and their freedom of religion. And the Swiss people saved thousands and thousands of refugees from the gas chambers. A well-regulated militia really was necessary to the security of a free state.

Winston Churchill and Adolph Hitler both understood how much Switzerland damaged the Axis cause—on both a military and a moral plane. Stephen Halbrook's excellent book—the first in English to tell Switzerland's history during the war—is the story of how a small, isolated nation, faced with mighty enemies and gigantic dangers, can demonstrate true greatness."
(See: http://www.davekopel.com/2A/Mags/TargetSwitzerland.htm)

I was curious, had no real way to poll law enforcement officially, was left with only to surmise that they would reject that subjugation and stand up to the powers trying to disarm all of America. One day, in a Mexican restaurant buying a burrito, I was there with a local detective who was ordering food. While we waited, I asked him who he was and he was local. So, I asked him that question, but the question was prefaced on what I had learned about Obama's agenda, the UN's role, and Interpol's mandate to take over all of law enforcement. After posing that agenda and its goals, I asked him what he would do as an officer of the law and protector of the Constitution he swore an oath too if subjugated under Interpol and told to go around and confiscate citizen firearms. He said that agencies sometimes gain control over other agencies, and that whoever the top boss was would be who called the shots for what the police would be tasked to do. He'd just continue to follow orders. I was so disappointed. Here was a police officer who swore an oath to uphold and enforce the law, an oath that included upholding the Constitution of the United States, who told me clearly that he would just follow orders (even if that meant participating in an agenda to destroy this country and usher in socialism, communism, or totalitarianism). I wish I had the facility to do a survey of police officers in every county in every state, and in every agency of government engaged in law enforcement, to see what they would say and do. Why is that important?

I had hoped that the law enforcement community was managed by, and staffed by, solid patriots of the United States, patriots who would enter or re-enter the military if there was a world war going on or an invasion of the USA, and fight for our country. I hoped that we patriots would be like the Swiss, not re-liant upon a separate military or "islands" of law enforcement agencies who might cave to the United Nations or any wanna-be socialist or tyrant. I hope this would be the case because historical review of what role the police play in a regime and/or ideological change shows that they simply "follow orders" even if that meant orders by an oppressive, murderous tyrant. Tyrants have taken control of countries and then used the police force to murder protestors and political enemies, and the police did so every time. I surmise it comes down to complying with the new regime completely, or ending up dead in some street or body of water. I reckon most people facing compliance or death would likely choose compliance. This is the nature of the human condition.

It is for these reasons that Americans must engage and embrace law enforcement at all levels now, before they are tasked with regime compliance or death, and while there is still a strong chance of pushing back the alt-Leftists fully engaged in their agenda to bring about Socialism and the destruction of Capitalism. We need to say to law enforcement that we taxpayers have paid their salaries and family benefits for a very long time, and we expect that when civil disorder breaks out from the Left they will respond against it to quell it, and we also expect them to see the citizens who support law enforcement as compatriots if and when civil war breaks out, i.e., patriots fighting to save America want to fight alongside those in law enforcement as a single, unified team, to restore America, not help destroy it. We need to tell them and receive mutuality on the idea that they are us and we are them, as citizens, and as patriots of this country. The badge is a symbol of their vocation, but the Constitution is a living symbol to our way of life to which they have sworn to uphold it against enemies, foreign or domestic. Patriotism is a single mindset expressed by unity of purpose in protecting our country.

We need our police forces to see that our survival as a nation may not occur at the hands of the politicians, many of whom are weak and inept, but by our own efforts fighting to keep America and its Constitution and our ideology. We patriot citizens need to know that we fight together against the overwhelming propaganda, civil unrest, or civil war. We need to agree that if a civil war does occur, we will NOT let the UN enter this country because its soldiers (many of whom are from hostile countries) will be not as peacekeepers but as destroyers of the patriots trying to save the country. The UN's agenda has long been the disarmament of Americans so that it would be easier to usher in the one-government world. Obama gave the UN authority to shoot to kill Americans who resist in any way the confiscation of firearms, and in methods of execution Obama suggested, "beheading" was at the top of his list. Obama hated America and Americans, and yet millions fawned over him like he was a Messiah because he was a smooth-talking orator. Liar liar, pants on fire!!! He was and still is a liar still involved in actions against this country. He should have been convicted of treason or treasonous conduct and imprisoned. Or worse.

The UN is an organization bent on bringing about a world centralized under a single government, and perhaps the UN intends to become that government if successful. But the UN is no friend of the American people. It is itself populated by many countries openly hostile to the United States and a capitalist democracy. Americans must see the UN itself as an enemy of the people of the United States; it is an "Obama Truth" where, like Obama who lied nearly every time he opened his mouth, the UN fostered and perpetuates the idea that the world should be "administered" under a single world government for the "welfare and benefits and public safety" of all.

More information on this subject can be found at the links at the end, in References, which are informative news articles, essays and videos exposing the "gun control" (i.e., civilian disarmament) agenda.

Those who think that all Americans should relinquish their firearms, particularly in this era where war and political violence is growing around the world, and where subversion, sedition, revolution, pro-socialism goals, and trading freedom and individualism for the false narrative of peace and security follows the lies told by prior socialist, fascist, and communist leaders (China's Chairman Mao Zedong, Russia's Joseph Stalin, German's Adolf Hitler (Jews only), Italy's Mussolini, Cambodia's Pol Pot, for example), they are living in a fantasy world believing in a Utopian one-government world. Their efforts to disarm Americans is taking us all not to Utopia but to a genocide that makes all other genocides like comparing the sinking of a small sailboat to the Titanic trans-atlantic passenger liner tragedy.

So, let's go back to the beginning of American independence, and just prior thereto.

History gives us clear reason to fight for our unalienable constitutional right to keep and bear arms, especially now. But let's look at some American history, bearing in mind that early American muskets and pistols were the latest in arms manufacturing also used by the British soldiers, while modern rifles, pistols, and shotguns in America mirror the firearms used by our enemies around the world, including the soldiers from other countries who definitely hate America who belong to the army of the United Nations who is already set to invade America to disarm us as established by former President Barack Obama if and when martial law is declared in America.

Contrary to some, including Ben Carson, Hitler and his leadership did not disarm Germans as he came to power. Rather, the Nazi Party inherited a 1928 gun registration law that had replaced a total ban on gun ownership on a defeated Germany after World War I. The 1928 law created a permit system to own and sell firearms and ammunition. According to Dagmar Ellerbrock, an expert on German gun policies at the Dresden Technical University, this order was rarely followed and most men, and many women, still owned the weapons they acquired before or during the first World War. After the 1928 registration law, only the new weapons became registered.

The Nazis did not seize German's gun. Rather, it outlawed guns possessed by Jew and those considered enemies of the Nazi Party. According to Ellerbrock, the Nazi Party used whatever gun records they had to seize those weapons, yet records showed that many Jews possessed guns well into the late 1930s. The Nazis did adopt a new gun law in 1938, loosening gun ownership in several ways (deregulating the buying and selling of rifles, shotguns and ammunition, making handguns easier to own by allowing anyone with a hunting license to buy, sell or carry one at any time, and extending the permit period from one year to three and gave local officials more discretion in letting people under 18 to acquire a gun). But it did impose new limits on the Jews. On November 11, 1938, the German Minister of the Interior issued "Regulations Against Jews Possession of Weapons" which said not only were Jews forbidden to own guns and ammunition, they couldn't own "truncheons or stabbing weapons." This clearly should have been an indicator that the future of German Jews might be in jeopardy. Hitler never did disarm Germans, with the exception of the Sturmabteilung, or Brownshirts (a founding Nazi street fighting organization) who were killed off by the Schutzstaffel (SS) because SS Commander Henrich Himmler felt the Brownshirts were plotting a coup against Hitler. (www.politifact.com/truth-o-meter/statements/2015/oct/26/ben-carson/fact-checking-ben-carson-nazi-guns/)

In affirmation of the above, I refer to Bernard E. Harcourt, writing for the University of Chicago Law School and Political Science Department, notes:

> If you read the 1938 Nazi gun laws closely and compare them to earlier 1928 Weimar gun legislation – as a straightforward exercise of statutory interpretation – several conclusions become clear. First, with regard to possession and carrying of firearms, the Nazi regime relaxed the gun laws that were in place in Germany at the time the Nazis seized power. Second,

the Nazi gun laws of 1938 specifically banned Jewish persons from obtaining a license to manufacture firearms or ammunition. Third, approximately eight months after enacting the 1938 Nazi gun laws, Hitler imposed regulations prohibiting Jewish persons from possessing any dangerous weapons, including firearms.

We should also not overlook such cautionary authors like Daniel D. Polsby & Don B. Kates, Jr., Of Holocausts and Gun Control, 75 Wash. U.L.Q. 1237 (1997). The authors contended that Americans underestimate their own susceptibility to tyrannical government and genocide: "But one cannot reason that an American tyranny is impossible simply from the fact that overwrought judgments on this subject are commonly and casually made, often by people who should know enough to weigh their words before speaking." Id., at 1255. Further, they said:

> To many Americans, genocide seems so remote a contingency that the relevance of policies meant to constrain it can simply be dismissed out of hand. This is one aspect of the theory of American exceptionalism – the idea that we Americans are different from and perhaps better than the other members of the human race. One is entitled to be skeptical whether this self-conceit is sound, especially given that one of the more terrifying aspects of genocide has been its prevalence among civilized, educated, cultured people. A reality check is in order for Americans who reflexively dismiss the relevance of genocide to their lives.

Id., at 1261-62.

The new 1938 policy on firearms extended not only to Jews and "enemies" within Germany, but was applied to other countries invaded by the Nazis. The bottom line is that gun bans and confiscation allowed the Jews to be completely disarmed before they were rounded up and sent to the gas chambers and other forms of genocide perpetrated upon them.

And then we have Stalinism. In Tsarist Russia, people loved guns. Officers, merchants, students, respectable dames, and young ladies all had a favorite handgun, sometimes more than one. However, by the end of the 1917 Revolution the authorities had restricted the right to carry firearms. Notwithstanding, before the Revolution, the gun regulations were about use of guns, not regulating ownership. Shooting a firearm indoors was a serious concern in 17th century Moscow, where almost all buildings were made of wood – a spark from a gunshot could start a fire very easily. In fact, such blazes were so common that in 1864 a Tsarist order prohibited pulling the trigger indoors. However, everyone seemed to ignore that order until 1845 when a new wave of restrictions also prohibited shooting outdoors in crowded places unless clearly necessary. But nobody threatened to take their guns away.

This all changed with the 1918 Bolshevik Revolution. The leaders of the revolution knew what the masses were capable of, especially if armed to the teeth, and so they moved to monopolize gun ownership. The Bolsheviks initiated a large-scale confiscation of civilian firearms, outlawing their possession and threatening imprisonment for up to 10 years for concealing a gun. The only exception was made for hunters who were allowed to only possess smoothbore (unrifled) weapons. Gun licenses were strictly regulated and only issued by the NKVD, the police organization known for its role in Joseph Stalin's political purges.

Thus, it was only a matter of time before Russia became an almost totally gun-free nation. Some people believed the Russians would regain their right to own guns after the collapse of the Soviet Union and under President Gorbechev, but despite firearms becoming available on the black market during the 1990s, the new government did not risk liberalizing the gun market for fear of the population uprising. Many Russians today see Gorbechev as a pawn of the United States because the collapse of Soviet Union caused widespread economic collapse and chaos, the rise of criminal cartels (some of which came into America cities and are considered some of the most violent), and generally the people were in a struggle to survive on a daily basis, while the United States turned a blind eye to their troubles.

Today, Russians can only legally buy smoothbore guns for hunting and sport, as well as pneumatic firearms for self-defense. Applying for a gun license also involves a rigorous background check.

Joseph Stalin, the butcher of Russians, died of natural causes (stroke) at age 73, in 1953. Soviet records indicate that Stalin was responsible for around 700,000 deaths of regular citizens, 14 million were relocated, deported or sent to gulags in his time, including the horrendous Siberian gulags. Stalin had a hatred for farmers, who did not want so much of their crops taxed, so he had them rounded up and killed or imprisoned, with the result that a great famine engulfed the Soviet Union where millions died of starvation and murder. So, while Stalin was responsible for some 400,000 murders, one should not overlook the millions who starved to death from his campaign against the farmers who produced the food to live on. The murder of the Kulak class triggered the Ukrainian famine, during which 3 million to 5 million peasants died of starvation.

Some figures show nearly a million of Stalin's citizens were executed, beginning in the 1930s. Millions more fell victim to forced labor, deportation, famine, massacres, and detention and 'interrogation' by Stalin's henchmen. Despite all that Stalin did, he somehow got a pass, while the Nazis, who did murder some 6 million Jews, a far less number than Stalin's death count, ended up in international courts prosecuting war crimes, yet Stalin died of old age. No one went after Stalin and his minions for war crimes, while Nazi hunters still today roam the world tracking down all known Nazis who managed to escape capture and prosecution at the end of WW-II. One of the problems in hunting down Stalin's party members is very simple: Every family had not only victims but perpetrators who either informed on them or worked for Stalin's party.

Also, during the short time Hitler and Stalin were talking about invading Poland, it cannot be said that Hitler was interested in Communism. He was not. Stalin was.

Vladimir Putin was one of the younger Russians who grew up in St. Petersburg during the famine crisis and suffered that famine personally. He did later join the KGB police, if only to find a way to survive.

In modern times we have seen, mass killings – we call genocide – in Rwanda, Cambodia, Darfur, and Bosnia. International courts consider genocide the crime of crimes, but nations still have tugs of war over the official definition of the word "genocide" itself – which mentions on national, ethnic, racial, and religious groups. The definition can determine, after all, international relations, foreign aid, and national morale, e.g., the international tussle over whether the 1915 Turkish massacre and deportation of the Armenians "counts" as genocide.

This question of definition also involves a book by Stanford history Professor Norman Naimark, entitled "Stalin's Genocides" (plural), where he argues a much broader definition of genocide is needed, one that includes nations killing social classes and political groups; his case in point was Joseph Stalin. Naimark argues that the Soviet elimination of a social class, the Kulaks (who were higher-income farmers), and the subsequent killer famine among all Ukrainian peasants – as well as the notorious 1937 order No. 00447 that called for the mass execution and exile of "socially harmful elements" as "enemies of the people" – were, in fact, genocide.

I also found it quite interesting that Naimark concluded there was more similarity between Hitler and Stalin than usually acknowledged, as Naimark wrote: "Both chewed up the lives of human beings in the name of a transformative vision of Utopia. Both destroyed their countries and societies, as well as vast numbers of people inside and outside their own states. Both, in the end, were genocidaires." Stalin was never charged or prosecuted for crimes against humanity, yet he killed more people than Hitler and Hitler's regime.

Finally, as to Stalin, it is interesting to note that toward the end of his life, Stalin may have had plans to act against Russia's own Jewish population; his concocted conspiracy about Jewish Kremlin doctors in 1952 would have resulted in the internal exile of the entire Jewish population, perhaps even more genocide. Whatever plans Stalin had died abruptly with his death in March of 1953, as rumors of Jewish deportations were swirling about. One of Stalin's colleagues recalled Stalin reviewing an arrest list (really, a death list) and muttering to himself: "Who's going to remember all this riff-raff in ten or twenty years' time? No one. ... Who remembers the names now of the boyars Ivan the Terrible got rid of? No one. ... The people had to know he was getting rid of his enemies. In the end, they all got what they deserved."

What lessons can we learn? In America right now, we have a growing revolutionary movement, richly funded by a totalitarian group wanting a totalitarian one-government world (New World Order), working towards the first step to that end, socialism. Voices are angry and accusatory, vilifying conservatives of any kind, Republicans, and white people. What if they create a civil war, inclusive of a racial genocide campaign against white people and anti-socialist political groups, and then they call upon the U.N. to come in to crush the side the Progressives are warring against, and disarm all Americans?

You see, that is the agenda Obama started when he went to the U.N. and made a deal with them to enter America if there was civil unrest and violence, and after martial law was declared, and disarm Americans. Obama gave the U.N. authority to shoot to kill all those who resisted disarmament. He gave authority to Interpol to take complete control of every police for, federal, state, and local, and force our own police to go against that portion of the citizenry who were patriots of American ideology and supporters of the Constitution. We were, and still are, facing genocide if we don't become active on a national scale. We still have the power, if we arise from our complacency, to take back this nation without firing a shot.

Self-conceit, a sense of invulnerability and self-superiority, must give way to reality, or America will see a flow of patriot blood across this nation begun from within our own borders and hastened and spread by enemies from without, including the United Nation's military forces from around the globe.

In 1999, the United Nations issued "Report of the Group of Governmental Experts on Small Arms" of August 19, 1999. The following excerpt is important for Americans who believe the Second Amendment is sacred and protectable; although I quoted it in a previous section about the U.N. I re-quote it here:

> "States should work toward the introduction of appropriate national legislation, administrative regulations and licensing requirements that define conditions under which firearms can be acquired, used and traded by private persons. In particular, they should consider the prohibition of unrestricted trade and private ownership of small arms and light weapons."

Review, as I have written about Obama and the U.N., not only did Obama go and make a deal with the U.N. to invade the USA if civil unrest occurred (which he and Hillary were cohorts in), and martial law was declared (which he and Hillary were also cohorts), for the purpose of disarming all U.S. citizens, with authority given by Obama to kill any American who resisted in any way (even by citing to the Constitution's Second Amendment), but the U.N. was actually invited in to do urban training exercises in confiscating firearms.

Review, as I already mentioned, citizens all over America saw hundreds of white U.N. vehicles during the Obama era as well as train cars miles long carrying military equipment like tanks, armed lighter vehicles, and troop carriers to various destinations around America. This was NOT because there was a concern about military invasion by other countries, but about enforcing martial law and about arresting millions of citizens for internment in the many new FEMA internment facilities suddenly thrown up by over 600 around the United States, with processing centers in former Walmart locations.

And, I might mention, the original old man of the Walmart family, during World War II, was the very person in charge of the Japanese internment camps in which Japanese-Americans were confined, eventually released, and never compensated for their huge personal and financial losses even though they were never charged with being pro-Japanese invaders. And, those who volunteered to fight in the military for America were sent, ill-equipped, right to the front lines where many were simply killed off. These were our own citizens who loved their country but who were simply discriminated against, vilified, and treated unfairly. Old man Walmart was part of that internment and oppression; post-War he created the most dominant chain store enterprise in America.

Let's take a look at what recently happened in Great Britain where the call for disarmament was successful.

In 2011-2012, the British government passed legislation to ban certain firearms, but called upon the citizenry to just turn in all their firearms, including ones just for hunting or sport-shooting, and even collections of antique firearms worth many thousands of dollars. Britains were shamed into relinquishing their weapons, after which Britain engaged in a total destruction of tons and tons of these weapons, making the confiscation permanent in a country where Islamism has gained considerable political control and engaged in unprecedented violence upon British citizens. Why? There can be only one answer. Despite the BREXIT movement, currently somewhat stalemated over whether to exit or seek a deal, there appears to be a concurrent rise towards the idea of joining the New World Order agenda and establish a one-world government under the United Nations's administration and management. Or so they think.

The original post-WW-II movement by European countries to create the United Nations and the European Union was one of common ground, i.e., to create a unity of nations so that it would be difficult or impossible for nations like Stalin's Russia or Hitler's Germany or Italy's Mussolini to invade and take over and subjugate other nations. The U.N. expected and encouraged America to create its own union with Mexico and Canada as a single entity, with the goal of joining the EU with that new entity so everyone could move towards a New World Order and one-government world. This United States/Canada/Mexico union did not, however, occur. (Perhaps you can see how the mass migration from Central and South America today seems bent on achieving that goal at the expense of Americans, while the Canadian Prime Minister Justin Trudeau, now turned Muslim, is seeking to create a Muslim caliphate of Canada while promoting Muslim migration in America as well.)

Can you see the pattern emerging?

The citizens of Great Britain were shamed into turning in their firearms by their own government and other pro-disarmament forces. In a video by LibertyInOurTime, published June 12, 2012, masses of citizens in England took to the streets in protests against their government, yet the mood of the crowds was somber as they marched quietly and dejectedly through the streets, as if they realized that they will never get back their right to defend themselves against any enemies, foreign or domestic. (www.youtube.com/watch?v=CC6aEx6xYFY.) Links with this video are Civilian Disarmament: Prelude to Tyranny (http://www.youtube.com/watch?v=1t8nfq6zyzA).

LibertyInOurTime also published on October 17, 2010, a video also listed above, titled Civilian Disarmament: Prelude to Tyranny, with John Birch Society speaker William Norman Grigg. Grigg is an award-winning investigative journalist and a Senior Editor for The New American magazine and author of the books The Gospel of Revolt and Freedom on the Altar. He has covered seven United Nations conferences, including UN world summits in Cairo, Egypt and Copenhagen, Denmark. His research into the issues of terrorism, organized crime, and the emerging police state has included in-person interviews with top federal officials, former agents of the Soviet KGB, members of the Chinese Communist Party, and leaders of groups such as the New Black Panther Party (the latter which calls for the extermination of "white people").

Produced in 2000 by the John Birch Society, it sums the video as follows:

> "The historical record clearly shows that civilian disarmament has been a precursor to tyranny and genocide. This is the grim reality that lurks behind the phrase "gun control." This video lays out the facts concerning the ongoing drive by the federal government and the United Nations for civilian disarmament, and explains how you can help prevent America's descent into a police state tyranny."

The John Birch Society was concerned about a growing political tendency to become a government over the people rather than a government by and for the people. This movement was not a "right wing" population, but a movement growing by Democrats, who are and have been the party of over-regulation, causing corporations moving out of the country and a concurrent loss of American jobs, and higher taxes on American citizens.

Citing the Bible, 1 Thessalonians 5:3, "For when they shall say, Peace and safety, then sudden destruction cometh upon them, as travail upon a woman with child, and they shall not escape." Grigg explained he began at his talk at this citation because "throughout history tyrants have made the offer of what we might call the "Devil's Bargain" today to those they would tyrannize. He emphasized that "One of the most important rights that men have to defend is the right to bear arms and defend themselves, their family, their right to their property, their liberty. We're being offered that "Devil's Bargain" today, as people say, in exchange for surrendering our God-given right to keep and bear arms, we can enjoy peace and safety guaranteed by an all-powerful state; it's a bad deal any way you look at it."

Grigg noted that one of the best expositions on the point of view of the "peace and safety" argument was made by Harold S. Herd, a retired Justice of the Kansas Supreme Court (he is a distinguished jurist in residence at the Washburn University School of Law), in a 1997 law journal article. He had the following things to say to those who cling to the increasingly un-fashionable view that free men and women have to have the right to keep and bear arms for defense:

> "It is time for America to act responsibly and stop the pro-liferation of arms. The more guns in private hands the more fear exists, with an increasing demand for more guns. The irrefutable facts are that gun-related violence is run-ning rampant in this country. That is sufficient impetus for an attempt to control guns in any way needed to halt the carnage. The statistics of firearms' violence in America is overwhelming, and the government has clearly had the power and authority to do something. Firearms, particu-larly handguns, are dangerous instrumentalities which gov-ernment has a duty to regulate for the health, safety, and welfare of the public. It is time for the debate to end. It is now time for government to discharge its duty and furnish public security."

Grigg noted that Judge Herd's view of those who continue to support the Sec-ond Amendment is this:

> "Extremists [who] refuse to accept majority rule, even on so-cial and economic issues where it clearly applies, [and who are united by\ the belief that the Second Amendment to the United States Constitution guarantees an individual right to bear arms, this right to bear arms is essential to extremists because they feel that the only way to protect their rights is by arming themselves. They never mention the rule of law

except to assert it in their efforts to oppose gun control. They are convinced that killing solves problems."

- Harold S. Herd
Kansas Supreme Court Justice (1979-93)
"Re-Examination of the Firearms
Regulation Debate and Its Consequences

Very interesting is Grigg's comment on Judge Herd's perspective:

"Now Judge Herd's perspective, which I am powerfully tempted to refer to as Herd poisoning, in recognition of [George] Orwell's term for status propaganda, is fact-starved and falsehood obese; it is also quite typical for what passes as scholarship in legal circles these days regarding the right to keep and bear arms. It also has some interesting historical resonance that parallels, both in ancient history and in more contemporary history. I think a 1770 proposal, which was written by William Knox, who was the Under-Secretary of State for the British Colonial Office. That proposal was entitled, "What Is Fit To Be Done With America?" I think that is sort of the "first draft" for the world view that Judge Herd represents. Here is a brief excerpt from the 1770 proposal from Secretary Knox, and I think that it is a quite interesting parallel to Judge Herd's comments. Quote:

The militia law should be repealed and not suffered to be re-enacted. And the arms of the people should be taken away and every piece of ordnance removed into the King's stores. Subjects will have but little need for such things for the future as the King's troops, ships, and forts will be sufficient to protect them from any danger.

"That is, any danger except that which is represented as individual freedom by the King's army. You will recall that our war for independence began on April 19, 1775 when a group

473

of militiamen refused – in Lexington, Massachusetts – refused to surrender their arms to the British redcoats or, if you will, to the peacekeepers of the time. Three days later, after the opening of our war for independence, British general Thomas Gage, ordered civic officials in Boston to conduct what is now commonly called a "gun turn-in program." A more contemporary expression for this is "micro-disarmament." That's the expression the United Nations likes to use. ... On July 6, 1775, the Continental Congress adopted a document written by Thomas Jefferson and John Dickinson entitled "The Declaration of Causes of Taking Up Arms." And, in that list of grievances, General Gage's disarmament of the Bostonian Patriots through deception was very prominently mentioned, as was one of the reasons why America had no choice but to withdraw from the British empire.

So, we can see that the "extremists" who presided over our war for independence and later went on to create our Constitution, in their world view it was understood that free men cannot be barred the use of weapons in defense of their liberties. A population of free men can be governed but it is difficult to rule. For those who would be free the right to bear arms would be indispensable. For those who would rule it is a nearly insurmountable obstacle to their ambitions.

And I think that is a necessary understanding as we continue our review of what's going on with respect to civilian disarmament, both nationally and internationally."

I strongly recommend that the reader check out the YouTube video by William Norman Grigg, (https://www.youtube.com/watch?v=1t9nfq6zyzA). It is 50 minutes, and goes into the controversial Brady Act which Grigg's points out was not to reduce crime but to reduce gun access. Follow-up statistics showed it had no measurable effect on crime but it did create an increased vulnerability of women who were raped; statistics showed a 3.6 percent rise in rapes of women, and a 3% increase in assaults against women, because they were unable to purchase a firearm to protect themselves. In addition, the Brady Act required background checks and criminalized those who attempted to obtain firearms by lying about their criminal records, but statistics showed there were only 29 arrests made of such criminals, so there was no negligible effect on such a problem. The Brady Act was couched as a prevention mechanism, but its true intent, made known by Gregory King of the Clinton regime, said very clearly the purpose of the Brady law was "to keep people from getting guns, not to increase federal prosecutions." The Brady law was deemed an indispensable public safety measure that should have had a dampening effect on murder and suicide, but a 2000 study by the American Medical Association disclosed that the Brady Act has no measurable impact on murder and suicide rates, as Grigg's noted.

Grigg noted that Gregory King, speaking for the Clinton administration, said that the purpose of the Brady law was <u>disarmament</u>, not public safety. As in the deceit by General Gage in 1775, the Clinton administration – now known for their pro-Socialist support – was engaged in efforts to disarm all Americans.

One of the things I really liked in Grigg's analysis. He pointed out that the unalienable right to defend oneself and his property does not depend exclusively on the Second Amendment and the abolition of the Second Amendment, however unwise that might be, does not given the central government the authority to take our guns away because that power was not delegated to the central government. Grigg's says:

> "The right to keep and bear arms, like the other rights mentioned and protected in the Bill of Rights is a natural or God-given right and it is a fundamental right which distinguishes free men from feudal serfs and citizens from slaves. It is, in fact, a duty of those who would be free to defend and exercise that right. By acknowledging the right of the People to keep and bear arms, the Framers of the Bill of Rights explicitly recognized a critical fact about the nature of our constitutional republic. Our government, almost uniquely in history, does not assume the state has a monopoly on the legitimate use of force. The government derives its just, limited, and

revocable powers from the consent of the governed. It does not confer limited and revocable rights upon its subjects. If the central government can monopolize the legitimate use of force, it stands to reason that it can and will absorb and abolish all other liberties as well. This has happened repeatedly in history, particularly in modern history. Invoking the desire for peace and safety, governments have disarmed their subjects only to visit them with sudden destruction of their lives and liberty. In many cases, visiting upon their hapless and abject populations the mass liquidation of those who are unsuitable for assimilation into the "new order."

One last thing from Will Grigg I would like to leave the reader with is this reference to Sir Walter Raleigh, who was charged and convicted of treason unjustly, then unjustly executed. His treatment led to significant reforms in Anglo-Saxon jurisprudence with respect to due process of law. Sir Walter Raleigh wrote a warning we all should be clear about, where he said the first goal of any would-be tyrant is "to un-arm his people of weapons, money, and all means by which they may resist his power."

Right now, the Democrat gun-grabbers are stepping up. Despite 95 counties in Virginia protesting they will not allow the new Governor and the Legislature to pass any laws that would violate the Second Amendment, the government there has done so, passing laws to criminalize citizens who did not comply, which is the vast majority of Virginians.

More recently, Arizona government has come up with a draconian gun-grabbing law even worse than California's, which has already imposed laws that, like Virginia, will likely not withstand court challenges. Arizona has nick-picked every aspect of just about every gun made, and would outlaw every gun that has any of these features. It criminalizes any citizen that owns guns after the law and all its features are implemented if they do not comply with every single detail. Essentially, guns will be outlawed in Arizona because what they will be allowed still suffers from severe regulations.

I will leave to you, the reader, to find this 50-minute video on YouTube or elsewhere and review the entire presentation. I urge you to listen closely to William Norman Grigg; I suspect he hopes that his message will be spread far and wide to all patriot Americans, and I definitely agree. If that video is no longer available, you should be able to contact Grigg at his blog: http://www.freedominourtime.blogspot.com.

Another thing you should know. While liberals and the LGBTQ group support the ban of firearms, it is interesting that liberals are arming themselves against the Second Amendment patriots, which is why I do not doubt the probability of a civil war occurring.

I also leave this subject with this truth. We are now engaged in a war for what this country is and becomes; it is a propaganda war. The anti-America pro-socialists are dangerous, display hatred and violence, and do have and will have guns to initiate their revolution if they see the need. We need to step up and stop totally this gun-grabbing agenda because for every little win they get, this becomes a platform for another grab, and they will do so until we have been disarmed. They, on the other hand, do not intend to be disarmed and may be purchasing weapons on the black market or in states that do not require registration of weapons purchased.

Don't acquiesce to giving up your firearms or the Second Amendment; this is all that stands between continued freedom and the new serfdom the puppeteers intend for us all. We give just one inch, they will take a mile, and another, and another, until they get it all. For these puppeteers, gun-confiscation will be the most important step in bringing about socialism and destroying America.

The difference between being free or becoming a slave or serf is the right to keep and bear arms. Why do you think the puppeteers are working so hard to disarm Americans? They want serfs and slaves, and they will be the rulers.

We are a country that believes in rights, freedoms, opportunity, and justice for all. Sometimes justice is obtained only through a strong enough demand.

PART 4. WHAT HAPPENS IF WE LOSE THE CONSTITUTION?

Author T.S. Lawrence, on Rebellion, once warned:

> Rebellions can be made by 2 percent, active in a striking force, and 98 percent passively sympathetic. The active rebels must have the qualities of speed and endurance, ubiquity and independence of arteries of supply.

Those rebelling against the USA and promoting Socialism have garnered a larger and larger percentage of the Democrat population. They are well-funded (by the globalist banks and other wealthy sources), they are well-organized and active in a striking force, while a large contingent of patriot Americans are passive and think socialism could not possibly occur by such efforts to take over politics and America. They are moving quickly with endurance, ubiquity and independence of arteries of money supply and people. Patriots are losing ground, mostly because patriots are NOT STANDING THEIR GROUND! So get busy, like the Virginians did.

The most important thing to realize and remember, pro-socialists think that achieving socialism is the end result; it is not. The end result is achieved in steps, from socialism, to communism, then to the totalitarianism of a one-government world, i.e., the New World Order. That is the end goal. The irony is this: if socialism were to occur and went to communism and totalitarianism, the protestors of today trying to bring America down will likely be the first bunch of people identified for extermination. Why? Because the new government will already know who the trouble-makers are, and they'll get rid of them

478

early on before they realize that they made a huge mistake in believing social-ism is Utopia.

The United States Constitution, inclusive of its Bill of Rights, separates us as a nation from most other countries, because it is a doctrine, an ideology, a way of life that puts the individual before government, which declares certain human rights do not come from man or the government, but as God-given birthrights as human beings. If we lose the Constitution, and we get disarmed, all that we are as human beings, all of our rights to exist, grow, thrive, pursue our dreams and livelihoods, and defend ourselves from all enemies domestic and foreign, all that will come to a halt. As with other socialist beginnings, millions will be killed off, one way or another.

Bill Gates believes "vaccines" will help depopulation, and he has already begun in India and Africa. India sued him for using a vaccine that killed thousands of children or caused them to become autistic. In Africa, his vaccines sterilized 500,000 females from age 15 to 35.

Others, like those characterized as "radical" Islamists, will love doing their Allah's work of beheadings, torturing, burning Americans, and bombing cities and places where Americans gather. Powerful and well-funded and well-armed drug cartels will likely invade (in our weakened state) to take part in the geno-cide intended for American patriots and non-Muslims (kafirs).

If we devolve into internal civil war, we'll be weak as a country, and the Con-stitution itself may get "suspended" until the anti-American forces can take American down, at which time the Constitution will cease to exist. We will see the army of the United Nations invade America, supposedly as a peace-keeping force, its soldiers from countries that hate America and Americans, and they are here to disarm us. And kill us if we resist, or if they just want to kill us. Life as we know it now will cease to exist, because kill us they will. Obama gave the U.S. that permission and, as far as I know, that permission has yet to be officially rescinded.

To sit back, complacent as if none of this horror is possible in America, is ac-quiescence to its destruction, because the powers-that-be, the enemy amongst us and without, are growing in power and numbers, already demanding that we surrender our guns and the Constitution and our Christianity. This enemy of America is domestic; they are already here, and active. We already know who the enemies are from other countries.

The Book of Revelation has warned us of these times. Christianity is on the chopping block. God is watching. Are we Christians going to turn the other cheek and let ourselves be slaughtered, or are we going to do God's work and save ourselves, our Christian beliefs and churches and members, our Constitution, and even our money which says, loud and clear, "In God We Trust"?

Even if these will not be the "end of days" predicted in Revelations, it will be the "end of days" of America and our ideology.

Chapter VI:

The Possibility of Civil War in America

There is a high likelihood that civil war in America is getting closer still. A war inside a country of those who believe one way and those who believe another is unwinnable in the sense that it will permanently damage civil and social discourse for many years. The fact of violence and death against each other is a permanent wedge that may never heal either side. But the real damage will come after martial law is declared, and it will be declared in a civil war situation, which is all that is needed to see the United Nations invade for "peacekeeping" they may say, but they are here to disarm Americans; that's all they care about. Many Americans, perhaps millions, are likely to be murdered by these U.N. forces. America may never recover under such circumstances, and they are highly likely to find themselves imprisoned in FEMA's new concentration camps, where our genocide is very likely to occur. As I said before, Obama set this all up, Clinton was to complete the plan, and only Trump interrupted that plan, which is why the Left attacked him, and continues to attack him to get him out by hook-or-crook.

There is a growing chorus from people of color against "white people" led by elitists/globalists pushing false narratives to create the divisiveness needed to marginalize or reduce "white people" who stand against socialism, communism, and totalitarianism. Why is it that so many people of color think that other ideologies are better than a market economy like in Western countries?

It's just not true, and they can easily look to countries predominantly people of color to see how much worse their lives are under those ideologies, yet they, here in America, push those same ideologies anyway. Are they just low IQ? Uneducated? What is it that makes them think so stupidly about converting America to a socialist country? How do you run from one in the home country to another which is better, and then want to convert it to what you just left?

In the event of a civil war, what will American patriots do? Escape to the forests? Ha! Not likely. In a poll I heard about several years ago, many people said they'd just pack up their camping gear and head for the forests and wilderness and live off the land. Sounds like just a vacation, doesn't it? So, if millions of people "escape" to America's 'wilderness', that means every lake will be fished dry within just a few months, all of the edible animals will have been killed off, and finding food will become more and more difficult. Planting crops takes a full season to develop, and then there are the looters, the hungry desperate for food. Experts say that if there was an EMP bomb attack to the American electrical grid, within six months 90% of Americans will die, many of starvation, many from violence as we kill each other in our desperation for food and survival.

I would say within 6 months millions will die, either murdered or through starvation – remember, Stalin killed millions of his own people by murdering the farmers, thus causing starvation of millions. Here, 95% of Americans are dependent upon grocery stores, not gardens. Grocery stores will fail within days, food supplies will stop arriving. Starvation will begin.

There is a growing number of very angry and volatile people: those on the alt-Left wanting socialism at any price, including violence and murder; those on the right who are steadfast against socialism or anything in that direction, willing to fight back with violence to avoid socialism and extermination or serfdom. A civil war is seen as a means to obtain socialism or to avert it. But America is moving closer and closer to that abyss.

As I have said before, I am certain there are millions of patriots in every political party, and despite our disagreements the overriding element is that the destruction of our country is a "common ground" matter that should unite us all; in this way we can easily defeat those alt-Left Progressives who are foolishly pushing for Socialism as America's ideology. Remember, if they achieve that, it is only the stepping stone the NWO folks wanted because from there, it's a fairly easily step to go from socialism to totalitarianism on the global level. If that occurs, we will NEVER see a free democracy or republic again.

What we will likely see for a long time are the bones of millions of unburied dead, empty towns and cities where the pallor of death holds sway, or burned out or bombed out buildings, of the faces of the death in their final agony. Are we immune from such a consequence? Citizens of other countries that crashed likely said such consequences could never happen in their country, yet they did.

So, this situation is a non-partisan condition, one that patriots of any Party can and should get behind to fight against. This is our mutual "common ground" talking point from which we can mutually agree on the solutions. We can't let the alt-Left control the narrative designed to indoctrinate any and every part of our population, especially our own children. We can't lose our guns, not now, not ever. The socialists, communists, and the globalists will never stop trying, no matter how many times we win against them. They'll only win if we are disarmed.

Chapter VII:

The Probability of Attack on America By Other Countries

There are numerous countries around the world that see the United States as the Number One terrorist country because of our going into various countries and engaging in war. Regardless of how we and our government view these incidents, how the rest of the world sees it is that it is none of our business and that we are just war-mongering. So, we have a growing list of enemies in countries around the world.

The U.S. invaded Iraq in 2003 because of the belief that Saddam Hussein was using weapons of mass destruction, particularly chemical weapons. But the U.S. turned a blind eye when Iraq attacked Iran using mustard gas, as well as against Syria. Saddam was believed to support and have ties to Islamic terrorists. Saddam was dethroned, convicted and hanged. Although Iraqis may be freer today, they are by no means pro-American. Fatality figures indicate between 2003-2017, there were some 650,000 fatalities, with some indications the actual number is much higher.

The U.S. went after Gaddafi in 2014, from 2014 to present, there were some 29, 859 – 42, 253 fatalities. The U.S. claimed Gaddafi was abusing his people. More credible sources revealed that he was changing from the petro-dollar to the gold standard for the sale of Libya's oil, which could have had devastating results for the American economy as well as those other countries who had no gold. It is a safe bet that Libyans are not pro-America either.

The Syrian death toll is estimated to be around 175,000 people. The "conflict" began in Syria in March of 2011, with demonstrations which came to be called "Arab Spring." They were protesting against President Bashar al-Assad and demanding he resign. In 2014 President Obama announced his intent to bomb targets in Syria and called on Congress to authorize a program to train and arm rebels who were fighting ISIL and the Syrian forces of Bashar al-Assad.

Our economic interests in North Africa seems to be the driving force for our interference and intervention. It appears the U.S. wants to control who gets to do business for oil in that region. Russia has an embassy in Damascus and Syria has an embassy in Moscow. Russia has enjoyed a historically strong, stable, and friendly relationship with Syria, as it did until the Arab Spring with most of the Arab countries. Our intervention in Syria did not improve our relations, or potential relations with Russia. In 2016, the United Nations Secretary-General Ban Ki-moon alleged Russian warplanes had attacked hospitals in Aleppo and were targeting medical facilities; considering Russia's deference and alliance with Syria, this does not seem credible; instead, it seems to be propaganda against Russia.

Iran and the U.S. have had no formal diplomatic relations since 1980. Iran has been somewhat unstable from within, and Iran's questionable relations with the U.S. ranges from explanations about the natural and unavoidable conflict between the Islamic Revolution on the one hand, and perceived American arrogance and desire for global hegemony on the other. As Iran has increasingly become a hotbed and supporter for Islamic terrorists, Iran is becoming an increasing threat to the U.S. and should be a top foreign policy priority. Only 13% of Iranians have a favorable view of the U.S., with 86% expressing a most-unfavorable view. The terrorist organization Hezbollah, a Shi'ite Islamist organization and client of Iran, has been responsible for attacks on Americans, including U.S. embassies.

And then there is the U.S. war in Afghanistan that seems never-ending. It public aims were to dismantle al-Qaeda and deny it and the Taliban power to grow.

Soviet Russia could not conquer it, and the U.S. – with all its military might – doesn't seem to be able root out of the caves and mountains the Taliban forces. It remains one of the most dangerous places in the world for tourist or non-Afghan travel because of critical levels of kidnappings, hostage taking, suicide bombings, widespread military combat operations, landmines, and terrorist and insurgent attacks, including attacks using vehicle-borne, magnetic, or other improvised explosive devides (IEDs), suicide vests, and so on. The goal of the Taliban is to turn the country into the world's purest form of Islam, banning many things, like education for girls, the use of make-up, and many forms of play and sports. In other words, a return to the Dark Ages.

Nearly every country in North Africa and South Asia are not pro-America, even if some of them remain our "allies" for political or economic reasons. For instance, the U.S. has some 50 of America's nuclear weapons stationed at Incirlik Air Base in Turkey, just 70 miles from the Syrian border, and Turkey, currently an ally, is being overtaken by Muslims in Turkey's regime. From a security point of view, it is a "roll of the dice" whether Turkey remains our ally, and what will happen with our nuclear arsenal if Turkey ceases to be an ally.

I point this all out because we Americans need to recognize that our government continues to get us involved in countries whose cultures and traditions span many centuries and who are unlikely to undergo any changes. They have demonstrated a mindset of fighting to the death to remain as they are. They see the West, and particularly America, as terrorists to them. Unfortunately for us, because of their large amounts of oil reserves and oil wealth, they are becoming emboldened and are infiltrating American-soil itself. They are not here to assimilate.

And then there is China, and it seems there is new information that China created the COVID-19 coronavirus to spread around the world, including here in the U.S., as a means of destabilizing the Western world, for what purposes I do not yet know, but I'm sure we'll find out soon enough. Communist China has, in fact, adopted a market-economy of sorts, and has capitalized on the Western corporations and manufacturers coming to China for cheaper labor. Allegations are that China wants to become the dominant world power. We now know China has been growing its population in numerous African countries, and it appears China intends to expand (conquer) its domain there.

And let us not forget the criminal cartels (both Islamic and Hispanic) in Central and South America. It is a safe bet that in case of civil unrest or civil war, they will gladly invade the U.S. too because they can, because they have the money, and because they have military-level weapons.

We have a lot of enemies.

So, what happens if we grow weak within our own ranks where the major Parties grow farther apart in a most hostile manner? What happens if we see an increase in civil disorder and political violence? What happens if that divisiveness becomes civil war? Will the UN invade us to "help" end the civil war? Who else might invade our soil with the idea of helping destroy this "superpower" called the United States, and also intending to carve out portions of the U.S. for themselves as new countries? What happens if the UN has disarmed all Americans? How can we defend ourselves?

We Americans need to consider that the majority of cultures and countries of the world do not embrace the same Christian ideals and morals the West does, and these have in fact been our strength. But the world's dissidents do not see Christianity as a benefit and benefactor of spiritual health and happiness. To them, Christianity is a blight that should be wiped out. So, Muslims are doing just that, and now we're seeing China doing that to its Christian population as well.

With the Marxists in America, and with the Islamic jihadists here in America, and with the atheists growing in America, and with nations around the world hating on America, we cannot afford to let our Constitution get dismantled and thrown out, nor can we afford to let the gun-grabbers destroy the Second Amendment and disarm all of America. Our right to own firearms may be all that stands between our right to exist and the intent of our enemies to destroy us all.

Just consider this: The gun-grabbers hang on to the subject of gun violence as the main reason to disarm all Americans so we can all be safe. The Crime Prevention Research Center published the following statistics, in 2018. More than half of all U.S. Murders occur in just 2% of counties, all of which are Democrat controlled. More than half of the 3,007 counties in the U.S. reported no murders in 2014, the latest year for which complete data is available. Another 10% of counties reported just one murder. But the worst 2% of counties logged 51% of all murders, and it's no secret where they are. Those same tough counties account for 28% of the population and included the largest U.S. cities, such as Los Angeles, Chicago, and Baltimore. Many of these cities have tough gun control laws, which have little to no effect. Drilling down even further, most of the murders occur in just a few neighborhoods within those cities. In the first several months of 2017, Chicago logged 222 murders. Among its 77 neighborhoods, 23 had zero murders, and 40 neighborhoods had just one. Twelve of the neighborhoods recorded at least 10 murders, and one neighborhood, Austin, record 25. In a study in the journal of Criminology, David L. Weisburd has a paper entitled, "The law of crime concentration and the criminology of place" that shows for eight cities 25% of violent crime occurred on one percent of the streets and that about half occurred on five percent of the streets. The biggest drivers of murder are gangs and drugs.

But let's look at another batch of statistics, just to put things in a broader perspective. Professor Lott at the University of Chicago, and is a noted expert on gun laws and statistics, provided much of the information below:

> There are 30,000 gun-related deaths per year by firearms, and this number is not disputed. The U.S. population is 324,059,091 as of June 22, 2016. Do the math: 0.00925% of the population dies from gun related actions each year. Statistically speaking, this is <u>insignificant</u>! What is never told, however, is a breakdown of those 30,000 deaths, to put them in perspective as compared to other causes of death:
>
> - 65% of those deaths are by suicide, which would never be prevented by gun laws.
> - 15% are by law enforcement in the line of duty and justified.

- 17% are through criminal activity, gang and drug related or mentally ill persons – better known as gun violence.
- 3% are accidental discharge deaths.

So technically, "gun violence" is not 30,000 annually, but drops to 5,100 (among the total population number). Still too many? Now let's look at how those deaths spanned across the nation in 2016.

480 homicides (9.4%) were in Chicago

344 homicides (6.7%) were in Baltimore

333 homicides (6.5%) were in Detroit

119 homicides (2.3%) were in Washington D.C (a 54% increase over prior years)

So basically, 25% of all gun crime happens in just **FOUR** cities. All 4 of those cities have VERY strict gun laws, so it is not the **lack** of law that is the root cause.

This basically leaves 3,825 for the entire rest of the nation, or about 75 deaths per state. That is an average because some States have much higher rates than others. For example, California had 1,169 and Alabama had only ONE.

Now, who has the strictest gun laws by far? California, of course, but understand, it is not guns causing this. It is a crime rate spawned by the number of criminal persons residing in those cities and states. So, if all cities and states are not created equal, then there must be something other than the tool causing the gun deaths. California has an extremely high number of illegal migrants, high numbers of those are gang-involved or simply criminals.

Are 5,100 deaths per year horrific? How about in comparison to other deaths? All death is sad and especially so when it is in the commission of a crime but that is the nature of crime. Robbery, homicide, rape, and assaults are all done by criminals. It is ludicrous to think that criminals will obey laws. That is why they are called criminals.

But what about other deaths each year?

40,000+ die from a drug overdose–THERE IS NO EXCUSE FOR THAT! (We already have laws about illicit drug use, as well as programs like AA and NA to help prevent that.)

36,000 people die per year from the FLU, far exceeding the criminal gun deaths. (I thought that was preventable with vaccines. What's up with "Big Pharma"?)

34,000 people die per year in traffic fatalities (exceeding gun deaths even if you include suicide). (Perhaps we should ban cars, trucks, motorcycles?)

Now it gets good:

200,000+ people die each year (and growing) from preventable medical errors. You are safer walking in the worst areas of Chicago than you are when you are in a hospital! (Well, perhaps we should ban hospitals?)

710,000 people die per year from heart disease. It's time to stop the double cheeseburgers!

So, what is the point? If the liberal loons and the anti-gun movement focused their attention on heart disease, even a

10% decrease in cardiac deaths would save twice the number of lives annually of all gun-related deaths (including suicide, law enforcement, etc.). A 10% reduction in <u>medical errors</u> would be 66% of the total number of gun deaths or 4 times the number of criminal homicides. Simple, easily preventable 10% reductions!

So, you have to ask yourself, in the grand scheme of things, why the focus on guns? It's pretty simple, and I'll say so again:

Taking away guns gives control to governments. The founders of this nation knew that regardless of the form of government, those in power may become corrupt and seek to rule as the British did by trying to disarm the populace of the colonies. It is not difficult to understand that a disarmed populace is a controlled populace. Already we're seeing the pro-socialist movement demanding censorship and absolutism; just look at Kamala Harris's campaign to see that. If we don't retain the Constitution and its Second Amendment, when our firearms have been confiscated, we WILL see socialist control in our own country. And then what? Do you want to just sit back and wait and see? If it goes down, it'll then be too late to do anything about it.

Thus, the second amendment was proudly and boldly included in the U.S. Constitution. It must be preserved at all costs. So, the next time someone tries to tell you that gun control is about saving lives, look at these facts and remember these words from Noah Webster: "Before a standing army can rule, the people must be disarmed."

So, understanding all that, where is the justification for disarming all law-abiding Americans who own over 300 million firearms and don't go around shooting everyone. Once again, the largest harbingers of death and violence in the U.S. are about gangs and drugs. Let's keep the Second Amendment and roll back restrictive regulations. Let's remove all laws and regulations that have been imposed federally and throughout the states that "infringe" upon the rights of all law-abiding citizens to own and bear firearms.

Americans need the Second Amendment in place without Leftist restrictions. Now, more than ever. Don't wait!

Chapter VIII:

Democrats & Replublicans:
Ending the Squabble

Chapter VIII: Democrats & Republicans: Ending the Squabble

As I mentioned earlier, in these trying and dangerous times, perhaps nothing is more important than the good, level-headed patriots in every political party, especially the Democrats and the Republicans, must find common ground issues and join together, in the same way as we join together as comrades when we go to the battlefield in war. And, as to that, let's remember too that despite the alleged racism in America, including the anti-white racism that is growing, in the military you will see soldiers of all races fighting alongside each other, having each other's back, taking risks for each other, and race is of no importance to them. We can all be like that today if we just think clearly about what is going on by the alt-Left and their propaganda and Orwellian lies.

You see, we patriots in every party are not really at war with each other, but we are in a pro-socialist/pro-communist war from the Far-Left Progressives, who are backed by forces that are determined to create a one-government world called the New World Order. They have infiltrated governments in every State, exist in some of our most powerful corporations, and are funded by the *globalist* rich who are behind all our problems on this planet. Until we each realize who the enemy in the "shadow government" is and what they intend to accomplish, we will continue to squabble with each other, like schoolchildren arguing over playgrounds.

In every country where socialism and communism occurred, the takeover was preceded by propaganda which included promises of a better, even Utopian, world, and the disarmament of its citizens under the guise of making everyone safer. What was the result of successful takeovers? Nothing more than equality of poverty and misery, what might be called Dystopia.

As a former Democrat, perhaps I shouldn't have jumped ship when I found out my Party had been hijacked by pro-socialists/pro-Communists; perhaps I should have joined a local Committee and protested, urging them to push back and reject this hijacking. But I didn't. I didn't know how bad it actually was. I found the Republicans ordinary people, most good, kind, and with a love and loyalty for their country. I know the same kind of people exist in the Democrat world; I lived among you, as did my parents.

When asked to speak recently to a Republican Women's Federation Committee, I said that the world and U.S. situation is such that Republicans need to reach over to the Democrats (moderate and conservative) and seek dialogue about "common ground" issues, like the health of this country, and mutual recognition and agreement that there are forces trying to destroy this country.

In the Democrat and Republican political parties, we can draw parallels and correlations to the West and Islam in the context of over-generalizing one another. Both political parties describe the other as if ALL of the members move as a cloud of fish, all moving one way and turning in unison with each other again and again, kind of like "brainwashing."

Democrats describe Republicans the same general way as "bad guys", yet if we actually look closely at what is going on, we find there are those in both parties who are devoutly patriotic, believe in the Constitution, the Bill of Rights, and in a kind and reasonably-tolerant nation. There is no party that can accurately be described as primarily-bad, although the Democrat party is fast-approaching that designation (unless patriot Democrats step up and reject the hijacking of their party by these Progressive socialists).

The greatest fault in both parties is that they are too easily swayed by the silver-tongued orator's "inspiring" presentations and promises rather than vet him or her on the basis of true character and values. Look at what happened with Obama; a wonderful speaker, able to manipulate audiences with charisma and powerful words that stirred the listener's emotions. His agenda was anti-American, and it still is. His own actions should have landed him in prison as a traitor to us all.

And then we have Trump, not an especially accomplished orator, but his down-to-earth everyday-man's man persona, rough around the edges, inspired the nation with his brashness and plain language enough to get him elected President. His MAGA slogan promised nothing more than fixing the nation with citizen help. He looked at the problems as a businessman, not as a political hack. After all, he did say, "together, we will make American great again," did he not? Are we "together" or not? If not, then we MUST get "together" on common ground issues.

There are millions of highly patriotic Americans on both sides of the political fence, people with whom the other party would generally, or even specifically, agree with on most "common ground" issues. Yet, we keep the "other side" at arm's length. We act like we are playing sports, where one team and its fans are totally committed against the other team and its fans, even to the point where violence breaks out between team players and between the fans. It's just a game! Have we simply gotten lost in the "home team game" concept that organized sports have so successfully brainwashed into sports fans, and adopted that silliness to divide us all? Life and national allegiance are not a game. Tolerance towards those who want to destroy us is not good game strategy, and it is NOT a game anyway. The Christian concept of "turning the other cheek" is no longer an option.

Understand the parallels and correlations on the local, state, national, and global levels, and the only conclusion that can be reached today is that we are already at war with each other locally, statewide, nationwide, and worldwide.

American patriots must fight back before we are rendered helpless by the brainwashing and the propaganda that "fundamental change" like Obama promised, is not necessarily a good thing. Obama was out to destroy America because he was a Marxist and an anti-colonialist; his legacy continues and America is directly in the crosshairs of our socialist and communist enemies within and without our own borders. And they are organized and powerful.

Numerous experts, or people in the know, believe that we are destined for a civil war like it or not. The violence from the Progressives/Antifa is growing, and the alt-Left is funding them, transporting them around the country to commit their protests and violence. Fortunately, we're beginning to see some pushback attempts. But we need to "body slam" them into the nearest prison as terrorists.

What if?

What if there is a civil war? Aside from the invasion by the UN and NATO (with soldiers from countries who hate America and Americans) if a civil war and martial law is declared – who intend to take everyone's guns and kill those who resist or even appear to resist – there is the initial problem of identifying who is the enemy. Uniforms of different sides seem unlikely, so how would you know your enemy? Will it divide along Party lines? Will moderate and conservative Democrats who are patriots defend America and its Constitution and ideology, or will they side with the Socialist-Progressives against the Republicans?

If they side with Republicans and Independents, working together to take back our country, then we on the Right will not be shooting them too. In such a situation, Party affiliation must give way to Americanism, i.e., the idea that we are all patriots in the same way for the same country and fight together to save her. If we proceed that way, in the end we'll likely recognize the serious need to fix the real problems that we could not theretofore agree on. Thereafter, we might even put aside our differences and learn to work together.

So, the problem of civil war is this: 'Lines in the sand' have to be very clearly marked so as not to be shooting another patriot ideologically on the same side.

For example, there you and your team are, observing a group of armed people walking down the street in urban-warfare fashion, and flying an American flag. Do you shoot them? Caution begs that you are able to ascertain if they are friends or foe (just flying a false flag). Making a mistake in judgment at that level is not acceptable. That would be akin to "friendly fire" in the war zone.

We are at war, with socialists, globalists, and Islamists. Right now, it is all about propaganda, including selling to the immature and inexperienced minds of our children the false narrative that socialism will be Utopian wonderful. With 80% of that polled young population believing socialism is good and capitalist democracy is evil, we patriots have a problem. You better talk with your kids about socialism, communism, and totalitarianism.

Plus, the socialists are today trying very hard to take down the Second Amendment and take our guns. And they are willing to let anyone who resists be summarily killed.

I write this book to alert everyone as to the threats to our very existence as a people, as a nation, and as the only ideology on the planet that has actually worked for its people, regardless of the ethical problems, these threats brought about by the need of some for total power and by those with unlimited money.

Saving America from socialism and the NWO is a non-partisan, common ground matter. It is so important to all of us that political differences must be set aside. We are in a leaky boat surrounded by deep waters and sharks. Do we debate ideology or strategies, or do we fix the boat? Simple as that. We have to do this together. The socialist/NWO forces are very powerful and determined.

Together, we can change all that. I beg you, then, as patriots of this country, open your minds and hearts – your future and your children's future is at stake – and be willing to establish meaningful dialogue on basic, common issues that, when resolved, benefit us all. We can do that, and we must do that. To be diametrically opposed to anything regarding the other Party is silly, immature, and dangerous. Democrats simply have an enemy within that has infiltrated it and taken over. Another analogy is this: We are together at a fire, our houses and neighborhoods are burning down, but burns to the ground because we can't agree who hooks up the water lines and who turns it on. That is where we are now. Forrest Gump, I'm sure you recall what he said, "Stupid is as stupid does." While we are squabbling, our country is being burned down by enemies from within, and the enemies outside the country are watching in fascination and awaiting opportunity to participate. If you don't understand this, you simply don't have a good understanding of human nature.

Chapter IX:

Complacency and Acquiescence Is The Enemy Of Freedom

If we do nothing, that is complacency. But complacency in this situation is inherently acquiescence to the threat against us and our nation. Sitting back and grumbling and then going on about the business at hand weakens all of us. Saying "But what can I do? I am nothing. I am not a politician. I don't have any money. I am just one, I can't make a difference.", and to that I say, I am just one, I am a nobody, I am not a politician, I don't have any money either, but, I love this country and I love the good-hearted people in it. Perhaps I can make a difference." I finally decided I CAN make a difference. I write well, my values are straight, and I know how to talk to people about this problem we have before us. This book, written after years of trying to discover how big this conspiracy against America really is and who is ultimately behind it, is my contribution. If it wakes you up to the truth, and helps inspire you to do something to help shut down this threat against us, then I can die satisfied that I have done something to help that effort. I can only do so much, but at least I am not complacent and I will not acquiesce to these evil socialists/communists trying to destroy my home. America is MY home, just as it is YOUR home. Would you fight for YOUR home?

Patriots have to first fight within civility, through the "system", dialogue and debate on common ground issues that are incompatible with socialism. Avoid violence. In time, if the socialists begin losing ground in the propaganda war, they will likely initiate the violence. Be calm. If Trump is President, give him the opportunity to employ whatever law enforcement agencies he has at his disposal, directly or indirectly. But stay prepared for the possibility that civil war might break out and initiated by the radical Left. Then the militia can act with full support from a Republican governance and agreement by all conservatives and, hopefully, moderate Democrats and other patriots. If all work together, it is likely that a civil war will not last very long at all. At any cost, patriots must not suffer the United Nations invading the USA with their soldiers, and we need President Trump to rescind, if he hasn't already, that agreement Obama made allowing the U.N. to invade if there is civil war. Some of you who read this book, and know personally President Trump, might ask him about rescinding that Obama anti-American UN agreement.

Chapter X:

Altering the Future

I am in California, in a state crippled by years of Democrat control, mostly by just four elitist families, Newsom, Brown, Pelosi, and Getty, and their rich friends. We have a large crime problem, 42 state prisons plus contracts with private prisons, very high welfare numbers, voter fraud, high taxes, one of the most regulated states in the Union, demands for open border and sanctuary cities and state, and a growing angst against conservatives of any party.

Right now, as of Monday, September 30th, Democrat Governor Gavin Newsom, will likely sign a bill into law that requires all groups of electors to possibly change their names. Here is the text. This is a clear fascist move against non-Democrat political parties and affiliates. It is carefully couched as a benefit and problem-solver; it is more dangerous than that.

SB696, Umberg. Elections: political parties.

Under existing law, a group of electors may qualify for a new political party by holding a caucus or convention at which temporary party officers are elected, by designating a party name, or by filing notice with the Secretary of State that the party has organized, elected temporary officers, and has declared its intent to qualify in a primary election. Existing law prohibits the name of a new party from being so similar to the name of an existing party so as to mislead the voters or from conflicting with the name of an existing political body that has previously filed notice with the Secretary of State.

This bill would prohibit the name of a party from including the phrase "no party reference" or "decline to state" or the word "independent" or a variation of that word or those phrases. The bill would require a party that is qualified on the effective date of the bill, but whose name includes a variation of the phrase "no party preference" or "decline to state" or the word "independent", to file a change of name notice with the Secretary of State by October 29, 2019. The Secretary of State would be required to disqualify, by October 30, 2019, any party that fails to so submit an appropriate change of name notice. The Secretary of State would be required to send related notices, as provided.

This bill would declare that it is to take effectively immediately as an urgency statute.

This Democrat action is nothing more than a political tool to move people into the "no party preference" category, which move could and likely would create confusion for the voters. This legislation removes Parties with the word "independent" in it; the Left can get rid of existing political parties over descriptive words, they can tell citizens in this legislation that the government can tell them what they can name their Party, and if they don't immediately comply, they will be moved into the "no party preference" category, a condition that could unlawfully and certainly unethically influence the elections by creating confusion of process. They started this in February 2019, and it is being enacted right now, just before the 2020 elections. It is a political ploy, done by those who control California politics, the Democrats. A recall petition is underway against new Democrat Governor Gavin Newsom, for reasons that include this SB696.

What will be next from the California socialist lawmakers, more direct indoc-ination of the public towards re-creating California as a full-blown socialist state? It is definitely heading that direction in fact, because to those in power, it is or will be a fact done eventually.

But right now, in the newly-convened Democrat-controlled House of Representatives into a bill to eliminate the electoral college. It seems that, since they didn't win the last presidential election under the rules that have existed for almost 250 years, they now want to change the rules. Here is why.

In their infinite wisdom, the Founders of the United States created the Electoral College to ensure all states were fairly represented. The premise was this: Why should one or two densely-populated areas speak for the whole of the nation?

The following list of statistics has been making the rounds on the Internet. I am simply bringing it forward. It should finally put an end to the argument as to why the Electoral College makes sense. This needs to be widely known and understood.

There are 3,141 counties in the United States. Trump won 3,084 of them. Clinton won 57. There are 62 counties in New York State. Trump won 46 of them. Clinton won 16. Clinton won the "popular vote" by approximately 1.5 million votes. In the 5 counties that encompass NYC, (Bronx, Brooklyn, Manhattan, Richmond & Queens), Clinton received well over 2 million more votes than Trump. Clinton only won 4 of these counties; Trump won Richmond. Therefore, these 5 counties alone more than accounted for Clinton winning the popular vote of the entire country. The United States is comprised of 3,797,000 square miles. When you have a country that encompasses almost 4 million square miles of territory, it would be ludicrous to even suggest that the votes of those who inhabit a mere 319 square miles should dictate the outcome of a national election. Large, densely-populated Democrat cities (NYC, Chicago, Los Angeles, Detroit, San Francisco, etc., DO NOT and SHOULD NOT speak dispositively for the rest of the nation. And, it's been documented and verified that those 319 square miles are where the majority of our nation's problems foment, especially extremely high rates of felony crimes. Democrat States like California, for instance, where the crimes in its "sanctuary cities" have skyrocketed, where its regulations strangled business and the economy, where its homeless problem is unbelievably high, where its employment rate is unbelievably low, and where its population on welfare is reaching 50% and promise to go higher, is nearly accomplishing full-blown socialism. The most densely populated of its cities are Democrat-controlled; should they dominate voter outcomes despite the many Republicans in the more rural counties.

At the national level, the 2020 elections are now critical. We must not allow the Electoral College to be taken down so that a few can ruin an entire country like the few elitist families are running California – into the ground.

As the 2020 elections approach, the Left is doubling down on criticisms of Donald Trump. Today, I am listening to the news that refugees from hurricane-torn Bahamas landed in Florida, but were turned away by immigration authorities. President Trump defended that decision saying among those were people who should not be here, i.e., drug dealers, criminals, gang members. Whether true or not, without vetting processes in place, we simply won't know. Our economy in this country, although recovering, still remains burdened by overwhelming numbers of welfare recipients and by illegal migrants in sanctuary cities and states, and that number is growing. America's citizens whose taxes are continually raised to cover the expense if the welfare systems are not happy. This, as Dr. Walter Williams pointed out, is direct theft from the citizens of their money to give to people it does not belong to, and which would be criminal if a citizen took money from another person directly to give it to another person who needed money. I support President Trump's decision to require a process before allowing refugees from anywhere to come into our country. It is simply common sense, and it is what the majority of other countries also require.

We patriots are at war. Regardless of political party, if you are a patriot and believe in the Bill of Rights and our Constitution, then we patriots all have common ground to unite together on to fight back this alt-Left effort to destroy our country. Right now, it's just a war of propaganda, spotted with a little violence here and there. But America is packed with problems of refugee and illegal migrants, increasing violence from pro-socialist advocates, the fight against open debate, and political-gerrymandering. Will it remain so?

Americans are facing many dangers. The enemies of our ideology are not ʼing to stop, until we stop them. Hoping they just get tired and go away is

NOT going to happen. They are well-organized and well-funded. They are out there active against us. Their propaganda is working successfully; just look at what they have already convinced the millennials of, i.e., that socialism is Utopia. And too, they are attacking us violently. We have to be rational and pragmatic, but we have to push back firmly; if in doing so we hurt their feelings, we can always offer them a boat ride to somewhere else.

So, the question is: how do we organize against this madness before us?

As a simple man, I don't think it is too complicated to figure out a plan. I suggest that we can alter the future, but the conservatives of Democrat, Republican, Libertarian, or Independent Parties need to help us out; if we lose this war, we all will lose too. The wealthy will lose all their wealth, just as did wealthy people in other countries where socialism or communism prevailed, i.e., China and Chairman Mao, Russia and Stalin, Germany and Hitler, Italy and Mussolini, Cambodia and Pol Pot. Need I say more?

Local Republican, Independent, Libertarian, and Democrat Committees should start organizing and meeting together on these common ground matters, work out an agreeable plan, network with other Committees of the State, form networks with Committees in other states, plan public rallies at their State Capitols, plan rallies in Washington DC, create "safe zones" for all meetings and events, put pressure on their lawmakers, kick out lawmakers who are supporting socialism, elect new ones who will fight as we want them to fight in state and federal legislatures, establish a strong central media, television, internet, and radio, and get these message out to as many people as possible. Demand legislation against the social media giants and technological corporations to force them to cease censorship of conservative voices. Go door to door, and let people know we are fighting against the destruction of our country and our homes and how they can help, if only by their votes. Tell them what socialism is actually about in reality.

I recently watch a video on YouTube entitled "Milton Friedman Speaks: Is Capitalism Humane." Dr. Friedman spoke on the morality of capitalism. He concluded the question was irrelevant. According to him, it comes down to this: capitalism per se is not humane or inhumane; neither is socialism. If we compare the two in terms of results, it is clear that only capitalism fosters equality and works toward social justice with a merit-based concept. The one is based on the principle of voluntary cooperation and free exchange, the other on force of position and power. In a free economy, it is hard to do good; you either have to use your own hard-earned money to do it or work hard to persuade others to your course. But by the same token, it is difficult to do harm because, by preventing a concentration of power, capitalism prevents people from committing sustained, serious harm. Is capitalism humane or inhumane? It is neither. But it tends to give free rein to the human values of human beings. That is not how socialism works at all. (See, www.youtube.com/ watch?v=27Tf8RN3uiM.) I urge you all to listen to what Milton Friedman had to say in his 45.18-minute speech to a college group. He also quoted Thoreau, "Philanthropy is an over-rated virtue. Sincerity is also an over-rated virtue. Heaven preserve us from the sincere reformer who knows what is good for you, and by Heaven he's going to make you do it whether you like it or not."

The essence of the Progressive movement is that they have increasingly accepted the tyrannical ideas of reduced private property rights and reduced rights to profits, and have become enamored with restrictions on personal liberty and control by the government.

We can't be lazy. But we can alter the future that we are facing right now. I recall, as the two planes crashed into the Twin Towers of the World Trade Center, what occurred in the hijacked Flight 93. Passengers were hearing on their phones what was going on, and realized their plane was likely headed for another large building target. Some realized they had to do something. We heard, on one of their phones, a determined man, say to others, "Let's roll!" as they attacked the hijackers. I'm sure they hoped to save themselves and the passengers on the plane as well as preventing it from being crashed into a populated building somewhere, but it is likely that they were too late from saving it from crashing into the rural ground. But they gave their lives trying. What are you willing to do to save America? All it takes is to get up out of your chair, join your local political party, and grow it in numbers and financing, and network with others, and network with parties in other states, grow, grow and grow. If you are a patriot, regardless of political party, then come together as ⸻riots first and foremost. I know patriotism by the millions exists in every

American Party except the Socialist Party. Survival of America supersedes Party lines. Bear in mind that we are SHORT OF TIME to do all this.

When our soldiers, white, black, brown, and so on, are sent into combat, they fight the enemy as a team, as brothers trusting each other, giving their life for one another in the battlefield. And our soldiers, in the battlefield under fire, they don't create politically-biased strategies independent to each other. They form a team, non-partisan, a fighting force against a common enemy.

But at home, it's a different story. Divisive forces reinforce racist narratives, promoting angst towards other races, primarily against the "white people" these days, even to the point of calling for white extermination. It makes me angry that the pro-socialists are using the race card, the fascist card, and "white privilege" card to instigate hate and violence for no other reason than to achieve their socialist and Islamic agendas. "Divide and Conquer" is exactly what these people are doing, and right now they seem to having a growing influence on people of color.

Should we patriots ignore all this, should we remain complacent? No, we shouldn't. This socialist agenda is an act of war against Americans, if only through their propaganda and, thus far, limited violence. But we are already seeing their violence is growing. Conservative and moderate patriots should put aside Party-bias and work together to win this war being fought against all of us right now. We've let it go on too long and it's only getting stronger and gaining ground with our younger people being brainwashed in our own schools by pro-socialist professors and teachers. Shut that down! We must somehow declare that our school system is ideologically-corrupted, that it has failed our own children over the last 20-30 years, and that legislation is needed to criminalize schools and teachers when they promote socialism or communism or fascism to our children. We must call for remedial education to try to roll-back the indoctrination damage that has already been done to our children, with re-education programs set forth in the public media domain that cannot be taken down by the social media platforms who have been banning conservative thought and ideas, programs that our current and past students can watch and understand the brainwashing they have received thus far.

I also think we should form a new organization for all patriots and call it the American Patriot Party. It would not be a political party for voting purposes, but a movement to encourage patriots of Americans to come together on "common ground" issues and concerns. The APP would transcend politics. Its goals would be simple: to protect the Constitution and the Bill of Rights, to ensure the continuation of the United States as a merit-based market-economy where the American Dream still lives, and to prepare against those enemies who are hell-bent on destroying our country.

While forming the APP, patriots need to be networking with each other, calling everyone, use your Party's online state political data banks and call everyone on the list that you can call. Phone bank. Create a brief narrative about the future if the socialists win, then argue why President Trump will not allow that to happen if we just vote him back in. He's already fighting against it. We need to re-elect Trump even if we don't like his tweets. We all "tweet" today; it is nothing more than a truncated message we all do on our phones. What matters is that Trump is, in his own way, a statesman who believes in the Constitution, our way of life, and our ideology. We don't know that about the candidates who run against him; they may be liars like Barack Obama. I think we should stick with someone we know.

Chapter XI:

Closing Thoughts

According to CNN (you know, the "fake news" channel), Biden is followed by Senators Elizabeth Warren (radical anti-Second Amendment person, for open borders), Bernie Sanders (radical Green New Deal and self-professed pro-Socialist), and Kamala Harris (pro gun-confiscation and anti-Second Amendment radical, and, apparently, another pro-socialist openly pushing for absolutism and censorship of speech; fortunately Harris dropped out).

The upcoming elections in 2020 represent an event in this century that will likely determine whether we lose this country as a constitutional democracy and capitalist republic. If we do not re-elect Trump, there is no other candidate with his stalwart ability to take on the powers that are even now working to destroy America and turn it into another failed socialist country from which it will become just another Orwellian state in the New World Order. Those Democrats running for President are running on the platform of socialism, thus they are and should be seen as enemies of the State. We have to rise against them at the polls, and I'm speaking also to moderate and conservative Democrats who are not pro-Socialism.

One other caution, and I think most level-headed women would agree: Women shouldn't vote for a woman just because she is in the race. It is smart, and shows character and wisdom, for everyone, including women, to choose a candidate on the basis of merit, not gender. A gender-only vote is a potential recipe for disaster, and when it comes to Warren and Harris, each of them will bring on disaster the likes from which America may not recover. Lots of women voted for Hillary who has turned out to be the epitome of political and criminal corruption.

If we end up as another state in the NWO, we'll never know freedom again. There will be two classes only: the rulers and the serfs. Like in Pink Floyd's "The Wall", we'll all just become just another brick in the wall, without individuality, without creative thought, without belief in something greater than ourselves, and without dreams and aspirations that could otherwise be achieved. I'm not willing to give up my country so easily. Are you?

I'll leave you with this thought about where Donald Trump stands on globalism.

At the U.N. General Assembly in New York on Tuesday, September 17, 2019, he called out allies in NATO over military spending, a point he made again at the United Nations, when he said:

> "We are also revitalizing our alliances by making it very clear that all of our partners are expected to pay their fair share of the tremendous defense burden, which the United States has borne in the past."

Trump's remarks also included sharp warnings for China and Iran. He lamented China's membership in the World Trade Organization, accusing Beijing of "gaming the system." He said, "As far as America is concerned, those days are over." Trump also called out Iran as "one of the greatest security threats" to peace-loving nations. The U.S. issued a new round of sanctions against Iran on Friday after the Tuesday meeting, after blaming Iran for an attack on a Saudi oil facility.

Trump also touched on immigration at the southern border, attempting to discourage migrants who may be thinking of making the trip to the U.S. without ~ropriate documents. Trump has been talking with leaders of those unfortunate countries from where these migrants originate, trying to get them to take care of their own populations. And he has said to all migrants:

> "Do not pay the coyotes. Do not put yourself in danger. Do not put your children in danger, because if you make it here, you will not be allowed in."

He is right, American taxpayers must not be required to accept unfortunate people from foreign lands as if they were our personal "extended family" which Americans are responsible for. That is literally stealing from taxpayer's pocketbooks to give their money to someone to whom it does not belong."

Most importantly, however, President Trump told world leaders to reject "globalism" and to look out for the interests of their own countries first. This, Trump's third address to the General Assembly as president, demonstrated, as he has done in the past, his position, and America's position, to the international organization to make the case for his "America first" style of diplomacy that puts nationalism ahead of multilateral efforts. Since entering the White House, Trump has pulled the U.S. out of several international agreements, including the Paris climate accords and the Iran nuclear deal. To the Assembly, and to the world, he said,

> **"The future does not belong to globalists;**
> **it belongs to patriots."**

Pete Seeger, a famous singer, wrote the lyrics that said, "Liberty is a hard-won thing, and every generation got to win it all over again." If we are to keep liberty alive, we must fight for it. It slips through our hands and out of our lives by complacency and acquiescence. Don't let the Left "guilt-trip" you into believing the world's problems are the fault and responsibility of Americans, and don't let anyone bully you into buying their false narratives and fantasies of a socialist Utopia. It has never, and will never exist because it always succumbs to some egomaniac or megalomaniac and despot who rules with an iron fist and hammer. The pro-Socialists seek socialism, and apparently do not know that the forces that fund them and drive their agenda intends to use socialism only as a stepping stone to the totalitarian

Dystopia called the New World Order, i.e., a one-government world ruled by a few globalist elites.

Remember, our Constitution makes the patriots of this country militia by default. You don't have to apply and sign a form requesting to become a person in the militia. We all are citizen soldiers in time of need. All you have to do is step up, coordinate with other militia persons, discuss strategy, and move forward as peacefully as possible. Do not advocate violence as the first solution; the Left will ultimately create that scenario and then self-defense is available. In times of crisis, it is the duty of patriots to defend this nation from all enemies, foreign and domestic. Our President Donald Trump is the one man whose finger is in the hole of the proverbial dike, holding back the flood waters, but the patriots are the millions who support him, and will defend against all efforts to destroy this nation. Patriots will not let the dam break and if it does after all other efforts have failed, patriots will fix the problem in the end. Right?

I want to include here our own Hollywood icon Clint Eastwood, who recently responded to criticism about his support of Trump. A stout patriot, he succinctly described our nation's problems:

> **The problem is not guns, it's hearts without God, homes without discipline, schools without prayer, and courtrooms without justice.**

He made this comment about Trump:

> People message me why I stick my neck out for Trump. Why do I tarnish my reputation with a man that's hated by so many? I don't care how much the media twists what he says. I don't care how bad he looks. I don't care about his sex life. At all. I don't even care that his language skills are not academic. I only look at what he does and what his policies accomplish. I see a booming economy. I see low unemployment rates. I see African Americans back at work. I see American companies that had fled overseas returning home. I see the

oldest President staying up till 3am in a suit on Airforce One waiting to greet our prisoners returning from Korea. I see China paying attention to him and returning to the negotiating table. I see him strengthening Israel, standing by Netanyahu, recognizing Jerusalem, saying Shehekhianu. I see him freeing Iran from a devastating regime. I see him tough on terrorism. I see a man who's delivering on every promise he made, not just talking to get votes. I see a lover of America. One who defends his men in uniform stronger than anyone I've ever seen. One who is proud of his flag, without feeling sorry, without excuses. I see an American hero. Let them say what they will. Trump is a hero. You will see. I love America. He loves America. I love him as our President. No one is without fault. We hired a man to do a job. He has surpassed my expectations in record time, single-handedly fighting the establishment. And he's doing it for free. Stop listening to talking heads. Look at policies. I'm proud to support Trump.

My viewpoint correlates with his. I see schools with socialists and atheists creating the policies and curriculum, throwing God and prayer out, taking down our flag, and instituting anti-God and pro-collectivism policies and ideals.

I see teachers encouraging not excellence but mediocrity so that the mediocre students do not have their feelings hurt from lower achievement levels.

I see schools that still teach reading by the known failure of the long-rejected Dewey-Mann methodology that leaves students unable to read or write properly, that does not prepare them for their future in America's marketplace or society, that leaves them embarrassed and guilt-tripped for even seeking excellence.

I see schools that turn a blind eye when students of color and even some white students vilify and guilt-trip white students as inherently racist, accusing Republican students as inherently fascist and racist, and shutting down free speech and even debate with conservative students, without any repercussions.

I see students of color guilt-tripping white girls telling they are racist if they date their own race, that they should be dating boys of color, and having their babies, not "white" babies. Guilt-tripped students, badgered and bullied, often accede to this pressure, not wanting to be "outed" so they acquiesce to the "party line" of the bullies as if they had become ashamed that they are white. Many of these guilt-tripped girls end up getting pregnant and having babies before they are even mature enough or adult enough to be a parent. Who suffer, if not both the young mother and her child.

I see schools that promote students who have not earned by their own merit the diploma they are given.

I see schools that will not fail students of color because of the destructive "affirmative action" view that they are systemically disadvantaged and it would be "racist" to fail them.

I see schools that discourage individualism and promote subjugation to the collective, as in Pink Floyd's "just another brick in the wall" concept.

I see schools banning debate and punishing students who speak for America while endorsing students the schools have turned into believers that socialism is a Utopian ideology, misguided students which are our next generation of politicians, bureaucrats, and voters.

I see schools promoting the new "political correctness" school of thought and speaking that is the cornerstone of Orwellianism.

I see schools banning conservative speakers and endorsing speakers who speak against the Constitution.

And, I see Trump as the bravest President ever, standing against the ugly forces that would destroy us all. He is stalwart, never giving an inch, as stubbornly patriotic as is possible, standing against a world ethos that wants a one-government world called the New World Order. Thank God for Donald Trump. We should all be like him in these times.

Voter apathy is what leads to bad politicians being elected. We already have the Deep State buying politicians campaigning for office. How do We the People vet these candidates?

Author Edmund Burke once cautioned: "The only thing necessary for the triumph of evil is for good men to do nothing." Tom Vaillancourt tomv@citizenstownhall.org, sent out a message, Thoughts at Large, which he suggested be forwarded to a friend. My 'friends' are American patriots, constitutionalists, and those who believe in God. I hope and trust that is you, the reader and, if not, that you will be enlightened enough to understand that perhaps being better informed is better than just going along with things that you don't know are true or not. Tom Vaillancourt writes:

> "Without the average American citizen taking personal responsibility and the proper action, our Republic will not survive."

> "How often do you hear these words?:
>
> - I do not discuss politics!
> - Who cares, they are all alike!
> - I don't know anything about politics!
> - No political discussions allowed at our house!

> But what is far worse is an institutional bias against any speaker or discussion or political issues.

> Try giving a speech at Rotary, Kiwanis, or any number of service clubs. You will be immediately shut down because they do not want to discuss anything that some of their members are in disagreement. The leaders of these organizations have effectively muzzled free speech.

> Religious organizations run from politics with blinding speed because they fear losing their tax exemption. Effectively muzzling free speech.

Why is it that the Democrat (Socialist) party can speak at any church function they want to, with no loss of tax exemption?

Whether we like it or not, politics is a part of everyone's life. It does not take long, after entering the work force, to figure out that corporate politics exists in every company, no matter what the size. A person will play to corporate politics every day because they think it directly affects their life. However, they pay no attention to government politicians who can pass laws that will take everything they have worked for from them. Shall we say California?

The percentage of registered voters who do not actually vote is staggering. How can the republic be saved if citizens do not complete the most basic civic duty, be an informed voter! ... There is a big difference between a voter who votes strictly along party lines or based on name recognition, and an informed voter!

A socialist government: With all decisions of importance in every American's life being made by the "ruling class." The everyday administration of those decisions being dictated by professional bureaucrats.

A government of "We the People": Made up of citizen legislators, the way our founding fathers envisioned; where the REAL POWER is in the hands of the everyday American!

END QUOTES.

VOTE WISELY IN 2020. DECIDE WISELY ABOUT THOSE WHO PROMISE SOCIALISM IS UTOPIAN. DECIDE WISELY ABOUT THOSE WHO WANT THE "NEW WORLD ORDER." DECIDE WISELY ABOUT

THOSE WHO TRULY WANT TO DO HARM TO THE AMERICAN IDEOLOGY; WHAT THEIR ALTERNATIVE OFFERS IS NOT WHAT THEY SAY IT IS. BE FULLY INFORMED. THIS IS THE ONE SINGLE VOTE IN OUR ENTIRE HISTORY AS A COUNTRY THAT TRULY MATTERS. FIND TRUTH, AND DISCARD PROPAGANDA. ETERNITY AWAITS YOUR DECISION. SO DO YOUR CHILDREN AND GRANDCHILDREN, AND THEIR CHILDREN.

Finally, I would like to pass on a good joke because it inspires one to want to understand the importance of evaluating and discerning truth and lie. Here goes:

While walking down the street a senator was tragically hit by a car and died. His soul arrives in Heaven and is met by St. Peter at Heaven's Gate. "Welcome to Heaven", says St. Peter. "Before you settle in, it seems there is a problem. We seldom see a high official around these parts, you see, so we're not sure what to do with you.:

"No problem. Just let me in", says the senator.

"Well, I'd like to, but I have orders from the higher ups. What we'll do is have you spend one day in Hell and one in Heaven. Then you can choose where to spend eternity."

"Really? I've made up my mind. I want to be in Heaven," says the senator.

I'm sorry, but we have our rules." And with that the senator goes down, down to Hell. The doors open and he finds himself in the middle of a golf course, in the distance a clubhouse and, standing in front of it are all his friends and other politicians who had worked with him. Everyone is very happy and in evening dress. They run to greet him, shake his hands and reminisce about the good times they had while getting rich at the expense of the people. They played a friendly round of golf and then dined on lobster, maliputo, caviar, Cebu lechon and the finest champagne.

Also present is the Devil who really is a very friendly guy and who is having a good time and telling jokes. They are all having such a good time that before the senator realizes it, it is time to go.

Everyone gives him a hearty farewell and waves while the elevator rises.

Now it's time to visit Heaven. So, 24 hours passed with the senator joining a group of contented souls moving from cloud to cloud, playing the harp, Cebu guitar and singing. They have a good time and before he realizes it the 24 hours have gone by and St. Peter returns. "Well then, you've spent a day in Hell and another in Heaven. Now choose your eternity."

The senator reflects for a minute before he answers: "Well, I would never have said it before, I mean Heaven has been delightful, but I think I would be better off in Hell."

So, he goes back down to Hell.

The elevator opens and he's in the middle of a barren land covered with waste and garbage. He sees all his friends, dressed in rags picking up the trash and putting it in trash bags as more trash falls from above. The Devil comes over to him and puts his arm around his shoulders.

"I, I, I don't, uh, I don't understand," stammers the senator. "The other day I was here and there was a golf course and clubhouse and we ate lobster, drank champagne, and we danced and had a great time. Now there's just a wasteland full of garbage and my friends look miserable. What happened?"

The Devil smiles at him and says, "Yesterday we were campaigning. Today you voted."

In closing, I would like to leave you with this thought:

> We should not await true patriotism to be borne in our country's darkest hours; rather, we should see the darkening coming and begin melding individual patriotism into a single spirit we all get behind. Complacency (sitting around ignoring what we see and know is moving against us), becomes acquiescence (allowing darkness to come upon us and destroy us) and both complacency and acquiescence are the harbingers that destroy our most fundamental freedoms as human beings. What is coming against us, if successful, likely cannot ever be undone. "1984" Orwellianism will be upon us for eternity. If that totalitarian system is the New World Order, mass genocide WILL occur and the world becomes rulers and serfs. If that totalitarian system is Islamic, mass genocide WILL occur as the Muslims kill off all "infidels" and turn "infidel" women into sex slaves to be killed later. This is war against humanity itself. No time to "turn the other cheek." No time to subsume oneself to a particular political Party; this is about "common ground" not politics. Join together, rebuild our country as it should be, based upon our venerable Constitution and Christian values.

May God guide your values and enhance your life, embrace us all in our time of need, and may you embrace the Golden Rule as your point of center and social foundation. May you see the Light.

I hope you enjoyed this book and learned something of value. If so, now act on it. I did a lot of research work, and I am no political expert. I am just John

Q. Citizen, a patriot, who is reasonably educated and fairly intelligent, so I am speaking to my American family of patriots regardless of Party affiliation. I changed parties from Democrat to Republican for good reasons, one of them being to find out who they really are and to see if they would agree that we need "common ground" dialogue with each other about a workable plan to stop this socialism attempt. I bailed out because the Democrat Party has been hijacked by socialists. I am just another patriot, one of you, and I want to do something to make a contribution to my country somehow, in a much-needed effort by all of us to save it from being destroyed from within. That's it. I'm not looking to be famous, just helpful.

The date is now into the new year. I had hoped this book could have been published by July of 2019, and in the stores and promoted by conservative media. I just didn't have the money to publish at the time. Also, I had to divide it into two volumes because it was too big for one volume, and I didn't want it priced beyond what my audience would likely not afford to pay. Again, I write to all patriots, regardless of Party, and to all enemies of America, domestic or foreign.

God bless you, God bless America, and may you be aligned with the Truth.

James Lewis, American Patriot, Christian, John Q. Citizen.

References

The following links provide additional information on this Yale organization that has gained so much influence in politics.

- Skull and Bones wiki - https://en.wikipedia.org/wiki/Skull_a...

- The 15 Most Powerful Members Of 'Skull And Bones' - http://www.businessinsider.com/skull-...

- The Order of Skull and Bones - http://www.bibliotecapleyades.net/soc...

- A brief history of the Skull and Bones Society - http://content.time.com/time/nation/a...

- The Order of the Skull and Bones: Everything you always wanted to know, but were afraid to ask - http://www.conspiracyarchive.com/NWO/...

- The Skull and Bones - Yale University - http://www.Bilderberg.org/skulbone.htm

- Skull and Bones - CBS News - http://www.cbsnews.com/news/skull-and...

- Skull and Bones - http://www.crystalinks.com/skullbones...

- Declassified 'Skull and Bones' Records from George W. Bush White House Set for Public Release - http://thefreethoughtproject.com/geor...

- George W. Bush White House's 'Skull and Bones' files due out - http://www.politico.com/blogs/under-t...

- Skull and Bones Tomb - http://www.atlasobscura.com/places/sk...

- Skull and Bones 322 - http://gnosticwarrior.com/322.html
- 10 Things in the Skull and Bones Society's Tomb - http://mentalfloss.com/article/21636/...

- George W. Bush's Skull & Bones Fraternity - http://mindprod.com/politics/bushbook...

- Skull and Bones Membership List (1833-1985) - http://www.mindfully.org/Reform/Skull...

- Yale's secret Skull and Bones society could be exposed - http://nypost.com/2016/05/10/yale-uni...

- The Secret Meaning of Number 322 Skull and Bones Illuminati Code Revealed - https://socioecohistory.wordpress.com...

ABOUT THE SECOND AMENDMENT AND GUN CONTROL:

- Civilian Disarmament: Prelude to Tyranny
  http://www.youtube.com/watch?v=1t9nfq6zyzA

- The Rise of the Robber State
  http://www.youtube.com/watch?v=hhO0QkVp5Qk

- The Untold Story of Gun Confiscation After Katrina
  http://www.youtube.com/watch?v=taU9d26wT4

- More Than A Right
  http://www.youtube.com/watch?v=EFpEbDNPeTE

- Enemy Public Number One: The Government, The People and The Militia Today
  http://www.youtube.com/watch?v=qnUfykk731c

- No Guns for Jews
  http://www.youtube.com/watch?v=Vjl2-ydZO9o
- Are Guns To Blame?
  http://www.youtube.com/watch?v=IjuLz_0o54

- Is The USA Next? Gun Control in Canada
  http://www.youtube.com/watch?v=PKE0NI-Djxs

- 2A Today for the USA
  http://www.youtube.com/watch?v=fsnGcJoNIXg

- Operation Fast and Furious Exposed
  http://www.youtube.com/watch?v=ONvmVcHIpP0

- Does the National Rifle Association Support Gun Owners?
  http://www.youtube.com/watch?v=oEVm6iyXaqM

- More Guns, Less Crime
  http://www.youtube.com/watch?v=nXTwAvE23ec

- Guns versus Crime
  http://www.youtube.com/watch?v=U2yhn80mR5k

- Firearms and Personal Defense
  http://www.youtube.com/watch?v=VGYttXa0d1k

- The Why of Gun Ownership
  http://www.youtube.com/watch?v=yvR3Vt80b-s

- Right to Bear Arms
  http://www.youtube.com/watch?v=RsY76EWmbWg

- Robert Williams and the 2nd Amendment
  http://www.youtube.com/watch?v=sKXbNis6IAE

- The UN: A Case for US Withdrawal
  http://www.youtube.com/watch?v=bTyvwUThKgY

- The UN's War on Firearms
  Taking advantage of Black Tuesday and the ongoing "war on terrorism," the United Nations is intensifying its own campaign against civilian ownership of firearms.
  http://tinyurl.com/7wx3xp9

- Disarmament and Destruction
  Under the guise of "peace and safety" the United Nations seeks to disarm entire populations. Never mind that disarmed populations invariably invite tyranny and genocide!
  http://tinyurl.com/8yxzz

- Dangerous Disarmament
  The drive to deprive Americans of privately owned firearms is part of a larger plan to render the U.S. helpless before a Russian-Chinese axis or a nuclear-armed UN.
  http://tinyurl.com/cvw45dd

- With UN Support, Socialist Chavez Disarms Civilians in Venezuela
  http://tinyurl.com/7f7h4ry

- Deadly Disarmament: U.N. Gun Control
  http://tinyurl.com/6wtjp2t

- UN-sponsored Civilian Disarmament in Brazil
  http://tinyurl.com/86jvqqq

- Bush Backs UN Global Disarmament Drive
  http://tinyurl.com/7jqarwl

- Gun Control Leads to Militarized Law Enforcement
  http://tinyurl.com/6s8dl5t

- Toward a Global Police State
  http://tinyurl.com/7tu8mjp

- Former UN Ambassador: Obama Will Target Gun Ownership in Second
  Term
  http://tinyurl.com/77wmcuw

- Obama's Anti-gun Agenda Shelved - for Now
  http://tinyurl.com/6u76s6r

- Second Amendment Rights Once Again at Risk
  http://tinyurl.com/85q82q3

- Gun Controllers Don't Want to Waste Tucson Tragedy
  http://tinyurl.com/6mrcw47

- The Shameful Manipulation of Murder: Gun Control and Tyranny
  http://tinyurl.com/83yv8n4

- Obama Planning Gun-control Legislation
  http://tinyurl.com/6n57ddb

- "Fast and Furious" Was Plot Against U.S. Gun Rights, NRA Chief Says
  http://tinyurl.com/cnw972p

- Gun Grab Revival
  http://tinyurl.com/6uxzvsr

James C. Lewis

- Gun Rights on Trial
  http://tinyurl.com/d43pnvb

- Second Amendment Solidified
  http://tinyurl.com/7c8e6bk

- Firearms and Freedom
  http://tinyurl.com/7pnxh24

- Defending the Home
  http://tinyurl.com/87apqcm
- Gun Ownership Up, Crime Down
  http://tinyurl.com/77glhoz

- The Darker Side of Gun Control
  http://tinyurl.com/857jkyz

- I Am Alive, No Thanks to Gun Control
  http://tinyurl.com/77yd729

- Shooting Down Faulty Arguments
  Collectivists cling to their worn-out gun control clichés, even though each
  one can be shot full of holes.
  http://tinyurl.com/6rlttl9

- Moms' Masquerade
  The Million Mom March was a carefully crafted revolutionary mobiliza-
  tion led by a political veteran.
  http://tinyurl.com/6ssnrak

- Citizen Soldiers: The Militia
  http://tinyurl.com/7tt6h3j

- Bearing Arms: A Right ... and a Duty?
  http://tinyurl.com/7dx58tg

- The American Rifleman in the Revolutionary War
  http://tinyurl.com/cyxoqtz

- No Compromise Against Gun Control: Aaron Zelman Interviewed
  http://tinyurl.com/c8g5dea

- The Impact of the Swiss Civilian Militia On Hitler's War Plans
  http://tinyurl.com/5lbjf4

- National Security, Swiss-Style
  http://tinyurl.com/2fnfm5
- Guns, Crime, and the Swiss
  http://tinyurl.com/crk6gl8

- Citizens in Arms: The Swiss Experience
  http://tinyurl.com/bq9z8oe

References below regarding quotes from Thomas D. Schauf, a national speaker to Certified Public Accountants and business leaders. Mr. Schauf's expertise includes banking, the economy, business appraisals, mergers, and acquisitions.

(1) "The Federal Reserve Bank", by H.S. Kenan, published by The Noontide Press

(2) National Committee to Repeal the Federal Reserve Act, P.O. Box 156, Westmont, IL 60559

(3) "The New World Order, Saving America", P.O. Box 1205, Middleburg, FL 32050-1205

(4) "Bulletin", February 1989 & November 1991 issues, P.O. Box 986, Ft. Collins, CO 80522 (Newsletter; $3 each)

(5) "The Most Secret Science", Betsy Ross Press, P.O. Box 986, Ft. Collins, CO 80522 (Book) States attempt to abolish the FED. $12.00

(6) "Insider Report", P.O. Box 84903, Phoenix, AZ 85071

(7) "Phoenix Journal Express", P.O. Box 986, Tehachap, CA 93581

(8) $16 trillion in government and private debt, much of which the FED printed and collected interest on (Reference 3)

(9) Northpoint Tactical Team, P.O. Box 129, Topton, NC 28781

(10) Christian Defense League, Box 449, Arabi, LA 70023

(11) "Bulletin", June 1992 issue, P.O. Box 986, Ft. Collins, CO 80522 (Newsletter; $3 each)

(12) "Savings and Loan Unethical Bailout" by Rev. Casimir F. Gierut

(13) "Dark Secrets of the New Age" by Texe Marrs

(14) "En Route to Global Occupation" by Gary H. Kah

(15) "One World" by John Amkerberg & John Weldon

(16) "The Spotlight", Liberty Lobby, 300 Independence Ave. S.E., Washington, D.C. 20003 (Newspaper)

(17) "Repeal the Federal Reserve Banks" by Rev. Casimir Frank Gierut

(18) The Constitution of the United States

(19) "Walls in Our Minds" by M.J. Red Beckman, Common Sense Press, P.O. Box 1544, Billings, MT 59103. A must read book - $2.50

(20) "The Law That Never Was" Volume I, Bill Benson & M.J. Red Beckman, P.O. Box 1544, Billings, MT 59103 or write to Bill Benson, P.O. Box 550, South Holland, IL 60473. Proof that the 16th Amendment (income tax) was never properly ratified.

(21) "New World Order: The Ancient Plan of Secret Societies" by William T. Still.

(22) "The Secrets of the Federal Reserve" by Mullins.

(23) "The Social Security & Pension Conspiracy" by Metz

(24) "The History of the Federal Reserve. How to Replace It or How to Reform It" by Metz - for references 23 & 24 write to Howard Metz, P.O. Box 341, Malverne, LI 11565

(25) "The New World Order" by Pat Robertson. On page 131 he states that we must abolish the FED.

(26) "Operation Vampire Killer 2000", highly recommended book. $6.00 ($8.00 for 2) from ACLA, P.O. Box 8712, Phoenix, AZ 85066 This is a must read book with quotes from well-known people. This book proves conspiracy. Your local police needs to read this book so they will protect you - not become United Nations Agents against you. This book will stop the New World Order plan to take over the U.S.A.

(27) "America Betrayed", Center For Action, 652 N. Glenview, Nesa, AZ 85213

For references 1, 12, and 17, contact The National Committee to Repeal the Federal Reserve Act (Reference 2)